Reconstructing Human Origins

Second Edition

Reconstructing
Human Origins
A Modern Synthesis

Second Edition

GLENN C. CONROY

Washington University
St. Louis

W · W · NORTON

NEW YORK · LONDON

W. W. Norton & Company has been independent since its founding in 1923, when William Warder Norton and Mary D. Herter Norton first published lectures delivered at the People's Institute, the adult education division of New York City's Cooper Union. The Nortons soon expanded their program beyond the Institute, publishing books by celebrated academics from America and abroad. By mid-century, the two major pillars of Norton's publishing program—trade books and college texts—were firmly established. In the 1950s, the Norton family transferred control of the company to its employees, and today—with a staff of four hundred and a comparable number of trade, college, and professional titles published each year—W. W. Norton & Company stands as the largest and oldest publishing house owned wholly by its employees.

Composition by GGS Book Services, Atlantic Highlands
Manufacturing by Maple-Vail

Library of Congress Cataloging-in-Publication Data

Conroy, Glenn C.
    Reconstructing human origins : a modern synthesis / Glenn C. Conroy.—2nd ed.
        p. cm.
    Includes bibliographical references and index.

    ISBN 0-393-92590-0 (pbk.)

    1. Human beings—Origin.   2. Fossil hominids.   3. Human evolution.   I. Title.

GN281.C587 2005
599.93′8–dc22   2004058307

W. W. Norton & Company, Inc., 500 Fifth Avenue, New York, N.Y. 10110
www.wwnorton.com

W. W. Norton & Company Ltd., 10 Coptic Street, London WC1A 1PU

2 3 4 5 6 7 8 9 0

To all creatures still wild and free,
I dedicate this book.
The success of human evolution has not been kind to you.

Brueghel's Two Monkeys

This is what I see in my dreams
about final exams:
two monkeys, chained to the
floor, sit on the window sill,
the sky behind them flutters,
the sea is taking its bath.

The exam is History of Mankind.
I stammer and hedge.

One monkey stares and listens
with mocking disdain,
the other seems to be dreaming
away—
but when it's clear I don't know
what to say
he prompts me with a gentle
clinking of his chain.

—Wislawa Szymborska

Contents

Preface

A waggish commentator once observed that the sciences could be conveniently lumped into three categories: the soft sciences, like political science and sociology; the hard sciences, like physics and chemistry; and then the really difficult sciences; like paleoanthropology. What makes paleoanthropology so "difficult" is the realization that human evolution is a unique evolutionary experiment—one that cannot be repeated. For this reason it is not unusual (or unreasonable) to encounter honest disagreements among knowledgeable paleoanthropologists about the nature, *but not the fact,* of human evolution. As in my previous book, *Primate Evolution* (Conroy, 1990), I have tried to convey this state of dynamic tension fairly and honestly without promoting my views to the exclusion of others. While I am certain that my own biases percolate through on occasion, I have made every effort to present the reader with what I take to be a balanced view of the major events and issues in human evolution. My hope is that by the time readers have reached the end of the book, they will have come away with a reasonable grasp of the fossil evidence for human evolution and how that evidence is interpreted in modern paleoanthropological research. I am less concerned, and I hope students agree, if my interpretation or emphasis differs somewhat from that of their own professors. After all, that is what teachers and books are for.

While this book is written mainly with anthropology undergraduate and graduate students in mind, anyone interested in the natural sciences can easily follow the major episodes of human evolution as outlined here by simply starting at the beginning and reading through to the end. Bearing in mind that the fossils themselves are the main "stars" of the book, I have tried to integrate the impact that recent advances in such areas as radiometric dating, functional morphology, molecular biology, and archeological inference have had on modern interpretations of how hominins lived and dispersed across the globe during the Pliocene and Pleistocene epochs (Plio-Pleistocene) of the last 5 million years or so.

ORGANIZATION OF THIS TEXT

Were the changes in human behavior that distinguish us from other primates causally related to the changes in morphology seen in the human fossil record? Can the emergence of humans be considered an evolutionary "revolution" or was it simply a gradual continuation of previously existing evolutionary change both in terms of morphology and culture? What were the selective advantages of the biocultural changes seen in the human fossil record that ultimately allowed us to become dominant in such a relatively short geological time span? These are the kinds of questions we will explore as we follow the course of human evolution through the Plio-Pleistocene.

We begin in Chapters 1 and 2 by putting human evolution into its proper anatomical, temporal, and paleoenvironmental contexts, first by considering the anatomical evidence uniting humans and other primates and then by reconstructing the geologic and paleoenvironmental history of the past 5 million years.

Chapter 3 begins with a general discussion of what an appropriate fossil site looks like and how paleoanthropologists go about their work. It is followed by an extensive review of the various dating methods used in paleoanthropological research, many of which prove critical to modern interpretations of the human fossil (and archeological) record discussed in later chapters.

Chapter 4 introduces three important topics in modern paleoanthropological research: (1) phylogeny reconstruction, (2) classification, and (3) the tempo and mode of evolution. We consider how failure to appreciate the distinction between phylogeny and classification can lead to confusion and misunderstanding in studies of human evolution. The underlying methods, principles, and assumptions of the two major schools of biological classification predominant in paleoanthropology today—evolutionary systematics and phylogenetic systematics (popularly known as cladistics)—are compared and contrasted.

If, as all modern biology suggests, humankind is part of a long evolutionary continuum, we need to know who, or what, preceded us in the evolutionary line. That is the question addressed in Chapter 5. If we seek humankind's antecedents we must search among the fossil hominoids, or primitive "apes," of the Miocene, the epoch preceding the Pliocene.

As the Miocene drew to a close, a major new episode in primate evolution unfolded as one of these Miocene "apes" began its adaptive radiation throughout Africa—and later the entire world. This unusual "ape" would begin to shape its world in ways no other organism had ever done before it. The story of this last major adaptive radiation in hominoid evolution, the evolution of the human lineage, begins in Chapters 6 to 8 with the appearance of the earliest undoubted hominins in the fossil record, the australopiths of southern and eastern Africa. Here we encounter for the first time evidence of hominization: the emergence of an animal who walked on two legs rather than four, used tools rather than teeth for tearing and cutting, had a relatively large brain, and had evolved behavioral and social mechanisms enabling it to survive the harsh environs of the African savanna. We discuss these trends in detail in Chapter 8.

In Chapter 9 we review the fossil evidence pertaining to the origins of our own genus, *Homo*. The genus *Homo* first appears in Africa about 2.4–2.0 million years ago (mya). This new genus reveals several important evolutionary distinctions from earlier (and contemporary) australopiths, including changes in the cranial and postcranial skeleton, more sophisticated stone-tool-making technology, and most important, new levels of cerebral organization in terms of both absolute size and complexity. These trends continue throughout the Plio-Pleistocene in the various *Homo* lineages, culminating in early members of our own species, *Homo sapiens*, over 100 thousand years ago (kya).

Over the past several decades an increasing number of fossils ascribed to early *Homo* have been discovered in both Africa and Eurasia; but as the pace of discovery has quickened, so have the inevitable questions such discoveries raise: How can early *Homo* be distinguished from australopiths? Is the range of morphological variation subsumed under the name *Homo habilis* too great for a single species? If all these specimens represent more than one species, what *other* taxa are represented in this heterogeneous sample? Does the definition of *Homo* need modification, and if so, how? Is *Homo habilis* really ancestral to *Homo erectus?* We explore these, and other, questions in this chapter.

In Chapter 10 we encounter a larger and more formidable hominin species, and certainly the first to spread out of Africa to populate much of the Old World, *Homo erectus* (or *H. ergaster* as some African specimens are now sometimes called). Prompted mainly by new, rigorous applications of cladistic techniques, some paleoanthropologists have recently begun to challenge some time-honored opinions about *H. erectus*. For example, is *H. erectus* simply an arbitrarily defined stage, or grade, of human evolution, temporally and morphologically sandwiched between Plio-Pleistocene *H. habilis* on the one hand and upper Middle Pleistocene hominins on the other? Or is it a "real" species with definable boundaries in time and space? Did *H. erectus* exist only in the Far East, where it was first discovered, or can it also be identified in Africa or Europe (e.g., *H. ergaster*)? Was Asian *H. erectus* simply an evolutionary dead end, contributing little to modern human evolution? In this chapter we consider these questions as we examine the fossil evidence for *H. erectus* and related forms.

By some 800–300 kya these populations were gradually being supplanted by, or evolving into, a highly varied group of hominins living throughout much of the Old World. These rather ill-defined or "transitional" fossil hominins of the Middle Pleistocene were often lumped together under the informal and unflattering designation of "archaic *H. sapiens*" because they had not yet evolved morphological features that could be considered typical of later anatomically modern *H. sapiens*. There has been a recent tendency among (most) paleoanthropologists to subdivide this rather motley assortment of hominins into a number of different species, including *H. antecessor, H. heidelbergensis, H. rhodesiensis,* and *H. neanderthalensis*—and even others. Throughout the Old World these hominins are usually associated with some form of the Developed Oldowan/Acheulean (chopper/handaxe) and/or prepared core (e.g., Levallois) tool complexes. The fossil record of this group is discussed in Chapter 11.

The issue of the biological and behavioral origins of "modern" humans remains one of the most contentious, and exciting, subjects for debate in contemporary paleoanthropology, and the last several decades have seen a virtual revolution in our thinking about modern human origins. This is the topic we fully explore in Chapters 12 and 13. Virtually all anthropologists agree that sometime during the Middle/Upper Pleistocene transition, important biological and cultural changes were taking place in human evolution between populations of (what are best called) "late early hominins" and "early modern humans." What is not uniformly agreed upon is exactly where, when, and how these "modern" humans first arose. In these last chapters we will discuss the molecular (Chapter 12) and fossil and archeological evidence (Chapter 13) that bears on a number of vexing questions about this important transitional period in human evolution. For instance, was the biocultural transition from late early hominins to early modern humans restricted in time and space, occurring first in Africa, then radiating outward, as the Out of Africa Model predicts, or did it develop independently in several different places across the continents, as the Multiregional Continuity Model predicts?

CHANGES IN THE SECOND EDITION

For those readers familiar with the first edition of *Reconstructing Human Origins,* this second edition embodies extensive updates and reorganizations, as well as numerous new illustrations. These updates and revisions, along with many new references, bring students up to date with the "state of the art" of paleoanthropology through the spring of 2004. First of all, it will be noted that whereas the first edition had 10 chapters, this second edition has now been expanded to 13 chapters. This increase results from both an abundance of new material and, just as important, a reorganization of chapter topics that I hope will create a more seamless and comfortable fit within the framework of a lecture course on human origins.

Some specific improvements include the following. The taxonomy of fossil hominins used in the text is made very explicit right up front in the preface in order to avoid any nomenclatural confusion in later chapters. Here the student will also find reference to the type specimen of each of the major fossil hominin species as well. The old Chapter 1 is now divided into two chapters. New Chapter 1 provides an introduction to basic primate dental and postcranial anatomy so that students can develop a general working vocabulary of some of the anatomical terms that show up later in the text when describing fossil hominins. New Chapter 2 now focuses on climatic aspects of the Plio-Pleistocene world that had a profound influence on the course of human evolution. I have divided old Chapter 2 into two separate chapters, Chapter 3 ("Finding and Dating Fossil Hominins") followed by Chapter 4 ("Naming and Classifying Fossil Hominins") in order to help students better focus on these distinct activities. Old Chapter 3 is now new Chapter 5 ("Before the Bipeds"), a chapter that has been extensively revised to provide a more synthetic overview of these important Miocene primates that preceeded the earliest hominins.

The discussion of the earliest hominins, the australopiths, is now divided into two chapters. Chapter 6 focuses on the earliest hominins from southern Africa and Chapter 7 focuses on those from eastern Africa. Chapter 6 now offers a gallery of representative hominins at the end, courtesy of J. K. McKee. In both chapters I first lay out the geological and paleoecological settings of the most important hominin sites, and then introduce the fossil hominins themselves. The newest fossil hominin discoveries from each of these regions are presented, including discussions of *Sahelanthropus, Orrorin, Ardipithecus, Kenyanthropuis,* and new species of *Australopithecus,* e.g., *A. garhi.* The paleobiology of the earliest hominins follows in Chapter 8 (old chapter 5). In Chapter 9 the "What Is Culture" section joins the discussion on the origins of *Homo* for better continuity.

Later chapters present new information on the oldest hominins from Europe, including those from Dmanisi (Republic of Georgia) and Atapuerca, Spain. Finally, Chapter 12 has been expanded to present a detailed, and I hope balanced, view about what the molecular evidence does, and does not, say about a number of important issues—such as the place of Neandertals in later human evolution and the Multiregional versus the Out of Africa hypotheses. Chapter 13 provides a "reality check" on what the actual fossils say about modern human origins.

I have also added a new section at the end of the book called "Brain-teasers." This is an essay I wrote for *Evolutionary Anthropology* several years ago on what I thought were some "hot issues" or "nonissues" in human evolution (Conroy, 1998). It is reproduced here as food for student intellects to munch on. I have had fun thinking about the issues they raise; I hope students do too. There is more to them than meets the eye, so tread carefully!

And finally, for ease of reference the extensive bibliography, current through spring 2004, is now presented as a single alphabetically arranged reference list at the end of the book in the style of the *American Journal of Physical Anthropology*.

TAXONOMY USED IN THIS TEXT

Most paleoanthropologists now follow some type of cladistic classification system in which the living great apes (gorillas, chimpanzees, orangutans) and certain fossil taxa (e.g., *Dryopithecus, Sivapithecus, Gigantopithecus*) are included together with humans in the family Hominidae (see Chapters 4 and 5). The student should be aware that while this is cladistically correct, it may lead to some potential confusion as to what is actually meant by the terms *hominid* and *hominin*. Since one of the most important attributes of any classification system should be ease of communication, the classification of higher primates used in this text is given below (Wood and Richard, 2000).

When referring solely to "humans" and their immediate fossil relatives, I will use the cladistically correct term *hominin*, a member of the tribe Homini, rather than the term *hominid*, a member of the family Hominidae, which includes the great apes. The names applied to some of these higher categories follow certain established rules.

For each of the hominin species listed below, its type specimen (i.e., the particular specimen to which the species name was first properly applied) is given.[1]

Superfamily: Hominoidea (hominoids)
   Family: Hylobatidae
      Genus: *Hylobates*
   Family: Hominidae (hominids)
     Subfamily: Ponginae
      Genus: *Pongo* (pongines)

---

[1]Note that some of these taxa are not universally accepted, but are included here for completeness (e.g., *A. crassidens, A. praegens, A. bahrelghazali*, and *H. neanderthalensis*). Also, the placement of late Miocene (about 6 mya) *Orrorin* and *Sahelanthropus* in the tribe Hominini is still debatable, and thus are considered here incertae sedis. Note also that in this text *Paranthropus* is considered a subgenus of *Australopithecus*.

Subfamily: Gorillinae
    Genus: *Gorilla* (gorillines)
Subfamily: Homininae (hominines)
  Tribe: Panini
    Genus: *Pan* (panins)
  Tribe: Hominini (hominins)
   Subtribe: Australopithecina (australopiths)
    Genus: *Ardipithecus*
      Ar. ramidus (ARA-VP-6/1; associated set of teeth)
      Ar. kadabba (ALA-VP-2/10; right mandible with M_3)
    Genus: *Australopithecus*
      A. anamensis (KNM-KP 29281; adult mandible)
      A. afarensis (L.H.-4; adult mandible)
      A. africanus (Taung; juvenile skull)
      A. garhi (BOU-VP-12/130; cranial fragments and maxilla)
      A. (Paranthropus) robustus (TM 1517; Adult partial cranium and mandible)
      A. (Paranthropus) boisei (OH 5; adult cranium)
      A. (Paranthropus) aethiopicus (Omo 18; adult mandible)
      A. (Paranthropus) crassidens (SK 6; adolescent mandible)
      A. bahrelghazali (KT 12/H1; adult mandible)
      A. praegens (KNM-T1 13150; adult mandible)
    Genus: *Kenyanthropus*
      K. platyops (KNM-WT 4000; adult partial cranium)
   Subtribe: Hominina (hominans)
    Genus: *Homo*[2]
      H. habilis (OH 7; partial calotte and hand bones)
      H. rudolfensis (KNM-ER 1470; adult cranium)
      H. ergaster (KNM-ER 992; adult mandible)
      H. erectus (Trinil 2; adult calotte)
      H. heidelbergensis (Mauer 1; adult mandible)
      H. neanderthalensis (Neanderthal 1; adult calotte and partial skeleton)
      H. antecessor (ATD6-5; partial mandible with teeth)
      H. sapiens (none)
  Tribe: Incertae Sedis
    Genus: *Orrorin*
      Orrorin tugenensis (BAR 1000'00, 1000a'00, 1000b'00 (fragmentary mandibles)
    Genus: *Sahelanthropus*
      Sahelanthropus tchadensis (TM 266-01-060-1 (partial cranium)

---

[2]It has recently been suggested that *H. habilis* and *H. rudolfensis* should be transferred to the genus *Australopithecus* (Wood and Collard, 1999b), a view that I tend to be sympathetic to and that will be explored further in Chapter 9.

For comparison, an alternative classification based solely on DNA data and following strict cladistic rules classifies the genus *Homo* as follows (Goodman et al., 2001; Wildman et al., 2003):[3]

Tribe: Hominini
   Subtribe: Hominina
      Genus: *Gorilla*
      Genus: *Homo*
         Subgenus: *H. (Pan)*
            H. (Pan) paniscus
            H. (Pan) troglodytes
         Subgenus: *H. (Homo)*
            H. (Homo) ramidus (Ardipithecus ramidus)
            H. (Homo) anamensis (Australopithecus anamensis)
            H. (Homo) afarensis (Australopithecus afarensis)
            H. (Homo) africanus (Australopithecus africanus)
            H. (Homo) boisei (Australopithecus boisei)
            H. (Homo) robustus (Australopithecus robustus)
            H. (Homo) habilis (Homo habilis)
            H. (Homo) erectus (Homo erectus)
            H. (Homo) sapiens neanderthalensis (Homo neanderthalensis)
            H. (Homo) sapiens sapiens (Homo sapiens)

Note that in this strictly cladistic molecular classification, both common and pygmy chimpanzees, plus all members of the human lineage, are classified within the genus *Homo* (but within separate subgenera, *Pan* and *Homo*, respectively). In addition, this classification scheme also places gorillas, chimpanzees, and humans all within the tribe Hominini (i.e., they would all be considered "hominins"). This is a legitimate, although still not widely adopted, alternative to the terminology used in this book. Indeed, some advocates of such strict molecular perspectives to hominin taxonomy suggest that there may have been only around 4 species, *in toto*, on the direct line to modern humans since the last common ancestor of chimpanzees and humans, and that only one species of human, *H. sapiens*, was in existence for most of the last 2 million years (Curnoe and Thorne, 2003).

Two other colloquial terms, *gracile* and *robust*, have often been used in the literature as a convenient shorthand label to refer to *Australopithecus africanus* and *A. afarensis* (gracile) on the one hand and *A. robustus* and *A. boisei* (robust) on the other. However, as we shall see in later chapters,

---

[3] The traditional taxonomic names for each taxon are given in parentheses. Approximately 95–99% of DNA base pairs are shared between chimpanzee and human DNA (Britten, 2002; Goodman et al., 2001; Wildman et al., 2003). Human-chimp DNA sequence divergence is roughly 10 times that between random pairs of humans. Initial studies suggest that genes relating to both olfaction and hearing have undergone distinct, rapid changes over the course of human evolution compared to chimpanzees (Clark et al., 2004).

these terms are potentially misleading and confusing because it is now thought that there was relatively little body size difference between the two groups. In fact, a cranium of *A. afarensis* from Hadar, Ethiopia, dated to about 3 mya is the largest australopith cranium (in terms of biasterionic width) yet discovered (Kimbel et al., 1994).[4]

In addition, recent fossil evidence, particularly from South Africa, clearly indicates that dental dimensions in some gracile australopiths greatly exceed those found in the type specimen of *A. robustus*. Therefore, the terms *gracile* and *robust* should probably be abandoned in the future; they are used in this text only for historical continuity with the older literature and are not meant to convey any formal taxonomic implications. Also, the term *australopithecine* has been abandoned in this text since it implies a subfamily ranking (Australopithecinae) for all its included taxa (as noted above, the correct subfamily designation for humans and their immediate fossil relatives is Homininae). Again, to keep some continuity with the older literature, I will use the term *australopiths* to refer to those early hominins that preceded the emergence of our own genus, *Homo* (i.e., all members of the subtribe Australopithecina).

Finally, a word about the practice of taxonomic attribution and nomenclature followed throughout this book, and in the literature, is in order. When a species can be identified, the taxonomic attribution is customarily recorded, as for example *Australopithecus africanus*, and both the genus and the species name are either underlined or italicized. When the abbreviation *cf.* (from the Latin "confer," to be compared to) is used, as in *Australopithecus* cf. *A. africanus*, this means that the specimen should be compared to *A. africanus*. Use of *cf.* in this context is taken to mean that while the preserved morphology suggests attribution to *A. africanus*, there is insufficient evidence to make an unequivocal judgment. A specimen that can only be identified at the generic level is indicated as, for example, *Australopithecus* sp. indet. (species indeterminate). Likewise, a specimen that can be referred only to family level is designated, for example, as Hominidae gen. et sp. indet. (genus and species indeterminate). If a fossil is the entire known material of a species available to a taxonomist, or hypodigm, that has affinity with, but is not identical to, another taxon, then the designation *aff.* (from the Latin, *affinis*) is used, for example, *Australopithecus* aff. *A. africanus*. If a specimen is damaged or incomplete but is none the less recognizable as part of such a hypodigm, it is referred to as cf. *Australopithecus* aff. *A. africanus*. *Aff.* is meant to suggest possible but inconclusive membership in a known species. A fossil whose taxonomic rank is uncertain is referred to as incertae sedis (Schenk and McMasters, 1936).

[4]Asterion is the point where the lambdoidal, parietomastoid, and occipitomastoid sutures meet low down on the lateral side of the cranium.

Writing a textbook can sometimes be a forbidding and lonely task. "Like fly-fishing, writing is an elaborate conspiracy to make lyrical an activity that is inherently a business of barbs and worms" (Fields, 1990). However, the process was made so much more pleasant by the congenial atmosphere provided by friends and colleagues within the anthropological community of Washington University, St. Louis (James Cheverud, Jane Phillips-Conroy, D. Tab Rasmussen, Richard Smith, Robert Sussman, Erik Trinkaus). I am grateful to them for sharing with me over the years their considerable and diverse insights into many of the topics discussed in this book.

The first edition of this book was completed while I was a Weatherhead Foundation Resident Scholar at the School of American Research (SAR) in Sante Fe, New Mexico. To the foundation and its then president, Douglas Schwartz, I am most grateful for the time spent under the pinyons. To all those who graciously gave of their time to review and improve various portions of the manuscript—David Begun, Robert Blumenschine, Russell Ciochon, Robert Eckhardt, David Frayer, Michael Little, Jim Moore, Jane Phillips-Conroy, D. Tab Rasmussen, John Relethford, Betsy Schumann, Jeffrey Schwartz, Richard Smith, Frank Spencer, Mark Teaford, Alan Templeton, Erik Trinkaus, and Tim White—I thank you for your strong words of encouragement and your gentle words of criticism.

I must add to this list my gratitude to my editors at W. W. Norton & Company over the years, particularly Jim Jordan for starting me down this path many years ago, and John Byram and Leo Wiegman, who saw the first and second editions, respectively, through to the end.

Finally, and most important, is the loving support provided on the home front. Sox the wonder dog was always waiting at the door when I came home late at night. And to my wife and colleague, Jane Phillips-Conroy—as Elton John wrote, *How wonderful life is, while you're in the world.*

Reconstructing Human Origins

Second Edition

CHAPTER 1

Humans as Primates

INTRODUCTION

The question of human origins and the immensity of time through which we have evolved has provoked humankind's collective imagination for as long as recorded history. Henry David Thoreau, in one of his musings at Walden Pond, expressed it quite beautifully (1854): "Time is but the stream I go a-fishing in. I drink at it; but while I drink I see the sandy bottom and detect how shallow it is. Its thin current slides away, but eternity remains." Indeed, interest in the subject is as pervasive today as it was in earlier times.

The modern study of human evolution encompasses many fields and is based on a large body of empirical research. Paleoanthropology is a subject that appeals to a remarkably wide range of people. There are a number of reasons why this is so. To some, much of its colorful history conjures up images of romance and adventure in far away and exotic places, a tale of dramatic discoveries and heated controversies amid the sound and fury of clashing egos. In others it evokes sublime reflections about our place in nature, about our collective past and future. And then there are those who simply believe in George Santayana's (1905) aphorism: "Those who cannot remember the past are condemned to repeat it."

The major emphasis in this book is on the discovery and interpretation of the fossil evidence for human evolution. To many dedicated students of human evolution, fossil discovery is the very heart and soul of paleoanthropology because fossils are the most *direct* and *unequivocal* evidence documenting the course of our evolutionary history. Fossil discoveries connect us to eternity, giving us the privilege of glimpsing, if ever so briefly and imperfectly, the blurred image of those who walked the earth hundreds of thousands, or even millions of years before us. We may not always be certain about their proper taxonomic label, or their exact place on the human evolutionary tree, but that does not diminish the wonder. We still recognize them as being a part of us, and us as being a part of them.

Even though it is fossil discovery that usually stokes the fire of public imagination, intellectual adrenaline flows into paleoanthropology from a number of other interrelated disciplines as well. Such diverse fields as geochronology, archeology, phylogenetic reconstruction, functional morphology, paleoecology, behavioral ecology, and molecular biology all play critical roles in modern paleoanthropological research. For this reason, one of the aims of this book is to integrate information from these, and other, fields into our ever expanding knowledge of, and appreciation for, the human fossil record.

Human evolution should not be considered to have a definite beginning or (barring a nuclear holocaust, "hot" virus disaster, or asteroid impact) a definite end. Humankind is part of an evolutionary continuum of primates stretching back to the origins of the order some 70–90 million years ago (mya). What we think of as "human" evolution has occupied only the last 5–7% of that time, approximately the last 5 million years or so, and that story is the subject matter of this book.

WHAT DISTINGUISHES HUMANS FROM OTHER PRIMATES?

Before launching into the story of human evolution, perhaps it is best to start with a more basic consideration. What distinguishes primates from other mammals and what distinguishes humans from other primates? Carolus Linnaeus, the originator of the modern scientific system of classifying and naming organisms, first put forward the definition of the mammalian order **Primates** in the 10th edition of his great work *Systema Naturae* (1758). He characterized primates as possessing several distinctive anatomical features, including (1) four cutting teeth, or **incisors,** at the front of the jaw; (2) two collarbones, or **clavicles;** (3) two mammary glands, or **mammae,** on the chest; and (4) at least two grasping, or **prehensile,** extremities that function as hands in the sense of being able to grasp objects by means of an opposable first digit. He divided the order into four genera, to which he gave the Latin names *Homo, Simia, Lemur,* and *Vespertilio.* Within *Homo* he distinguished between *Homo diurnus* (which included European, Native American, Asian, and African humans) and *Homo nocturnus* (the orangutan) (Cela-Conde and Ayala, 2003). *Simia* included monkeys and the rest of the apes, *Lemur* included lemurs and other "lower," less human-like forms, and *Vespertilio* included various species of bats.

Linnaeus's taxonomic lumping together of humans and apes did not meet with universal approval and a succession of eighteenth- and nineteenth-century comparative anatomists devoted much effort and ingenuity to devising anatomical and behavioral criteria that could convincingly distinguish the two groups. They pointed not only to measurable anatomical characters, such as bone structure and dentition, but also to such qualitative traits as the human capacity for speech, reason, and what were called other "higher" brain functions (McCown and Kennedy, 1972; Owen, 1858). None of their alternative classification schemes made much headway, however, and the Linnaean formulation stood more or less unchanged for more than a century.

The true evolutionary link between apes and humans finally received scientific validity in the mid-nineteenth century through the writings of Charles Darwin and Thomas Huxley, among others. Having established the general principles of his theory of natural selection in *The Origin of Species* (1859), Darwin went on to apply them specifically to the question of human evolution in *The Descent of Man* (1871). He wrote:

> It is notorious that man is constructed on the same generalized type or model with the other mammals. All the bones in his skeleton can be compared with the corresponding bones in a monkey, bat or seal. So it is with his muscles, nerves, blood vessels and internal viscera. The brain, the most important of all the organs, follows the same law. . . . It is, in short, scarcely possible to exaggerate the close correspondence in general structure, in the minute structure of tissues, in chemical composition and in constitution, between man and the higher animals, especially the anthropomorphous apes.

Darwin even speculated on the likely geographic region where the human species most likely emerged. He noted that

> in each great region of the world the living mammals are closely related to the extinct species of the same region. It is therefore probable that Africa was formerly inhabited by extinct apes closely allied to the gorilla and chimpanzee; and as these two species are now man's closest allies, it is somewhat more probable that our early progenitors lived on the African continent than elsewhere.

The first significant post-Darwinian modification of the Linnaean system of primate classification was proposed in 1873 by the English anatomist St. George Mivart. Removing bats and colugos ("flying lemurs") from the order, he reorganized the remaining members into two suborders: the primitive **Prosimii,** or "premonkeys" (lemurs, lorises, and the like), and the more advanced **Anthropoidea** (monkeys, apes, and humans). He also proposed an expanded list of traits to further distinguish primates from other mammals. Primates, he wrote, were

> unguiculate [having nails or claws], claviculate [having clavicles], placental mammals, with orbits [eye sockets] encircled by bone, three kinds of teeth [incisors, canines, and molars], at least at one time of life; brain always with a posterior lobe and a calcarine fissure [a transverse groove along the medial surface of that lobe]; the innermost digit of at least one pair of extremities opposable; hallux [big toe] with a flat nail or none; a well-developed caecum [a pouchlike part of the large intestine]; penis pendulous; testes scrotal; always two pectoral mammae.

Although none of these characters, it turns out, are peculiar to primates, their *combination* has long been accepted as diagnostic of the order.

An alternative approach to the problem of defining the primates, advocated chiefly by the English anatomist Sir Wilfred Le Gros Clark (1959) nearly a half century ago, sought to characterize the order in terms of a complex of evolutionary *trends* rather than a simple listing of morphological traits. According to this view, the distinctive evolutionary trends that set the early primates apart from other placental mammals included progressive enlargement of the brain, convergence of the axes of vision, shortening of the snout, atrophy of the olfactory sense, prolongation of the postnatal growth period, and specializations of the extremities for grasping. Most of these trends, it was thought, were related to a tree-living, or **arboreal,** way of life.

More recently, a much more elaborate definition of the living primates has been proposed that takes into account such diverse factors as geographic distribution, habitat, means of locomotion, influence of major sense organs on the shape of the **cranium,** relative brain size, reproductive biology, and dental patterns (Martin, 1986). For example, living primates are typically arboreal animals living mainly in tropical and subtropical ecosystems (there are some obvious exceptions, such as the more savanna-dwelling baboons of Africa and the temperate forest-dwelling macaques of Asia). Anatomical features of the hands and feet, the **manus** and **pes,** respectively, are adapted for prehension (grasping). This is clearly evidenced in the foot by the widely divergent big toe, or **hallux,** in all primates except humans. In addition, the digits have nails instead of claws, which serve as supportive structures for the tactile cutaneous ridges on the fingertips that reduce slippage on arboreal supports.

In all modern primates the visual sense is emphasized over the olfactory sense. For this reason the eyes are usually relatively large and are protected either by a **postorbital bar** (typical of lemurs and lorises) or by a complete bony cup, a condition referred to as **postorbital closure** (typical of monkeys, apes, and humans). The emphasis on vision has other anatomical consequences. For example, the orbits have become enlarged and have moved from a more lateral-facing to a more forward-facing position in the cranium. This feature is associated with **binocular vision,** by which both eyes focus on the target object and thereby allow it to be perceived with greater depth perception (Fig. 1.1).

Compared with most other mammals the primate brain is enlarged relative to body size. Indeed, primates are unique among living mammals in that the brain constitutes a significantly larger proportion of body weight at all stages of gestation. Modern primates have long gestation periods relative to maternal body size, and both fetal and postnatal growth is characteristically slow in relation to maternal size. Consequently, sexual maturation is attained late, and life spans are correspondingly long relative to body size. In sum, it takes longer for modern primate populations to reproduce themselves than is the case for populations of most other mammals (Martin, 1986).

In many respects, what distinguishes humans from other primates is simply an extension of what distinguishes primates from other mammals.

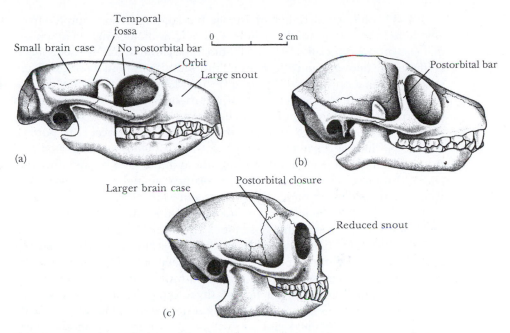

Fig. 1.1. Several morphological features distinguishing modern primate and non-primate skulls. (a) Insectivoran (hedgehog); (b) prosimian (*Lepilemur*); (c) New World monkey (*Callithrix*). Note the relative sizes of the brain and snout, development of the postorbital bar and postorbital closure, and position of the eye sockets. (Conroy, 1990.)

For example, the trends noted above toward increased brain size, delayed maturational periods, and specializations of the hand for object manipulation reach their most extreme development in modern humans.

Harvard anthropologist David Pilbeam (1992) nicely summarized some of the features that distinguish humans from other primates, in other words, some of the things that "make us human." For example, he notes that in terms of population size and distribution and genetic structure modern human populations are found in virtually every environment on the planet, far exceeding the tropical and subtropical ranges characteristic of most nonhuman primate populations. Humans can accomplish this enormous range extension only because we, in a sense, provide our own microenvironments wherever we go (e.g., clothes, shelters, and climate-control contraptions like furnaces and air-conditioners).

Compared to other primates, humans are a genetically uniform species, with most of our genetic variation occurring within single populations (so-called within-group diversity as opposed to between-group diversity), so much so that even if all human populations were to disappear except one, about three quarters of the world's total human genetic diversity would still be preserved (Lewontin, 1972).

It has been calculated that an average human population sampled from anywhere in the world would include 85% of all human variation at autosomal (i.e., nonsex) loci and 81% of all human variation in mtDNA sequences. Differences among populations from the same continent contribute another 6% variation; only 9–13% of genetic variation differentiates populations from different continents. As far as variation in the Y chromosome is concerned, an average population includes only 36% of the world's Y chromosome variation; most Y chromosome variation (53%) occurs in populations from different continents. Since mtDNA is maternally inherited and the Y chromosome paternally inherited, these differences between mtDNA and Y chromosome patterns are best explained by higher migration rates among females than among males (Owens and King, 1999).

One method commonly used to quantify within-to-among population genetic diversity is through the F_{st} statistic. This statistic ranges from 0 to 1, where 0 indicates that all the genetic diversity within a species is shared equally by all populations and there are no genetic differences among populations and 1 indicates that all genetic diversity within a species is fixed among populations and there is no genetic diversity within populations. This statistic in human populations is about 0.156, indicating that most human genetic diversity exists as differences among individuals within populations. Major human "races" differ genetically by only about 15% (Templeton, 1999).

We are also distinguished from most other primates by our feeding habits. Whereas most nonhuman primates have fairly restricted or specialized dietary preferences (e.g., fruit eating, or frugivory; leaf eating, or folivory; insect eating, or insectivory), human populations are eclectic in their feeding preferences, selecting from almost every type of plant and animal food available. As we shall see in later chapters, the type of foods our ancestors ate, and the way they procured and processed those foods, had a tremendous influence on human evolution. Many features of our ancestor's cranial and dental anatomy directly reflect the types of stresses generated by powerful chewing (masticatory) muscles (Fig. 1.2a). In addition, the development of increasingly sophisticated tool technologies beginning about 2.5 million years ago has clearly been influenced by food procurement strategies throughout much of human evolution. Indeed, probably the most distinctive feature of modern humans compared to other primates is our now complete reliance on material culture (i.e., tools) for survival.

Fig. 1.2. There are many anatomical and behavioral distinctions between humans and other primates.   (a) The size and shape of the human cranium have changed dramatically over the past 4 million years. Most of these changes relate to (1) the gradual reduction in the size of the teeth, jaws, and chewing muscles and (2) the threefold increase in brain size. (b) Adaptations of the pelvis and lower limbs for bipedal walking are another one of the major anatomical distinctions between humans and other primates. In this model of *Australopithecus afarensis* (dated to over 3 mya), many of these unique adaptations were already well under way. (Photos courtesy of David Brill. Weaver, 1985.)

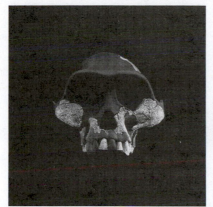

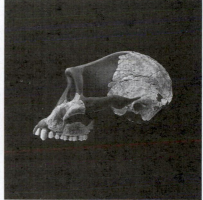

Australopithecus afarensis (composite specimen)

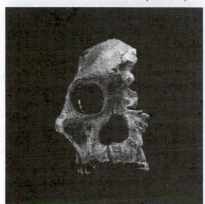

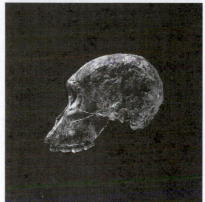

Australopithecus africanus (Sts 71)

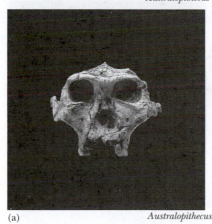

(a)　　　　　　*Australopithecus robustus* (SK 48)

(Continued)

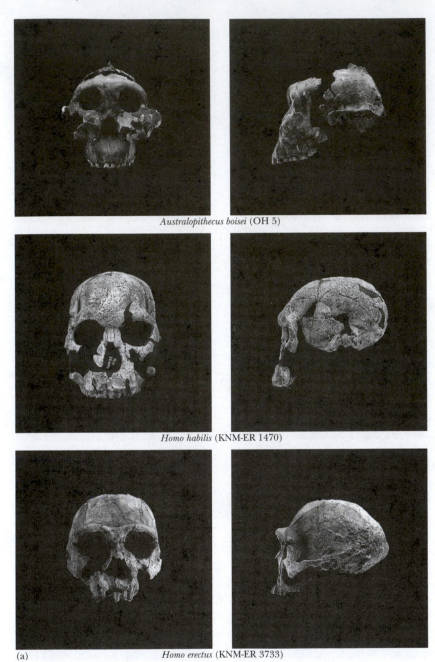

Australopithecus boisei (OH 5)

Homo habilis (KNM-ER 1470)

(a)   *Homo erectus* (KNM-ER 3733)

Fig. 1.2.   *(Continued)*

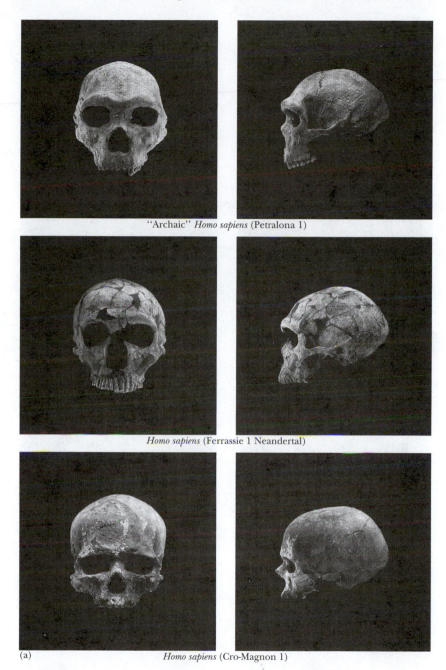

"Archaic" *Homo sapiens* (Petralona 1)

Homo sapiens (Ferrassie 1 Neandertal)

(a)

Homo sapiens (Cro-Magnon 1)

Fig. 1.2. *(Continued)*

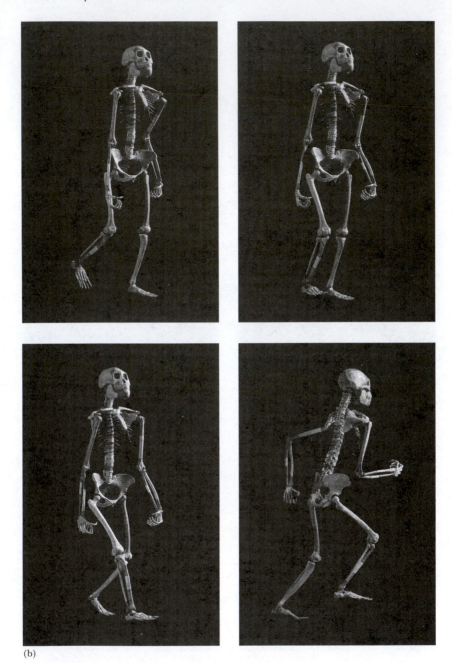

(b)

Fig. 1.2.   *(Continued)*

Box 1.1 Some Features Characterizing Living Primates That (in General) Distinguish Them from Other Mammals

1. Lifestyle is typically arboreal; range is mainly restricted to tropical and subtropical forest ecosystems.
2. Extremities are adapted for prehension; sensitive tactile pads are present on the digits.
3. Locomotion is hindlimb dominated, with the center of gravity of the body located closer to the hindlimbs.
4. The visual sense is greatly emphasized, and the olfactory sense is reduced.
5. The bony housing for the middle ear is formed by a separate bone called the petrosal bone.
6. The brain is moderately enlarged relative to body size (at all stages of gestation) and has a true lateral, or Sylvian, sulcus separating the frontal and parietal lobes from the temporal lobe and a triradiate calcarine sulcus.
7. Males are characterized by early descent of the testes into a scrotal sac.
8. Gestation periods are long relative to maternal body size, and small litters of precocial neonates (i.e., infants born with at least a moderate covering of hair and both ears and eyes open at birth) are produced.
9. Both fetal and postnatal growth are characteristically slow in relation to maternal size; sexual maturity is attained late, and life spans are correspondingly long relative to body size (i.e., reproductive turnover is slow).
10. The dental formula exhibits a maximum of two incisors, one canine, three premolars, and three molars in each quadrant of the upper and lower jaws.

SOURCE: Martin (1986).

The unique skeletal adaptations distinguishing humans from other primates are those of the pelvis and lower limb that permit our unusual type of locomotion, bipedalism (Fig. 1.2b). The reason(s) for the origin of bipedalism remain one of the intriguing mysteries of human evolution, and we will discuss it fully in later chapters. For now, let us just note that bipedalism frees the hands from the locomotor functions that characterize all other primates, thereby allowing the hands to be used in other critical roles such as making tools, holding infants, and gathering food.

As noted above, a number of life history variables distinguish humans from other primates. Modern humans have long gestation periods relative to maternal body size as well as prolonged periods of infant dependency. Sexual maturation occurs relatively late and life spans are correspondingly long. Therefore, compared to other primates, human females have a much longer postreproductive phase to their life cycle. Unlike other primates that usually have peak periods of sexual receptivity, or **estrus,** human females remain receptive throughout the duration of their monthly reproductive cycle.

Finally, one of humanity's most distinguishing characteristics is the evolution of language and the type of symbolic thinking associated with it. Without language, much of our social behavior and interactions would be impossible. The evolution of articulate human speech involved major structural reorganization in both the brain and the laryngeal apparatus (i.e., the voice box). As Pilbeam (1992) notes, language "makes possible sharing, exploitation and the delay of reward or punishment; the structuring of relationships; propaganda; art; the division of labour; warfare; and the aggregation and socialisation of masses of people. Its most essential feature is that it allows human behavior to be governed by the complex and subtle rules that together make up human culture."

BASIC PRIMATE MORPHOLOGY

Virtually all human fossil material studied by paleoanthropologists consists of cranial, dental, and/or postcranial (skeletal) remains. For this reason, interpretation of the human fossil record necessarily demands a basic understanding of primate morphology (particularly skeletal biology) and odontology. To better prepare the reader for discussions of the fossil record that follow in later chapters, we begin by reviewing some basic aspects of primate cranial, dental, and skeletal anatomy. Many of the items mentioned in this brief overview will be more fully discussed in later chapters when they become relevant to interpretations of the fossil evidence.

Cranial Morphology

The primate cranium[1] serves a number of critical functions: it houses and protects the brain and special sense organs such as those of hearing, vision, and smell; it forms the anchoring structure for the upper dentition; and it provides the bony surface attachment area for both the chewing (masticatory) muscles and the muscles of facial expression. The main osteological features of the ape and human cranium are compared in Figure 1.3 and the main osteological landmarks of the human mandible are identified in Figure 1.4.

[1]By definition, the anatomical term *skull* refers to a specimen containing both the cranium and the lower jaw, or mandible; the term *cranium* refers to the skull without the mandible; and the term *calvaria* refers to the domelike roof of the cranium, or "skullcap." The term **calotte** is sometimes used for *skullcap*. The term *calvarium* is an incorrect term for *calvaria*.

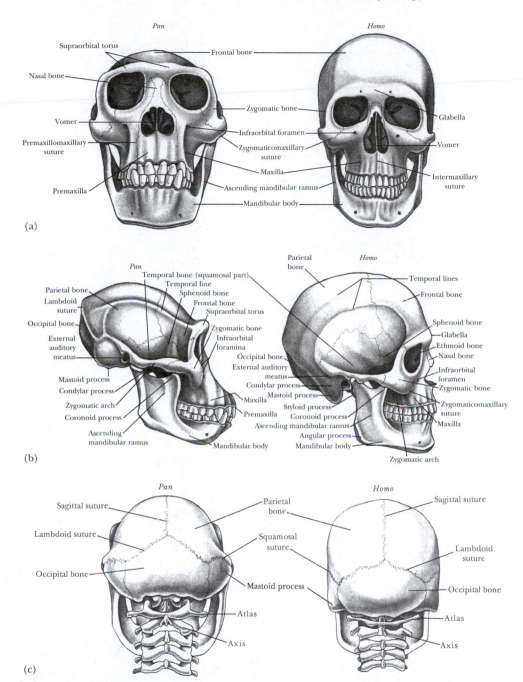

Fig. 1.3. Comparison of the skull in chimpanzees (*left*) and modern humans (*right*), with the major bones and bony landmarks identified. (a) Frontal view. (b) Lateral view. (c) Posterior view. (d) Basal or occlusal view.

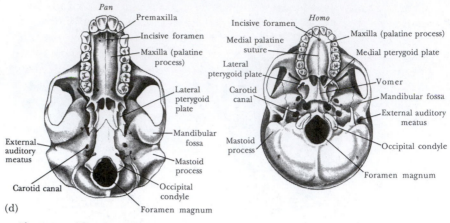

Pan

Premaxilla

Incisive foramen

Maxilla (palatine process)

Lateral pterygoid plate

Mandibular fossa

External auditory meatus

Carotid canal

Mastoid process

Occipital condyle

Foramen magnum

(d)

Homo

Incisive foramen

Maxilla (palatine process)

Medial palatine suture

Medial pterygoid plate

Lateral pterygoid plate

Carotid canal

Vomer

Mandibular fossa

External auditory meatus

Mastoid process

Occipital condyle

Foramen magnum

Fig. 1.3.   *(Continued)*

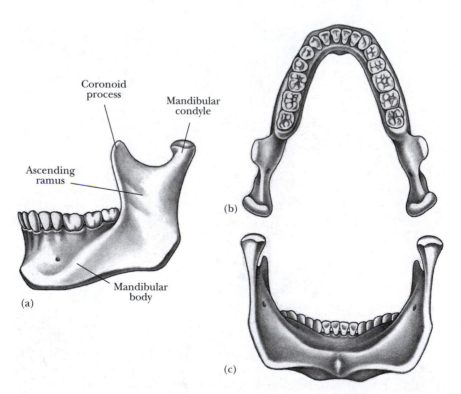

Coronoid process

Mandibular condyle

Ascending ramus

Mandibular body

(a)

(b)

(c)

Fig. 1.4.   Important bony landmarks of the human mandible.   (a) Lateral view. (b) Occlusal view. (c) Posterior view.

To a large extent, the overall shape of the cranium in various primates reflects the relative degree of enlargement or specialization of these various functions. For example, primates that rely more on the sense of smell, or olfaction, tend to have longer snouts than those that rely more on vision. Likewise, those primates with well-developed chewing muscles often have accentuated bony crests or muscular markings on the cranium, for instance temporal lines or sagittal crests marking the origin of the temporalis muscle, that serve as sites of attachment for those powerful muscles.

Posture, or how the head is carried on top of the vertebral column, may also affect cranial morphology. For example, the hole at the base of the cranium for passage of the spinal cord, the **foramen magnum,** tends to face more inferiorly than posteriorly in primates that routinely hold their trunk more erect in both resting and locomotor postures. There are, however, other factors affecting the relative position of the foramen magnum. In humans such factors may include (1) the relatively large degree of cranial base flexion that brings the face to a position below, rather than in front of, the brain case and (2) the relative enlargement of the **occipital lobes** of the brain that results from an expansion of the visual cortex of the cerebral cortex.

The thin bones forming the roof of the cranium, the **calvaria,** consist of the frontal bone anteriorly, the occipital bone posteriorly, and the parietal, temporal, and sphenoid bones laterally. These bones are joined to one another by fibrous joints called **sutures.** All of the upper teeth are housed in the maxilla except for the incisors, which are housed in the premaxilla. All the lower teeth are contained in the mandible.

Dental Morphology

The dentition is one of the most informative parts of the human body as far as paleoanthropologists are concerned. Of all the skeletal elements teeth are the most resistant to biological, chemical, and/or physical destruction and, therefore, are generally the most common skeletal element found in fossil assemblages. The important clues about past and present human adaptations provided by the dentition pertain to diet, age, sex, health, and phylogenetic relationships.

A major characteristic of the human dentition is that our teeth are regionally differentiated to serve special functions, a condition known as **heterodonty.** Thus, on each side of the upper and lower jaws, starting at the front, are two teeth adapted for cutting and cropping, the **incisors,** followed by a single-pointed, tusk-like tooth, the **canine,** which in turn is followed by the postcanine dentition consisting of two **premolars** and three **molars,** teeth whose complex chewing surfaces are adapted for grinding and crushing. Therefore, all adult fossil and modern humans normally have 8 teeth in each quadrant of the upper and lower jaws, giving a total of

32. A shorthand way to write the **dental formula** for humans is 2.1.2.3. Teeth in the upper and lower jaws are usually identified with superscripts and subscripts, respectively. For example LM^1 is shorthand for a left upper first molar, whereas RM_1 is shorthand for a right lower first molar. One point of potential confusion is that the two premolars in each quadrant of the upper and lower jaws are usually referred to as the third and fourth premolars (P3 and P4) and not as the first and second premolars as one might expect. Actually, there is a good evolutionary reason for this terminology; more ancient primates once had four premolars in each quadrant, but during the course of primate evolution the ancestors of higher primates, including humans, lost the first and second premolars. Thus the two remaining premolars are actually premolars three and four of the original set of four.

The adult dentition is preceded by the milk, or **deciduous,** dentition consisting of two incisors, one canine, and two premolars, sometimes referred to as "milk molars," in each quadrant. The three permanent adult molars are not preceded by any deciduous teeth. Shorthand notation for the deciduous dentition would be, for example, Rdi_2 and Ldm^1 for the right deciduous lower second incisor and left deciduous upper first molar, respectively.

The proper anatomical orientation is very important when referring to teeth. A crown, or **occlusal,** view refers to the chewing surface of the tooth. The **buccal** side of the tooth faces laterally toward the cheek and the **lingual** side of the tooth faces medially toward the tongue. The side of the tooth facing the front of the mouth is the **mesial** surface, and the side facing the back of the jaw is the **distal** surface. These orientations are labeled in Figures 1.5 and 1.6.

Teeth consist of two main parts: crowns and root(s). The crowns project into the oral cavity and the roots are anchored in the bony socket, or **alveolus,** of the mandible or maxilla. The crowns are covered by an avascular layer of mineralized tissue called **enamel** (Fig. 1.5). Enamel is the hardest biological structure in the human body. Roots are covered by a thin bone-like layer, the **cementum.** Beneath these surface layers, and forming much of the tooth's bulk, is another very resilient connective tissue, the **dentine.** Dentine differs from enamel in that it is not as highly mineralized a tissue (approximately 70% versus 97% mineralization by weight). The **pulp cavity** is the neurovascular space deep to the dentine that extends for a variable distance into the roots.

In humans the incisors are relatively simple, single-rooted teeth having a somewhat spatulate crown. The single-rooted canine is still a somewhat pointed, tusk-like tooth, but it is not the long, sharp weapon that it is in some other primates like baboons. Functionally, the human canine has become more incorporated into the incisor tooth row. Humans use these teeth in diverse ways, from cutting and cropping foods to holding objects.

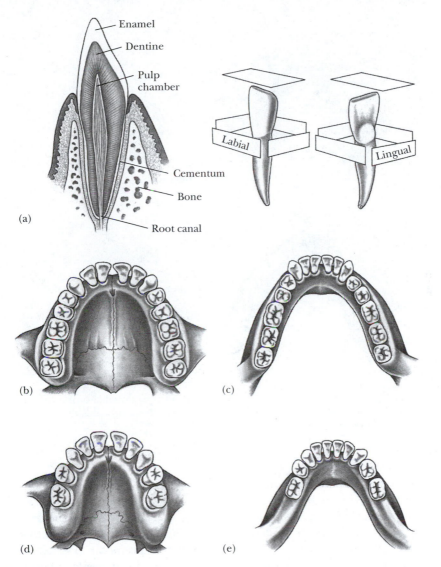

Fig. 1.5. (a) Cross section through a human incisor tooth to show the different tissues (*left*) and its proper orientation (*right*). (b) Occlusal view of the upper permanent dentition. (c) Occlusal view of the lower permanent dentition. (d) Occlusal view of the upper deciduous dentition. (e) Occlusal view of the lower deciduous dentition.

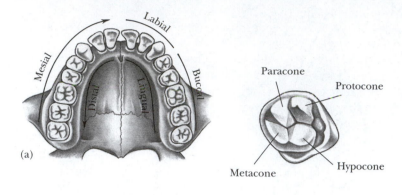

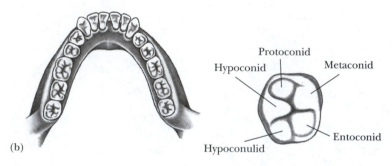

Fig. 1.6. (a) Occlusal view of the upper dentition plus detail showing the major cusps of the right M^1. (b) Occlusal view of the lower dentition plus detail showing the major cusps of the left M_1.

The premolars may have one or more roots and are also relatively simple teeth having two main cusps, which is why they are sometimes referred to as **bicuspids.** There is often a thickened ring of enamel around the base of the tooth, called the **cingulum.** In some primates with large, stabbing upper canines like baboons, the anterior lower premolar (P_3) acts as a honing stone to sharpen the posterior edge of the upper canine every time the two teeth come into contact. Such an adaptation is referred to as a **sectorial** premolar. The loss of the honing C/P_3 complex is a characteristic of hominins, in contrast to other primates, and evolved very early in human evolution.

The upper molars of humans have four main cusps: **protocone, paracone, metacone,** and **hypocone.** Looking at the occlusal surface of an upper molar, the protocone is the main cusp on the mesiolingual side, the paracone is the main cusp on the mesiobuccal side, the metacone is the main cusp on the distobuccal side, and the hypocone is the main cusp on the distolingual side (Fig. 1.6). Enamel crests often connect the main cusps; these crests are adaptations for slicing food between the molars during occlusion.

The lower molars of humans consist of two parts: an anterior portion, the **trigonid,** and a posterior, heel-like projection, the **talonid.** The three main cusps of the trigonid are the mirror image of the cusps of the upper molar trigone: the **protoconid** on the buccal side and the **paraconid** (which is usually absent in higher primates, including humans) and **metaconid** on the lingual side. Note that the names of the lower molar cusps end in *-conid,* whereas those of the upper molars end in *-cone.* The talonid is usually a basin-like structure surrounded by a raised enamel rim with two main cusps: the **hypoconid** buccally and the **entoconid** lingually. Often there is an additional cusp, the **hypoconulid,** toward the middle of the distal margin of the rim, which can be well developed on lower third molars. During chewing, the protocones of the upper molars fit into the talonid basins of the corresponding lower molars, like the action of a pestle in a mortar.

Postcranial Morphology

The postcranial skeleton is composed of an **axial skeleton,** consisting of those bones forming the central axis of the body (including the vertebrae, sacrum, ribs, and sternum) and an **appendicular skeleton,** consisting of those bones making up the upper and lower limbs (including their respective limb girdles). The postcranial skeleton provides the overall scaffolding that holds up the body as well as the site of attachment for the muscles that move the body. The skeleton acts as a system of levers that facilitate, indeed make possible, movement powered by muscles.

In many respects, the primate skeleton retains many basic mammalian postcranial features. For example, primates, including humans, retain five fingers and toes; a relatively mobile shoulder joint for free movement of the upper limb in all directions; grasping, or prehensile, capability in both hands and (in nonhuman primates) feet; a well-developed collarbone, or clavicle; and completely separate bones of the forearm (radius and ulna) and leg (tibia and fibula).

Primates also have developed highly sensitive friction pads on the hands and feet, and in most modern primates the distal finger and toe bones, or phalanges, are covered by flattened nails instead of sharp, curved claws. These nails and friction pads provide an efficient mechanism for both grasping and manipulating objects.

The skeleton of humans and apes consists of the same basic bony elements, although the size and shape of many of these bones, of course, vary, depending on the different functional demands placed on them (Fig. 1.7).

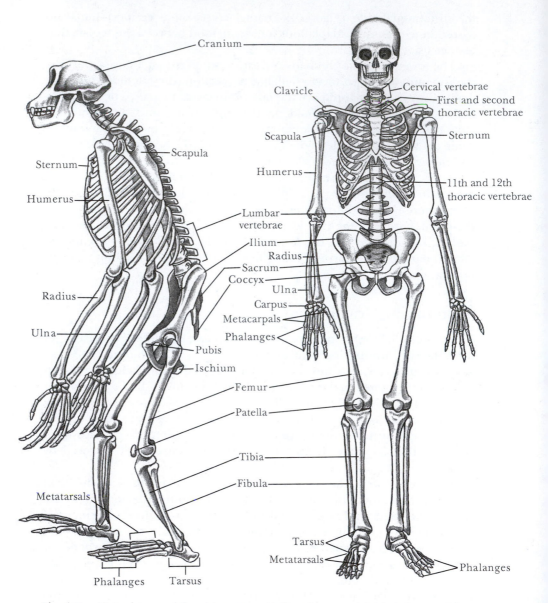

Fig. 1.7. Major bones of the chimpanzee (*left*) and human (*right*) skeleton. Note in the human that the right hand is pronated (palm facing backward), whereas the left hand is supinated (palm facing forward).

These differences are particularly marked in the parts of the skeleton related to locomotion (e.g., the pelvis and lower limb), brain size (e.g., cranial size and shape), and masticatory stresses (e.g., dental size and shape, cranial crests). We will be discussing each of these in much greater detail in later chapters as they pertain to the fossil evidence for human evolution.

CHAPTER II

The Plio-Pleistocene World

RECONSTRUCTING THE PLIO-PLEISTOCENE WORLD

Darwin realized around 150 years ago that organisms evolve adaptations to better suit them to their habitats, including both the plants and the animals they eat and the climates they inhabit. Perhaps nothing sums up this Darwinian world better than this line from Stephen Sondheim's musical *Sweeney Todd, the Demon Barber of Fleet Street* (1979) "The history of the world, my sweet, is who gets eaten and who gets to eat."

Primates, the mammalian order to which humans belong, have been evolving over the past 70–90 million years or so of earth history. The interval of geologic time over which most of this process has taken place, the **Cenozoic Era,** began about 65 mya and is subdivided into the Paleocene, Eocene, Oligocene, Miocene, Pliocene, and Pleistocene **epochs** (Fig. 2.1). The last 10,000 years are sometimes considered a separate epoch, the Holocene. The Quaternary is the most recent period of the Cenozoic Era, comprising the Pleistocene and the Holocene. The story of human evolution mainly unfolds over the last two of these epochs, the 5 million years or so collectively referred to as the Plio-Pleistocene.

The major divisions of earth history that we recognize today—eras, epochs, and others—derive from the work of early geologists who had no way of determining the actual ages of the different rocks they studied. Instead, geological divisions were defined either by the kinds of fossilized animals found in the rocks or by evidence of major climatic changes. For example, the name of the last epoch of the Cenozoic Era, the Pleistocene (meaning "most recent"), was introduced by Sir Charles Lyell in 1839 to describe those sediments in which 70% or more of the molluscan fauna consisted of extant, or living, species. Soon thereafter, however, other mid-nineteenth-century geologists began the misleading practice of equating the Pleistocene with the "glacial period," a concept that developed out of

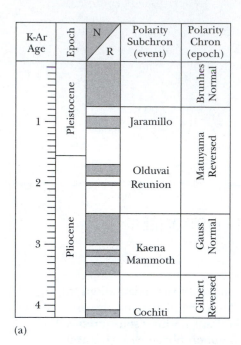

Fig. 2.1. The paleomagnetic chronology of human evolution over the Plio-Pleistocene.   The Earth's geomagnetic field is known to have gone through a series of complete reversals in its polarity. At various times in the geologic past, its magnetic field has been directed, as it is today, toward the north (normal polarity) and at other times toward the south (reversed polarity). Short-term magnetic reversals of opposite polarity within each paleomagnetic "epoch" are called "events." In (a), the normal magnetic polarity epochs and events are shaded; reversed magnetic epochs and events are white. Shown expanded in (b) are the Alpine glacial sequences and corresponding temperatures over the past 500,000 years (see text and Table 2.2). (F. Brown, 1992.)

an emerging **Glacial Theory** that held that extensive glaciers had formerly covered much of the Northern Hemisphere. Thus began the era of defining the Pleistocene and its subdivisions on the basis of glacial stratigraphy rather than on Lyell's original faunal concept.

EVIDENCE OF CLIMATIC CHANGE FROM GLACIAL STRATIGRAPHY

The Pleistocene was, in fact, a time of highly variable global climate and is characterized by abundant geological evidence of alternating periods of glacial ice advances, or **glacial periods,** and retreats, or **interglacial periods.**

Irregular but well-defined episodes of somewhat milder climatic conditions occurring during glacial periods, so-called **interstadials,** are also known from this epoch. It has been discovered from analyses of ice cores drilled in central Greenland that extreme climatic instability characterized both interglacial and glacial periods, with abrupt climatic changes beginning rapidly and lasting in some cases from only decades to centuries (Anklin et al., 1993; Dansgaard et al., 1993; Field et al., 1994; Grootes et al., 1993; Kotilainen and Shackleton, 1995; Taylor et al., 1993; Weaver and Hughes, 1994). In addition, pollen samples from southern Europe during the last glacial period show that numerous vegetation changes (e.g., from forest or wooded steppe biomes to steppe biomes and vice versa) were incredibly rapid, frequently occurring in less than 200 years (Allen et al., 1999).

Glacial periods were about 7°C colder than interstadial periods, and 12–13°C colder than present temperatures (Johnsen et al., 1992). It is interesting that deep-sea sediments of Middle Pleistocene age dating from 400 to 300 kya, the time of the so-called mid-Brunhes climatic event, reveal a transition to more humid or "interglacial" conditions in equatorial Africa while more "glacial" ocean conditions were prevailing in the Northern Hemisphere, thereby suggesting that global climatic changes sometimes had opposite effects in the two hemispheres (Jansen et al., 1986). For example, from November 1978 through December 1996, the areal extent of sea ice decreased by about 2.9% per decade in the Arctic but increased by about 1.3% per decade in the Antarctic (Cavalieri et al., 1997). In addition, climatic changes occurred on average some 1000–2500 years earlier in the Antarctic than in Greenland—at least during the last major glacial cycle (Blunier et al., 1998).

Glacial periods had a significant climatic impact even on geographical regions at low altitudes far removed from the glaciers themselves. Evidence from the continental interior of Australia indicates that average air temperatures dropped by at least 9°C between 45 and 16 kya during the last glacial maximum (LGM). It is hypothesized that this cooling may have been induced by reduction in atmospheric water vapor content during this glacial maximum (G. Miller et al., 1997). The LGM has also been correlated to times of peak Late Quaternary aridity, when desert systems expanded up to five times their present extent (Stokes et al., 1997).

Alternating episodes of glacial advance and retreat profoundly affected worldwide sea levels, with glacial advances leading to lowered sea levels as seawater was increasingly locked up in the ice sheets, and glacial retreats leading to elevated levels as seawater was increasingly released from melting ice sheets (Shackleton, 1987). During Pleistocene glacial ages, the total area covered by glaciers was up to three times as great as today, and many glaciers were 2–3 km thick. The total volume of water contained in glaciers outside Greenland and Antarctica is not known precisely, but it is probably equivalent to a sea level rise between about 0.3 and 0.7 m. The global sea level has risen some 10–20 cm over the last century as mountain glaciers have retreated in most parts of the world. Modeling of modern glaciers suggests that the area-weighted glacier mass balance will decrease

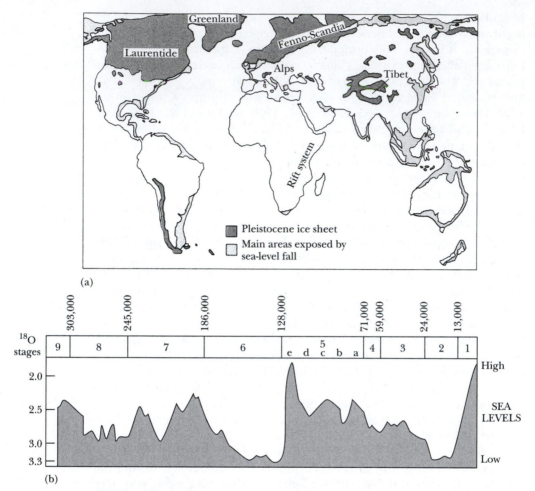

(a)

(b)

Fig. 2.2.   (a) During the last Ice Age, glacial ice covered extensive areas of the Northern Hemisphere, causing sea levels to fall by more than 100 m. This lowering of the sea level dramatically changed coastlines worldwide by exposing shallow continental shelves. (Adapted from Roberts, 1992.) (b) Variations in ice and sea levels over the past 300,000 years are recorded in this ^{18}O record. The last interglacial (isotopic stage 5e) is notable for its high sea level. Conversely, low sea levels (indicating maximum glacial conditions) are seen in stages 2 and 6, especially. (Stringer and Gamble, 1993.) (c) Representation of the vegetation during an interglacial and during a glacial period, in a north–south section through Europe. (Van der Hamman et al., 1971.)

by 0.40 m per year for every 1° K warming, which corresponds to a sea level rise of 0.58 mm per year (Oerlemans and Fortuin, 1992). Of course, as sea levels dropped, more of the continental shelf became exposed and more land corridors were opened up for migrating animals, including early humans. It is estimated that sea levels may have fallen by as much as 100–140 m during glacial periods and risen by as much as 20 m above present-day lev-

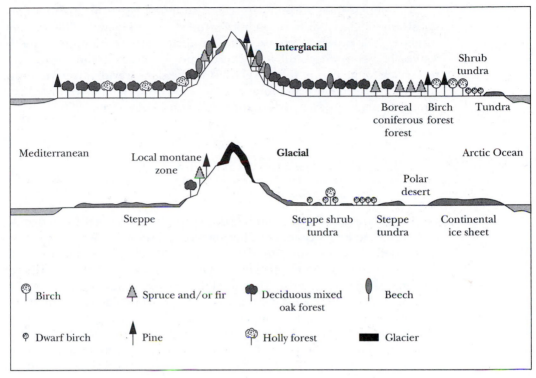

Interglacial

Shrub
tundra

Boreal   Birch   Tundra
coniferous forest
forest

Mediterranean   Local montane   Glacial   Arctic Ocean
                        zone

                                                        Polar
                                                        desert

Steppe   Steppe shrub   Steppe   Continental
                                        tundra   tundra   ice sheet

⚇ Birch   ▲ Spruce and/or fir   ● Deciduous mixed   ▮ Beech
                                                   oak forest

☿ Dwarf birch   ▮ Pine   ⚇ Holly forest   ▰ Glacier

(c)

els during interglacial periods (Bard et al., 1990a; Flint, 1971; Richards et al., 1994; Rohling et al., 1998) (Fig. 2.2).

Simply put, glacial ice accumulates whenever snow has not had time to completely melt before the next season's snow begins to accumulate. This is why, given sufficient time, glacial ice buildup can occur in places like Antarctica even though the total annual precipitation there is no greater than in the Mojave Desert.

The power of glaciers to transform the landscape is everywhere manifest, from the gouging out of vast inland lakes, such as the Great Lakes, to the hollowing out of steep cliffs and gorges on mountainsides and the scooping out of mountain valleys like Yosemite and the fjords of northern Europe. Driven by the force of gravity, glaciers leave other signs of past climatic change, including (1) characteristic striations in bedrock inscribed by rocks in the base of overriding glaciers, (2) deposits of rock material transported by glacial ice and then "dumped" by the melting ice on the land surface (**glacial drift**), (3) ridges of glacial drift built up from the material riding on the ice that delineates the melting zones along the margins and bottom of the glacier (**moraines**), and (4) extensive deposits of wind-blown glacial dust produced by the grinding down of boulders within glacial ice against bedrock (**loess**).

Sometimes when currents are calm, stratified layers in lake bottoms consisting of glacial drift, or **till,** may settle out in thin layers. These layers of glacial till, known as **varves,** reflect annual cycles of summer melt-off. Varves have proven useful in reconstructing prehistoric time scales (at least back to the end of the last glacial) in the same way that tree rings, in the science of **dendrochronology,** have been used in the southwestern United States and other parts of the world (Kuniholm et al., 1996).

SUMMARY OF PLIO-PLEISTOCENE GLACIATIONS

Geologists are continually refining the dates for the epoch immediately preceding the Pleistocene, the Pliocene. The base of the Pliocene is currently defined at its type site at Capo Rosello, Sicily, at about 5.3 mya, roughly corresponding to the Thvera/Gilbert boundary of the paleomagnetic time scale (see below). Thus the Pliocene essentially coincides to the time interval from the end of the so-called **Messinian salinity crisis** at about 5.3 mya, when sea levels dropped worldwide, producing the temporary desiccation of the Mediterranean Sea, to the base of the Lower Pleistocene at about 1.6 mya. A number of factors, including the sudden increase in global ice volume caused by the expanse of Antarctic glaciers, brought about the drastic lowering of sea levels that precipitated the Messinian crisis (Brain, 1981a, 1983; Deacon, 1983; Hodell et al., 1986; Hsu et al., 1977). The complete drying up of such a large body of water had profound biological and geological consequences. Of particular interest is the fact that the expanded dry-land connections between Africa and Europe permitted the free exchange of faunas and floras, including increased selection for annuals in the herbaceous flora of the Mediterranean region.

It now seems apparent that substantial glaciation events were already well under way in Greenland by the late Miocene, perhaps as early as 8 mya (Sugden et al., 1995). Records of ice-rafted debris in deep-sea sediments indicate the presence of substantial continental ice masses adjacent to both the North Atlantic and the Pacific Oceans as early as 5.5 mya, although major intensification of Northern Hemisphere glaciation did not begin until around 2.7 mya (Clemens and Tiedemann, 1997). There is also evidence suggesting that globally significant climatic perturbations were generating glaciers in other parts of the world at about this same time, including the Southern Hemisphere, where glaciers were probably present in Antarctica and in Patagonia (Argentina) 7–6 mya (Larsen et al., 1994).

By the middle Pliocene, about 3.5 mya, these Antarctic ice sheets had retreated in the face of somewhat warmer temperatures as sea levels rose. However, some evidence suggests that the east Antarctic ice sheet, although experiencing extensive deglaciation, may have endured for at least 4.3 million years (Barrett et al., 1992; Dowsett et al., 1992; Marchant et al., 1993).

Table 2.1   Glaciation during the Plio-Pleistocene

6.0–4.3 mya: Global ice volume fluctuated about a constant mean with an average amplitude of about 0.5%

4.3–2.8 mya: Ice volume fluctuated around a smaller mean

2.8–2.4 mya: Global ice volume began a cyclic but steady increase, culminating in an abrupt increase about 2.4 mya to a volume significantly larger than had been attained in the preceding 4 million years

2.4–2.1 mya: Global ice volume decreased steadily

2.1–0.9 mya: Global ice volume stabilized

0.9–0.7 mya: Global ice volume increased abruptly to a new maximum about 700 kya

700 kya–present: Large amplitude, approximately 100,000-year fluctuations in ice sheet volume

---

Prentice and Denton (1988).

But by about 2.5 mya the cold cycle was back and brought with it the return of lowered temperatures and advancing ice sheets (Shackleton et al., 1984). It was this cold phase for which geologists first find evidence of mountain glaciation in the western United States and Canada. These periodic swings between warmer and colder conditions continued into the later Pliocene and reached their peak in the Pleistocene. The main events leading up to and including the Plio-Pleistocene global ice volume retreats and advances are summarized in Table 2.1.

EVIDENCE OF CLIMATIC CHANGE FROM DEEP-SEA CORES

It is becoming increasingly common in modern geological work to investigate Plio-Pleistocene climates using information gleaned from deep-sea cores rather than glacial stratigraphy because deep-sea sedimentation occurs continuously, whereas continental sedimentation does not. For example, **oxygen-isotope studies** from ocean sediments indicate that there have been nearly two dozen glacial advances just within the Pleistocene, many of which would not have been picked up in the terrestrial stratigraphic record (Fig. 2.3a). Today, the powerful technique of analyzing oxygen isotope ratios in the calcareous shells of deep-sea marine organisms is increasingly used because the oxygen isotope composition of calcite reflects both ice volume and ocean temperature.

In theory at least, oxygen isotope analysis is relatively simple and is based on the fact that there are two isotopes of oxygen in ocean water: the heavier ^{18}O and the lighter ^{16}O (^{18}O being about 12.5% heavier). The differential weight of the isotopes has two useful consequences for the study of ancient environments: As ocean water evaporates into the atmosphere, more of the heavier isotope is left behind in the ocean, and the ^{18}O that does evaporate tends to precipitate out before the ^{16}O. The result is that precipitation over the interior of continents is relatively deficient in ^{18}O and relatively enriched in ^{16}O, as compared to seawater. Since the overall quantity of the two isotopes is unchanging on Earth, more of ^{16}O tends to be locked up in continental ice during glacial periods, making less available in the oceans. Over time this process leads to an increase in the $^{18}O:^{16}O$ ratio of seawater during glacial periods. For example, $^{18}O:^{16}O$ ratios from tropical Atlantic Ocean sediments indicate ocean temperatures 4°C colder than present during the LGM (Schrag et al., 1996).

Since some marine organisms incorporate oxygen when forming their calcareous shells, the $^{18}O:^{16}O$ ratios preserved in their shells reflect past ocean temperatures—the lower the temperature, the higher the ^{18}O content. Thus shells of marine organisms recovered from deep-sea sediments provide information about past ice volume *and* ocean temperatures. For this reason, oxygen isotope stratigraphy can be used to subdivide deep-sea sediments into stages of relatively high and low oxygen isotope ratios that reflect alternating cold and warm climatic cycles (Fig. 2.3b).

Analyses of carbon isotopes in marine fossils provide another independent measure of climatic change with which to cross-check results from oxygen isotope data. Increases in ocean temperature are associated with increases in atmospheric carbon dioxide: Present data indicate a 40% increase in atmospheric carbon dioxide (CO_2) since the last glacial period (Jasper and Hayes, 1990). During periods of ocean warming, the lighter isotope of carbon, ^{12}C (compared to the heavier ^{13}C), is preferentially evaporated out of the ocean and into the atmosphere as a component of carbon dioxide for the same reason as noted above for the lighter isotope of oxygen. This increase in ^{12}C concentration passes from the atmosphere to land plants as they take up the carbon dioxide and may be detectable in the teeth and bones of animals that feed on the plants (Koch et al., 1992).

It is now abundantly clear from both oceanic and terrestrial evidence that marked, progressive global cooling began in the early Eocene and culminated in the Ice Ages of the Pleistocene. For example, atmospheric CO_2 concentrations can be inferred from the size of fossil leaf **stomata,** the minute

Fig. 2.3. (a) The Pleistocene oxygen isotope column as recorded in a deep-sea core from the Pacific Ocean. Note how the amount of ^{18}O isotope varies with the depth of the core. At the 1200-cm level, the sediments show a change in magnetic polarity that is dated by radiometric means to about 780 kya. The variation in ^{18}O (e.g., $-0.5‰$, $-1.0‰$) represents changes in the average $^{18}O:^{16}O$ ratio found in bottom-living foraminifera (the ratio increases, i.e., approaches $-0.5‰$ during glacial periods and decreases, i.e., approaches $-2.0‰$ during interglacial periods). (Stringer and Gamble, 1993). (b) The respective enrichments and depletions of oxygen isotopes 18 and 16 during glacial and interglacial cycles. (Dawson, 1992).

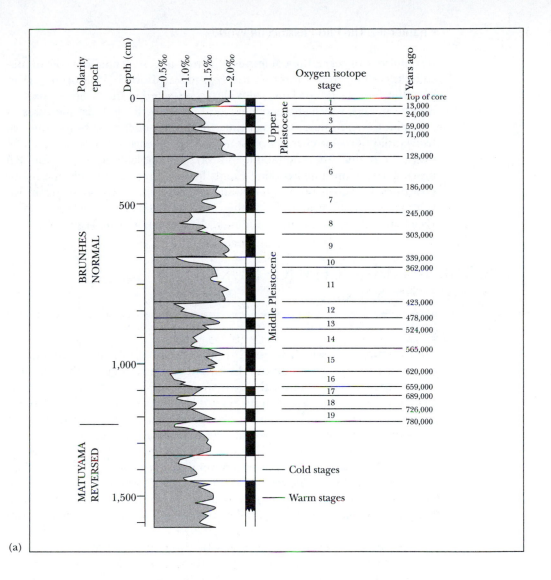

(a)

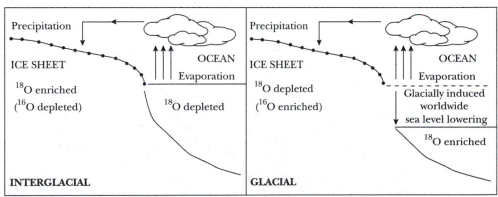

(b)

33

respiratory orifices in the epidermis of leaves, and such studies show unmistakable cooling trends through the **Neogene** (Miocene–Pleistocene) (Van Der Burgh et al., 1993). This is also clearly reflected in the Cenozoic oxygen isotope record, which shows unequivocal evidence for gradual increases in ^{18}O values (i.e., cooling) through time that were punctuated by several relatively rapid ^{18}O value changes, most notably in the early Oligocene (about 36 mya), the middle Miocene (about 14 mya), and the late Pliocene (about 2.5 mya). These more rapid cooling events likely correlate with the first major growth of ice sheets on Antarctica and further subsequent increases in ice volume in Antarctica and in the Northern Hemisphere, respectively (Buchardt, 1978; Raymo and Ruddiman, 1992; Zachos et al., 1992, 1997).

CAUSES OF CLIMATIC CHANGE DURING THE PLIO-PLEISTOCENE

For over a century scientists have hypothesized about the forces that drove these Late Cenozoic cooling trends. Ample evidence suggests that patterns of the Earth's orbit around the Sun were a major factor affecting Pleistocene climates. The Pleistocene record shows that there were about 15 major and 50 minor cold advances over the past 1.5 million years, or about 1 major cold advance every 100,000 years. Virtually all models of the orbital (Milankovitch) hypothesis of climatic change hold that the **obliquity,** or tilt, of the Earth's axis, the **eccentricity of the orbit of Earth,** and the **precession of the equinoxes** are the controlling variables that influence these climatic cycles. Each does so through their impact on planetary **insolation,** the geological effect of solar rays on the surface materials of the Earth (Gallup et al., 1994; Hays et al., 1976).

The influence of these factors may be thought of in the following way. Perturbations of the Earth's orbit are produced by gravitational forces of other planets and periodically alter the geographic distribution of incoming solar radiation. These gravitational forces produce three main perturbations having five primary periods (Fig. 2.4 [pp. 36–37]):

- The Earth's orbit around the Sun varies between near circularity and more pronounced ellipticity at periods of about 100,000 years and 400,000 years. This is known as the eccentricity of the orbit (Fig. 2.4a). When the orbit is most elliptical the Northern Hemisphere reaches extremely cold temperatures, which may trigger maximum glacial advances. One model suggests that the ice ages are driven by a different orbital mechanism—namely, changes in the inclination of Earth's orbit relative to the plane of the solar system. It is theorized that such orbital shifts would periodically dip Earth into a climate-altering cosmic dust cloud. The theory is based on the observation that Pleistocene ice volume seems to vary with a single period of about 100,000 years, exactly the period over which the plane of

Earth's orbit moves a few degrees above and below the plane of the solar system (Muller and MacDonald, 1997).

• The obliquity, or tilt, of the Earth's axis varies between about 22° and 25° with a period of about 41,000 years (Fig. 2.4a).

• The third effect, precession, changes the distance between the Earth and the Sun at any given season. There are two components of precession: (1) **axial precession,** in which the Earth's axis of rotation "wobbles" like that of a spinning top (the North Pole describes a circle in space with a period of 26,000 years) (Fig. 2.4b), and (2) **elliptical precession,** in which the elliptical orbit itself rotates slightly (Fig. 2.4c). The net effect of these two precessions is referred to as the precession of the equinoxes in which the equinoxes (March 20 and September 22) and the solstices (June 21 and December 21) shift around the Earth's orbit with a period of 22,000 years (Fig. 2.4d). The equinox is the time when the sun crosses the plane of the earth's equator, making night and day all over Earth of equal length; the solstice is the time of year when the Sun is at its greatest distance from the equator. The precession can cause warm winters and cool summers in one hemisphere while having just the opposite effect on the other hemisphere. Presently, the point of closest approach of the Earth to the Sun, or **perihelion,** occurs in northern winter (January). Thus portions of the winter hemisphere receive as much as 10% more insolation than they did 11 kya when perihelion occurred in the summer (Crowley and North, 1991). There is now little doubt that these planetary effects of low orbital insolation correlate quite well with some of the main glacial advances (Fig. 2.4e).

Other theories also implicate localized tectonic forces as important factors causing major climatic changes. One such force, **continental drift,** is a consequence of powerful convective currents in the Earth's upper mantle. This force causes the top 70-km layer of the Earth (**lithosphere**), which includes oceanic and continental crust, to move slowly over the underlying layer (**asthenosphere**), which is 70–200 km below the surface. The lithosphere consists of independently moving plates, hence the term **plate tectonics.** Probably the single most important factor causing plates, and the continents they bear, to move is the extensive volcanic activity along the mid-oceanic ridges. Along these ridges new crustal rock is continually being formed and the new rocks are carried to each side of the ridge by plate-tectonic convection (Storey, 1995). Soon after plate tectonics and continental drift became established facts in geological thinking by the late 1960s, it was proposed that drift of continental plates over the poles may have been a contributing factor in climatic change. As an aside, it turns out that the basic elements of the theory of continental drift were first suggested by Abraham Ortellus in 1596, antedating by more than 150 years other writers credited with early formulations of the theory (Romm, 1994).

Another idea was that tectonic movements in critical locations resulted in the formation of ocean gateways that accelerated rapid cooling and glaciation in the Cenozoic by spilling the colder, less salty, and hence lighter waters of the Arctic Ocean over the North Atlantic, eventually covering the entire ocean surface with a layer of low-temperature, low-salinity water (Gartner and McGuirk, 1979; Herman and Hopkins, 1980). Another such example speculates that the development of a cold circum-Antarctic current was produced when Antarctica separated from South America and Australia (Kennett, 1977). The relationship between the emergence of the Isthmus of Panama and the initiation of Northern Hemisphere glaciation is unclear, however. The formation of the isthmus seems to predate widespread Northern Hemisphere glaciation by 2.0–0.5 million years (Raymo and Ruddiman, 1992).

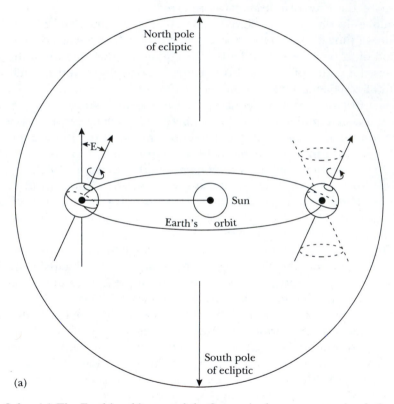

(a)

Fig. 2.4.   (a) The Earth's orbit around the Sun varies between near circularity and more pronounced ellipticity at periods of about 100,000 years and 400,000 years (eccentricity of the orbit). When the orbit is most elliptical the Northern Hemisphere reaches extremely cold temperatures, which may trigger maximum glacial advances. The obliquity, or tilt, of the Earth's axis (E) varies between about 22° and 25° at periods approximating 41,000 years. (b) There are two components of precession: axial precession, in which the Earth's axis of rotation "wobbles" like that of a spinning top (the North Pole describes a circle in space with a period of 26,000 years), and (c) elliptical precession in which the elliptical orbit itself rotates slightly. (d) The net effect of these two precessions is referred to as the precession of the equinoxes (see text). (e) Planetary effects of low orbital insolation correlate quite well with some of the main glacial advances. (Crowley and North, 1991.)

Axial precession or "wobble"

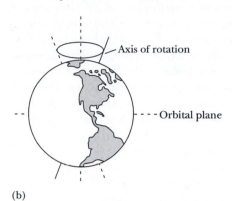

(b)

Precession of the equinoxes

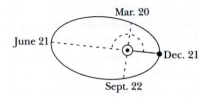

Today

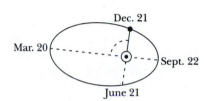

5,500 years ago

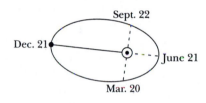

11,000 years ago

● Earth on December 21
⊙ Sun

Precession of the ellipse

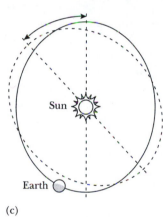

(c)

(d)

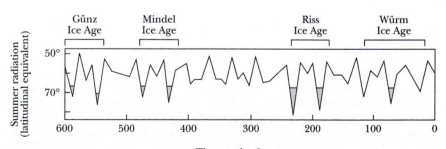

Thousands of years ago

(e)

More recently formulated Ice Age theories have focused on the possible climatic effects caused by uplift and erosion of mountain ranges and plateaus during the Cenozoic (Molnar and England, 1990). Several such models consider the uplift of the Himalayas and the Tibetan Plateau to be *the* main driving force of Cenozoic climate change (Raymo and Ruddiman, 1992; Zhisheng et al., 2001). Although Cenozoic uplift has occurred in other regions of the world (e.g., the Alps, East Africa, and parts of the cordillera of North and South America), nowhere has it reached the immense scale seen in the Himalayas and Tibetan plateau. Formed as a result of the collision between the Indo-Australian and Asian plates beginning in the middle Eocene (52–44 mya), with further significant increases in altitude occurring 10–8 mya and continuing today, the Tibetan plateau is the most imposing topographic feature on the planet, having a mean elevation of 5 km and an area half that of the continental United States (Chung et al., 1998).

The modern Tibetan plateau is so vast that its weather drives not only the regionally intense monsoon circulation but also perturbs atmospheric circulation on a hemispheric scale. Computer-simulated climate models that factor in the effects of changing Tibetan plateau topography successfully predict climatic trends progressing from the equable, moist temperate climates characteristic of the Early and Middle Cenozoic to the periodic cold/warm and dry/wet regional patterns seen today in the Northern Hemisphere (Prell and Kutzback, 1992; Raymo and Ruddiman, 1992). However, such models show that high topography alone is not sufficient to initiate the growth of large terrestrial ice sheets in both hemispheres but is just one of the factors contributing to these climatic changes. These models propose that over the past 40 million years or so, uplift of the Tibetan plateau resulted in stronger deflections of the atmospheric jet stream, more intense monsoonal circulation, increased rainfall on the front slopes of the Himalayas, greater rates of chemical weathering, and ultimately, lower atmospheric CO_2 concentrations.

Before the rise of the plateau, the Earth's climate was more equable, warmer, and more temperate. However, hot air can gather at the top of an uplifted plateau each year, rise, and then be displaced by moist, cooler air from the Indian Ocean, thereby driving the annual monsoon rains. This continual cycle produces a chemical-weathering phenomenon: the heavy monsoonal rain contributes to the removal of vast amounts of carbon dioxide from the atmosphere; the carbon dioxide in the rain reacts with silicate rocks that are exposed as the plateau rises; and the heavy rain weathers the rock, ultimately washing the minerals downriver into the ocean. There they are incorporated into the shells of marine animals and eventually deposited as limestone on the ocean floor. The Tibetan plateau and the Himalayas produce up to a quarter of the rock sediment released into the world's oceans, though they make up only 5% of the Earth's landmass. The removal of so much carbon dioxide from the atmosphere over millions of years has helped cool the Earth's temperatures by reducing the **greenhouse effect,** the trapping of heat in the Earth's atmosphere by carbon dioxide. Indeed, climate modeling studies have shown that greater mean South Asian summer monsoonal rainfall and warmer surface temperatures are associated with increases in atmospheric carbon dioxide concentration (Meehl and Washington, 1993).

Even though elevation of the Himalayas was initiated in the early Tertiary, the full ecological and climatological impact of the Tibetan plateau uplift has been fully manifest only since the Middle to Late Miocene (Burbank et al., 1993; Coleman and Hodges, 1995; Turner et al., 1993; Wang et al., 1982; Zhisheng et al., 2001). We now know that a dramatic ecological shift of plant species occurred worldwide at that time, reflected in the transition from predominantly C_3 plants to those exhibiting C_4 metabolism (see below). Indications of the predominance of these photosynthetic pathways are gained through **carbon isotope analyses,** specifically by comparing the relative abundance of two carbon isotopes, ^{12}C and ^{13}C.

CARBON ISOTOPE ANALYSES

Carbon isotope analysis is one type of stable (i.e., nonradioactive) isotope analysis. Stable isotopes of several common elements (e.g., hydrogen, carbon, nitrogen, oxygen, sulfur, flourine, calcium, phosphorous, strontium) are found in organisms. Stable isotope studies are based on the observation that in various biochemical reactions involving such isotopes, the lighter isotope (e.g., ^{12}C as opposed to ^{13}C or ^{14}N as opposed to ^{15}N) has a faster reaction rate than the heavier one, thereby producing reaction end products whose isotope ratios differ from those of the starting components, or substrate, of the reaction. For example, each of the constituent amino acids of bone collagen is a biochemical reaction end product derived from an original substrate composed of food and metabolites from an animal's own tissues. Consequently, the $^{15}N : ^{14}N$ ratio in the product (bone collagen) is different from the same ratio in the substrate (the nitrogen in the animal's diet and metabolites). In this example, bone collagen is normally enriched in ^{15}N relative to its substrate, the diet, because more ^{14}N is excreted relative to ^{15}N. Conversely, excretion materials are normally depleted in ^{15}N compared to the original diet. This difference in isotope ratio between product and substrate is known as fractionation.

As noted above, one of the most useful stable isotopes in paleoanthropological studies is the carbon isotope ratio ($\delta^{13}C$) (Schoeninger, 1995). Much of the world's active cycling carbon is sequestered in the ocean as dissolved carbonate, and when this oceanic carbon pool is exchanged with atmospheric carbon dioxide, the ^{13}C in the atmosphere is depleted through a process known as equilibrium isotope fractionation (a type of fractionation in which the reaction is caused by some physical property such as temperature or evaporation). A further depletion of ^{13}C occurs in the transfer of CO_2 from the atmosphere to plant tissues during photosynthesis. However, the $\delta^{13}C$ values in plants are also determined by the plants' own photosynthetic pathway as well as by atmospheric CO_2 and, as we have mentioned, these are referred to as C_3 and C_4 pathways.

The C_3 photosynthetic pathway is named after the three carbon atoms in the first metabolic product of this reaction, phosphoglyceric acid; the C_4 pathway is named after the four carbon atoms in the first metabolic product of its reaction, asparate. Today, C_4 plants have $\delta^{13}C$ values around $-12\%o$ (parts per million; ppm), whereas most C_3 plants have values around $-26\%o$.[1] In temperate regions most plants follow the C_3 pathway, although some grasses may follow a C_4 pathway. However, in tropical regions vegetation can usually be divided into herbaceous C_3 vegetation and trees and C_4 grasses.

As we have noted, distinct carbon isotope "signatures" are passed along the food chain from the plants to the tissues, including tooth enamel, of herbivores. In warm savanna environments, trees, shrubs, forbs, corms, and tubers are C_3 plants, whereas grasses are mainly C_4 plants. Browsers, for example, display a C_3 isotope signature because of the dominance of foliage from trees, shrubs, and forbs in their diets. Grazers, on the other hand, display a mostly C_4 signature, reflecting their more **graminivorous,** or grass-eating diet. Most trees, shrubs, forbs, corms, tubers, and grasses that require cool, wet growing seasons exhibit the C_3 pathway and were dominant before the uplifting of the Tibetan plateau, whereas most grasses that require hot, dry growing seasons exhibit the C_4 pathway and rose in abundance late in the Miocene (Pagani et al., 1999). The transition from C_3 to C_4 ecosystems is first detected in the Asian interior (e.g., Pakistan, India, China) about 8 mya, with C_4 grasslands dominating by the Plio-Pleistocene. This transition also occurs in North and South America and in Africa about the same time (Cerling et al., 1997; Morgan et al., 1994). Also about this same time large-bodied hominoids were being replaced by cercopithecids in both South Asia and East Africa. The advent of C_4 plants in the fossil record of Asia signals the initial development of increased aridity and the Asian monsoon system of long, dry seasons punctuated by periods of massive rains (Lee-Thorp et al., 1989; Quade et al., 1989; van der Merwe, 1982; Zhisheng et al., 2001). In order to illustrate some of these principles, the basic carbon isotope signature of modern East African ecosystems is compared with that of Olduvai Gorge (Bed II) in Figure 2.5.

The utility of stable carbon isotopes in paleoanthropological studies lies in the facts that (1) there is a positive correlation between animals and their substrate diets and (2) the isotope signal from C_3 or C_4 plants is recorded in animals that feed on one or the other of these plant types or on other animals that predominantly feed on one of these plant types. Thus, for exam-

---

[1]$\delta^{13}C$ values are defined as: $\delta = [R_{sample}/R_{std} - 1] \times 1000$ (ppm), where R is the isotope ratio (e.g., $^{13}C{:}^{12}C$) and *std* is the internationally recognized standard. A negative value indicates that the sample is depleted in the heavier isotope relative to the internationally recognized standard; a positive value indicates the sample is enriched relative to the sample.

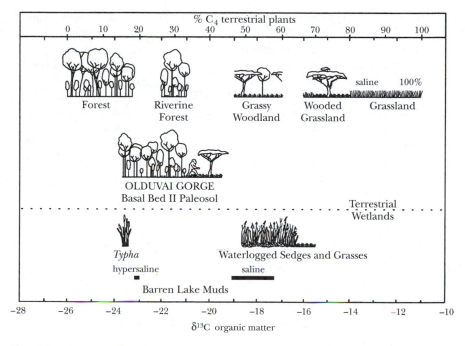

Fig. 2.5. An example of the carbon isotope signature of Olduvai Gorge. The upper horizontal scale indicates the approximate equivalent percentage of C_4 flora. The lower horizontal scale indicates that basal Bed II at Olduvai supported a relatively closed riverine forest to grassy woodland habitat. (Sikes, 1994.)

ple, a C_3 isotope signal would be expected if early hominins were eating mainly browsers, whereas more of a C_4 signal would be expected if they were eating mainly grazers. However, tubers, nuts, and berries also have a characteristic C_3 signal, thus complicating dietary interpretations somewhat. For example, studies on South African "robust" australopiths have revealed a mixed carbon signal: about 75% C_3 and 25% C_4, suggesting that *Australopithecus robustus* had a generalized, rather than a specialized, graminivorous diet. A C_3 signal in "gracile" australopiths suggests the main protein source for these hominins may have been young leaves and/or fruit or grasses and sedges and/or the animals that ate these plants. The C_4 signal found within the *Homo* lineage may indicate that the main protein source for these hominins was the meat of grazing mammals (Lee-Thorp and Beaumont, 1995; Lee-Thorp and van der Merwe, 1993; Lee-Thorp et al., 1994, 2000; Schoeninger, 1995; Sponheimer and Lee-Thorp, 1999).

Studies of soils and tooth enamel from sites around the world indicate that C_4 ecosystems underwent a global expansion about 7–5 mya. Large mammals older than 8 mya all had diets compatible with a pure C_3, or C_3-dominated diet; however, by about 6 mya equids and other large mammals from South Asia, Africa, and North and South America all had C_4-dominated diets. It is interesting that no evidence is found suggesting a significant C_4 component in the diets of large mammals from western Europe at any time in the Tertiary. The modern pattern of C_4 and C_3 grasses shows that C_4 grasses dominate in tropical and subtropical regions, that the transition to C_3 grasses takes place between 30° and 45° latitude, and that C_3 grasses dominate at high latitudes (Cerling et al., 1997).

Fully understanding the forces driving climatic change is difficult by any standard. But we can conclude from this discussion that, taken as a whole, such factors as change in the tilt of the Earth's axis, continental drift, mountain building, and glacial sedimentation all may have initiated strong positive-feedback loops to global cooling (Burbank et al., 1993; Raymo and Ruddiman, 1992). The review of glacial and oxygen isotope evidence of climatic change leads the way for a more detailed look at the geological events and chronology of the Plio-Pleistocene.

THE PLIO-PLEISTOCENE TIME SCALE

As noted earlier, geologists usually divide geological history into divisions that reflect major climatic changes and/or changes in fossil flora and fauna. Today, the base of the Pleistocene is defined at its type locality at Vrica, Italy, by the first occurrence there of cold water–adapted mollusks that are today restricted to the North Sea and the Baltic. This abrupt appearance of cold water–adapted mollusks, and hence by definition the base of the Lower Pleistocene, is presently dated to about 1.64 mya and reflects the onset of climates far colder than those of the preceding Pliocene. This Plio-Pleistocene boundary datum coincides quite closely with other more modern indicators that we will discuss below (Combourieu-Neubout et al., 1990; Harland et al., 1990).

The Pleistocene is traditionally subdivided into **Lower, Middle,** and **Upper** (or **Late**) **Pleistocene** time intervals, though there is little evidence now that these original divisions have global significance since they were originally applied to undefined stratigraphic sediments in the Bavarian Alps (Flint, 1971). Much work in the past few decades has gone into refining the Pleistocene time scale using recent advances in glacial stratigraphy, geomagnetic polarity reversal stratigraphy, deep-sea oxygen isotope stratigraphy, and radiometric dating techniques. Using global glacial criteria, modern stratigraphers correlate the onset of the Middle Pleistocene to the first evidence of continental glaciation in Europe, about 900 kya, and its termination to the end of the next-to-last glacial (Riss or Saale) in Europe and (Wisconsinian I) in North America about 127 kya (Van Couvering and Kukla, 1988) (Fig. 2.1b). Thus, on the basis of glacial stratigraphy, the Lower Pleistocene lasted from about 1.6 to 0.9 mya, the Middle Pleistocene from about 900 to 127 kya, and the Late Pleistocene from about 127 kya to the present or to 10 kya if one recognizes the Holocene.

However, more recently it has been proposed that Pleistocene subdivisions are better correlated to the geomagnetic polarity record (see below) and to the marine oxygen isotope record than to glacial stratigraphy, since continental glacial stratigraphy is both incomplete and not applicable worldwide. Accordingly, it has been recommended that the Lower/Middle Pleistocene boundary be set at the Matuyama/Bruhnes magnetic polarity reversal about 780 kya (Baksi et al., 1992) and that the Middle/Late Pleistocene boundary be set at the beginning of the last interglacial incursion of the sea over land about 125 kya years ago (Butzer and Isaac, 1975)—a change known as a **transgression,** that converts initially shallow-water conditions to deeper-water conditions. This latter date corresponds quite closely to the beginning of marine oxygen isotope stage 5e (Harland et al., 1990; Slowey et al., 1996; Szabo et al., 1994) (Fig. 2.2b).

THE CONTRIBUTION OF GEOMAGNETIC REVERSAL STUDIES

The first indications that the Earth's magnetic field may have reversed its polarity was presented in 1906 by the French physicist Bernard Brunhes, after whom the Brunhes normal polarity epoch was named (Fig. 2.1). Twenty years later, M. Matuyama concluded that the Earth's magnetic field had a reversed polarity during the early Pleistocene and that it has been normal ever since, hence the term Matuyama reversed polarity epoch.

The geomagnetic field is known to have gone through a series of complete reversals in its polarity lasting from about 10^4 to 10^7 years (Faure, 1986). At various times in the geologic past the Earth's magnetic field has been directed, as it is today, toward the north, or normal polarity, and at other times toward the south, or reversed polarity. The cause(s) of these reversals in the magnetic field are not yet clearly understood but are thought to originate from electric currents in the Earth's outer core, which consists mainly of liquid iron. In addition, the possibility exists that the Earth's magnetic field shifts by following preferred (i.e., predictable) paths along longitudinal meridians, and these patterns of change may eventually provide insights into the causes of the changes themselves. For example, over the past 5 million years or so there has been a tendency for the polarity reversals to be characteristically biased along two longitudinal bands, one centered over the Americas and the other over East Asia and Australia, rather than being uniformly distributed around the geographical North Pole (Constable, 1992; Langereis et al., 1992).

Magnetic minerals in rocks preserve a magnetic vector indicating the orientation and intensity of the global magnetic field within which they formed, and this vector can be detected and used to indicate the relative time and position of the rock's formation. The processes by which sediments are magnetized are thought to depend on several factors, including magnetic mineralogy, duration of the transitional field state, and sedimentation rate (Jackson, 1992). Hundreds of magnetic field reversals are now well documented in the geological record. In general, it takes about 5000 years for a total reversal to occur. However, on occasion the magnetic field can undergo extremely rapid changes during a reversal, up to about 6° per day (Coe et al., 1995). The magnetic histories of rocks and sediments are used to construct a **geomagnetic polarity reversal time scale** of a field or region that consists of extended intervals called **polarity epochs,** during which the field has predominantly one polarity, interrupted by shorter **polarity events** of opposite polarity. By convention, polarity epochs are named after scientists who made significant contributions to studies of the Earth's magnetic field (e.g., Brunhes, Matuyama) and polarity events are named after the location at which a reversal was first recognized (e.g., Olduvai, Jaramillo). The geomagnetic polarity reversal time scale for the past 5.8 million years contains four epochs—starting with the present: **Brunhes** (normal), **Matuyama** (reversed), **Gauss** (normal), and **Gilbert** (reversed)— and several events. These palemagnetic epochs and events are dated as shown in Table 2.2 (Fig. 2.1).

Paleontologists can use magnetic profiles if they can fit a sequence of fossiliferous sediments of interest into a **paleomagnetic column,** or magnetostratigraphic profile of a region. A viable column requires that the ages of the actual magnetic reversals represented in the profile be dated by independent means, usually by a radiometric technique (discussed later). A radiometrically dated column allows the age of the fossils to be determined within the limits of resolution of that column. For example, if a fossil were found in sediments of normal polarity dated to between about 1.7 million years (end of Olduvai normal event) and 780 thousand years (beginning of Brunhes normal epoch), it could be reliably inferred to date to the Jaramillo normal event between 0.990 and 1.070 mya.

Measurements of past reversals in the Earth's magnetic field are important to paleoanthropologists for another reason: They document the progress of continental drift, a phenomenon that has had a profound impact on the distribution of plants and animals, including primates, and hence on their evolution. Volcanic activity at the midoceanic ridges is continually creating new crustal rocks, which, as they spread and cool to both sides of the ridge, become magnetized in the direction of the prevailing geomagnetic field. This process results in the phenomenon known as sea-floor spreading. In effect, sea-floor spreading can be likened to a tape recording of changes in polarity of the Earth's magnetic field on both sides of the ridge. Geologists can play back this recording to reconstruct the past positions of the continents. This paleomagnetic record of sea-floor spreading can be extended back to rocks dating to the middle Jurassic, about 180 mya (Kappelman, 1993; Tarling, 1980).

Table 2.2 Polarity Intervals

Million years	Polarity[a]
0.000–0.780	**BRUNHES**
0.780–0.990	MATUYAMA
0.990–1.070	**Jaramillo**
1.070–1.770	MATUYAMA
1.770–1.950	**Olduvai**
1.950–2.140	MATUYAMA
2.140–2.150	**Reunion**
2.150–2.581	MATUYAMA
2.581–3.040	**GAUSS**
3.040–3.110	Kaena
3.110–3.220	**GAUSS**
3.220–3.330	Mammoth
3.330–3.580	**GAUSS**
3.580–4.180	GILBERT
4.180–4.290	**Cochiti**
4.290–4.480	GILBERT
4.480–4.620	**Nunivak**
4.620–4.800	GILBERT
4.800–4.890	**Sidufjall**
4.890–4.980	GILBERT
4.980–5.230	**Thvera**
5.230–5.894	GILBERT

Data from Cande and Kent (1995). Also see Fig. 2.1.
[a]Boldface, normal polarity; all capital letters, epoch.

THE ARCHEOLOGICAL TIME SCALE

Over the years, archeologists have developed their own definitions for subdividing the (late) Plio-Pleistocene into **Early** (or **Lower**), **Middle,** and
Late (or **Upper**) **Paleolithic** based mainly on stone-tool complexes. It
should be emphasized that these terms refer to cultural complexes of early
humans and are *not* synonymous with the chronostratigraphic terms Early,
Middle, and Late Pleistocene, as defined above. It is interesting to note
that the Paleolithic (Old Stone Age) was originally defined as the period
when early humans were contemporary with now-extinct fauna, whereas
the Neolithic (New Stone Age) was originally defined as the period in
which stone implements were more skillfully made, more varied in form,
and more polished. Thus the Neolithic was defined in terms of stone tools
and the Paleolithic in terms of ancient faunas (Chazan, 1995a).

   To add to the confusion, the terms Early, Middle, and Late Stone Age
have often been used for subdivisions of the African sub-Saharan Stone

Age. The approximate chronological arrangement of these major cultural divisions and their characteristic tool types as well as inferred behavioral traits are shown in Figure 2.6.

The Lower Paleolithic spans the interval between the first evidence of stone-tool manufacture about 2.5 mya in East Africa and the first appearance, or predominance, of prepared-core flake technologies and flake tools 300–40kya, depending on the location.

Depending on the particular time and place, these Lower Paleolithic industries are characterized by choppers and flakes (e.g., Oldowan industry), **handaxes** and/or **cleavers** (e.g., Acheulean industry), and unspecialized flakes (e.g., Clactonian industry) (Brooks, 1988a) (Fig. 2.7a–d). The main difference between a handaxe and a cleaver is that the former has a

Age and Main Division	Stone Technology		Some Other Tools[a]	Behavioral Traits
	General	Specific		
Present Late Stone Age 0.035 mya	Specialized composite tools Abstractions Cave art	Many regional traditions Many functionally specific tool sets	Shaped	Population expansion Small bands Intensive seasonal resource use in smaller areas Cohesion for ceremonies and exchange
0.04 mya Middle Stone Age 0.15 mya	Simple compound tools Hafting begins	Several regional traditions and chronological sets		Seasonal herding of livestock Resource and task-specific camps Regular reoccupation by large bands in large territories
0.2 mya Early Stone Age II Acheulian and Developed Oldowan 1.8 mya	First standard tool forms	Large cutting bifacial tools Chopper/light-duty complex	Digging sticks — Carrying trays, etc. — Spears — Throwing sticks — Bone tools: opportunistic — Fire ?	Organized hunting of large animals Scavenging and planned collecting Widely adapted sites reoccupied
2.0 mya Early Stone Age I Oldowan 2.5 mya	Selected opportunistic tools	Choppers Spheroids Light duty Heavy duty Small cutting tools		Scavenging and hunting of small animals Collecting insects, eggs, and plant foods from brief stopovers
No known flaked stone tools 5.0 nya	Simple opportunistic tools (sticks, etc.)?	Manuports?		Collecting plant foods, insects, and small mammals

[a] - - -, inferred; ———— confirmed.

Fig. 2.6.   The approximate chronological arrangement of the major cultural divisions of the Plio-Pleistocene. (Adapted from Clark, 1985.)

more or less pointed end whereas the latter has a straighter cutting edge. More will be said about these early tool industries in later chapters.

The Middle Paleolithic (300–40 kya) is often referred to (in Europe at least) as the **Mousterian** after the site of Le Moustier in France where it was first recognized. It is characterized by increasing sophistication of stone-tool technology, particularly in the use of flake tools made from prepared cores (e.g., **Levallois cores**). A Levallois core is one that is extensively pre-shaped to produce one or more flakes having a predetermined shape (Fig. 2.7e). The first appearance of Middle Paleolithic tools is not a synchronous event throughout the Old World. Mousterian sites are dominated by side scrapers and denticulates that have little regional specificity and are difficult to sort into discrete, nonoverlapping categories. In Europe, the only fossil hominins found at Mousterian sites are Neandertals; however, skeletal material associated with Middle Stone Age (Middle Paleolithic) industries of southern and eastern Africa (e.g., Klasies, Herto) and the Near East (e.g., Skhul and Qafzeh) appear much less Neandertal like,[2] more closely approaching anatomically modern humans (Brooks, 1988a; Klein, 1992; White et al., 2003).

A stone-tool-making technique usually associated with Late Pleistocene modern humans is the fashioning of stone inserts by blunting flakes and blades for making composite tools (e.g., by preparing hafts). However, it is now recognized that these so-called backed tools form a small, but significant, part of some early Middle Stone Age sites of south central Africa (e.g., Lupemban industry of Zambia at about 300 kya). This tends to support the emerging view that some modern-like behaviors were emerging by the later Middle Pleistocene in Africa, far earlier than in Eurasia (Barham, 2002; Barham and Smart, 1996; McBrearty and Brooks, 2000).

In fact, emerging evidence suggests that many of the so-called components of the human revolution claimed to first appear around the Middle/Late Paleolithic (40–50 kya in Eurasia) are actually found tens of thousands of years earlier in the Middle Stone Age of Africa. Such features include blade and microlithic technology, bone tools, specialized hunting, exploitation of aquatic resources, long-distance trade, and the use of pigments in art and decoration. Taken together, these suggest that a gradual evolution of modern human behaviors first occurred in Middle Stone Age Africa, which was later "exported" to other regions of the Old World (McBrearty and Brooks, 2000). More recent discoveries

---

[2]For trivia buffs, British (and older American) authors usually spell Neandertal with an *h* (Neanderthal). Virtually everyone else, including contemporary American authors, now spell it without the h (Neandertal). In 1863 an account of the cranium from Neandertal was read by Professor W. King to the Geological Association for the Advancement of Science at Newcastle-upon-Tyne. His address was published using the new specific name *Homo neanderthalensis* in 1864. According to the International Rules of Zoological Nomenclature, Article 19, "The original orthography of a name is to be preserved unless an error of transcription, a *lapsus calami,* or a typographical error is evident. Since none of these conditions applies, the scientific name of this species (for those who consider it a distinct species) must be *neanderthalensis,* although in colloquial and adjectival forms the name can be modified to Neandertal (Oakley, 1958b).

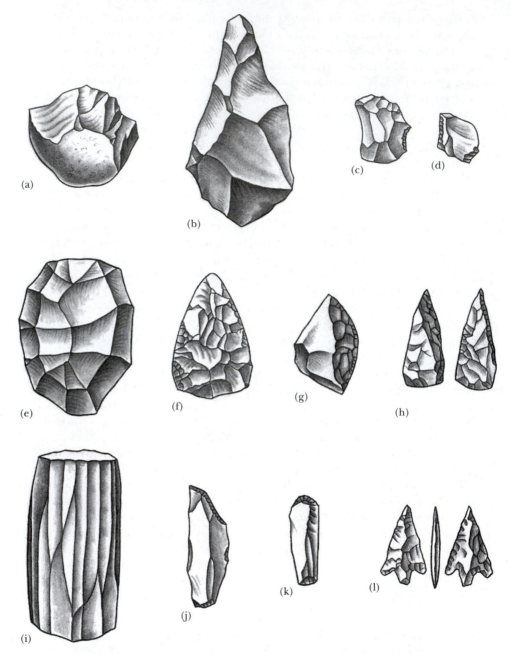

Fig. 2.7. Representative stone tools of the Paleolithic. Lower Paleolithic: (a) Oldowan chopper, Africa; (b) early Acheulean handaxe, Africa; (c) Clactonian flake tool, Europe; (d) flake tool, China. Middle Paleolithic: (e) Levallois core with flakes removed from it, Europe; (f) Mousterian handaxe, France; (g) Quina convex scraper, Europe; (h) Pietersburg bifacial point, South Africa. Upper Paleolithic: (i) prismatic blade core; (j) burin on blade; (k) Perigordian end scraper; (l) Solutrean tanged point.

from the Semliki Valley, Zaire, also show that finely made bone tools were being manufactured in the western rift valley of Africa some 90–75 kya (Brooks et al., 1995; Yellen et al., 1995). This early occurrence of bone tools in Africa is intriguing, particularly given the somewhat surprising announcement that two abstract representations engraved on pieces of red ochre as well as shell beads have been recovered from Middle Stone Age layers at Blombos Cave, South Africa, in association with nearly a dozen hominin teeth. The date of about 75 kya for these engravings, if confirmed, would imply that the emergence of modern human behavior in Africa (at least in the form of engravings, bone tools, etc.) occurred some 35,000 years *before* the start of the Upper Paleolithic in Eurasia (Grine and Henshilwood, 2002; Henshilwood et al., 2001, 2002, 2004; Jacobs et al., 2003). We shall have much more to say about this in a later chapter.

The Upper Paleolithic (40–10 kya) is characterized by the predominance of well-made **blades** (by definition, any flake that is at least twice as long as it is wide), microliths, distinctive bone points, and the use of **burins** (tools with a chisel-like point) and other tools to work bone, antler, ivory, teeth, and shells. Although as one might expect, many Middle Paleolithic tool types continued with diminished frequency into the Upper Paleolithic as well (Fig. 2.7i–l) (Brose and Wolpoff, 1971; Straus, 1995). As is true of Middle Paleolithic tools, the first appearance of Upper Paleolithic tools is not a synchronous event throughout the Old World. The oldest Upper Paleolithic technology in Europe comes from the Balkans (e.g., Bacho Kiro and Temnata, Bulgaria) dated to 40–45 kya and also appears in both Spain (Castillo) and Belgium (Magrite) by at least 40 kya (Straus, 1994). Some Upper Paleolithic assemblages from Siberia (e.g., Kara-Bom) and the Russian Arctic also date to this same time frame, indicating that Upper Paleolithic hominins were fully capable of inhabiting sites located at extremely high latitudes by this time (Goebel et al., 1993; Goebel and Aksenov, 1995; Pavlov et al., 2001; Pitulko, 2004).

Decorative beads, pendants, and other items of personal adornment became much more common in Upper Paleolithic sites. Raw materials such as stone, ivory, and shell were traded over long distances, and graves were becoming more elaborate (Fig. 2.8) (Binford, 1989; Soffer-Bobyshev, 1988). Of particular interest is the first use of nets for hunting and the appearance, at least in Eurasia, of more elaborate dwellings such as mammoth-bone huts (Oliva, 1988; Pringle, 1997). Upper Paleolithic tool complexes also tend to exhibit greater degrees of regional specificity than those of the preceding Lower or Middle Paleolithic. In the Late Stone Age (Upper Paleolithic) of southern Africa, one finds clear evidence for better utilization of marine resources (e.g., fishing, capture of fur seals) (Klein, 1979, 1987, 1989a; Klein and Cruz-Uribe, 1996). At least one South African Middle Stone Age site, Klasies River, also shows evidence of extensive marine resource exploitation.

In terms of variety and sophistication of tool types, richness of symbolic and artistic expression, and successful exploitation of ever-increasing and diverse food resources, the transition from the Middle to Upper Paleolithic

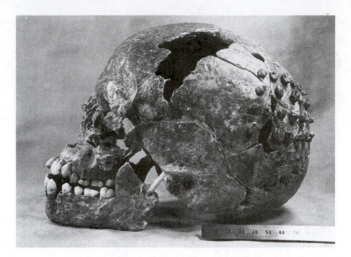

Fig. 2.8.   Side view of an adolescent cranium from the Upper Pleistocene burial site of Grotte des Enfants, Grimaldi, Italy.   Many Upper Pleistocene skeletons, like those at Grimaldi, were deliberately buried and their bones colored with red ocher. Shell ornaments and other decorations often surrounded the skeletons. Note the coiffe, or headpiece, made from pierced shells on the back of this adolescent's cranium. (Photo courtesy of B. Schumann.)

about 40 kya documents a radical transformation in human behavior, one that Stanford archeologist Richard Klein (1992) considers "the most dramatic behavioral shift that archeologists will ever detect . . . [one that] almost certainly marks the advent of the fully modern way of doing things or, more precisely, of the fully modern ability to manipulate culture." Klein (2000) attributes this dramatic behavioral shift to some (unknown) genetic mutation (a gene for language perhaps?) that occurred in human ancestry about this time, a genetic change he considers "the most significant mutation in the human evolutionary series, for it produced an organism that could alter its behavior radically without any change in its anatomy and that could cumulate and transmit the alterations at a speed that anatomical innovation could never match."[3]

Upper Paleolithic industries are usually associated with anatomically modern humans, although two sites in France are exceptions: At Arcy-sur-Cure and Saint-Césaire, Neandertal remains are found in association with early Upper Paleolithic Châtelperronian tools. However, as noted above, many of these so-called Upper Paleolithic behaviors were already gradually appearing much earlier in the Middle Stone Age of Africa.

---

[3]One might argue that humans managed far greater technological innovations between the nineteenth and the twentieth centuries (horse-drawn buggies to walking on the Moon) than anything seen between the Middle and the Upper Paleolithic—all without recourse to any genetic mutations.

EFFECTS OF MIOCENE AND PLIO-PLEISTOCENE CLIMATES ON HOMININ EVOLUTION

Events at the end of the Miocene may have had far-reaching implications for hominin paleobiology during the succeeding Plio-Pleistocene. For instance, during the Antarctic ice-cap buildup cold, upwelling water flowed along the west coast of Africa and, by drawing moisture-laden air off the land, increased the aridity of the coastal areas of southern Africa (Ward, 1983). Any flora or fauna strongly dependent on high rainfall patterns would have suffered during this period as more open, drought-resistant forms spread. This trend, which we will review in greater detail in later chapters, must have put pressure on the late Miocene arboreal hominoids in Africa, since the equatorial forests were undoubtedly shrinking. The continuation of this process greatly enlarged the area of the transitional ecological zone between forest and adjacent savanna. It is tempting to view this transitional ecological zone, which is neither forest nor savanna, as the area in which behavioral and anatomical changes were initiated in early hominin evolution. These changes, which will be examined in detail in later chapters, ultimately led to the terrestrial bipedalism of early hominins from the arboreal quadrupedalism of preceding Miocene "apes" (Stanley, 1992).

Increasing aridity in east Africa 3–4 mya may also have been exacerbated by the closing of the Indonesian seaway about this time (Cane and Molnar, 2001). The source of seawater flow through Indonesia from the warm South Pacific to the relatively cold North Pacific waters may have been switched due to the northward displacement of New Guinea about 5 mya. This would have had the effect of decreasing sea-surface temperatures in the Indian Ocean, thereby leading to reduced rainfall over eastern Africa. Such sea-surface temperature changes in the equatorial Pacific may have reduced atmospheric heat transport from the tropics to higher latitudes, thereby stimulating global cooling and the eventual growth of ice sheets about 2.5 mya. And as we noted earlier, the climatic affects of ice sheet formation on Late Cenozoic climates, whether direct (e.g., by topographic and ice albedo forcing) or indirect (e.g., sea-level changes and freshwater discharge) cannot be overestimated. The Late Cenozoic waxing and waning of Northern Hemispheric glaciations (and all their consequences) with the same periods (100, 41, and 23 thousand years) as the orbital parameters eccentricity, obliquity, and precession, respectively, as modeled by the Milankovitch Theory, were undoubtedly the most influential climatological factors influencing hominin evolution over the Plio-Pleistocene (Clark et al., 1999).

Several ecological models concerning the evolution of hominin bipedalism stress the importance of such fringe environments as they arose in Africa 12–5 mya. For example, one such model speculates that at the time the African apes and australopiths split from their common ancestor, the initial ecological niche available to both would most likely have been rather broad, including dense to fairly open savanna and even some more densely forested areas (Wolpoff, 1982). The result of the growth of the fringe environment might have been to lessen competition between the new sibling species by partitioning the niche occupied by the parent species into two narrower and less overlapping adaptive zones: The australopiths would have gravitated to the more open areas and the African apes would have moved into the more densely forested regions. This fringe environment model goes on to predict that competition would have been further reduced if the apes and australopiths had developed their own special dietary, dental, and loco-motor adaptations. Such specializations of early hominins would have included the evolution of a powerful masticatory apparatus, bipedalism, the use of rudimentary tools and weapons, and a set of social changes, including the use of home bases, the division of labor, and food sharing.

Recent research casts some doubt on this rather neat scenario purporting to "explain" the origins of bipedality as an adaptive response to the transition from forested to more open habitats. For example, analyses of stable carbon isotopes from soils in Kenya's East African Rift Valley indicate that a heterogeneous environment persisted for the last 15 million years in the region and that open grasslands never did dominate this portion of East Africa. In addition, paleoecological reconstructions suggest that one of the earliest australopith species, *Ardipithecus ramidus*, existed in fairly wooded, well-watered environments (WoldeGabriel et al., 1994). The change from closed to open habitats occurred gradually from about 4 to 1.8 mya, over which time there was a major increase in arid and grazing adapted mammals. For example, the earliest bovids adapted to secondary grasslands, as opposed to seasonally flooded valley (edaphic) grasslands, occurred about this time. Therefore, the appearance of open savannas alone is not enough to explain hominin origins or the evolution of bipedalism for, as we shall see in later chapters, both occurred long before the evolution of open grasslands. Our own genus, *Homo*, seems to be the first hominin completely adapted to open, arid environments (Reed, 1997; Spencer, 1997).

Thus there appears to be little evidence for a sudden or dramatic shift from more forested to more grassland habitats during this early phase of hominin evolution. If hominins evolved in East Africa during the late Miocene, they clearly did so in an ecologically diverse setting (Kingston et al., 1994). And, as noted, recent discoveries in Ethiopia also suggest more wooded habitats for the earliest hominins from that region of East Africa (White et al., 1994; WoldeGabriel et al., 1994). Finally, we should note that recent long-term observations indicate that rain forest–dwelling chimpanzees from West Africa use more tools, make them in more different ways, hunt more frequently and more often in groups, and show more frequent cooperation and food sharing than their savanna–dwelling relatives do—all behaviors that we tend to associate with models of early hominin behavior (Boesch-Achermann and Boesch, 1994). We shall come back to a more detailed discussion of these early hominins and the origins of bipedality in Chapter 8.

A number of hypotheses have been developed that attempt to relate widespread climatic and associated environmental change to important events in Plio-Pleistocene hominin evolution, particularly the widespread cooling that occurred around 2.5 mya that affected faunas and floras worldwide (Bobe et al., 2002). These hypotheses are collectively referred to as **climatic forcing models,** and much of the data relating to these models are summarized in Figure 2.9. In general, these models conclude that major speciation events in early African hominins (as well as other African mammals) are coincident with shifts to more arid, open conditions in Africa around 2.8, 1.7, and 1.0 mya—time periods that seem correlated with the growth and subsequent expansion of ice sheets in the higher latitudes. The model's hypothesis is supported by data from many locales, including records of African climate variability from deep-sea drilling of marine sedimentary sequences off the African coasts (deMenocal, 1995). In southern Africa changes in fossil bovids reflect a shift from moderately moist, or mesic, and bush-covered environments to more arid and open ones (Vrba, 1988). In East Africa this conclusion is supported by changes in micromammals (Wesselman, 1985), pollen assemblages (Bonnefille, 1976), and bovids that all reflect expansion of arid and open grasslands. Many of the larger African mammals, including elephants, pigs, horses, rhinos, and "robust" australopiths, all show trends toward increasingly high-crowned teeth, or **hypsodonty,** and/or hypermasticatory development, adaptations associated with grassland diets of tougher and perhaps more abrasive foodstuffs (Turner and Wood, 1993a). Tundra-like open vegetation also first appears in northern-central Europe and the major glaciations in the Northern Hemisphere begin. In China one finds widespread and thick loess deposits (Kukla, 1987), and in the mountains of Colombia there is evidence for a significant lowering of the tree line (Hooghiemstra, 1986).

The climatic cooling noted at about 2.5 mya also marks the appearance in Europe of a distinctive mammalian fauna that includes animals particularly well adapted to highly seasonal, drought-resistant grasslands. This fauna characterizes the **Villafranchian** mammal age and is recognized by the presence of mammoths (*Mammuthus*), true bovines (cattle, bison, buffalo), and one-toed horses (*Equus*). None of the widespread Miocene hominoids of Eurasia (e.g., *Dryopithecus, Pliopithecus, Sivapithecus*) survived into the Pliocene of Europe, and only *Gigantopithecus* and fossil gibbons and orangutans persisted in Asia. (We will review the Miocene hominoid fossil record in Chapter 5). Likewise, none of the vast array of African Miocene hominoids is known from the Pliocene of that continent, although hominoids must, of course, have existed somewhere in Africa at that time, since their modern descendants, chimpanzees and gorillas, still survive there. Instead, what we do find in the Pliocene of Africa are the first undoubted hominins in the fossil record, the subject of Chapters 6–8.

But how well does the climatic forcing model hold up when compared and contrasted to another general model of speciation, the

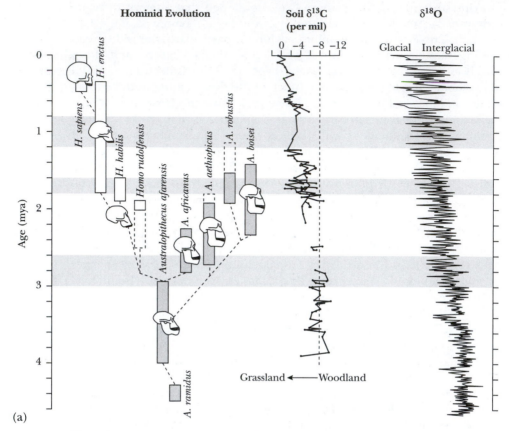

Fig. 2.9. (a) Temporal relations between changes in one scenario of hominin evolution, East African vegetation, and glacial ice volume. Step-like increases in African aridity at about 2.8, 1.7, and 1.0 mya may be related to significant speciation events in early hominin evolution. Increased regional aridity near 1.7 mya is supported by soil carbonate stable isotopic evidence (^{13}C values), and general cooling trends through the Plio-Pleistocene are evident in the oxygen isotope ^{18}O values. (From deMenocal, 1995.) (b) The climactic forcing model and Plio-Pleistocene hominin evolution.

Red Queen Model, which holds that evolutionary change leading to new species is driven by competition among populations that share the same habitat and that sexual recombination evolved to augment a population's capacity to evolve quickly (Van Valen, 1973)? In contrast to the climatic forcing model, the Red Queen Model would not predict a tight relationship between major climatic change and speciation events but would instead predict evolutionary change to continue even during periods of relative climatic stability. Two studies compared speciation events in hominin evolution to climatic patterns over the past 5 million years to see if any

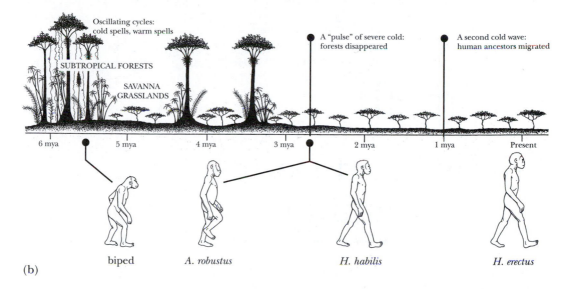

Oscillating cycles: cold spells, warm spells

SUBTROPICAL FORESTS

SAVANNA GRASSLANDS

A "pulse" of severe cold: forests disappeared

A second cold wave: human ancestors migrated

| 6 mya | 5 mya | 4 mya | 3 mya | 2 mya | 1 mya | Present |

biped   A. robustus   H. habilis   H. erectus

(b)

correlation between the two emerged (Foley, 1994; McKee, 1994). The results were unequivocal: Not a single statistically significant correlation was obtained between the first appearance of hominin taxa (speciation) and any climatic variable. This is not to say that climate does not affect hominin evolution, it most certainly does, particularly on levels of taxonomic diversity and extinction patterns. What it does say is that climatic forcing *alone* cannot explain the pattern of hominin evolution and that such patterns are probably best viewed as resulting from both climatic and intraspecific and interspecific competition.

Another hypothesis, referred to as variability selection, also attempts to relate widespread Plio-Pleistocene climatic and associated environmental change to important events in early hominin evolution (Potts, 1998). However, unlike other hypotheses that tend to stress the consistent selective effects associated with specific habitats or directional environmental change through time (e.g., reduction of woodland, savanna expansion), variability selection holds that wide climatic fluctuations through the Plio-Pleistocene created a growing disparity in adaptive conditions, eventually causing habitat-specific adaptations to be replaced by structures and behaviors more responsive to complex environmental change. According to this hypothesis, key hominin adaptations emerged during times of increased environmental variability and not during times of long-term, directional, environmental change like that envisioned by the various climate forcing models mentioned above.

Now that we have placed the study of human evolution within a general temporal and paleoenvironmental framework, it is time to launch into a more detailed discussion of how paleoanthropologists actually find, date, and name fossil hominins.

CHAPTER III

Finding and Dating Fossil Hominins

56

INTRODUCTION

Establishing plausible scenarios to explain how fossil hominins relate one to another is a central problem in the study of human evolution and the aspect of evolutionary study most prone to controversy. Before delving into the technicalities of hominin phylogeny and classification, we will first look at some examples of what paleoanthropologists do in the field and laboratory. Nearly all aspects of human paleontology—which include interpreting hominin fossils, establishing phylogenies, and speculating about the tempo and mode of human evolution—depend on some understanding of how and where fossils are found, and on how they are dated. In addition, we will come to appreciate just how infinitesimally short, in a geological sense, our presence on this planet has been. As the writer John McPhee expressed it (1998): "With your arms spread wide . . . to represent all time on earth, look at one hand with its line of life. The Cambrian begins in the wrist, and the Permian Extinction is at the outer end of the palm. All of the Cenozoic is in a fingerprint, and in a single stroke with a medium-grained nail file you could eradicate human history."

FINDING FOSSIL HOMININS

How *do* the remains of once-living animals end up as fossils, or to put it another way, how do bones that were once part of the biosphere end up as stones or part of the lithosphere? In trying to decipher the hominin fossil record, paleoanthropologists almost quite literally try to squeeze blood from a stone. The science that concerns itself with the process of fossilization is called **taphonomy,** which literally means "laws of burial" (Effremov, 1940; Olson, 1980). Fossilization usually takes place over thousands or millions of years, and much of the original geological and biological information is lost during the process (such as the ancient environmental context of the site or the form and function of soft tissues, like muscles). Thus one of the main objectives of modern paleoanthropological research is to reconstruct as much of this lost information as possible. In order to do so, the geological and biological conditions responsible for the creation of the particular fossil assemblage under study must be investigated (Fig. 3.1).

Both geological and biological factors determine what type(s) of environment(s) best preserve fossil bones after death (Bishop, 1980). Various geological factors include (1) the geometry and lithology of the sediments (e.g., their thickness, composition, and grain size); (2) sedimentary structural and/or dynamic properties that could depend, for example, on the existence of former streams or lake beds; and (3) depositional compositions that alter bone chemistry itself. Biological factors affecting fossil preservation may include the presence of predators (e.g., leopards) and bone scavengers (e.g., hyenas and porcupines). Geologists refer to the

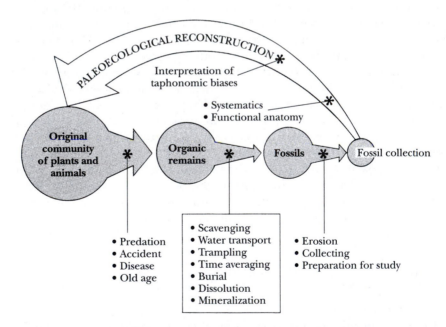

Fig. 3.1. Taphonomy is the study of how fossil samples are related to the original plant and animal communities of the past.   In order to reconstruct these past communities, the biological and geological conditions responsible for the creation of the particular fossil assemblage under study must be investigated. (Behrensmeyer, 1992.)

sum of the physical, chemical, and biological changes affecting fossil bearing sediments as **diagenesis.** Sedimentary diagenesis involves a temporal element as well: Were the fossils deposited over a relatively long or short period of time, or even over a geologically "instantaneous" period of time through a single catastrophic event, like a volcanic eruption or flash flood?

Because the factors that prevent bones from fossilizing far outnumber those that are conducive to fossilization, the chances that any one previously living hominin individual would ever become fossilized are exceedingly small, much less that it would be discovered thousands or millions of years later by paleoanthropologists.[1] And yet there have been many hominin fossil discoveries, some fortuitous and others the result of dogged persistence in the field. However, the study of taphonomy has led to an improved ability to predict the unique terrains and conditions in which hominin fossils are most likely to be recovered, and these predictions tend to correlate with the history of hominin finds.

Virtually all hominin fossils have been discovered in one of four main depositional environments: (1) volcanic deposits associated with large-scale tectonic forces such as rift valley formation; (2) lake, or lacustrine, deposits; (3) river, or fluviatile, deposits; and (4) cave deposits.

Box 3.1 Two Examples of Depositional Environments in Which Early Hominins Have Been Found

---

Let's consider the set of circumstances associated with fluviatile environments in East Africa, as illustrated in Figure 3.2a. In this case, an early hominin dies alongside a river fringed by riverine forest. The carcass is dismembered and scattered by predators, such as jackals, hyenas, and vultures. Some of the bones are washed downstream in a flash flood and then covered by successive layers of sediment, including ash from a nearby erupting volcano. Gradually, all the organic material in the bone disappears and is replaced by water-soluble minerals in the soil that ultimately turn the bone to stone. Suppose, in this example, that over hundreds of thousands (or perhaps millions) of years the environment changes into a stream-dissected region of eroding sediments with little vegetative cover, a topography referred to as **badlands**. A keen-eyed paleoanthropologist walking over these sediments might be fortunate enough to notice a small piece of fossilized bone or tooth eroding out of one of the many gullies in the region. And if he or she is fortunate enough to be able to match bits of sediment, or matrix, still attached to the fossil to some nearby stratigraphic layer, then a clue may be provided as to the location of the exact stratigraphic level from which the fossils are eroding. This would be a good place to start a test excavation in the hope of finding more of the fossil still embedded in the sediments. Geologists may also be able to radiometrically date the overlying and/or underlying volcanic ash and thereby provide a minimum or maximum age for the fossil. These dating techniques will be discussed more fully later in this chapter.

---

[1] It is estimated that only about 7% of all primate species that ever existed are known from fossils (Tavaré et al., 2002).

(a)

Fig. 3.2.   (a) One example of how a hominin might become fossilized and then later discovered in a fluviatile deposit in East Africa by paleoanthropologists. (Weaver, 1985.) (b) Four stages in the formation of the Swartkrans Cave site. Leopards are often attracted to the trees near entrances to dolomitic caves as safe retreats to bring their kills. Cave entrances characteristically support several large tree types that flourish there as a result of protection afforded to them from frost and fire. Thus many of the fossilized bones found in the cave breccias, including some of the early hominins, were probably part of leopard meals that were stored in these trees near the cave's entrance. (From Brain, 1970, 1993b.)

A very different environment in which fossil hominins have been discovered are the cave sites of southern Africa, first explored by paleoanthropologists early in the twentieth century. Most of the australopith-bearing South African cave sites are formed out of two kinds of Precambrian rock: magnesium-containing, or **dolomitic,** limestone and calcareous deposits, known as **tufas,** which are chemical sedimen-

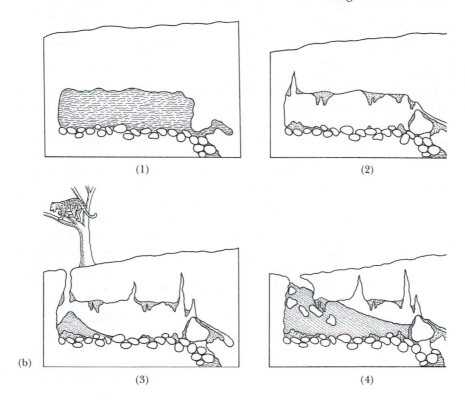

(1) (2)

(b)

(3) (4)

tary deposits rich in calcium carbonate typically occurring as incrustations around the mouths of springs (Brain, 1981b; McKee, 1993b).

Swartkrans Cave in South Africa (Fig. 3.2b) was initially formed by the solution of dolomite in groundwater, the contours of the cave being determined by planes of weakness in the rock (panel 1). As the water level in the region dropped, the cavern filled with air, and rainwater caused joints or other natural planes of weakness in the rock to form in the dolomite overlying the cave (panel 2). Eventually, one or more of the joints broke through to the surface, thereby providing a direct passageway between the cave and the surface. In caves of this sort, sediment containing the bones of animals that have washed in from the surface usually begins to form beneath the joint into what is called a **talus cone** (panel 3). When the sediment is calcified by lime-bearing solutions dripping from the roof, the resulting deposit is known as a **cave breccia.** Ultimately, the cavern fills almost completely with breccia; but over thousands or millions of years, surface erosion removes much of the dolomitic roof of the ancient cave, thereby exposing the fossil-bearing breccia at the surface (panel 4). The South African early hominin sites of Sterkfontein, Kromdraai, Swartkrans, and Makapansgat are currently at this stage of development. Because these cave sites were rich in limestone, they were early targets for mining activity—and, in fact, it was the miners who first noted fossil bones in most of these cave deposits.

DATING FOSSIL HOMININS

The technology of dating fossil sites has improved dramatically in recent years, making it possible to construct complex scenarios of geological, floral, and faunal transitions at a given site. Understanding the biological and/or cultural implications of a hominin fossil or artifact often requires two types of dating: **relative dating,** which seeks to put fossils and artifacts into a temporal context with other locally associated archeological, faunal, and floral materials; and **absolute dating,** which ties a fossil or artifact to an absolute time scale in years and therefore to other fossils or artifacts discovered at other sites. As we will see, time is an indispensable factor in any construct of relatedness and evolutionary change. Even though some, like strict cladists, disregard time when determining phylogenetic relationships (see below), the validity of any phylogenetic analysis depends on its being consistent with temporal considerations. For example, any phylogenetic analysis that concluded that Australian aboriginals were more closely related to *Homo erectus* than to modern Europeans would obviously be absurd based on what we know about the history of these groups in both time and space. Likewise, if we wish to explore how various phases of human evolution relate to major climatic cycles or changes, we need to know when in human history these climatic events occurred. Finally, cultural traditions (as seen in the archeological record) evolve just as biological systems do; therefore, accurate dating is imperative in order to understand the connections between biological evolution and cultural evolution through the Plio-Pleistocene. In later chapters we will see many examples of the relevance of dating techniques to all these issues. Ultimately, dating is really the only independent measure of the validity of any evolutionary scenario.

RELATIVE DATING

Before the advent of absolute dating techniques, paleoanthropologists were limited mostly to relative dating methods, and in some cases they still are today. Relative dating simply orders objects of interest (fossils, archeological assemblages, etc.) into temporal sequences relative to one another (i.e., older or younger than) and are often applicable only at the local or regional level. For example, if fossils can be securely placed into a local stratigraphic sequence, the so-called **Law of Superposition** dictates that the fossils contained in the lower strata will be older than those higher up in the stratigraphic sequence, assuming the strata are relatively undisturbed. It is also assumed that fossils found in the same stratigraphic level are roughly contemporaneous, the degree of contemporaneity depending on how quickly that particular strata was laid down. Of course, if younger fossils are redeposited in older sediments (e.g., in certain burials) then these assumptions are violated.

An example of relative dating at several important early hominin sites in southern Africa is shown in Figure 3.3. None of these sites contains rocks suitable for precise radiometric dating, yet by identifying the fossil mammals

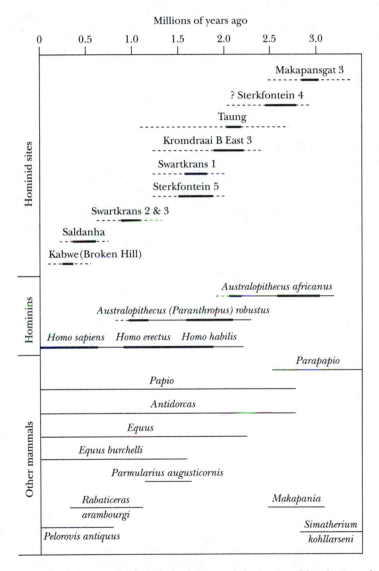

Fig. 3.3. Relative dating of fossil hominin sites and associated hominin and mammal fossils from southern Africa. Estimated time ranges of fossil hominin species and of some of the mammals used to date them are also shown. Numbers after the site names denote stratigraphic units (Members). *Parapapio* and *Papio* are baboons, *Equus* is the zebra, and the others are bovids (buffaloes and antelopes). (From F. Brown, 1992.)

associated with these early hominins and then comparing them to similar species from radiometrically dated sites in East Africa, paleoanthropologists are able to place these sites into a reasonably secure temporal framework. For example, the bovids from Makapansgat are similar to those found in several East African sites radiometrically dated to 3.7–2.5 mya, suggesting that the Makapansgat sediments are roughly equivalent in age.

Relative dating often relies on chemical and geological information. Several chemical tests widely used in paleoanthropology measure the concentrations of fluorine, uranium, and/or nitrogen within fossil bones found together in the same deposit to determine their relative ages. The **nitrogen test** is based on the fact that the nitrogen-containing amino acids in collagen break down at a predictable rate as bone fossilizes. Thus the amount of nitrogen remaining in the bone indicates how long the bone has been fossilizing. The **fluorine test** is based on the fact that bones absorb flourine from surrounding groundwater that then combines with bone calcium to form the compound fluoroapatite. The longer the bone has been in the ground, the more fluoroapatite is present. Fluorine and nitrogen relative dating tests are complementary in that bones deposited recently would have higher nitrogen contents and lower fluorine contents than more ancient bones. These chemical tests are site specific, meaning that the amount of nitrogen lost or fluorine absorbed depends on geological and environmental factors at each particular site. For this reason, these tests usually cannot determine the relative ages of fossil bones found at sites whose conditions of deposition are different.

A notable early success in using these tests was the unmasking of the infamous Piltdown forgery. Flourine dating tests determined that the calvaria had much more fluorine than the "associated" mandible; of course, had they both been in the deposits at Piltdown for the same amount of time they would have absorbed approximately equal concentrations of fluorine. Because of this discrepancy, the fossils were more carefully examined, and it was found that the mandible was actually that of a female orangutan whose molars had been filed down to obscure its true identity (Spencer, 1990; Weiner, 1955).

ABSOLUTE DATING: RADIOMETRIC AND OTHER TECHNIQUES

Contrary to popular belief, most **radiometric dating** techniques do not date the fossil bones themselves but rather the geological strata associated with the fossil bones. (As we discuss in detail below, the major exception to this is carbon-14 dating, which can date fossil bones only younger than 50–70 kya, the normal outside limit of the technique.) Ideally one would like to date the actual fossiliferous layer of sediment, but when there is any question about the relation between the fossil and the sediment from which it came, one brackets the fossil by dating strata above and below it (if possible) in order to provide minimum and maximum ages. This is accomplished by one of several different dating techniques.

Radiometric dating techniques are indispensable to the study of human evolution. All such techniques are based on the principle that when atoms of a radioactive element emit radiation, these "parent" atoms decay at a known constant rate into "daughter" atoms of another element. In such cases, the age of the sample is determined by measuring the ratio of parent to daughter atoms remaining in the sample. This procedure is employed when the radioactive atoms included in newly formed rock contain none of the daughter atoms, the initial daughter to parent ratio thereby being set at zero.

The principles behind radiometric dating are determined by the chemical behavior of atoms. Many atoms are unstable and change spontaneously to a lower energy state by radioactive emission or decay within the nucleus itself. Two atoms that have the same number of protons, and hence the same **atomic number,** but a different number of neutrons, are called **isotopes.** For instance, two commonly used isotopes of uranium (atomic number 92) are ^{235}U and ^{238}U. The superscripts represent the **atomic mass number,** or total number of protons and neutrons. Radioactive decay may occur through one of the following processes, depending on the characteristics of the atom:

- **Alpha decay.** The nucleus of the parent atom loses two protons and two neutrons; thus its mass number decreases by four and its atomic number decreases by two. An example of alpha decay is the decay of uranium to thorium: ^{238}U to ^{234}Th.
- **Beta decay.** One of the neutrons in the nucleus turns into a proton; in this case the atomic number increases by one but the mass number remains unchanged. An example of beta decay is the decay of rubidium to strontium: ^{87}Rb to ^{87}Sr.
- **Electron capture.** A proton in the nucleus turns into a neutron, thus decreasing the atomic number by one. As in beta decay the mass number remains unchanged. An example of electron capture is the decay of potassium to argon: ^{40}K to ^{40}Ar.

All radioactive elements are inherently unstable and each has a characteristic decay behavior and a unique constant rate of decay. Thus if a radioactive element is incorporated into a mineral or rock when it forms, the amount of the radioactive element that decays into its daughter atoms is controlled only by the elapsed time since formation. The principle of radiometric dating can be likened to sand in an hourglass; the amount of sand in the top chamber compared to the amount of sand accumulated in the bottom chamber always provides a measure of the time that has elapsed since the glass was turned. Just as the hourglass is sealed so that extraneous sand cannot enter or leave the system, so too must the atomic structure of the mineral be "sealed" so that neither the parent nor the daughter atoms can enter or leave from any external source (Eicher, 1976).

Each individual atom of a given radioactive isotope has the same probability of decaying within any given year, and this probability remains the same no matter how long the material being dated has been in existence. This probability of decay is termed the **decay constant** (let us call it K) and is simply that proportion of atoms of a particular element that always decays within any given year. The number of atoms that will actually decay is $K*N$, where N is simply the number of radioactive parent atoms still present in the system at the beginning of the year. At the beginning of the following year, the number of radioactive parent atoms is obviously smaller, having decreased by the amount $K*N$. Thus the number of radioactive parent atoms decreases with each succeeding year. The time required for half of the atoms of any particular radioactive element to decay is termed its **half-life,** and each radioactive element has its own specific half-life that may last seconds or millions of years.

The end of one half-life marks the beginning of the next one. Thus, if N_0 represents the initial number of atoms, then half that number $(N_0/2)$ remain after the first half-life, half of those $(N_0/4)$ remain after the second half-life, half of those $(N_0/8)$ remain after the third half-life, and so on. If one plots the number of surviving parent atoms as a function of time, the result is a curve like that shown in Figure 3.4. This relationship forms the

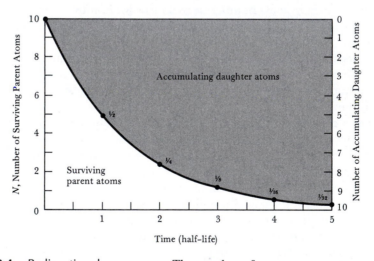

Fig. 3.4. Radioactive decay curve. The number of parent atoms present when the rock was formed (N_0) is arbitrarily taken here to be 10 units. The points along the curve (N/N_0) represent the ratio of surviving parent atoms to the initial number of parent atoms. Using the right-hand vertical axis, one can also read off the number of daughter atoms present at any given time. (From Conroy, 1990.)

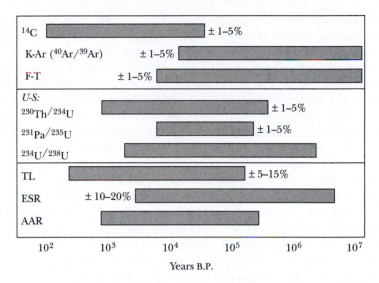

Fig. 3.5. The main dating methods used in paleoanthropology. (From Schwarcz, 1992a.)

basis for most radioactive clocks. As a simple illustration, suppose one wants to determine the age of a sample in which the parent to daughter ratio is found to be 1:32 and the half-life of the element is known to be 1 million years. Since 1:32 equals $(1/2)^5$, this means that the sample has undergone five half-life cycles and is thus 5 million years old.

A number of conditions are required to use radiometric techniques in paleoanthropological studies, including the following:

- The radioactive decay process of the samples must not have reached completion too early; if it has, the sand will all be in the bottom of the hourglass—that is, the isotope will have completely decayed into its daughter isotopes.
- All materials to be dated (e.g., bones, artifacts, pottery, minerals) must lie in a well-defined stratigraphic context.
- Any analytical methods used to detect the products of radioactive decay must be sufficiently refined to give dates within statistically acceptable margins of error.

The main dating methods used in paleoanthropology are shown in Figure 3.5, along with their approximate dating ranges.

Carbon-14

One of only two techniques that can be applied to fossil bone directly, carbon-14 (^{14}C) dating is important and widely used. This technique can date many once-living carbon-containing materials, like wood, charcoal, bone, shell, and peat, within a range of about 300 to 50,000 years ago, and in exceptional cases, up to about 70 kya (Hughen et al., 2004; Taylor, 1996). It is customary to express radiocarbon dates in terms of years before the present (B.P.) where "the present" is taken to be 1950. A useful rule of thumb is that it takes about 83 years for 1% of radiocarbon to disappear and about 3 days for a millionth part to disappear. The limitations on the young end of the time scale are a consequence of three factors: (1) recent significant variability in ^{14}C production rates due to rapid changes in solar magnetic intensity since the seventeenth century, (2) the effect of the combustion of large quantities of fossil fuels beginning in the late nineteenth century, and (3) the production of artificial ^{14}C as a result of the detonation of nuclear and thermonuclear devices in the atmosphere beginning in the 1950s (Leute, 1987).

Carbon-14 is continuously produced in the upper atmosphere by the interaction of cosmic-ray neutrons with stable isotopes of nitrogen (^{14}N).[2] The radioactive atoms of ^{14}C, along with those of the much more numerous nonradioactive isotopes of carbon, ^{12}C and ^{13}C, are rapidly incorporated into atmospheric carbon dioxide (CO_2) (Gillespie, 1984). Generally, the ratio of ^{14}C:^{12}C in the atmosphere remains relatively constant—that is, the continuous production of ^{14}C is offset by its continuous radioactive decay, a condition referred to as steady state. All living organisms in equilibrium with the atmosphere maintain a small natural concentration of radiocarbon; carbon dioxide enters plants through photosynthesis and/or root absorption and is passed on to animals through the plants they eat. But when an organism dies, or when any carbon-containing compound can no longer exchange carbon freely with the atmosphere, ^{14}C is no longer absorbed, and its concentration declines as a result of radioactive decay (the half-life of ^{14}C is 5730 $\pm$ 40 years). By comparing the atmospheric ^{14}C:^{12}C ratio to that of the dead organism and by knowing the half-life of ^{14}C, the time since death can be calculated (Fig. 3.6).

Working with Carbon-14 Samples   A number of potential uncertainties are involved in ^{14}C dating. For example, has the activity of ^{14}C in plant and animal tissues been constant and independent of time during the past 70,000 years or have there been fluctuations in levels of absorption? Are ^{14}C values independent of geographic location? Do ^{14}C values vary with the species of plant or animal whose tissues are being dated? Have the samples themselves been contaminated with modern ^{14}C or are they in other ways impure?

Recent studies indicate that there have been systematic variations in atmospheric radiocarbon content in the past that could make radiocarbon dates inaccurate unless the fluctuations are taken into account. For example, the higher radiocarbon content of plants and animals in the polar regions may result from a rate of ^{14}C production that is significantly greater in

---

[2]Expressed as $n + {}^{14}N \rightarrow {}^{14}C + H$, where n is the neutron and H is the proton that is emitted by the product nucleus.

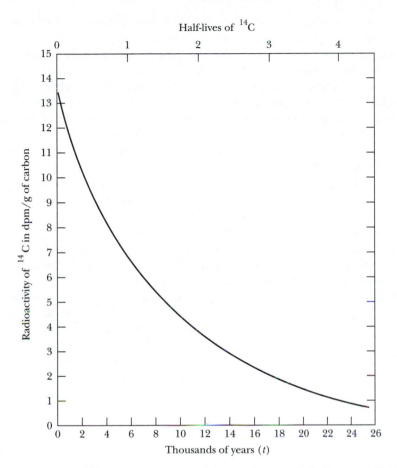

Fig. 3.6. Decay of ^{14}C in plant or animal tissue that was initially in equilibrium with $^{14}CO_2$ in the atmosphere (or hydrosphere). When the plant or animal dies, the exchange stops and the activity due to ^{14}C decreases as a function of time (the half-life of ^{14}C is about 5730 years). (From Faure, 1986.)

the polar atmosphere than at the equator. Also, the radiocarbon content of the Earth's atmosphere is influenced by the intensity of both solar activity and the Earth's magnetic field. Finally, the introduction of fossil fuels into the Earth's atmosphere since the Industrial Revolution has also influenced ^{14}C activity in the atmosphere, as has radiation from atomic bombs.

How do geochronologists deal with these potential sources of error in ^{14}C dating? One way is to calibrate the variation of the atmosphere's radiocarbon content by analyzing the carbon content of wood from ancient trees like the sequoia (*Sequoia gigantea*) or the bristlecone pine (*Pinus aristata*). Trees grow by adding a layer of woody tissue to the circumference of their trunks and branches each year thereby isolating the underlying woody layers from atmospheric ^{14}C. Therefore, the concentration of ^{14}C in the underlying woody tissues decreases over time because of radioactive decay. Variations in the radiocarbon content of the atmosphere over the past several thousand years can thus be measured by analyzing wood samples whose age is established by counting annual growth rings—that is, by dendrochronology. The age-corrected deviations of the radiocarbon content of such trees can then be used to calculate corrections to conventional radiocarbon dates. Unfortunately, such adjustments to the ^{14}C time scale cannot be accurately calibrated by dendrochronology much before about 10 kya due to the lack of suitable fossil trees for such dating. However, paired uranium and thorium (^{234}U/^{230}Th) and ^{14}C samples from cores drilled into coral formations now extend the ^{14}C calibration curve back to about 20 kya. Even so, it does appear that ^{14}C ages are consistently younger than true ages for objects dated to beyond about 9 kya (Bard et al., 1990b).

The advent of accelerator mass spectrometry (AMS) technology in the 1980s made possible improvements in ^{14}C dating: (1) smaller sample sizes can be analyzed from grams to milligrams of carbon and (2) major reductions in counting times are possible. It was hoped that the applicable dating time frame could be increased from the currently routine 40–70 kya to as much as 100 kya, but this last goal has yet to be realized (Taylor, 1996).

A novel application of radiocarbon dating has been to date rock art in both North America and Europe. For example, charcoal used in prehistoric paintings at Altamira and El Castillo Caves in Spain and at the Niaux Caves in France have been dated to about 14 kya and 13 kya, respectively (Valladas et al., 1992). Organic carbon found in paint pigment in southwestern Texas rock art has been dated to 4 kya (Russ et al., 1990).

Potassium-Argon and Argon-Argon

Two of the most important radiometric techniques in paleoanthropology are potassium-argon (K-Ar) and the closely related argon-argon (^{40}Ar-^{39}Ar) methods. Conventional K-Ar dating relies on the decay of ^{40}K (about 0.01% of all potassium) through a complex sequence of intermediate steps into ^{40}Ar. Consolidated volcanic ash, known as **tuff,** and certain **igneous rocks,** like basalt, that flow in a molten state to the Earth's surface from deeper in the crust are the samples most widely used for K-Ar dating. With a half-life of just under 1.3 billion years, K-Ar decay can date the oldest rocks on Earth as well as rocks dating to less than 100 kya.

Conventional K-Ar dating requires the processing of at least two samples. The first sample has to be chemically processed to measure the amount of stable potassium-39 (^{39}K) it contains, and a second sample has to be melted to measure the amount of ^{40}Ar present. Since the ^{40}K:^{39}K ratio is constant from rock to rock, the amount of ^{39}K in the sample reflects the amount of radioactive ^{40}K originally contained within the rock. These separate procedures may lead to various degrees of imprecision.

Conventional K-Ar dating also requires that all of the argon must be extracted from the sample that is to be dated.

Two types of errors are associated with K-Ar dating that, if not accounted for, may lead to distorted dates: Discrepantly high ages may occur if any ^{40}Ar is incorporated into the rock or mineral to be dated at the time of its formation, and discrepantly low ages may occur if ^{40}Ar is lost from the rock or mineral due to diffusion or various other chemical reactions (Fitch, 1972).

More recently, a spinoff of conventional K-Ar dating, the ^{40}Ar-^{39}Ar method, has been developed that overcomes some of the limitations of conventional K-Ar dating by allowing both potassium and argon to be measured from a single sample and by requiring the measurement of isotope ratios of argon only. It is one of the most precise dating methods available. Under ideal circumstances (e.g., using potassium-rich volcanic minerals like sanidine), age precision of 0.5% or better is possible for samples in the 100,000–10,000,000 year range (Deino et al., 1998; Ludwig and Renne, 2000). The technique is based on the assumption, noted above, that the isotopic proportions of both ^{39}K and ^{40}K are essentially constant in natural terrestrial materials. Samples for this type of dating are first irradiated in a nuclear reactor, which converts a portion of the ^{39}K to ^{39}Ar by bombardment with fast neutrons. Thus ^{39}Ar serves as a proxy for the amount of ^{40}K in a sample. A standard of known age must also be analyzed along with the sample to be dated in order to calculate the age of the sample. This standard, known as the monitor mineral, provides a measure of neutron flux, which in turn permits calculation of the parameter J in the following age-determination formula:

$$t = \frac{1}{\lambda} \ln \left(1 + J \frac{^{40}Ar}{^{39}Ar} \right)$$

where t is the age of the sample, λ the radioactive decay constant, and ^{39}Ar the amount of ^{39}Ar produced by neutron bombardment from ^{39}K. The ability to derive the ^{40}K and ^{40}Ar contents directly from the same material avoids the problem of sample splitting found in conventional K-Ar dating. Another advantage over conventional K-Ar dating is the ability to use very small amounts of material, even down to single grains, for dating.

The recent dating of the Vesuvius eruption by ^{40}Ar-^{39}Ar techniques to 79 C.E. (1925 ± 94 years ago) shows the potential of this method for dating events into the Holocene (Renne et al., 1997).

Working with K-Ar and ^{40}Ar-^{39}Ar Samples   When potassium-bearing rocks are experimentally subjected to neutron irradiation, a series of reactions are set up that result in the formation of several isotopes of argon. The most important of these reactions produces ^{39}Ar from ^{39}K. Of course, the number of atoms of ^{39}Ar produced is directly proportional to the number of atoms of ^{39}K present in the original sample. As noted above, the atoms of ^{40}Ar in the sample are produced by the radioactive decay of ^{40}K atoms. In one variation of the ^{40}Ar-^{39}Ar method, all the argon gas is extracted at once, yielding dates that are comparable to conventional K-Ar dates; still, they are based only on measurements of isotopic ratios of ^{40}Ar:^{39}Ar and do not require a separate determination of the potassium concentration. However, argon can also be released by irradiating samples at ever-increasing temperatures, thereby allowing ages to be calculated for each fraction of the argon gas released from the sample. In this way, a spectrum of dates can be calculated from the ^{40}Ar:^{39}Ar ratio for each step until finally an age plateau is reached that provides the best overall age estimate for the sample (Faure, 1986).

One final variation of the ^{40}Ar-^{39}Ar technique that is becoming more widely used in paleoanthropology is the **single-crystal fusion** method. In this method, a laser is used to melt crystals to release the argon gas. This technique has two important advantages over the methods mentioned above: (1) because the laser beam allows such a localized heating of the crystals there is much less chance of background atmospheric argon confounding the final age calculations, and (2) it greatly reduces the amount of sample needed for the age determination (F. Brown, 1992).

Fossil-bearing strata associated with volcanic events can also be correlated using geological "fingerprints" characterizing individual volcanic episodes. Since products of volcanic explosions like ash, lapilli, and pumice are collectively known as **tephra,** this is referred to as tephrostratigraphy. Tephra provide a key to both dating and correlation. Some tephra can be directly dated. In addition, the glass component of many ashes has a geochemical fingerprint that is unique to a particular volcanic eruption, thereby defining an isochronous marker layer within the stratigraphic record. By identifying characteristic geochemical signatures, geologists can correlate sequences and establish time relationships among distant fossiliferous localities. Many important Plio-Pleistocene hominin localities in East Africa have been established using such tephrostratigraphic frameworks (Feibel, 1999).

Uranium Series

Uranium is present as a trace element in virtually all naturally occurring materials, thereby providing a very large potential sample for radiometric dating and for building up fossil chronologies. Uranium series (U-S) dating includes several techniques based on the radioactive decay of either ^{238}U or ^{235}U through a series of intermediate steps to various daughter isotopes. The entire uranium series of radioactive elements and isotopes, only some of which are useful in radiometric dating, is shown in Figure 3.7a. The different sets of daughter isotopes used for dating purposes are thorium-uranium (^{230}Th-^{234}U, or simply Th-U), protactinium-uranium (Pa-U), and ^{234}U-^{238}U. The first of these is the most widely used (Schwarcz, 1992a, 1992b).

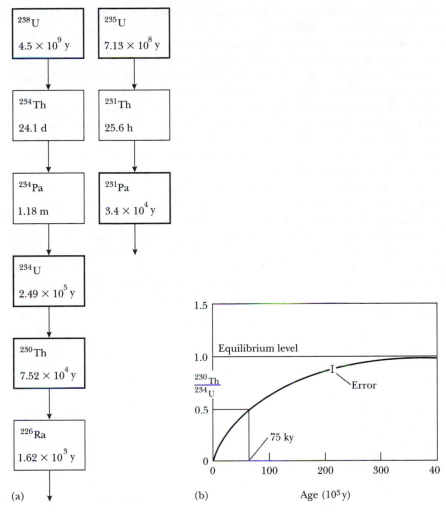

Fig. 3.7. (a) The decay series of each of the parent isotopes of uranium. Heavily outlined boxes represent isotopes having half-lives long enough to be useful in dating fossil hominins. The numbers under the elements refer to their half-lives. *m,* minutes; *d,* days; *y,* years. (b) The ^{230}Th:^{234}U activity ratio as a function of the age of a sample. The origin of the graph assumes the sample was initially precipitated with a zero content of thorium. The error bar is an example of the magnitude of typical errors in this dating technique. In this example, a ^{230}Th:^{234}U ratio of 0.50 corresponds to an age of 75 kya (75 ky in the figure). (From Schwarcz, 1992a.)

Working with U-S Samples   All U-S dating methods are based on the observation that unaltered uranium-containing material contains a certain proportion of each daughter isotope. Most important, in any uranium-bearing material that has lain undisturbed for millions of years, the radioactive decay rate of each daughter isotope equals the decay rate of all other daughter isotopes in the same sample. Such a sample is said to be in **secular radioactive equilibrium.**

For example, if atoms of ^{238}U are decaying at the standard decay rate of 1 disintegration unit per minute (dpm) per gram of sample, then all its daughter isotopes (e.g., ^{230}Th, ^{226}Ra) will decay at 1 dpm per gram as well. The decay rate (in dpm/g) is proportional only to the concentration of uranium in the sample and does not depend on any other chemical or physical property of the sample. However, when a sample is altered or disturbed by some physical or chemical process, it departs from secular radioactive equilibrium, and millions of years may elapse before equilibrium is reestablished. For radiometric dating purposes, this state of disequilibrium is most important because it preserves a record of the time when the sample was disturbed. It is the age of the disturbance that is measured in U-S dating. The following example may help clarify the method.

While most geological material at hominin sites are ancient rocks that are in, or close to, equilibrium, other materials such as stalagmites, bones, teeth, or shells may have arrived, or been formed, at the site de novo. Imagine that one wishes to date a calcium carbonate deposit that is associated with a fossil or stone-tool assemblage. Further suppose the deposit is a **travertine,** a crystalline calcium carbonate deposit precipitated in solution in ground or surface water by inorganic chemical processes. As we might expect, the travertine contains a concentration of uranium that can be used to date the sample. However, when freshly deposited, travertine contains no ^{230}Th because this isotope, unlike the uranium that produces it, is relatively insoluble in water and, therefore, cannot be precipitated within the structure of the travertine. Thus the $^{230}Th{:}^{234}U$ ratio in the travertine will be zero on the date of its formation: With the passage of time, some ^{234}U decays to ^{230}Th, and the $^{230}Th{:}^{234}U$ ratio increases (Fig. 3.7b). Remember that equilibrium is defined as the equal radioactive decay rate of each daughter isotope with its parent atom. Thus, in equilibrium, ^{230}Th decays at the same rate it forms by the decaying ^{234}U. As the travertine approaches equilibrium, the $^{230}Th{:}^{234}U$ activity ratio approaches a limiting value of 1.0; in the curve shown in Figure 3.7b the degree of approach to equilibrium is used as a measure of the time elapsed since the sample was formed. The date at which this ratio approaches 1.0 is the effective upper age limit for this dating technique, in this case approximately 350 kya. The minimum age is typically a few hundred years. Depending on the procedures used, the accuracy of such dates ranges from approximately 1% to 5%.

The principal materials datable by U-S techniques include various types of chemically or biologically precipitated calcium carbonate ($CaCO_3$; calcite or aragonite), such as:

• travertines: crystalline calcium carbonate deposits formed by chemical precipitation from solution by inorganic processes (e.g., flowstone or dripstone in caves, tufa near springs)

- **speleothems:** any variously shaped mineral deposits formed in caves by the action of water (e.g., stalagmites, stalactites, and flowstones)
- **calcretes:** calcitic deposits formed in soils of arid regions
- **biogenic carbonates:** skeletons or shells of some marine organisms made of aragonite or calcite (unfortunately, molluscan shells are unsuitable for U-S dating, but stromatolitic [algal] calcite and coral are well suited for U-S dating)

Studies are still being done to see if other materials can be used for U-S dating, including **apatite** (the phosphate found in teeth and bones), wood, and peat. Tests using the U-Th dating method on corals from Barbados have confirmed the high precision of the technique for dating at least the past 30,000 years. In fact, precision of U-Th dating is often better than that achieved for most ^{14}C dating for materials older than 10 kya. These results suggest that U-Th dating may be used as a first-order tool to calibrate the ^{14}C time scale beyond the range of dendrochronological tests (Bard et al., 1990b).

Fission Track

Although fission track (F-T) dating relies on the principle of radioactivity, it differs from the methods previously discussed in that it measures the side effects of **spontaneous fission** within the atomic nucleus of ^{238}U. During spontaneous fission, the nucleus splits into two or more high-energy fragments, and these fragments leave damage tracks within the rock crystals that can be enlarged and studied. Instead of measuring parent to daughter ratios, F-T dating counts the number of tracks left behind by the naturally recoiling atoms in the sample; the more tracks per unit volume, the older the sample. Over time a uranium-bearing sample accumulates spontaneous fission tracks, and if all of the tracks were made since the sample was formed (or was fired, in the case of pottery) the number of fission tracks would be a measure of the sample's age. It must be kept in mind, however, that the density of fission tracks is a function of both the sample's age and its uranium content and that fission tracks can fade over time and at elevated temperatures. Given the right kind of sample, F-T dating can be applied to common minerals such as micas, apatite, and zircon, ranging in age from a few decades to 3.5 billion years, the age of the oldest rocks on earth (Wagner, 1996). The technique has been particularly useful in archeology for dating pottery and obsidian tools. For example, when clays used in making pottery contain crystals of zircon, the fission-track "clock" of the zircon would be set to zero when the pottery was "fired" (MacDougall, 1976). Likewise, if an obsidian artifact was heated when made, the fission tracks would date the age of its manufacture. Successful F-T dating is based on the assumptions (1) that ^{238}U decays at a constant rate (^{238}U decays by spontaneous fission with a half-life of 8.2×10^{15} years), (2) that fission tracks are produced and retained with 100% accuracy, and (3) that the concentration of uranium in any specimen remains constant through time.

Thermoluminescence and Electron Spin Resonance

Many sediments containing common minerals like quartz or feldspar have weak levels of radioactivity, since most contain at least some traces of the radioactive elements uranium, potassium, and/or thorium. In addition, various types of ionizing radiation, such as gamma rays, cosmic rays, and even sunlight, sometimes interact with atoms in soils in such a way that electrons are removed and trapped within the crystal lattice of the material. Because these electrons retain the excess energy they received from the radiation source, heating these solids induces the trapped electrons to return to their stable energy states and liberates the excess energy as light in the process. The light emitted by such thermal activation is called **thermoluminescence** (TL), and the intensity of the emitted signal is a measure of the trapped electrons in the mineral. In TL dating, the signal is stimulated by heat, whereas in optically stimulated luminescence (OSL) dating the signal is stimulated by light from a lamp or a laser (Aitken and Valladas, 1992). Since minerals within fossiliferous sediments may contain some of these trapped electrons, their radioactive signal may be detected with appropriate instrumentation (Aitken and Valladas, 1992; Ciochon et al., 1990; Feathers, 1996).

A prerequisite for successful TL dating is that at some time in the past the trapped electron population of the material was zero. Some materials may be "zeroed" or "reset" when they are heated to upward of 450^0C or occasionally when exposed sufficiently to daylight. Thus, for burnt stones (e.g., burnt flint or quartz tools) and pottery, the "resetting date" is the time of firing; for unfired calcite, it is the time of crystallization; and for sediments, it is the time of deposition subsequent to exposure to sunlight. As in other radiometric tests, electrons accumulate in the lattice at a standard rate, and the amount of accumulated energy is a measure of the duration of time since the solid was originally formed or subsequently zeroed.

In order to transform the dating signal into years, it is first necessary to measure the amount of total radiation that has accumulated in the sample (the accumulated dose) and the amount of radiation the sample receives in 1 year in that particular sedimentary environment (the dose rate). Determining the accumulated dose, or total radioactive signal of the sample, is a two-step process. The radioactivity of the sample is first measured in a spectrometer. To calibrate the result, the sample is given a dose of radioactivity of known intensity, after which the radioactivity of the sample is measured a second time. From these two tests, one is able to calculate the original level of radioactivity in the sample (or the measure of radiation to which the sample has been exposed since it was last zeroed; i.e., last heated to about 450^0C). The annual radiation dose, or the dose rate per year that the sample has been receiving while buried, is determined from the concentrations of radioactive uranium, thorium, and potassium in the parent rock. The time elapsed since the last heating is thus given by the simple relationship:

$$\text{age} = \frac{\text{accumulated radiation dose}}{\text{annual radiation dose}}$$

TL dating is still somewhat problematic. Although TL has been successful in dating archeological materials such as pottery, glass, bones, shells, and flint heated by fires, its use in dating sediments exposed to sunlight is much more equivocal (Aitken and Valladas, 1992; Cook et al., 1982). There is little doubt that heat from fire can set the TL clock back to zero in the case of pottery or burnt stones, but it is not so clear whether the clock is set to zero in sediments containing quartz or feldspar simply by exposure to sunlight. Although some electrons may require only a few minutes of sunlight to be thoroughly bleached (i.e., freed from their electron traps), others may require hours or even days of ultraviolet light for this to occur. Thus for sediments blown into an archeological site by wind, the minerals would probably be exposed to enough light to be entirely bleached and thus TL dating would be appropriate; however, for sediments deposited by river or glacial action this may not be the case. TL dating of sediments at archeological sites under the latter conditions could produce misleadingly old TL dates (Gibbons, 1997).

The presence of unstable electrons in solids can also be detected by **electron spin resonance** (ESR) (Grün, 1993; Schwarcz and Grün, 1992). Unlike TL dating, in which the number of trapped electrons is determined by heating and the emission of light, in ESR dating, the number of trapped electrons is determined by measuring their absorption of microwave radiation. The radiation exposure age of a sample dated by ESR is calculated using the same formula as noted above for TL dating. The theoretical age range of ESR dating is from a few thousand years to more than 1 mya, but in practical terms most age estimates beyond about 300 kya are very uncertain.

For paleoanthropologists, the most useful material for ESR dating is tooth enamel. After an animal dies, its enamel starts to record the radioactivity of the environment in which it is buried. This radioactive signal emanates from minute concentrations of radioactive elements that are in the environment (e.g., uranium, thorium, and potassium) as well as from cosmic rays. Unfortunately, bone and other components of teeth, such as dentine and cementum, are not suitable for dating; but the technique has been successfully applied to calcite in cave deposits, fossil shells, and corals (Grün et al., 1990a, 1990b, 1991; Ikeya and Miki, 1980; Porat and Schwarcz, 1994).

One advantage of ESR over TL dating is that TL measurements remove the age information from the sample, whereas an ESR measurement can be taken a number of times on the same sample.

Amino Acid Racemization

Amino acid racemization is a nonradiometric test that has been used to date such diverse materials as fossil bone, mollusk shells, and ostrich eggshell, ranging from a few centuries to several hundred thousand years old (Bada, 1985; Bada et al., 1974; Brooks et al., 1990; Goodfriend, 1992; Miller et al., 1992).

The bones of living animals consist of 25–30% organic material, most of which is protein. At death, these proteins begin to break down into free amino acids through predictable biochemical pathways. The one property of amino acids that makes them potentially useful for dating is that most of them exist in at least two configurations that have the same molecular formula. Two amino acids that have different structures but identical formulas are called **optical isomers** and are designated D and L forms. Only the L-amino acids are commonly found in living organisms, although some D-proteins are found in certain bacteria (Bada, 1985). However, over long periods of time these L-amino acids slowly undergo a conversion from the active L-amino acid form into the inactive D-amino acid form, a process known as **racemization.** Thus the ratio of D- to L-amino acids remaining in a fossil increases through time, and the rate of this reaction is slow enough to be useful in geochronology. Aspartic acid has one of the fastest amino acid racemization rates, and for this reason it has generally been used for dating Holocene and Upper Pleistocene fossils. Isoleucine, on the other hand, has a racemization rate about 10 times slower than aspartic acid and is used to date older fossil bones.

Amino acid racemization rates are very sensitive to both temperature and the physical/chemical environment in which the material to be dated has been deposited. For example, the half-life of amino acids undergoing racemization ranges from a few days at 100^0C to thousands of years at 20–25^0C. For this reason, formulas that convert the degree of racemization to geological age must first be empirically "calibrated" to account for variations in paleotemperatures and other relevant environmental factors of the locality over the time period of interest. In order for amino acid racemization dating to be practical, the fossil to be dated must have been kept at a relatively constant temperature over time and the amino acids in the sample must have been separated from any environmental contamination (Bada, 1985; Bada et al., 1974; Brooks et al., 1990; Goodfriend, 1992; Miller et al., 1992; Turekian and Bada, 1972). Environments that come closest to meeting these criteria are deep-sea sediments, where there has been relatively constant cold-water temperatures over long periods of time, and deep sealed caves, in which the temperature remained relatively constant during the various Ice Age cycles.

It is fair to say that the validity of the technique is the subject of intense debate, particularly because of this dependence on temperature and on the physiochemical environment (Blackwell and Rutter, 1990).

SUMMARY OF ABSOLUTE DATING TECHNIQUES

The most widely used dating methods in paleoanthropology today are those just discussed: carbon-14, uranium series, potassium-argon, argon-argon, fission-track, thermoluminescence, electron spin resonance, and amino acid racemization (Figure 3.5). Of these, carbon-14, uranium series, potassium-argon, and fission-track are all based on the radioactive decay of specific isotopes. Thermoluminescence and electron spin resonance use aspects of ionizing radiation and require additional information about paleoenvironmental factors that may affect their results. Since fission-track and potassium-argon dating are applicable only where volcanic rocks are present, and carbon-14 is applicable only for ages less than about 70 kya at best, electron spin resonance, thermoluminescence, and uranium-series have the most potential for dating stages of human evolution in locations where volcanic rocks are scarce or absent. Amino acid racemization and carbon-14 are the only techniques able to date fossil bone directly.

Now that we have explored potential hominin sites and the dating methods used to age hominin fossils, how, and what, do we name them?

CHAPTER IV

Naming and Classifying Fossil Hominins

INTRODUCTION

Two important goals of modern paleoanthropological research are the phylogenetic reconstruction of the human lineage and the classification of human fossils. As the novelist and ecoterrorist guru Edward Abbey once wrote (Abbey 1989): "We are all ONE, say the gurus. Aye, I might agree—but one What?" Often the failure to appreciate the distinction between phylogeny and classification leads to much confusion, controversy, and misunderstanding in human evolution studies. **Classification** is simply the process of establishing, defining, and ranking taxa within some hierarchical series of groups (Lincoln et al., 1990). **Phylogeny**, on the other hand, concerns the evolutionary history of organisms and includes both cladogenetic and anagenetic information (Ashlock, 1974). **Cladogenesis**, or dendritic evolution, refers to a branching type of evolutionary process involving the splitting and subsequent divergence of populations. **Anagenesis**, or phyletic evolution, refers to the evolutionary process of gradual accumulation of changes in ancestor-to-descendant lineages through time.

The controversy arises when the relationship between classification and phylogeny is considered. All biological systematists agree that the criteria chosen upon which a classification is based should reflect some aspects of phylogeny but there is great disagreement about which details to emphasize. As one evolutionary biologist commented: "That there should be any controversy at all might . . . seem strange. The principle of classification, considered superficially, might seem too straightforward to be controversial: you simply have to define groups by taxonomic characters. . . And if taxonomists are observed superficially that is what they appear to do" (Ridley, 1986). However, as we shall see, the processes by which taxonomic characteristics are selected and employed in classification are more complex, bringing in theoretical and philosophical considerations of a more subjective sort.

THREE ANALYTICAL LEVELS OF CLASSIFICATION AND PHYLOGENY

Implicit in any Darwinian system of classifying organisms is a set of underlying evolutionary principles, and the classification of any group of organisms, including hominins, depends upon which organizing principles are adopted. Most hypotheses about human evolution can ultimately be boiled down to three analytical levels each having its own degree of complexity. The first, or simplest, level is represented by the **cladogram,** which is a branching diagram of the distribution of unique character states, a **character** being any feature chosen for study. Membership in a **clade** means that the members have specific characters in common with each other and with their most recent common ancestor but not with earlier ancestors. These characters, because they can be identified only with immediate ancestors and with members of the same clade, are called shared derived, or **synapomorphic**, characters (characters *B* and *C* in Fig. 4.1a). A character may evolve through several character states, and each state is derived from the one preceding it. Although the common possession of such derived character states (see below) among different taxa implies that they share some type of evolutionary relationship, *the exact nature of the evolutionary relationship is not specified in the cladogram* (Eldredge and Tattersall, 1975; Tattersall, 1986; Tattersall and Eldredge, 1977).

The second, more complex analytical level is represented by the **phylogram,** or phylogenetic tree, which adds information not present in a cladogram by depicting the nature of the hypothesized evolutionary relationships among the various taxa. For example, the evolutionary relationship may be an ancestor-descendant lineage or a forked lineage of two daughter species derived from one parental species after a speciation event (Fig. 4.1b). Furthermore, phylogenetic trees convey more information because they depict not only extinct and extant taxa but also ancestor-descendant relationships and degrees of divergence among taxa. By convention, the branches in a phylogenetic tree represent lineages, forks in the branches represent speciation events, the slant and length of the branches reflect the rapidity with which divergence took place, and the branch end points indicate terminal taxa, either extant or extinct (Fig. 4.2). In pictorial terms, the main difference between a cladogram and a phylogram is that the former has no time dimension.

To summarize, a phylogram may add to the information contained in a cladogram by specifying the nature of the evolutionary relationships postu-

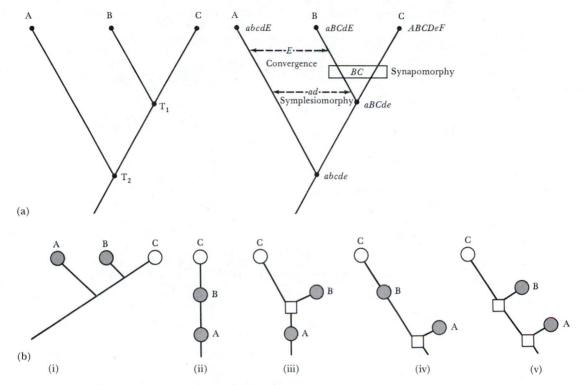

Fig. 4.1. (a) In the simple cladogram on the left, hypothetical taxa B and C are more closely related to one another than either is to taxon A, since they share a more recent common ancestor (T_1). Thus taxa B and C together make up a clade that is the sister group of taxon A. In the simple cladogram on the right, characters observed in three taxa and inferred in their common ancestors are given beside each group. Lower-case letters signify primitive (plesiomorphic) characters and capital letters signify derived (apomorphic) states of those same characters. Taxa B and C are linked by shared derived (synapomorphic) character states *B* and *C*. Characters *a* and *d* linking taxa A and B are shared primitive (symplesiomorphic) characters and thus do not indicate any special relationship between those two taxa. Character *F* is an autapomorphic character (one that arose for the first time in that group) in taxon C. (Adapted from Patterson, 1987.) (b) Cladograms and phylograms compared for information content. Open circles represent recent taxa, filled circles represent fossil taxa, and squares represent postulated common ancestors. The four phylograms (ii–v) are all consistent with the given cladogram (i) and provide more information about hypothesized ancestor-descendant relationships than does the cladogram. (From Szalay, 1977.)

lated as well as the temporal sequence of the taxa, provided reliable data can be obtained from fossil-bearing rock layers. The comparative information content of cladograms and phylograms is illustrated in Figure 4.1.

The third and most complex level is the scenario. A **scenario** is not a diagram at all but an historical narrative that attempts to describe not only

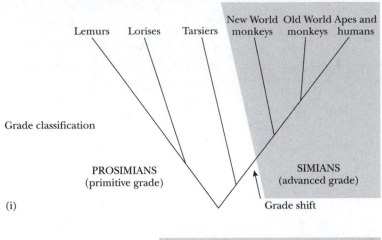

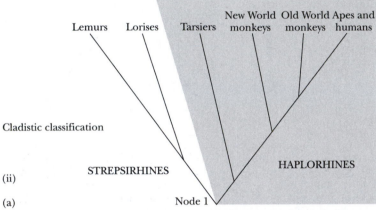

Fig. 4.2. (a) Two approaches to the classification of living primates. (i) In the classical (or grade) classification, the classification is based on the general grade of organization of the animal. In this phylogram primates that have retained a relatively high proportion of primitive features are allocated to a lower grade (Prosimii), whereas those primates characterized by a higher proportion of advanced features are allocated to a higher grade (e.g., simians or Anthropoidea). (ii) By contrast, in a cladistic classification, divisions are based solely on the sequence of branching within the tree rather than preservation of the general features of the group. Node 1 represents the point at which organisms ancestral to lemurs and lorises—the strepsirhines—became genetically isolated from the ancestors of the other primates—the haplorines. Individual groups in the cladogram are, therefore, considered clades rather than grades. (From Simpson, 1963a.) (b) Contrasting classifications of living hominoid primates. (i) Cladists classify groups solely according to the branching sequence of phylogeny, and sister groups are given the same taxonomic rank. For example, if *Pongo* is placed in the family Pongidae, its sister group (comprising *Pan, Gorilla,* and *Homo*) must also be included in a family, Hominidae. (ii) Evolutionary systematists take the same phylogenetic information but classify the taxa differently, by taking into account the unique morphological and behavioral features of *Homo* compared with those of the other great apes. Thus *Homo* is placed in its own family, the Hominidae and the great apes are placed in a separate family, the Pongidae. From (From Martin, 1992a.)

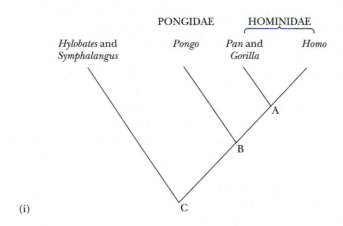

(i)

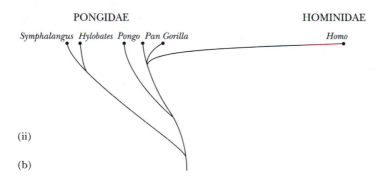

(ii)

(b)

phylogenetic relationships among taxa but also the ecological and/or evolutionary forces that most directly influenced the character state(s) under discussion. More abstract, hypothetical, and interpretive than the cladogram or phylogenetic tree, the scenario also inspires the greatest number of verbal fisticuffs in paleoanthropology (Hull, 1979; Landau, 1984, 1991).

TWO SCHOOLS OF CLASSIFICATION

The two main schools of biological classification popular in paleoanthropology today, **evolutionary systematics** and **phylogenetic systematics** (**cladistics**), make different uses of the analytical tools outlined above and sometimes arrive at differing classifications. The more traditional approach, evolutionary systematics, evaluates the observed similarities and differences among organisms in terms of their presumed line of evolutionary descent, or phylogeny. In cladistics, the phylogenetic relationship is defined solely by "recency of common ancestry." There are two points of agreement between the schools. First, both agree that branching sequences are important, though the evolutionary systematist believes that classification should reflect more than just branching sequences. Second, both agree that analyses of morphological characters must be taken into account before a classification may be accepted and that some morphological characters are better suited than others for biological classification. Morphological characters that are considered better clues than others to evolutionary relationships are given greater weight in both systems, a practice known as **character weighting**. But this is where the similarities end. The pictorial representation of evolutionary systematics is the phylogenetic tree, which, as we have already noted, shows *both* the branching patterns of ancestor-descendant lineages and the degree of divergence of the descendant branches (Fig. 4.2). In this approach, the systematist takes into account not only the branching pattern of phylogeny but the subsequent evolutionary fate of each branch as well (Mayr, 1981). Phylogenetic systematics (cladistics), on the other hand, employs the cladogram and tries to represent phylogenetic relationships in a very formalistic way, which we will examine in detail.

The underlying philosophy of phylogenetic systematics (cladistics) was best expressed by its founder, the German entomologist Willi Hennig (1965), as follows:

> New species originate exclusively because parts of existing reproductive communities have first become externally isolated from one another for such extended periods that genetic isolation mechanisms have developed which make reproductive relationships between these parts impossible when the external barriers which have led to their isolation are removed. Thus, all species (= reproductive communities) which exist together at a given time . . .have originated by the splitting of older homogeneous reproductive communities. On this fact is based the definition of the concept, "phylogenetic relationship": under such concept, species B is more nearly related to species, C, than to another species, A, when B has at least one ancestral species source in common with species C which is not the ancestral source of species A.

Thus in cladistics the degree of phylogenetic relationship is defined solely by "recency of common ancestry" (the more recent ancestry of B and C above) and pictorially represented in the cladogram. The sole aspect of phylogeny that cladists represent is the *order* of branching sequences among taxa, which in turn reflects the distribution of certain characters within a clade or group of related organisms. As noted earlier, members of a clade possess shared derived characters, or synapomorphies, (i.e, characters they share in common with each other and with their most recent common ancestor but not with earlier ancestors). An important distinction needs to be drawn between groups of organisms having a common genetic origin (clade) and those characterized by a certain level of organization and/or adaptation, or **grade** (Fig. 4.2) (Huxley, 1958; Wood and Chamberlain, 1986).

To the cladist, phylogeny is simply a sequence of dichotomies, or splitting evolutionary branches, with each fork of the branch representing the splitting of a parental taxon into two daughter taxa known as **sister groups**. The clade stemming from the most recent common ancestor of sister taxa with extant representatives (i.e., the clade containing only living taxa and their last common ancestor) is called a **crown clade;** the clade that includes all species, living or extinct, that are more closely related to the living members of that group than to any other living taxon is called a **stem-based clade**. The taxon Anthropoidea refers to what can be termed a "closed descent community," including both a stem-based lineage and a crown group. Most paleoanthropologists who use the term are referring to the stem-based clade that includes the living and fossil platyrrhines (New World higher primates) and catarrhines (Old World higher primates) as well as the fossil taxa that are more closely related to those groups than either is to *Tarsius* (Williams and Kay, 1995; Wyss and Flynn, 1995).

In its strictest form, cladism demands that sister groups occupy the same taxonomic rank—that is, the same genus, family, superfamily, etc.—and that the parent taxon ceases to exist after it splits into its two daughter taxa. Because of this, a cladistic classification can be read directly off a cladogram simply by ranking sister groups in a hierarchical fashion. However, what is sometimes overlooked is the fact that cladistic classifications do not necessarily represent the branching order of sister groups per se but rather the order of emergence of unique derived characters, whether or not the development of these characters happens to coincide with speciation events (Hull, 1979).

THE PROBLEMS OF CLASSIFICATION

The first step in cladistic analysis, or any classification scheme, is to cluster together those species that seem morphologically similar. However, morphological resemblance cannot be the sole criterion by which phylogenetic relationships are determined because morphological similarity may have several causes. More specifically, two groups of organisms may resemble each other in a given character state for any one of the following reasons:

- The similar character existed in the ancestry of the two groups before the evolution of their nearest common ancestor. This is a shared *primitive* character, or **symplesiomorphy.** In Figure 4.1a, *a* and *d* represent symplesiomorphic characters. Clearly, characters can remain unchanged through a number of speciation events. Therefore, the common retention of shared primitive characters cannot be used as evidence of a close phylogenetic relationship. If one associates in a group taxa whose similarities are based on shared primitive features, then one may create a group that consists of taxa derived from a single ancestral taxon but does not contain all the descendants of that most recent common ancestor, a so-called **paraphyletic** group (Fig. 4.3).

• The similar character originated in a common ancestor of the groups and is shared by all of that ancestor's descendants. In this case, the character is a shared *derived* character, or synapomorphy. In Figure 4.1a, *B* and *C* represent shared derived characters. Note that *B* and *C* are *not* present in the ancestor of all three taxa A, B, and C, but only in the immediate ancestor to B and C. By contrast, two groups may differ from each other because one possesses a character that arose for the first time in that group. This type of unique derived character is an **autapomorphy.** Such characters are acquired by a phylogenetic line *after* it has branched off from its sister group. In Figure 4.1a, *F* is such a unique derived character. The supposition that two or more taxa are more closely related to one another than to any other taxon can be confirmed only by demonstrating their common possession of synapomorphic characters. Two or more such taxa constitute a **monophyletic group** (Fig. 4.3).

• The similar character arose independently in several descendant groups. This is a convergent character. A taxonomic group whose resemblances are based on convergences is called a **polyphyletic group.** A polyphyletic group consists of taxa derived from two or more distinct ancestral taxa and is a taxonomic category based on convergence rather than on common ancestry (Fig. 4.3).

(a) One paraphyletic group   (b) Two monophyletic groups   (c) One polyphyletic group

Fig. 4.3. Three different ways of forming taxonomic groups. (a) Paraphyletic group. If a taxonomic grouping is based on shared primitive features (symplesiomorphies), the group may consist of taxa derived from a single ancestral taxon but not contain all the descendants of that most recent common ancestor. (b) Monophyletic group. These groups are based on the common possession of shared derived (synapomorphic) features and include the ancestral species and all descendant species. (c) Polyphyletic group. A taxonomic group whose resemblances are based on convergences. A polyphyletic group consists of taxa derived from two or more distinct ancestral taxa and is a taxonomic category based on convergence rather than common ancestry. (From Hennig, 1965.)

The similarities in form or structure that are of interest to systematists in building classifications are called **homologous** structures when they are shared among two species and their common ancestor. An example of homology is pentadactyly, as in the five-fingered hand of chimpanzees and humans. Depending upon the school of classification they adhere to, systematists attempt to deal with several other factors in choosing and weighting characters. The opposite of homology, **homoplasy,** is any resemblance not due to inheritance from a common ancestry—that is, similarities due to parallel evolution, convergent evolution, or analogy. **Parallel evolution** is the independent acquisition in two or more related descendant species of similar character states evolved from a common ancestral condition; **convergent evolution** is the independent evolution of structural or functional similarity in two or more unrelated or distantly related lineages or forms that is not based on genotypic similarity; and **analogy** is functional similarity due to convergent evolution rather than to common ancestry—that is, a similarity of form or structure shared between two species but not shared with their nearest common ancestor. An example of such a structure would be the wings of birds and bats.

One of the main problems systematists encounter in character analysis arises in the case of **polymorphic** characters, those that change gradually over a continuum of forms, or **morphocline**, from one species to another. The problem is to determine the **polarity** of the morphocline; in other words, which end of the continuum is primitive and which end is derived? For example, the mammalian forefoot can have from one to five digits (e.g., horses versus humans). Which of the two character states is actually the primitive mammalian condition and which is the derived one?

There are several ways of dealing with this problem. If a given morphological character state is typical of a large number of relevant taxa and particularly if the state is shared with other closely related taxa of similar taxonomic rank, then it is reasonable to regard that state as primitive. Another alternative is to rely on developmental, or **ontogenetic** data. Although the old notion that ontogeny recapitulates phylogeny is no longer accepted in the literal sense, morphological characters typical of an early stage of an organism's development are still generally considered more primitive than features appearing at a later stage. Thus in the case of the mammalian forefoot, five digits are regarded as the primitive condition and any reduction in this number is considered a derived state.

Strictly speaking, cladists do not weight characters. Rather, they discard from their analysis any characters that are not synapomorphies. For example, among prosimian primates (lemurs and lorises) the possession of a shared derived trait, like the special alignment of canines and incisors for fur grooming known as the **dental comb,** has more taxonomic significance than the possession of a shared primitive trait, such as a comparatively small brain. In this view the common possession of such derived characters proves the common ancestry of a particular group, whereas the common possession of primitive characters has little, if any, taxonomic value.

Harvard zoologist Ernst Mayr (1981) succinctly summed up the distinction between the two taxonomic schools (Mayr, 1981):

> The main difference between cladist and evolutionary taxonomists is in the treatment of autapomorph characters. Instead of automatically giving sister groups the same rank, the evolutionary taxonomist ranks them by considering the relative weight of their autapomorphies as compared to their synapomorphies. For instance, one of the striking autapomorphies of man (in comparison to his sister group, the chimpanzee) is the possession of Broca's center in the brain, a character that is closely correlated with man's speaking ability. This single character is for most taxonomists of greater weight than various synapomorphous similarities or even identities in man and the apes in certain macromolecules such as hemoglobin or cytochrome C. The particular importance of autapomorphies is that they reflect the occupation of new niches and new adaptive zones that may have greater biological significance than synapomorphies in some of the standard molecules.

Even though humans may actually be very similar to apes in certain molecular characters such as in overall protein and DNA structure, the two groups differ so much in mental capacity that no less a figure than famed biologist Julian Huxley once proposed that humans should be placed in a separate kingdom—the Psychozoa!

But what do paleoanthropologists mean by the term *species*? There are actually a number of species concepts current in the evolutionary biology literature:

- *Biological species concept*: A group of actually or potentially interbreeding natural populations that are reproductively isolated from other such groups (Mayr, 1963).
- *Evolutionary species concept*: A lineage (an ancestral-descendant sequence of populations) evolving separately from others and with its own unitary evolutionary role and tendencies (Simpson, 1963b).
- *Recognition species concept*: The most inclusive population of biparental organisms that share a common fertilization system (Patterson, 1986).
- *Cohesion species concept*: The most inclusive population of individuals having the potential for phenotypic cohesion through intrinsic cohesion mechanisms (Templeton, 1989).
- *Phylogenetic species concept*: The smallest diagnosable cluster of individual organisms within which there is a parental pattern of ancestry and descent (Cracraft, 1983).
- *Concordance principle*: If several independent lines of genetic evidence converge on a single partition, then species status for the populations in question is suggested if the inferred reproductive barrier is intrinsic, but subspecies status is suggested if they are solely extrinsic (geographic) (Avise, 1994).

The biological species concept (based on actual or potential reproductive isolation) that describes living species is not applicable to fossils because actual or potential interbreeding has ambiguous anatomical

Box 4.1   Two Examples of Cladistic and Evolutionary Systematics Classifications

---

To illustrate the differences between evolutionary and phylogenetic systematics, let's consider how each school would approach the classification of two very different types of animals—crocodiles and birds. Although crocodiles and birds took very different evolutionary pathways and have obvious morphological differences, a strict cladist would have to classify them as sister groups because they share characters derived from a common reptilian ancestor. In fact, birds have sometimes been referred to as "glorified reptiles" for, with the exception of feathers, almost every character in their skeleton can be matched to that of archosaurian reptiles. They would also have to be classified at the same taxonomic rank, even though one sister group, the crocodiles, still looks very much like the ancestral reptilian group whereas the other, birds, obviously does not.

Looking at the same organisms, an evolutionary taxonomist would take into account the different evolutionary history of each group. Accordingly, the two groups would be assigned to different taxonomic ranks, with crocodiles being classified as an order within the class Reptilia and birds as an altogether separate class, Aves (Mayr, 1981). In general, the evolutionary systematist considers the fossil record to be an important arbiter as to whether or not an inferred primitive group is the true one or not. As eminent paleontologist George Gaylord Simpson (1975) once noted, "primitiveness and ancientness are not necessarily related, but they usually are."

Consider how the contrasting schools approach the relationships among humans and apes. A cladist would interpret the cladogram in Fig. 4.2b.i to mean that humans, chimpanzees, and gorillas (*Homo, Pan,* and *Gorilla*) share a more recent common ancestor with one another than they do with orangutans (*Pongo*). Thus *Homo* forms a clade that is the sister group of the clade formed by *Pan* and *Gorilla,* and together these three genera form a clade that is the sister group of *Pongo*. These four genera would in turn make up the sister group of a clade consisting of gibbons (*Hylobates*) and siamangs (*Symphalangus*). The classification would necessarily reflect this branching pattern, as follows: If the orangutan clade were classified at the family level, say as Pongidae, then humans, chimpanzees, and gorillas would also have to be classified together at the family level as Hominidae, since sister groups must have the same taxonomic rank (Fig. 4.2b.i). To put a finer point on it, then, a cladistic interpretation suggests that the term *hominid* should be used to refer to humans as well as chimpanzees and gorillas. To avoid any confusion however, we use the term *hominin* in this text to refer only to humans and their immediate fossil relatives (e.g., the genera *Homo* and *Australopithecus*).

An evolutionary systematist might derive a very different classification from the same cladistic relationships, depending upon how much emphasis is placed on unique derived, or autapomorphic, characters. For example, as we see above the strict cladist classifies chimpanzees and humans as sister groups and accords them the same taxonomic rank, even though chimpanzees presumably look much more like the ancestral group than modern humans do. In other words, since diverging from chimpanzee-like ancestors, humans as a lineage have developed an extensive suite of autapomorphies—large brains, bipedal posture, language, delayed maturation, and elaborate tool use among others—that the evolutionary systematist takes into account in the phylogram (Fig. 4.2b.ii). Evolutionary systematists, therefore, usually classify all the apes in the family Pongidae and humans in the family Hominidae, even though chimpanzees share a more recent common ancestor with humans than with some of the other apes, such as orangutans and gibbons. The justification is that humans have reached a higher grade of evolution (Panchen, 1992). In short, evolutionary classifications reflect the adaptive and morphological attributes of a taxon rather than their strict cladistic relationships.

correlates that are not easily observable in fragmentary fossils. A morpho-species is defined by anatomical differences. Adding a time dimension results in the phylogenetic species concept, which holds that species can be diagnosed (1) by sharing at least one feature unique to them (synapomorphy) and (2) by having a unique pattern of descent from a single ancestor within the group and no descendants outside of it (monophyly). According to this concept, the phylogenetic species is easy to recognize in the fossil record because each so-called species is defined by the presence of one or more unique features (e.g., *Homo erectus, H. ergaster, Homo neanderthalensis*).

Unfortunately, there is little if any necesssary relationship between the biological species concept and the phylogenetic species concept. Because of this problem, another species concept, the evolutionary species concept, has been described. The evolutionary species retains the essence of the biological species: reproductive isolation. Evolutionary species are identified not by the amount of variation per se but rather by the pattern of variation—how it is distributed over space and how it changes through time. In this concept, species are created and ended by lineage splits or extinctions and are not arbitrarily defined by comparing the variation from their beginning to end with the variation across the range of an extant species. The variation over the life of a species has a temporal dimension and is controlled by accidents of cladogenesis and extinction. Variation over the range of species has a spatial dimension and is controlled by the adaptive potential of the gene pool and the ecological range of the species. In this view, for example, *Homo erectus* would be seen simply as an early version of *H. sapiens* (Tattersall, 1994; Wolpoff, 1994; Wolpoff and Caspari, 1997).

THE TEMPO AND MODE OF HUMAN EVOLUTION

Two important components in debates about hominin phylogeny and classification concern the rate (**tempo**) and process (**mode**) by which hominin evolution actually occurred. Determining the tempo and mode of hominin evolution is a formidable challenge since neither aspect of the evolutionary process is obvious from a human fossil record in which fossilization has occurred by chance and in which many organic changes in organisms have not necessarily been preserved. As George Gaylord Simpson (1953) put it:

> Looking more closely into the pattern of evolution, we see that it involves also the organic changes that have occurred in the (branching) sequence and the rates at which these changes have occurred. Trying to see how these (organic changes) arose, were transmitted, and became what they did, we find ourselves grappling finally with every factor and element that is in life or that affects life.

There are currently two principal models concerning tempo and mode in hominin evolution. The first, sometimes referred to as **phyletic gradualism**, holds that a daughter species usually originates through a progressive series of small, gradual transformations of a parental species—the process we have previously described as anagenesis. There are several main attributes of this model: (1) new species arise by the gradual modification of an ancestral population, (2) the transformation is generally slow, (3) the transformation may involve most of the ancestral population but more commonly involves **allopatric** populations (i.e., populations occupying different and disjunct geographical areas), and (4) the transformation takes place over all or at least a large part of the ancestral population's geographic range.

An alternative model, **punctuated equilibrium**, holds that the creation of a new species (speciation) is more often than not a comparatively rapid event. Furthermore, its advocates believe this is the mode that best describes the kinds of major evolutionary changes paleoanthropologists study and that the hominin fossil record contains (Eldredge and Gould, 1972; Gould and Eldredge, 1993). The model is based on the idea that most evolutionary change is concentrated in comparatively rapid speciation events in small isolated subpopulations of the ancestral species, a process known as **allopatric speciation.** A species that originated in such a small, isolated population and then spread to invade the territory of the parental population would appear to paleoanthropologists as having arisen abruptly in the fossil record; thus speciation in such populations would appear to be essentially instantaneous in terms of geologic time.

What is novel about the punctuated equilibrium model is the idea that most evolutionary change within lineages is concentrated in these rapid speciation events and that the rest of most species' life histories—the time before or after the actual speciation event itself—is characterized by little change, or **stasis.** Thus the *equilibrium* part is as important to this model as the *punctuated* part. There are several main attributes of this model (Levinton and Simon, 1980): (1) most new species arise from the splitting of existing lineages; (2) most new species develop rapidly, then stabilize; (3) a small subpopulation of the ancestral species gives rise to the new species; (4) the new species originates in a very small, isolated part of the geographic range of the ancestral species; and (5) once they arise, species do not change much throughout their remaining history.

Both of these models of tempo and mode have important implications for interpreting the fossil hominin record (Cronin et al., 1981; Gingerich, 1991, 1993; Godfrey and Jacobs, 1981). For example, a phyletic gradualist might interpret the many obvious morphological discontinuities in the fossil hominin lineage as mere gaps in the fossil record, perhaps using them as convenient temporal boundaries for dividing the fossil lineage into different species, say for example, between *Homo erectus* and *H. sapiens.* A punctuationist, on the other hand, would regard the same fossil data as a reflection of the normal evolutionary process: long periods of morphological stasis interrupted by rapid speciation events. To the punctuationist, the process of change from *H. erectus* to *H. sapiens* would not be seen as a slow, gradual species-wide evolution but rather as resulting from allopatric speciation in which a *H. erectus* subspecies, as a peripheral isolate of the *H. erectus* parental species, rapidly evolved and ultimately replaced its parental population by migration. In this view, unlike phyletic gradualism, the main body of the *H. erectus* species does not undergo the gradual change to a new *H. sapiens* species. Thus what is considered missing data by a phyletic gradualist is considered evidence for a critical evolutionary event by a punctuated equilibriumist. In the equilibriumist interpretation, one has to ask what the chances are that a given series or sequence of fossils found at a particular site just happen to coincide with the point of geographic isolation of a subspecies from the parental population.

Strict gradualists, in emphasizing the importance of steady morphological change within fossil lineages, interpret speciation as a special case of phyletic evolution. They see species as arbitrary units conveniently defined by gaps in the fossil record. Strict punctuationists, in arguing that morphological change is dominated by abrupt speciation events, see species as discrete units having a beginning and an end in time. Thus, although strict proponents of both models agree that both slow and rapid changes are manifested in the fossil record, they interpret the data quite differently (Fig. 4.4).

Increasingly, paleoanthropologists and biologists alike seem to view these two models of speciation as opposite ends of a continuum of possibilities, with some lineages being better described by one model and some tending toward the other in their pattern of speciation, but few species being exclusively defined by either.

Now that we have looked at some of the ways paleoanthropologists find, date, and name fossils, we are ready to delve into the fossil record itself. If, as all modern biology suggests, humankind is part of a long evolutionary continuum, we need to know who or what preceded us in the evolutionary line. That is the question we address in the next chapter.

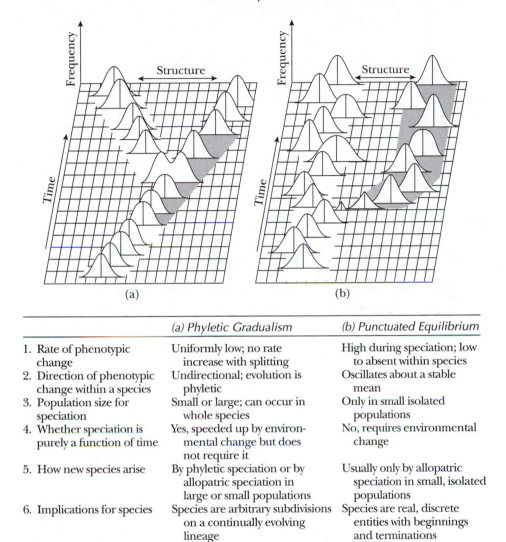

	(a) Phyletic Gradualism	(b) Punctuated Equilibrium
1. Rate of phenotypic change	Uniformly low; no rate increase with splitting	High during speciation; low to absent within species
2. Direction of phenotypic change within a species	Undirectional; evolution is phyletic	Oscillates about a stable mean
3. Population size for speciation	Small or large; can occur in whole species	Only in small isolated populations
4. Whether speciation is purely a function of time	Yes, speeded up by environmental change but does not require it	No, requires environmental change
5. How new species arise	By phyletic speciation or by allopatric speciation in large or small populations	Usually only by allopatric speciation in small, isolated populations
6. Implications for species	Species are arbitrary subdivisions on a continually evolving lineage	Species are real, discrete entities with beginnings and terminations

Fig. 4.4. Major differences between (a) phyletic gradualism and (b) punctuated equilibrium.   Different species are denoted by stippling. The bell curves simply represent the morphological variability within the populations at any point in time. (From Vrba, 1980a.)

CHAPTER V

Before the Bipeds: Human Antecedents among the Miocene Hominoids

INTRODUCTION

In Cormac McCarthy's haunting novel of the American Southwest, *Blood Meridian*, the "Judge" remarks: "Whatever in creation exists without my knowledge exists without my consent" (1985). The Judge wasn't referring to Miocene hominoids, but the sentiment fits. Certainly our knowledge of human antecedents in the Miocene is murky at best and consensus is lacking about the identity of the "missing link" between Miocene "apes" and succeeding early hominins.

Legend has it that the wife of the Bishop of Worcester was heard to exclaim after someone explained Darwin's new theory to her: "Descended from the apes! My dear, let us hope that it is not true, but if it is, let us pray that it will not become generally known." Whether this story is true or not, I do not know, but if it is the Bishop's wife need not have worried. Humans are not descended from chimpanzees—that would be unkind to chimpanzees. We do, however, share a common ancestor somewhere back in the Miocene. But if the earliest hominins didn't spring full blown, as Minerva did from Jupiter, from the head of a chimpanzee or gorilla around 7 million years ago, then where *did* they come from? The story of human evolution unfolds mainly over the last two epochs of the Cenozoic Era—the Pliocene and the Pleistocene. But to understand humankind's deeper history, which is the subject of this chapter, we must search among the fossil hominoids (or primitive "apes") of the preceding epoch, the Miocene. **Hominoid primates** encompass the lesser apes (gibbons and siamangs of eastern Asia), the great apes (chimpanzees and gorillas of Africa and the orangutan of Southeast Asia), and humans (as well as their fossil relatives). The Miocene was the heyday of hominoids for it was during this epoch that they reached their greatest abundance and diversity, and there is little doubt that human origins lie somewhere within this group.

A major rethinking of Miocene hominoid phylogeny began to emerge by the late 1970s, reflecting new fossil discoveries, developments within the field of molecular anthropology, and a wave of enthusiasm for cladistics. The results of these studies led paleoanthropologists to conclude that the traditional taxonomic scheme of hominoid primates prevalent in the 1960–1970s (i.e., that modern ape taxa had already diverged by the Early/Middle Miocene) was incorrect. Accumulating data were making two things increasingly clear: (1) the African apes (chimpanzees and gorillas) were more closely related to humans than either one was to the orangutan, and (2) the evolutionary lineages leading to each of the modern African apes (and humans for that matter) could not have diverged as long ago as the Early/Middle Miocene (Andrews, 1978; Andrews and Cronin, 1982; Goodman et al., 1983, 2001; Pilbeam, 1996; Pilbeam et al., 1980; Sarich, 1971; Sarich and Cronin, 1976; Sarich and Wilson, 1967; Sibley and Ahlquist, 1984, 1987; Templeton, 1984, 1991; Wildman et al., 2003). This rethinking of hominoid phylogeny ultimately led to the classification scheme presented in Table 5.1.

The purpose of this chapter is not to examine in detail each of the myriad genera and species of Miocene hominoids but rather to briefly describe and focus on those more relevant to discussions surrounding human origins. Although it is impossible to present a coherent overview of Miocene hominoids within a universally accepted taxonomic and phylogenetic framework, Table 5.1 provides a general consensus classification of Miocene hominoids relevant to discussions in this text.

In addition to this formal classification scheme, several more informal clusters of Miocene hominoids are sometimes recognized: (1) primitive Early Miocene hominoids of East Africa, characterized by molar enamel with high dentine penetrance forming dentine pits and many other primitive catarrhine features of the cranial and postcranial skeleton (e.g., *Proconsul*); (2) Middle and Late Miocene hominoids of Africa and Eurasia, characterized by thickened molar enamel and many other cranial (but not necessarily postcranial) similarities to *Pongo* (e.g., *Kenyapithecus, Sivapithecus, Ankarapithecus*); and (3) Middle Miocene hominoids of Eurasia, which share some cranial and postcranial features with later hominins (e.g., *Dryopithecus, Ouranopithecus*). These will all be discussed in greater detail throughout this chapter.

Table 5.1 Taxonomy of Some Miocene Hominoids Mentioned in the Text

Infraorder: Catarrhini
 Superfamily: Hominoidea
  Family: Proconsulidae
   Subfamily: Proconsulinae
    Genus: *Proconsul*
   Subfamily: Afropithecinae
    Genus: *Afropithecus*
    Genus: *Otavipithecus*
  Family: Griphopithecidae
   Subfamily: Griphopithecinae
    Genus: *Griphopithecus*
    Genus: *Kenyapithecus*
    Genus: *Equatorius*
  Family: Hominidae
   Subfamily: Homininae
    Tribe: Dryopithecini
     Genus: *Dryopithecus*
     Genus: *Ouranopithecus*
    Tribe: *incertae sedis*
     Genus: *Orrorin*
     Genus: *Sahelanthropus*
   Subfamily: Ponginae
    Genus: *Sivapithecus*
    Genus: *Ankarapithecus*
    Genus: *Gigantopithecus*
    Genus: *Lufengpithecus*
   Subfamily: Oreopithecinae
    Genus: *Oreopithecus*

(Also see "Taxonomy Used in This Text" in the Preface.)

AFRICA IN THE MIOCENE

The Miocene epoch lasted nearly 20 million years, from about 24 to 5 mya (Harland et al., 1990). Primitive Old World hominoids first appear in the late Oligocene/Early Miocene fossil record of East Africa about 25 mya and become abundant and diverse in a number of East African faunas 22–17 mya (Harrison, 2002). By the Middle Miocene, approximately 16–11.5 mya, this situation changes dramatically, with monkeys becoming more abundant in the fossil record and hominoids less so, a trend that continues to this day. The Early/Middle Miocene, about 16.5 mya, was also the time when African hominoids first emigrated to Eurasia. For

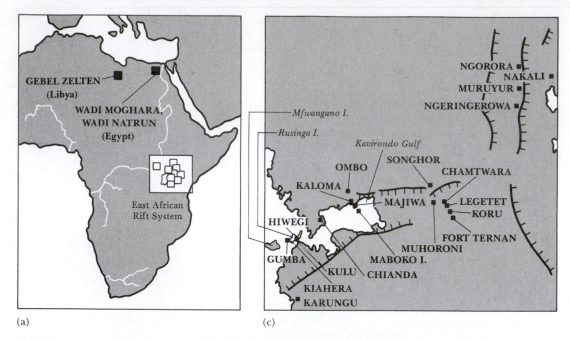

(a)

(c)

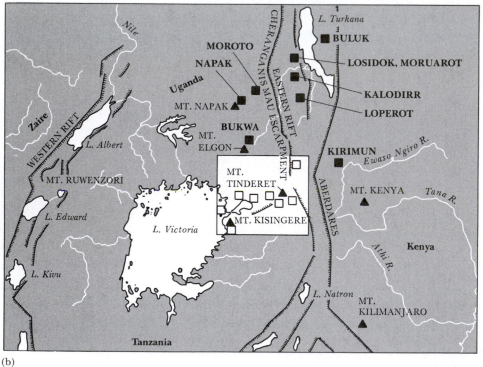

(b)

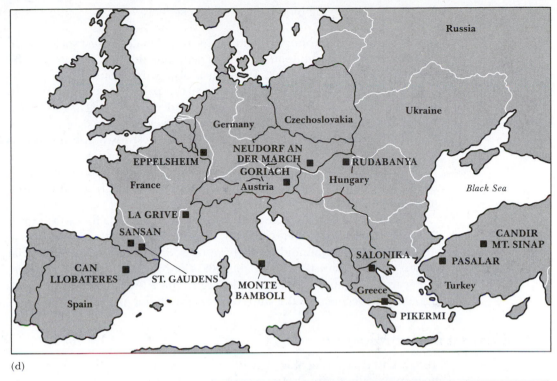

(d)

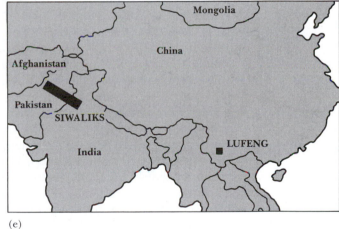

Fig. 5.1. Geographic distribution of Miocene hominoids from Africa and Eurasia. (a) Sites in North and East Africa. (b) Sites in East Africa (the area in the square in panel a). Triangles represent ancient volcanoes. (c) Sites in western Kenya (the area in the square in panel b). (d) Miocene hominoid sites in Europe and Asia Minor. (e) Miocene hominoid sites in southern and eastern Asia. (From Conroy, 1990.)

(e)

reasons that are still unclear, hominoids become extremely rare in the African fossil record by the Late Miocene (approximately 11.5–5.0 mya), although pockets of them survived in some abundance in southern Asia and China until about 7 mya (Fig. 5.1). The absence of fossil chimpanzees or gorillas in Africa has led some to suggest that rain forests are not conducive to fossil bone preservation. This cannot be the total story, however, since taphonomic studies in the Kibale Forest of western Uganda show that chimpanzee bones can, and do, accumulate on the forest floor (Peterhans et al., 1993). It is also worth noting that literally thousands of ape fossils are known from the paleoforests of Lufeng in southern China, Rudabánya in Hungary, and various *Oreopithecus* localities of Tuscany. These were densely forested, even swampy, ecological settings that, nevertheless, preserved some of the best fossil ape specimens ever found.

By the end of the Miocene very different apelike creatures first appear in the African fossil record—the early hominins. We will begin their story in the next chapter.

With the exception of recent discoveries from Namibia in southwestern Africa (*Otavipithecus*) and Chad in central Africa (*Sahelanthropus*), all African Miocene hominoid fossils have been discovered in the equatorial region of East Africa (Brunet et al., 2002; Conroy et al., 1992). Therefore, our search for human origins should begin with a brief sketch of the geology and paleoecology of this important region of the African continent.

East Africa in the Miocene

Today, East Africa is ecologically isolated from Eurasia even though it has been physically connected to the Arabian Peninsula since the Miocene (Bernor et al., 1988; Thomas, 1985). The dominant feature of the landscape is the great **East African Rift System,** which stretches all the way from the Red Sea in the north to the southern end of Lake Malawi (bordering Mozambique, Tanzania, and Malawi) in the south. The East African Rift is continuous with tectonic spreading centers in both the Red Sea and the Gulf of Aden, and all three began to form in pre-Miocene times (Omar and Steckler, 1995). In fact, volcanic activity in southwestern Ethiopia began some 40–45 mya and by 32–25 mya was widespread throughout the Red Sea, Gulf of Aden, and Ethiopian plateau. Actual seafloor spreading commenced about 20 mya and propagated into the Afar region by about 5 mya (Ebinger and Sleep, 1998).

Rift valleys are formed when continental crust is subjected to tension, usually the result of tectonic uplifting. A rift valley can be likened to a fractured arch that has been pulled apart by tension so that the keystone has dropped en bloc or in strips (Fig. 5.2) (Gregory, 1986; Holmes, 1965). East African Early Miocene landscapes were characterized by large-scale volcanic activity, with some volcanoes rising 1000 m or more above the surrounding countryside. By the Late Miocene flood-like volcanic eruptions had spread over much of the area. The main source of Early Miocene hominoid fossils in East Africa is the tuffaceous sedimentary sequences below the Miocene lavas of the Tinderet and Kisingiri volcanoes along the eastern shores of Lake Victoria in Kenya (Fig. 5.1b). This association with volcanic lavas and tuffs allows many of these Miocene hominoid–bearing

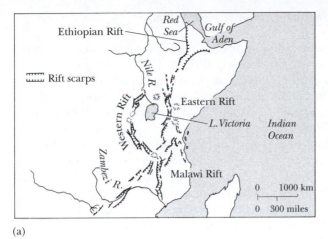

(a)

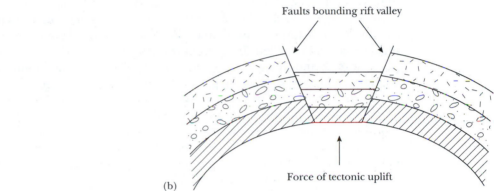

Faults bounding rift valley

Force of tectonic uplift

(b)

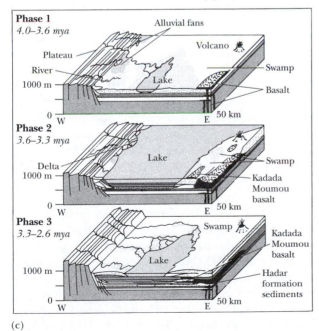

(c)

Fig. 5.2. (a) The East African rift system stretches some 4000 km from Mozambique in the south to the Red Sea in the north. Most of the major Miocene hominoid localities are in Kenya and Uganda, between the eastern and western rifts. Highlands form the shoulders of both major rifts. (b) Rift systems are caused by underlying tectonic uplift that produces surface cracks in the overlying continental crust. The resulting subsidence of crustal blocks between these fracture lines in the Earth's crust produces a long, narrow trough bounded by faults. (c) Three phases of rift formation using the site of Hadar in Ethiopia as an example. Phase 1, 4.0–3.6 mya; phase 2, 3.6–3.3 mya; phase 3, 3.3–2.6 mya. (Adapted from Wood, 1992b.)

sites in East Africa to be radiometrically dated using techniques discussed earlier (e.g., potassium-argon dating) (Bishop, 1978; Bishop et al., 1969; Van Couvering and Miller, 1969; Van Couvering and Van Couvering, 1976). Most of the hominoid fossils associated with the Kisingiri volcano (e.g., Rusinga Island, Kenya) are about 17–18 million years old and those associated with the Tinderet volcano (e.g., Songhor and Koru, Kenya) are about 19 million years old. Several ancient volcanic regions in Uganda have also yielded important Early Miocene hominoid fossils (e.g., Bukwa), and these may be as old as 23 million years (Bishop, 1964, 1967; MacLatchy et al., 1995; Walker, 1969). Unfortunately, Miocene deposits in the western rift valley have not yet been radiometrically dated but some of the Plio-Pleistocene volcanic tuffs there have been correlated to dated tuffs in the Lake Turkana Basin (Pickford et al., 1991) (see Chapter 7).

Many of the Early Miocene faunas show similarities to present-day African lowland forest communities. For example, the fauna at Songhor includes several excellent forest-indicator species like flying squirrels, elephant shrews, and prosimians (Nengo and Rae, 1992). In addition, over a half-dozen primate species are present at the site. In modern African faunal communities, this number of primate species is usually found only in fully forested conditions. As mentioned above, cercopithecoids (Old World monkeys) are rarer than hominoids in these Early Miocene faunas, so it seems probable that Early Miocene hominoids were occupying many of the ecological niches that later came to be more fully exploited by monkeys (Andrews, 1981; Evans et al., 1981).

Several important Middle Miocene sites in this area of western Kenya lie stratigraphically below a 12-million-year old lava flow that flooded the region from the northwest. Hominoid fossils from several of the most important Middle Miocene sites, Maboko Island, Fort Ternan, and the Tugen Hills region of Lake Baringo, date to about 15–12 mya (Andrews et al., 1981; Benefit, 1995; Feibel and Brown, 1991; Gitau and Benefit, 1995; McCrossin, 1992; Shipman et al., 1981b; S. Ward et al., 1999). These, and other, Middle Miocene sites are significant because they document the unfolding of a major ecological shift in East Africa from forested environments to more open-country ones (Benefit and McCrossin, 1989; Cerling, 1992; Cerling et al., 1991; Pickford, 1981, 1983; Retallack et al., 1990, 1995). This is evident, for example, in the greater proportions of open-country mammals like bushbucks, buffalo, gazelles, and giraffids in these Middle Miocene faunas (Gentry, 1970). It is important, however, that there were still pockets of rain forest and woodland in the East African rift valley as recently as about 12 mya, in contrast to the savanna-like conditions found there today (Cerling et al., 1991; Hill, 1987; Jacobs and Kabuye, 1987). And, as we will discuss in a later chapter, the earliest undoubted hominin species yet discovered, *Ardipithecus ramidus* and *Ar. kadabba*, from deposits in Ethiopia dated to about 5.8–4.4 mya, are associated with fauna and flora more typical of African woodlands (Begun, 2004; Haile-Selassie,

2001; Haile-Selassie et al., 2004b; White, 2002; White et al., 1994, 1995; WoldeGabriel et al., 1994, 2001).[1]

Unfortunately, East African Late Miocene faunas are poorly known, making it difficult to infer paleoecological information for that time period. There are some reasonable faunal samples from Sahabi (Libya), Ngorora (Kenya), and Morocco between about 10 and 7 mya, indicating these areas were forested as well. We do know, however, that the climatic trends toward cooling and drying seen in the Middle Miocene continued in the Late Miocene and into the Pliocene. The new hominin-bearing site of Toros-Menalla (*Sahelanthropus*)—dated to about 6–7 mya—may be instructive in this regard. While both paleoecological and sedimentological reconstructions suggest the presence of a lake (e.g., fish, crocodiles) associated with gallery forest and savanna-like conditions (e.g., primates, rodents, elephants, equids, bovids), there is also evidence for the nearby presence of sandy desert (fossil dunes). If so, this would be the oldest record of desert conditions in the Neogene of northern central Africa (Vignaud et al., 2002).

Today's East African climate is greatly affected by the highlands bordering the eastern and western rifts, mainly because these highlands prevent both Atlantic and Indian Ocean rainfall from reaching the inter-rift region of the interior. Rainfall in the west, brought by warm prevailing winds of the South Atlantic, penetrates inland to equatorial western and central Africa only as far as the shoulder of the western rift valley. In the east, the northeast monsoon and the year-round southeast trade winds bring moisture to East Africa from the Indian Ocean, but this moisture precipitates predominately at the coast and over the highlands bordering the eastern rift. The result of these rainfall patterns is that much of the inter-rift area is deprived of rain. Since rainfall is heavy where moisture-bearing winds from the sea are forced up over mountain ranges, the land on the leeward (or rainshadow) side of the two mountain ranges is usually dry, thereby causing the semiarid conditions found today in the interior rift valley.

The climate of eastern equatorial Africa was probably wetter in the Early Miocene than it is at present because the surrounding highlands had not yet formed (Andrews and Van Couvering, 1975; Kortlandt, 1983) and rainfall in the inter-rift region was unlikely to have been as severely restricted as it is today. The prevailing rainfall patterns probably started to change as the highlands began to form in the Middle to Late Miocene, therefore, Early Miocene East African climate and vegetation probably resembled what we see today in the forested volcanic mountains and lowlands along the western rift (Fig. 5.2).

---

[1]Two recently discovered genera, *Orrorin* and *Sahelanthropus*, from sediments dated to about 6–7 mya in Kenya and Chad, respectively, may, with further study, turn out to be the earliest hominins yet recovered from Africa (Brunet et al., 2002; Senut et al., 2001; Vignaud et al., 2002).

EURASIA IN THE MIOCENE

The landscapes of Eurasia, like Africa, have changed dramatically since the Miocene, mostly as a result of the mountain-building forces of the Alpine and Himalayan systems and the regression of the **Tethys Sea** to form the Mediterranean, Black, Aral, and Caspian sea basins. The Tethys Sea was initially a broad waterway that divided the northern supercontinent **Laurasia** (consisting of what is now North America, Europe, and Asia) from the southern supercontinent **Gondwanaland** (South America, Africa, Antarctica, India, Madagascar, and Australia). From about 25–20 mya, southwestern Eurasia was inundated by the extensive Tethys seaway that acted as an effective faunal barrier preventing African mammals, including hominoids, from reaching Eurasia.

Approximately 20 mya, as the Tethys Sea began to recede, the first significant emigration of African land mammals into Eurasia evidently occurred through a corridor linking the two landmasses. Miocene hominoids first appear in Europe about 16–17 mya and radiated throughout Eurasia for at least 10 million years (Begun, 2002; Heizmann and Begun, 2001; Kelley, 2002). In Europe, as in East Africa, more seasonal environments and the evolution of more open-country woodland habitats are in evidence by the Middle Miocene. As the Tethys Sea continued to regress the Mediterranean, Black, Caspian and Aral sea basins assumed the form we recognize today.

The period about 10–5 mya was characterized by major faunal turnover in Eurasia. As environments became increasingly seasonal, the geographic ranges of Eurasian hominoids began to shrink, so that by about 7 mya most of them had disappeared, leaving only residual, or relict, populations in the subtropical and tropical environments of Southeast Asia and Tuscany (Bernor, 1983; Bernor et al., 1988; Harrison and Rook, 1997). The expansion across Asia of more open-country faunas and plants with thickened cell walls better adapted for resistance to water loss, so-called **sclerophyllous vegetation,** coincided with these hominoid extinctions.

We mentioned earlier the tremendous effect the rising Himalayas had on worldwide climates (Zhisheng et al., 2001). The continuing uplift and subsequent erosion of the Himalayas were important for another reason—namely, the resulting thick sequence of fossiliferous sediments that were deposited at their base. These sediments, known as the **Siwalik Group,** and the Miocene hominoid fossils derived from them, have played a very important historical role in discussions of human origins (Fig. 5.1e) (Conroy and Pilbeam, 1975; Kelley, 2002; Pilbeam, 2002). We will come back to them later in the chapter.

OVERVIEW OF MIOCENE HOMINOIDS

As pointed out earlier, hominoids first appear in the Late Oligocene/Early Miocene fossil record of East Africa (northern Kenya) approximately 25 mya and become quite abundant and diverse in Early Miocene faunas dated to about 22–17 mya. By contrast, hominoids first appear in Eurasia only about 16–17 mya and, with few exceptions, most disappear from Eurasia about 7 mya.

Fossil hominoids were first discovered in East Africa in 1926 at Koru, Kenya. Shortly thereafter (1931–1932) two other richly fossiliferous Kenyan Miocene sites, Songhor and Rusinga Island, were discovered. Subsequent work has resulted in the discovery of several thousand specimens, representing a number of Miocene hominoid genera from these and other East African sites (Fig. 5.1). Although most of these specimens consist of teeth and jaws, one genus at least, *Proconsul,* is well represented by both cranial and postcranial material.[2] Since this is the best known of the Early Miocene hominoids, we shall use it as our general model of early hominoid morphology and adaptation.

CHARACTERISTICS OF EARLY MIOCENE HOMINOIDS (*PROCONSUL*)

The temporal and geographical distribution of Early Miocene hominoids is limited mainly to Late Oligocene/Early Miocene sites of northern and western Kenya, including Rusinga and Mfwangano Islands, Songhor, and Koru (Fig. 5.1) (Boschetto et al., 1992; Harrison, 1989).

The genus *Proconsul* was first described in 1933 from fossils discovered at Koru (Hopwood, 1933). *Proconsul* was a highly successful genus that diversified into several species in the Early Miocene of East Africa, including *P. africanus, P. heseloni, P. nyanzae,* and *P. major* (Harrison, 2002; Walker, 1992; Walker et al., 1993). *Proconsul* was considered to be a fossil great ape when it was first described. In fact, it was commonly held well into the 1970s that an ancestor-descendant relationship existed between *P. heseloni* (formerly known as *P. africanus*) and chimpanzees and between *P. major* and gorillas (Pilbeam, 1969; Simons, 1972; Simons and Pilbeam, 1965; Walker and Rose, 1968). However, later studies in both paleontology and

---

[2]Much of the more complete postcranial material belongs to the species *Proconsul heseloni* (formerly referred to as *P. africanus* (Walker et al., 1993).

molecular biology clearly demonstrated the improbability that any modern great ape lineage was already distinct by the Early Miocene.

P. heseloni and *P. africanus* are the smallest of the *Proconsul* species, being intermediate in dental size between gibbons (*Hylobates*) and pygmy chimpanzees (*Pan paniscus*). Body weight estimates for these smaller *Proconsul* species range from about 9 to 12 kg. *Proconsul nyanzae* is a much larger, sexually dimorphic, species with male body weights estimated at 35–38 kg and females at 26–28 kg (Conroy, 1987; Ruff, 2003; Ruff et al., 1989; Teaford et al., 1993; Walker and Pickford, 1983). *Proconsul major* is the largest species, with a dental size approaching that of a female gorilla. Unfortunately, little is known about the postcranial skeleton of this species.

Proconsul is generally associated with forested paleoenvironments, and its species are recognized as a group by their common possession of a number of mainly ancestral features of the cranium and dentition that characterize Old World monkeys, apes, and humans generally. *Proconsul* is, however, linked specifically to hominoid primates, apes, and humans, on the basis of several postcranial characters, which are discussed below.

Generally speaking, *Proconsul* had rather lightly built, or gracile, jaws and thinly enameled teeth, whereas most Middle to Late Miocene taxa, such as *Kenyapithecus*, *Griphopithecus*, *Ouranopithecus*, and *Sivapithecus* had more robust jaws and thicker-enameled teeth (Begun, 2002; Kelley, 2002). Some exceptions to this general rule include the genera *Dryopithecus* and *Otavipithecus*, both of which appear to have had teeth more thinly enameled than other Middle Miocene hominoids (see below). By the Middle/Late Miocene most of the thinner-enameled proconsulines were clearly on the wane and thicker-enameled taxa such as the pongines *Sivapithecus* and *Ankarapithecus* were becoming more common in the fossil record. This suggests that hominoid craniodental morphology was adapting coincidentally with dietary changes resulting from the ecological factors we noted earlier—namely the replacing of foodstuffs associated with wetter, more forested environments of the Early Miocene (e.g., soft fruits, young leaves) by foodstuffs associated with drier, more woodland-bushland conditions of the Middle to Later Miocene.

One of the finest Early Miocene hominoid specimens ever discovered is the beautifully preserved cranium of *P. heseloni*, found by Mary Leakey at Rusinga Island in 1948 (Fig. 5.3). The cranium is lightly built and lacks both browridges, or **supraorbital tori,** and strong muscular markings. The lower portion of the face projects forward, a condition known as **facial prognathism.** When originally found, the back or occipital portion of the cranium did not articulate with the rest of the specimen because large parts of the intervening cranium were missing. Incredibly, 35 years later two of the missing pieces of the cranium were found, thereby making it possible to attach the main cranial fragment to the occipital portion. As a

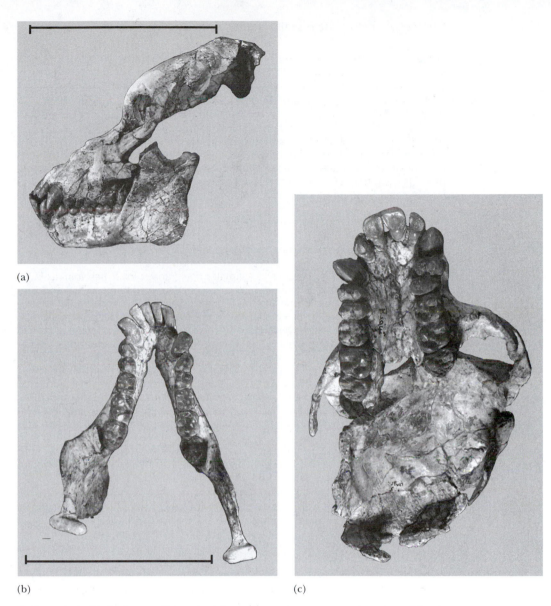

(a)

(b)   (c)

Fig. 5.3. Skull of *Proconsul heseloni* from the early Miocene of Rusinga Island, Kenya. (a) Lateral view (b) Occlusal view of lower jaw (c) Occlusal view of the upper jaw. (Courtesy of P. Andrews.)

result of this fortuitous circumstance, a reasonably accurate cranial cavity, or endocranial, volume of 167 cc has been calculated for this specimen.

The postcranial skeleton in Early Miocene *Proconsul* is relatively well known (Napier and Davis, 1959; Walker and Pickford, 1983; Walker et al., 1993). (Some of the specimens originally attributed to *P. major* have been

Box 5.1   Encephalization Quotients: How Do Paleoanthropologists Interpret Endocranial Volume?

How do researchers determine and interpret a cranial volume of 167 cc for *P. heseloni?* Is that a large volume, a small volume, or something in between? Part of the answer depends on how large the animal in question is. After all, a cow will have a much larger brain than a mouse in absolute terms, but will the cow have a relatively larger brain than the mouse if body size is taken into account? Biologists have devised a very useful index, called the encephalization quotient (EQ), to explore this question. EQ is designed to measure relative brain size in mammals and is calculated by dividing the endocranial volume of the specimen in question by the endocranial volume expected of a living mammal of the same body size. For example, one (of several) such empirically derived formulas for EQ is

$$EQ = \text{observed brain weight (g)}/0.0991\,[\text{body weight g}]^{0.76}$$

Given the body weight and brain size estimates noted above for *P. heseloni*, its EQ is approximately 1.5 by this formula. An EQ of 1.5 is interpreted to mean that endocranial volume in this species is one and a half times larger than the endocranial volume we would expect to see in a living mammal of the same approximate body size.[a]

Relative brain size in *Proconsul* can also be expressed as a percentage of human relative brain size by dividing its EQ value by 2.87, the EQ for *Homo sapiens* determined from this same formula (note that other formulas result in different values for EQ). The corresponding value for *P. heseloni* is about 52% and for chimpanzees, orangutans, and gorillas is about 41%, 32%, and 17%, respectively. Similar calculations for various New and Old World monkeys range between 23% and 82%. Therefore, one might conclude that, on this scale, the gorilla has the smallest relative brain size of all higher primates and that there is some overlap in relative EQs between monkeys and apes. It is important to note, however, that relative EQs in monkeys of about the same body size as *P. heseloni* range from 23% to 41%, indicating that *P. heseloni* had a relatively bigger brain than modern monkeys of comparable body size (Walker et al., 1983).

[a]A later Miocene hominoid from Hungary, *Dryopithecus brancoi*, has an endocranial capacity estimate of 305–329 cc and an EQ estimate of 2.0–2.3, the latter well within the range of values for extant great apes and near that for some australopiths (Kordos and Begun, 1998).

transferred to a new taxon, *Morotopithecus bishopi* [Gebo et al., 1997]). It exhibits a unique mosaic of rather generalized higher primate features combined with a few shared derived features characteristic of living hominoids, most notably the absence of both a tail[3] and an enlarged bony expansion of the ischium, or **ischial tuberosity** (Figs. 5.4 and 5.5). The absence of enlarged ischial tuberosities indicates that Early Miocene hominoids, as in living great apes, lacked the enlarged fatty sitting pads known as **ischial callosities** found on the ischium of all Old World monkeys and gibbons.

[3]The claim that *Proconsul* lacks a tail has been challenged by a claim that two caudal (tail) vertebrae discovered on Rusinga Island probably belong to *Proconsul* (Harrison, 1998). The recent description of a caudal vertebra attributed to *Nacholapithecus* indicates that *Nacholapithecus*, at least, most probably did not have a tail (Nakatusukasa et al., 2003; Ishida, 2004).

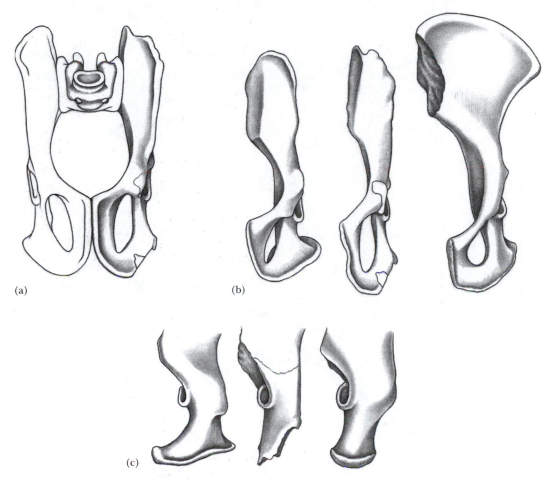

Fig. 5.4.   (a) Ventral view of a reconstruction of a *Proconsul* pelvis. Note the very narrow overall shape of the pelvis. (b) Ventromedial views (from left to right) of *Papio* (baboon), *Proconsul*, and *Pan* (chimpanzee) hip bones. Note the widely flaring iliac blade of *Pan*, absent in *Papio* and *Proconsul*. The width of the iliac blade reflects the mediolateral breadth of the torso. *Proconsul* probably had a narrow torso like *Papio*. (c) Dorsal view (from left to right) of *Papio*, *Proconsul*, and *Pan* left ischia. Note the flaring ischial tuberosity of *Papio*, with its broad, flat surface, and the flaring of the ischial ramus cranial to the tuberosity. *Proconsul* exhibits virtually no flaring, even less than does *Pan*. This indicates that *Proconsul* did not have ischial callosities. (From Ward et al., 1993.)

The ratio of upper limb length to lower limb length, the **intermembral index,** is a crude predictor of overall locomotor behavior in many living primates. For example, low intermembral indices (e.g., those less than 70%) typify vertical clinging and leaping primates, such as tarsiers and bushbabies; moderate indices (e.g., 70–100%) typify most arboreal quadrupedal

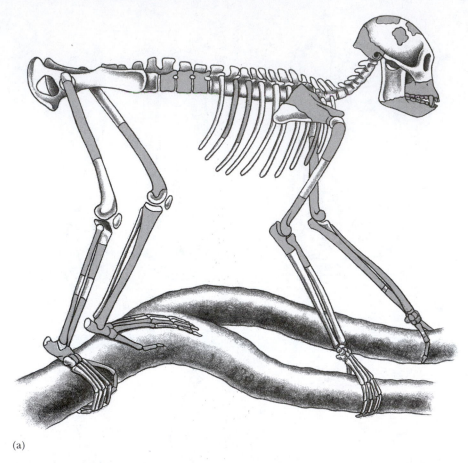

(a)

Fig. 5.5. (a) Reconstruction of the skeleton of *Proconsul heseloni* (about 20% actual size). Nonshaded areas represent reconstructed regions. Limb proportions are most similar to those found in some Old World monkeys. The intermembral index is about 87 [length of forelimb/length of hindlimb] × 100. (From Walker and Pickford, 1983.)

monkeys, like rhesus macaques and baboons; and high indices (e.g., 100–150%) typify hominoids that engage in some degree of suspensory locomotion, like chimpanzees and gibbons. The intermembral index in *Proconsul* was about 85–90%, squarely within the set of values for general arboreal quadrupedal monkeys (Fig. 5.5a).

Proconsul hand and foot proportions were also more similar to those of arboreal monkeys than to apes (Fig. 5.5b, c). The size and shape of their finger bones suggest that they were primarily above-branch arboreal quadrupeds. It is interesting that the thumb was relatively long and was clearly adapted for rotation and opposition, as in extant great apes. There

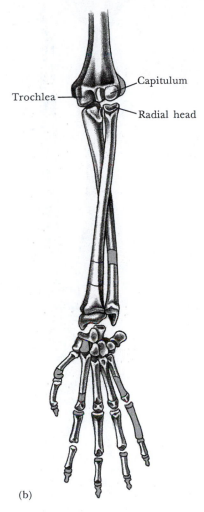

Capitulum

Trochlea

Radial head

(b)

(b) The hand and forearm bones of *P. heseloni* (about 40% actual size). (From Walker and Pickford, 1983.)

is no indication of any knuckle-walking adaptations in the wrist or finger bones (Beard et al., 1986).

Based on a partial skeleton of *P. nyanzae*, it appears that *Proconsul* had a number of monkey-like features of the trunk as well, including a long, flexible vertebral column, a narrow rib cage or torso, and an habitually **pronograde** posture—in other words, it most likely walked with its palms flat on the ground. These features are very different from the short, inflexible vertebral column (particularly in the lumbar, or lower back, region), broad and shallow torso, and knuckle-walking postures seen in modern African great apes (Fig. 5.6). Thus the overall impression we are left with is

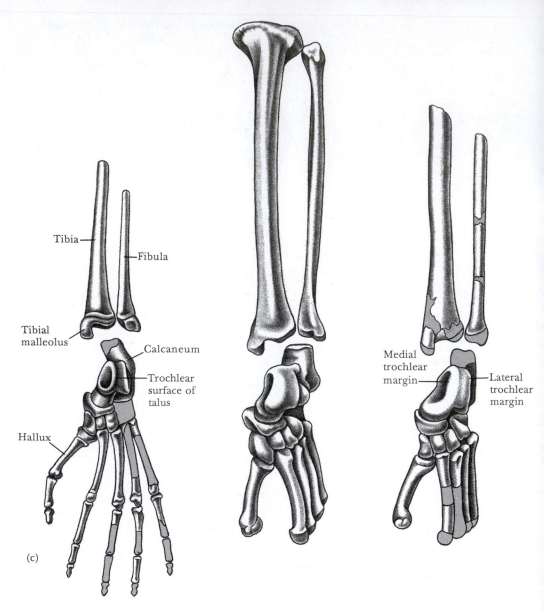

Fig. 5.5. (c) Comparison of the lower leg (from left to right) of *Proconsul heseloni*, *Pan*, and *P. nyanzae* (about 33% actual size). Note the opposable, grasping hallux in all three. (From Walker and Pickford, 1983.)

of an animal having a unique mosaic of monkey-like and ape-like postcranial features, quite unlike any primate living today. Probably, these morphological features represent the ancestral higher primate or catarrhine postcranial condition (Beard, 1990; Begun et al., 1994; Harrison, 2002; Rose, 1988, 1992; Ward, 1993; Ward et al., 1991, 1993).

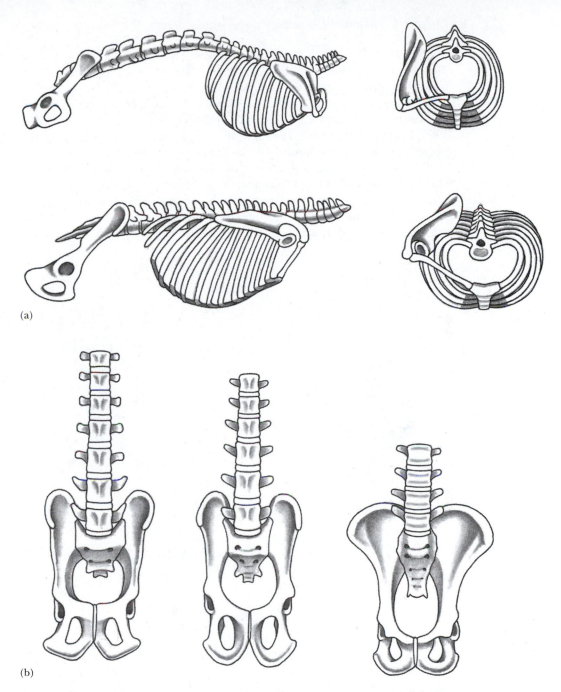

Fig. 5.6. Postcranial comparisons between monkeys and apes. (a) Trunk and pelvis (top to bottom) of *Macaca* and *Pan,* in lateral (left) and superior (right) views. Note the different orientations of the shoulder joints and the different shapes of the thorax. (b) Anterior views of the pelvis and lumbar vertebral column (left to right) of *Macaca, Proconsul,* and *Pan.* Note the longer lumbar region in the macaque monkey. (From Rose, 1994.)

Discoveries from a number of other Early Miocene sites around Lake Turkana (e.g., Kalodirr, Buluk) and Lake Baringo (e.g., Kipsaramon) attest to the great diversity of Early Miocene hominoids (Fig. 5.1). The described genera include *Afropithecus*, *Simiolus*, and *Turkanapithecus* (Hill et al., 1991; Leakey and Leakey, 1986a, 1986b, 1987; Leakey and Walker, 1985; Leakey et al., 1988a, 1988b; Rose et al., 1992). Based on faunal comparisons, most of these hominoids date to about 18–16 mya.

One of these taxa, *Afropithecus turkanensis*, is particularly interesting (Fig. 5.7). It is known from a number of specimens, including a partial cranium, several mandibles, isolated teeth, and associated postcranial bones. It appears to be a rather distinctive species, quite unlike any other Miocene hominoid. It is particularly distinctive from other Miocene homi-

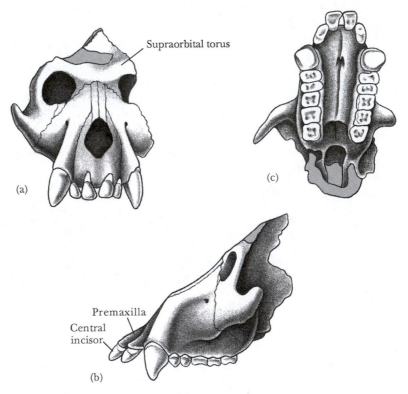

Fig. 5.7. Cranium of *Afropithecus turkanensis* from Kalodirr, Kenya. Front (a), side (b), and basal (c) views of the upper jaw and face. Note the small supraorbital tori, the long premaxilla, and the procumbent incisors, all traits shared with *Sivapithecus*. It differs, however, from *Sivapithecus* in its more linear midface profile. Scale about 33% actual size. (From Leakey et al., 1988a.)

noids in the basal flare of the upper cheek teeth, which has the effect of making the cusp tips appear more closely packed together than the cusp bases, and in its very thick enamel (Martin, 1995; T. Smith et al., 2003). Although it resembles some Eurasian Middle Miocene hominoids like *Sivapithecus* in some ways (e.g., in the large, forwardly projecting, or procumbent, central incisors coupled with relatively small, asymmetrical lateral incisors; small supraorbital tori with high hafting of the cranial vault onto the face; and molars with thickened enamel and more flattened occlusal surfaces), its overall facial shape differs markedly from them. It looks more like a blown-up version of the primitive Oligocene anthropoid *Aegyptopithecus* from Egypt (Leakey et al., 1991). These similarities between Oligocene *Aegyptopithecus* and Miocene *Afropithecus* pose three interesting questions: (1) Do they simply represent a retention of primitive facial features for more than 14 million years of hominoid evolution? (2) Do they mean that *Afropithecus* represents the last of a long lineage of primitive Oligocene hominoids from North Africa that survived into the Miocene of East Africa? (3) Do they mean that *Afropithecus* has phylogenetic affinities with other Middle Miocene genera such as *Sivapithecus, Griphopithecus, Kenyapithecus,* and *Otavipithecus* (see below)? Finally, we should note that because some craniodental features shared by Miocene *Afropithecus* and Oligocene *Aegyptopithecus* also characterize the Middle Miocene cercopithecoid *Victoriapithecus,* some paleoanthropologists suspect that many aspects of the craniofacial anatomy of Miocene large-bodied hominoids are in fact primitive catarrhine features rather than synapomorphies linking them with the great ape and human clade (Benefit and McCrossin, 1997). We cannot confidently answer any of these questions as yet, but in posing them we demonstrate just how complex Miocene phylogenetic relationships really are.

CHARACTERISTICS OF MIDDLE TO LATE MIOCENE HOMINOIDS

Middle Miocene hominoids are found at a number of sites throughout Eurasia (e.g., Spain, France, Germany, Austria, Greece, Hungary, Georgia, Turkey, India, Pakistan, Nepal, China) and a few sites in Africa (e.g., Fort Ternan, Tugen Hills, and Maboko in Kenya and the Otavi Mountains of Namibia) (Fig. 5.1). *Dryopithecus* and *Sivapithecus* cross the Middle/Late Miocene boundary but the others are exclusively either Middle or Late Miocene. The exact number of, and phylogenetic relationships among, these Middle Miocene hominoid taxa are matters of ongoing and spirited debate (Begun, 1994b, 1995, 2002; Conroy, 1994; Hartwig, 2002; Ward and Duren, 2002). For example, some propose that *Dryopithecus* may be among the earliest members of the great ape–human clade (Begun, 1992, 1994a, 2002), whereas others propose that *Ouranopithecus* may be directly ancestral to later humans (de Bonis and Koufos, 1993, 1995; de Bonis et al., 1990) (see below). For our purposes, however, it is not necessary to discuss all of these phylogenetic machinations in great detail. Rather, our objective is to highlight some of the more general features of this rather heterogeneous group of Middle Miocene hominoids and to discuss how some of them have influenced discussions about human origins.

One of the most widespread of these Middle Miocene Eurasian homi- noids that affect discussions on hominin origins is *Dryopithecus*. It is known from a number of sites in Europe, and specimens include both upper and lower teeth and jaws as well as reasonably complete cranial and postcranial material (Begun, 2002; Begun and Kordos, 1997). The better preserved specimens are mainly from Hungary (Rudabánya), Spain (Can Llobateres, Can Ponsic), and France (St. Gaudens, La Grive). Species range from about 15 to 45 kg, with some exhibiting marked sexual dimor- phism. The discovery of a 9.5-million-year-old partial *Dryopithecus* skeleton from Can Llobateres provides convincing evidence that orthograde pos- tures had already evolved in this lineage by this time and that its overall body structure resembled extant African apes in many important features, such as (1) a shorter and stiffer vertebral column, (2) a broader thorax with more dorsally shifted scapula, (3) a relatively high intermembral index, and (4) very large hands adapted for powerful grasping (Moya- Sola and Kohler, 1996). A number of other cranial features also seem to be shared between *Dryopithecus* and living African apes, including detailed similarities in the premaxilla and subnasal regions as well as overall cra- nial shape. Because of these and other similarities with living African apes, *Dryopithecus* (and the closely related *Ouranopithecus*) are now gener- ally classified within the subfamily Homininae (Table 5.1), thus making them, cladistically at least, members of the African great ape clade, to the exclusion of the Asian great ape clade (e.g., *Sivapithecus, Pongo*) (Begun, 1994a, 2002).

One of the most controversial of these Eurasian Middle Miocene taxa is *Ouranopithecus macedoniensis* known from a number of sites in Greece dated to about 10–9 mya. What makes this female gorilla–size taxon partic- ularly relevant to a text on human evolution is the claim by its discoverers that it is the sister group of *Australopithecus* and *Homo* (de Bonis et al., 1990; de Bonis and Koufos, 1993, 1995). This claim is based on several general similarities between *Ouranopithecus* and *Australopithecus*, such as low-crowned and thick-enameled molars; broad, shallow mandibular bod- ies; the overall appearance of the rounded and swollen molar cusps; and the trend toward both canine and P_3 honing facet reduction.

According hominin status to *Ouranopithecus*, representing it as the sister group of *Australopithecus* and *Homo*, harks back to views prevalent in the 1960s—namely, that the human lineage had diverged from the African apes by the Middle Miocene. This claim for *Ouranopithecus*, however, has the earliest member of the human lineage appearing in Greece, rather than Africa! This view has not gone unchallenged (Andrews, 1990).

Can another spin be put on the apparent similarities between *Ouranopithecus* and *Australopithecus*? First, because sexual dimorphism in body weight and canine size in primates decreases exponentially with decreasing body size (Leutenegger, 1982; Leutenegger and Cheverud, 1985), the reduced canines could be accounted for if the relevant *Ouranopithecus* specimens are shown to be females instead of males. Second, as we noted earlier in our review of basic primate dental morphology, the relative size of P_3 honing facets is functionally related to the size of the upper canine, because these honing facets serve to sharpen the back edge of the upper canine; if upper canine size is reduced, the associated P_3 honing facets will be as well. Third, the morphology of the "rounded and swollen molar cusps" is indistinguishable from that of other thick-enameled Middle Miocene hominoids such as *Sivapithecus*.

Thus it is probably safe to conclude that while the roots of Western civilization may rightly be traced back to Greek soil, the same cannot be said, at least yet, about human origins.

Other Eurasian Middle Miocene hominoid samples that have affected discussions of human origins come from sites in South Asia (Pakistan, India), Turkey, and China. In the twentieth century, the most extensively explored area for the recovery of Middle Miocene hominoids was the Siwalik Hills of Pakistan and India. Assorted craniodental and postcranial remains representing hundreds of Miocene hominoids have been found in this extensive area. Unlike the Miocene tuffaceous deposits of East Africa, the Siwalik sediments are generally not amenable to direct radiometric dating. Consequently, most of the Siwalik hominoids have been dated on the basis of paleomagnetic stratigraphy and faunal correlations (Pilbeam et al., 1997). Specimens allocated to *Sivapithecus* first appear in South Asia about 13–10 mya in the Chinji Formation, reach their peak of abundance and diversity about 10–8 mya in the Nagri Formation, and disappear about 8–5 mya after the Dhok Pathan Formation (Barry, 1986; Kappelman et al., 1991; Kelley, 2002; Pilbeam et al., 1977; Raza et al., 1983).

Probably the single most important *Sivapithecus* specimen recovered from the Siwaliks is a cranium preserving much of the face and lower jaw (Fig. 5.8) (Pilbeam, 1982; Pilbeam and Smith, 1981). This important specimen provides a number of specific details about *Sivapithecus* facial architecture that demonstrate a more remarkable similarity to orangutans than to *Proconsul* or to any living African great ape. Such orangutan-like features include the deep and widely flared zygomatic process, marked prognathism,

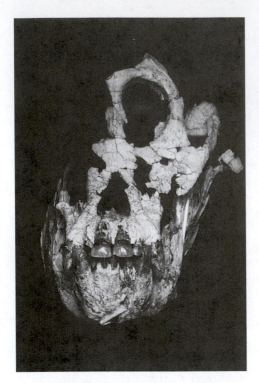
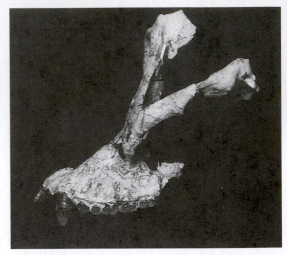

Fig. 5.8.   Cranium of *Sivapithecus indicus* from the Middle Miocene of Pakistan. In the shape of the eye socket, the construction of the bony ridge over the orbits, the dimensions of the incisors, and the detailed anatomy of the lower face, *Sivapithecus* can be seen to resemble the orangutan more closely than any other modern hominoid. (Photo by W. Sacco; courtesy of D. Pilbeam.)

short upper face, narrow interorbital distance, relatively large first incisor compared to the second incisor, and overall shape of the orbits and facial profile.

Differences in the anatomy of the lower face distinguish early from Middle Miocene hominoids, and the same differences, in general, also distinguish African apes from orangutans. The differences relate primarily to the disposition of the incisive canal, the passageway in the front of the hard palate for small arteries and nerves running between the nasal and oral cavities, as well as to the morphology of that portion of the premaxilla that houses the roots of the upper incisors, the subnasal alveolar process (McCollum and Ward, 1997; Ward and Kimbel, 1983; Ward and Pilbeam, 1983). As shown in Figure 5.9, the pattern found in Middle Miocene hominoids like *Sivapithecus* resembles the pattern found today in orangutans. We shall come back to this morphology in a later chapter when we look at early hominin facial architecture in more detail.

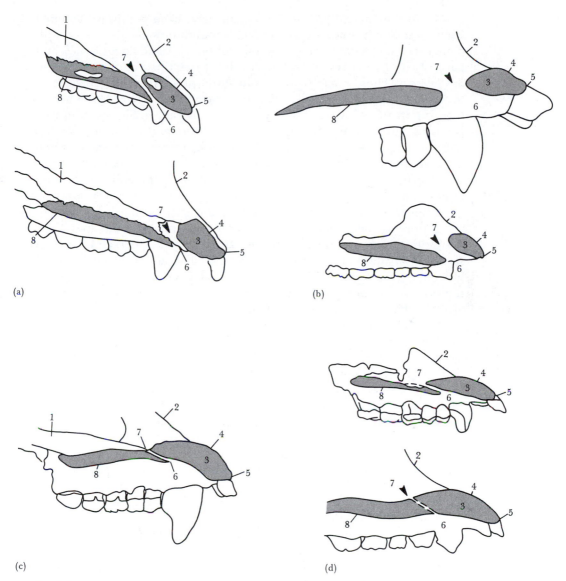

Fig. 5.9. Anatomy of the lower face in Miocene and extant hominoids. Sagittal sections through the premaxilla and palate (shaded areas). (a) *Pan* (top) and *Gorilla* (bottom). (b) *Morotopithecus bishopi* (top) and *Rangwapithecus vancouveringi* (bottom). (c) *Pongo*. (d) *Sivapithecus indicus* (top) and *S. meteai* (bottom). Anatomical parts: *1*, vomer; *2*, lateral margin of nasal aperture; *3*, subnasal alveolar process; *4*, nasoalveolar clivus; *5*, prosthion; *6*, oral incisive fossa; *7* and arrowhead, nasal incisive fossa; *8*, hard palate. Note that in both specimens in panel b the premaxilla is broadly separated from the palate. (Adapted from Ward and Kimbel, 1983.)

Very few hominoid postcranial remains have been positively identified from these South Asian sites, and none is found in direct association with dental remains. A distal femur, several foot bones, some finger bones, and parts of the humerus and radius have been described and attributed to *Sivapithecus.* These range in size from those of a pygmy chimpanzee to those of a female gorilla. The articular surfaces of the finger bones are interesting in that they resemble those found in palmigrade, quadrupedal primates. However, the degree of shaft curvature and robustness implies that the fingers were also subjected to tensile stresses, for instance when hanging from branches. Several of the bones, including several phalanges, a navicular, and large pollex and hallux, are all compatible with a powerful grasping hand and foot, indicating that *Sivapithecus* engaged in arboreal quadrupedalism such as vertical climbing and clamboring behaviors but not antipronograde behaviors such as those practiced by extant apes. However, some features of the limb bones, particularly the lateral, rather than straight, curvature of the proximal humeral shaft, are ancestral *Proconsul*-like characters rather than modern orangutan ones, which complicates the tidy picture of a direct *Sivapithecus*-orangutan relationship (Madar et al., 2002; Pilbeam et al., 1980, 1990; Rose, 1986, 1989).

The richest of the Turkish sites, Pasalar in northwestern Anatolia, has yielded over 700 isolated teeth, several maxillary and mandibular elements, and about a dozen postcranial fragments dated by faunal correlation to about 15 mya. These have been provisionally grouped into two separate genera: *Griphopithecus* and a new as yet unnamed genus. As is typical of Middle Miocene hominoids generally, the molar enamel is relatively thick. Dental dimensions in the larger species are about the same size as those in the larger *Sivapithecus* species from the Siwaliks but, unlike most Siwalik hominoids, the lower molars have a prominent buccal cingulum reminiscent of the condition found in *Proconsul* and *Griphopithecus* from another locality in Turkey (Çandir) and several sites in Slovakia and Germany. The smaller Pasalar species is similar in having well-developed molar cingula; low, rounded molar cusps; and thick molar enamel (Alpagut et al., 1990; Andrews and Martin, 1991; Bernor and Tobien, 1990; Kelley, 2002; Martin and Andrews, 1991, 1993).

A particularly important Turkish specimen discovered from the Sinap Formation northwest of Ankara is a lower face of *Ankarapithecus*, a taxon closely related to *Sivapithecus* and *Pongo*, that includes the complete palate with all the upper teeth (Andrews and Tekkaya, 1980; Begun and Gülec, 1998). This specimen, and the Pakistan specimen mentioned above, are the two most significant fossil discoveries linking *Sivapithecus* to the orangutan clade and support the argument that the orangutan clade had already diverged from the other great apes by at least 13 mya (Fig. 5.10). The importance of these discoveries to the history of human evolution studies is that they provide one of the most widely cited divergence dates by which molecular anthropologists set their molecular clocks and in their

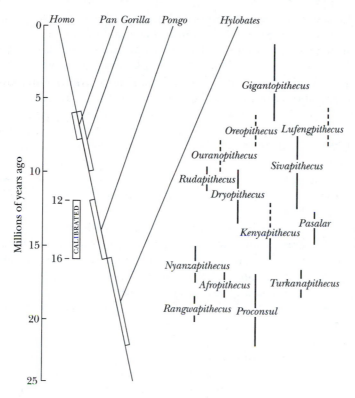

Fig. 5.10.   Time of branching sequences of living apes as determined from comparative genetics and based on calibration dates between 16 and 12 mya for the origin of the orangutan lineage.   Temporal ranges of fossil apes are shown to the right. Solid lines reflect relatively well-known times ranges and dashed lines reflect uncertain temporal positions within a probable time interval. (From Kelley, 1992.)

disproving of the 1960s and 1970s idea that *Sivapithecus* and the closely related specimens referred to at one time as *Ramapithecus* were on the human evolutionary lineage.

Recently, however, this view linking *Ankarapithecus* to the orangutan clade has been challenged by the discovery of a more complete *Ankarapithecus* face and mandible (and several postcranial fragments) from the Sinap Formation securely dated to about 10 mya. This new specimen reveals a combination of features such as a relatively narrow interorbital region, extensive frontal and maxillary sinuses, moderately developed supraorbital tori, square orbits, robust mandibular corpus, and incisor heteromorphy quite unlike anything found in other hominoids, living or fossil (Alpagut et al., 1996). This combination of features suggests to some that *Ankarapithecus* more likely represents a stem member of the great ape and human clade rather than being specifically related to the orangutan clade (Begun and Gülec, 1998).

In the last few decades important Late Miocene hominoid samples have also been recovered from lignite beds at Lufeng in south-central China in deposits representing lake and swamp environments (Guoqin, 1993; Wanyong et al., 1986; Woo, 1957). Extensive excavations since the 1970s have produced a wealth of hominoid material, which includes jaws, crania, teeth, and a few postcranial bones (Wood and Xu, 1991; Wu et al., 1981, 1983, 1984; Xu and Lu, 1979). Chinese paleoanthropologists initially divided this hominoid sample into two genera, *Sivapithecus* and *Ramapithecus*, and considered the latter genus to be an early representative of the human lineage. As we shall see, there is some uncertainty about whether these fossils belong to one or two genera, but they are now recognized as distinct from South Asian fossil great apes and are generally placed in the genus *Lufengpithecus*.[4]

The Lufeng crania have a number of features in common. The two supraorbital tori are poorly developed and the region of the frontal bone between the two browridges, the area of the cranium known as **glabella,** is concave. The orbital contours are squarish with rounded corners and the nasal aperture is narrow and pear shaped. It is interesting that many of the craniodental features found in these specimens are similar to those found in orangutans (Schwartz, 1990).

A few postcranial remains, including a scapula and clavicle, have also been descibed as orangutan-like (Wu et al., 1986). In contrast, the finger bones are described as being less orangutan-like—for example, the articular surface for flexion and extension is less extensive than in orangutans, suggesting that this movement is more extensive in modern orangutans than in the Lufeng hominoids. However, it seems clear that the fossil finger bones, or phalanges, were adapted to grasping and hanging, as they are very long and strongly curved.

Many of the morphological differences noted between the larger and smaller crania from Lufeng that were originally placed in the two genera *Sivapithecus* and *Ramapithecus* are similar to those found between male and female orangutans, so it is very likely that these two "genera" simply represent the males and females of a single, sexually dimorphic genus (Kelley, 1993; Schwartz, 1990). Another possibility is that the Lufeng sample includes two separate genera that have very different patterns of dental sexual dimorphism, with one more similar to *Pongo* and the other more similar to *Homo* (Lieberman et al., 1985).

Only a few fossil specimens document the existence of hominoids in the Middle Miocene of Africa. Most of these specimens come from the Kenyan sites of Fort Ternan, Maboko Island, Nachola, Tugen Hills, Majiwa, and Kaloma (Andrews and Walker, 1976; Benefit and McCrossin, 1989; Leakey, 1962; McCrossin and Benefit, 1993; Pickford, 1982), and one

---

[4]English translations of many of the original Chinese articles dealing with these fossils can be found in Etler (1984).

comes from northern Namibia (Conroy et al., 1992, 1993). The East African specimens are mainly referred to the genera *Kenyapithecus, Equatorius,* and *Nacholapithecus* (Hill, 2002; Ward and Duren, 2002; S. Ward et al., 1999), and the Namibian specimen has been referred to the new genus *Otavipithecus.* These fossils date from about 16 to 12 mya.

Probably the richest of these Middle Miocene sites is Maboko Island, where at least five hominoid genera have now been recovered, all dating to about 16–14 mya (McCrossin and Benefit, 1994).[5] One of these, referred by some to *Kenyapithecus* and by others to either *Equatorius* or *Griphopithecus,* is of particular interest because for many years it was considered, along with *Ramapithecus,* a direct ancestor of the human lineage (Leakey, 1967a; Simons and Pilbeam, 1978). Many of the morphological features of *Kenyapithecus* are similar to those already noted for other Middle Miocene hominoids—for example, the broad, shallow, robust mandibles; low-crowned and thick-enameled molars lacking cingula; differential molar-wear gradients from M_1 to M_3; and canines that are relatively reduced in size. These features of mandibular robustness, molar morphology, and differential molar-wear gradients are markedly different from the complex of morphological features characterizing most Early Miocene hominoids. Once again we note that these morphological differences undoubtedly signify a change in diet from relatively soft and easily chewed foods to more resistant foodstuffs. For example, craniofacial features in *Kenyapithecus* are most similar to those of the bearded saki (*Chiropotes*) and the uakari (*Cacajao*) among extant primates, primates that use their robust upper canines, enlarged premolars, and robust and strongly procumbent lower incisors to break open tough outer coats of nuts and fruits with hard seeds.

Craniodental similarities among these genera include: (1) root of maxillary zygomatic process positioned anteriorly at M^1; (2) upper incisors strongly heteromorphic; (3) upper canine robust and tusk-like; (4) mandible with strongly proclined symphyseal axis with well-developed inferior transverse torus and robust corpus; (5) procumbent, narrow lower incisors; and (6) molars with low, rounded cusps and crenulated enamel (McCrossin and Benefit, 1997). This is consistent with the paleoenvironmental evidence indicating that these Middle Miocene sites were more open woodland environments compared to the earlier Miocene sites.

The postcranial sample associated with the genera of thickly enameled Middle Miocene East African hominoids has improved dramatically over the past decade or so (McCrossin and Benefit, 1997; S. Ward et al., 1999). In general, their postcranial skeleton is similar to other Miocene hominoids in lacking modern ape-like suspensory adaptations of the forelimb. An important distinction, however, is that the Maboko taxon's skeleton seems

[5]*Micropithecus, Limnopithecus, Kenyapithecus, Nyanzapithecus,* and *Mabokopithecus.*

more adapted to semiterrestrial digitigrade locomotion than the more ar-boreally adapted *Proconsul* skeleton. Such semiterrestrial features include the following: (1) greater tubercle of humerus projects proximal to the ar-ticular surface of the humeral head; (2) humeral head faces posteriorly rather than medially; (3) medial humeral epicondyle is short and poste-riorly directed; (4) olecranon is relatively long and moderately retroflected; (5) humeral/femoral index of about 95 indicates forelimbs and hindlimbs were used fairly equally during locomotion; (6) short, stout phalanges; and (7) adducted hallux (big toe), not abducted as in more arboreal primates.

An interesting inference from some studies of Miocene hominoids is that if the many skeletal specializations shared by living humans and apes evolved only once, then the apparent absence of such features in many currently known Middle Miocene apes suggest that none of them could be in the modern ape-human clade. Instead, they must have actually diverged before the last common ancestor of living apes, which is dated to about 14 mya according to the molecular timescale (Kumar and Hedges, 1998; McCrossin and Benefit, 1997).

Recently, our knowledge of Middle Miocene East African hominoids was greatly increased by the discovery of a new genus, *Equatorius africanus*, from the Tugen Hills of north-central Kenya (Ward and Duren, 2002; S. Ward et al., 1999). Some researchers have concluded on the basis of this more recently discovered and more complete material that it is the same taxon as the large Maboko hominoid and different from a related form from the somewhat later site of Fort Ternan, the type locality for *Kenyap-ithecus*. Thus these researchers reserve the name *Kenyapithecus* for the Fort Ternan fossil and *Equatorius* for Maboko and Tugen Hills specimens. The specimen consists of a partial skeleton from deposits just over 15 mya.[6] This is the first African Middle Miocene hominoid found with associated dental and postcranial remains. Body mass is estimated at about 27 kg based on regressions of dental and long-bone size. *Equatorius* shares many primitive hominoid features with Early Miocene *Proconsul* and *Afropithecus*, such as the broad, flat sternum; posteriorly oriented humeral head; long ulnar styloid process that contacts the proximal carpal row; and long, flexi-ble vertebral column. There are, however, a number of features that also distinquish *Equatorius* from these earlier Miocene hominoids: reduced pre-molar and molar cingula, reduced and relatively straight clavicle, posteri-orly deflected humeral medial epicondyle, and femoral head projecting proximal to the greater trochanter. This new discovery reinforces the view of considerable hominoid diversity in the Middle Miocene.

Late in the twentieth century, the first Miocene hominoid ever discov-ered from the African continent south of equatorial East Africa was reported (Figs. 5.11 and 5.12) (Conroy et al., 1992, 1993; Pickford et al., 1997a).

---

[6]This new genus now incorporates all material previously referred to *Kenyapithecus africanus*.

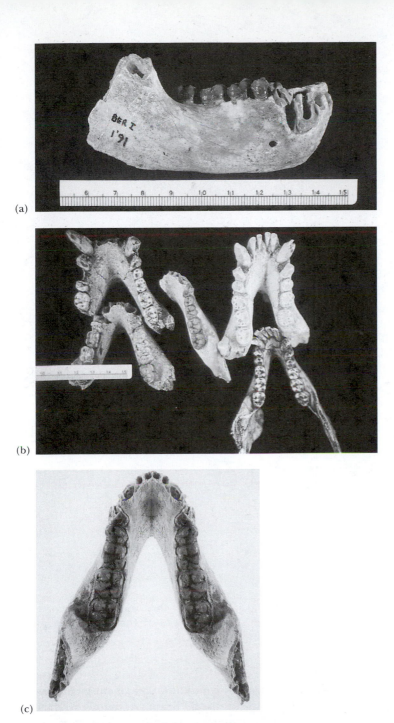

(a)

(b)

(c)

Fig. 5.11. Holotype mandible of *Otavipithecus namibiensis,* the only known
Miocene hominoid from subequatorial Africa.   (a) Lateral view. (b) Occlusal view
of *Otavipithecus* (middle) compared to *Proconsul nyanzae* (upper left), *Dryopithecus
fontani* (upper right), *Sivapithecus sivalensis* (bottom left), and *P. heseloni* (bottom
right). (c) Reconstructed mandible of *Otavipithecus.* (Photos by G. Conroy.)

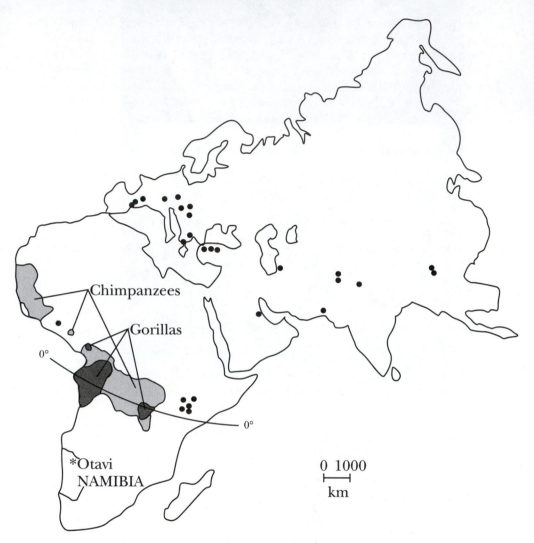

Fig. 5.12. Distribution of Middle and Late Miocene Hominoidea (black dots) and extant African apes (shading). Asterisk indicates site of *Otavipithecus* discovery. (From Conroy et al., 1992.)

This discovery demonstrated a previously unknown major range extension of Miocene hominoids in Africa to latitude 20°S, approximately 10° farther south than the limit of extant African apes. As we have seen, most previously known Miocene hominoids are found in southern Eurasia between latitudes 23°N and 50°N, extending from Spain in the west to China in the east, and in East Africa (Fig. 5.1). *Otavipithecus namibiensis* exhibits a unique constellation of characters that differentiate it from other Middle Miocene hominoids of Africa and Eurasia and represents the only fossil evidence documenting a pre-australopith stage of hominoid evolution in southern Africa. *Otavipithecus* has been dated by faunal analyses to the latter part of the Middle Miocene, approximately 13 mya. The faunal analyses also suggest that Namibia experienced a relatively humid climate during the Middle and Late Miocene, which contrasts strongly with the desertic and semiarid conditions that characterize the region today (Pickford et al., 1994a, 1997).

With the exception of the Plio-Pleistocene hominins, which we discuss in the following chapters, there are no other hominoids from southern Africa with which to compare *Otavipithecus*. *Otavipithecus* is clearly not an australopith; moreover, its dental and mandibular morphology and proportions differ from Early Miocene proconsulids. More appropriate comparisons are with Middle Miocene hominoids of East Africa and Eurasia such as *Kenyapithecus*, *Sivapithecus*, and *Dryopithecus*.

As noted earlier, *Kenyapithecus* and the closely related *Sivapithecus* are known from a number of sites in Kenya and Eurasia. Both differ from *Otavipithecus* in having molar teeth that are characterized by thick enamel and marked differential wear and by mandibles that are quite robust with broad ascending rami that obscure most of the third molar in lateral view.

In spite of the fact that *Otavipithecus* and *Dryopithecus* share several characteristics—including relatively thin enamel, reduced or absent buccal cingula, and a moderately developed shelf-like buttress of bone on the inside of the mandibular symphysis, the **inferior transverse torus**—there are enough clear distinctions to identify *Otavipithecus* as a separate genus (Pickford et al., 1994b).

Statistical tests relating molar size to body weight in modern anthropoids suggest that *Otavipithecus* weighed 14–20 kg—that is, about the same body size estimated for small *Proconsul* or *Dryopithecus* species but smaller than the 30- to- 35 kg size of living female pygmy chimpanzees. The minimal differential wear on the molars, combined with the thinness of the enamel, suggests that *Otavipithecus* most likely subsisted on nonabrasive foods. The narrowness of the incisor, or symphyseal, region of the lower jaw also argues against a specialized fruit-eating, or frugivorous, diet of tough-skinned fruits, but neither molar size nor molar shape shows any adaptations to a specialized leaf-eating, or folivorous, diet. It is most likely that *Otavipithecus* subsisted on foods such as leaves, berries, seeds, buds, and flowers—that is, foods that did not require extensive preparation by the incisor teeth before mastication.

Because the timing of dental eruption, as inferred from molar wear patterns, is related to the length of the maturational process within major groups of primates, it is reasonable to conclude that the molars of *Otavipithecus* emerged in rapid succession as they do in living chimpanzees.

Estimation of the age at death using chimpanzee maturation rates suggest that this individual died at about 10 years of age (Conroy and Mahoney, 1991; Kuykendall et al., 1992).

SUMMARY OF CRANIODENTAL ADAPTATIONS OF MIDDLE MIOCENE HOMINOIDS

Although the phylogenetic affinities of many Miocene hominoids are still subject to debate and revision, there seems little doubt that, as a group, most Early Miocene forms can be distinguished from most Middle and Late Miocene forms and that human origins trace back to one of these later Miocene groups. Distinguishing characteristics of most Middle/Late Miocene hominoids include: (1) molars that are thick enameled with low, rounded cusps (bunodont); (2) relatively low-crowned and robust canines; (3) relatively deep, robust mandibular bodies and symphyses; (4) laterally flaring zygomatic arches; (5) anteriorly abbreviated mandibles and pre-maxillas, suggesting a relatively nonprojecting, or orthognathous face; and (6) lower first molars enlarged relative to third molars.

These features are relevant to discussions about human origins because, as we shall see in the next chapter, most of them foreshadow the conditions found in the earliest hominins, the australopiths. As we shall document, these morphological changes undoubtedly relate to increased masticatory stresses in these animals as they began to exploit the new ecological niches of the African savanna.

THE ROLE OF MOLECULAR CLOCKS IN HOMINOID CLASSIFICATION

Comparisons of biomolecular data in modern apes and humans have been crucial in confirming that (1) African apes (chimpanzees and gorillas) are more closely related to humans than either one is to the orangutan and (2) the evolutionary lineages leading to each of the modern African apes (and humans for that matter) could not have diverged as long ago as the Early/Middle Miocene (Figs. 5.13 and 5.14) (Ruvolo, 1994; Wildman et al., 2003). These molecular tests fall into several categories, depending on the resolution of the test: (1) those that measure differences in whole proteins without knowledge of the specific changes in the protein structure, like immunodiffusion and electrophoresis; (2) those that determine

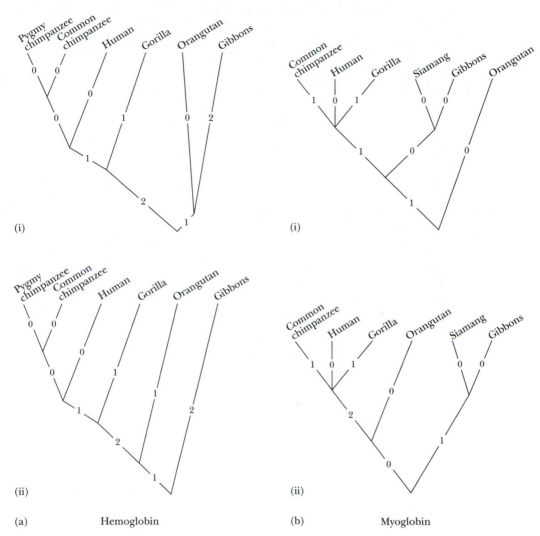

Fig. 5.13. (a) Evolutionary tree for humans and apes based on sequencing of hemoglobins. (i) Relatedness between groups as a function of the lowest number of amino acid replacements needed. For example, gibbons and orangutans differ by two amino acids, whereas gibbons and humans differ by six amino acids; therefore, the most parsimonious classification of humans and apes based solely on hemoglobin sequences would group gibbons and orangutans together. However, evidence from a number of different molecular lines of evidence place orangutans closest to the chimpanzee-human-gorilla clade, as shown in (ii). (b) Trees vary depending on the molecular character chosen; shown is the evolutionary tree for humans and apes based on myoglobins. (i) Lowest number of amino acid replacements needed. (ii) Amino acid replacements constrained by other molecular evidence. (From Goodman, 1992.)

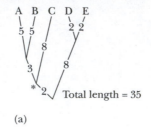

(a)

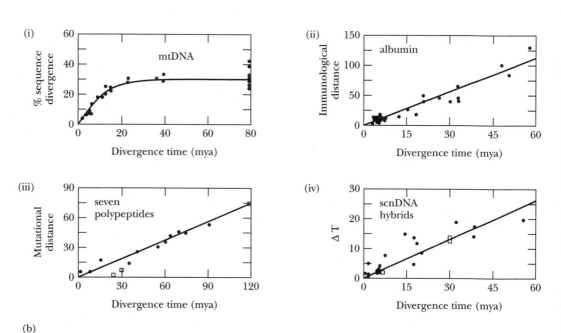

(b)

Fig. 5.14. (a) Calibrating the molecular clock based on a uniform rate of molecular change over time. This hypothetical evolutionary tree shows the number of changes of some particular molecular event along each branch of the tree. Note that the same number of steps are involved as one follows any pathway from a given branch point to the tip of the tree. For example, from the branch point marked with an asterisk it is 3 + 5 = 8 steps to taxon A, 8 steps to taxon B, and the same to taxon C. This tree can be drawn against a time scale if a single uniform rate of molecular change is assumed over the whole tree in that the number of changes on each branch reflects the time, in relative units, that has elapsed on that branch. To convert relative time to absolute time, all that is needed is the absolute date for just one branch point. For example, if we knew from the fossil record that the common ancestor of taxa A, B, and C (at the asterisk) dated to 40 mya, then we could infer that one molecular change occurred every 5 million years (e.g., 8 changes occurring over 40 million years). Therefore, taxa A and B must themselves have diverged 25 mya (5 changes in each since their divergence); the root of the entire tree would be 50 mya (10 changes) and the divergence of species D and E would be 10 mya (2 changes). (From Friday, 1992.) (b) Examples of various molec-

Box 5.2   DNA Hybridization

DNA hybridization has had a particularly profound, if controversial, influence on studies of hominoid phylogeny (Marks et al., 1988; Sibley, 1992; Sibley and Ahlquist, 1987). The technique itself is relatively straightforward. When double-stranded DNA is heated, the bonds between the nitrogenous base pairs adenine-thymine and guanine-cytosine are broken down so that single strands of DNA are produced. When the single strands are allowed to cool, they tend to reassociate into double strands. When single strands of DNA from two different species are combined, they tend to produce what are known as hybrid double-stranded DNA molecules. These hybrid DNA molecules will contain a number of mismatched base pairs, depending on how genetically different the two species are from one another. The more mismatches, or genetic differences, there are in the hybrid DNA molecule, the lower the temperature needed to disassociate it again into two strands. Thus hybrid DNA from two closely related species will disassociate at higher temperatures than hybrid DNA from two more distantly related species.

---

the specific amino acid sequences of proteins, like amino acid sequencing; (3) those that determine the nucleotide sequences of DNA, like DNA sequencing; and (4) those that detect differences in DNA molecules without indicating exactly which nucleotides have changed, like DNA hybridization.

Data from such studies show a fairly consistent branching sequence within hominoid evolution: first, the separation of gibbons from the great ape–human clade; second, the separation of the orangutan from the African great ape–human clade; and third, the separation of gorillas, chimpanzees, and humans after a long common evolutionary pathway since separation from the orangutan (Fig. 5.10). The details and timing of this last split among chimpanzees, gorillas, and humans are still the subject of active study and debate. Some molecular anthropologists conclude that

---

ular clock "calibrations" for different types of molecular genetic data. All dates along the abscissa are derived from fossil or biogeographic evidence. (i) Mitochondrial DNA sequence divergence for various mammals. The slope of the linear portion of the curve gives the conventional mtDNA clock calibration of approximately 2% sequence divergence per million years between recently separated lineages (note that beyond about 20–15 mya, mtDNA sequence divergence begins to plateau, presumably as the genome becomes saturated with substitutions at the variable sites). (ii) Albumin immunological distances (as estimated by microcomplement fixation) from various carnivorous mammals and ungulates. (iii) Accumulated codon substitutions in seven proteins (cytochrome c, myoglobin, α- and β-hemoglobin, fibrinopeptides A and B, and insulin) for various mammalian species. The two squares below the curve involve primate comparisons. (iv) Delta T values from DNA hybridizations of carnivores (circles) and primates (squares). (After Avise, 1994.)

Box 5.3   Molecular Clocks

In order to see how molecular clocks work, let us suppose two taxa differ in some molecular parameter by X units and that they diverged Y million years ago, judging by the fossil record. Thus, assuming relatively constant rates of change, X number of molecular changes have occurred over Y millions of years, and this relationship sets the clock. It is then a relatively simple matter to calculate the divergence times of other taxa by measuring how much the taxa differ in the same molecular parameter. For example, suppose two taxa that diverged 60 mya differed by 20 units of some molecular parameter. Change in this parameter is thus assumed to occur at the rate of 1 unit per 3 million years. Consequently, the divergence date of two taxa differing by 10 such units would be estimated at 30 mya, 5 units at 15 mya, and so on. A number of such molecular clocks have been proposed for calculating divergence times within hominoid evolution. Many of the clocks have been calibrated by placing the split between Old World monkeys and apes, the cercopithecoid-hominoid split, at about 25 mya; but this split could be several million years older than this. In general, molecular clock studies suggest the following: (1) separation of the gibbon from the great ape and human clade about 12–15 mya; (2) separation of the orangutan from the African ape–human clade about 10–12 mya; and (3) separation of African apes from humans about 4–7 mya.

It is obvious, then, that if any of these dates are even remotely correct, the Early/Middle Miocene divergence dates for chimpanzees, gorillas, and humans offered by paleoanthropologists in the 1960s and early 1970s are significant overestimations. Be that as it may, while molecular biology has provided paleoanthropology with invaluable insights into evolutionary processes and with more testable means of assessing phylogeny and cladogenesis, it is still by no means the panacea that some claim for it.

There are several general points that should not be lost sight of in any discussion about molecular clocks. First, the debate is not whether molecular clocks keep time metronomically, like a watch—they do not. At best their "clock-like" behavior is stochastically constant, analogous to the situation in radioactive decay. Second, there is little doubt that different DNA sequences evolve at markedly different rates (Avise, 1994; Britten, 1986; Goodman et al., 1983; Strauss, 1999). There is also little doubt that molecular clocks tick at different rates in different lineages and at different times. Rates can fluctuate over time even on a single branch of a phylogenetic tree. For example, a single stretch of DNA within the *Drysophila* male fertility gene (*Ods*) has changed more in the past 500,000 years than in the preceding 700 million years. If researchers had assumed a standard rate of change in this particular marker, they would have concluded that the last 500,000 years spanned a longer time than the previous 700 million years! Third, molecular anthropologists sometimes have difficulty in ascertaining which molecular configurations are primitive and which are derived for the taxa under study. In such cases, similarity in molecular structure, in and of itself, may be no more informative about phylogenetic relationships than similarity in morphological structures would be if their polarities were unknown. And finally, there is one other little problem—molecular anthropologists do not even agree among themselves about what their data reveal about the "true" phylogeny of hominoid primates.

---

humans and chimpanzees are more closely related to one another than either one is to the gorilla (humans and chimpanzees differ by only about 1–5% of their genomic DNA sequences, depending on how these differences are estimated) (Britten, 2002; Navarro and Barton, 2003; Wildman et al., 2003). Others conclude that chimpanzees and gorillas are more closely related to one another than either is to humans, and still others conclude that this three-way split, or trichotomy, is unresolvable, at least with present molecular techniques (Deinard and Kidd, 1999; Goodman et al., 1994, 2001; Green and Djian, 1995; Marks, 1994, 1995; Rogers, 1994; Rogers and Comuzzie, 1995; Ruvolo, 1994, 1995; Saitou, 1991; Samollow et al., 1996; Templeton, 1985).

Regardless of how this trichotomy is ultimately resolved, molecular anthropologists have still attempted to date each of these major cladogenic events by devising various **molecular clocks**. The use of molecular clocks is based on the premise that many molecular differences among taxa are neutral mutations that accumulate at a relatively constant rate when averaged over geologic time (Fig. 5.14). Therefore, the larger the molecular difference, the earlier the inferred date of divergence. The irony, at least as far as paleoanthropologists are concerned, is that molecular clocks must ultimately be calibrated against the fossil record.

Fortunately, the results of molecular anthropology are bolstered by more traditional anatomical and paleontological studies that also support the broad outline of the three major cladogenic events noted above (Andrews and Martin, 1987). For example, most paleoanthropologists agree that the hominoid primates (gibbons, chimpanzees, gorillas, orangutans, and humans) are a monophyletic group. Within this group there are numerous postcranial features, particularly in the wrist, shoulder musculature, and trunk that also attest to the linkage between the great apes and humans to the exclusion of gibbons. Within the great ape–human group there is also strong morphological evidence linking gorillas and chimpanzees to the exclusion of orangutans, particularly in the many anatomical specializations for knuckle-walking (Jenkins and Fleagle, 1975; Tuttle, 1967, 1970). Increasingly, anatomical studies have also supported a chimpanzee-human clade to the exclusion of gorillas, a conclusion consistent with most molecular studies (Begun, 1992). It is interesting that many of these relationships were deduced decades ago by such early morphologists as Thomas Huxley, G. Elliot Smith, and William Gregory.

SPECULATIONS

Finally, let's return to the question posed at the beginning of this chapter. If the earliest hominins didn't spring full-blown from the head of a chimpanzee or gorilla 5 mya, then where *did* they come from? Did Darwin (1871) have it right when he wrote over a century ago:

> In each great region of the world the living mammals are closely related to the extinct species of the same region. It is therefore probable that Africa was formerly inhabited by extinct apes closely allied to the gorilla and chimpanzee; and as these two species are now man's closest allies, it is somewhat more probable that our early progenitors lived on the African continent than elsewhere.

But one question keeps raising its ugly head: If Darwin was right that extinct relatives of chimpanzees and gorillas would most likely be found in Africa, then *where are they?* To date, no fossils have been recovered from the Middle/Late Miocene of Africa that can be confidently linked to living chimpanzees and/or gorillas.[7]

However, if one accepts the paleontological, morphological, and molecular evidence indicating that African apes and humans are closely related sister groups that have only recently diverged from one another (say 10–5 mya), it may be pushing the envelope to argue that the earliest members of this clade are to be found anywhere else but in the Middle/Late Miocene of Africa. But some researchers are now doing just that. As we saw above, for example in the case of *Ouranopithecus*,[8] there is a long tradition in paleoanthropology of attempting to identify early members of this clade somewhere other than in Africa. Over the past few years new fossil discoveries and interpretations have led some to the novel and intriguing suggestion that the earliest members of this clade may actually be found within the European Middle Miocene *Dryopithecus* group. As noted earlier, *Dryopithecus* shares a number of cranial and postcranial features with later African hominins. In addition, it has not gone unnoticed that while most Late Miocene African localities lack hominoids, many Eurasian sites do not. This has led to the suggestion that the ancestor of the African ape–human clade may have actually evolved in the Miocene of Eurasia, not Africa, and then back-migrated into Africa (thereby accounting for its absence in the Late Miocene fossil record of Africa). This hypothesis has received some support from several sources, including: (1) known patterns of biogeographic dispersal of a few other mammalian lineages in the Miocene (e.g., some other African mammalian lineages like the bovid *Eotragus* and the muroid rodents are thought to have Eurasian origins), (2) evidence of climatic change in the circum-Mediterranean region at the time, and (3) some evidence from molecular biology (Begun, 2002; Heizmann and Begun, 2001; Stewart and Disotell, 1998).

However these issues are ultimately resolved, one thing seems clear. As the Miocene epoch drew to a close, a major new episode in primate evolu-

---

[7]Unless that is what *Orrorin* or *Sahelanthropus* turn out to be!

[8]Not to mention the long saga of *Ramapithecus*!

tion began to unfold: One of these Miocene hominoid species began an adaptive radiation throughout Africa and began to shape its world in ways no other primate had even approached. The story of the last major adaptive radiation of this weird ape, the evolution of the human lineage, is the subject of the rest of this book.

CHAPTER VI

The Earliest Hominins (Part 1): The Australopiths of Southern Africa

INTRODUCTION

It is quite remarkable that while there are literally hundreds of prehuman "apelike" fossils from Miocene deposits in eastern Africa, there are virtually none from the succeeding Plio-Pleistocene (Conroy, 1990). What do we find instead? Creatures "wholly at venture, primal, provisional, devoid of order. Like beings provoked out of the absolute rock and set nameless and at no remove from their own loomings to wander ravenous and doomed and mute as gorgons shambling the brutal wastes of Gondwanaland in a time before nomenclature was and each was all" (McCarthy, 1985). Not at all. Instead we find in the Plio-Pleistocene of Africa the rather sudden appearance of a very unusual higher primate, one that walked on two legs rather than four, used tools rather than teeth for tearing and cutting, had a relatively large brain, and survived, indeed even thrived, in the harsh environs of the African savanna by virtue of newly evolved behavioral and social mechanisms.

In this chapter we introduce these new creatures on the African landscape, the australopiths. Because they were first discovered in southern Africa, we begin our story there.[1] In the next chapter we move on to the australopiths of eastern Africa, who are at present the oldest known hominins in the fossil record. Then, having introduced the australopiths and their paleoenvironmental and geological settings, we turn in Chapter 8 to a more general discussion of the paleobiology of the fossils themselves and what they can tell us about early hominin lifestyles.

[1]At the end of this chapter, on pages 178–83, is a gallery of photographs of early hominins from the Plio-Pleistocene epochs in southern Africa.

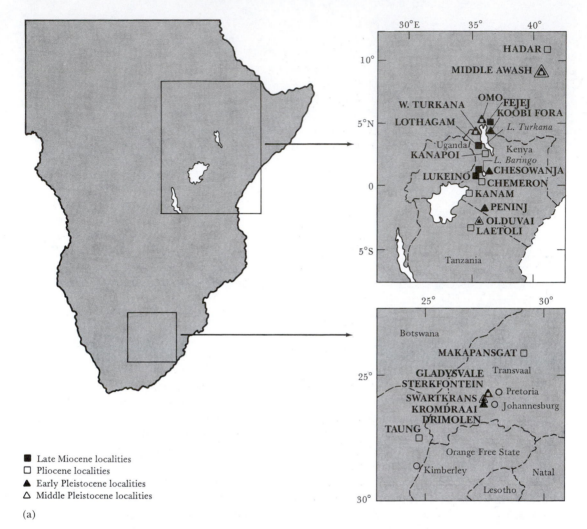

Late Miocene localities
Pliocene localities
Early Pleistocene localities
Middle Pleistocene localities

(a)

Fig. 6.1. (a) Australopith sites of eastern and southern Africa. Middle Awash sites include Maka, Belohdelie, and Aramis. The australopith species *Ardipithecus ramidus* and *Ar. kadabba*, discovered at several Middle Awash sites in Ethiopia, are dated to about 5.8–4.4 mya and may be the stem group from which all later hominins evolved. *Australopithecus anamensis* is dated to about 4 mya. All three newer South African australopith sites, Gladysvale, Gondolin, and Drimolen, are found within a few kilometers of the well-known sites of Sterkfontein, Kromdraai, and Swartkrans. (b) A general chronology of major Plio-Pleistocene hominins discussed in the text. Note that the genus *Paranthropus* is retained in Wood's view. The species marked with an asterisk were all unknown a decade or so ago. (From Wood, 2002.)

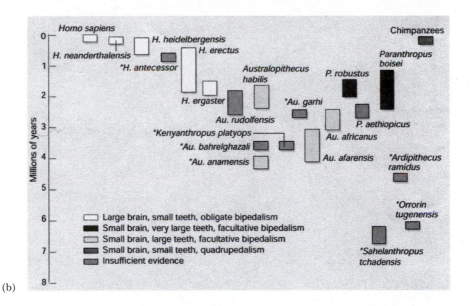

(b)

These earliest hominins on the African landscape, the australopiths (meaning "southern apes"), first appear in eastern Africa around 5.8 mya, in southern Africa around 4 mya, and possibly as early as 7 million years ago from the Sahara Desert of Chad (Burnet et al., 2002; Haile-Selassie, 2001; Haile-Selassie et al., 2004b; Partridge et al., 2003). Thus far, australopiths are known only from sites in Africa (the major australopith sites are shown in Figure 6.1). As we shall see in a later chapter, claims for the presence of australopiths in Southeast Asia (e.g., Java) are generally not given much credence (Kramer, 1994; Tobias and von Koenigswald, 1964). Many popular accounts of human evolution give the misleading impression that these early hominins were small brained and/or of small size. Although they are smaller than modern humans (Fig. 6.2a), australopiths had brains roughly three times larger than those of Miocene "apes," and their body size was within the range of modern chimpanzees, which are very formidable animals indeed and quite capable of hunting and killing a diverse array of other mammals, including red colobus monkeys, bushpigs, and bushbucks (Stanford, 1995; Stanford et al., 1994).

Claims for the earliest appearance of our own genus, *Homo*, date to about 2.4 mya in East Africa (Kenya and Malawi) and to slightly less than 2.0 mya in southern Africa, although some of these earliest specimens are difficult to distinguish from the more "gracile" forms of australopith, which we will discuss below (Brain, 1988; Hill et al., 1992b; Howell et al., 1987; Kimbel et al., 1996, 1997; Schrenk et al., 1993).[2] It appears that

[2]The claim for the earliest evidence of *Homo* at 2.4 mya in East Africa, a temporal bone fragment (KNM-BC1) from the Chemeron Formation of Kenya (Hill et al., 1992b), has been disputed by several workers (Falk and Baker, 1992; Feibel, 1992; Tobias, 1993a).

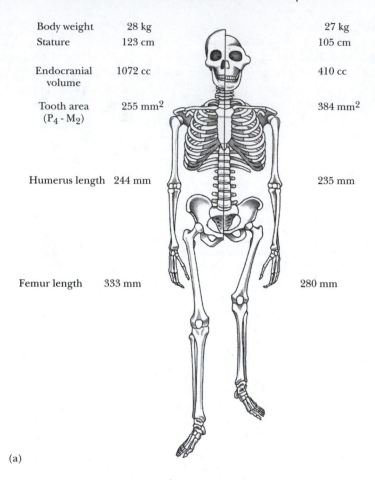

Body weight	28 kg		27 kg
Stature	123 cm		105 cm
Endocranial volume	1072 cc		410 cc
Tooth area (P_4 - M_2)	255 mm^2		384 mm^2
Humerus length	244 mm		235 mm
Femur length	333 mm		280 mm

(a)

	Body Weight (kg)		Stature (cm)		
	Male	Female	Male	Female	EQ
A. afarensis	45	27	151	105	2.4
A. africanus	41	30	138	115	2.6
A. robustus	40	32	132	110	3.1
A. boisei	49	34	137	124	2.7
H. habilis	52	32	157	125	3.1
H. erectus (African)	68		180	160	3.3
H. sapiens	65	54	175	161	5.8
P. troglodytes	54	40			2.0

(b)

Fig. 6.2.   (a) Estimated body proportions of an early hominin, *A. afarensis* ("Lucy") (right) compared to those of a modern human pygmy (left). (b) Estimated male and female body weight, height, and encephalization quotient (EQ) of several early hominin species compared to those of modern chimpanzee (*Pan troglodytes*). (After McHenry, 1992b.)

Australopithecus and *Homo* may have coexisted in eastern and southern Africa for more than a million years, from about 2.4 to 1.2 mya (Suwa et al., 1997; White, 1988). The newer genus, *Homo*, reveals several important evolutionary distinctions from australopiths, including more gracile jaws and teeth, more frequent use of stone-tool technology, and, most important, new levels of cerebral organization reflected in both absolute brain size and increased complexity (Falk, 1990; Tobias, 1987; Toth, 1987). These trends continued throughout the Plio-Pleistocene in the *Homo* lineage(s), culminating in early members of our own species, *H. sapiens*, several hundred thousand years ago. We shall discuss the evolutionary journey of *Homo* in more detail in later chapters.

Although most paleoanthropologists recognize a number of australopith taxa, including *Ardipithecus ramidus, Ar. kadabba, Kenyanthropus platyops, Australopithecus anamensis, A. afarensis, A. garhi, A. africanus, A. robustus, A. boisei,* and *A. aethiopicus,* it is fair to say that there is no unanimity of opinion (and probably never will be) about the exact number of australopith species, or even genera, or about the classification of individual australopith specimens (White et al., 1994, 1995). In addition, there has also been a tendency in recent years for some authors to resurrect the genus name *Paranthropus* for both *A. robustus* and *A. boisei,* a practice we do not follow in this text.[3]

Traditionally, australopith species have often been distinguished from one another by inferred body and craniodental type as either **gracile** (lighter, smaller toothed) or **robust** (heavier, larger toothed). Two different taxonomic schemes reflecting this somewhat artificial, or at least overlapping, dichotomy are presented in Table 6.1. While the terms *gracile*

Table 6.1 Two Schemes for the Nomenclature and Taxonomy of Australopiths

Form	One Genus (Australopithecus)	Three Genera (Ardipithecus, Australopithecus, Paranthropus)
Gracile forms	A. ramidus	Ar. ramidus
		Ar. kadabba
	A. anamensis	A. anamensis
	A. africanus	A. africanus
	A. afarensis	A. afarensis
Robust forms	A. robustus	P. robustus
	A. boisei	P. boisei
	A. aethiopicus	P. aethiopicus

[3]Much of this often spirited debate about the number of early hominin genera and/or species might appear to the uninitiated like the paleoanthropological equivalent of how many angels could dance on the head of a pin.

australopith and *robust* australopith may be convenient shorthand labels, a number of studies strongly suggest that body size and dental dimensions of these species may not differ as much as previously thought (Fig. 6.2b) (Feldesman and Lundy, 1988; Jungers, 1988b; McHenry, 1988, 1992a, 1992b). In fact, most of the differences may be restricted to the gracility or robustness of the cheek teeth and chewing apparatus rather than overall body size, although it is evident that some specimens allocated to "gracile" forms, like *A. africanus,* actually have larger teeth than some of those allocated to *A. robustus.* In this text we shall therefore use the terms *gracile* and *robust* only as informal convenient shorthand labels to provide some continuity with pre-existing literature.

One major generalization about australopith evolution in Africa seems warranted: Most of the so-called gracile australopiths like *Ardipithecus ramidus, Ar. kadabba, Kenyanthropus platyops, Australopithecus anamensis, A. afarensis,* and *A. africanus* are known before about 2.6 mya, whereas most of the so-called robust australopiths like *A. robustus, A. boisei,* and/or *A. aethiopicus* first appear about 2.6 mya and survive until about 1.0 mya (Fig. 6.1b). As we shall see later, this generalization has had a significant impact on theories of australopith phylogeny.

Current evidence suggests that australopiths were confined to the African continent with most of their fossil remains being recovered from widely separated sites in East Africa, southern Africa (including Malawi), and central Sahara (Chad). What this suggests is that australopiths were actually distributed throughout most of Africa during the Plio-Pleistocene but have been discovered only in these particular regions due to the accidents of geology and luck. The East African deposits generally consist of lake and riverine sediments that bear occasional layers of volcanic tuff. Many of these tuffs have been radiometrically dated by the methods presented earlier. The South African cave breccias, on the other hand, are not easily dated radiometrically, and dates for them are usually based on faunal comparisons to other radiometrically dated African sites. The other sites are dated mainly by faunal comparisons.

THE AUSTRALOPITHS OF SOUTHERN AFRICA: THE SETTING

Australopith fossils have been recovered from several South African cave sites. Of the major australopith-bearing sites, five (Sterkfontein, Kromdraai, Swartkrans, Gladysvale, Drimolen) are located within 10 km of one another, just a few miles outside Johannesburg; one, Makapansgat, is located in the Limpopo Province (formerly known as the Transvaal); and one, Taung, is located on the edge of the Kalahari Desert, north of Kimberley in the western Cape. What follows is a brief overview of the history of discovery and the geological setting of the major South African cave sites shown in Figure 6.1, beginning with the earliest finds.

Taung

Taung, in the local language, means "the place of Tau (or Tao), the Lion." Located some 130 km north of Kimberley, it is the most southwesterly site on the African continent from which australopiths have been recovered.

In May 1924, a friend of Josephine Salmons, a young medical student at the University of Witwatersrand in Johannesburg, showed her the cranium of a fossil baboon that had come from the limeworks at Taung. She, in turn, brought the fossil to her anatomy professor, Raymond Dart. Australian by birth, Dart had just assumed the chair of anatomy at the new medical school in Johannesburg. Before arriving in South Africa, Dart had spent a year as a Rockefeller Fellow in the anatomy department at Washington University in St. Louis under the guidance of Robert J. Terry and had also worked on fossil human skulls under the tutelage of G. Elliot Smith in London. Both Terry and Smith had strong anthropological interests, which were undoubtedly passed on to the young Dart, who later admitted that "circumstances thrust anthropology upon me after I had chosen to follow even more useless trails as a neurological embryologist" (1949). The fossil baboon piqued Dart's latent anthropological interest. Reasoning that a site yielding fossil baboons might also contain fossil hominins, Dart discussed the fossil find with R. B. Young, a professor of geology, who was about to visit the vicinity of Taung to do some economic geology research.

When Young arrived at Taung in November of that year, the limeworks manager, A. E. Spiers, showed him part of another fossilized skull that had recently been blasted out of the limeworks and that was now lying around in his office. Knowing Dart's interest in fossil primates, Young brought the fossil back to Johannesburg and handed it over to Dart on November 28, 1924 (Tobias, 1984). Over the next 40 days Dart extracted the fossil from its rocky matrix, analyzed it, and then sent his preliminary conclusions to the British scientific journal *Nature* for publication (Dart, 1925a).

The specimen he extracted from the rock consisted of most of the face, lower jaw, and half of a brain endocast of a young "child" he named *Australopithecus africanus* ("southern ape of Africa"). In his short article (which appeared in *Nature* on February 7, 1925), despite the name he gave the fossil, Dart described its many *human*-like qualities. Dart proposed that his new specimen be regarded as a man-like ape and in keeping with this view proposed that a new family, Homo-simiadae, be created for it. Because of this, and because this was the first truly ancient hominin fossil ever found on the African continent, his article triggered an intellectual revolution about human origins that continues unabated to this day.

One might think that the human-like qualities of the Taung skull noted by Dart in his 1925 article would have been accepted with open arms by a worldwide anthropological community obsessed with finding the "missing link" between apes and humans. However, the reaction to the Taung skull (and to the claims of human-like qualities for australopiths in general) ranged from total neglect (Leakey, 1935), to ridicule (Hooten, 1946),[4] to extreme criticism in the most influential textbooks of the day (Keith, 1931). Clearly, Dart's little skull was not consistent with the preconceived notions of Victorian paleoanthropologists—namely, that early hominins must have had large brains (at least 750 cc according to one eminent anatomist of the day)[5] and that early man must have evolved in Europe or Asia but surely not in the Dark Continent of Africa. Since the skull was obviously that of an immature individual, critics were quick to point out that if and when adult specimens were found they would certainly look more like apes than humans, since immature living apes look more human-like than adult apes do.[6] Perhaps European society was just not prepared to accept the view that Africa was the "cradle of mankind," as Dart had referred to it when he exhibited the skull at the 1925 British Empire Exhibition at Wembley. Dart's Taung child remained in taxonomic limbo until adult australopiths began showing up in other South African sites in the 1930s and 1940s. As we shall see, southern African australopiths eventually received recognition through the discoveries of Robert Broom and John T. Robinson and the subsequent efforts of C. K. (Bob) Brain, Phillip V. Tobias, and Ronald Clarke, among others.

Because the exact site of discovery of the only *Australopithecus* specimen from Taung was destroyed by limestone quarrying in the 1920s, precise biostratigraphic information for use in dating the fossil remains problematic. Earlier geological and uranium-isotopic investigations suggested an age of about 1 million years for the Taung child (Partridge, 1986); however, this was clearly at odds with the faunal dating, particularly of the cercopithecids, or Old World monkeys, which suggested an age of 2.0–2.5 mya (Delson, 1984, 1988). In fact, it is now known that the younger radiometric date based on U-S dating can be considered only a minimum age. The older age is more consistent with that of other *A. africanus* specimens from Sterkfontein (member 4) and Makapansgat (members 3 and 4),

---

[4]"Cried an angry she-ape from Transvaal,
  Though old Doctor Broom had the gall
        To christen me Plesi-
        anthropus, it's easy
  To see I'm not human at all" (Hooten, 1946).

[5]Sir Arthur Keith, English anatomist extraordinaire, has even been alleged to have been the brains behind the Piltdown forgery (Spencer, 1990; Tobias, 1992), although more recent evidence suggests the forger was Martin A. C. Hinton, a curator of zoology at London's Natural History Museum (Gee, 1996).

[6]A phenomenon referred to as *neoteny*, whereby a descendant species will have an adult shape more similar to that of a juvenile in the ancestral species.

which date to about 3.0–2.4 mya (see below) (McKee, 1993a, 1993b; McKee and Tobias, 1994; Tobias et al., 1993).

An analysis of the Taung sediments suggest that they formed under semiarid conditions similar to those in the area today. The cycle of cave filling that entrapped the hominin seems to have marked the onset of more humid conditions. Paleontological excavations resumed at Taung for a few years in the 1990s, but, alas, no further hominin remains were discovered. Taung is, therefore, unique among South Africa's australopith-bearing caves in that it has yielded only the one single hominin specimen. The associated fauna is unique as well, consisting mainly of small-size animals, many of which display unusual damage to the bones and crania. While early accounts interpreted these characteristics of the Taung assemblage as being due to the carnivorous activities of australopiths (or of other carnivorous mammals) (Dart and Craig, 1959), a more recent suggestion is that a large bird of prey with hunting habits analogous to living African black, martial, or crowned eagles may have been the taphonomic agent responsible for the collection of most of the Taung fossils, including the Taung child itself (Berger and Clarke, 1994, 1996; Hedenstrom, 1995).

Sterkfontein

In a 1935 guidebook to places of interest around Johannesburg, the owner of the Sterkfontein caves suggested visitors come to Sterkfontein and find the missing link. On Monday, August 17, 1936, the South African paleontologist and physician Robert Broom did just that by finding the first adult australopith!

Earlier that year, two of Dart's former students, G. Schepers and W. Le Riche, alerted Broom to the fact that fossil baboons had been found in the cave breccias of Sterkfontein. Broom, who had joined the staff of the Transvaal Museum in Pretoria only 2 years before, was understandably excited by these discoveries and paid his first visit to Sterkfontein on August 9, 1936. Eight days later, he was rewarded by the discovery of an adult fossil hominin. In a series of brief communications to *Nature*, Broom initially described this material as *A. transvaalensis* (Broom, 1936, 1937, 1938) but later described it as a new genus, *Plesianthropus*. It turned out to be the first adult australopith known to science.[7] The specimen consisted of the anterior two-thirds of a brain cast (endocast), the cranial base, parts of the parietal bones, a right maxilla containing the P^4–M^2, portions of the frontal bone, and a partial lower jaw with teeth.

Following this initial find, Broom made many discoveries at the site until the outbreak of World War II interrupted his fieldwork. After the war,

---

[7]Actually, the first adult australopith specimen ever found was a lower canine from Laetoli found by Louis Leakey in 1935. However, its hominin affinities were recognized only in 1979 (White, 1981).

Broom was assisted by John T. Robinson, also of the Transvaal Museum, and discovered many other australopiths at the site (Broom and Robinson, 1947). For many years the onsite director of excavations at Sterkfontein was Alun Hughes. Work continues there today under the supervision of Phillip Tobias and Ronald Clarke of the University of the Witwatersrand, and over 600 hominin specimens have now been found at the site (including seven partial crania, two dozen well-preserved but isolated cranial bones and mandibles, and numerous postcranial elements) (Lockwood and Tobias, 1999). The overwhelming majority of the specimens are attributed to *A. africanus*, but a cranium attributed to *Homo habilis* has also been recovered as have several teeth tentatively identified as *A. robustus* (Kuman, 1994a, 1994b; Tobias and Baker, 1994).

The Sterkfontein deposits have been subdivided (from oldest to youngest) into stratigraphic units, or **members,** numbered 1 to 6. Fossil hominins have thus far been found in members 2 (and Jacovec Cavern), 4, and 5 (Fig. 6.3). The oldest hominins from member 2 include four articulating foot bones ("Little Foot") and an extraordinarily complete skeleton (Stw 573) as well as new remains from Jacovec Cavern (Clarke and Tobias, 1995; Partridge et al., 2003) (see below). The bulk of the *A. africanus* sample is from member 4. Thus far, remains of both *Homo habilis* and (tentatively) *A. robustus* seem restricted to member 5. The small sample of robust australopith teeth from member 5 includes a lower right first molar and an upper incisor and canine, all heavily worn. Ironically, the earliest representative of the genus *Homo* in southern Africa, the *H. habilis* cranium Stw 53, was discovered on August 9, 1976, by Hughes, some 40 years to the day after Broom's first visit to Sterkfontein (Hughes and Tobias, 1977).[8] As we will see in a later chapter, Jonathan Leakey (Louis and Mary Leakey's son) had already discovered the type specimen of *H. habilis* at Olduvai Gorge, Tanzania, in the mid-1960s. The Latin name *H. habilis* was actually suggested to Louis Leakey by Dart to indicate a hominin that was presumably handy or skillful with tools.

The member 4 *A. africanus* sample includes remains of at least 50 individuals, represented by crania of varying degrees of completeness, maxillas, mandibles, isolated teeth, two partial skeletons, and various isolated postcranial bones. Remarkably, a middle ear bone (stapes) was recovered from one partial cranium (Stw 151) (Moggi-Checchi and Collard, 2002). However, the substantial size and morphological variation of the sample suggest to some that more than one hominin species may be present in member 4 (Clarke, 1988, 1994a; Conroy and Vannier, 1991b). For example, one specimen in particular (Stw 252) has large, ape-like incisors and canines in combination with cheek teeth that are larger than many specimens from both eastern and southern Africa attributed to *A. robustus* and/or *A. boisei*. In fact, Stw 252 looks remarkably similar to a recently discovered *A. afarensis* cranium from Hadar (Kimbel et al., 1994).

---

[8]This specimen is regarded by Kuman and Clarke (2000) as *Australopithecus* sp.

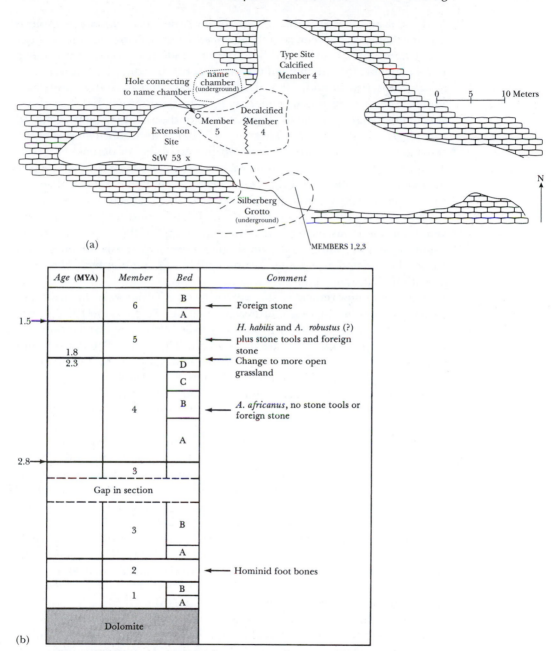

Fig. 6.3. (a) Sterkfontein excavation plan showing areas referred to in text (Clarke, 1994b). (b) Stratigraphic sequence of the Sterkfontein cave site. Note positions of *A. africanus* and *H. habilis*. Several isolated teeth tentatively assigned to *A. robustus* have also been recovered from member 5 as have large collections of Oldowan and Acheulean tools. The total depth of the section is about 27.5 m. (Tobias, 1980.)

Dental and cranial variability in the member 4 *A. africanus* sample is greater than that between some *Homo habilis* and *A. boisei* specimens. However, several recent studies of hominin craniodental remains from member 4 conclude that the bulk of the material can be confidently assigned to *A. africanus* (Lockwood, 1999; Lockwood and Tobias, 2002). The taxonomic identity of several specimens cannot be determined, but at least two specimens suggest the possibility that a second taxon may be present. To investigate whether the Sterkfontein member 4 hominin material represents a single species, one study tested the variability in dental characters compared to several modern reference samples, one having a high degree of sexual dimorphism and the other having an extreme degree of sexual dimorphism. The analysis found excessive (i.e., statistically significant) variation in a few of the features but noted that a consistent pattern of elevated variation was evident in most characters in the member 4 fossil hominin sample. Thus, while the single-species hypothesis for member 4 cannot be rejected, the results are compatible with a multiple-species interpretation (Calcagno et al., 1997).

Of great importance is the recognition of what may be southern Africa's earliest stone-tool cultures in member 5 (Kuman, 1996). Both Oldowan and early Acheulean tool types have been recognized, and some of the more diagnostic tools are illustrated in Figure 6.4. The three robust australopith teeth are associated with the Oldowan tools, and faunal comparisons suggest the Sterkfontein Oldowan of member 5 may date to about 2.0–1.7 mya. Several specimens tentatively identified as early *Homo* (e.g., Stw 80) are associated with Acheulean tools (Kuman and Clarke, 2000).

The Oldowan tools are characterized by simple tool-making methods that use more easily flaked raw materials, such as quartz. The most distinctive tool types are two chopper-like cores, a discoid-like core, and a proto-biface. These tools presumably accumulated at the site as a result of repeated visits by hominins to an open site favored for its shelter and for the nearby gravels used for tool making.

The Sterkfontein early Acheulean compares well with East African Acheulean assemblages dated to approximately 1.5 mya. The *H. habilis* cranium was found about 6 feet from the limit of the early Acheulean tool distribution of member 5 so it is still not clear whether or not *H. habilis* was the Acheulean tool maker (Kuman, 1994a, 1994b).

Unfortunately, the paleomagnetic stratigraphy of Sterkfontein is still poorly resolved. Based on faunal comparisons, the hominins from member 4 are estimated to date from about 3.0 to 2.0 mya and those from member 5 to about 1.8–1.5 mya (Vrba, 1982).[9] Electron spin resonance (ESR) has been used to date bovid tooth enamel from member 4 and gives

---

[9]For a somewhat different view of the age of hominin bearing deposits at Sterkfontein, see Berger et al. (2002) and the response by Clarke (2002b).

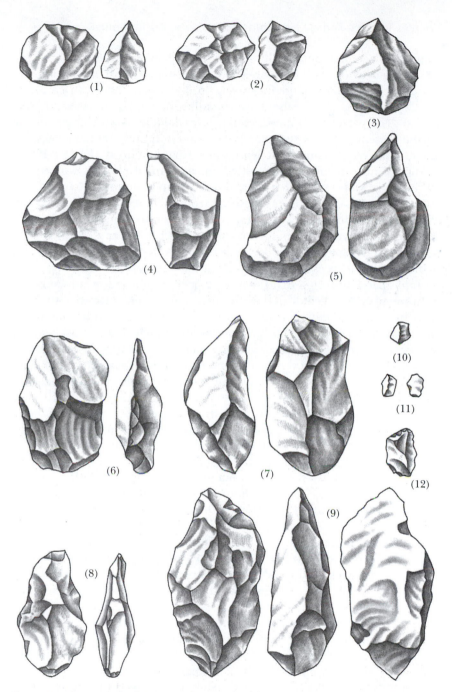

Fig. 6.4. Stone tools from member 5, Sterkfontein. *Oldowan tools*: (1) quartz chopper-core, (2) quartz discoid-core, (3) quartz irregular core, (4) quartz chopper-core, (5) quartzite proto-biface, (10, 11) utilized quartz flakes, (12) retouched quartz flake. *Acheulean tools*: (6) quartzite cleaver on a large flake, (7) quartzite cleaver on a large flake or other detached piece, (8) small chert bifacial handaxe, (9) quartzite unifacial handaxe on a large flake. (From Kuman, 1994a.)

an average age of about 2 million years for this member (Schwarcz et al., 1996). Analysis of fossil antelopes from the site suggests a transition to more open grasslands and increasing aridity in southern Africa about 2.5–2.0 mya—that is, at about the member 4/5 interval (Vrba, 1980b, 1985a). The presence of fossilized lianas in member 4 provides evidence for the presence of large supporting trees and indicates that the local vegetation must have included at least some riparian forest (PARU, 1994). Studies of micromammals suggest the mean annual precipitation in the Sterkfontein Valley varied between about 310 and 550 mm (Avery, 2001). No stone tools have yet been recovered from member 4. The distribution of the fossil hominins, as well as that of the fossil wood in the partly calcified breccia, suggests that member 4 sediments formed as a talus cone beneath a vertical shaft and that large carnivores were dropping in the bones as they fed in the trees above the cave entrance (Clarke, 1994b).

It has been suggested that the low proportion of juvenile animal bones from member 5 indicates that some meat was scavenged rather than actively hunted by hominins (Vrba, 1975). The presence of indisputable cut marks on the shaft of a small bovid humerus implies that at least some of the bones in member 5 represent hominin food remains. This conclusion must be tempered, however, by the observation that there are no obvious cut marks on any of the bones associated with the Oldowan tools, suggesting that hominins were not the accumulating agent for the bulk of the fauna. At least some of the bone tools from the site were probably used as instruments for digging up edible bulbs and/or termite mounds (Backwell and d'Errico, 2001; Brain, 1981b).

As mentioned earlier, over 600 hominin remains have been recovered from Sterkfontein. The member 4 mammalian remains include a moderate number of arboreal species (about 3.5%) and a high percentage of frugivorous ones (above 17%). There are no aquatic mammals and only about 3% of species are fresh-grass grazers. This suggests a habitat of more open woodland interspersed with bushland and thicket areas. The majority of the bones in member 5 were most likely accumulated by *Homo* and/or porcupines. About 44% of the mammals are grazing species, and there are no arboreal or frugivorous species in this member. These numbers suggest more open or wooded grasslands or plains for member 5 as compared to member 4 (Reed, 1997).

Of great interest is the recent discovery of the oldest virtually complete hominin skeleton from Africa. The 4-foot-tall skeleton, cataloged as Stw 573, was recovered from Sterkfontein's Silberberg Grotto (member 2) and has recently been redated to approximately 4.0 mya using a new technique of the radioactive decay of cosmogenic aluminum (Al^{26}) and beryllium (Be^{10}) in cave sediment quartz (Partridge et al., 2003). The specimen includes associated cranium and lower jaw, foot bones, and both lower and upper limb bones (Clarke, 1998, 1999, 2002a), but has yet to be fully excavated from its enclosing breccia. All that one can say at the moment is that the cranium has a massive zygomatic arch unlike known crania of *A. africanus*. The temporal line approaches the midline of the low frontal squamae and continues as a small sagittal crest on the parietals. The nuchal plane faces backward as in chimpanzees, not downward as in humans. The proximal radius and ulna are moderately large, and the radius has a pronounced tuberosity. The heads of these bones are said to be more ape-like than human-like. The metacarpals do not appear to be elongated as in apes but are similar in length to those of other australopiths and modern humans. The first metacarpal and proximal phalanx indicate a robust thumb whose proportions to the rest of the hand seem to resemble those of modern humans. The proximal phalanges of the thumb and forefinger are curved as in *A. afarensis*. The length of the complete left upper limb and complete right lower limb seem to be coequal. These dimensions, together with the long thumb and relatively short fingers, suggest that this individual was not a knuckle-walker or likely derived from one.

The skeleton belongs to the same individual as an earlier find of several articulating foot bones (talus, navicular, medial cuneiform, and proximal half of the first metatarsal) dubbed "Little Foot" (Clarke and Tobias, 1995). These fossils, and the newly discovered hominins from Jacovec Cavern, are of approximately the same age as East African *A. anamensis*.

Additional hominin remains recently recovered from Sterkfontein's Jacovec Cavern include much of a cranial vault (Stw 578), isolated teeth, proximal half of a left femur (Stw 598), lumbar vertebrae, a hand phalanx, distal end of a left humerus (Stw 602, and lateral half of a left clavicle (Stw 606). The cranium shows some interesting features such as the presence of a pronounced sagittal keel on the frontal bone and a posteriorly wide cranial vault (in superior view). Perhaps the most unusual feature is the steeply sloping tympanic plate, which is more reminiscent of *Pan* than the vertically inclined orientation seen in all other australopiths from Sterkfontein member 4. The Jacovec femur is the most complete known from Sterkfontein. It has a small head and a long, thick neck. In these features it more closely resembles two *A. robustus* femora from Swartkrans (SK 82 and SK 97) and one from member 4 (Stw 99). However, it differs from other Sterkfontein femora such as Stw 522, also from member 4. Does this suggest two different hominins in the Sterkfontein sample or simply normal variation in this population? The clavicle is chimpanzee-like in having a pronounced conoid tubercle, which marks a strong anterolateral angulation of the shaft at that point.

Stable carbon isotope analyses of enamel from 10 *A. africanus* specimens from member 4 show that dietary variation in this taxon was highly variable. Carbon isotope signals are compatible with mainly C_4 based foods—either C_4 grasses and sedges and/or the insects and vertebrates that ate them (van der Merwe et al., 2003).

Kromdraai

The first robust australopith was discovered at Kromdraai in 1938 under somewhat unusual circumstances (Berger et al., 1994). The site itself is situated only 1.5 km east of Sterkfontein. The limeworks manager at Sterkfontein, G. W. Barlow, sold Broom a well-preserved palate with a molar tooth of a fossil hominin but at first refused to tell him where it had come from. Broom eventually extracted from Barlow the information that the specimen had been found nearby by a schoolboy, Gert Terblanche. Broom took the young boy back to the place he had found the specimen where he soon discovered much of a hominin cranium, including part of a palate, most of the left side of the face, almost the whole left zygomatic arch, the left side of the base of the cranium, a portion of the parietal bone, and the greater part of the right mandible with most of the teeth. Broom (1938) made this cranium (TM 1517)[10] the type specimen of a new genus and species that he named *Paranthropus robustus*. Subsequent excavations carried out by personnel from the Transvaal Museum have now recovered a minimum of six robust australopith individuals from member 3 of the Kromdraai B East (KBE) Formation, also referred to as the Kromdaai Australopith Site (Fig. 6.5). The fossil hominin sample includes the partial cranium and dentition of the type specimen, isolated teeth, a proximal ulna, distal humerus, second metacarpal, proximal hand phalanx, talus (or ankle bone), and ilium. Faunal comparisons suggest an age of about 1–2 million years, and this is consistent with the reversed polarity (tentatively correlated to the Matuyama reversal) of the Kromdaai stratigraphic column.

For many years, only one questionable stone-tool flake was known from the site (Brain, 1981b). However, recent excavations have recovered a sizable assemblage of approximately 100 artifacts and manuports of Early Acheulean/Developed Oldowan tools from Kromdraai A ("faunal site") (Kuman et al., 1997).

Sedimentological analyses suggest a more humid environment than that prevailing during deposition of member 4 at both Makapansgat and Sterkfontein. A wooded local environment is evident from the fauna of KBE member 3, whereas the pollen recovered from the boundary of KBE members 2 and 3 suggests that a more open savanna characterized the area at that time (Vrba, 1981).

A. robustus is the only hominin from Kromdraai B. This deposit consists entirely of terrestrially adapted animals and likely represents an open grassland environment. However, there is also a relatively high proportion (20%) of frugivorous species, indicating some patches of riparian woodland in the vicinity (Reed, 1997).

---

[10] *TM* stands for Transvaal Museum.

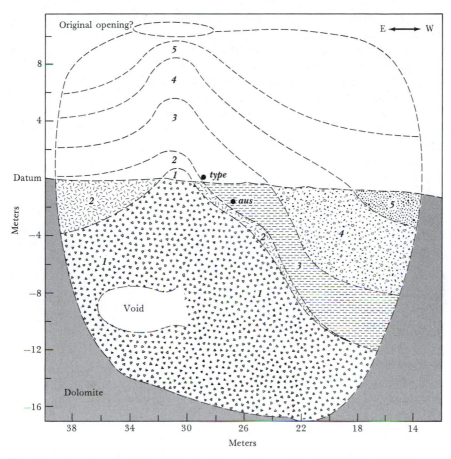

Fig. 6.5. Stratigraphy of the Kromdraai cave site; section through the KBE Formation (Kromdraai Australopith Site). The scale (left) gives meters above and below the present land surface (*datum*). Dotted lines above datum show hypothetical original cave contours before erosion. Successive breccia members are labeled 1 to 5. *Type,* possible source of type specimens of *A. (Paranthropus) robustus; aus,* mandible of a juvenile *A. robustus* (Vrba, 1985b).

Makapansgat

Located in Limpopo Province, the Makapansgat hominin site is a cavern of almost pure limestone that was mined for a decade starting in 1925. Approximately 30 specimens (representing about a dozen individuals) of *A. africanus* have been recovered from the site, which are, with the possible exception of the new hominins from Sterkfontein member 2, the oldest known remains of this taxon from the fossil record of Africa.[11] During these mining operations a local mathematics teacher, Wilfred Eitzman, drew Dart's attention to the abundance of fossil bones being blasted out of the cave breccia by limeworkers (Dart, 1925b). Inexplicably, Dart did not investigate the site thoroughly until 1947, at which time he discovered that many of the vertebrate fossils contained free carbon, leading him to speculate that the bones had been intentionally burned by early hominins inhabiting the cave (subsequently, the carbon test was shown to be spurious, the black color instead being attributable to manganese staining). In September 1947, one of Dart's researchers, J. W. Kitching, discovered the back, or occipital, portion of an australopith cranium on one of the limeworkers' dumps. Reasoning that this early hominin might have been responsible for some of the "burned" bones in the deposit, Dart (1948b) named the new hominin *A. prometheus* after the Titan Prometheus, the mythological hero who stole fire from the gods. By the mid-1960s, however, most workers concluded that the majority of australopith fossils previously described as *Plesianthropus* (named for Broom's adult specimen from Sterkfontein) as well as *A. prometheus* should be included in the single taxon, *A. africanus* (Tobias, 1967b).

Other important hominin discoveries were made at the site in 1948, including an adolescent mandible, an infant's right parietal bone, several craniofacial fragments and isolated teeth, and two fragments of an adolescent pelvis (Dart, 1948a). The discovery of the pelvis was critical since it proved conclusively that *A. africanus* walked bipedally. Several stone tools were also recovered from the site (Brain et al., 1955).

Dart also noticed that many of the vertebrate fossils from the site seemed to be artificially fractured and that some animal parts were more commonly preserved than others. This suggested to him that the hominins were in some way responsible for the bone accumulation, and he proposed the idea that many of the bones and jaws at Makapansgat had been utilized as tools by the early hominins at the cave: teeth as saws and scrapers, long bones as clubs, and so on (Dart, 1957). He named this the **Osteodontokeratic** (bone-tooth-horn) **Culture.** Dart's theory became the inspiration for the "killer ape" theory made famous by the dramatist Robert Ardrey in his book *African Genesis* (1961). However, later taphonomic studies have cast doubt on this interpretation, suggesting instead that many of these bone accumulations were the product of carnivore scavengers such as hyenas (Brain, 1981b; Shipman and Phillips, 1976; Shipman and Phillips-Conroy, 1977).

---

[11]A second cave (the Cave of Hearths) is located about 1 km from the Makapansgat limeworks cave and contains what is probably the most complete archeological record of continuous habitation (up to 220,000 years from the earliest stone age to recent historical times) in Africa.

A paleomagnetic record for this site extends from the base of member 1 to the lower levels of member 4 (Fig. 6.6), but the calibration of the paleomagnetic record at Makapansgat is open to several different interpretations. Member 1 shows reversed polarity as does the lower member 2. The upper part of member 2 is normal. Member 3 is poorly magnetized, but member 4 shows two narrow reversed zones followed by a normal sequence. This, in conjunction with the faunal evidence, supports an age in

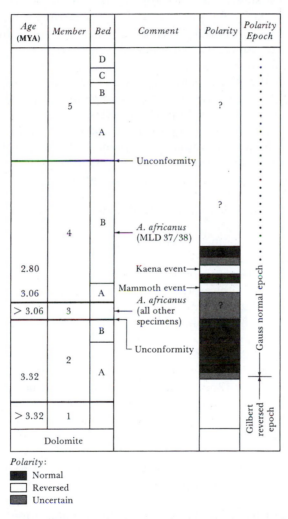

Fig. 6.6.   One interpretation of the relative dating of the Makapansgat cave site; stratigraphic and paleomagnetic sequence of the Makapansgat Formation, showing the location of the major australopith discoveries from that site. An unconformity represents an interruption of deposition. (From Tobias, 1980.)

the middle of the Gauss normal polarity epoch, involving the Kaena or Mammoth events, suggesting an age close to 3 mya. However, the possibility of lateral facies variation makes precision impossible (Cooke, 1997; McFadden and Brock, 1984). The fossil hominins, all assigned to *A. africanus,* are known only from members 3 and 4 and have been variously dated to about 3.0–2.4 mya (Delson, 1984; Partridge, 1986; White et al., 1981). Faunal correlations using fossil bovids (antelope, buck, buffalo, etc.), suids (pigs), and cercopithecoids (monkeys) indicate that member 3 faunas are most similar to East African faunal assemblages dated to between about 3.0 and 2.6 mya (Vrba, 1985a). Such comparisons assume, of course, that East and South Africa had similar enough environments to support the same fauna and that similar faunas are truly contemporaneous (Turner and Wood, 1993b).

The bulk of the mammalian bones from member 3 (more than 30,000 specimens, including at least two dozen hominins) were accumulated in the cave by fossil hyenid and porcupine species. Among the bones are a relatively high percentage of both frugivorous (about 15%) and arboreal species (about 5.5%), indicating the proximity of bushland and medium density woodlands. The presence of both fresh-grass grazers (about 3.5%) and aquatic mammals (about 2%) indicate the nearby presence of a river and some edaphic grassland as well. Overall, the fossil mammalian fauna suggests a habitat mosaic that contained riparian woodland, bushland, and edaphic grassland.

In contrast, the member 4 deposits contain only three hominins out of about 250 mammalian specimens. The bulk of the specimens are cercopithecines (about 80%), and the likely accumulators were birds of prey and leopards. There are, however, greater percentages of arboreal (7%) and frugivorous (20%) species than in member 3, suggesting more wooded habitats (however, this may simply be a function of smaller sample size and predation bias, e.g., birds of prey as opposed to hyenas) (Reed, 1997).

Taphonomic, palynological, and sedimentological studies suggest fluctuating climatic and vegetational conditions during the period of sedimentation at Makapansgat (Zavada and Cadman, 1993). Studies of fossil pollen suggest that when australopiths occupied the area the region may have had higher rainfall patterns that supported patches of subtropical forest and thick bush as well as savanna. Evidence of more episodic rainfall patterns begins to appear after the middle of member 4, with the presence of a higher proportion of grazing mammals, signaling the onset of more open, drier conditions about this time (Cadman and Rayner, 1989; Rayner et al., 1993).

As noted in Chapter 2, the role of stable carbon isotope analyses is assuming increasing importance in paleoanthropological studies. This is based on the observation that there is a positive correlation between animals and their substrate diets. Isotope signals from C_3 or C_4 plants are recorded in animals that once fed on one or the other of these plant types or who once fed on animals that predominantly ate one of these plant types. Thus, if early hominins were eating mainly browsers, a C_3 isotope signal would be expected, whereas if they were eating mainly grazers then more of a C_4 signal would be expected. However, tubers, nuts and berries also have a characteristic C_3 signal, complicating dietary interpretations. Stable carbon analyses of tooth enamel from *A. africanus* at Makapansgat reveals that this early hominin ate not only fruits and leaves but also large quantities of carbon-13 enriched foods such as grasses and sedges and/or animals that ate these plants. These early hominins must have regularly exploited open woodland or grassland environments for food (Lee-Thorp and van der Merwe, 1993; Lee-Thorp and Beaumont, 1995; Lee-Thorp et al., 1994, 2000; Schoeninger, 1995; Sponheimer and Lee-Thorp, 1999).

Swartkrans

Toward the end of 1948 Broom decided to investigate Swartkrans, a new cave site less than a mile from Sterkfontein. The excavations had an auspicious beginning: The very first dynamite blast yielded an australopith tooth. By the end of the first week a mandible (SK 6) was found, which Broom (1949) described as a new species of robust australopith, *Paranthropus crassidens* (now usually lumped together with the Kromdraai specimens as *A. robustus*). Soon afterward, in April 1949, a very different hominin was discovered, first named *Telanthropus capensis* but later reclassified as *Homo erectus* (Broom and Robinson, 1950; Clarke et al., 1970). This was the first evidence for the coexistence of *Australopithecus* and *Homo* in the fossil record of Africa (Olson, 1978). We shall have more to say about African *H. erectus* in a later chapter.

Broom died in Pretoria in April 1951, but the work he initiated at Swartkrans was continued by his colleague John Robinson. Since the 1960s the site has been investigated by C. K. Brain and associates from the Transvaal Museum who have recovered a large number of robust australopiths and a lesser number of *Homo* specimens. The hominin sample from the site now includes several hundred specimens, representing over 100 individuals and including cranial remains, mandibles, numerous isolated teeth, and limb bone fragments. Remains of *A. robustus* have come from member 1 (about 98 individuals), member 2 (about 17 individuals), and member 3 (about 9 individuals). Temporal coexistence with *Homo* cf. *erectus* is indicated by the fact that four individuals of this hominin were found in member 1, two in member 2, but none as yet in member 3 (Brain, 1994). It is interesting that approximately 40% of the hominins represent immature individuals (Grine, 1989, 1993b; Grine and Daegling, 1993; Grine and Strait, 1994; Grine and Susman, 1991; Grine et al., 1993; Susman, 1988, 1989, 1993; Susman and Brain, 1988).

There are several major rock units defined at this cave site, designated members 1–5 (Fig. 6.7) (Brain, 1993b; Brain and Watson, 1992). Both

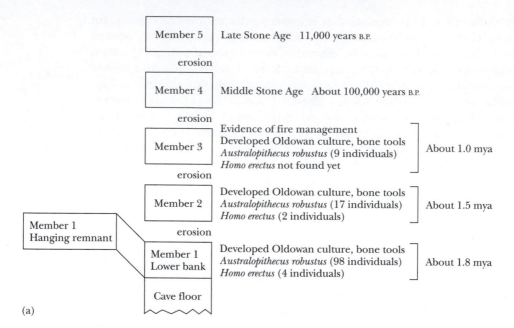

(a)

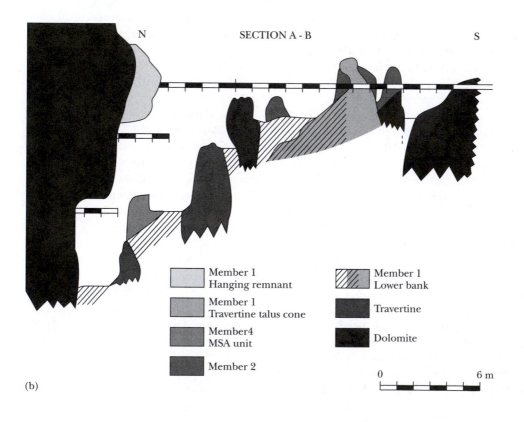

SECTION A - B

Member 1
Hanging remnant

Member 1
Lower bank

Member 1
Travertine talus cone

Travertine

Member4
MSA unit

Dolomite

Member 2

0   6 m

(b)

members 1 and 2 contain stone and bone tools and, as noted above, remains of both *A. robustus* and *Homo* cf. *erectus*. Similar tools and *A. robustus* remains are also known from member 3. Evidence for the earliest use of fire also comes from this member (Brain, 1993a; Brain and Sillen, 1988; Sillen and Hoering, 1993).

Faunal analyses suggest that member 1 is between about 1.5 and 1.8 million years old and that the faunas from members 2 and 3 do not differ significantly from member 1. Direct ESR dating of a small piece of enamel from SK 11 (*A. robustus*) from member 1 is consistent with this age (Curnoe et al., 2001). The artifact assemblages from members 1–3 also show no significant differences, and all are classified in the core/chopper/flake tool tradition, sometimes referred to as the Developed Oldowan. In addition to the stone tools, several fossil bones have been discovered from all three members that appear to have been used as digging tools, and some may have even been modified for preparing animal skins (Brain and Shipman, 1993; Clark, 1993). It is interesting that one delicate bone flake from member 3 had been fashioned into a pointed awl-like tool similar to those used for the piercing of animal hides. Middle Stone Age artifacts have been recovered from member 4, although no hominin fossils are known from this level. It is now thought that members 1–3 date from about 1.8–1.0 mya. Thermoluminescence dating of quartz sands gives ages of about 1.2 million years for the breccia of member 2 and about 1.6 million years for the breccia of member 1 (Vogel, 1985). Paleomagnetic results have not proven useful at the site so far.

As noted, both *A. robustus* and *Homo* are found in Swartkrans member 1. There are no arboreal species in this member, but the number of fruit and leaf eaters (about 14%), aquatic species (about 6%), and fresh-grass grazers (about 3%) suggest open habitats with riverine woodland or forest in the vicinity. *A. robustus* and *Homo* are also found in member 2. There is some decline in the number of fruit and leaf eaters from member 1 (down to about 9%), and there are no fresh-grass grazers. There are both aquatic (about 6%) and terrestrial carnivores (9%). The increase of grazing animals (about 32%) suggests a somewhat drier habitat than in member 1.

Fig. 6.7. (a) Stratigraphic sequence of the Swartkrans cave site. Hominin remains have been found in members 1–3: *A. robustus* and *H. erectus* in both members 1 and 2, but only *A. robustus* in member 3. Stone tools have been found throughout the sequence, and the earliest evidence of fire comes from member 3. The oldest deposit, member 1, is divided into two discrete masses: the hanging remnant clinging to the cave's north wall and the lower bank resting on the cave floor, both thought to date from 1.8 to 1.5 mya based on faunal considerations. Members 1–3 probably fall within a time range of 1.8–1.0 mya, and members 4 and 5 are probably less than 100,000 years old. (b) A section running north-south through the filling of the Outer Cave at Swartkrans, showing the vertical relationships among the various members. It now appears that members 1 and 2 occupied much of the Outer Cave south of the hanging remnant. Note that members 3 and 5 are not shown in this section. *MSA*, Middle Stone Age. (Brain, 1993b.)

Only *A. robustus* has thus far been recovered from member 3. There is a further decrease in fruit and leaf eaters (about 6%) and a decrease in grazing animals as well (about 25%). Fresh-grass grazers increase in abundance to about 4%. The abundance of aquatic animals stays about the same (6%). These are all indicative of open grassland with a river or stream supporting edaphic grasslands. The paleoenvironment throughout the depositional history of the cave seems to have been very similar to that of today—one of highveld grassland and riverine woodland savanna in the vicinity of the Blaaubank Stream, which currently flows near the site (Reed, 1997; Watson, 1993).

Based on analyses of mammalian skeletal parts preserved at the site, as well as by carbon isotope analyses, it appears that large cats, leopards, and sabre-toothed cats, particularly *Megantereon* and *Crocuta*, were the main bone-collecting agents at Swartkrans, including many of the hominins (Lee-Thorp et al., 2000). However, evidence of controlled use of fire and butchering in member 3 suggests that hominins could also have been responsible for at least some of the bone accumulation. Analyses of microscopic wear patterns on modified bone "tools" from Swartkrans (and also from Sterkfontein and Drimolen) suggest that hominins at these sites used at least some of these tools to dig into termite mounds (Backwell and d'Errico, 2001). Since *Homo* and *A. robustus* have both been identified at all three sites, it is unclear who actually made and used the tools. However, if these analyses are correct, this would be the earliest evidence of insectivory in hominin diets.

This "termite-eating hypothesis" is further strengthened by carbon isotope analyses. A significant proportion of dietary carbon from C_4 plants indicative of a protein component to the diet have been found in the remains of *Homo*, *A. robustus*, and *A. africanus*. In fact, carbon isotope data confirm that proportions of C_3 and C_4 foods in the diets of Swartkrans *Homo* and *A. robustus* did not differ significantly (Lee-Thorp et al., 2000). The presence of a strong C_4 plant signal for these taxa has sometimes been interpreted to mean that they were mainly vegetarian. However, there may be another explanation—C_4 plant carbon may be incorporated into these species by the ingestion of grass-eating herbivores or grass-eating termites.

Newer Sites: Gladysvale, Drimolen, Gondolin

Although only two early hominin teeth have been described thus far from Gladysvale (an upper premolar and molar), the site was the first new australopith-bearing locality to be found in southern Africa since Broom discovered the remains of *A. robustus* at Swartkrans in 1948. The fauna, preliminarily dated to 2.5–1.7 mya, indicates that savanna conditions prevailed during deposition of the cave deposits. The teeth have been designated as *A.* cf. *africanus*. More recently, several other Gladysvale hominin fossils attributed to early *Homo* have been reported from deposits thought to be of early Middle Pleistocene age (Berger and Tobias, 1994; Berger et al., 1993).

Of greater interest is the recent discovery of new hominin fossils from the nearby site of Drimolen (Keyser, 2000; Keyser et al., 2000). This site has already yielded a number of isolated australopith teeth as well as a mandible and cranium of a female *A. robustus* with almost complete dentition and, next to it, a mandible of a male *A. robustus*. Five bone tools, comparable to those published from Swartkrans, have also been recovered (PARU, 1995). Hominin fossils are tentatively dated to between 1.5 and 2.0 mya.

Even more remarkable is the discovery of the bones of two infants, one 2–3 years of age at the time of death and the other only 8–10 months of age. The older infant may be a member of the genus *Homo* and the younger one *A. robustus*. The two were found fairly close together at a depth of 4.2m in the cave. The remains of the older child include the lower jaw with two milk teeth and the first permanent molar, which had not yet erupted. Next to the jaw were the bones of the forearm, the radius and ulna. Some cranial fragments were also recovered. The remains of the younger child consist of both maxillae, two milk teeth, and the frontal bone. The Drimolen infants help resolve a particularly vexing problem— whether or not the skeletal traits used to identify early hominin adults can be found in infants as well. For example, the frontal bone of the Drimolen infant is clearly identifiable as *A. robustus* by its thin browridges and by the slight depression at glabella, thus confirming that it is possible to tell the difference between *A. africanus* and *A. robustus* infants (Keyser, 2000; Keyser et al., 2000).

The site of Gondolin is located about 4 km southwest of the town of Broederstroom in South Africa's Northwest Province (Menter et al., 1999). The site was worked briefly in 1979 by Elisabeth Vrba, then of the Transvaal Museum, and given a maximum date of approximately 2 mya, based on the occurrence of the suid *Metridiochoerus andrewsi*. During a brief test excavation in November 1997, two fossil hominin teeth were recovered from one of the extensive mining dumps at the site. One of the teeth is a complete left M_2. Its most notable trait is its enormous size. It may signal the first evidence of a hyper-robust australopith in southern Africa (*A. boisei?*). The tooth shows both proximal and distal interproximal wear facets, and its occlusal surface is worn flat. The uncorrected mesiodistal and buccolingual diameters—18.4 and 17.8 mm, respectively—exceed those of any recorded robust australopith M_2 from South Africa and place the tooth well within the upper range of so-called hyper-robust *A. boisei/aethiopicus* specimens from East Africa. Leaving aside the varied and controversial issues in robust australopith systematics, the two most likely alternative taxonomic interpretations for the Gondolin M_2 are that it is an unusually large South African specimen belonging to either *A. robustus* or *A. crassidens* or that it represents an extreme southern population of an East African hyper-robust taxon such as *A. boisei*. More conclusive statements await recovery of additional and more complete specimens from this site.

The second tooth is a fragmented molar that may be *Homo*—it is relatively small, shows very uneven wear, and has much more relief to the cusps than would be expected for a robust australopith tooth. Thus if these identifications hold up with further discoveries it will be only the third site in southern Africa at which *Homo* and *Australopithecus* co-occur (the others being Swartkrans and the Malawi Rift) (Brain, 1993c; Kullmer et al., 1999).[12]

SUMMARY OF SOUTHERN AFRICAN SITES

Throughout most of the time that *A. africanus* was present in southern Africa, the region was characterized by greater humidity and thicker bush cover than it is today. A major ecological change apparently occurred 3.0–2.0 mya that led to increasing dryness and to the spread of more open grassland conditions. Sedimentological and faunal evidence suggests that a more cyclic (and probably seasonal) rainfall pattern emerged after this time and persisted throughout the Pleistocene. However, none of these subsequent fluctuations between wet and dry climates was as dramatic as the event about 2.5 mya that initiated them. For the most part *A. africanus* was replaced in southern Africa by populations of *A. robustus*, which co-existed at first with *H. habilis* and later with *H. erectus*.

Thus the three major sites near Johannesburg (Sterkfontein, Swartkrans, and Kromdraai) suggest changing patterns of vegetation cover and cave filling over the approximately 2 million years of australopith evolution in southern Africa. Among fossil bovids, the Alcelaphini (e.g., hartebeests) and Antilopini (e.g., springboks) are useful faunal markers for inferring past vegetation cover because both are indicative of open plains and grassland environments (Skinner and Smithers, 1990; Vrba, 1974). These bovids make up anywhere from 25% to 90% of the bovid remains at these sites. Although the percentage of these bovids generally increases over time, an abrupt increase apparently occurred about 2.5–2.0 mya. This shift seems to fit well with the idea of a general faunal change in southern Africa in the late Pliocene, including the shift from gracile to robust australopiths about this time in the Sterkfontein Valley (Fig. 6.8).

Although various climate forcing models (see Chapter 2) have become very popular over the past few years in "explaining" hominin speciation in the Plio-Pleistocene, more recent computer simulations of faunal change in both East and South Africa indicate that such models may not fully ex-

---

[12]*Homo* and *Australopithecus* may also co-occur at Sterkfontein, but in different members.

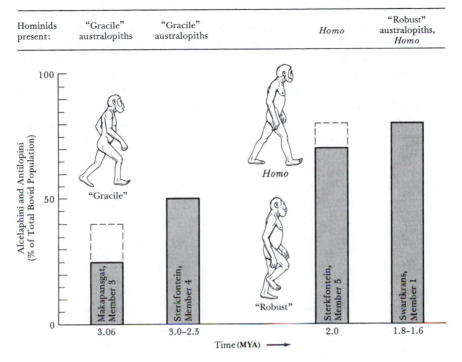

Fig. 6.8. Among fossil bovids, the Alcelaphini (e.g., hartebeests) and Antilopini (e.g., springboks) are useful faunal markers for inferring past vegetation cover since both are indicative of open plains and grassland environments. These bovids make up anywhere from about 25% to 90% of the bovid remains at South African hominin sites. Although the percentage of these bovids generally increases over time, it appears an abrupt increase occurred about 2.5–2.0 mya. This shift seems to fit well with the idea of a general faunal change in southern Africa in the late Pliocene, including the shift from gracile to robust australopiths about this time in the Sterkfontein Valley. The sites are arranged from left to right according to their estimated chronological sequence. The dotted lines represent uncertainty due to possible faunal admixture from several stratigraphic layers. (After Vrba, 1985a).

plain the complexity of the situation (Behrensmeyer et al., 1997b; McKee, 1997). Climate forcing models imply that ecological catalysts drove mammalian evolution and may have been responsible for the origin of *Homo*, whereas models of more gradual or constant faunal turnover rates allow for models of interspecific competition, or autocatalysis, to be postulated for the origins of *Homo*. Computer-simulated models of faunal turnover and fossilization have now been tested for both the southern and the eastern African fossil record and show little evidence for a faunal "pulse" between 2.8 and 2.5 mya; indeed, in East Africa, at least, the most significant period of faunal change began after 2.5 mya and continued through about 1.8 mya. It now appears that models of constant, rather than climatically induced pulses, of faunal turnover best fit the empirical data.

To sum up, the australopith-bearing sites in southern Africa can be lumped together in the following general way: Taung, Makapansgat, and Sterkfontein members 2 and 4 as older than 2.5 million years (the so-called Sterkfontein Faunal Span) and Swartkrans, Kromdraai, Sterkfontein member 5, Drimolen (and possibly Gladysvale and Gondolin) as younger than 2.5 million years (the so-called Swartkrans Faunal Span). More specifically, these sites can be arranged (from oldest to youngest) in the following sequence: Sterkfontein member 2, Makapansgat member 3, Makapansgat member 4, Taung, Sterkfontein member 4, Sterkfontein member 5 and Kromdraai B, Kromdraai A and Swartkrans member 1, Swartkrans member 2, and Swartkrans member 3 (McKee et al., 1995). In general, *A. africanus* seems restricted to the older sites and *A. robustus* to the younger ones. As we shall see, this has been used as partial support for the view that *A. africanus* and *A. robustus* were both part of a single evolving robust australopith lineage.

THE AUSTRALOPITHS OF SOUTHERN AFRICA: THE PLAYERS

Australopithecus africanus

Age: about 3–2 mya
Sites: Taung, Makapansgat, Sterkfontein

A. africanus was the first australopith ever discovered (Dart, 1925a). The species is restricted to the South African sites of Taung, Sterkfontein member 4 (and possibly member 2, depending on the ultimate identification of Stw 573), Makapansgat members 3 and 4, and possibly Gladysvale. The type specimen from Taung consists of the right side of a natural brain endocast, the face, and most of the mandible of an immature "man-like ape." Based on the shape of the mandibular body and inferior symphysis, the specimen is most likely that of a young male (Loth and Henneberg, 1996). All the deciduous teeth are in place, and the first permanent molars had recently erupted (Fig. 6.9). Based on an analogy with modern children, Dart originally considered the Taung child to be about 6 years old when it died. As we shall see later, it was most likely closer to 3–4 years of age at death (Conroy, 1991; Conroy and Vannier, 1987, 1988, 1991a).

Let's consider what made Dart proclaim in 1925 that he had found "an extinct race of apes intermediate between living anthropoids and man." First, there is the long and narrow, or **dolichocephalic,** cranium which is more human-like than ape-like. Second, there are no browridges, or supraorbital tori, as there are in even young apes. Third, the orbital region has a human-like shape: The orbits are circular in outline, not squarish as in apes; the interorbital distance is very small; and the bones associated with the olfactory apparatus situated between the eyes, the ethmoids, are not

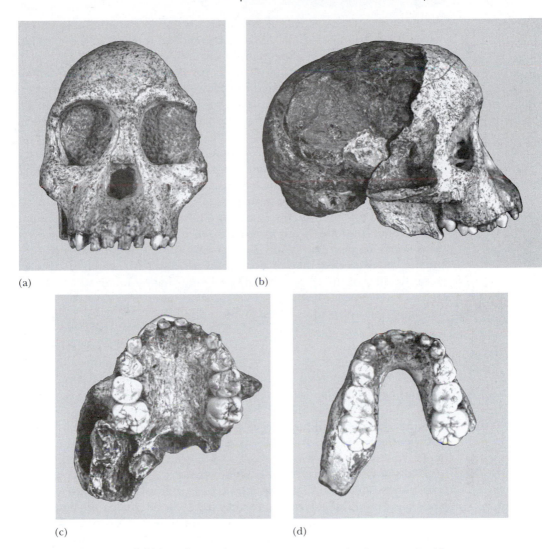

(a)

(b)

(c)

(d)

Fig. 6.9. The Taung child (*A. africanus*).   This specimen was the first australopith ever discovered. (a) Frontal and (b) lateral views of the cranium and brain endocast; (c) upper and (d) lower jaws. Note the long, narrow cranium, the lack of supraorbital tori (browridges), the narrow interorbital distance, the small canines, the parabolic dental arch, and the lack of a simian shelf. Scale approximately 60% actual size. (Photos by G. Conroy.)

inflated laterally as in modern African apes. Fourth, all the other facial bones are delicate structures, and the anterior projection of the face, or facial prognathism, is relatively slight.

Even though the specimen was a juvenile, Dart was able to see that the dentition and mandible were distinctly human-like. He noted in particular the small canines and the absence of a diastema between the lower canines and premolars (i.e., absence of any indication of a canine honing mecha-nism); the parabolic shape of the **dental arch;** and the lack of the so-called **simian shelf** at the back of the mandible's midline (Fig. 6.9).

Dart also remarked on the relatively forward position of the foramen magnum, which to him indicated the "poise of the cranium upon the ver-tebral column," and "the assumption by this fossil group of an attitude ap-preciably more erect than that of modern anthropoids." This more vertical posture suggested to him that the hands were freed from their primitive function as accessory organs of locomotion and were becoming better adapted as organs of manipulation and tool use.

Finally, Dart pointed to some unusual features of the surface of the brain as revealed by the endocranial cast. An **endocranial cast** is produced in a fossilized cranium when the inside of the braincase fills with sediment that hardens, thereby forming a replica, or cast, of the inner surfaces of the cranial bones. The brain size of the diminutive Taung creature equaled or exceeded that of gorillas many times its overall body size. Other features of the endocast suggested neuronal reorganization. For ex-ample, Taung's ratio of cerebral to cerebellar matter is greater than in go-rillas and the **association areas** of the parietal and temporal lobes, the regions of the cerebral cortex involved with complex functions of compre-hension, communication, and consciousness, seemed to be enlarged com-pared to apes (Fig. 6.10). The significance of the enlargement of these so-called association areas in the Taung specimen became the subject of a vigorous and somewhat inconclusive debate in the literature (Falk, 1983b, 1985, 1989, 1991b; Holloway, 1984, 1991). Overall, however, the shape of the brain and the configuration of the grooves on the side of the brain, or **sulcal patterns,** on the Taung endocast are ape-like, not human-like, par-ticularly in the frontal and temporal lobe regions (Falk et al., 1989).

Dart's original claims for the hominin status of *Australopithecus* were ulti-mately vindicated years later by discoveries of adult australopith cranial, dental, and postcranial remains, particularly at Sterkfontein and Makapans-gat (Fig. 6.11). It became evident from these later discoveries that *A. africanus* had reduced canines, walked bipedally, made stone tools, and had large brains relative to body size—all as Dart had predicted back in 1925.

A great deal of cranial and postcranial evidence is now available for *A. africanus,* including two partial skeletons from Sterkfontein. In Chapter 8 we will consider this evidence in more detail and discuss their bearing on the paleobiology of these early hominins.

Australopithecus robustus

Age: about 1.7 mya
Sites: Kromdraai, Swartkrans, Drimolen, Gondolin

Only 13 years after Dart's publication of the Taung child in 1925, Broom (1938) announced the discovery of a much more robust australopith from

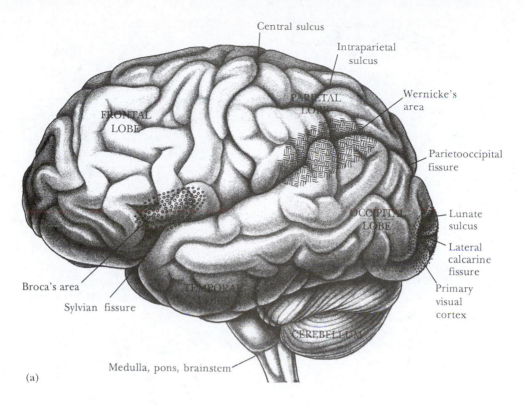

(a)

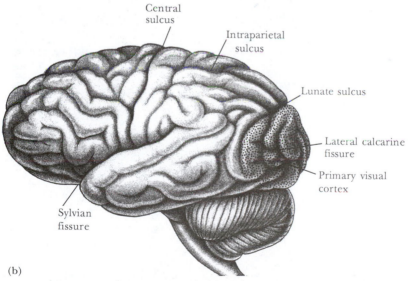

(b)

Fig. 6.10. Comparison of the (a) human and (b) chimpanzee brain. The lunate sulcus divides the primary visual cortex posteriorly from the association areas of the parietal and temporal lobes. Note that expansion of the association areas has resulted in a more posterior displacement of the lunate sulcus in the human brain. Two very important association areas in the human brain involved with speech comprehension and production are labeled *Wernicke's area* and *Broca's area*, respectively. (From R. Holloway in Tattersall et al., 1988.)

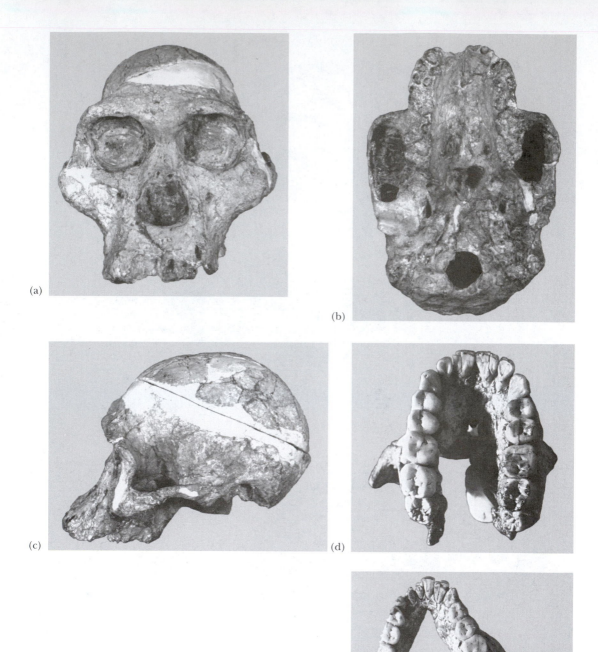

Fig. 6.11. Craniodental remains of adult *A. africanus* specimens from Sterkfontein. (a) Frontal, (b) basal, and (c) lateral views of Sts 5 ("Mrs. Ples"), (d) Upper and (e) lower jaws of Sts 52. Scale about 60% actual size. (Photos by G. Conroy.)

(a)

(b)

(c)

(d)

(e)

Kromdraai, South Africa. This specimen became the type of a new genus and species of australopith, which Broom originally named *Paranthropus robustus*. Since 1948 the other site in South Africa that has proven to be an exceptionally rich source of *A. robustus* specimens is Swartkrans.

Robust australopiths are also known from a number of sites in East Africa (Omo, Koobi Fora, East and West Lake Turkana, Olduvai, Peninj, Chesowanja, Middle Awash) dating to about 2.6–1.0 mya (Fig. 6.1). The robust australopiths from East Africa are usually put in the species *A. boisei* (or *A. aethiopicus*). Only the South African robust australopiths from Kromdraai, Swartkrans, and Drimolen are currently allocated to the species *A. robustus*. As mentioned earlier, the site of Gondolin may indicate the presence of *A. boisei* in South Africa (Menter et al., 1999).

As the name implies, the major distinction between *A. africanus* and *A. robustus* is one of greater size and overall robustness in the craniofacial and dental features of the latter. Recent analyses have shown, however, that endocranial capacity does not differ significantly between the two groups; endocranial capacity estimates for 11 robust australopiths (*A. robustus*, *A. aethiopicus*, *A. boisei*) average 450 cc, whereas estimates for 7 gracile australopithes (*A. africanus*) average 451 cc (Conroy et al., 1990, 1998; Falk et al., 2000). Average brain size in both australopith groups is still relatively small compared to later hominins of the genus *Homo*.

The brain is housed in a cranium that is more massive than that of *A. africanus* but less so than that of *A. boisei*. The cranial vault is thin walled and normally has well-developed sagittal and nuchal crests. The facial skeleton is hafted onto the calvaria at a relatively low level—that is, the forehead rises only slightly above the upper margins of the orbit. The browridges are well developed and the face is broad with prominent anterior pillars to withstand large chewing stresses passing through the face (Figs. 6.12 and 6.13). Both *A. africanus* and *A. robustus* have a long external ear canal, the **external auditory meatus**, which contrasts with the short meatus found in modern humans. However, while *A. robustus* has a more conical meatus, the meatus in *A. africanus* is more tubular (Rak and Clarke, 1979). The functional significance of this, if any, is presently unknown.

The dentition is a very distinctive feature of the robust australopith lineage: The incisors are relatively small, whereas the premolars and molars are large crushing and grinding teeth with thick enamel and flat surfaces (Conroy, 1991; Grine and Martin, 1988; Kay, 1985; Schwartz, 1997). *A. robustus* displays absolutely and relatively thicker enamel, especially at the cusp tips, than other South African australopiths.

The canines tend to be functionally incorporated into the incisor row and thus are not the kind of projecting, pointed, stabbing teeth found in so many other primates (Fig. 6.14) (Greenfield, 1992; Plavcan and Kelley, 1996). The high incidence of anterior dental crowding, particularly in the Swartkrans *A. robustus* sample, strongly supports the notion that anterior tooth reduction in robust autralopiths was spurred on by posterior tooth

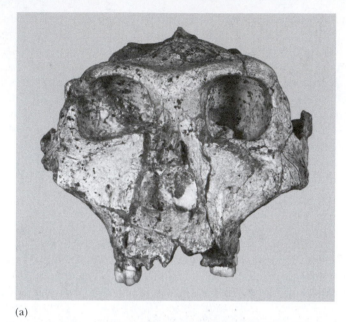

(a)

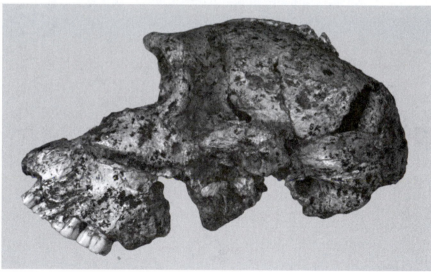

(b)

Fig. 6.12.   Craniodental remains of adult *A. robustus* from Swartkrans.   (a) Frontal view of SK 48. (b) Lateral view of SK 46. (c) Upper jaw of SK 13. (d) Lower jaw of SK 12. Scale about 60% actual size. (Photos by G. Conroy.)

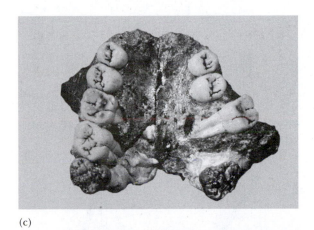

(c)

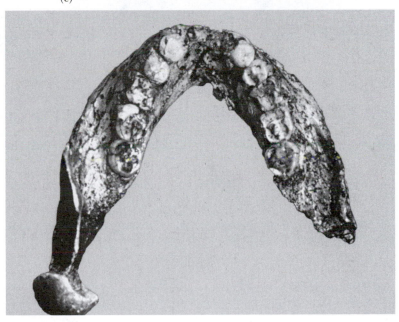

(d)

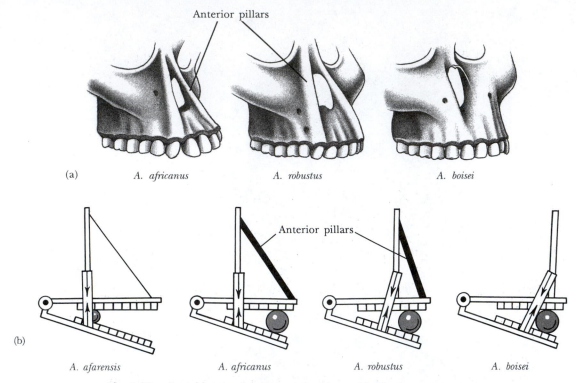

Fig. 6.13.   Facial buttressing in australopiths.   (a) Three-quarter view of the facial region in *A. africanus*, *A. robustus*, and *A. boisei*. Note the increased extent of the bony buttressing along the lateral side of the nasal cavity. In both *A. africanus* and *A. robustus* this buttressing takes the form of distinct anterior pillars. (b) The mechanical forces requiring facial buttressing. The vertical columns represent the infraorbital region and the opposing arrows, the contracting masseter muscle. As the occlusal load of food to be crushed by the molars (shaded circle) increases and is extended forward from the infraorbital region, additional buttressing in the form of anterior pillars becomes necessary. In *A. boisei* the whole infraorbital region has moved forward sufficiently to functionally replace the anterior pillars. (From Rak, 1983, 1985.)

expansion and that canine reduction may be related to the need to expand the cheek teeth within given limits of jaw size (Calcagno, 1995). As one might expect, the mandibles are also large and robust because they house these large teeth; serve as sites of attachment for the powerful chewing muscles; and withstand the large chewing stresses generated during mastication of tough, fibrous vegetation. Both qualitative and quantitative studies show that the gracile australopith dentition is better adapted to diets consisting primarily of leaves and/or fleshy fruits, whereas the robust australopith dentition is better adapted to a diet consisting of harder food items like seeds, nuts, roots and tubers (Grine and Kay, 1988; Kay and Grine, 1988; Teaford and Ungar, 2000).

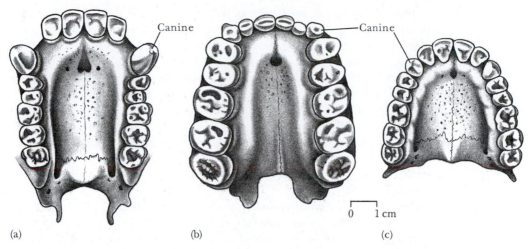

(a)   (b)   (c)

Fig. 6.14. Upper dentition of (a) modern chimpanzee, (b) *A. boisei*, and (c) modern *H. sapiens*. Note the relative size differences between anterior and posterior teeth in *A. boisei* compared with those of the other genera.

This last dietary conclusion has been tempered somewhat by evidence from both strontium to calcium (Sr:Ca) ratios and stable carbon isotope studies of *A. robustus* teeth from Swartkrans. In theory, Sr:Ca ratios should be lower in carnivores than in folivores. Since vertebrate digestive systems discriminate against strontium in favor of calcium, the Sr:Ca ratios in their tissues, including bone, should be lower than the Sr:Ca ratios in the food they eat (Fig. 6.15). For example, herbivores have lower Sr:Ca ratios than

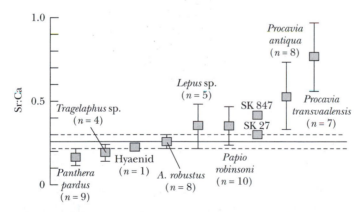

Fig. 6.15. Mean Sr:Ca ratio ± 1 standard deviation for *A. robustus* and *Homo* sp. (SK 847, SK 27) from Swartkrans member 1. *Panthera*, leopard; *Tragelaphus*, kudu; *Lepus*, hare; *Papio*, baboon; *Procavia*, hyrax. Note the general trend of higher Sr:Ca ratios from left to right as one goes from more carnivorous (leopard) to more folivorous (hyrax) mammals and the higher ratio in the *Homo* sp. specimens compared to the *A. robustus* sample. (From Sillen et al., 1995.)

the plants they eat, and carnivores have lower ratios than the meat they eat, and these differences are preserved in the Sr:Ca ratio of their bones. When applied to humans, the Sr:Ca ratio is assumed to inversely reflect the contribution of meat to the diet. Data suggest that the *A. robustus* diet may have been more omnivorous than previously supposed and probably included both animal matter and fibrous vegetation. By comparison, the elevated Sr:Ca ratios found in early *Homo* samples from Swartkrans suggest that its ecological niche may have included intensive exploitation of underground plant resources, since roots and rhizomes have higher Sr:Ca ratios than leaves from the same plants (Burton and Wright, 1995; Lee-Thorp and van der Merwe, 1993; Lee-Thorp et al., 1994; Sillen, 1992; Sillen et al., 1995).

One other intriguing possibility exists, however. The differences in Sr:Ca ratios between *A. robustus* and early *Homo* (e.g., SK 847) at Swartkrans may reflect physiological differences between males and females and not necessarily differences in diet. Sr:Ca ratios are typically higher in females than in males because calcium is reduced in bones of pregnant and lactating females (Carter et al., 1997). According to this interpretation, SK 847, a specimen often referred to as early *Homo*, may in fact be a female of the same species represented by specimens with low Sr:Ca ratios usually identified as *A. robustus* (Sillen, 1996; Thackeray, 1995). In this regard, we should note that part of the cranium of SK 847 was initially described as *A. robustus* before it was fitted to cranial fragments that had been earlier attributed to early *Homo* (Clarke et al., 1970).

Stable carbon isotope values for *A. robustus* demonstrate an overall reliance on C_3-based foods with, however, a substantial contribution from C_4 foods as well. The latter signal most probably derives, at least indirectly, from eating grass-eating animals rather than grass itself, since dental evidence precludes *A. robustus* from being an exclusive grass eater. This evidence indicates that *A. robustus* was a generalized rather than a specialized feeder (Lee-Thorp and van der Merwe, 1993). As we will see later, however, recent studies of bone tools at Swartkrans suggest that grass-eating termites may also have been an important component of early hominin diets, thereby helping explain the high C_4 dietary signal in *A. robustus* (Backwell and d'Errico, 2001).

Remains of the pelvis, ankle bone (talus), and metatarsal of the first toe, or hallux, are more human-like than ape-like, indicating that robust australopiths were bipedal, although not identical to modern humans in their bipedalism (Susman and Brain, 1988; Susman and Stern, 1991). Studies on hand bones from Swartkrans suggest that *A. robustus* was capable of using and making stone tools (Susman, 1988, 1989, 1994).

Features such as stature, body weight, and body proportions are very poorly known. Body weight estimates based on the diameter of the femoral heads suggest that male and female *A. robustus* cluster around 40 and 30 kg, respectively (McHenry, 1992b; Susman et al., 2001). This degree of body weight sexual dimorphism is greater than that seen in modern humans, chimpanzees, or bonobos, but less than that found in orangutans and gorillas.

Now that we have introduced the early hominin setting and its players from southern Africa, we will next turn to their peers in eastern Africa.

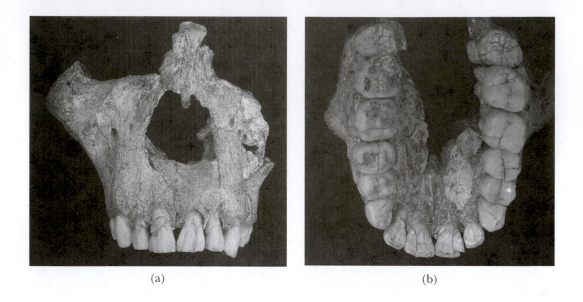

(a)   (b)

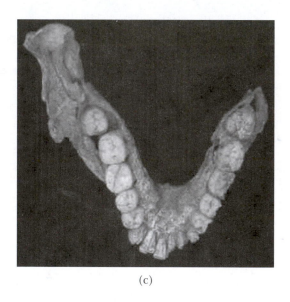

(c)

Plate A   Australopith hominins from the Plio-Pleistocene of southern Africa: (a) maxillary fragment, (b) upper dentition, and (c) lower dentition of *A. africanus* (Sts 52) from Sterkfontein. (The photographs on pp. 178–83 are courtesy of J. M. McKee, University of Witwatersrand, and the Transvaal Museum.)

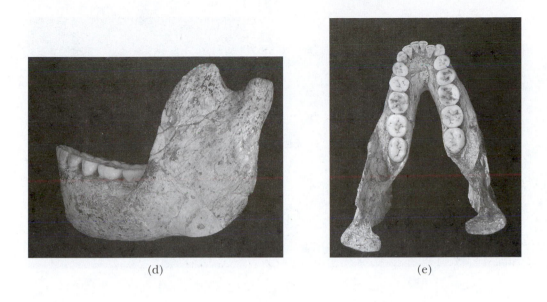

(d)   (e)

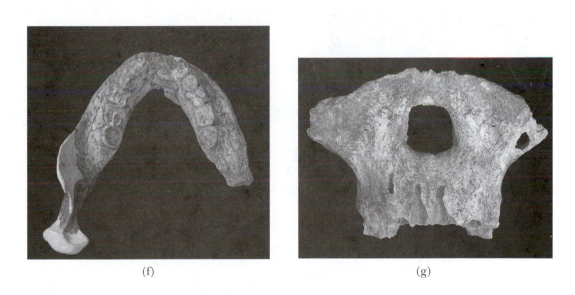

(f)   (g)

Plate B   Australopith hominins from the Plio-Pleistocene of southern Africa: (d) lateral and (e) occlusal views of an *A. robustus* mandible from Swartkrans (SK 23), and (f) mandible and (g) facial fragment of *A. robustus* from Swartkrans (SK 12).

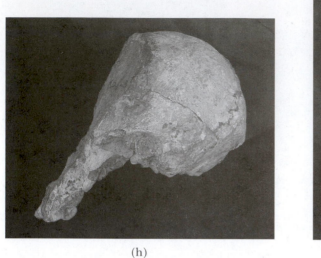

(h)

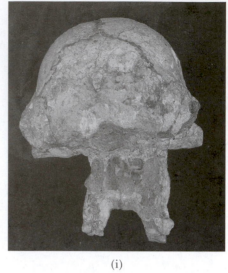

(i)

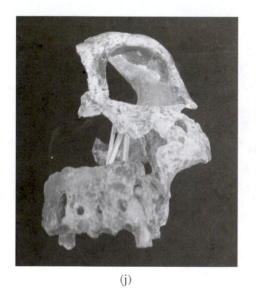

(j)

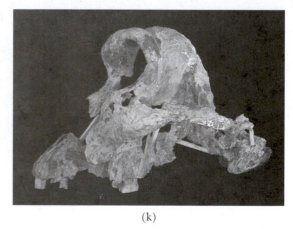

(k)

Plate C   Australopith hominins from the Plio-Pleistocene of southern Africa: (h) lateral and (i) occipital views of an *A. africanus* cranium from Makapansgat (MLD 37/38)—note that the face has been sheared off by erosion; (j) frontal and (k) lateral views of a partial early *Homo* cranium from Swartkrans (SK 847).

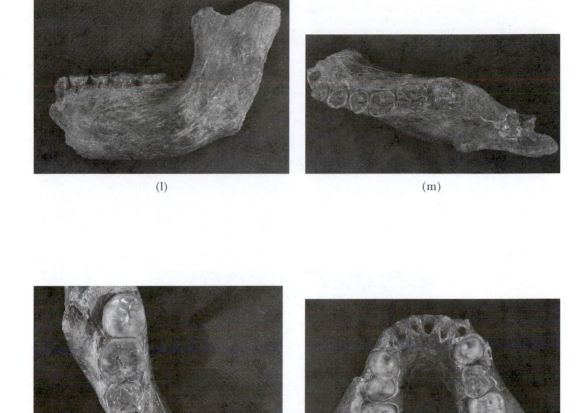

(l)　　　　　　　　　　　　　(m)

(n)　　　　　　　　　　　　　(o)

Plate D　Australopith hominins from the Plio-Pleistocene of southern Africa: (l) lateral and (m) occlusal views of an *A. africanus* mandible from Makapansgat (MLD 40); (n) occlusal view of an *A. africanus* mandible from Makapansgat (MLD 18); (o) occlusal view of an *A. africanus* mandible from Makapansgat (MLD 2).

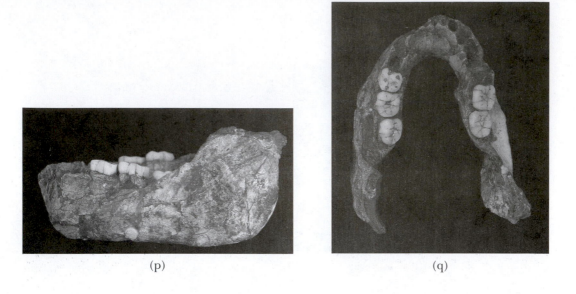

(p)   (q)

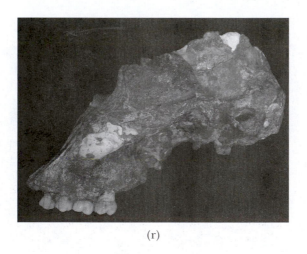

(r)

Plate E Australopith hominins from the Plio-Pleistocene of southern Africa: (p) lateral and (q) occlusal view of the type specimen of *Telanthropus capensis* (now considered a form of early *Homo*) from Swartkrans (SK 15); (r) lateral view of the type cranium of *A. robustus* (TM 1517).

182

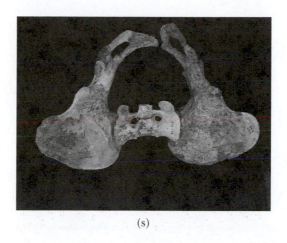

(s)

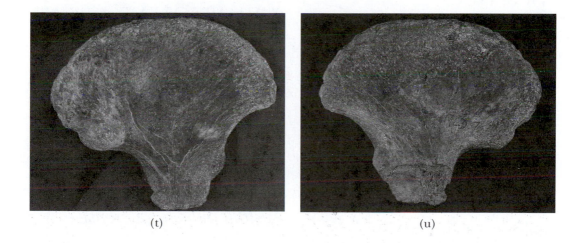

(t)   (u)

Plate F Australopith hominins from the Plio-Pleistocene of southern Africa: (s) pelvis of
A. africanus from Sterkfontein (Sts 14); (t) medial and (u) lateral views of an *A. africanus* ilium
from Makapansgat (MLD 7).

183

CHAPTER VII

The Earliest Hominins (Part 2): The Australopiths of Eastern Africa

THE AUSTRALOPITHS OF EASTERN AFRICA: THE SETTING

The East African rift system is part of a single tectonic system extending from the Zambesi River in southern Africa to the Dead Sea in the Near East. Beginning in the late Eocene, several major episodes of crustal warping and uplift, accompanied by volcanism and faulting, occurred as large volcanic domes arose in East Africa. Then, in the Miocene, flood-like volcanic eruptions covered much of the area. But the East African rift system underwent its greatest transformation during the Plio-Pleistocene, when major uplift combined with faulting and affected the entire length of the rift (Baker and Wohlenberg, 1971).

Australopith-bearing deposits associated with the East African rift system are concentrated at Omo and a number of Middle Awash sites in Ethiopia, around Lake Turkana and Lake Baringo in Kenya, at Olduvai and Laetoli in Tanzania, and at Chiwondo in Malawi. Several early hominins have also been found in the central Sahara of Chad some 2500 km west of the rift valley. One of these australopith specimens includes much of the anterior mandibular dentition (canines, premolars, and a lateral incisor) as well as an upper premolar. The specimen was originally assigned to *A. afarensis* but is now sometimes placed in a new species, *A. bahrelghazali* (Brunet et al., 1995, 1996). More recently, six hominin specimens, including a nearly complete cranium and fragmentary lower jaws, have been recovered from Late Miocene (6–7 mya) deposits at Toros-Menalla (Chad). These have been assigned to a new genus and species, *Sahelanthropus tchadensis*, that may be the earliest hominin from the fossil record of Africa (Brunet et al., 2002).

Opinions vary among paleoanthropologists but over a half dozen East African australopith species are now generally recognized: *Ardipithecus ramidus, Ar. kadabba, Australopithecus anamensis, A. afarensis, A. garhi, A. boisei* (and possibly *A. aethiopicus* which is considered here as part of *A. boisei*), and *Kenyanthropus platyops*. Fossils identified as early *Homo* (*H. habilis, H. ergaster, H. rudolfensis, H. erectus,* etc.) have been found at sites at Omo, Lake Turkana, Olduvai, Eritrea, and the Middle Awash. These will be reviewed in subsequent chapters. What follows is an introduction to the East (and Central) African early hominin fossil record.

Some Early Pliocene Hominin Sites from East Africa: Lothagam, Lukeino, Ngorora, Tabarin, Fejej

With the exception of the *Ardipithecus* sample discussed in more detail below, some of the oldest, although poorly known, East African hominins come from scattered sites in Kenya and Ethiopia (e.g., Lothagam, Lukeino, Ngorora, Tabarin, Fejej) (Fig. 6.1).

In 1967 an expedition to the Lothagam area of Kenya discovered a right mandibular fragment preserving the crown and root system of M_1 and the broken roots of M_2 and M_3. The specimen comes from the lower layer designated Lothagam-1 (now known as the Apak member of the Nachukui Formation), which is bracketed by radiometric dates of 8.3–3.7 mya (Behrensmeyer, 1976; Brown et al., 1985b; Leakey et al., 1996; Patterson et al., 1970; White, 1986a). Biostratigraphic analyses suggest that the mandible may in fact be from the late Miocene since it appears to be older than 5.6 million years—but the dating is still uncertain (Hill et al., 1992a). The specimen was originally assigned to *A. africanus* although some considered it a possible ape (Eckhardt, 1977) or a form close to the lineage of a hypothetical ancestral hominin (Corruccini and McHenry, 1980). More recent assessments of the fossil demonstrate its similarity to *A. afarensis* or *A. anamensis*, particularly since it shows some adaptations to increased masticatory power and enlarged cheek teeth, or megadontia, characteristic of later australopiths (Hill and Ward, 1988; Hill et al., 1992a; Kramer, 1986). If either assessment is correct, it would be the earliest known member of either of these two species.

Two early Pliocene hominin fossils have been recovered from the site of Tabarin in the Chemeron Formation near Lake Baringo, dated to approximately 5 mya: a right mandibular fragment preserving M_1 and M_2 and a proximal humerus. Both have been tentatively assigned to *A. afarensis* (Hill and Ward, 1988; Pickford et al., 1983; Ward and Hill, 1987).

Several teeth from a single individual have also been recovered from deposits at Fejej in southern Ethiopia that may also date to about 4 mya.

These have also been tentatively assigned to *A. afarensis* (Fleagle et al., 1991; Kappelman et al., 1996).

Some researchers have pointed to a couple of isolated teeth from two sites in the Lake Baringo area of northern Kenya, Lukeino and Ngorora, as evidence of a hominin presence in East Africa before about 5 mya. However, these claims are questionable because it is sometimes very difficult to assign single hominin teeth at the species or even genus level (Hill, 1994; Hill and Ward, 1988; Ungar et al., 1994). It is of some interest, however, that a piece of mandible and several isolated teeth described from deposits in East Lake Turkana and dated to about 4 mya include an M_1 that is said to resemble the Lukeino molar (Coffing et al., 1994).

Orrorin and *Sahelanthropus*: The Earliest Hominins?

The identity of these few Lukeino teeth become more interesting given that they may actually belong to the recently named Late Miocene genus and species, *Orrorin tugenesis*, considered by its discoverers to be the earliest hominin (Pickford and Senut, 2001; Senut et al., 2001).[1] *Orrorin* is said to differ from other australopiths by (1) its smaller and less mesiodistally elongated molar teeth and (2) the presence of a shallow, narrow, vertical groove on the mesial face of the upper canine (also seen in Miocene and extant apes). It also differs from *Ardipithecus* in possessing thicker enamel. Features of the proximal femur—such as its slightly anteriorly rotated spherical head, presence of an intertrochanteric groove, and elongated neck—are alleged to be more human-like than those of other australopiths or African apes and indicative of a bipedal gait for this taxon (these claims have not been independently verified). The proximal manual phalanx is curved as in *A. afarensis*, a feature often linked to climbing adaptations.

If *Orrorin* proves to be the earliest bipedal hominin, as its original describers suggest, it will indicate that small, thick-enameled molars are primitive for the hominin lineage and that bipedalism evolved far earlier than presently thought. If correct, this scenario would remove thin-enameled *Ardipithecus* from its current ancestral hominin position. Until postcranial remains of *Ardipithecus* are published, its locomotor behavior cannot be evaluated. The jury is still out on the hominin status of *Orrorin*.

The recent announcement of new hominin discoveries from Chad has generated great excitement in the field of paleoanthropology—both for the remarkably old dates for the fossils and for the totally unexpected location of the discoveries (the Sahara Desert) (Brunet et al., 2002; Vignaud et al., 2002).[2] The site of Toros-Menalla is located in the Djurab Desert of

---

[1] The name *Orrorin* means "original man" in the local Tugen language.

[2] The holotype is sometimes referred to as "Toumaï"; in the Goran language of this region of the Djurab Desert this name is given to babies born just before the dry season and means "hope of life."

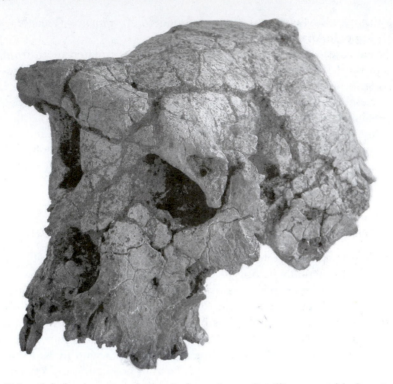

Fig. 7.1. *Sahelanthropus tchadensis* from 6- to 7-million-year-old deposits at Toumai (Chad) may be the earliest hominin in the fossil record.   (Photo courtesy of M. Brunet.)

northern Chad. Associated fauna indicates an age of between 6 and 7 mya for the hominins, slightly older than that indicated for the Lukeino *Orrorin* site. Thus, if correctly identified, these six specimens of the new genus and species, *Sahelanthropus tchadensis*, represent the earliest known members of the hominin clade.[3]

The cranium of *Sahelanthropus tchadensis* is virtually complete but quite distorted (Fig. 7.1). It reveals a hominin with an orthognathic face and slight subnasal prognathism; a small endocranial cavity (estimated at only 320–380 cc); and a long, narrow basicranium. The interorbital region is wide, and a very large, thick, and continuous supraorbital torus is present above the orbits. Postorbital constriction is marked. Both a sagittal crest and well-developed compound temporal-nuchal crest are present. The compound temporal-nuchal crest is actually much larger than that seen in male *A. afarensis* (e.g., AL 444-2). Mastoid processes are large and occipital condyles relatively small. The zygomatic process emerges above M[1] and is, therefore, more posterior relative to the cheek teeth than in most other

[3]For a dissenting view see Wolpoff et al. (2002).

australopiths. As in *Ar. ramidus,* the bicarotid chord intersects basion. As also found in *Pan, Australopithecus,* and *Ardipithecus,* the orientation of the petrous portion of the temporal bone is oriented at an angle of approximately 60° relative to the bicarotid chord, instead of the 45° more typical of robust australopiths.

Both incisors and canines are small. There is no diastema between the canine and P_3 and thus no canine-honing mechanism is present. The dental arcade is U-shaped. The cheek teeth are small and within the size range of *Ar. ramidus.* Molar enamel thickness is intermediate between that found in chimpanzees and other australopiths.

As the above points emphasize, the most notable features of *Sahelanthropus* are to be found in the mixture of primitive and derived features of the face—particularly the combination of a short, moderately prognathic face surmounted by a massive browridge. Somewhat surprising, even though the cranium of *Sahelanthropus* is much smaller than that of a modern male gorilla, its supraorbital torus is both relatively and absolutely thicker. Assuming this is a male specimen, the presence of a massive browridge combined with small canines suggests that canine size was probably not strongly sexually dimorphic in this species.

Whatever the final taxonomic label of these specimens, their discovery clearly underscores two important points: First, early hominins (or "prehominins") were much more widespread in Africa than previously appreciated.[4] Second, there is absolutely no reason to believe that the earliest phases of hominin evolution were necessarily restricted to the East African rift valley, whose famous sites are well known only because of the accidents of geology, resulting from the processes of continental drift slowly tearing apart eastern Africa along the fault lines of the Red Sea, rift valley, and Gulf of Aden.

Major Sites of the Middle Awash (Ethiopia): Aramis, Belohdelie, Maka, Konso, Hadar

The famous site of Hadar and others along the Middle Awash River valley are located within the Afar depression of Ethiopia—a hot, desolate area of badlands situated at the confluence of the East African, Red Sea, and Gulf of Aden rift systems (de Heinzelin, 1994; Kalb, 1993; Kalb et al., 1982a, 1982b, 1984; WoldeGabriel et al., 1994, 2000, 2001). Volcanic activity in southwestern Ethiopia was initiated early in the Tertiary, about 40–45 mya and between about 32 and 25 mya was widespread throughout the Red Sea, Gulf of Aden, and Ethiopian plateau. Sea-floor spreading began approximately 20 mya and propagated into the Afar region by about 5 mya (Ebinger and Sleep, 1998; Renne et al., 1999).

---

[4]Although the unexpected discovery of a Miocene "ape" in Namibia (*Otavipithecus*) should have made this point obvious to most observers long ago (Conroy et al., 1992).

The two individuals most responsible for initiating paleoanthropological explorations in the Middle Awash valley, and for originally finding many of its now famous fossil localities, were geologists Maurice Taieb and Jon Kalb, both of whom were investigating the geological evolution of the Awash River (Kalb, 2001). In 1972 their first short geological and paleontological surveys of the area were undertaken, and the following year the first hominin remains from Hadar were recovered, an associated knee joint consisting of a distal femur and proximal tibia and fragmentary right and left proximal femora (Johanson and Coppens, 1976). And the rest, as they say, is history.

The Middle Awash region of Ethiopia is undoubtedly the most important of the world's early Pliocene hominin areas. Some of the most significant discoveries of hominins more than 4 million years old are the dental, cranial, and postcranial elements of *Ardipithecus ramidus* from Pliocene deposits dating to about 4.4 mya at Aramis (White et al., 1994a, 1995; Wolde-Gabriel et al., 1994) and the even older (if less complete) fossils from several other nearby sites dating to about 5.8 mya and recently considered a separate species, *Ar. kadabba*, based mainly on evidence of an "ape-like" canine–third premolar honing complex (Begun 2004, Haile-Selassie, 2001; Haile-Selassie et al., 2004b; WoldeGabriel et al., 2001). The antiquity and primitive morphology of the specimens suggest that *Ar. ramidus* may represent the potential root species of all later hominins. In fact, the name *ramidus* is from the local Afar language in which *ramid* means "root."

The published specimens from Aramis include most of the teeth of one individual, several associated postcranial elements, two partial cranial bases, a child's mandible, and other associated and isolated teeth. Further discoveries at the site have added a number of additional cranial and postcranial specimens to the *Ar. ramidus* sample, including mandibular fragments and teeth, humeri, hand and foot bones, and a fragmentary adult skeleton that includes cranial, mandibular, vertebral, and upper and lower limb elements (Asfaw et al., 1995). The older *Ar. kadabba* sample includes a proximal foot phalanx, several hand phalanges, humerus and ulna, clavicular fragment, a right mandible with M_3 and associated teeth, and a number of isolated teeth. We will have more to say about the morphology of *Ardipithecus* in the next chapter.

A rich fossil fauna and flora has also been recovered from Aramis, including thousands of *Canthium* seeds, a genus common in African woodlands and forests. The presence of these seeds, plus the predominance in the fossil fauna of medium-size colobine monkeys and kudus (as well as the sedimentological record) suggest that *Ar. ramidus* may have inhabited relatively wet, closed, wooded habitats (WoldeGabriel et al., 2001).[5] If true, it would indicate that *Ar. ramidus* may have lived before the expansion of

---

[5]A similar wooded habitat has also been suggested for the about 6.0 mya *Orrorin* fossils (Pickford and Senut, 2001).

hominins into the more open grassland environments that later hominins like *A. afarensis* more typically favored. However, the caveat should be noted that similar floral and faunal elements are found along the river in the Middle Awash region today—one of the driest, hottest, most inhospitable regions in the world and hardly one that conjures up the popular image of a "wet, closed, wooded habitat."

Before the discovery of the Aramis *Ardipithecus* hominins, the oldest fossil hominins from Ethiopia had come from Fejej and the Belohdelie and Maka regions of the Sagantole Formation in the Middle Awash valley south of Hadar (Clark et al., 1984; Renne et al., 1999; White et al., 1993). The Belohdelie hominins date to about 3.8 mya and the Maka hominins to about 3.4 mya. The Belohdelie hominin cranial fragments consist of a large part of the right frontal bone and a small segment of a left parietal bone. Although the incomplete fragments are chimpanzee-like in size, they are not chimpanzee-like in shape. The Belohdelie frontal bone has a much flatter side-to-side, or **coronal,** profile; therefore, the cranium would have had less narrowing behind the orbits, or **postorbital constriction,** than is found in extant apes and other early hominins. The specimen is very robust, with the thickness at **bregma** (the point on the top of the cranium where the sagittal and coronal sutures intersect) falling outside the range of all other australopiths and early *Homo* (but within the *H. erectus* range) (Asfaw, 1987; White, 1984).

A number of important craniodental and postcranial fossils have been described from Maka (White et al., 1993, 2000). Several mandibular specimens and isolated teeth have been recovered that show certain morphological and metrical resemblances to *A. afarensis* from Hadar and Laetoli. In addition, the site has also yielded several postcranial bones, including a proximal femur, humerus, and proximal ulna. The humerus is large and robust, much more so than the humerus of "Lucy" (AL 288-1 from Hadar), and is taken to support the view that *A. afarensis* was a highly sexually dimorphic species. The Maka femur shares a number of morphological features with other specimens attributed to *Australopithecus* that differ from later *Homo*. It, along with the Kanapoi tibia of *A. anamensis* (see below), provides the earliest anatomical evidence documenting the evolution of upright walking (Leakey et al., 1995; White, 1984). We shall discuss these, and other, anatomical correlates of bipedal locomotion in more detail in the next chapter.

Over 250 australopith specimens representing a minimum of 35 individuals have been recovered from Hadar since the 1970s by members of the Institute of Human Origins now based at Arizona State University. Undoubtedly, the most spectacular of these finds include the skeleton nicknamed "Lucy" (AL 288-1) and the partial remains of at least 13 individuals from site AL 333 (the "first family"), both dated to about 3.2 mya (Johanson et al., 1982) (Fig. 7.2). It is unusual to discover so many individuals at one site—maybe these 13 individuals were part of a hominin social group

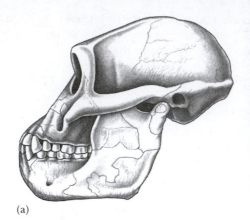

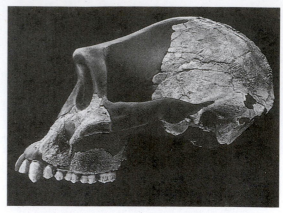

(a)

Fig. 7.2. (a) Side view of an adult cranium of *A. afarensis* reconstructed by W. Kimbel and T. White. (Courtesy of Institute for Human Origins.) (b) The skeleton of AL 288-1 (Lucy) discovered at Hadar, Ethiopia, in 1974. (c) The skeleton of Lucy contrasted with the skeleton of a modern human female of average height in walking position.(From Wood, 1992b.) Although Lucy was only about 105 cm (3 feet, 5 inches) tall, other *A. afarensis* individuals have been found up to 150 cm (4 feet 11 inches) tall. Note Lucy's relatively long arms. (d) Partial skeleton of *A. africanus* from Sterkfontein (Sts 14). (Photo by D. Panagos courtesy of the Transvaal Museum, Pretoria.)

that was overcome, buried, and preserved by a sudden flood (Johanson and White, 1979; Radosevich et al., 1992). Several more field seasons beginning in 1990 have yielded more than 50 additional australopith specimens, including the first cranium of *A. afarensis* (Kimbel et al., 1994).

Most workers attribute all the Hadar australopiths to a single species, *A. afarensis.* However, a few workers have questioned whether or not there may be more than one hominin taxon present in the Hadar sample. Such questions have been raised based on aspects of cranial venous sinus patterns (Falk and Conroy, 1983; Falk et al., 1995) or on considerations of body size and/or other morphological considerations (Häusler and Schmid, 1995; Olson, 1985; Senut and Tardieu, 1985). If this entire sample does represent one species, then most would agree that there is a great deal of size disparity (sexual dimorphism) between presumed male and female specimens assigned to *A. afarensis.*

New faces of *A. afarensis* include AL 444-2 (male?) and AL 417-1 (female?). Both are associated with mandibles. The larger male face lacks any trace of robust australopith specializations (Rak et al., 1997). The specimens display a great deal of sexual dimorphism, including moderate canine dimorphism. Comparable size differences in mandibles, humeri, and proximal femora are rarely observed in modern humans or chimpanzees but may be approximated in the most sexually dimorphic living primates, orangutans and gorillas (Lockwood et al., 1996; Richmond and Jungers, 1995). However, part of the reason for a great deal of the size variation in

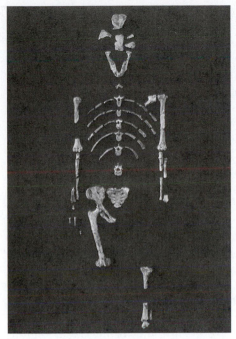

(b)

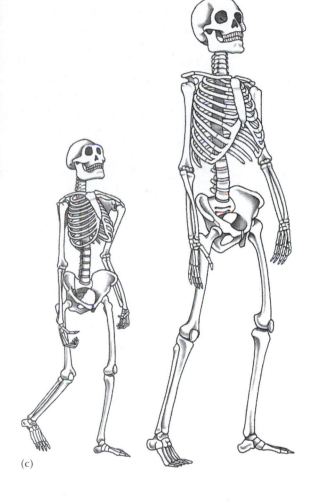

(c)

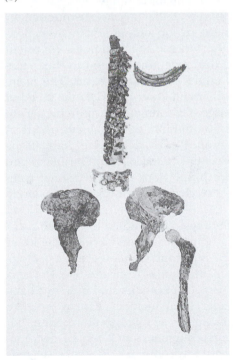

(d)

this taxon may simply be due to temporal trends in certain metric characters, particularly in the mandible and dentition. In other words, size in *A. afarensis* may not be static over time; rather the species may undergo some directional size changes. This is most noticeable in the distinct mandibular corpus size increase in later *A. afarensis* specimens. It is interesting that this is a size increase that occurs without a similar increase in tooth size. Thus a combination of secular trends in mandibular size *combined with* a large degree of sexual dimorphism may simply act to "inflate" apparent size variation beyond levels seen in single populations of African apes today (Lockwood et al., 2000).

The Hadar hominins derive mainly from the Sidi Hakoma, Denen Dora, and lowermost Kada Hadar members of the Hadar Formation (Aronson and Taieb, 1981; Haileab and Brown, 1992) (Fig. 7.3). Recent geological work has shown that the Sida Hakoma Tuff near the bottom of the australopith time range at Hadar correlates with other tuffs in East Africa dated to about 3.4 mya (e.g., the Tulu Bor Tuff at Koobi Fora). Therefore, the Hadar hominin sample ranges from about 3.4 to 2.9 mya, some 1 million years or so younger than the *Ardipithecus* hominins from Aramis and some 200,000–600,000 years younger than the oldest of the Laetoli hominins (see below) (Walter, 1994; Walter and Aronson, 1993).

While a number of stone tools have been found in the Hadar region, none is definitely associated with skeletal remains of *A. afarensis*.

Analyses of the Hadar sediments reveal that a lake surrounded by marshy environments once existed in the region and was fed by rivers flowing off the Ethiopian escarpment. In general, the sediments represent marshy, lake margin, and associated fluvial deposits related to the extensive lake that periodically filled the entire sedimentary basin. The mammalian fauna of the upper Basal member and lower Sidi Hakoma member also suggest primarily marshy, lake-edge environments. A little higher up in the Sidi Hakoma member a transition to more open habitats occurs in apparent association with lake regression. Clearly, a mosaic of habitats existed through time that included closed and open woodland-bushland and grassland. It appears that the relative proportions of these habitat types varied through time in response to the changes in local climatic conditions and/or lake-basin regression.

Two significant paleoecological findings can be noted from Hadar: (1) significant faunal turnover, including hominins, occurs between the lower and upper parts of the Kada Hadar member and coincides with a geological disconformity; and (2) analyses of the faunas from the Sidi Hakoma and Denen Dora members indicate that *A. afarensis* existed in wetter habitats than did *Homo* in the upper Kada Hadar member. Faunas dated to around 2.3 mya contain *Homo* and mammals adapted to more open, but fairly mesic habitats, whereas later faunas ranging from 2.3 to 1.7 mya contain animals indicating more open, arid environments. Evidence suggests that the environment in the Hadar region became significantly drier between about 2.9 and 2.3 mya (Reed and Eck, 1997).

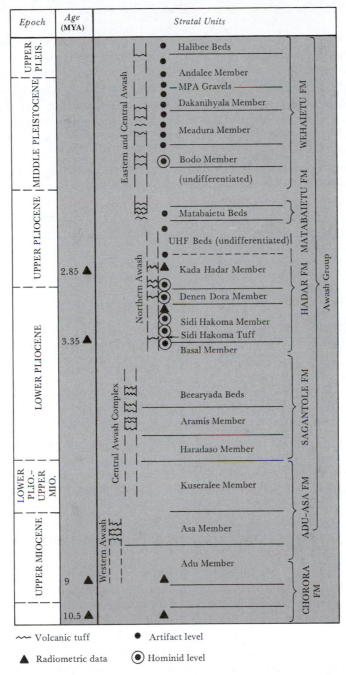

Epoch	Age (MYA)	Stratal Units	

Eastern and Central Awash

~~ Halibee Beds

Andalee Member
— MPA Gravels —
Dakanihyala Member

Meadura Member

Bodo Member

(undifferentiated)

WEHAIETU FM

Matabaietu Beds

UHF Beds (undifferentiated)

Kada Hadar Member

Denen Dora Member

Sidi Hakoma Member
Sidi Hakoma Tuff
Basal Member

MATABAIETU FM

HADAR FM

Northern Awash

2.85

3.35

Beearyada Beds

Aramis Member

Haradaso Member

Kuseralee Member

Asa Member

Adu Member

SAGANTOLE FM

ADU-ASA FM

CHORORA FM

Awash Group

Central Awash Complex

Western Awash

9

10.5

UPPER PLEIS.
MIDDLE PLEISTOCENE
UPPER PLIOCENE
LOWER PLIOCENE
LOWER PLIO.- UPPER MIO.
UPPER MIOCENE

~~ Volcanic tuff   ● Artifact level

▲ Radiometric data   ◉ Hominid level

Fig. 7.3. Composite stratigraphic section of the Hadar Formation indicating distribution of *A. afarensis* hominin specimens. Dating of volcanic tuffs indicate that no Hadar hominin is older than about 3.40 million years and establish ages of about 3.18 million years for the AL 288-1 (Lucy) skeleton and about 3.20 million years for the AL 333 hominin assemblage ("the first family"). The temporal range of *A. afarensis* at Hadar thus extends from about 3.4 to 3.0 mya *MIO.*, Miocene; *PLEIS.*, Pleistocene. (Adapted from T. White in Tattersall et al., 1988.)

195

Fossils were first discovered at the Middle Awash site of Konso (formerly known as Konso-Gardula) in 1991. Hominin remains include a mandible of *H. erectus*, nine specimens of *A. boisei* (including the first skull of this species), and the oldest firmly dated Acheulean assemblage from Africa. All are securely dated to about 1.4 mya and provide clear evidence for the co-existence of *A. boisei* and *H. erectus* at this place and time. The presence of Acheulean tools at Konso is in striking contrast to their absence in beds containing both these hominins at east Lake Turkana (Asfaw et al., 1992; Suwa et al., 1997). All the *A. boisei* specimens were recovered from a single locality (KGA 10) with an associated mammalian fauna dominated by alcelaphine bovids (e.g., wildebeests, hartebeests, blesbok), equids, and several suid species, highly indicative of extensive dry grasslands. The *A. boisei*–bearing sediments are interpreted to be portions of an alluvial fan deposited into a nearby lake.

Major Lake Turkana Sites: Kanapoi, Allia Bay, Koobi Fora, Nachukui (Kenya)

During the first field season (1967) of the International Omo Expedition, Richard Leakey chartered a helicopter to explore the northeastern shores of Lake Turkana (known then as Lake Rudolph). Almost immediately he found stone tools similar to those from Bed I at Olduvai Gorge (see below). Buoyed by the prospects of new discoveries, he pulled out of the Omo Expedition and organized his own expeditions to Lake Turkana in 1968. These explorations continue on both the east and west sides of the lake and have been enormously successful (Leakey and Lewin, 1992).

Leakey's first hominin discovery at Lake Turkana was the virtually complete cranium of a robust australopith (KNM-ER 406, which stands for Kenya National Museum-East Rudolf, specimen number 406) (Fig. 7.4a). Many other australopith specimens (Fig. 7.4b,c) have since been found as well as representatives of both *Homo* aff. *H. habilis* and *Homo* aff. *H. erectus*. These fossils will be discussed in later chapters.

Lake Turkana is one of many African lakes that developed in depressions formed by crustal downwarping and faulting during the Cenozoic. While there is no geological evidence for an extensive and long-lived lake throughout the entire Plio-Pleistocene in this region, there were intervals of lacustrine deposition over restricted areas that were associated with significant lake-level fluctuations (Brown and Feibel, 1988). This history has resulted in the deposition of more than 500 m of lake, deltaic, and fluvial sediments that record the gradual shift of the lake's eastern shoreline. These sediments, now known as the Koobi Fora Formation, are further subdivided into eight members (most of which are defined by volcanic tuffs and were given names, rather than numbers) (Fig. 7.5). Fossil hominins from the Koobi Fora Formation have been recovered from the

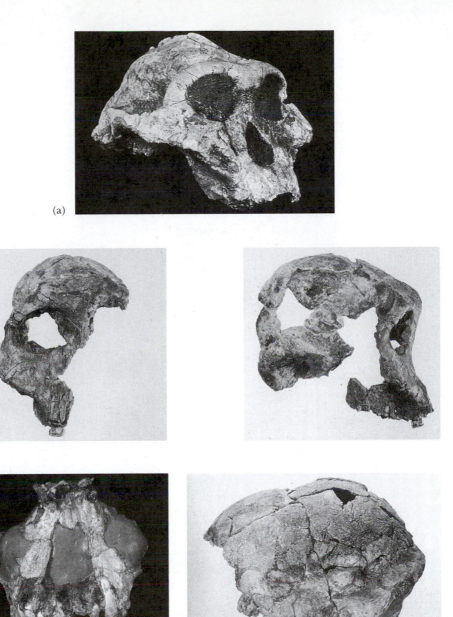

(a)

(b)

(c)

Fig. 7.4. Examples of early hominins recovered from Lake Turkana in northern Kenya. (a) Fronto-lateral view of KNM-ER 406, generally classified as *A. boisei*. The cranium has well-developed sagittal and nuchal crests and a wide, robust face. Endocranial capacity has been estimated at 510 cc. (b) Front and side views of KNM-ER 732, possibly female *A. boisei*. Endocranial capacity estimated at 500 cc. (c) Front and side views of KNM-ER 1805. Since it has proven difficult to assign this cranium to a particular species, it is often referred to as *Australopithecus* sp. (Photos courtesy of Kenya National Museum.)

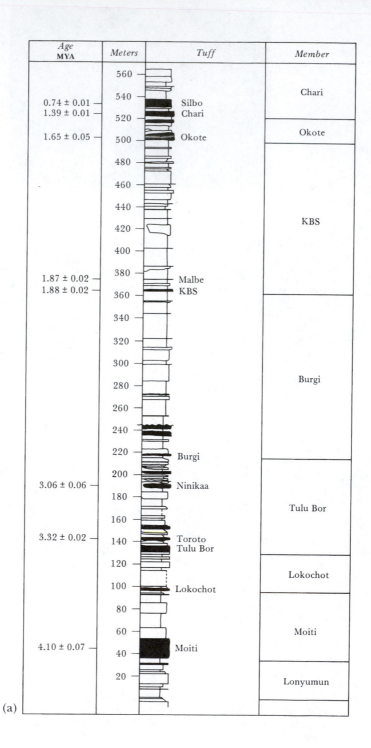

(a)

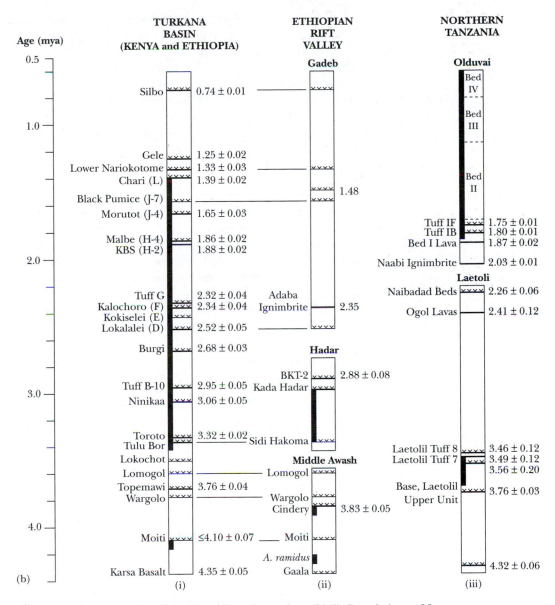

Fig. 7.5. (a) Stratigraphy of the Koobi Fora Formation. (b) (i) Correlations of fossil hominin sites in the Turkana Basin of Kenya and Ethiopia (e.g., Koobi Fora, Omo). (ii) Sites in the middle Awash valley (e.g., Hadar). (iii) Sites in northern Tanzania (e.g., Olduvai, Laetoli). The heavy dark line on the left edge of each column indicates a time interval from which fossil hominins have been recovered. Note the stratigraphic position of the new species *Ar. ramidus*, just above the Gaala tuff in the Ethiopian rift valley. *Ar. kadabba* is dated to about 5.8–5.2 mya. Radiometrically dated levels are given to the right of each column. (After Brown, 1994.)

Lonyumun, Lokochot, Tulu Bor, upper Burgi, KBS, and Okote members and span a time range from just over 4.0 to 1.4 mya, although the great majority of Koobi Fora hominin specimens are less than 2.0 million years old (F. Brown, 1992, 1994; Brown and Feibel, 1986; Feibel et al., 1989).

The paleoenvironmental setting for hominins at Koobi Fora was one of fluctuating spatial shifts in ecological zones as lake levels rose and fell. For this reason, paleoecological models have been inconsistent. For example, one paleoecological model found that *A. boisei* from both Koobi Fora and West Turkana appeared to be closely associated with closed/wet habitats, such as those found today at national parks like Hwange (Zimbabwe), Umfoloze (South Africa), and Kafue (Zambia). This model also suggested that early *Homo* was associated with less restricted habitats, including open and dry bushy areas as well as closed/wet habitats, and that *A. robustus* from southern Africa may have preferred more open, arid habitats (Shipman and Harris, 1988). However, a more recent paleoecological study at Turkana concluded that *A. boisei* occurred less frequently than expected in faunas with arboreal monkeys whereas nonrobust australopiths appeared to be more common than expected in such faunas. This suggests that nonrobust australopith habitats included riverine forest, whereas robust australopiths were associated with more open vegetation (Behrensmeyer et al., 1997a).

Studies of the Lake Turkana region indicate that Plio-Pleistocene environments were generally comparable to the modern environment of the area even though temperature and rainfall fluctuations have certainly occurred over the past 4 million years. For example, bovids from Koobi Fora and Olduvai both have postcranial similarities to modern bovids that have varied environmental "signatures" ranging from primarily open conditions to more closed conditions with, however, limited evidence for dense forest (Kappelman et al., 1997). However, the recovery at Koobi Fora of two plant taxa characteristic of the central African rain forests from a restricted chronostratigraphic layer dating to about 3.4–3.0 mya suggests that the general pattern of environmental stability in East Africa was punctuated at times by brief but significant rain forest expansions (Williamson, 1985).

Two Kenyan sites near Lake Turkana, Kanapoi and Allia Bay, have yielded several postcranial pieces (distal left humeral fragment, radius, capitate, phalanx, partial right tibia) and jaws and teeth of a newly named australopith species, *A. anamensis*, dating to between about 4.2 and 3.9 mya (Leakey et al., 1995, 1998; Patterson and Howells, 1967; C. Ward et al., 1999, 2001). This species is temporally intermediate between *Ar. ramidus* and *A. afarensis* and may turn out to be a descendant of the former and an ancestor of the latter. The tibia is particularly important, as it appears fully adapted to bipedalism (e.g., tibial shaft oriented vertically to the ankle joint surface, thereby placing the knee directly over the foot in bipedal stance) and, if correctly interpreted, would be the oldest anatomical evidence for upright walking in the fossil record. Many features of the jaws and teeth, such as enamel thickness and lower first deciduous molar morphology, seem intermediate between *Ar. ramidus* and *A. afarensis*. Other specimens attributed to this new species have been recovered from the Allia Bay region of east Lake Turkana.

A nearly complete left radius of *A. anamensis* was recovered from Middle Pliocene sediments near Allia Bay. Unlike the tibia from Kanapoi, this specimen includes a number of ape-like characteristics and has a distal articular surface (for articulation with the wrist bones) that is arranged like that found in quadrupedal climbers, thus supporting the argument that vertical climbing was a significant component of the total locomotor repertoire of early hominins (this is a debate we take up in the next chapter) (Heinrich et al., 1993). The radius is relatively long and suggests that some *A. anamensis* individuals had forearms as long as those of modern males over 6 feet tall. It seems apparent that both *A. anamensis* and *A. afarensis* had relatively long forearms (C. Ward et al., 1997, 1999, 2001).

Plio-Pleistocene sediments on the western side of Lake Turkana make up the Nachukui Formation. As in the Koobi Fora Formation, members within the Nachukui Formation are named for volcanic ash layers at the base of each member. Over a dozen hominins have been collected from this formation thus far, the most important being the 2.5 million-year-old cranium of a hyper-robust australopith (WT 17000; the "Black Skull"), a beautifully preserved *Homo erectus* skeleton (WT 15000; "Turkana Boy"), and the cranium of a new australopith genus and species, *Kenyanthropus platyops*. Stone tools have also been found on both sides of the lake, the oldest ones dating to just over 2.0 mya.

Extensive geological and paleontological research over the past decades has refined the original radiometric ages first proposed for these sediments (Behrensmeyer, 1978; Brown et al., 1978; Cooke, 1976; Curtis et al., 1975; Fitch et al., 1974, 1996; Gleadow, 1980; Hillhouse et al., 1977; McDougall, 1981; McDougall et al., 1980; White and Harris, 1977). Precise correlations between radiometrically dated tuffs in the Omo Group and the Middle Awash valley (see below) have been achieved (Fig. 7.4b) (Brown, 1994; Brown and Feibel, 1986; P. Brown et al., 1985; Haileab and Brown, 1992).

Omo Group: Northern Turkana Basin (Kenya and Ethiopia)

First visited by European big-game hunters in the late 1880s, the Omo area produced its first fossils in 1902. In 1933 the French paleontologist Camille Arambourg established a rudimentary geological sequence for the Omo area and published a paleontological survey of the region.

Detailed paleoanthropological studies at Omo began in 1966 under the auspices of the International Omo Research Expedition headed by

F. Clark Howell from the United States, Yves Coppens from France, and Richard Leakey from Kenya. Conceived as a multidisciplinary effort involving geologists, paleontologists, anatomists, and archeologists, this expedition was one of the first, and most successful, cooperative paleoanthropological efforts ever undertaken in Africa. The Omo Group of sedimentary deposits is now one of the most continuous and well-dated fossil hominin–bearing sequences in Africa.

R. Leakey's (1969) Kenyan team first explored some of the younger deposits in the area and discovered two hominin crania dating to about 100 kya. As we shall see in a later chapter, these fossils have important implications for the origins of modern humans. Meanwhile, the French and American teams explored the older deposits dated to about 3–1 mya and recovered several hundred early hominin specimens from nearly a hundred separate localities (Feibel et al., 1989). Initial assessments of these hominins suggested the presence of both gracile and robust australopiths as well as early *Homo* (Howell and Coppens, 1976; Howell et al., 1987).

The Omo Group deposits that yield the bulk of the hominin fossils are part of the depression of the eastern rift valley and are exposed around the northern half of Lake Turkana in Kenya and in the lower Omo River valley of Ethiopia. These Plio-Pleistocene sediments include the Mursi, Usno, and Shungura Formations of the lower Omo River valley, Ethiopia, and the Koobi Fora and Nachukui Formations on the eastern and western shores, respectively, of Lake Turkana, Kenya. At last count, nearly 500 fossil hominins have been recovered from the Omo Group sediments, most of which come from the Koobi Fora, Usno, and Shungura Formations. The Mursi Formation has yet to yield any hominin fossils.

Shungura and Usno Formations (Ethiopia)

A number of important hominin fossils have been recovered from the Shungura Formation. These sediments consist of over 700 m of stream (fluvial), lake (lacustrine), and deltaic deposits that are divided into 11 members (labeled from oldest to youngest as members A–L) on the basis of widespread volcanic ash layers at the base of each member. Each member is named for the volcanic ash layer at its base and includes that tuff and all overlying sediments up to the base of the next volcanic ash layer. There is no member I. Hominin fossils are known from Shungura members B–H, K, and L and from levels of the Usno Formation equivalent to Shungura member B (Fig. 7.6).

It was originally thought that hominins from the Usno Formation, and from Shungura Formation members B–G, were similar to specimens of *A. africanus* from southern Africa. Even early on, however, it was perceptively noted that some of the oldest specimens (notably those from the Usno Formation) might ultimately prove, with additional material, to represent a distinct but related species, possibly *A. afarensis*. Other specimens from Shungura Formation members E–G were attributed to robust australopiths

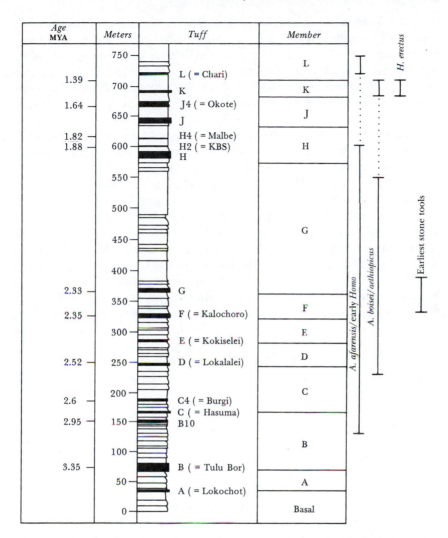

Fig. 7.6. Stratigraphy of the Shungura Formation, Omo Basin, Ethiopia. The height of strata above the bottom of the basal member is given in meters; the names of tuffs, in parentheses, refer to field names in the Koobi Fora Formation at eastern Lake Turkana. Hominins have been recovered from members C–H, K, and L (hominins from the Usno Formation correlate with Shungura member B). The approximate age of the fossil hominins and the appearance of earliest stone tools are indicated to the right. (Modified from Feibel et al., 1989.)

and compared to *A. boisei* and/or *A. aethiopicus*. A few localities in Shungura Formation members G and H (and perhaps L) have yielded teeth and cranial parts that are similar to those attributed to *H. habilis* and some cranial fragments from (the uppermost) member K suggest the presence of *H. erectus* (Hunt and Vitzthum, 1986).

F. Clark Howell suggested that the more gracile specimens from the Usno and Shungura Formations previously assigned to *A. africanus* probably belong to *A. afarensis* and/or *H. habilis*. The fragmentary nature of the material makes it difficult to assign many of these specimens with any great degree of confidence. In Howell et al.'s (1987) view, many of the more robust specimens previously assigned to *A. boisei* may actually belong to *A. aethiopicus*.

There is little consensus on the taxonomic placement of all the Usno and Shungura hominins, so a summary statement is difficult. However, the following general chronology can be offered (Grine, 1993a; Suwa, 1988; Suwa et al., 1996; Wood et al., 1994). Australopiths (possible *A. afarensis*) first appear at Omo in the Usno Formation just over 3 mya. Gracile hominins (*A. afarensis* and/or early *Homo*) are present in members B–H and L of the Shungura Formation, thus spanning a time range from about 2.7 to 1.4 mya. Robust hominins provisionally referred to *A. boisei* and/or *A. aethiopicus* are from members C–G and K, although the allocation of some of these specimens from below tuff G to *A. boisei* is questionable. The robust Shungura specimens from members C–F are now allocated to *A. aethiopicus*, with *A. boisei* emerging about 2.3 mya in member G (Alemseged et al., 2002). Thus the robust time range at Omo extends from about 2.7 to 1.5 mya. This implies that gracile and robust lineages are sympatric by about 2.7 mya in these sediments. Several gracile specimens from members E–G show similarities to early *Homo* indet. One specimen referred to *H. erectus* from member K is dated to about 1.5 mya.

The earliest stone tools, mainly quartz flakes, are found in members F and G and date to about 2.4–2.3 mya (Feibel et al., 1989). These, and the more recently discovered Oldowan tools from Gona, Ethiopia, dated to about 2.6 mya, are among the oldest stone tools yet discovered from Africa. In fact, these earliest tools at Gona represent the first direct association of stone tools and broken animal bones with cut marks seen in the archeological record (Semaw et al., 1995, 1997, 2003). In only two instances are hominin fossils found at these early Omo archeological sites but, unfortunately, none of them is found in direct association with the tools, so it is uncertain which hominins were the toolmakers.

Only about two dozen isolated teeth have been recovered from the Usno Formation (from the Brown and White Sands localities). This part of the Usno Formation correlates to the lower portion of the Shungura Formation (member B) and thus the hominin fossils are just over 3 million years old.

What do the Usno and Shungura Formations reveal about the paleoenvironments in which these early hominins lived? Their rich fossiliferous deposits provide a continuous and well-dated sequence of fossil mammals within which to examine environmental change. In the Omo Group the relative abundance of bovids, cercopithecids, and suids changed gradually from about 3.5 to 2.8 mya with a more abrupt change occurring about 2.3 mya near the base of member G. This faunal change is characterized by more open and edaphic grassland as the predominant vegetative type and generally correlates with the appearance of *A. boisei* in these sediments (Alemseged, 2003). *A. afarensis* is present in the earlier part of the sequence before 2.8 mya; robust australopiths appear shortly after this faunal break, followed by specimens of *Homo* later on. The faunal break reflects a transition from wet and wooded environments to a mosaic of drier woodland-grasslands and edaphic grasslands. *A. robustus* and *Homo* are more closely associated with fauna from this latter environment (Bobe, 1997).

The earlier Pliocene in this region was dominated by an extensive freshwater pre-Turkana lake with a diverse fish and molluscan fauna. The presence of fossil wood signifies dry wooded or bush savanna habitats in the region as well. By the mid-Pliocene a major north to south flowing river system had emerged with numerous east and west flowing tributaries. Fossil wood and pollen suggest that more humid riparian forest and more open forest/wooded savanna habitats existed at this time. Many of the associated small mammals have equatorial African forest affinities. The reduction in arboreal pollen and the substantial increase of grasses is strong evidence for a change in vegetation and drier conditions about 2.5–2.0 mya. This change to more arid climates and expanding grasslands is also documented in the gradual turnover of the mammalian fauna to more grazing, open-country, and **xeric** (dry) adapted species, particularly bovids and suids. As we have seen, this parallels paleoclimatic inferences reached for the South African sites (Bonnefille, 1976; Gentry, 1976).

Laetoli (Tanzania)

The oldest well-documented sample of australopiths from Tanzania comes from Laetoli, a site some 50 km south of Olduvai Gorge in northern Tanzania (Fig. 6.1). Laetoli is most renowned for studies conducted there by Mary Leakey and associates from 1974 to 1979. The Pliocene deposits of this area are known as the Laetolil Beds, and all the hominins from these beds (including the type specimen of *A. afarensis*) are attributed to *A. afarensis* (Johanson and White, 1979; Johanson et al., 1978).

Louis Leakey actually discovered East Africa's first australopith fossil, an isolated lower left canine, at Laetoli in 1935, though its australopith affinities were not recognized until 1979 (White, 1981). The first fossils from Laetoli to be recognized as hominins were unearthed in 1939 by Ludwig Kohl-Larsen's German expedition and consisted of a maxillary fragment with P^{3-4} (from Garusi I) and tooth sockets, or alveoli, for the canine and incisors, an isolated M^3 (Garusi II), and various other cranial fragments among which was a large occipital fragment that has apparently since been lost (Protsch, 1981; Puech et al., 1986). The maxillary fragment and isolated molar probably belong to different individuals since dental wear suggests the former is from a young individual and the latter from a much older and smaller individual. These hominins were originally named *Meganthropus africanus* because of their alleged similarity to the genus *Meganthropus* described from Java (Weinert, 1950). More recent mineralogical analyses indicate that these specimens come from the same level in the Laetoli Beds as the *A. afarensis* specimens discovered in the 1970s by Mary Leakey and her team, and there now seems little reason not to allocate them to *A. afarensis* as well.

The most famous and unusual "fossil" from the site is the trail of hominin footprints discovered in 1978 (Fig. 7.7). These fossil footprints are preserved because of a unique combination of climatic, volcanic, and mineralogical conditions. Approximately 3.6 mya a series of light ashfalls from a nearby volcano coincided with a series of rainshowers. The carbon-

Fig. 7.7. Laetoli footprints. These footprints, dated to approximately 3.6 mya, are entirely human-like in form. This 10-m stretch of trackway shows two hominin trails made by three individuals. The single hominin trail (G1) is on the left and the double hominin trail (G2/3)—made by two hominins, the second stepping directly within the tracks of the first—is on the right. Traversing the hominin trail at the lower right are two trails of the extinct equid, *Hipparion*, and its foal. (Photo by T. Moon and reprinted by permission of the J. Paul Getty Trust, copyright 1995.)

ate in the ash then hardened as it dried in the sun. Fortunately, several hominins appear to have crossed the ash layer while it was still wet, preserving very human-like tracks (Leakey and Hay, 1979). These famous footprints provide the most incontrovertible evidence to date that by about 3.6 mya early hominins were bipedal (Day, 1985; Tuttle, 1985, 1987; White and Suwa, 1987). We shall have more to say about the Laetoli footprints in the next chapter.

The Laetolil Beds are subdivided into two units, the lower one approximately 70 m thick and the upper one 45–60 m thick. Almost all the vertebrate fossils, including the hominins, are from the upper unit, which consists principally of **aeolian,** or windblown tuffs. The hominin-bearing strata in the upper unit are well dated to 3.76–3.46 mya (Fig. 7.5b) (Leakey and Harris, 1987).

Several paleoenvironmental reconstructions of Laetoli have been developed from sedimentological analyses. The aeolian deposits suggest an environment in which vegetation was sufficient seasonally to prevent extensive windblown transportation of sand-size ash particles. The nature of the weathering of these Laetoli tuffs further indicates the presence of a saline, alkaline soil. Perhaps the closest modern analogy to the Pliocene at Laetoli is the eastern semiarid-arid part of the Serengeti Plain, an area of grassland savanna with scattered bush and acacia trees with a dry season and a rainy season averaging about 50 cm per year.

The fossil vertebrate and invertebrate fauna from Laetoli reinforce this model of a semiarid climate: The absence of hippopotamus, crocodile, and other water-dwelling animals characterizes an upland savanna distant from a permanent water source. The fossil fauna is, in fact, quite similar to the fauna living in the area today. Fossil rodents are particularly useful paleoenvironmental indicators because they do not migrate through the year as larger mammals do, and most species live within quite restricted ecological niches. Laetoli fossil rodents also suggest an environment of open grassland with occasional acacia trees, and the presence of the naked mole rat in particular implies that the climate in the Laetoli area was even warmer then than it is today (Hay, 1981).

Olduvai (Tanzania)

Olduvai Gorge is a large gash in the Serengeti Plain of northern Tanzania (Fig. 6.1). Louis Leakey—the husband of Mary Leakey and father of Richard Leakey—enjoyed telling the story of its "discovery" in 1911 by Professor Wilhelm Kattwinkel, an absentminded German butterfly collector, who nearly plunged to his death down the gorge in pursuit of some elusive lepidopterous specimen. Recovering from his fall, Kattwinkel descended into the gorge and discovered fossil bones along its slopes.

The elder Leakey first visited the site that was to make him world famous in 1931. Within hours of setting up his camp he discovered stone tools in the gorge. During his explorations at Olduvai in the 1930s, Leakey discovered a number of promising sites for the recovery of stone tools. In 1935 his young research assistant, Mary Nicol, discovered fragments of a hominin cranium among the remains of antelopes and pigs and some stone tools. Louis and Mary were married in 1936 and thus began one of the most productive husband and wife collaborations in the annals of science.

Constraints of time, money, and other research projects kept the Leakeys away from Olduvai until the early 1950s. During that decade they found and described a number of tool sites and uncovered a few hominin teeth but nothing particularly newsworthy. That all changed on the morning of July 17, 1959. Louis remained in camp recovering from a bout of influenza while Mary went off to revisit the area where the first stone tools had been found in 1931. When she arrived at the site she noticed some teeth and parts of a hominin cranium just eroding through the surface of the slope. After brushing away the dirt to reveal some of the teeth, she found that she had uncovered the most complete hominin cranium ever found at Olduvai. It was a beautifully preserved cranium of a robust australopith that Louis Leakey named *Zinjanthropus boisei* (*Zinj* for the ancient name of East Africa, *anthropos* meaning "man," and *boisei* to honor Charles Boise, one of the Leakey's financial benefactors). "*Zinjanthropus*" would turn out to be only a temporary taxonomic label—but the discovery of this "Nutcracker Man," as the press was quick to nickname him, would soon change the course of fossil hominin discoveries in Africa by turning the spotlight away from South Africa and on to East Africa (Fig. 7.8) (Leakey, 1959, 1967b).

It was immediately clear that "Zinj" represented a taxon distinct from *A. africanus*. The question of whether or not it represented a distinct genus, however, was (and still is) open to debate (Leakey, 1960; Robinson, 1960). The original describer of the cranium, Phillip Tobias (1967b)—Dart's successor at Witswatersand University—felt that this robust australopith should be classified only as a distinct species within the genus *Australopithecus*, appropriately named *A. boisei*. However, over the past decade or so the taxonomic pendulum has begun to swing back to the view that the robust australopiths should be separated at the generic level from the gracile australopiths and that the name *Paranthropus* should be retained for such robust forms.[6] Although we do not follow that trend in this text, readers should know that it is a legitimate and widespread view within some paleoanthropology circles today.

A few hundred meters north of the Zinj site, the Leakey's eldest son, Jonathan, found another interesting fossil hominin. Excavations yielded fragments of a rather thin-walled cranium, several hand and food bones, and a mandible of a hominin very different from *Zinjanthropus*. In fact,

---

[6]It seems the more things change, the more they stay the same!

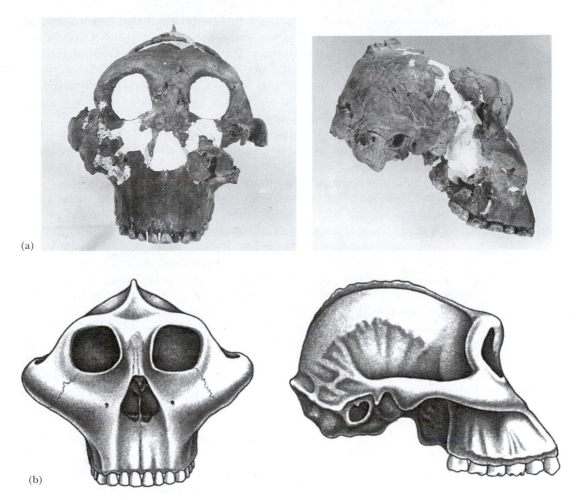

Fig. 7.8. Crania of *A. boisei.* (a) *Zinjanthropus* cranium from Bed *I* of Olduvai Gorge. (Photo by R. G. Klomfass, by permission of P. V. Tobias.) (b) Reconstruction based on specimens from Olduvai Gorge and Koobi Fora (Lake Turkana). Note the massive face and attachment areas for the powerful chewing muscles, particularly the size of the sagittal crest for the origin of the temporalis muscle and the size of the zygomatic arch for origin of the masseter muscle. (Redrawn from Howell, 1978.)

what Jonathan had discovered were the fossils that would later be made the type specimens for *Homo habilis,* the subject of the following chapter (Leakey et al., 1964).

The Olduvai sediments are labeled (from oldest to youngest) Beds I to IV, with additional Pleistocene beds above Bed IV (Fig. 7.5b). Olduvai has been an unusually rich hominin site. In addition to the numerous *A. boisei* and *H. habilis* fossils recovered from Beds I and II, it has also yielded specimens of *H. erectus* from upper Bed II and lower Bed IV, thus marking the appearance of this species at about 1.2 mya at this site. Louis Leakey himself found the first of these *H. erectus* specimens at Olduvai (OH 9). Considering how strongly the public associates his name with early hominin discoveries, it is ironic that this specimen was the only hominin fossil he personally ever found at Olduvai. We will have a lot more to say about *H. erectus* in following chapters.

Because australopiths are restricted to Beds I and II (as are most early *Homo* specimens), the following comments on the Olduvai paleoenvironments will concentrate on these two beds.

The Olduvai Gorge is between 45 and 90 m deep where the lowest unit of the beds (Bed I) is exposed. Varying between 30 and 54 m in thickness, Bed I is probably the most firmly dated of any hominin Upper Pliocene/Lower Pleistocene site: the fossils are on the order of about 1.7–1.8 million years old and the fossiliferous part of Bed I may represent a time span of only some 50,000–100,000 years (Walter et al., 1991). Bed I can be subdivided into five lithologically different deposits: lake, lake margin, alluvial fan, alluvial plain, and lava flows. The lake deposits accumulated in a shallow, perennial lake in the lowest part of the basin at the western foot of the volcanic highlands. The lake either did not have an outlet or overflowed infrequently, resulting in fluctuating lake levels. The perennial part of the lake was saline and alkaline. The lake-margin sediments were laid down on a broad expanse of low-lying, relatively flat terrain periodically flooded by the lake. Hominin fossils in Bed I are concentrated in these lake-margin deposits at the eastern end of the lake (Hay, 1973).

Fossilized leaves and pollen are rare in Beds I and II, but swamp vegetation is evident by abundant vertical root channels and casts probably made by some kind of reed. Fossil rhizomes of papyrus also suggest the presence of marshland and/or shallow water. Other structures, such as diatoms and traces of algae, point to fluctuating lake levels and saline conditions. The climate was probably semiarid, although wetter than at Olduvai today, as indicated by the presence of ostracods, freshwater snails, fish, and aquatic birds. Climatic fluctuations may have been seasonal or may have lasted a few decades. Studies relating habitat preferences in modern antelopes (Bovidae), pigs (Suidae), and rodents to similar fossil animals from Olduvai indicate that Bed I paleoenvironments may have been more wooded than previously suspected, since no modern grassland-dominated ecosystem contains as many closed and intermediate habitat animals as the Bed I assemblages (Bishop and Plummer, 1995; Fernández-Jalvo et al., 1998).

The paleogeography of the region represented by Bed II was similar to that of Bed I, at least until faulting began, after which time the perennial lake in the basin was reduced to perhaps a third of its former size. This paleogeographical event accounts for the change in mammalian faunas that occurred about this time whereby swamp-dwelling animals decreased in number and plains-dwelling animals, such as horses, increased in abundance (Hay, 1971).

SUMMARY OF EAST AFRICAN SITES

As we have seen, the earliest undisputed hominins appear in the fossil record of East Africa as various fragments of *Ar. kadabba* from the Middle Awash dated to about 5.8 mya. However, the more complete *Ar. ramidus* material from Aramis, Ethiopia, dated to about 4.4 mya, gives us the best glimpse of what the earliest hominins in the fossil record looked like. The combination of relatively thin enamel and large canine size, together with a primitive P_3 morphology, suggests a canine/premolar complex morphologically and functionally like the presumed ancestral ape condition (a conclusion strengthened by the honing canine/P_3 complex seen in the older *Ar. kadabba* material). Slightly younger than the *Ar. ramidus* material are the hominin specimens from Kanapoi and Allia Bay (East Lake Turkana) allocated to the new species, *A. anamensis*, dating to about 4 mya. Of these, the tibial fragment from Kanapoi is particularly important in showing that bipedal adaptations of the hindlimb had commenced very early in hominin evolution, a view dramatically supported by the discovery of fossil hominin footprints at Laetoli dated to about 3.6 mya.

Beginning with the site at Laetoli at about 3.6 mya and continuing through the sites of Hadar, Omo, Lake Turkana, Bouri, and Olduvai, the fossil record of East African australopiths is impressive up to about 1 mya, when it ceases. As we have seen, the most common hominins in the earliest part of this fossil record, from about 5.8 to 2.5 mya, are *Ar. ramidus*, *A. anamensis*, and *A. afarensis*, which actually may form a series of ancestor-descendant species over this time frame. By about 2.5 mya a new australopith species comes on the scene, *A. garhi*. As we will see below, this species has some features that make it as good a candidate as any to be ancestral to early *Homo*, which in turn first appears in East Africa just before about 2 mya. Also at about this same time an early hyperrobust australopith, designated as either *A. boisei* or *A. aethiopicus*, appears in the fossil record and was evidently contemporaneous with early *Homo* from about 2.4 to 1.4 mya at Omo, about 2.0 to 1.5 mya at Lake Turkana, and about 1.8 to 1.2 mya at Olduvai (White, 1988). *Homo erectus* (or *H. ergaster* as it is sometimes called in Africa) first appears about 1.5 mya in East Africa and is known from sites at Lake Turkana, Omo, and Olduvai (Fig. 6.1). *H. erectus* and *A. boisei* clearly co-existed at several of these sites, for example at Konso about 1.4 mya (Suwa et al., 1997).

With the possible exception of Laetoli, most East African early hominin sites are associated with water sources of one sort or another, from the ancient lake margins at Olduvai to the dense riverine forests along the Omo Valley. Proximity of hominins to water would be expected, especially if the sites represent campsites or home bases where families or groups gathered repeatedly. The cave sites in South Africa, in contrast, have yielded bones that may have been accumulated by hominins and/or other carnivores.

Grazing mammalian species make up about 15–25% of most East African fossil localities until about 1.8 mya, after which time the percentage increases to approximately 45% (the pattern seems similar in southern Africa as well). The high number of arboreal species in East African sites around 3.5 mya suggests more closed woodland at this time; however, the percentages begin to fall to levels indicative of more closed/open woodland until around 1.8 mya, after which time they drop further, indicating more shrubland and grassland habitats (the percentages of frugivorous mammals in East African communities also follows this same general trend). These faunal inferences also support evidence of an expansion of modern C_4 type grasslands in Africa and evidence of drier environments and seasonality around this time (Cerling, 1992).

In general, gracile australopiths are more common in fossil assemblages indicative of fairly wooded regions, whereas robust australopiths are more common in ones indicative of slightly more open habitats, including wetlands. Early *Homo* appears just before 2 mya and is associated with habitats that also support robust australopiths. Later *Homo* species are also found in faunal communities indicative of extremely arid and open landscapes. Therefore, if resource partitioning characterized these co-existing hominin groups, it may be that robust australopiths inhabited more edaphic grassland and wetland areas, whereas *Homo* utilized the more open woodland and grassland habitats (Reed, 1997). Aramis, and the earlier *Ar. kadabba* localities, stand out as the only early hominin sites possibly associated with closed woodland environments.

The presence of australopiths in Chad some 2500 km west of the rift valley strongly suggests that hominins were already widely distributed throughout the woodland and savanna belt from the Atlantic Ocean across the Sahel of Africa (Brunet et al., 1995, 1996, 2002). Vegetation types inferred from pollen studies of various East African hominin sites are summarized in Figures 7.9 and 7.10.

In this chapter we have encountered evidence of "hominization" for the first time in the fossil record of Africa—that is, the evolution of an animal that walked on two legs rather than four, used tools rather than teeth for tearing and cutting, had a relatively large brain, and had evolved behavioral and social mechanisms enabling it to survive the harsh realities of the African savanna. We have placed these early hominins into their proper geological and paleoenvironmental context. Now we turn to the fossils themselves and to what they tell us about the paleobiological adaptations of our earliest ancestors.

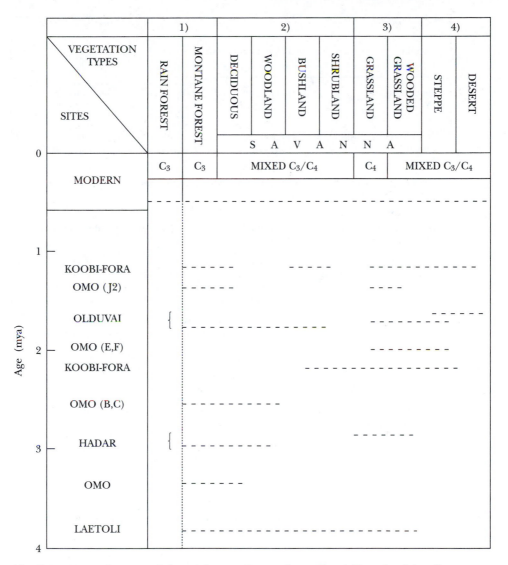

Fig. 7.9. Vegetation types inferred from pollen studies at East African fossil localities. 1) Rain forest: a closed stand of trees of several strata, large trees 40–60 m high, with an interlaced canopy. Montane forest: an evergreen forest with a smaller height of trees and a homogenous composition above 1300 m. 2) Woodland: a stand of trees up to 18 m height with an open or continuous canopy cover of more than 20%; at least 40% grasses and herbs dominate the ground cover. 3) Grassland: land dominated by grasses and occasionally other herbs, sometimes with widely scattered or grouped trees and shrubs; canopy cover not exceeding 2%. 4) Steppe: vegetation with short grass, abundant annual plants between widely spaced perennial herbs, and scattered trees (*Acacia* and *Commiphora* are the most common trees in East Africa). In a broad sense, the term *savanna* includes all categories between woodland and desert. (Adapted from Bonnefille, 1994.)

Locality (mya)	Paleoenvironment
Tabarin, Kenya (5.0–4.0)	Lake margin, with locally variable savanna elements
Middle Awash, Ethiopia (4.5–3.9)	Fluvial conditions, with extensive tectonic activity associated with the formation of the East African rift
Laetoli, Tanzania (3.7–3.2)	Savanna woodland, with well-defined wet and dry seasons
Hadar, Ethiopia (3.6–2.6)	Lake and associated floodplain, with braided streams and rivers
Omo, Ethiopia (Shungura) (3.3–1.4)	After 2.1 mya, dry savanna flanking river banks with gallery forest and dry-thorn savanna; before this date, the environment was probably forested
Koobi Fora, Kenya (3.3–1.4)	Before 1.6 mya, a freshwater lake with floodplains, gallery forest and dry-thorn savanna; during later times, the lake fluctuated from fresh to brackish
Olduvai, Tanzania (1.9–<1.0)	Salt lake with surrounding floodplains with seasonal streams and rivers and dry woodland savanna; tectonic changes after 1.5 mya resulted in the drying up of the lake
Transvaal, South Africa (Makapansgat 3, Sterkfontein 4 and 5, Swartkrans 1, Kromdraai and Taung) (3.0–1.4)	All were mosiac environments, with Makapansgat member 3 and Sterkfontein member 4 being less open (more bush/woodland) than Swartkrans member 1 and Sterkfontein member 5; this suggests a trend from wetter to drier conditions through time

Fig. 7.10.   Early hominin environments in Africa.   (From Andrews, 1992.)

THE AUSTRALOPITHS OF EASTERN AFRICA: THE PLAYERS

Ardipithecus ramidus and *Ar. kadabba*

Age: about 5.8–4.4 mya
Sites: Middle Awash, Ethiopia

As mentioned above, some of the most important additions to the early Pliocene fossil hominin record include the dental, cranial, and postcranial elements of the australopith species *Ar. ramidus* and *Ar. kadabba*, from several sites in the Middle Awash, Ethiopia. The bulk of the fossils come from the site of Aramis and derive from a thin stratigraphic interval immediately above the Gaala Vitric Tuff Complex (GVTC) dated by Ar-Ar to approximately 4.4 mya (Fig. 7.4b) (White et al., 1995; WoldeGabriel et al., 1994). The antiquity and primitive morphology of the specimens suggest that *Ar. ramidus* may represent the potential root species of all later hominins. The Aramis specimens include most of the teeth of one individual, several associated postcranial elements, two partial cranial bases, a child's mandible, and other associated and isolated teeth. An older, but more fragmentary, *Ar. kadabba* sample includes a proximal foot phalanx, several hand phalanges, humerus and ulna, clavicular fragment, a right mandible with M_3 and associated teeth, and a number of isolated teeth. This sample comes from various Middle Awash sites dated to between 5.2 and 5.8 mya (Begun, 2004; Haile-Selassie, 2001; Haile-Selassie, et al., 2004b). As noted earlier, all *Ardipithecus* samples come from sites suggestive of wet, wooded paleoenvironments.

A number of features distinguish *Ardipithecus* from other australopiths, including the larger upper and lower canines relative to postcanine teeth; the narrow and obliquely elongated lower first deciduous molar (in fact, the Aramis dm_1 is more similar to that of chimpanzees than it is to any known hominin); the thin enamel on both molars and canine teeth; the marked inclination of the distal radial articular surface; the strong lateral condylar ridge on the distal humerus; and the elongate, superoposteriorly extended lateral humeral epicondyle. The combination of relatively thin enamel and large canine size together with the primitive P_3 morphology suggests a canine/premolar complex both morphologically and functionally like the presumed ancestral ape condition (Fig. 7.11). In terms of the size of the molar teeth, the *Ardipithecus* sample is significantly smaller than *A. afarensis* and thus shows no evidence of the postcanine megadontia that characterizes all later australopith species.

The cranial material also displays a mosaic of ape-like and hominin-like features. For example, the marked pneumatization of the temporal bone that invades the root of the zygomatic bone is quite chimpanzee-like, whereas the shortened basioccipital component of the cranial base is more hominin-like.

Published postcranial remains include portions of all three bones (humerus, radius, ulna) from the left forelimb of a single individual. These bones are larger than some of the same bones in *A. afarenesis* (see below). The arm also seems to display a mosaic of hominin/great ape features. Further discoveries have added a number of other cranial and postcranial specimens to the *Ar. ramidus* sample, including additional mandibular portions and teeth, humeri, hand and foot bones, and a fragmentary adult skeleton that includes cranial, mandibular, vertebral, and upper and lower limb elements (Asfaw et al., 1995). However, it would be premature to attempt to infer locomotor behavior for this australopith species until these lower limb

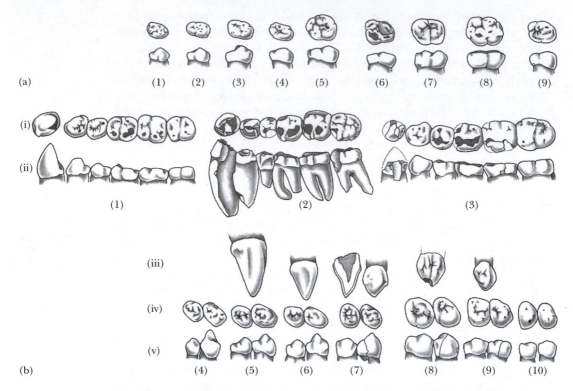

Fig. 7.11. (a) Metric and morphological comparisons of deciduous first molars showing the differences between the dm$_1$ of *Ar. ramidus* and other early hominin species. (1) *Dryopithecus*, (2) *Pan paniscus* (pygmy chimpanzee), (3) *Pan troglodytes* (chimpanzee), (4) *Ar. ramidus*, (5) *A. afarensis*, (6) *A. africanus*, (7) *A. robustus*, (8) *A boisei*, (9) modern *Homo sapiens*. The dm$_1$ of *Ar. ramidus* is much more like that of chimpanzees, both in terms of size and morphology, and represents a good ancestral morphotype for all later hominin species. (b) Comparisons of upper canine/lower premolar complexes and tooth rows. Rows i and ii: occlusal and lateral views of (from left to right) the lower canines, premolars, and molars of (1) *P. troglodytes*, (2) *Ar. ramidus*, (3) *A. afarensis*. Shaded areas represent dental wear. Rows iii–v: lingual views of upper canines and occlusal and buccal views of lower third and fourth premolars of (4) *Dryopithecus*, (5) *P. troglodytes* (male), (6) *P. troglodytes* (female), (7) *Ar. ramidus* (holotype ARA-VP-6/1), (8) *A. afarensis* (LH-3); (9) *A. afarensis* (AL 400); (10) *A. afarensis* (AL 288-1, Lucy). Note the absence of upper canines in specimens 4 and 10. (From White et al., 1994a.)

bones have been fully analyzed and published. However, several derived craniodental features shared with all other hominins—such as the anterior placement of the occipital condyles for articulation with the first cervical vertebra (atlas); the anterior placement of the foramen magnum for passage of the spinal cord; and the more incisiform canine, indicating reduced sexual dimorphism—may correlate with bipedality, but that remains to be demonstrated.

Australopithecus anamensis

Age: about 4.2–3.8 mya
Sites: Kanapoi and Allia Bay, Kenya; ?Fejej and ?Galili, Ethiopia

The recently named species *A. anamensis* is known from over 50 cranial, dental, and postcranial specimens recovered from Kanapoi and Allia Bay (East Lake Turkana), Kenya, dated to about 4.2–3.8 mya (Fig. 7.12) (Leakey et al., 1995, 1998; C. Ward et al., 1999, 2001). The species is described as having a mosaic of primitive and derived features, suggesting that it may be a possible ancestor to *A. afarensis*. Dentally it is most similar to the Laetoli *A. afarensis* sample. Some of the features by which it differs from other australopith species include nearly parallel mandibular bodies and tooth rows, long sloping axis of the mandibular symphysis, sexually dimorphic canines with very long and robust roots, asymmetrical lower third premolar, molars with more sloping buccal sides, and small elliptical external ear hole (acoustic meatus). In other features, such as enamel thickness, first deciduous molar morphology, and buccolingual expansion of the molars, it appears to be a good structural intermediate between the earlier *Ar. ramidus* and later *A. afarensis* specimens.

As noted earlier, the right tibia (which is larger than the largest *A. afarensis* tibia from Hadar) shows several features associated with bipedalism, most notably the size and shape of the proximal articular surfaces for articulation with the distal femur, the relatively straight tibial shaft (although part of the midshaft region is missing), and the configuration of the distal articular facets for articulation with the ankle. Using

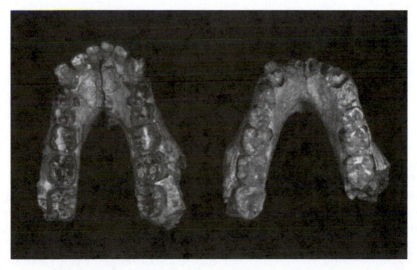

Fig. 7.12. Australopith mandibles. Type specimens of *A. anamensis* (KNM-KP 29281) (left) and *A. afarensis* (LH 4) (right). (Photo courtesy of C. Ward.)

regression analyses based on human tibial size, the body weight of this individual is estimated to be 47–55 kg. A distal humerus from the same site
is basically similar to that of other australopiths in its combination of
chimpanzee-like and human-like features, exhibiting no special affinities
to either *A. afarensis* or to modern humans (Lague and Jungers, 1996).

The capitate differs from all other hominins in having a laterally,
rather than obliquely, directed facet for the second metacarpal, an ape-like
feature. The obliquely oriented facet seen in other australopiths and *Homo*
permits some degree of rotation of the second metacarpal at this joint.

Further remains of *A. anamensis* have also been recovered from
Kanapoi and Allia Bay, Kenya, and include a manual phalanx, maxilla,
mandible, associated maxillary and mandibular dentitions, and numerous
isolated teeth. The phalanx, like the other previously described postcranial bones, is similar to that of *A. afarensis*. The *A. anamensis* maxillas and
mandibles have parallel postcanine tooth rows, like great apes, rather than
the posteriorly diverging tooth rows typical of all later hominins. Canine
root size dimorphism exceeds levels seen in *A. afarensis* and seems closer to
levels found in gorillas. Molar size comparisons suggest body size dimorphism similar to that of *A. afarensis* (C. Ward et al., 1997, 1999, 2001).

Australopithecus afarensis

Age: about 3.6–2.9 mya
Sites: Laetoli, Tanzania; Koobi Fora and West Turkana, Kenya; Omo, Maka,
    and Hadar, Ethiopia

By far the best known of the East African early australopith species is *A.
afarensis*, a taxon well sampled from the period between about 3.6 and 2.9
mya. If the Lothagam mandible mentioned in the previous chapter is correctly identified, the species dates back to more than 5 mya. *A. afarensis* has
been recovered only from sites in East Africa, including Laetoli, Lake
Turkana, Omo, Hadar, Maka, and a few other Middle Awash sites. At present, however, the 3.6 million-year-old Laetoli sample is the earliest undoubted sample of the species.

The craniodental morphology of *A. afarensis* is known from a number of
adult and juvenile specimens and, as a whole, seems intermediate between
apes and later hominins (Figs. 7.2, 7.13, and 7.14; Table 7.1) (Johanson and
White, 1979; Kimbel et al., 1994; Ryan, 1979; Skelton and McHenry, 1992;
Skelton et al., 1986; White et al., 1981, 2000). Much of the postcranial skeleton is also known and reveals an interesting mosaic of human-like and nonhuman-like features (Langdon et al., 1991; Latimer, 1991; Latimer and
Lovejoy, 1989, 1990a, 1990b; McHenry, 1991b; Stern and Susman, 1983).
The most complete adult skeleton is Lucy (AL 288-1). Dated to about 3.2
mya, this small female was probably no more than 1.1–1.2 m in height (approximately 3 feet, 5 inches) and about 30 kg in weight.

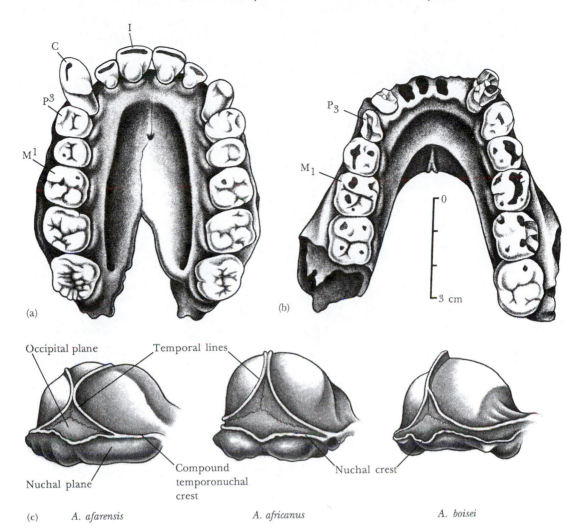

Fig. 7.13. Craniodental features of *A. afarensis.* AL 200-la from Hadar; a partial maxilla with a full adult dentition. Note the wide central incisors with worn dentine; the slightly projecting canines with a worn area for honing the lower third premolar; the distinct space, or diastema, between the upper incisor and canine; and the shallow palate with long, narrow, straight-sided dental arcades. (b) The type specimen of *A. afarensis,* the mandible LH 4 from Laetoli. Several features appear to be quite primitive, for example the large dominant cusp on the lower third premolar and the rather parallel-sided tooth rows. (c) Comparison of posterior view of *A. afarensis, A. africanus,* and *A. boisei* showing the compound temporonuchal crest which is absent in all but a few specimens of later australopiths. (From Johanson and White, 1979; Rak, 1983; White, 1977.)

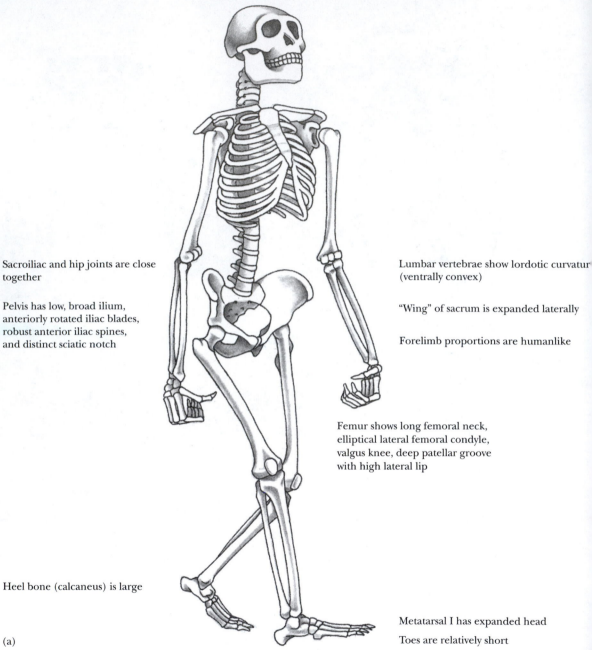

Sacroiliac and hip joints are close together

Pelvis has low, broad ilium, anteriorly rotated iliac blades, robust anterior iliac spines, and distinct sciatic notch

Lumbar vertebrae show lordotic curvatur (ventrally convex)

"Wing" of sacrum is expanded laterally

Forelimb proportions are humanlike

Femur shows long femoral neck, elliptical lateral femoral condyle, valgus knee, deep patellar groove with high lateral lip

Heel bone (calcaneus) is large

Metatarsal I has expanded head

Toes are relatively short

(a)

Fig. 7.14.   (a) Postcranial synapomorphies of *A. afarensis* and *H. sapiens*. (b) Primitive postcranial traits of *A. afarensis*. (From McHenry, 1991b.)

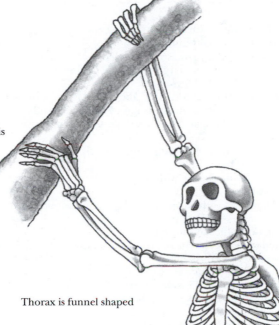

Wrist bones are ape-like

Proximal phalanx of thumb is attenuated

Proximal phalanges II–V are slender and curved

Metacarpal I has attenuated shaft

Metacarpals II–V have large heads and bases, and curved shafts

Thorax is funnel shaped

Scapula has a more cranial orientation

Lumbar vertebrae are small

Iliac blades are more laterally flaring

Middle phalanges are relatively long

Proximal phalanges are long and curved

Hindlimbs are relatively short

Metatarsal I has rounded head

Femur is short

Knee has wide intercondylar notch

(b)

Table 7.1   Features Listed as Diagnostic for *Australopithecus afarensis*

Cranium
  Strong alveolar prognathism with convex clivus
  Palate shallow, especially anteriorly
  Dental arcade long, narrow, straight sided
  Facial skeleton exhibiting large, pillar-like canine juga separated from zygomatic
      processes by deep hollows
  Large zygomatic processes located above P^4/M^1 and oriented at right angles to
      tooth row with inferior margins flared anteriorly and laterally
  Occipital region characterized by compound temporonuchal crest (in larger
      specimens)
  Concave nuchal plane short anteroposteriorly
  Large, flattened mastoids
  Shallow mandibular fossae with weak articular eminences placed only partly
      under braincase
  Occipital condyles with strong ventral angulation
Mandible
  Ascending ramus broad, not high
  Corpus of larger specimens relatively deep anteriorly and hollowed in region of
      low menal foramen that usually open anterosuperiorly
  Moderate superior transverse torus
  Low rounded inferior transverse torus
  Anterior corpus rounded and bulbous
  Strong posterior angulation of symphseal axis
  Postcanine teeth aligned in straight rows
  Arcade tends to be subrectangular, smaller mandibles with relatively narrow
      incisor region
Dentition
  Upper central incisors relatively and absolutely large
  Upper central and diminutive lateral incisors with strong lingual basal tubercles
  Upper incisors with flexed roots
  Strong variation in canine size
  Canines asymmetric, lowers with strong lingual ridge, uppers usually with
      exposed dentine strip, along distal edge when worn
  P_3 occlusal outline elongate oval in shape with main axis mesiobuccal to
      distolingual at 45–60° to tooth row
  P_3 with dominant mesiodistally elongated cusp and small lingual cusp often
      expressed only as inflated lingual ridge
  Diastemata often present between $I^2/\underline{C}$ and $\overline{C}/P_3$
  $\underline{C}/P_3$ complex not functionally analogous to pongid condition

$\underline{C}$, upper canine, $\overline{C}$, lower canine

The measure of the ratio of the length of the humerus divided by the
length of the femur multiplied by 100, known as the **humerofemoral
index,** is approximately 85 in *A. afarensis,* a value that is higher than in
modern humans (about 75). Comparing these two figures gives an intu-
itive sense of the unique body proportions in *A. afarensis,* which generally
had a longer humerus in proportion to its lower limbs than modern humans (Jungers, 1982, 1991; Jungers and Stern, 1983). More recently dis-

covered upper limb bones at Hadar also confirm that the *A. afarensis* forearms were relatively long as well (Kimbel et al., 1994). For example, the
ulna/humerus index of about 92% is much closer to values typical of modern chimpanzees than to those of modern humans. The finger and toe
bones also differ from those of modern humans, particularly in their more
marked longitudinal curvature (Susman et al., 1984). The significance of
these, and other, postcranial features will be discussed below in the context of general postcranial trends in early hominin evolution.

As noted earlier, there is a great deal of presumed sexual dimorphism
in specimens assigned to *A. afarensis*, assuming that all the specimens are
correctly identified as belonging to a single species. The association between inferred body weight, degree of sexual dimorphism, and primate social systems in living primates has even been used to argue that *A. afarensis*
probably did not have a monogamous social structure but more likely lived
in large, kin-related multimale groups with females who were not kin-
related, an inference that is tenuous at best (Foley and Lee, 1989; Richmond and Jungers, 1995).

This view of *A. afarensis* sexual dimorphism has been recently challenged. Drawing on advances made in statistical modeling and using body
mass estimates derived from Al 288-1 (Lucy) and the Al 333 sample, Reno
et al. (2003) argue that *A. afarensis* had only slight to moderate levels of
sexual dimorphism, more like those seen in *Homo* or chimpanzees, rather
than in gorillas. Monomorphic species of living primates tend to show
minimal male–male competition, whereas dimorphic species tend to express relatively higher levels of competition. Thus sexual selection is one
explanation for high levels of dimorphism in primates. Chimpanzee
males, although aggressive to "outsiders," tolerate each other, live in multimale kin groups and evidence a fair degree of collaborative behavior, particularly in hunting. Thus this type of multimale, cooperating kin group
may be a better model of monomorphic *A. afarensis* society. However, *A.
afarensis* has lower canine dimorphism than chimpanzees, which may indicate a different kind of social organization. Reno et al. suggest that *A.
afarensis* may have had a monogamous, rather than polygynous, mating system with strong intermale competition. They believe that the low amount
of canine and body size dimorphism in *A. afarensis* is more consistent with
pair bonding and the behaviors associated with it. It is fair to say, however,
that this view of limited sexual dimorphism in *A. afarensis* is a decidedly minority one.

A number of important craniodental and postcranial fossils have been
described from Maka, Ethiopia, that may predate much of the Hadar material (White et al., 1993). Four mandibular specimens and several isolated
teeth have been recovered from deposits dated to about 3.4 mya that show
certain morphological and metrical resemblances to *A. afarensis* from
Hadar and Laetoli. These include such features as large canines and incisors compared to later hominins, asymmetrical third premolars, and a

diastema between the canine and P_3. However, it is clear that *A. afarensis* was functionally and developmentally hominin in its incisor/canine/premolar complex. For example, it differs from all extant apes, as well as the more primitive *Ardipithecus*, in its relatively small canine size (but not compared to later hominins) and its relatively large, thick-enameled postcanine dentition (megadontia). In addition, the canine/P_3 complex lacks the functional honing seen in extant and extinct apes. The Maka *A. afarensis* sample also reflects the wide range of size variation in the species.

Maka has also yielded several postcranial bones, including a proximal femur, humerus, and proximal ulna. The humerus is large and robust, much more so than the humerus of Lucy (AL 288-1 from Hadar) and is taken to support the view that *A. afarensis* was a highly sexually dimorphic species. It is important that the Maka femur (and the tibia attributed to *A. anamensis*) provide some of the earliest anatomical evidence of upright walking (White, 1984).

Australopithecus garhi

Age: about 2.5 mya
Sites: Bouri and ?Omo, Ethiopia; ?Baringo-Chemeron, Kenya

The newest addition to the pantheon of australopith species is *A. garhi*, recently described from sites in the Middle Awash Bouri Formation dated to about 2.5 mya (Asfaw et al., 1999; de Heinzelin et al., 1999).[7] The species may be descended from *A. afarensis* and is considered a possible ancestor for early *Homo*. Specimens include both craniodental and postcranial elements. A partial hominin skeleton (BOU-VP 12/1A-G) includes fairly complete shafts of a left femur and right humerus, radius, ulna, partial fibular shaft, proximal foot phalanx, and base of the anterior portion of the mandible. Several hundred meters from this site other partial crania and postcrania were also found. These finds are of particular importance since the East African hominin record between about 3.0 and 2.0 mya is poorly sampled and it is during this time that (presumably) the genus *Homo* first emerged from some australopith ancestor. Unfortunately, the best-preserved Bouri partial cranium (BOU-VP 12/130) cannot be definitely linked to the partial skeleton, so the diagnosis of the new species is based solely on the craniodental remains.

A. garhi is distinguished from *A. afarensis* by its absolutely larger postcanine dentition and upper third premolar morphology. It also lacks the many derived features found in the craniodental complex of robust australopiths. The lower face is prognathic, the clivus contour is convex, and the incisors are procumbent. Molar enamel is thick. A sagittal crest is present in (presumed) males. Both the anterior (e.g., central incisor and ca-

---

[7]The name *garhi* means "surprise" in the local Afar language.

nine breadths) and postcanine dentitions are large being at, or beyond, dimensions known for all gracile australopiths and *A. robustus* (postcanine dentition) and for all australopiths and early *Homo* (anterior dentition). Thus the proportions of the anterior and postcanine dentitions are very different from those found in all robust australopiths. The palate is vertically thin and the zygomatic roots originate above P^4/M^1 (rather than the P^4/P^3 position more common in robust australopiths. Cranial capacity is estimated at about 450 cc.

The Bouri VP 12/1 partial skeleton is only the third Plio-Pleistocene hominin in which reasonably accurate limb length proportions can be determined (the other two being AL 288-1 Lucy and KNM-WT 15000). *A. garhi* postcranial proportions are unique for early hominins. The human-like humeral/femoral ratio marks the earliest appearance of femoral elongation characteristic of later *Homo* seen in the hominin fossil record. It is somewhat surprising that the brachial index (upper arm length to lower arm length) is ape-like, even exceeding values for chimpanzees (Richmond et al., 2002). The earliest fossil hominin with a more modern brachial index was *H. erectus (ergaster)* (KNM-WT 15000). Clearly, the limb proportions of *A. garhi* are unlike anything yet known from the fossil record.

At Bouri the mixture of associated grazers and other water-dependent fauna suggests mainly lake marginal paleoenvironments. Zooarcheological remains from the site show that hominins (presumably *A. garhi*) acquired both meat and marrow by 2.5 mya (de Heinzelin et al., 1999). Near the hominin partial skeleton locality a number of mammalian bones show evidence of cut marks and percussion marks clearly made by stone tools. The bone modifications indicate that large mammals were disarticulated and defleshed and that their long bones were broken open to extract marrow, presumably a new food resource in hominin evolution. It is ironic that the Bouri hominin sites seem devoid of stone tools and the raw materials to make them, but clearly stone tools were being used for meat and marrow recovery. This opens up the intriguing possibility that early hominins were actually "importing" stone tools from other sites to carry on their butchery work at Bouri.

Australopithecus boisei

Age: about 2.3–1.4 mya
Sites: Chiwondo, Malawi; Olduvai and Peninj, Tanzania; Chesowanja, Koobi
  Fora, and West Turkana, Kenya; Omo and Konso-Gardula, Ethiopia

The hyperrobust hominin *A. boisei* is well known from a number of East African Plio-Pleistocene sites, including Olduvai Gorge, eastern Lake Turkana (Koobi Fora Formation), Omo Basin, Konso, and west of Lake Turkana (Fig. 6.1). More recently, specimens referred to *A. boisei* have been found as far south as Malawi and possibly South Africa (Kullmer et al., 1999; Menter et al., 1999). These specimens are dated to about 2.3–1.4 mya. The earliest representatives of East African hyperrobusts from Omo and West Turkana are considered by some to be a distinct species, *A. aethiopicus.*

By most appearances, *A. boisei* simply represents a more robust version of *A. robustus* (Fig. 7.8). The cranium is the most robust of any australopith and is characterized by accentuated sagittal and nuchal crests. Pneumatization of the cranium is more extensive than in *A. africanus* or *A. robustus,* browridges are well developed, the forehead is low or absent, and the face is very long and flat. The jaws and postcanine teeth are extremely large, as are the parts of the cranium where the chewing muscles attach, for example, the zygomatic arches for the attachment of the masseter muscles and the lateral pterygoid plates for the attachment of the medial and lateral pterygoid muscles. Substantial variation exists in mandibular size and shape among specimens attributed to this taxon. In fact, the degree of mandibular size variation in this taxon is never observed in modern human and chimpanzee samples and is rarely seen in gorillas (it does, however, fall within the range of variation sometimes seen in orangutans) (Silverman et al., 2001).

Clearly, selection pressures favored increased occlusal surface areas for both *A. robustus* and *A. boisei* since in both species molars and premolars are much larger compared with incisors and canines; the differential is greatest in *A. boisei* (Fig. 6.14). Variations in cranial and dental size in specimens attributed to *A. boisei* suggest that the species was markedly sexually dimorphic in body size, with males averaging 49 kg and females 34 kg.

Probably the most spectacular *A. boisei* fossil ever found in terms of overall robustness is WT 17000 from West Lake Turkana (Fig. 7.15) (Walker et al., 1986). At 2.5 million years old, it is the oldest representative of *A. boisei* yet known, although, as noted above, it is sometimes classified as a distinct species, *A. aethiopicus.* Its cranium reveals a very flat and shallow palate and a premaxilla showing pronounced subnasal prognathism. The small size of the braincase, combined with the development of enormous chewing muscles (particularly the posterior fibers of the temporalis muscle), has produced a compound temporonuchal crest and a large sagittal crest. Like all robust crania, the forehead is rather low and flat and pneumatization of the cranial bones is extensive, particularly in the lateral portions of the cranial base.

The first skull (i.e., cranium and lower jaw) of *A. boisei* was reported from the site of Konso, Ethiopia (Suwa et al., 1997). What is most interesting about this find is its demonstration of a considerable amount of morphological variation within this species. While the overall morphology of the Konso cranium and dentition clearly warrant taxonomic allocation to *A. boisei,* other features resemble other australopith taxa. For example, the configuration of the large sagittal crest, which originates behind bregma and contin-

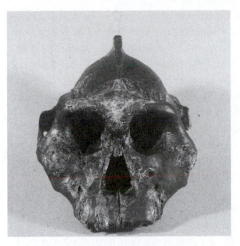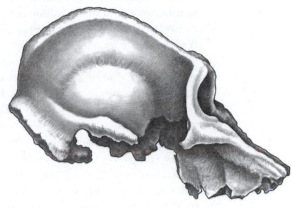

Fig. 7.15. Frontal and lateral views of a hyperrobust cranium of *A. boisei* (WT 17000) from deposits west of Lake Turkana dated to about 2.5 mya. Some researchers consider it to be a distinct species, *A. aethiopicus.* Note the prognathic face, large sagittal crest, low, flat forehead, and small brain size (about 410 cc). (Photo courtesy of A. Walker and National Museums of Kenya.)

ues past lambda, most closely resembles *A. aethiopicus* (which is not considered a separate species in this text); the broad, anteroposteriorly short palate most closely resembles *Homo;* and the relatively laterally facing zygomatic surface most closely resembles *A. robustus.* An endocranial capacity estimate of 545 cc for this *A. boisei* cranium is slightly larger than those recorded for other *A. boisei/robustus* specimens (Falk et al., 2000). This may be due to the younger geologic age of the Konso hominin (1.4 mya), indicating some small degree of increased encephalization in the robust lineage over time or simply an example of relatively minor intraspecific variation.

The Konso *A. boisei* material reminds paleoanthropologists (who really shouldn't need to be reminded) that many details of craniodental features used in early hominin systematics may "vary between populations in a manner consistent with random genetic drift . . . [and that] excessive atomization of morphological features and their individual evaluations may then lead to erroneous phylogenetic and simplistic functional interpretations" (Suwa et al., 1997). Thus, for taxonomic "lumpers," much of the variation seen in various hominin taxa are interpreted to be the result of intraspecific variation due to individual, age-related, temporal and/or geographic factors having little, if any, taxonomic significance (which is the general philosophy evident in this text).[8] It is important to emphasize, however, that any consideration of intraspecific craniodental variation in fossil hominins should maintain a functional and developmental perspective (Strait, 2001). For example, it has

---

[8]For an excellent statement of the opposing taxonomic "splitters" credo, see Tattersall (1986).

been shown that intraspecific variation in variables from the cranial base, **neurocranium,** and face that are not subject to high levels of masticatory strain usually have lower levels of intraspecific variation than variables from regions of the face subject to higher levels of strain—thus not all variables are equally useful for testing hypotheses about taxonomic heterogeneity without some knowledge of functional and developmental demands on those structures (Wood and Lieberman, 2001). When these factors are taken into account, it appears that *A. boisei* is unexceptional in terms of its intraspecific variation, being more variable than highly dimorphic genera like *Gorilla* and *Pongo* only in several palatal and mandibular variables subject to high mechanical loads and, therefore, of lower taxonomic utility.

A. boisei is currently represented primarily by craniodental specimens. A few isolated limb bones (partial humerus, femur, tibia) have been attributed to *A. boisei;* however, it is difficult to assign postcranial material to this species with any certainty since skeletal parts have not been recovered in direct association with any teeth or crania attributed to *A. boisei.*

Kenyanthropus platyops

Age: about 3.5 mya
Sites: west Lake Turkana (Lomekwi), Kenya

Interpretations of australopiths got murkier with the recent announcement of a new genus and species, *Kenyanthropus platyops,* from about 3.5-mya sediments from Lomekwi, Nachukui Formation, west Lake Turkana (Leakey et al., 2001). The new finds include a temporal bone; two partial maxillas; isolated teeth; and a largely complete, though distorted, cranium that is said to show a unique combination of derived facial and primitive neurocranial features.[9] Until this discovery, only two australopiths species were recognized in the 4 to 3 mya time period: *A. afarensis* and its possible ancestor, *A. anamensis.*

The cranium differs from its near contemporary, *A. afarensis,* in having a smaller external acoustic meatus (similar in this respect to *Ar. ramidus* and *A. anamensis*), an absence of an occipital/marginal venous sinus system (Falk and Conroy, 1983), a more orthognathous facial architecture (e.g., anteriorly positioned zygomatic process, more vertically oriented clivus, lack of anterior facial pillars, flat transverse facial contour), and smaller molars. In fact, the flat, orthognathic face of *K. platyops* is most reminiscent of KNM-ER 1470 and many robust australopiths. If the size of the M^2 is any indication, *K. platyops* teeth fall at the bottom of the size range for *A. anamensis, A. afarensis,* and *H. habilis* and are below the ranges for other African early hominins. Molar thickness is comparable to that seen in *A. anamensis* and *A. afarensis.*

---

[9]See White (2003) for a discussion about how this distortion may have affected the taxonomic assessment of this specimen.

Of interest is the apparent similarity of the derived facial aspects of *K. platyops* with that of KNM-ER 1470, the type of *H. rudolfensis*—possibly suggesting a close phylogenetic relationship between the two despite the time difference of about 1.5 million years. As we will see later, there is growing sentiment for removing *H. rudolfensis* from the genus *Homo* and transferring it to the genus *Australopithecus* (Wood and Collard, 1999a, 1999b).

All in all, *K. platyops* reveals a strange mix of primitive and derived hominin features, particularly the combination of small cheek teeth with a large flat face and an anteriorly positioned zygomatic arch. These latter facial features are usually found in early hominins with megadontia. In some features it resembles chimpanzees and *A. anamensis* (e.g., small ear hole), in others it shares other primitive hominin features with *A. afarensis* and *A. anamensis* (e.g., thick molar enamel, small brain, and flat nasal margins), while in others it shares more derived facial features with *H. rudolfensis* (e.g., anterior origin for the root of the zygomatic arch on the upper jaw, the flat face).

COMPARISON OF GRACILE AND ROBUST AUSTRALOPITHS

What, if anything, distinguishes "gracile" from "robust" australopiths? Do they represent two distinct lineages, one ancestral to *Homo* (the graciles) and the other doomed to extinction (the robusts)? Are they part of one evolving robust australopith lineage (*A. africanus–A. robustus–A. boisei*) or are they simply size variants of the same animal? To put these phylogenetic issues into perspective in order to discuss them later on, we need a clear understanding of the morphological differences between the two groups. The person most responsible for first emphasizing distinctions between them and for relating these distinctions to inferred behavior and ecology was the Transvaal Museum's John T. Robinson (1956, 1963, 1972).

Robinson pointed out many years ago that in "robust" australopiths the relatively small anterior teeth (incisors and canines) are set in a flattish, or **orthognathous,** face whereas the massive postcanine teeth are set in dense bone of the upper and lower jaws. It is obvious that this animal generated large chewing stresses through the cranium via these enormous teeth. This is confirmed by the thickened bone in several areas where these forces would have been dissipated throughout the cranium: the robust zygomatic process, the anteriorly thickened palate, and (in *A. robustus* at least) the robust anterior pillars (McCollum, 1994, 1997, 1999; McCollum and Ward, 1997; McCollum et al., 1993; Rak, 1983).

The large masticatory muscles also left their mark on cranial architecture. The presence of a sagittal crest on most robust crania indicates the large size of the temporalis muscle in relation to the overall size of the braincase. The strong development of the lateral pterygoid plates for attachment of the lateral and medial pterygoid muscles and the zygomatic arch for attachment of the masseter muscle also indicate the hypertrophy of these chewing muscles. The combination of large, strongly flaring zygomatic arches with relatively small anterior dentitions gives most of these robust forms a flattish, even dished, facial appearance. The absence of a true forehead, the great postorbital constriction to accommodate a large temporalis muscle, the sagittal crest, and the large browridges combine to give this form a cranial shape unique among hominins. Muscle markings indicate that the neck muscles were also powerful. Their size undoubtedly contributes to the fact that in posterior view the broadest part of the cranium is low down across the mastoid region.

There are other unique features of the robust australopith cranium that relate to powerful masticatory stresses. In both juvenile and adult *A. boisei* specimens there is an extraordinary degree of overlap along the edges of the temporal and parietal bones at the squamosal suture. This overlap is a bony adaptation to offset the forces produced by the combined effect of the massive temporalis muscle acting from a relatively anterior location and the masseter muscle acting from a relatively lateral location. The excessive pressure created along the squamosal suture by this unique masticatory system would otherwise loosen the contact between the temporal and parietal bones (Rak, 1978).

In Robinson's model, the total morphological pattern of gracile australopiths is very different from that of robust australopiths. In the gracile form, the anterior teeth are relatively larger, the postcanine teeth relatively smaller, the face more prognathous, and the cranial vault higher than in the robust form. This implies relatively lower chewing stresses in the gracile species, since the great ruggedness of the bones, including sagittal cresting, is for the most part absent. It is interesting to note that even though the overall appearance of the cranium in both forms is of a rather rugged creature, the actual cranial bones themselves are quite thin.

To Robinson, these craniodental differences reflected considerable differences in diet and behavior between the two groups. The larger anterior teeth in the gracile forms were seen as an adaptation to diets that included meat eating, whereas the emphasis on the postcanine dentition in the robust forms was seen as an adaptation to tough vegetarian diets utilizing roots, tubers, and bulbs. Robinson considered *A. africanus* so human-like in both morphology and implied hunting behaviors that he eventually reclassified it as *Homo africanus.* Robinson's insights have been reinforced by other studies. For example, an analysis of incisor microwear indicated that *A. africanus* used its incisors to process a greater variety of foods, including larger, more abrasive items, than *A. robustus* (Ungar and Grine, 1991).

Many of these craniodental distinctions between gracile and robust australopiths are summarized in Table 7.2.

Table 7.2   Differences between Southern African Gracile (Sterkfontein) and Robust (Swartkrans) Australopiths

Feature	Gracile	Robust
Cranial		
Overall shape	Narrow, with "unmistakable" forehead; higher value for supraorbital height index	Broad across the ears; lacking a forehead; low supraorbital height index
Sagittal crest	Normally absent	Normally present
Face	Weak supraorbital torus variable degree of prognathism, sometimes as little as robust form	Supraorbital torus well developed medially to form a flattened "platform" at glabella; face flat and broad, with little prognathism
Floor of nasal cavity	More marked transition from the facial surface of the maxilla into the floor of the nasal cavity; sloping posterior border to the anterior nasal spine and lower insertion of the vomer	Smooth transition from facial surface of maxilla into the floor of the nasal cavity; small anterior nasal spine that articulates at its tip with the vomer
Shape of dental arcade and palate	Rounded anteriorly and even in depth	Straight line between canines, deeper posteriorly
Pterygoid region	Slender lateral pterygoid plate	Robust lateral pterygoid plate
Dental		
Relative size of teeth	Anterior and posterior teeth in "proportion"	Anterior teeth proportionally small posterior teeth proportionally large
dm_1	Small, with relatively larger mesial cusps; Lingually situated anterior fovea; large protoconid with long, sloping buccal surface	Larger, molariform, with deeply incised buccal groove and relatively large distal cusps
P^3 roots	Single buccal root	Double buccal root
Upper canine	Large, robust, and symmetrical crown with slender marginal ridges and parallel lingual grooves	Small, *Homo*-like, with thick marginal ridges and lingual grooves converging on the gingival eminence
Lower canine	Asymmetric crown with marked cusplet on the distal marginal ridge and marked central ridge on the lingual surface	More symmetric crown with parallel lingual grooves, weak distal enamel ridge

CHAPTER VIII

Australopith Paleobiology and Phylogeny

INTRODUCTION

Having introduced the australopiths and reviewed their paleoenvironmental and geological settings in the last two chapters, we now turn to a more general discussion concerning the paleobiology of the australopiths themselves and what they can tell us about early hominin lifestyles. We will be concerned particularly with two of the most important trends in Plio-Pleistocene hominin evolution: the increase in brain size and the development of bipedalism. The following sections focus first on paleobiological inferences to be drawn from craniofacial morphology. In the sections that follow we will look in closer detail at the postcranial evidence for the evolution of bipedalism.

As noted earlier, popular accounts of human evolution often use the colloquial terms *gracile* and *robust* as a convenient shorthand for referring to *A. africanus* (and by extension all other "nonrobust" taxa as well) on the one hand and *A. robustus*, *A. boisei/aethiopicus* on the other (but remember the caveat we noted about body size differences among these species). At present, *Ar. kadabba*, *Ar. ramidus*, *A. anamensis*, *A. afarensis*, *A. garhi*, and *Kenyanthropus* are restricted to East African sites, whereas *A. africanus* and *A. robustus* are restricted to South African ones. *A. boisei* has been found in East Africa, Malawi, and possibly South Africa (Gondolin) and *A. bahrelghazali* (if it is a separate species) is known only from Chad. Some gracile hominins in East Africa have also been attributed to *A. africanus* (Tobias, 1980) but this is debatable, and most workers now assign these specimens to either *A. afarensis* or early *Homo*. Therefore, both East and South Africa contain at least one gracile and one robust australopith species.

Documenting evolutionary trends requires that we determine the chronological order of the species as best we can. As a first-order approximation, the following australopith species can be listed chronologically (from oldest to youngest) as *Ar. kadabba, Ar. ramidus, A. anamensis, K. platy-ops, A. afarensis, A garhi, A. africanus, A. robustus,* and *A. boisei.*[1] In general, the gracile species precede the robust species in the fossil record, although early forms of *A. boisei* in East Africa evidently co-existed with later forms of *A. africanus* in South Africa. Not only do the two robust species overlap in time but their accepted chronological relationship may eventually be reversed based on the discovery of the *A. boisei* specimen from west Lake Turkana (WT 17000), which, at about 2.6 mya, is much older than any specimens of *A. robustus.* This point is still open to debate (Kimbel et al., 1988; Walker and Leakey, 1988).

CRANIOFACIAL MORPHOLOGY

Compared to modern humans, australopiths are characterized by relatively small brains, ranging from approximately 400 to 530 cc, housed in cranial bones that are generally quite thin (Conroy et al., 1998; Falk et al., 2000; Gauld, 1996). In spite of small actual brain size, australopith encephalization quotients (EQs) are relatively high (compared to other mammals), ranging from 2.4 in *A. afarensis* to about 3.1 in *A. robustus* (Figs. 6.2b and 8.1). In addition, trends toward some neural reorganization, like expansion of the temporal lobes of the brain, are evident through time (Falk, 1980, 1987b; Holloway, 1983; Vrba, 1994).

As australopith crania become generally larger and more robust in later species, other cranial trends become evident. The robust cranium carries forward the adaptive trends already seen, albeit in less-developed form, in the gracile australopiths: (1) faces become shorter, deeper, and more massive; (2) the dentition is characterized by increasing postcanine megadontia and relative reduction in incisor and canine size; (3) the lower molars develop accessory cuspules and thickened enamel; (4) sagittal and compound temporal/nuchal crests are common; (5) the zygomatic arch is positioned high above the occulsal plane; (6) the zygoma is forwardly placed; (7) the mandible is robust and has a tall ascending ramus; (8) the hard palate is thick; (9) the infraorbital region is vertically tall with a correspondingly low position of the infraorbital foramen; (10) the face is hafted high onto the neurocranium; (11) the frontal region is depressed behind the supraorbital torus (frontal trigone); (12) there is strong postorbital constriction; and (13) cranial bones tend to become more **pneumatized** (filled with air spaces) in order to reduce the weight of the

---

[1]However, if some of the hominin material from member 2, Sterkfontein, is ultimately attributed to *A. africanus* and if the older dates of about 4 mya are confirmed for this member (Partridge et al., 2003), then this chronological sequence will need some modification.

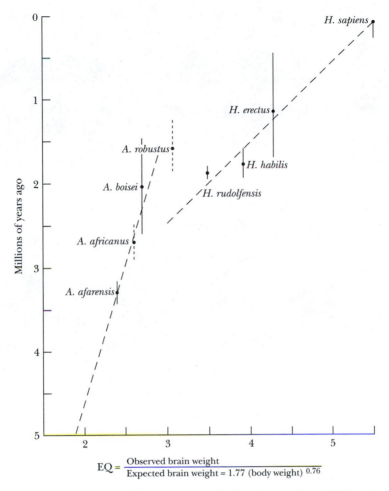

Fig. 8.1. Evolutionary trends in hominin encephalization quotients (EQs). Dots represent mean EQ values for each taxon; lines extending from each taxon along the time axis indicate estimated age ranges for each taxon. (From Vrba, 1994.)

enlarged cranium (a process that had already begun in *Ar. ramidus*) (Fig. 8.2) (Kay, 1985; McCollum, 1999; Tobias, 1967a).

Almost all of these characteristics of the robust cranium may result from the developmental consequences of having extremely large postcanine teeth and relatively small anterior teeth. The massive molars require a tall, vertical ascending ramus to anchor them, as well as to anchor the massive muscles of mastication that insert on this part of the mandible (e.g., masseters, lateral and medial pterygoids, temporalis). The small front teeth alter the configuration of the floor of the nose. The interface between the nose and the mouth, the hard palate, has to readjust its orientation and

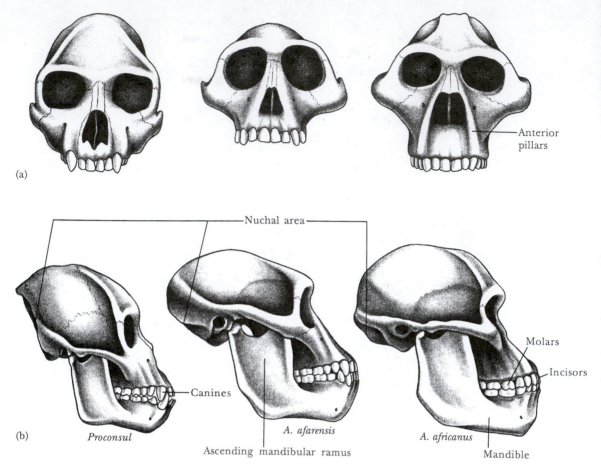

Fig. 8.2. General craniodental trends in australopiths. Frontal (a) and lateral (b) views of a Miocene ape and four australopiths. Note that many morphological features associated with powerful chewing and grinding are more accentuated in robust than in gracile australopiths: faces become shorter, deeper, and more massive, often with strong anterior pillars; crania may show pronounced sagittal crests; lower jaws become thickened with high ascending mandibular rami; incisors become smaller relative to molars; canines become more incisiform; molars become massive; and the temporal fossa becomes larger for the increased size of the temporalis muscle.

thicken during development, thereby setting off a cascade of interrelated ontogenetic patterns that ultimately define the robust australopith face and neurocranium. There is an important lesson in this for primate systematists: One must try to understand the developmental interrelationships among morphological characters before "atomizing" them into discrete characters for phylogenetic analyses in any cladistic study (McCollum, 1999, 2000). It may often be the case that long lists of character traits used in such analyses (such as those enumerated above for the robust australo-

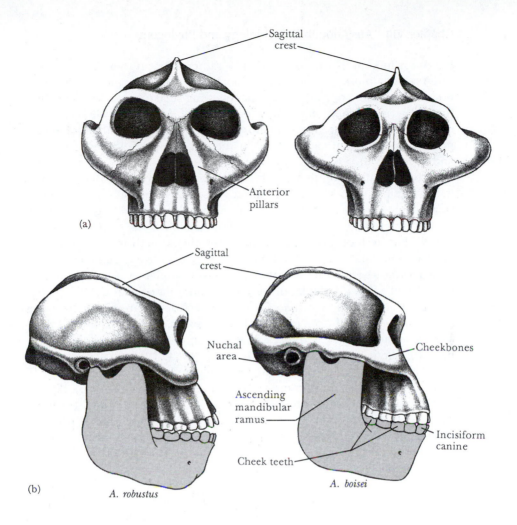

(a)

Sagittal
crest

Anterior
pillars

(b)

Sagittal
crest

Nuchal
area

Cheekbones

Ascending
mandibular
ramus

Incisiform
canine

Cheek teeth

A. robustus

A. boisei

pith cranium) may actually reflect only a small number of developmental variables. These far fewer variables, if properly understood, should be the ones used in cladistic studies, not the original atomized list of characters.

The need to generate powerful masticatory forces probably influenced the evolution of australopith cranial morphology more than any other single factor. Since the power of a muscle is directly related to its physiological cross-sectional area, one way to increase the bite force of major masticatory muscles, like the temporalis muscle, is to enlarge its cross-sectional area, an evolutionary change that is documented in the increased size of the **temporal fossa** through which this muscle passes to its insertion on the coronoid process of the mandible (Fig. 8.2). Changes in cranial shape, in particular the realignment of the jaw to a position more directly beneath the midface and braincase, also serves to improve the mechanical advantage of some of the masticatory muscles, allowing them to generate greater bite force along the tooth row. Finally, since hominins rely on their hands for food preparation and uptake rather than on their anterior dentition alone, more of the entire tooth row can become "molarized," thereby increasing overall masticatory chewing surfaces. Many of these features are carried to an extreme in robust australopiths, in whom the mechanical advantage of the masticatory muscles and the molarization of the premolars (and even canines) reach their greatest development (Demes and Creel, 1988).

Trends in australopith cranial morphology can be correlated to trends in postcanine tooth size. For example, absolute postcanine dental size is smallest in *Ar. ramidus*, *A. afarensis*, and *Kenyanthropus*, and largest in *A. boisei*. In terms of size, early *Homo* is indistinguishable from *A. afarensis* in this regard. Furthermore, the size of the lower cheek teeth in *A. africanus* reveals an unusual pattern in that the M_1 is similar in size to *A. afarensis* (and early *Homo*), whereas the M_2 and M_3 are more similar in size to *A. robustus* (Suwa et al., 1994). Calculation of the megadontia quotient (MQ)[2] shows that in *A. afarensis* and *A. anamensis* the cheek teeth are about 1.7 times larger than expected from estimated body weight, in *A. africanus* and *A. robustus* they are about 2.0 and 2.2 times larger, respectively, and in *A. boisei* they are about 2.7 times larger (McHenry, 1984, 1985). These compare with MQ estimates of about 1.6 for *H. habilis* and about 1.0 for African *H. erectus*, *H. sapiens*, and common chimpanzees (McHenry, 1988, 1992b). These studies reveal two important things: (1) all australopiths (with the possible exception of *Ardipithecus* and *Kenyanthropus*) are characterized by postcanine megadontia and (2) relative cheek-tooth size tends to increase through time from *A. afarensis* to *A. boisei* and to decrease through time in the *Homo* lineage.

Even though australopith molars can be generally described as large and relatively flat, gracile australopiths (e.g., *A. africanus*) generally tend to have a little more occlusal relief, as well as lower incidences of enamel pitting, than robust australopiths (e.g., *A. robustus*), again indicative of some dietary differences between the two. However, these earliest hominins may have been less efficient in breaking down tough, pliant foods such as soft seed coats and the veins and stems of leaves because of this lack of strong molar shearing crests—although they were probably capable of processing buds, flowers, shoots, roots, tubers, etc. Ironically, meat is the other food type they would have had trouble breaking down in mastication (Teaford and Ungar, 2000).

The size and shape of the postcanine dentition are not the only clues to hominin dietary preferences—the relative size of the incisors is important as well. If one looks at the relative size of maxillary central incisor breadth compared to body size in various primates, one is struck by the

---

[2]MQ is a measure of relative tooth size and compares the size of the tooth area of the specimen in question to that of a mammal of about the same body size. It is calculated by the formula: MQ = P4-M2 tooth area$/12.15$ (body weight)$^{0.86}$.

fact that cercopithecines have relatively large incisors while colobines (predominantly leaf eaters) have relatively smaller ones (Hylander, 1975). As far as apes are concerned, the more frugivorous chimpanzees and orangutans have relatively larger incisors compared to the less frugivorous gorillas and gibbons. Relative incisor size for most gracile australopiths resembles that of gorillas more than chimpanzees, suggesting that these early hominins used their incisors for ingestion in similar ways—that is, far less than the more frugivorous extant apes (Teaford and Ungar, 2000). In other words, gracile australopiths were probably eating foods that demanded much less incisal preparation such as those with thick husk and/or those with flesh adherent to large, hard seeds. Robust australopith incisors are even relatively smaller.

Larger teeth require larger jaws, which in turn require larger muscles to move them. The larger muscles then need larger bony attachments to the cranium and jaw. These include (1) prominent **sagittal** and **nuchal crests** for the attachment of powerful chewing and neck muscles, respectively, and (2) bony struts in the face to withstand powerful chewing stresses set up through the massive jaws and teeth. One pair of struts, the **anterior pillars,** are massive bony columns that support the anterior portion of the palate on both sides of the nasal aperture (Fig. 8.2) (McKee, 1989; Rak, 1983).

So what can we conclude about early hominin diets based on the australopith craniodental complex? The combination of (1) relatively small to moderate size incisors and canines; (2) large, flat premolars and molars with little shear potential; (3) thickened tooth enamel (except in the earliest forms like *Ardipithecus*); and (4) thickened mandibular corpora all point to animals that were most efficient at breaking down and crushing hard, brittle, and abrasive foods (e.g., underground storage items like roots, tubers, corms) rather than tough fruits, leaves, meat or other foods requiring a great deal of incisal preparation (e.g., husked fruit). The robust australopiths carried this trend of small incisors and large postcanine teeth to an extreme.

Two further features of cranial morphology deserve mention here, the first of which relates to vocalization. The upper respiratory system of modern humans is unique among mammals (Fig. 8.3). Although humans share homologous upper respiratory tract features with other mammals, the positions of structures such as the larynx and pharynx have become markedly altered during human evolution. These anatomical changes have determined our breathing and swallowing patterns and have provided the physical basis necessary for the production of the full variety of human speech sounds, or phonation (Lieberman, 2002; Lieberman et al., 1992). Phonation is the result of laryngeal activity, in particular the activity of the vocal cords. Movement of the vocal cords produces "puffs" of air into the airspace above the vocal cords, an area known as the **supralaryngeal vocal tract** (SVT).

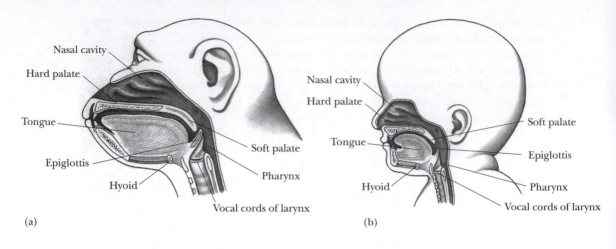

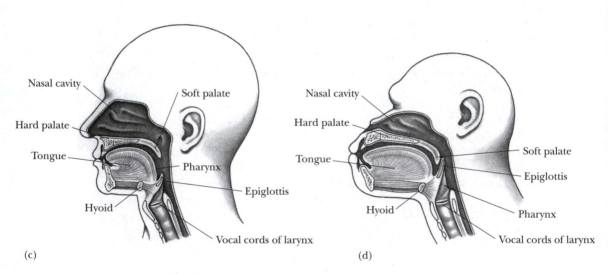

Fig. 8.3.   Comparative views of the primate airway. (a) Chimpanzee. (b) Human infant. (c) Adult human. (d) Australopith.   In the chimpanzee the tongue is situated entirely within the oral cavity whereas in the adult human its rounded posterior border forms the anterior boundary of the oropharynx. Also note that the larynx (epiglottis) is high in the neck in the chimpanzee, reaching the level of the soft palate. This morphology reduces the amount of space in the airway above the vocal cords, the supralaryngeal vocal tract. In the adult human the larynx is lower in the neck (the epiglottis does not reach the level of the soft palate), thereby increasing the size of the supralaryngeal vocal tract. The human infant and the reconstructed australopith appear more like the chimpanzee. (From Laitman and Heimbuch, 1982; Lieberman, 1992.)

Several specific anatomical changes occurred in human evolution that directly affected the configuration of the SVT. In fact, analysis of phonation capabilities in fossil hominins has been based almost entirely on reconstructions of the SVT. The most important of these evolutionary changes is the increased flexion of the cranial base resulting in a larynx that has "descended" in the neck relative to the position of the soft palate, thereby increasing the size of the SVT. In addition, the human tongue now lies within both the oral and the pharyngeal cavities, whereas the nonhuman primate tongue lies almost entirely within the oral cavity. The primary linguistic function of the SVT is that of an acoustic filter. Therefore, even though nonhuman primate SVTs can produce most of the sounds of human speech, albeit with nasalization, only the human SVT can produce the entire range of vowels and consonants. In nonhuman primates, the size and shape of the SVT is incapable of producing velar stop consonants (like [g] and [k]) and quantal vowels (like [i], [u], and [a]).[3]

Several analyses of the australopith cranial base, the **basicranium,** indicate that the unique morphology of modern humans had not yet evolved in these hominins, and by extension the australopith SVT was probably more similar in overall structure and function to that of living apes than to modern humans (Laitman, 1984, 1985; Laitman and Heimbuch, 1982; Laitman et al., 1979). While the correlations among basicranial anatomy, laryngeal position, and language capabilities are highly complex and somewhat equivocal (Gibson and Jessee, 1994; Lieberman et al., 1998), it seems reasonable to conclude that australopiths were probably not capable of speech as we know it but were limited to the range of vocalizing seen in modern apes (Fig. 8.3). The issue remains controversial, however, since some recent studies suggest that *A. africanus, H. erectus,* and both early and modern *Homo* all have more flexed basicrania than other nonhuman primates do (Ross and Henneberg, 1995) and that chimpanzees also are characterized by some descent of the larynx during their early ontogenetic development (Nishimura et al., 2003).

Gracile and robust australopiths can also be generally distinguished by their differing vascular patterns for draining venous blood from the brain. Although their function is debated, these venous patterns may have evolved in response to the changing gravitational pressures associated with bipedalism: Gracile australopiths (and *Homo*) tend to employ a transverse/sigmoid sinus system in combination with a widely dispersed network of veins that pass through and within the cranial bones (the **diploic** and **emissary veins**, respectively), whereas robust australopiths, as well as the Hadar *A. afarensis* hominins, employ blood channels that are described as the **occipital/marginal venous sinus** system (Fig. 8.4) (Falk, 1986;

---

[3]Velar consonants are ones that form a constriction at the midpoint of the SVT. Computer modeling studies do show, however, that chimpanzees have the anatomy to produce nasalized vowels like [I], [ae], and [e] and consonants like [t], [d], [b], and [p] (Lieberman, 1989).

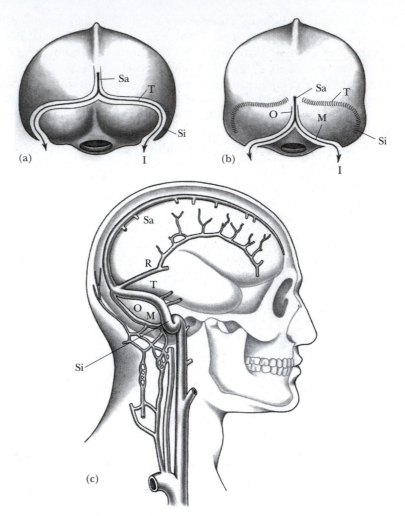

Fig. 8.4.   Posterior views of typical cranial venous sinus systems in (a) gracile australopiths and modern humans and (b) robust australopiths and the Hadar hominins. In (a), blood flows from the superior sagittal sinus (*Sa*) to the transverse (*T*)-sigmoid (*Si*) sinuses and then exits the cranium via the internal jugular veins (*I*). In (b), this transverse-sigmoid system is reduced or missing. Instead, a large portion of blood is drained through the occipital (*O*)-marginal (*M*) sinus system to the vertebral plexus of veins that are near the foramen magnum. The O-M sinus can also deliver blood to the internal jugular vein, depending on postural and respiratory constraints. (c) Venous sinuses and emissary veins. Emissary veins traverse the cranium and communicate with the vertebral plexus of veins around the foramen magnum. *R*, rectus or straight sinus. (From Falk, 1990; Falk and Conroy, 1983.)

Taxon	n	Mean (cm³)	95% Confidence Limits (to nearest cm³)
A. afarensis	3	?413.5	352 – ?500
A. africanus	6	440.3	383 – 499
A. robustus	1	530.0	—
A. boisei	7	463.3	332 – 595
H. habilis	6	640.2	429 – 852
H. erectus erectus	7	895.6	667 – 1125
H. erectus pekinensis	5	1043.0	731 – 1355
H. erectus (Asia and Africa)	15	937.2	647 – 1228
H. sapiens soloensis	5	1151.4	896 – 1407

Fig. 8.5. Endocranial capacity estimates for various early hominin species. There is a 95% chance that the "true" endocranial mean value of each species falls within the interval denoted by the 95% confidence limits. n = sample size. (From Tobias, 1994.) More recent analyses show that 11 endocranial capacity estimates of robust australopiths (*A. robustus, A. aethiopicus, A. boisei*) average 450 cc and 7 endocranial capacity estimates for gracile australopiths (*A. africanus*) average 451 cc (Conroy et al., 1990, 1998; Falk et al., 2000).

Falk and Conroy, 1983; Falk et al., 1995; Spoor and Zonneveld, 1999; Tobias and Falk, 1988).[4]

Why such different cranial vascular patterns characterize gracile and robust australopiths is not intuitively obvious, but one intriguing theory is that the venous network pattern that ultimately emerged in both gracile australopiths and *Homo* acted as a radiator to help cool the heat-sensitive brain. This theory is based on the observation that under conditions of heat stress, or hyperthermia, in modern humans, cooler blood in the scalp flows *inward* through the cranium and toward the brain through tiny emissary and diploic veins. A corollary to this theory, then, is that the gracile vascular pattern of brain cooling released a thermal constraint in *Homo* that had previously kept brain size in check in earlier hominins (Fig. 8.5) (Falk, 1990, 1991a). Certainly the dense concentration of sweat glands in the face and scalp leaves little doubt that the head continues to function as a specialized evaporative cooling and heat-dissipating structure (Porter, 1993; Wheeler, 1994b). These and other thermoregulatory cooling mechanisms must have been critical to the emerging bipedal hominins who remain the only mammal capable of sustained running, with the possible exception of pronghorn antelopes and the modern horse.[5]

[4]The true situation is somewhat more complex in that some robust australopiths (e.g., KNM-ER 23000) and some gracile australopiths (e.g., Taung) have both types of vascular patterns (Brown et al., 1993).

[5]Modern hunter-gatherers like the Kalahari Bushmen and the Tarahumara of Mexico have been known to pursue animals for hours, even days.

BODY SIZE AND BRAIN SIZE

Early hominin body size assumes great importance in paleoanthropological research because of its relationship to a number of important life-history parameters, including brain size, feeding behavior, habitat preferences, and social behavior. How do paleoanthropologists determine australopith body size? One statistical method used by researchers is regression analysis, a statistical method that compares some osteological variable to body weight in modern animals to see how good a body weight predictor that variable might be when applied to the fossil record. Since in bipedal animals the body weight must be transmitted through the vertebral column, a good test might measure the cross-sectional area of several vertebrae as a predictor of body weight. Using a formula relating vertebral cross-sectional area to body weight in modern humans, the body weights of *A. africanus* and *A. robustus* were estimated to range from about 28 to 43 kg and from about 36 to 53 kg, respectively (McHenry, 1975, 1976). Different techniques give different results, and body weight estimates have ranged from about 30 to 80 kg for *A. afarensis*, about 33 to 67 kg for *A. africanus*, about 37 to 88 kg for *A. robustus*, and about 33 to 88 kg for *A. boisei* (Hartwig-Scherer, 1993; Jungers, 1988b; McHenry, 1988). Other estimates based on hindlimb joint size are given in Figure 6.2. Estimates of height can be determined using similar principles (McHenry, 1991a, 1992b, 1992a).

If these body weight estimates are reasonable, then EQs can be calculated for early hominins in exactly the same way as they are for nonhuman primates (Martin, 1981; Tobias, 1994). Relative brain size calculations are presented in Figures 6.2 and 8.1.

What can we conclude from these EQ data? An obvious difference between modern humans and apes is the relative and absolute size of the brain. In absolute terms, *Homo sapiens* has a cranial capacity about three times that of great apes. However, the EQ values reveal that modern humans have a brain size nearly six to seven times that expected of a similar size mammal living today, whereas australopiths and chimpanzees have a brain size only about two to three times that expected of a similar size mammal.

However, it is quite clear from the fossil record that brain expansion per se was not an early trend in human evolution, since brain size in some of the oldest australopiths, such as *A. afarensis*, was well within the range of extant apes (in both absolute and relative terms). In this regard, it is interesting to note that the pelvis of *A. afarensis* has a birth canal whose size and shape show little or no adaptations for passage of an enlarged fetal cranium, adaptations that so clearly dominate the form of the modern human pelvis (see below) (Lovejoy, 1981, 1988; Rosenberg, 1992). As we shall see in later chapters when we discuss the evolution of the genus *Homo*, it appears that marked expansion of the human brain took place only within the last 1–2 million years of human evolution (Fig. 8.5) (Conroy et al., 2000).

BIPEDAL LOCOMOTION: MORPHOLOGY AND BIOMECHANICAL PRINCIPLES

It is self-evident that at some early stage in human evolution a highly unique form of bipedal locomotion evolved from some type of quadrupedal locomotion. The exact type of locomotion employed by this quadrupedal ancestor is still open to debate. Was it like the knuckle-walking of the African ape, the fist-walking of the orangutan, more like the upright posture of the gibbon, or something altogether different (Begun, 1992; Richmond and Strait, 2000, 2001; Richmond et al., 2001; Tuttle, 1974, 1994)? No matter what type of quadrupedalism was practiced by these "prehominins," it is important to understand what morphological changes were necessary to change a quadruped into a biped (Fig. 8.6).

Box 8.1   Laetoli Footprints

From 1977 to 1979 at Laetoli, Tanzania, a team led by Mary Leakey uncovered the trails of four bipedal individuals that had been made in volcanic ashfalls about 3.6 mya. At site G there are two trails representing three individuals. A fourth individual was represented at site A, about 1.5 km from site G. While there is little doubt that the G trails were made by bipedal hominins, there is some question of whether trail A was made by a bear or some other animal. Remarkably, the feet that made the G trail seem indistinguishable from those of modern humans: The great toe, or hallux, was adducted, or aligned with, the lateral toes and left a deep impression in the ash that is typical of the final toeing-off before the swing phase seen in human bipedal walking; the four lateral toes were not particularly long and did not project beyond the level of the hallux; the foot was not "flat-footed" as in quadrupedal primates but had both medial longitudinal and transverse plantar arches. The foot impressions also indicate that the transfer of weight during the stride was fully human-like in that weight was initially borne by the heel and lateral sole of the foot, then shifted medially onto the ball of the foot and hallux before toe-off. It is interesting that it is difficult to reconcile the long, curved pedal phalanges evident in the *A. afarensis* foot bones from Hadar with the footprints found at Laetoli (unfortunately, no foot bones have yet been found at Laetoli). Based on comparisons of foot size and height in modern humans, the individual designated as G1 was probably between 3 feet 8 inches and 4 feet 4 inches tall, individual G3 was probably between 4 feet 4 inches and 4 feet 11 inches tall, and the individual from site A was between 2 feet 11 inches and 3 feet 6 inches tall. (See pp. 205–07, above.)

As we have seen, the fossil evidence reveals significant postcranial adaptations to bipedalism very early on in human evolution (by at least about 4.0 mya, based on the evidence from the tibia of *A. anamensis*). This conclusion receives unequivocal support from the fossilized hominin footprints discovered at Laetoli dated to about 3.6 mya (Day, 1985; Feibel et al., 1996; Tuttle, 1985, 1987; White and Suwa, 1987). These adaptations to bipedalism occurred long before any significant brain expansion or evidence of stone tool making. In a metaphorical sense, then, humans evolved like a breech delivery—"feet first."

In this section we will consider some of the basic biomechanical principles of bipedal locomotion and examine the morphological evidence for bipedalism in australopiths; in the following section we will consider some of the behavioral pressures that may have contributed to the evolution of this unique mode of locomotion in our ancestors.

There are a number of basic requirements for effective and efficient bipedal posture and locomotion, two of the most important being (1) the body's center of gravity must be lower than it is in quadrupeds and balanced above the points of contact of the feet on the ground not only while standing but also during the "single support phase"—that is, the portion of the stride when only one limb is supporting the body; and (2) the lower limb must be able to move quickly through a relatively wide arc to provide propulsive force to the stride. We will shortly see that such adaptations were already under way in the Pliocene.

The ability of humans to maintain trunk balance derives in large part from the large muscles of the vertebral column (the erector spinae group), the abdominal muscles (external and internal obliques), and the muscles of the gluteal region, particularly the gluteus medius and minimus muscles. It is important to note that all these muscles attach to the pelvis, specifically to the iliac blades (Fig. 8.7). If one were to take an imaginary cross section through the pelvis, the resulting picture would

Fig. 8.6.   A number of anatomical changes are associated with bipedal walking and can be seen when comparing the human skeleton to that of apes.   (a) The head is more balanced on the vertebral column, and the foramen magnum through which the spinal cord connects with the brain is shifted forward. Because the head is better balanced, there is less need for massive neck muscles to keep it in position. (b) Humans have developed a more barrel-shaped rib cage. (c) Secondary curves of the cervical and lumbar vertebral column. (d) The pelvis has become rearranged so that the distance between the sacroiliac joint and the hip joint has been reduced and the iliac blades run in a more sagittal direction. (e) The legs are longer than the arms and constitute a greater proportion of body weight, thus lowering the center of gravity. Numbers indicate percentage of total body weight represented by each body segment. (f) The knee is brought medially well under the body and closer to the line of action of the body weight. (g) The big toe (hallux) is not opposed to the other toes, so the foot has lost its grasping function. (From Martin, 1992b.)

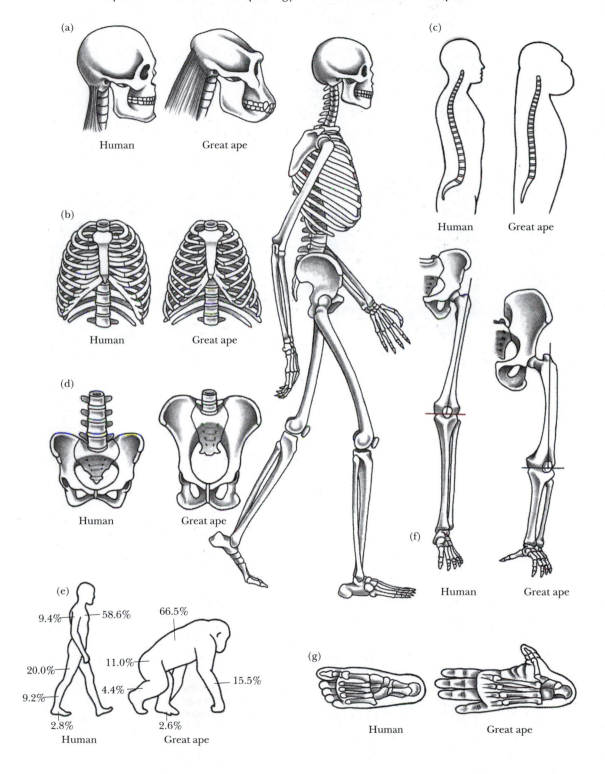

(a) Human   Great ape

(b) Human   Great ape

(c) Human   Great ape

(d) Human   Great ape

(e)
9.4%   58.6%   66.5%
20.0%   11.0%
9.2%   4.4%   15.5%
2.8%   2.6%
Human   Great ape

(f) Human   Great ape

(g) Human   Great ape

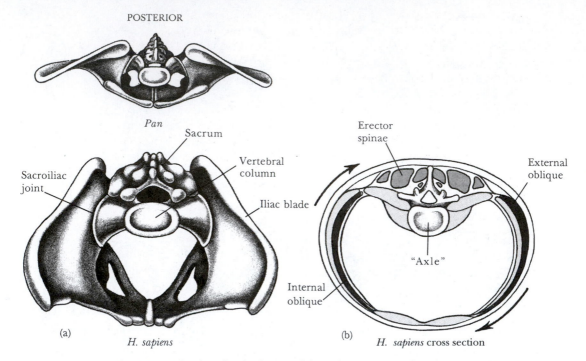

Fig. 8.7. Wheel-and-axle design of the pelvic region in hominins. (a) Overhead view of chimpanzee and human pelves. In chimpanzees the external surfaces of the ilia face dorsally (backward), whereas in modern humans they face laterally and "wrap around" the vertebral column, resulting in a more wheel-like morphology for muscle attachment. (b) Cross section of the human trunk shown at about the first lumbar vertebra. The force of the erector spinae is applied directly to the vertebral column ("axle") and the force of the oblique abdominal muscles is applied to the ilia ("wheel").

look something like a steering wheel and column, the column being the vertebral column at the center and the steering wheel being the iliac blades at the periphery. If the hip bones are twisted like a steering wheel, the vertebral column rotates around its axis as well.

A wheel-and-axle is a simple machine in a class with levers, pulleys, and inclined planes. The gluteal and abdominal muscles act on the wheel (the ilium) and the erector spinae group acts directly on the axle (the vertebral column). From simple physics, it is known that the leverage of the forces acting on the wheel (gluteal and abdominal muscles) will be greater the farther their line of force is from the center of rotation (the axle, or vertebral column). Thus a clear adaptation to improved stability in both lateral and front-to-back directions is to "wrap" the ilium around the vertebral column at an ever increasing distance.

If we compare the pelvis of modern humans and apes, this is exactly what we see (Fig. 8.8). The ape ilium is rather long and narrow, and the iliac blades flare out to the sides so that their flat inner surfaces face more anteriorly. Humans, on the other hand, have short, broad ilia that curve around the vertebral column so that their flat inner surfaces face more medially.

The most critical muscles for lateral stability in bipedal walking are the lesser gluteal muscles (gluteus medius and minimus) that run from the lateral surface of the ilium to the greater trochanter of the femur (Fig. 8.8a and b). Their attachments to the femur allow them to function as abductors of the lower limb. Every time a bipedal hominin lifts a foot off the ground to take a step, it teeters on the verge of disaster. The gluteal abductors on the opposite side must contract to hold the hip steady otherwise the hip would collapse to the unsupported side during each stride and walking would require lurching over sideways (i.e., laterally bending the trunk) to maintain the center of gravity over the leg that is on the ground. This is the type of gait seen today in humans with paralysis of these muscles or with dislocated hips. It is also the type of gait typically seen in apes when they walk bipedally because their lesser gluteal muscles are positioned to act not as effective hip abductors but rather as extensors and medial rotators of the hip (Stern and Susman, 1981; Tardieu, 1991).

During an individual's lifetime bones will remodel themselves in response to biomechanical stresses passing through them. The ilium is no exception and will come to reflect the large stresses generated by body weight that are counterbalanced by the lesser gluteal muscles. This stress results in the formation of an iliac pillar, a supporting bony buttress in the form of a thickened outer table of bone along the ilium between the iliac crest and the acetabulum (hip socket). The presence of this pillar is important osteological evidence of the efficient lateral balance control mechanism required by bipedalism (Macchiarelli et al., 1999). In another bony adaptation to bipedalism, the ilium becomes broader from front to back in order to increase the leverage of hip flexors and extensors around the hip joint. These morphological changes result in the development of a sciatic notch and prominent anterior and posterior iliac spines (Fig. 8.8d).

Another important aspect of balance control in humans is that the body's center of gravity is closer to the hip joints than it is in quadrupeds (Tardieu et al., 1993). The human pelvis accomplishes this in several ways: (1) by reducing the overall height of the ilium; (2) by moving the part of the ilium that articulates with the sacrum, the sacroiliac joint or auricular surface, closer to the hip joints; (3) by increasing the relative size of the lower limbs; and (4) by the development of a lumbar curve, or lordosis, that effectively brings the upper portion of the trunk back over the pelvis without blocking the birth canal (Kummer, 1991).

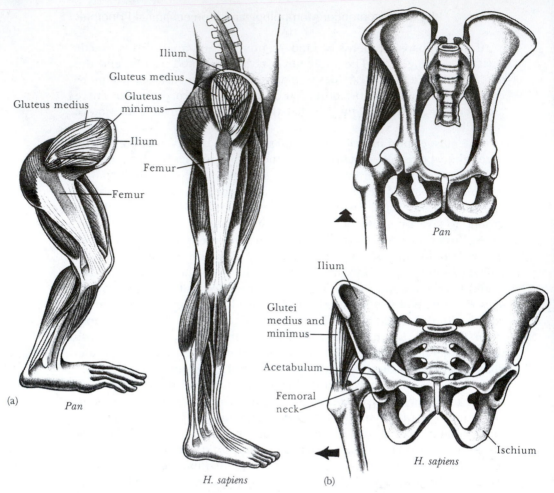

Fig. 8.8. Muscle configuration in the pelvic region of apes and humans. (a) Lateral and (b) frontal views of the gluteal muscles in *H. sapiens* and *Pan*. In chimpanzees, the gluteus medius and minimus are extensors and medial rotators of the hip. In humans, these muscles are critical for maintaining lateral stability during walking: The abductors on the side of the body supporting the body during a stride contract to prevent the hip joint from collapsing to the opposite (unsupported) side. (c) During walking and running, the force of body weight times the distance from its line of action to the center of the hip joint must be balanced by the abductor muscle force times its distance from the center of the hip joint. Making the femoral neck longer and/or the distance between the hip joints shorter improves the mechanical advantage of the abductor muscles. But narrowing the distance between the hip joints decreases the diameter of the birth canal (dashed lines). *Ab*, line of action of the abductor muscles (gluteus medius and minimus). (From Lovejoy, 1988; Walker, 1993.) (d) Comparison of the right hip bone in chimpanzees and humans. In response to increased stresses passing through the bipedal hip joint, the human pelvis has developed a prominent iliac pillar and anterior and posterior spines not evident in the chimpanzee. In addition, the human ilium is shorter to help lower the center of gravity, and wider, to enlarge the attachment area of flexor and extensor muscles of the hip. This alteration in shape results in a distinctive sciatic notch. (Redrawn from Jolly and Plog, 1986.)

250

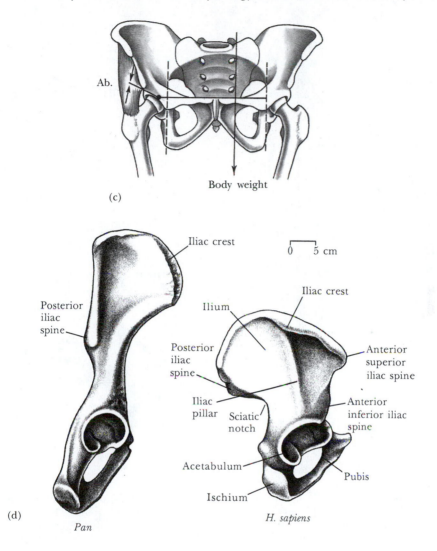

Ab.

Body weight

(c)

Iliac crest

0 5 cm

Iliac crest

Posterior
iliac
spine

Ilium

Anterior
superior
iliac spine

Posterior
iliac
spine

Iliac
pillar   Sciatic
notch

Anterior
inferior iliac
spine

Acetabulum

Pubis

Ischium

(d)

Pan

H. sapiens

In apes that try to walk or stand bipedally, the center of gravity is well forward of the hip joint (Fig. 8.9a). For this reason, ape bipedality is very inefficient, because the natural tendency for the body to fall forward over the hip joints has to be resisted by powerful muscular activity. In humans, the center of gravity has shifted downward and backward relative to overall height so that it is slightly above and behind the hip joint (Fig. 8.9b). In fact, there is even a slight tendency for the human trunk to fall backward over the hip joint in erect posture, a tendency easily resisted by the **iliofemoral ligament,** which runs from the anterior inferior spine of the ilium to the proximal femur (Fig. 8.9c). Thus humans expend little muscular energy in maintaining an erect posture.

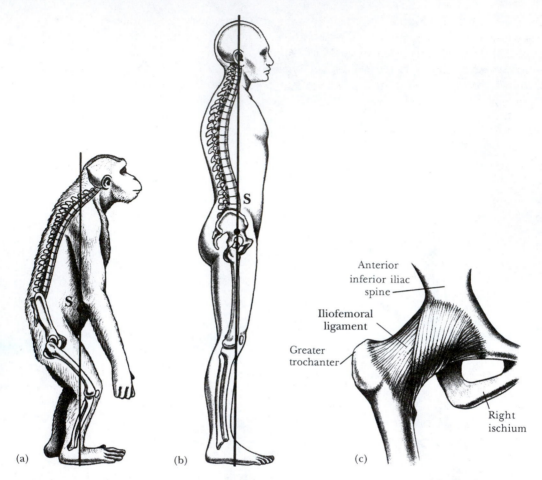

Fig. 8.9.   (a) Chimpanzee and (b) modern human in a bipedal posture. Note that in the upright human the line of the center of gravity falls very close to the hip, knee, and ankle joints whereas it is far forward of the hip joint in the chimpanzee. *S,* center of gravity. (From Kummer, 1991.) (c) Human hip joint seen from the front. Tension in the iliofemoral ligament helps keep the trunk from falling backward when standing upright.

Another general principle of mammalian morphology (including humans) is that larger animals tend to support their body weight on less bent limbs than smaller mammals do. This shift in posture seen in bipeds further decreases the magnitude of muscle forces needed to support the animal while standing or walking (Biewener, 1990).

With the assumption of erect posture, more body weight must be supported and propelled by the hindlimbs, increasing the stresses on both the pelvic and the hindlimb joints. In bipeds, the lower limbs account for less than one-third of the total body weight and must alone carry the remaining two-thirds. As a percentage of total body weight, the upper limbs of humans are only 60% as heavy as those of chimpanzees, whereas the lower limbs are nearly twice as heavy (Zihlman and Brunker, 1979). This redistribution of body weight contributes to a more stable posture because it shifts the center of gravity lower in the pelvis (Fig. 8.6).

Origins of Bipedalism: The Fossil Evidence

Precise information about the morphology and body proportions of early hominins is crucial for accurate functional and phylogenetic interpretations of early human evolution. We shall now examine some early hominin features that have a bearing on their mode of locomotion. Unfortunately, lower limb specimens associated with the *Ar. ramidus* discoveries have yet to be fully analyzed and published. Therefore, the partial skeleton of *A. afarensis* from Hadar ("Lucy") still provides the best information regarding body size, limb proportions, and skeletal allometry in ancestral hominins predating about 3 mya (Figs. 7.2, 7.13, and 7.14).

Locomotor Adaptations in *A. afarensis*

By using allometric relationships between limb lengths and body weights in monkeys and apes for comparison, it has been shown that the limb proportions of *A. afarensis* (Lucy) are unique among hominoids. *A. afarensis* had already attained forelimb proportions similar to those of modern humans but had hindlimbs that were relatively much shorter. Lucy's very short hindlimbs (particularly the femur) are proportioned much like those of small-bodied African apes and outside the known human range. By contrast, relative humerus length in relation to body size is similar to that seen in modern human pygmies. A similar combination of relative limb lengths appears to exist in the larger individuals of *A. afarensis* and possibly other gracile australopiths as well. Clearly, relative and absolute hindlimb elongation represents one of the striking evolutionary changes in later human evolution and first appears in material associated with *A. garhi* about 2.5 mya (Asfaw et al., 1999). The body proportions of Lucy are not incompatible with bipedal locomotion but her locomotion was clearly not identical to the bipedal gait of modern humans. Reduced relative stride length in *A. afarensis* probably implies both greater relative energy cost and relatively lower peak velocities of bipedal locomotion in *A. afarensis* than in later hominins (Jungers, 1982, 1988a; Jungers and Stern, 1983).

    As noted in the previous chapter, the partial skeleton of *A. garhi* shows postcranial proportions unique for early hominins. Its human-like humeral to femoral ratio marks the earliest appearance of femoral elongation characteristic of later *Homo* seen in the hominin fossil record and in this regard is significantly different from the same proportions in OH 62 (*H. habilis*) or AL 288-1 (*A. afarensis*). However, its human-like humeral to femoral ratio is combined with an ape-like brachial index (Richmond et al., 2002). A more modern brachial index is not seen until the appearance of early *H. erectus* (KNM-WT 15000) (Walker and Leakey, 1993).

It has been argued that the upper limb of *A. afarensis* retained a number of features indicating an adaptation to, or retention of, movement in the trees (Heinrich et al., 1993; Marzke, 1983; Senut, 1989; Senut and Tardieu, 1985; Stern and Susman, 1983; Susman et al., 1984; Tuttle, 1981). For instance, several of the wrist and metacarpal bones are markedly chimpanzee-like, and the finger and toe bones (phalanges) are slender and curved as in apes (Paciulli, 1995; Smith, 1995). In general, arboreal primates have greater phalangeal curvature than their more terrestrial relatives (Corkern, 1997). These features of the hand (and foot) suggest well-developed grasping capabilities compatible with suspensory behavior. It is also particularly significant that some features of the wrist (particularly the distal radius) in both *A. anamensis* and *A. afarensis* purportedly show some vestiges of knuckle-walking ancestry, suggesting that knuckle-walking may be a derived feature of the African ape/human clade (Corruccini, 1978; Richmond and Strait, 2000, 2001).[6] It is important to emphasize that this does *not* mean, however, that *A. afarensis* and *A. anamensis* (and by extension other australopiths) were themselves knuckle-walkers—they almost certainly were not—only that they were descendant from ancestors that were.

The hand of *A. africanus*, known from specimens at Sterkfontein, seems similar to that of *A. afarensis*, and both were presumably well adapted for powerful manual tasks, including gripping sticks and stones for vigorous pounding and throwing (Marzke, 1983, 1997; Marzke and Shackley, 1986; Ricklan, 1987). The hands do not, however, show all the morphological features associated with human-like precision grasping (Susman, 1994). What are some of these morphological adaptations?

First, some definitions. The term *precision grip* refers to any grip that involves the thumb and one or more fingers with or without the palm serving passively as a prop; the term *power grip* refers to a grip in which objects are strongly squeezed by the fingers alone or squeezed by the fingers, thumb, and actively by the palm.

There are at least eight morphological features that would predict precision grip capabilities in early hominins and that differentiate them from nonhuman primates (Marzke, 1997): (1) broad ungual tufts on the distal phalanges (the tufts support pads whose large surfaces distribute pressure during forceful grasping and whose mobility allows accommodation of the pads to uneven surfaces as well as fine-tuning in the positioning of objects),

---

[6]For a different opinion, see Dainton and Macho (1999) and Lovejoy et al. (2001).

(2) a long thumb relative to the length of the fingers, (3) proportionately well-developed intrinsic thumb muscles, (4) proportionately large flexor pollicis longus muscle, (5) radial orientation of the third metacarpal head, (6) marked asymmetry of the second metacarpal and fifth metacarpal heads, (7) orientation of the second metacarpal joints with the trapezium and capitate away from the sagittal plane, and (8) spines on the ungual shafts. Of these eight features, *A. afarensis* (Hadar) shares features 2, 6, and 7; *A. africanus* (Sterkfontein) shares features 1, 4, and 8; *A. robustus* (or early *Homo*) (Swartkrans) shares features 1 and 4; and early *Homo* (Olduvai) shares feature 1.[7]

Thumb/hand proportions in *A. afarensis* are higher than in chimpanzees (i.e., the thumb is relatively longer) and much closer to values found in humans (Alba et al., 2003). This also seems to be the case with StW 573, the new skeleton from Sterkfontein member 2 (Clarke, 1999). This would suggest that the thumbs of *A. afarensis,* and presumably *A. africanus,* if that is what StW 573 turns out to be, were probably long enough to permit pad-to-pad precision grips (note, however, that the relative elongation of the thumb in *A. afarensis* and later hominins is due more to relative shortening of the fingers than to elongation of the thumb). Since both of these taxa predate the first evidence of stone tool making, it seems clear that the human-like proportions of the hand did not first evolve for stone-tool-making capabilities but rather for other manipulative and tool-making behaviors involving nonlithic material.

Two stages in the evolution of hominin tool-using behavior can be defined (Marzke, 1997). The first corresponds to the use and modification of natural objects with hands primarily adapted for locomotion as seen today in chimpanzees. This stage would have been present in the common ancestor of chimpanzees and humans. The second stage shows evidence of increasing use of natural objects of varying sizes and shapes as tools. This tool use would be facilitated by the evolution of new and distinctively human morphological features, like those noted above, and would also include the appearance of more human-like thumb/hand proportions. This stage would characterize the hand of *A. afarensis.*

Other upper limb characteristics are more equivocal as to whether some arboreal adaptations were retained in early hominins like *A. afarensis.* For instance, it was initially suggested that the **glenoid cavity,** the socket on the scapula that articulates with the head of the humerus, is directed in a more cranial orientation than is typical in modern humans, suggesting use of the upper limb in elevated positions as is common during climbing behavior (Stern and Susman, 1983; Susman et al., 1984). However, a more recent study using larger human and ape samples and more appropriate statistical techniques concludes that this feature of the

[7]But see Susman (1998) for a critique.

scapula is not tightly correlated with locomotor behavior and, therefore, cannot be reliably used as a morphological signal of arboreal behavior in small-bodied hominoids (including Lucy). In fact, this scapular feature in Lucy looks exactly like that predicted for a small modern human having the same body size as Lucy (Inouye and Shea, 1997).

When we examine the pelvis and lower limb, *A. afarensis* clearly shows a mosaic of human-like and ape-like features (Fig. 7.14). Some of the distinctly human-like features of the pelvis include: (1) a low, broad ilium with a deep sciatic notch; (2) a prominent anterior inferior iliac spine for attachment of the rectus femoris muscle, a powerful flexor of the hip; and (3) an ischial surface for the origin of the hamstring muscles that is divided by a vertical ridge into lateral and medial portions (*A. afarensis* had a relatively long hamstring moment arm but one that did not fall outside the range of human variation).

There are also a number of pelvic and lower limb features that differ somewhat from those seen in modern humans (Berge, 1994; Lovejoy, 1975; Stern and Susman, 1983; Susman et al., 1984). For example, the articular surface of the acetabulum lacks the large contribution from the pubic bone that characterizes modern humans (Fig. 8.8). Functionally, this feature suggests the absence of full, human-like extension at the hip joint during bipedal locomotion. Other nonhuman-like features of the pelvis and lower extremity include: (1) the extreme width of the pelvis at the level of the iliac crests and at the level of the hip sockets (interacetabular width), (2) the more lateral orientation of the iliac crests, and (3) the relatively shorter femur with a long femoral neck.

Lucy's axial skeleton is represented by portions of seven thoracic vertebrae, two lumber vertebrae, and a sacrum. The ventral concavity of the sacrum is only slightly developed, and the first segment of the sacrum lacks well-developed transverse processes. These features suggest poorly developed sacrotuberous ligaments, which bind together the sacrum and the ischium. This implies a less well developed mechanism for sacroiliac stabilization when the trunk is in an erect position. The cross-sectional area of the lower back vertebrae, particularly the lumbar and sacral vertebrae, are also extraordinarily small, suggesting that they were not adapted for the bearing of heavy loads associated with full upright postures (Fig. 8.10a) (McHenry, 1991b). It is interesting that the ventral surfaces of some lumbar vertebrae in both *A. afarensis* and *A. africanus* (e.g., Stw H8) show osteophytic lesions normally associated with either arthritis or mechanical trauma. *A. afarensis* clearly had a significant lumbar lordosis, as evidenced by the wide lumbar interfacet distance between the presumed second lumbar and first sacral vertebra. A lumbar lordosis is an unequivocal indicator of habitual upright postures and even occurs, although to a much lesser degree, in modern nonhuman primates trained to walk bipedally (Ward, 2002).

In *A. afarensis,* the orientation of the iliac blades is similar to that seen in chimpanzees—that is, their external surfaces face more posterolaterally than laterally (Schmid, 1991; Stern and Susman, 1991). The ilium also shows the typical australopith trait of a laterally flaring anterior superior iliac spine far removed from the anterior inferior iliac spine. Taken as a whole, the pelvis of *A. afarensis* reveals that the "wrapping" of the iliac blades around the vertebral column had already begun but had not yet reached the degree of curvature seen in modern humans (Fig. 8.10b–e). Some workers take this, and the more anterior placement of the iliac pillar, to mean that the mechanism of lateral pelvic balance during bipedalism in *A. afarensis* was more similar to apes than to humans (i.e., a more bent-knee gait). These views must be tempered, however, with the knowledge that other, more human-like, pelvic features in *A. afarensis* (and also in *A. africanus* (Sts 14), *A. robustus* (SK 3155 and SK 50), and *Homo erectus* (KNM-WT 15000)—such as the strong development and dorsal reflection of the posterosuperior iliac spine for origin of the erector spinae muscles—indicate that the functional demands of these muscles to resist forward flexion of the trunk were already well developed (Sanders, 1998).

One remarkable feature of Lucy's pelvis is the extreme width of her pelvic inlet, particularly considering her small body size (Fig. 8.10e). The functional significance of this feature is that in combination with horizontal rotation of the pelvis it minimizes unwanted vertical displacement of the center of mass during bipedal walking. Later humans reduced this unwanted vertical displacement another way—by elongating the lower limbs (Fig. 8.11). This latter "solution" may have been partly responsible for the reduction of inlet width in later hominins. However, while pelvic rotation may increase stride length at walking speeds, it apparently does not do so at running speeds. Pelvic rotation seems to contribute relatively little to running stride length but does add to walking stride length in subjects with wide pelves (Cartmill and Schmitt, 1997). In the words of one researcher, "Lucy's pelvis . . . does not represent simply an intermediate stage between a chimpanzee-like hominoid and *Homo sapiens* , nor is it essentially a modern human pelvis. Although clearly bipedal and highly terrestrial, Lucy evidently achieved this mode of locomotion through a solution all her own" (Rak, 1991).

Fossil evidence also indicates that the toe bones of *A. afarensis* from Hadar are both longer and much more curved than those of modern humans (Fig. 8.12). For some, this again reinforces evidence for some arboreal activity in *A. afarensis,* since it is easier for feet to grip tree branches with long, curved digits. However, this neglects the obvious point that it is not so easy for feet to grip tree branches without an opposable big toe! Consider this equally valid alternate view: Given the loss of the opposable big toe in *A. afarensis,* which mitigates against climbing, any climbing adaptations in Lucy's forelimb should be *more* accentuated than in chimpanzees,

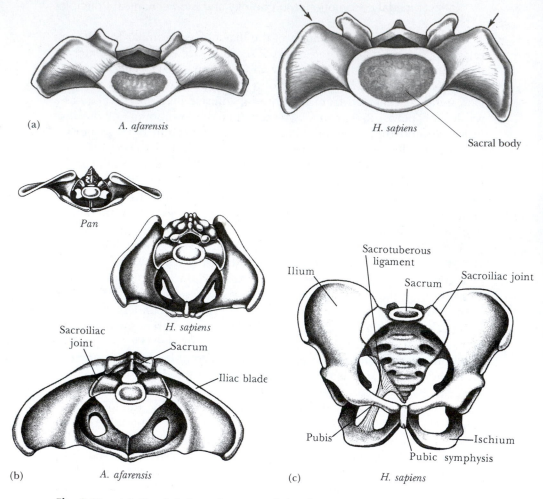

(a) *A. afarensis*

H. sapiens

Sacral body

Pan

H. sapiens

Sacroiliac
joint

Sacrum

Iliac blade

(b) *A. afarensis*

Ilium

Sacrotuberous
ligament

Sacrum

Sacroiliac joint

Pubis

Ischium

Pubic symphysis

(c) *H. sapiens*

Fig. 8.10. (a) Cranial view of sacrum of *A. afarensis* (left) and modern human (right). In the human note the lateral expanse of the upper lateral angles (*arrows*) to which powerful sacroiliac ligaments attach. This lateral expansion is greatly reduced in *A. afarensis*. Also note the much larger cross-sectional area of the body of the sacrum in humans. (b)–(e) Comparison of the pelves in *A. afarensis*, *Pan*, and *H. sapiens*. (b) Cranial view. Note that the iliac blades in *A. afarensis* are beginning to curve around the vertebral column, as in the modern human, but the blade angle is still closer to that seen in the chimpanzee. (c) Anterior view of the human pelvis. Strong sacrotuberous ligaments in the human (shown on one side only) help stabilize the sacroiliac joint when the body is erect. Features of the sacrum in *A. afarensis* suggest it lacked well-developed sacrotuberous ligaments. (d) Anterior view of the full pelvis in *A. afarensis* with smaller views of *Pan* and *H. sapiens* for comparison. The gluteal muscles are acting as partial abductors in *A. afarensis*, providing some lateral stability. Note, however, that the ball-and-socket joint in the australopith is shallower than in the human, due to less contribution to the acetabulum from the pubis. (e) *A. afarensis* pelvis (Lucy) superimposed on a pelvis of a modern *H. sapiens* female, both scaled to body weight. Note that although the anteroposterior length of the two pelvic inlets is similar, the width of Lucy's pelvic inlet is considerably greater. (From Rak, 1991; Stern and Susman, 1983.)

258

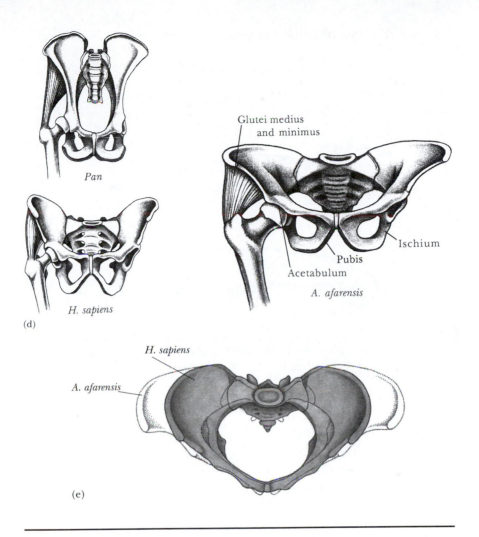

Glutei medius
and minimus

Ischium

Pubis

Acetabulum

A. afarensis

Pan

H. sapiens

(d)

H. sapiens

A. afarensis

(e)

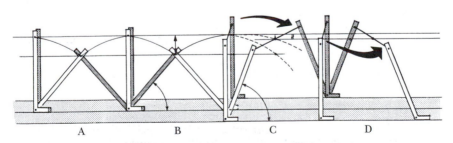

A   B   C   D

Fig. 8.11. Two models of a biped walking the same step length. A–B represent a condition in which the hip joints are separated by a narrow pelvis, and C–D represent an individual with a wide pelvis (like Lucy). Note that the individual with the wide pelvis (C–D) shows less vertical displacement of the hip joint for the same stride length. Another way to achieve the same result would be to lengthen the legs. (From Rak, 1991.)

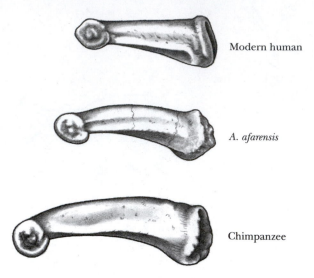

Modern human

A. afarensis

Chimpanzee

Fig. 8.12.   Lateral view of proximal pedal (toe) phalanges from the third toe.   Similarities between *A. afarensis* (AL 333-115H) and the chimpanzee are seen in their curvatures and overall lateral profiles. The same phalanx in the human has a thick base relative to a thin distal portion. (From Susman et al., 1984.)

not *less*, as they appear to be, for the simple reason that possession of slightly curved fingers and toes by themselves are inadequate adaptations for climbing in an animal lacking opposable, grasping big toes. In other words, without the opposable big toe, the lower limbs of *A. afarensis* might have been nothing but dead weight in such arboreal activities. Perhaps they had curved toes for the same reason they had five toes—these are simply primitive features carried over with no particular survival value, positive or negative, from more "ape-like" ancestors. Interpreting why australopiths retained many such "primitive" postcranial features is really at the heart of the debate of whether or not australopiths retained significant arboreal capabilities (Ward, 2002). And there is one other little problem: Some workers have suggested that the *A. afarensis* feet typified by the remains at Hadar could not have made the very human-like Laetoli footprints (Tuttle, 1985, 1994; Tuttle et al., 1991).

One further piece of evidence used to argue that *A. afarensis* was still a capable climber comes from analyses of the joints of the metatarsals and phalanges. The orientation of these joints indicates that the toes of *A. afarensis* were still capable of significant degrees of plantarflexion, an adaptation for arboreal locomotion (Duncan et al., 1994). In addition, overall proportions of the *A. afarensis* foot bones may suggest some arboreality. For example, the tarsus makes up 51% of foot length in modern humans, 35% in *Pan* and 38% in *A. afarensis*. In the same groups, the metatarsus makes up 26%, 29%, and 39%, respectively, of foot length, and the phalanges 23%, 36%, and 30%, respectively, of foot length. These same approximate percentages are observed in the Laetoli footprints (Deloison, 1997).

A comparison of the smaller, presumably female, specimens to the larger, presumably male, specimens suggests sexual differences in locomotor behavior linked to marked size dimorphism. This has led some to hypothesize that the males were probably less arboreal than females and engaged more frequently in terrestrial bipedalism (Stern and Susman, 1983).

A very different viewpoint about *A. afarensis* locomotion is expressed by a number of other researchers who consider it, and by extension other australopiths, to be fully adapted bipeds (Langdon et al., 1991; Latimer, 1991; Latimer and Lovejoy, 1989, 1990a, 1990b; Lovejoy, 1988; Ohman et al., 1997). They identify a number of adaptations to human-like bipedalism found in *A. afarensis:* (1) a knee positioned close to the midline to minimize side-to-side shifting of the center of gravity during locomotion; (2) raised lateral lip of the patellar groove to prevent lateral displacement of the kneecap, or patella, during extension of the leg; (3) a well-developed iliofemoral ligament, which, as we have noted, helps keep the erect trunk from falling backward; (4) a long abductor muscle moment arm for the gluteus medius and minimus for lateral stability in the hip joint during walking; (5) a posterior position of the gluteus maximus, which acts as an extensor of the lower limb; (6) the uniquely hominid-like distribution of cortical bone in the femoral neck; and (7) most significant, the lack of an opposable, grasping big toe or hallux.

While almost all researchers agree that *A. afarensis* was bipedal to a significant degree, the question still remains: did it walk erect or with a more bent-knee, bent-hip gait? Was its bipedal gait somehow less efficient than that of modern humans?

Dynamic modeling techniques provide several insights regarding these questions. First, Lucy's proportions are incompatible with the kinematics of chimpanzee bipedalism. They are, however, compatible with both the kinematics of either an erect or a bent-knee, bent-hip human gait. However, in a bent-knee, bent-hip gait, neither the ankle nor the knee joint could have contributed substantial mechanical work for propelling the body forward, therefore making it unlikely that Lucy would have walked with this type of gait. Second, although Lucy's shorter legs (compared to modern humans) may have resulted in less energy expenditure at walking speeds than comparable energy expenditures in modern humans, this energetic advantage would come at a price: Her preferred transition speeds from walking to running would have been lower, possibly resulting in smaller daily ranges and natural walking velocities than in longer-legged modern humans (Crompton et al., 1998; Kramer and Eck, 2000; Wang et al., 2003).

In the midst of these competing schools of thought, what can we conclude about the locomotor proclivities of *A. afarensis*? We see that Lucy is fundamentally different from apes only in features directly related to bipedalism. We also see more ape-like retentions in Lucy than in us. But it would be wrong to simply consider Lucy as half-ape, half-human, since she bears characteristics that are not present in apes or in humans. The majority of the morphological changes we do see in Lucy are in the direction of bipedalism. If it is true that "natural selection, when viewed within the animal's historical context, can be said to have a direction vector" (Latimer, 1991), then we must conclude that such a direction vector in *A. afarensis* was clearly pointing toward bipedalism. Figure 7.14 summarizes some of the important postcranial features of *A. afarensis*.

LOCOMOTOR ADAPTATIONS IN OTHER AUSTRALOPITHS

A good deal of postcranial material of *A. africanus* is available from which to extrapolate locomotor behavior in that species, including two partial skeletons from Sterkfontein (Stw 431 and Sts 14) (Robinson, 1972). With few exceptions, the postcranial skeleton seems generally similar to that described above for *A. afarensis*, although important differences may exist between these two species in terms of some body proportions (see below and Figure 7.1).

The most complete *A. africanus* specimen yet excavated and fully published, the adult female from Sterkfontein (Sts 14), consists of much of the vertebral column (including the lumbar vertebrae and sacrum), a few ribs, almost the complete pelvis, and much of the femur (Fig. 7.1d). The ribs; vertebral bodies; and the femoral head, neck, and shaft are all slender, indicative of a small, gracile animal. The stature of this individual is estimated at 122–137 cm (4 ft. to 4 ft. 6 in.) (Robinson, 1972). Robinson initially described the presence of six lumbar vertebrae in Sts 14 (and in another *A. africanus* specimen, Stw 431). This would be unusual in that modern humans normally have five lumbar vertebrae and African apes no more than three or four (Schultz, 1968). More recent studies suggest, however, that both of these australopith specimens most likely have five lumbar vertebrae as in modern humans (Häusler et al., 2002; Toussaint et al., 2003).[8] Another recently described *A. africanus* specimen, Stw H8/H41, preserves two thoracic and four lumbar vertebrae.

---

[8]The *Homo erectus* skeleton from West Lake Turkana (KNM-WT 15000) has also been described as having six lumbar vertebrae (Latimer and Ward, 1993); but again, this is questionable (Häusler et al., 2002).

Although the morphology of the australopith vertebrae shows some signs of adaptation to the weight-bearing demands associated with terrestrial bipedality, for example the increase in size from proximal to distal vertebral segments (Ward and Latimer, 1991), the cross-sectional areas of the lower back vertebral bodies (lumbar and sacral) are still very small. This is an important point. Human vertebrae are characterized by several unique adaptations to bipedal posture: (1) the surface areas of the lower lumbar vertebral bodies and cross-sectional areas of their pedicles are large relative to body size, (2) the anterior portion of the vertebral arch is large relative to body size, and (3) the lower lumbar pedicles are wider relative to length and to body size than are those of nonhuman quadrupedal primates. It is interesting that the last lumbar vertebra of Sts 14 does not exhibit any of these human-like vertebral features—its pedicles and body surface areas are relatively small and its pedicles are relatively short (Shapiro, 1993). However, while still not fully modern in appearance, it is important to emphasize that the lumbar vertebrae of *A. africanus* show no specific adaptations toward monkey-like pronograde quadrupedalism. In addition, there are no specific traits that can be associated directly, or exclusively, with modern ape-like climbing or suspensory behaviors. Instead, their morphology is compatible with a dominance of bipedal activity over other locomotor modes though perhaps of lesser structural soundness than is found in modern human vertebrae (Sanders, 1998).

Another interesting feature of the Sts 14 skeleton is the distribution of trabecular bone within the ilium. As previously noted, both the direction and the density of trabecular bone patterns are related to stresses passing through the ilium, and in humans this pattern clearly reflects stresses associated with bipedalism. The ilium of Sts 14 shares some features of trabecular pattern with those of modern humans and is quite different from the pattern seen in chimpanzee ilia (Macchiarelli et al., 1999).

All postcranial evidence from Sterkfontein and Makapansgat suggests that *A. africanus* was a gracile animal. However, on the basis of a recently described proximal femur from Makapansgat, it seems that the pattern of sexual dimorphism in *A. africanus* may be similar to that in *A. afarensis* (Reed et al., 1993). Estimated femur length from one individual (Sts 14) was initially suggested to be about the same relative to overall body length as that in modern humans. From this information it was concluded, probably erroneously (see below), that in *A. africanus* the lower limbs were about the same length relative to upper limbs as in modern humans (Robinson, 1972). If true, this would be in clear contrast to the proportions calculated for *A. afarensis*, with its relatively reduced lower limb length, and would presumably predate the evidence from *A. garhi* about when femoral elongation first appeared in the fossil record.

But it appears not to be true. Over the past few decades, a number of new postcranial remains of *A. africanus*, including a partial skeleton (Stw 431), have been recovered from member 4, Sterkfontein. Body proportions of this individual seem quite unlike those of earlier *Australopithecus* species like *A. afarensis* and *A. anamensis*. Specifically, forelimb joint sizes of StW 431 are in the range of modern humans weighing 41–62 kg, whereas hindlimb joint sizes are in the range of modern humans weighing 27–45 kg (in contrast, forelimb and hindlimb joint sizes of *A. afarensis* and *A. anamensis* more closely resemble the human pattern). If these body proportions are typical of *A. africanus*, they reveal a primitive pattern of joint size (and perhaps limb proportions) more typical of apes than humans. This is particularly interesting in light of the more ape-like limb proportions in the two known associated partial skeletons of *H. habilis* (OH 62 and KNM-ER 3735) and certainly complicates our understanding of early hominin evolution (McHenry and Berger, 1996).

The more ape-like body proportions of *A. africanus* compared to the more human-like *A. afarensis* proportions (deduced from joint sizes, not actual limb lengths) are just the opposite of what is inferred from the craniodental evidence. For example, in such craniodental features as reduced canines, larger brains, shortened faces, deeper temporomandibular joints, more bicuspid lower third premolars, and more vertical mandibular symphyses, *A. africanus* appears more *Homo*-like than *A. afarensis*. Thus we are left with the rather paradoxical situation in which forelimb to hindlimb joint sizes in the geologically older and more primitive (at least craniodentally) *A. afarensis* are within the range of modern *H. sapiens*, whereas the geologically younger and more craniodentally *Homo*-like *A. africanus* is more ape-like in these same joint size proportions. Did the *Homo*-like craniodental features in *A. africanus* evolve in parallel with the *Homo* lineage or did the *Homo*-like limb proportions in *A. afarensis* (and possibly *A. anamensis*) evolve in parallel with the *Homo* lineage? A great deal of homoplasy (parallel evolution) must have been involved in whichever scenario is chosen (McHenry and Berger, 1998a, 1998b).

The *A. africanus* pelvis, similar in many respects to that described for *A. afarensis*, is clearly approaching the modern human pelvis in terms of overall morphology and muscle attachment sites (Fig. 8.13) (Häusler and Berger, 2001). Moreover, *A. africanus* has been described as showing a well-developed, human-like lumbar curve, which suggests that the posture was more like that found in modern humans than in apes (Robinson, 1972). Another bipedal feature, the carrying angle of the femoral shaft, demonstrates that the knees, and therefore the feet, were close together during standing and walking, an important adaptation to minimize sway while striding.

In the mid-1990s four articulating hominin foot bones, tentatively assigned to *A. africanus*, were recovered from Sterkfontein member 2. Recent new dating techniques suggest that the bones may be about 4 million years old (Partridge et al., 2003). While the foot clearly belongs to a bipedal hominin, it has been described as having a medially divergent and strongly mobile hallux, as in apes (Clarke and Tobias, 1995). This, in conjunction

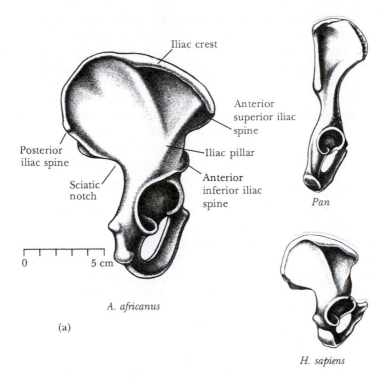

A. africanus

(a)

Pan

H. sapiens

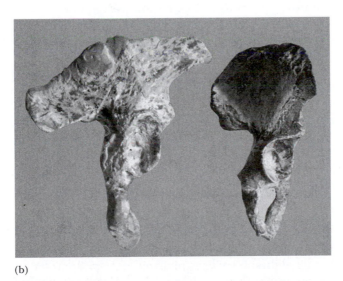

(b)

Fig. 8.13. Pelves of South African australopiths. (a) Hip bone in *A. africanus*; smaller views of *Pan* and *H. sapiens* are provided for comparison. (b) Lateral view of the right pelvis of *A. robustus* from Swartkrans (left) and *A. africanus* from Sterkfontein (right). Both pelves have broad, short ilia with well-developed sciatic notches. Scale about 33% actual size. (From Robinson, 1972.)

with a recently described chimpanzee-like *A. africanus* tibia from Sterkfontein member 4 reinforces the view that *A. africanus*, like *A. afarensis*, may have retained some degree of arboreal behavior as part of its total locomotor repertoire (Berger and Tobias, 1996). However, one must temper that conclusion by noting the locomotor proclivities of *A. afarensis*, as discussed above.

The postcranial evidence is less satisfactory for *A. robustus*. We know little about such features as lumbar curvature or body proportions for this species. Only a few isolated vertebrae, and one vertebral series (SKW 14002) consisting of four lumbar vertebrae, are known. However, we do know that the ilium shows some important adaptations to bipedalism, such as the reduction of iliac height and the development of an iliac pillar. It also appears that in some features *A. robustus* was simply a more robust and heavily built creature than *A. africanus* (Fig. 8.13), although, as noted earlier, body size apparently did not differ much between the two (in this regard, one *A. robustus* lumbar vertebra, SK 3981b, is said to fit very well on the lower end of the *A. africanus*, Stw-H8, lumbar vertebral series). As in all australopiths, the femoral neck is relatively long and the femoral head is small (Ruff et al., 1999). This suggests greater moment arms for the hip abductors (gluteus medius and minimus) and relatively less weight being borne directly on the femoral heads.

A complete metatarsal of the big toe attributed to *A. robustus* has been recovered from Swartkrans that has features suggesting human-like foot postures and ranges of extension. Examination of the toe joints suggests human-like toe-off, or stride, mechanisms. Most important, the great toe in *A. robustus* was a nongrasping structure and incapable of ape-like opposition.

Unlike the condition in *A. afarensis*, the broad apical tuft of the distal thumb phalanx is human-like, not ape-like. It has also been shown that the first metacarpal bone of the modern human thumb is characterized by a broad head in relation to its length, a feature found in *A. robustus*, *Homo erectus*, and Neandertals, but, interestingly enough, not in *A. afarensis* (Susman, 1988, 1989, 1993, 1994). This feature of the thumb may be correlated with tool-making abilities, and, if so, it is interesting to note that *A. afarensis* spans a time period (about 3.8–3.0 mya) that is devoid of any evidence of stone and bone tool making.

Based on relative apical tuft breadth and morphology of the flexor pollicis longus (FPL) insertion region, some have concluded that *A. robustus* and *H. habilis* were stone tool makers whereas *A. africanus* was not. However, the terminal thumb (pollex) phalanx of *A. africanus* (Stw 294) resembles that of modern humans, *A. robustus*, and *H. habilis* much more so than that of the African apes in having a markedly expanded apical tuft and well-defined FPL insertion. In addition, electromyographical studies show that there is no statistical difference between peak FPL activity in either tool making and tool using or during precision and power grasping.

Therefore, FPL muscle activity cannot be said to distinguish precision grasping per se. FPL muscle activity increases as resistance is applied to the thumb's volar pad during any type of grasping activity using the thumb such as during hammering, cutting, and stone-tool knapping behaviors. On the other hand, FPL activity appears minimal during fine manipulation of food items, making slender wooden probes, or when using these probes as tools. Since human-like pollical adaptations apparently developed before stone tool making appeared in the fossil record, it suggests that tool using, not necessarily tool making, may have been a critical factor in their development and that the FPL initially functioned to stabilize the terminal pollical phalanx during the frequent and forceful use of unmodified stones as tools (Hamrick et al., 1997, 1998).

Even less can be said about the postcranial adaptations of *A. boisei*. Few skeletal parts have been found and even fewer in association with teeth or crania—thus making attribution tentative at best. However, because *A. robustus* and *A. boisei* are judged to be so closely related, most workers assume similar postcranial adaptations in both species. Fortunately, a fragment of mandible and partial associated skeleton (KNM-ER 1500) has been identified as *A. boisei*, as have several other specimens from the Lake Turkana region (Grausz et al., 1988). The KNM-ER 1500 specimen reveals forelimbs that are relatively large and hindlimbs that are relatively small in comparison to modern humans and in overall limb proportions most closely resemble AL 288-1 (Lucy).

Based on the distribution of subchondral bone on the femoral head and/or acetabulum in *A. afarensis*, *A. africanus*, and *A. robustus*, all of these species had a preponderance of articular surface area on the anterior aspect of the femoral head, a morphology associated with moderate hip mobility and an adducted femur. In fact, the presence of a high femoral bicondylar angle suggests that walking with an adducted knee occurred very early in the life of all australopiths (Tardieu, 1999; Ward, 2002). In this they differ from the condition seen in chimpanzees in which the articular surface area is more uniformly distributed about the femoral head. With the exception of Lucy, the superior acetabular articular surface of these early hominin species was expanded, indicative of a greater habituation to the cranially directed forces generated by a bipedal gait (although even Lucy had an adducted hip and a limited range of abduction more similar to modern humans than to chimpanzees) (MacLatchy, 1996).

Another anatomical system that may reveal important clues about bipedal locomotion in australopiths is the inner ear, specifically the size and shape of the semicircular canals, which, together with their associated neurological structures, mediate perception of angular velocity and balance. The anterior and posterior canals in great apes are smaller than in modern humans, and this is presumably the primitive condition for this feature (Fig. 8.14). If so, the larger and characteristically shaped canals of modern humans must have been selected for during the course of the

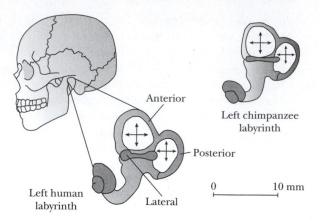

Fig. 8.14. Relative size of semicircular canals in the human and great apes. (From Shipman, 1994.)

transition from quadrupedalism to bipedalism and presumably in response to the need for fine neuromuscular control mechanisms of the musculoskeletal system, a crucial adaptation for habitual bipedal locomotion. What is particularly interesting is that the size and shape of the semicircular canals in both *A. africanus* and *A. robustus* are more great-ape-like than modern human-like,[9] and it is not until we reach the *Homo erectus* stage of human evolution that the semicircular canals take on an essentially modern human-like appearance (e.g., OH 9, Sangiran 2 and 4). This supports an interpretation drawn from the postcranial evidence that bipedal behavior of australopiths and (perhaps) early *Homo* was less specialized in terms of obligatory bipedalism than that of modern humans and that the locomotor repertoire of these hominins included a substantial nonbipedal, or arboreal, component (Spoor, 1993; Spoor et al., 1994).

What explains some of the morphological rearrangements of the pelvis observed during early hominin evolution? One suggestion is the rapid encephalization, or brain growth, that took place in hominins during the Pleistocene. If this were the case, there would have been significant selective pressure on the female to maintain adequate pelvic breadth both to provide balance during walking and to allow parturition, despite the constantly increasing size of the fetal cranium.[10] There is certainly a maximum total pelvic breadth that can be maintained in a biped. The australopith

[9]Some specimens referred to *Homo* aff. *habilis*—namely Stw 53—have canal dimensions unlike those seen in any hominins or great apes.

[10]However, in *A. afarensis* and *A. africanus*, at least, neonatal brain size (and the corresponding neurocranial dimensions) were smaller than in modern chimpanzees and smaller than in the corresponding pelvic dimensions of AL 288-1 (Lucy) and Sts 14, respectively, indicating little, if any obstetrical constraints in these two early hominin species (Leutenegger, 1987).

Box 8.2 Summary of Trends in Hominin Pelvic Morphology

Since the anatomy of the pelvis is so critical for interpreting locomotor behavior in fossil hominins, let us summarize the salient points. Distinctive features of the modern human pelvis include the following:
- A low, broad ilium
- A short distance from the center of the acetabulum to the articular surface of the sacrum
- A deep sciatic notch
- A more lateral orientation of the iliac blades
- The presence of an iliac pillar

Fossil evidence clearly indicates that pelvic reorientation from a typically ape-like configuration to a more human-like one had already commenced several million years ago. That this pelvic transition to the modern condition was still incomplete in australopiths, however, is demonstrated by the fact that they had
- A relatively small area on the sacrum for articulation with the ilium
- Relatively small femoral heads
- Incomplete rotation of the iliac blades, whose orientation was more dorsolateral than is characteristic of modern humans (this last feature seems to indicate that the hip abductor mechanism, discussed earlier, did not yet function as it does in modern humans, although this is still a point of contention).

pelvis was already broad because of the laterally flared ilium and the broad interacetabular distance relative to that in quadrupeds. Because of increasing fetal cranial dimensions, adjustments that enlarged the pelvic opening but did not increase total pelvic breadth would have been favored. If stature and total pelvic breadth were to remain unchanged relative to one another and the dimensions of the birth canal were to increase, the only avenue of change would have been to increase the interacetabular width and reduce the length of the moment arm of the hip abductors. Such changes would have led to an increase in the muscle force of the abductor mechanism (because of its reduced moment arm) and would have required a commensurate increase in the iliac pillar and general robustness of the ilium. It is precisely these changes, in addition to those discussed earlier, which can be seen between the hip complex of *Australopithecus* and *H. sapiens*.

PALEOPEDIATRICS: AUSTRALOPITHS AND OBSTETRICS

Both the size and the shape of the female pelvis strongly influence the human birth process, and this morphology is constrained by several exclusively human attributes: bipedalism, a large brain, and "secondary altriciality," or the birth of the infant in a helpless state. In most primate species the sagittal dimensions of the pelvic inlet, midplane, and outlet are all longer than the transverse dimensions. In humans, however, the greatest breadth at the inlet is in the transverse dimension, and the outlet is largest in the sagittal dimension. For this reason, the orientation of the fetal head as it enters the birth canal is different between nonhuman primates and humans; in the former it usually faces forward or backward and in the latter it faces sideways (Fig. 8.15). The change in orientation of the fetal head as it passes through the birth canal is also different: that of nonhuman primates rotates to a variable degree but emerges facing forward with the head flexed, while that of humans rotates to exit facing backward with the head extended. Because the human fetus emerges from the birth canal facing in the opposite direction

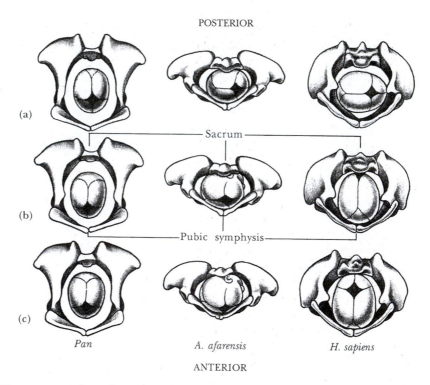

Fig. 8.15. Pelvic dimensions, encephalization, and parturition in apes and hominins. The fetal head is shown passing through the (a) inlet, (b) midplane, and (c) outlet of the birth canal, seen from below. The membrane-covered "soft spot" in the infant's incompletely ossified cranium, known as the anterior fontanelle, is marked in black to indicate fetal orientation. In *A. afarensis* the birth process was probably more difficult than in the chimpanzee because, although the birth canal was broad, it was constricted from front to back; the infant's cranium could pass through only if it first turned sideways and then tilted. During the human birth process the canal is even more constricted, and a second rotation of the fetal cranium within the birth canal is required. (From Lovejoy, 1988.)

from its mother, it is difficult for the mother to reach down to clear a breathing passage for the infant or to remove the umbilical cord from around its neck as nonhuman primate mothers often do. If a human mother tries to assist in delivery by guiding the infant from the birth canal, she risks damaging the infant's spinal cord. It has been suggested that this may be one reason why human mothers often seek assistance at childbirth, whereas nonhuman primate mothers do not (Rosenberg and Trevathan, 1996).

Accurate dimensions of the australopith pelvis are known from only two specimens: AL 288-1 (*A. afarensis*) and Sts 14 (*A. africanus*). Both specimens are usually thought to be females. Among humans there are a number of anatomical features related to obstetrics by which female pelves differ from those of males: (1) the iliopectineal line is greater in females, reflecting the increased size of the pelvic inlet; (2) the long axis of the sacrum is oriented more horizontally in females, thereby increasing the dimensions of the pelvic midplane and outlet; (3) the ischial spines are everted in females, thereby widening the transverse diameters of the lower pelvic planes; and (4) the inferior border of the ischiopubic ramus is concave in females, which helps widen the subpubic angle. It is interesting to note that, with the exception of the length of the iliopectineal line, all other features of Lucy's pelvis are more typical of males (Tague and Lovejoy, 1986).

In fact, some have even suggested that the obstetrical constraints apparent in the pelvis of AL 288-1, in particular the protruding sacral promontory, make it more likely that Lucy was a male rather than a female. According to these arguments, if AL 288-1 were the female of a very sexually dimorphic species, then she would have had to give birth to a child with a neonatal brain size of around 200g, basically an obstetrical impossibility given her pelvic dimensions. If she were a female of a species with low sexual dimorphism, she would still have had to give birth to a child with a neonatal brain size between about 140 and 160g, a delivery judged to be more difficult and complicated than in modern humans. If, on the other hand, AL 288-1 were the male of a rather small, nonsexually dimorphic early hominin species, then the female of this species would have had childbirth difficulties little different from that experienced by modern humans. By contrast, it was calculated that Sts 14 could have given birth to a child with a brain weight up to 237g, some 30% larger than Lucy was capable of (Häusler and Schmid, 1995, 1997).

However, a reanalysis of Lucy's pelvic anatomy has reinforced the view that AL 288-1 and Sts 14 are the same sex and that both individuals would have been obstetrically adequate as females. The identification of Lucy as female, however, is based not so much on pelvic anatomy but rather in the belief that there is only one sexually dimorphic species present at Hadar and that her small body size logically implies that "she" was female (Tague and Lovejoy, 1998). It is fair to say that Lucy's sex is still a matter of contention.

Obstetrical measurements on these specimens indicate that, relative to newborn brain size, the australopith pelvic inlet was more spacious than in modern humans and thus obstetrical constraints were minimal in early hominins (Leutenegger, 1987). However, pelvic inlet shape does differ from modern humans, being much wider from side to side and narrower from front to back—that is, more **platypelloid,** particularly in AL 288-1. A platypelloid shape minimizes the actual space available for fetal entry into, and descent through, the birth canal, and for this reason some have suggested that delivery may have been more difficult in *A. afarensis* than in *A. africanus* (Tague, 1991). This more platypelloid pelvis, in contrast to the twisted birth canal of modern humans, resulted in a birth canal that maintained the same shape from inlet to outlet and, in this sense, would have been similar to the straight passageway seen in the nonhuman primate birth canal (but with the significant difference in the orientation of its longest diameter). Therefore, the australopith infant cranium would have had a human-like transverse orientation at the pelvic inlet, but since the birth canal had a constant shape throughout, the infant's head would have remained in this orientation through the entire birth canal. In such a pelvis, human-like cranial rotation would have been impossible.

BEHAVIORAL THEORIES FOR THE EVOLUTION OF BIPEDALISM

As we have seen, australopiths had evolved unmistakable adaptations to bipedalism by 4 mya. But why did bipedalism develop at all? Why are two legs better than four? At first glance, bipedalism might seem to be an unusual mode of locomotion for a mammal because it has the disadvantages of reducing speed, agility, and energy efficiency.

Many theories have been advanced to explain the evolution of bipedalism: (1) it frees the hands for tool use, (2) it allows for new feeding adaptations, (3) it allows for behaviors such as carrying food and infants and using the hands for display, (4) it evolved from bipedal threat/appeasement displays, (5) it is more bioenergetically efficient than quadrupedalism, or (6) some combination of these (Fig. 8.16) (Jablonski and Chaplin, 1993). However, in recent years the fossil record has made it clear that bipedalism predated the use of stone tools, the modern hominin dental complex, and increased encephalization.

Could bipedalism be more energy efficient than quadrupedalism? Empirical studies have shown that, at maximum running speeds, human bipedalism costs twice as much energy per kilogram per kilometer as predicted for a mammalian quadruped of the same size. It has also been shown that for chimpanzees and capuchin monkeys the energy costs of

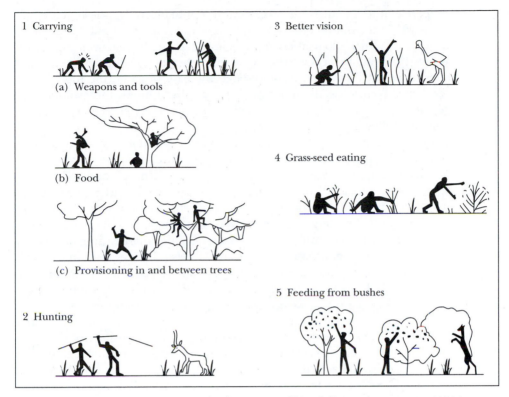

1 Carrying

(a) Weapons and tools

(b) Food

(c) Provisioning in and between trees

2 Hunting

3 Better vision

4 Grass-seed eating

5 Feeding from bushes

Fig. 8.16.   Rival theories to account for the origins of bipedalism.   (From Isaac, 1983.)

traveling quadrupedally and bipedally are about the same. Is energy efficiency then not a good argument for the evolution of human bipedalism (Taylor and Rowntree, 1973; Taylor et al., 1970; Tuttle, 1994)?

Of course, there are degrees of bipedalism and varying degrees of energy efficiency: bipedal *posture* turns out to be an important factor in energetics models of bipedal locomotion. For example, studies using Japanese macaques indicate that these animals expend about 30% less energy during upright walking when they shift from postures with deeply flexed lower limb joints and forwardly inclined trunks to more upright postures (humans expend up to 50% less energy by walking fully upright rather than with flexed lower limb joints) (Ishida, 1991).

It is important to note that while bipedal *running* may be energy intensive, bipedal *walking* in modern humans is more efficient than quadrupedalism in like-size quadrupeds, including modern apes (Leonard and Robertson, 1997a, b; Steudel, 1996; Taylor et al., 1982). One can imagine a scenario in which energy efficiency in terms of food-gathering strategies would actually have increased through bipedalism. The climatic fluctuations in the Miocene resulted in changing distributions of forests and open country. In places where the forests were receding, food sources would no longer have been as concentrated; ancestral australopith populations in these marginal areas would thus have had to travel farther to forage for food. One might argue that morphological changes to improve quadrupedalism may have evolved instead in order to increase efficiency at moving between food sites; however, this would have lessened the ease of gathering food at the food sites themselves. By modifying only the hind limbs, the evolution of bipedalism provided for the possibility of improved efficiency of travel while still allowing for arboreal feeding.

The energetic cost of locomotion forms a substantial fraction of an animal's total daily energy expenditure and, therefore, influences such things as dietary requirements, foraging strategies, and the amount of energy that can be allocated to other needs such as growth and reproduction. Two terms must first be defined: locomotor *efficiency* and locomotor *economy*, the former referring to the ratio of work done to energy expended and the latter to the thrifty use of resources. Thus a larger animal may be more energy efficient than a smaller animal, even it if requires more total energy to travel a given distance, if the amount of needed energy per unit work is less. Usually, however, larger animals are less economical than smaller ones because they use more energy during locomotion.

Animal studies have found that the cost of locomotion increases linearly with speed since increasing speed requires increases in stride length and/or stride frequency. However, it seems that the rate at which cost increases with speed actually decreases in larger animals—that is, it costs a larger mammal less per kilogram to increase its speed by 1 m per second than it costs a smaller mammal.

The question that interests us is whether bipedalism is more energetically efficient than quadrupedalism and, if so, was this a key selective factor in the evolution of upright posture and gait in early hominins? The experimental evidence is somewhat equivocal. Some studies find little difference in the cost of locomotion between bipedal and quadrupedal walking in trained chimpanzees and capuchin monkeys (Taylor and Rowntree, 1973).[11] Others question these results and conclude that humans are able to travel a given distance at a lower mass-specific energy cost than chimpanzees and see energetic efficiency as particularly advantageous in an ecosystem in which food resources are more dispersed (Rodman and McHenry, 1980). It is interesting that other studies have shown some quadrupedal primates (e.g., patas monkeys) are actually more efficient than humans or chimpanzees at speeds in the middle of the range over which cost was measured (Mahoney, 1980; Taylor et al., 1982).

It was also found that while hominin bipedalism (particularly at walking, not running, speeds) may be more cost efficient than chimpanzee knuckle-walking or quadrupedal locomotion in similar-size animals, it may not necessarily be more so than in some smaller primate quadrupeds. So

---

[11]A rather silly experimental design in that "bipedal" postures in such animals are highly energetically inefficient given their skeletal and muscular adaptations to quadrupedalism.

even though locomotor efficiency per se may not be the main factor in the origin of bipedal posture, one may think that once such postures were achieved there would be selection for increased efficiency, such as by increasing lower limb length. In studies of human walking there seems to be no significant correlation between limb length and cost of locomotion. There is, however, a modest but significant relationship between limb length and maximum running speed. It thus appears that the single most important variable determining locomotor efficiency and economy in early hominins is body size. Calculations have shown that if *A. afarensis* were a very sexually dimorphic species (which seems to be the case) then total locomotor cost would be approximately 30% greater in males than in females, although locomotor efficiency would have been relatively less in males than in females (Steudel, 1994).

The experimental evidence on which many of these conclusions were based has recently been reviewed, with interesting results (Steudel-Numbers, 2003). It turns out that bipedality could not have originated in the human lineage as a strategy to mitigate the high cost of locomotion characteristic of nonhuman primates (and thus our ancestor) since estimates of locomotor cost in nonhuman primates are actually similar to those of generalized endotherms. However, the data do show that human *walking* is relatively efficient compared to both other primates and generalized endotherms. Human running, on the other hand, is less efficient than in generalized endotherms. This makes sense when one thinks about modern human hunter-gatherer hunting practices. Humans aren't cheetahs—they don't run their prey to ground.[12] Human hunter-gatherers stalk, or trap, their prey and follow wounded animals over long distances. Human hunter-gatherers basically walk their prey to death! In this type of hunting strategy, the cost efficiency of bipedal walking would be an obvious advantage.

SEED-EATING, SEX, REPRODUCTION, AND LEARNING

During the 1970s and 1980s probably the two most creative and influential models for the evolution of bipedalism were Clifford Jolly's (1970) **seed-eating hypothesis** and C. Owen Lovejoy's (1981) **sexual-and-reproductive-strategy model**. Both have had their critics, yet both stand as landmark

---

[12]Likewise, when the predator/prey roles are reversed, humans are very seldom able to outrun predators when they themselves are the prey. Anyone who doesn't believe this has never been left standing alone on the African savanna. And don't think clambering up a small acacia bush would do you much good. If australopiths (or anyone else) tried to outrun contemporary carnivores, they would end up as supper.

Table 8.1   Adaptive Characters of Early Hominins and *Theropithecus* (gelada baboons and their fossil relatives)

Character	A	B	C
Behavior			
Open-country habitat, not forest or woodland	X	—	—
Trees rarely or never climbed when feeding	(X)	—	—
One-male breeding unit	(X)	—	—
Foraging mainly in sitting position	?	—	—
Small daily range	?	—	—
More regular use of artifacts in agonistic situations	X	X	—
Regular use of stone cutting tools	X	X	—
Most food collected by index-pollex precision grip	?	—	—
Postcranial structure			
Hand more adept, opposability index higher	X	—	—
Index finger abbreviated	?	—	—
Hallux short and weak	—	—	X
Hallux relatively nonabductible	X	—	—
Foot double-arched	X	X	—
Phalanges of pedal digits two to five shorter	(X)	—	—
Ilium short and reflexed	X	X	—
Sacroiliac articulation extensive	X	X	—
Anterior-inferior iliac spine strong	X	X	—
Ischium without flaring tuberosities	X	X	—
Accessory sitting pads (fat deposits on buttocks) present	(X)	—	—
Femur short compared with humerus	?	—	—
Distal end femur indicates straight-knee "locking"	X	X	—
Epigamic hair about face and neck strongly dimorphic	(X)	—	—
Female epigamic features pectoral as well as perineal	(X)	—	—
Cranium and mandible			
Foramen magnum basally displaced	X	X	—
Articular fossa deep, articular eminence present	X	X	—
Fossa narrow, postglenoid process appressed to tympanic	X	—	—
Postglenoid process often absent, superseded by tympanic	X	X	—
Postglenoid process long and stout	—	—	X

(*Continued*)

attempts to synthesize anatomical and behavioral observations on living primates into plausible scenarios of human origins and adaptations.

The seed-eating hypothesis draws an analogy between anatomical and behavioral characters shared by living papionins, particularly gelada baboons (*Theropithecus gelada*), and early hominins (Table 8.1) (Jolly, 1970, 2001). It suggests that early hominin populations relied on small-object feeding, that this dietary specialization resulted in a suite of adaptations

Character	A	B	C
Basioccipital short and broad	X	—	—
Mastoid process regularly present	X	—	—
Temporal origins set forward on cranium	X	—	—
Ascending ramus vertical, even in largest forms	X	—	—
Mandibular corpus very robust in molar region	X	—	—
Premaxilla reduced	X	—	—
Dental arcade narrows anteriorly	X	—	—
Dental arcade of mandible parabolic, simian shelf absent	X	X	—
Dental arcade (especially in larger forms) V-shaped; shelf massive	—	—	X
Teeth			
Incisors relatively small and allometrically reducing	X	—	—
Canine relatively small, especially in larger forms	X	—	—
Canine incisiform	X	X	—
Male canine "feminized," little sexual dimorphism in canines	X	X	—
Third lower premolar biscupid	X	X	—
Sectoral face of male P_3 relatively small and allometrically decreasing	—	—	X
Molar crowns more parallel sided, cusps set toward edge	X	—	—
Cheek teeth markedly crowded mesiodistally	X	—	—
Cheek teeth with deep and complex enamel invagination	—	—	X
Cheek teeth with thick enamel	X	X	—
Canine eruption early relative to that of molars	X	—	—
Wear plane on cheek teeth flat, not inclined buccolingually	X	X	—
Wear on cheek teeth rapid, producing steep M_1–M_3 "wear gradient"	X	—	—

A, characters distinguishing early hominins from *Pan* and other apes; B, features of the hominin complex not seen in *Theropithecus*; C, features of the *Theropithecus* complex not seen in hominins; X, presence of character; (X), assumed presence of character.
From Jolly (1970).

to feeding in grassland savanna, and that bipedalism developed in response to such feeding posture. This model fits quite well some of the dental specializations seen in the robust australopiths, but the more generalized dentition of *A. afarensis* or later *A. garhi* is more difficult to fit, unless of course *A. afarensis* represents the beginning of this new adaptation to savanna living and to small-object feeding, a scenario that is quite possible.

The sexual-and-reproductive-strategy model presents a somewhat different view of human origins based on an undeniable trend toward prolonged life span in the primate evolutionary record (Fig. 8.17). An increased primate life span has implications for primate physiology, population dynamics, and behavior, all of which bear, as we shall see, on the issue of hominin origins.

A number of trends in primate physiology, such as prolonged gestation, single rather than multiple births, and successively greater periods between pregnancies, correlate well with longer periods of infant dependency. According to Lovejoy's hypothesis, the progressive extension of primate life phases might be accounted for by an evolutionary strategy in which populations devote more energy to the care and survival of fewer young. The increase in primate life span would then be accompanied by both a proportionate delay in the onset of reproductive readiness and greater spacing between births. This requires a female to survive to an older age in order to maintain the same reproductive potential or to give birth to a second offspring before the first is independent, thereby producing a "serial litter." However, to accomplish the latter, she would (ideally) need male help. Increased longevity depends on strong social bonds,

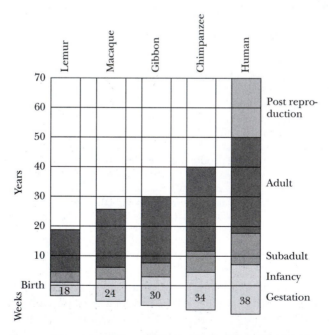

Fig. 8.17. Progressive prolongation of life phases and gestation in primates. Note the proportionality of the four indicated phases. The postreproductive phase is restricted mainly to humans and is probably a recent development. (From Lovejoy, 1981; Schultz, 1969.)

high levels of intelligence, intense parenting, long periods of postnatal learning, and other such developments to reduce the potential for environmentally induced mortality of the newborn. The emergence of successful hominins in the Pliocene strongly suggests that major changes in reproductive strategies were in fact evolving as hominins came to occupy new environments. Yet neither brain expansion nor significant material culture appear at this time and were presumably not responsible for the shift (unless the material culture was not preserved).

Lovejoy (1993) suggests a novel behavioral pattern that could have evolved from typical primate survival strategies in which males and females had nonoverlapping feeding areas and the females and infants had a much reduced day range to minimize injury to the infants. Such a division of feeding areas, however, would not genetically favor males unless it specifically reduced competition with their own biological offspring and did not reduce their opportunities for having consort relationships. **Polygynous** mating, the mating of several males with one female, would not be favored by this adaptive strategy, though **monogamous pair bonding** would be. Sexual division of labor would develop, with the male provisioning the female and his biological offspring at some type of **home base,** an area to which hominins return to meet other group members, share food, and make tools. This scenario could also account for a social system capable of supporting multiple dependent offspring rather than, or in addition to, a reproductive strategy of one offspring at a time. In this model, such male provisioning is also seen as an impetus to the evolution of bipedalism since distances would have to be traveled while bearing food.

As we noted earlier, Lovejoy ascribes the reduced degree of sexual dimorphism in australopiths (indicated by the lack of sexual dimorphism in *A. afarensis* canines) to a reduced intensity of sexual selection.[13] Based on analogies with extant primates, this implies to Lovejoy a more monogamous mating system, since the strength of sexual selection is roughly correlated to the degree of polygyny in primates species (Fleagle et al., 1980; Plavcan and Van Schaik, 1994). This is explained in the following way. In monogamous primate species, males presumable do not compete for access to females any more than females compete for access to males, so dimorphism should be minimal. However, males do compete for access to females in polygynous species, resulting in potentially large differences in male reproductive success and strong selection for the development of weaponry (e.g., canines) and/or increased body size. However, Lovejoy interprets the evident dimorphism of australopith body size as a result of males and females occupying different feeding niches.

---

[13]This seems to ignore the problem that if all the craniodental and postcranial hominin material from both Hadar and Laetoli are correctly assigned to the single species, *A. afarensis*, then this species would be one of the most sexually dimorphic primate species known.

These findings are not universally accepted. Some studies show a disso-
ciation between body weight and canine size dimorphism in various
species of *Australopithecus* and suggest that different selective forces must
have acted on body weight and canine size (Leutenegger and Shell, 1987).
In addition, there is little evidence in extant primates that body size dimorphism can be linked to males and females occupying different feeding
niches. Instead, australopith body weight dimorphism is seen as a function
of intrasexual and intersexual competition typical of polygynous, not
monogamous, mating systems. This interpretation explains the lack of canine sexual dimorphism in australopiths as a consequence of a "developmental dental crowding" model in which canine size and canine
dimorphism reduction results from selection for increased premolar chewing surface areas accompanied by the space restrictions of tooth sockets
for late erupting hominin canines.

There are still other factors affecting canine sexual dimorphism in primates that should be considered in this context. For example, canines are
relatively larger in both males and females of those species in which agonistic interactions are most likely to occur. In such cases, the size of the canine teeth of both sexes is influenced by selection of canines as weapons.
Conversely, it has also been shown that where aggressive interactions are
resolved between coalitions of individuals, selection pressures for enlarged
canines are reduced even though agonistic competition can still be intense. That female primates form such coalitions much more commonly
than do males may partially explain why canine size is less in females than
in males (Plavcan et al., 1995).

Lovejoy's model also addresses the critical notion of extended periods
for learning and infant dependency. In modern humans the course of development from conception to maturity requires nearly twice the time as
in modern apes (Conroy and Mahoney, 1991; Conroy and Vannier,
1991b). This extended period of maturation in humans is usually regarded
as a major evolutionary advance because enhanced learning reduces environmentally induced mortality. This view was best expressed by the prominent population geneticist and evolutionary biologist Theodosius
Dobzhansky (1962):

> Although a prolonged period of juvenile helplessness and dependency would,
> by itself, be disadvantageous to a species because it endangers the young and
> handicaps their parents, it is a help to man because the slow development pro-
> vides time for learning and training, which are far more extensive and impor-
> tant in man than in any other animal.

Lovejoy's model assumes that, relative to monkeys, long periods of
learning already existed in the early lifetimes of Pliocene hominins. This
assumption relied heavily on the pioneering work of Alan Mann (1975)
who concluded that "a long childhood dependency period . . . which the
evidence . . . seems to indicate for *Australopithecus*, would provide the time

necessary for the skills associated with tool-making to be developed in the young."

How can we determine whether long learning periods really occurred in australopiths? As Mann pointed out, it would be crucial to know how old individual australopiths were when they died. He estimated their age by examining their teeth. Nearly all mammals have one set of deciduous teeth that are first formed and then replaced by permanent teeth in a predictable sequence. A jaw with some deciduous teeth in it reveals fairly precisely at which point along the way to adulthood the individual died. The key is translating the relative ages of the fossil into actual time spans in years and months. The crucial question is whether australopiths developed on a human-like or an ape-like timetable. The difference is significant. Based on an analysis of the timing of tooth eruptions in a small sample of mainly *A. robustus* teeth, Mann concluded that australopiths showed a human-like pattern of dental development and so he based his age estimates on the human timetable. Thus it was thought that alterations in the timing of growth and development occurred very early in hominin evolution, indicating that a long maturational period had already evolved in Pliocene hominins older than *A. robustus*.

Mann's work proved to be very influential, and it became widely accepted that human-like traits of sociality, enhanced intelligence, elaborate communication, and so on arose quite early in the hominin lineage. Subsequent work has shown, however, that the situation is more complicated (Bromage, 1987; Bromage and Dean, 1985; Conroy and Vannier, 1987, 1991a, 1991b; Smith, 1986).

For example, B. Holly Smith (1986, 1994) of the University of Michigan, using many more specimens than were available to Mann, aged all the teeth separately for each fossil jaw she studied. She then statistically compared the dental age ranges of the jaw as determined by the individual teeth to chimpanzee and human dental calibration standards to see which group the fossil most closely resembled. Theoretically, all the teeth in the jaw should follow a standard pattern and rate of development for that species. For example, if the incisors are in a state of maturation that is typical of a 6-year-old human, the molars should be as well. Surprisingly, her results showed that only the robust australopiths followed, at least superficially, a human-like pattern, while *A. afarensis* and *A. africanus* (and *H. habilis*) showed an ape-like pattern.

Actually, this "superficially" human-like pattern in robust australopiths, which concerns the relative rate of eruption of the first permanent central incisors and molars, was first noted by Broom and Robinson (1951) a half century ago and has been the subject of periodic debate ever since (Conroy, 1988; Dean, 1985; Grine, 1987; Wallace, 1972). In *H. sapiens*, permanent central incisors and first molars erupt with little time in between. In apes, eruption of the first permanent incisors is often delayed more than 2.5 years after the first molars erupt (Fig. 8.18) (Conroy and Mahoney, 1991;

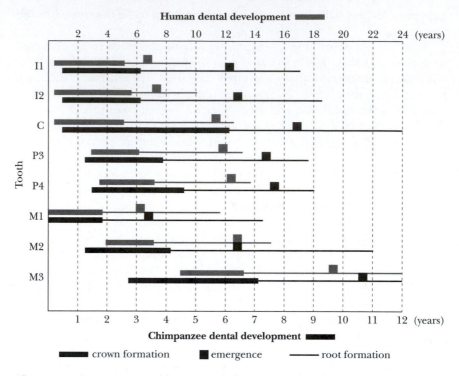

Fig. 8.18.   A comparison of human and chimpanzee dental development drawn to same scale of dental completion.   Note that while chimpanzee and human first molars erupt at about age 3 and 6 years of age, respectively, they both erupt at about the same *relative* time in the total dental development cycle of each species. This is not true of the incisors, canines, and premolars, all of which erupt relatively earlier in humans. (From Kuykendall, 1992.)

Kuykendall et al., 1992). Part of the difficulty in resolving this issue is that the developing teeth most crucial to solving this debate, particularly the incisors in some of the fossils, had never been clearly visualized by conventional radiographic techniques because of heavy mineralization. However, studies using high-resolution CT scans showed that patterns of dental development differed between *A. robustus* and *A. africanus*, even though the length of time for dental development may have been relatively short in both (Fig. 8.19) (Conroy and Kuykendall, 1995; Conroy and Vannier, 1991a, 1991b).

Several other anthropologists have used a totally independent method of analysis to age australopiths at death (Beynon and Dean, 1988; Bromage and Dean, 1985; Dean, 1985, 1987; Dean et al., 1993; Ramirez-Rozzi, 1993). These studies count the daily microscopic increments, or **cross striations**, and near weekly increments, the **striae of Retzius** or **perikymata**, of enamel laid down as teeth are formed (Fig. 8.20). In modern humans, this

Fig. 8.19. (top) A geometrically accurate three-dimensional image of the Taung cranium created from 2-mm, thin contiguous CT scans. (bottom) A 2-mm, thin CT scan taken through a parasagittal plane of the cranium (at the crosshairs in the top picture) showing the state of calcification of the developing teeth. (Image created by G. Conroy and M. Vannier.)

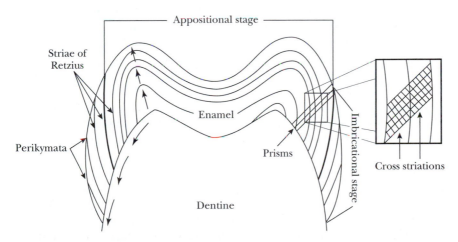

Fig. 8.20. The various incremental growth markers in the enamel of a molar tooth. Cross striations are produced in enamel formation, with seven to nine cross striations being the most common interval between adjacent striae of Retzius. Stria of Retzius that reach the enamel surface form perikymata, or ridges, on the surface of the tooth. The first stria of Retzius that reaches the enamel surface is taken as the limit between the appositional and imbricational stages of enamel growth. Arrows indicate the two directions of enamel formation. (From Ramirez-Rozzi, 1994.)

technique shows that the lower or cervical third of an incisor tooth crown takes more than three times as long to form as the upper or incisal third, a general pattern that is also seen in *A. afarensis* (LH 2), *A. africanus* (Sts 24), and early *Homo* (KNM-ER 820, OH 6). However, none of these fossil hominins has as great a total number of perikymata on the surface of the tooth as modern humans do. It is interesting that incisor teeth of robust australopiths from southern Africa tend to have widely spaced perikymata even at the cervix, unlike the modern human condition. Since lower incisors of robust australopiths are similar in height to those of modern humans, their lower total perikymata counts indicate that crown formation must have been much faster in these fossils.

These results independently confirm that many of the earlier australopith age determinations using modern human timetables were too old by a factor of about two; in other words, australopiths generally followed an ape-like maturational process, not a human-like one. These studies suggest that many of the immature australopiths apparently died between the ages of 2.5 and 3.5 years old (Conroy and Kuykendall, 1995; Conroy and Vannier, 1991a, 1991b). An interesting avenue for future research would be to see whether these newer estimates for ages at death are related to weaning stresses in australopith populations (Shipman, 1987). In addition, obstetrical studies on the australopith pelvis provide no evidence of selection for human-like delayed maturation at this early stage of human evolution.

It is difficult to be certain just when the modern human maturational pattern finally emerged. Modern human enamel develops rather slowly because the earliest formed enamel closest to the enamel-dentine junction is secreted in small increments for a longer period of time. Enamel growth trajectories in apes, australopiths, *H. habilis, H. rudolfensis* and *H. erectus* all fall outside the range seen in modern humans. The *H. erectus* specimen from Nariokotome in West Turkana dated to about 1.5 mya, some *H. antecessor* specimens from Atapuerca (Gran Dolina) in Spain dated to about 800 kya, and some *H. heidelbergensis* specimens from Atapuerca (Sima de los Huesos) dated to about 350 kya all suggest that while the *sequence* of dental maturation may be more human-like than ape-like, the actual *timing* of events may not be (Dean et al., 2001; de Castro and Rosas, 2001; de Castro et al., 1999b; Smith, 1993; B. Smith et al., 1995). Early *Homo* seems to have had maturation rates intermediate between ape-like australopiths and more human-like *Homo erectus* (R. Smith et al., 1995). The slow rate of enamel growth that is characteristic of the extended growth periods of modern humans is not seen in the hominin fossil record until the appearance of the larger-brained Neandertals (e.g., Gibraltar 2, Tabun) (Dean et al., 2001; Smith, 1986, 1994).

Two uniquely human life history events occur at opposite ends of our normal life cycle: At one end we have long maturational periods for infants to learn and at the other end we have long postreproductive (postmenopausal) life spans. We have already noted above some of the positive aspects (in an evolutionary sense) of long maturational periods, but why the long postreproductive life span? One interesting suggestion is that it may have evolved with mother-child food-sharing practices to allow aging females to enhance their daughters' fertility (Hawkes et al., 1998). Although mother-child food sharing occurs in many primate species, human mothers are unique in providing a substantial fraction of their weaned children's diets. This allows mothers to use resources that they themselves can gather at high rates but that their children cannot (e.g., young children cannot efficiently extract deeply buried tubers). Postmenapausal women (grandmothers), having no young children of their own, can help feed their daughters' and nieces' offspring, particularly when their daughters' foraging abilities are limited by the arrival of a newborn. This would have the long-term evolutionary effect of increasing the reproductive success of their daughters.

Such a support system most probably evolved by the time *H. erectus* came onto the scene. *H. erectus* females were over 50% heavier than average australopith females and their energetic costs would have been proportionally larger as well, particularly those energetic costs incurred during gestation and lactation. One way to reduce such costs per offspring would be by shortening the interbirth interval. However, if females adopted such a strategy it would necessarily imply a revolution in the way they obtained and utilized energy to support their increased energetic requirements, since the mother would now have to incur the cost of caring for more dependent offspring (Aiello and Key, 2002). The evolution of "grandmothering" at this stage of hominin evolution may have been one such behavioral mechanism.

Another interesting hypothesis for the evolution of human bipedality uses evidence from both primate field ecology and functional morphology to suggest that ecological conditions that produce episodes of bipedal behavior in living chimpanzees may provide clues to the selection pressures leading to hominin bipedalism. More specifically, living chimpanzees seem to adopt bipedal postures much more commonly when feeding on the small fruits of low, open-forest trees. Chimpanzee bipedalism suggests that hominin bipedalism may have evolved in conjunction with arboreal adaptations like arm-hanging as a specialized feeding adaptation, permitting more efficient harvesting of fruits among open-forest or woodland trees, an idea that seems compatible with what we know about the anatomy of early hominins. For example, we have seen that *A. afarensis* has features of the hand, shoulder, and torso that relate to arm-hanging postures. And though the australopith hip and hindlimb clearly indicate significant advances toward bipedalism, they also indicate a less than optimal adaptation to bipedal locomotion compared to modern humans. This lends support to the idea that bipedalism may have evolved more as a terrestrial feeding posture than as a walking adaptation (Hunt, 1994).

PHYLOGENY AND CLASSIFICATION:
CURRENT ISSUES AND DEBATES

Attempts to identify direct lineages between Miocene hominoids and present-day apes and hominins have not been particularly successful. The reason for this is quite straightforward: There is simply little decent fossil evidence for hominoid evolution in Africa from the critical time period of about 12 to 5 mya. Presumably this is when various African Miocene hominoids were differentiating into the African great apes and early hominins (Conroy, 1990). However, recent discoveries of *Orrorin* and *Sahelanthropus* are at least beginning to fill in this enormous temporal gap.

Although no likely Miocene candidates for direct ancestry of the first hominins can be confidently advanced, a number of plausible scenarios for relationships among the various early hominin groups that we have been discussing have been proposed, which are summarized below.

In this text we have followed a taxonomically conservative approach by recognizing only five australopith genera (*Ardipithecus, Australopithecus, Kenyanthropus, Orrorin, Sahelanthropus*) containing 11 species: *Ar. kadabba, Ar. ramidus, A. anamensis, A. afarensis, A. garhi, A. africanus, A. robustus, A. boisei, K. platyops, O. tugenensis, and S. tchadensis*). However, the debate continues about the actual number of genera and species represented in this fossil sample and about what their phylogenetic and ecological relationships are to one another and to *Homo* (Aiello and Collard, 2001; Asfaw et al., 1999; Curnoe and Thorne, 2003; Lieberman, 2001; Senut et al., 2001; Wood, 2002). The significance of the "gracile" vs. "robust" distinction and its role in hominid evolution has also been controversial.

At the moment most paleoanthropologists would probably accept that *Ar. kadabba, Ar. ramidus–A. anamensis–A. afarensis* form a reasonably good ancestor-descendant series. There is nothing in their morphology that would preclude such a scenario, and their respective geological ages fall into line as well. The main debate is over what happens after *A. afarensis*. Here we summarize six hypotheses that have been offered in the literature (Figs. 6.1 and 8.21).

- *Hypothesis One:* The hominins from Hadar and Laetoli, which some classify as *A. afarensis*, are really a geographically separate subspecies of *A. africanus*, which in turn is the last common ancestor of both the robust australopith and *Homo* lineages (Tobias, 1988).

- *Hypothesis Two: A. afarensis* represents the ancestral species from which both the *Homo* and robust australopith lineages emerge. In this scenario, *A. africanus* is situated near the base of the robust australopith lineage (Johanson and White, 1979; Rak, 1983; White et al., 1981).

- *Hypothesis Three: A. afarensis* represents the ancestral species from which *A. africanus* evolved. This latter species, or one very similar to it, is the common ancestor of both later robust australopith and *Homo* lineages (Skelton and McHenry, 1992; Skelton et al., 1986).

- *Hypothesis Four:* The Hadar and Laetoli hominins represent two species, one related to the robust australopith lineage (called *Paranthropus*) and the other to the *Homo* lineage. Therefore, the robust australopith lineage can be traced back through an *A. afarensis*–like ancestor (Falk and Conroy, 1983; Olson, 1985; Senut and Tardieu, 1985; Zihlman, 1985).
- *Hypothesis Five:* A. *afarensis* represents the ancestral species from which both hyper-robust East African australopiths and an *A. africanus*–like form evolved. Both *Homo* and *A. robustus* emerge out of this *A. africanus*–like ancestor (Walker et al., 1986).
- *Hypothesis Six:* A. *afarensis* is the last common ancestor of a monophyletic robust australopith lineage (called *Paranthropus*) and a *Homo* lineage, the latter passing through an *A. africanus*–like stage (Grine, 1988) or perhaps an *A. garhi*–like stage (Asfaw et al., 1999).

These rather bewildering alternatives (and their uncertainties as represented by the profusion of question marks) are summarized in Figure 8.21.

The relationship between two of the oldest australopiths, *A. afarensis* and *A. africanus*, is anything but clear. Are they geographic variants of the same species (Hypothesis One), or is *A. afarensis* the stem hominin species (Hypotheses Two, Three, Five, Six)? The latter is refuted by the discovery of *Ar. ramidus*, which is now considered the most likely candidate for the stem hominin species. Owing to their antiquity, it is not surprising that *A. afarensis* and *A. africanus* share a number of primitive craniofacial characteristics. Some have argued that the primitive craniofacial plan of *A. africanus* represents a derived morphological composite, making it an excellent structural and phylogenetic intermediate between *A. afarensis, A. robustus*, and *A. boisei* (Johanson and White, 1979; Rak, 1985; White et al., 1981). These authors would exclude *A. africanus* from direct ancestry of *H. habilis* because of the apparent fact that it is specialized in the direction of robust australopiths (Hypothesis Two). Such specializations revolve around the stronger molarization of its premolars, large relative size of its postcanine dentition, and increased buttressing and robustness of its mandibular body. Other features are all closely related to the increased size of the posterior dentition. Larger postcanine teeth are functionally associated with greater mandibular buttressing, more strongly developed muscle attachment areas on the cranium, a shift forward of the center of action of the temporalis muscle, and midfacial buttressing.

It has also been pointed out that although *A. afarensis* is remarkably primitive in many features, *A. africanus, A. robustus*, and *A. boisei* more closely resemble *H. habilis* in many of those same features (McHenry, 1985). In fact, *H. habilis* and the later species of *Australopithecus* share an extensive suite of derived traits not present in *A. afarensis* at all. This implies that the immediate ancestor of *H. habilis* also probably shared these traits. If *A. afarensis*, rather than *A. africanus*, were the immediate ancestor of *H. habilis*, then a great deal of parallel evolution would have to be postulated. From this point of view, it is clearly more parsimonious to assume

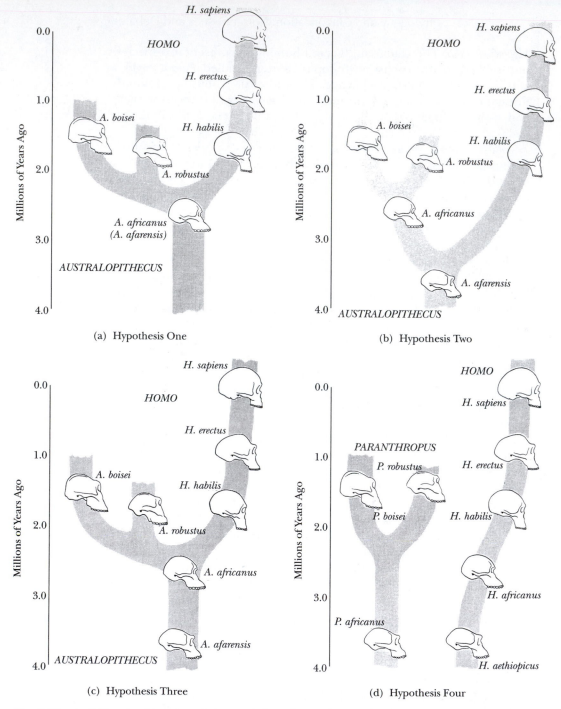

Fig. 8.21. (a–f) The six alternative phylogenetic hypotheses about early hominin evolution discussed in the text. *Ar. ramidus* would appear very close to the root of all later hominins in these phylogenetic trees. *A. anamensis* may be descendant from *Ar. ramidus* and ancestral to *A. afarensis* in all these scenarios. Note that *Paranthropus* is regarded as a separate genus in some of these scenarios. (From Grime, 1993a.) (g) A summary of the hypotheses. Note that question marks indicate hypothetical or conjectural relationships; horizontal bars indicate uncertainty in the species' temporal spans. (From Lieberman, 2001.)

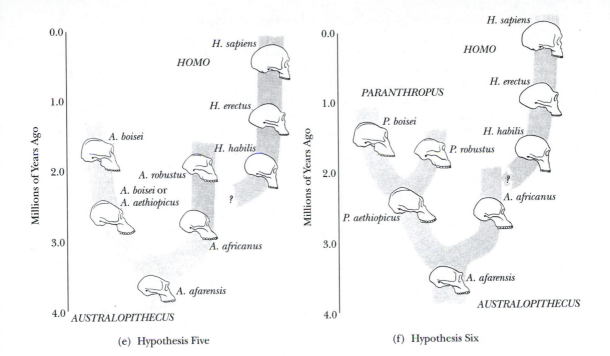

(e) Hypothesis Five

(f) Hypothesis Six

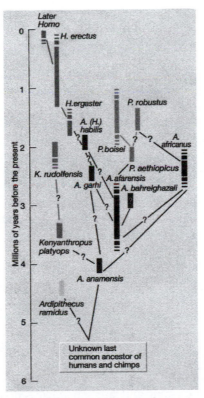

(g) A summary of the hypotheses.

that the hominin species immediately predating the appearance of *Homo*, *A. africanus*, is the immediate common ancestor not only of *H. habilis* but also of *A. robustus* and *A. boisei* (Hypothesis Three).

What is the relationship between *A. africanus* and *A. robustus*? Both are found in South African sites and, as we have seen, J. T. Robinson (1963) viewed them as occupying separate ecological niches based on dietary preference, *A. africanus* being omnivorous and *A. robustus*, vegetarian. Presumably he considered dating of the fossils to be indeterminate enough that the two species could have overlapped in time as well as geographic area; however, most proposals for dating the South African sediments place the earliest *A. robustus* specimens at least a half million years *after* the last *A. africanus* specimens. In any case, Robinson considered these two groups distinct enough to assign them to separate genera, renaming the gracile hominin *H. africanus* because of its similarity to other *Homo* species.

Some have advocated an ancestor-descendant relationship between *A. africanus* and *A. robustus*, with the latter then giving rise to *A. boisei*. This view is based in large part on an analysis of the structure and function of the australopith face (Rak, 1983, 1985). This follows the evolutionary scheme similar to that shown in Hypothesis Two, in which the origins of the robust clade are in *A. africanus*, which is thereby removed from consideration as a human ancestor. To those who see *A. africanus*–*A. robustus*–*A. boisei* as a single evolving lineage, the beginnings of specialization characterizing the robust australopiths are already manifest in almost every aspect of the masticatory system of *A. africanus*. Evidence for this viewpoint includes the presence of anterior pillars in both forms. This buttressing is viewed as a structural response to the greater occlusal load arising from the incipient molarization of the premolars. In *A. africanus* this molarization process was just beginning, but the still considerable protrusion of the palate relative to the more peripheral facial frame increased the need for such incipient pillars. The anterior pillars and the advancement of the inferior part of the infraorbital region (where the masseter muscle originated) played a major role in molding the facial topography of *A. africanus*. The presence of such pillars in *A. africanus* is considered evidence linking it to the robust australopith clade. The absence of the pillars in *A. afarensis* has led some to conclude that its face was the most primitive among the australopiths (McKee, 1989; Rak, 1985).

This scenario was gaining widespread acceptance before the discovery of the 2.5-million-year-old *A. boisei* cranium (WT 17000, "Black Skull") from west of Lake Turkana (Fig. 7.13) (Walker et al., 1986). This specimen shows that the *A. boisei* lineage was established before the well-dated *A. robustus* specimens from southern Africa and that, in robustness and tooth size, at least some members of the early *A. boisei* population were as large or larger than the later ones. Previously, most workers had suggested that within the robust australopith lineage there was a trend toward increasing size and robustness of the crania and jaws. This view is no longer tenable. Two possible phylogenetic schemes involving this new specimen are shown in Hypotheses Five and Six (here labeled as *A.* [or *Paranthropus*] *aethiopicus*).

A. robustus shares with younger examples of *A. boisei* several features that are apparently derived from the condition seen in WT 17000. These features include: (1) the cresting pattern with emphasis on the anterior and middle parts of the temporalis muscle, (2) the orthognathic face, and (3) the deep temporomandibular joint with a strong bony projection, or articular eminence, anterior to the mandibular fossa on which the mandibular condyle slides as the jaw opens. Thus WT 17000 suggests that *A. robustus* may be a related, smaller species that was derived from ancestral forms earlier than 2.5 mya and/or had evolved independently in southern Africa, perhaps from *A. africanus.*

Although WT 17000 shows characteristics of robustness and tooth size usually thought to be typical of later robust australopiths, it also has a number of craniofacial features that are more primitive than those in *A. africanus* and similar to those in *A. afarensis.* Some of the primitive features it shares with *A. afarensis* include strong upper facial prognathism; a flat cranial base; a flat temporomandibular fossa; extensive pneumatization in the temporal bone; a large anterior tooth row; a flat, shallow palate; and a maxillary dental arch that converges posteriorly.

In spite of these primitive features, WT 17000 seems clearly to be a member of the *A. boisei* clade. Is it possible that the Hadar sample from which *A. afarensis* comes actually consists of two species, one of which gave rise to *A. boisei?* Features of the nasal region suggest that at least one of the juvenile crania from Hadar has features associated with robust australopiths, while patterns of cranial venous circulation and some postcranial evidence also suggest the same. The phylogenetic implications of this conclusion can be seen in Hypothesis Four. These lines of evidence, however, are not unequivocal and have been challenged by some researchers (Eckhardt, 1987; Kimbel, 1984).

A more recent cladistic analysis, based solely on craniodental characters, concludes that robust australopiths form a well-defined clade and that *A. afarensis* is the sister taxon of all other hominins. The relationship between *A. africanus* and *H. habilis* was determined to be phylogenetically unstable and resulted in the genus *Australopithecus* (e.g., *A. robustus* and *A. africanus*) becoming a paraphyletic taxon. This conclusion follows from *A. africanus* being positioned as the sister taxon of a joint *Homo* + robust australopith clade. To a strict cladist, all clades must be monophyletic, so they suggest that in this case the only taxonomic alternative is to refer all robust australopiths to a monophyletic genus, *Paranthropus;* reserve the name *Australopithecus* for *A. africanus* only; and refer all specimens previously named *A. afarensis* to a new, monophyletic taxon, *Praeanathropus africanus* (Strait et al., 1997).[14]

---

[14]Since this study did not include *A. anamensis* or *Ar. ramidus* in the phylogenetic analyses, and since the inclusion of these taxa would surely influence the conclusions, it would be premature to act on this nomenclatural suggestion.

In analyzing the differences between the gracile and robust australopiths, two related questions come to mind that return us to basic principles of variation. First, how much intraspecific and interspecific variation can we expect to find in the two forms? Second, are the differences between gracile and robust forms the product of real functional and biological differences or are they merely the differences one would predict in two similar animals of different body size? In other words, are robust australopiths merely "blown-up" versions of gracile australopiths or are they morphologically, behaviorally, and/or ecologically different, as Robinson first suggested? These critical questions are too often ignored in taxonomic arguments about early hominins.

As mentioned earlier, Robinson believed the two forms to be distinct at the generic level and proposed a dietary hypothesis to explain these differences. But how distinct in quantitative terms are these forms? How does their morphological variability stack up against known variability in living hominoids? In postcanine dental area, the gracile species are about 88% the size of the robust species. Is this a great difference? By absolute and percentage measures, gracile and robust australopiths are more similar in this dimension than many modern human populations are. According to Robinson's dietary hypothesis, gracile australopiths are supposed to have had smaller posterior dentitions because of their presumably more omnivorous diet. However, gracile australopith cheek teeth are not really as small as Robinson implies. After all, their size lies completely within the range of dental variation of modern gorillas, in spite of the fact that gracile australopith body size is only a fraction of that of living gorillas.

Another way to look at cheek tooth size is to ask the question: What is the relative size of the cheek teeth in *Australopithecus* in comparison to body size? As we saw earlier, the megadontia quotient of all australopith species (except *Ardipithecus*) is large. The sequence *A. afarensis–A. africanus–A. robustus–A. boisei* shows strong positive allometry indicating increasing megadontia through time (McHenry, 1984, 1985, 1992b).

The question of whether gracile species and robust species were merely allometric variants of one another was first directly addressed by David Pilbeam and Steven Gould (1974) who argued that the three species, *A. africanus, A. robustus,* and *A. boisei,* simply represented the "same" animal expressed over a wide range of body size: "In other words, size increase may be the only independent adaptation of these animals, changes in shape simply preserving the function of the smaller prototype at larger sizes." They came to this conclusion after examining the relationships between brain size and body size and between tooth size and body size in the three species. Intraspecific plots of brain size versus body size have been carried out for numerous birds and mammals. (Here *intraspecific* includes not only individual adults or races within a species but also very closely related species displaying the "same" body plan over a wide size range.) The slopes of these plots range from 0.2 to 0.4. The slope for the three australopith species calculated by Pilbeam and Gould is about 0.33, well within this intraspecific range.

When tooth areas are plotted against body weights, a slope of 2/3 is the expected value of geometric scaling for constant proportions throughout the size range. Any value greater than 2/3 indicates that larger animals have relatively larger postcanine teeth than smaller members of the series. The value calculated by Pilbeam and Gould for *A. africanus, A. robustus,* and *A. boisei* is 0.7 and that for pygmy chimpanzee, chimpanzee, gorilla is 0.85. This would confirm that in both these groups the larger species has relatively larger cheek teeth. Based on similar data from other mammals, including rodents, pigs, deer, and monkeys, however, they concluded that positive allometry might be expected in sequences of related mammals that vary in size but not in basic design. Perhaps the observable increase in cheek tooth size in these species is more closely correlated with increasing metabolic rate than with mere geometric similarity.

As we leave the australopiths behind us, we emerge on the brink of humanity. As we've seen, it's unclear which, if any, of these currently recognized australopith species gave rise to the earliest known species of *Homo,* although it was most probably a gracile form. Although the traditional interpretation of the genus *Homo* is that *H. habilis, H. erectus,* and *H. sapiens* are chronologically successive species that slowly graded one into another, we shall see in the following chapters that the situation is now thought to be far more complex.

At what point did our hominin ancestors become truly "human"? This question, the subject of the next chapter, remains the most difficult to answer. We can say that many of the biological and environmental forces that helped shape the genetic makeup of modern humans were operating by at least the Pliocene. And whatever the actual selection pressures were for the traits that distinguish us from the other primates—bipedal locomotion, reduced canine teeth, enlarged brains, parental care of the young, home bases, food sharing, verbal communication skills, savanna-adapted diets, cooperative hunting and scavenging, tool use, opposable thumbs, and division of labor, among others—they were certainly in evidence by the mid-Pleistocene.

It is easy to assume that the more recent the fossil being studied, the more confident paleontologists are about its line of descent. And so it may surprise the reader to learn that the source, timing, and area of differentiation—in short, the origin—of our own kind, *H. sapiens,* the last bipedal, large-brained primate species to arrive on the scene, is still largely unknown. Although there is no unanimity of opinion on the timing of the transition to *H. sapiens* from earlier forms, it is probably fair to say that it took place sometime in the middle Pleistocene, most likely less than 500 kya. Because of the morphological continuity between *H. sapiens* and earlier *Homo* species, the dividing line for humanity will perhaps always remain somewhat ambiguous.

These are just some of the interesting issues that we will tackle in the following chapters.

CHAPTER IX

The Emergence of Culture and the Origins of the Genus *Homo*

INTRODUCTION

It is important to recognize that models of human origins must address both the morphological and the behavioral differences separating humans and apes. We have already looked at how dietary and/or reproductive behavior has been used to model theories of human evolution. Now we shall examine the emergence of culture—tool use, tool making, and the use of fire. This will lead us on to the beginnings of our own genus, *Homo*.

WHAT IS CULTURE?

What is culture and when did it begin to play a dominant role in hominin evolution? Definitions of culture have always been elusive and changeable as ethologists and anthropologists learn more about extant and extinct hominins. In a broad sense, **culture** indicates a system of shared meanings, symbols, customs, beliefs, and practices that are learned by teaching or by imitation and used to cope with the environment, to communicate with others, and to transmit information through the generations. Culture also determines the production of human artifacts. A behavior is considered culture only if differences in its distribution among populations are independent of any environmental or genetic factors. By these definitions then, the distribution of various behavior patterns, including tool use, grooming, and courtship behaviors among populations of African chimpanzees can be construed as "culture" in these nonhuman primates (Boesch-Achermann and Boesch, 1994; Boesch et al., 1994; Whiten et al., 1999).

Most people regard tool use, tool making, and the use of fire as three important types of cultural behavior. Certainly they are some of the earliest examples of culture among fossil hominins for which there is evidence. It is important to recognize, however, that tool use and even rudimentary tool making have been documented among living primates other than humans. For example, chimpanzees are known to adapt thin branches for extracting termites from the ground, to use leaf "sponges" for sopping up water in the hollows of trees, and to extract sap from oil-palm trees with a "pestle" and then drink it using a "fiber sponge." A captive bonobo (*Pan paniscus*) has even been taught the basic skills required to produce usable stone flakes and fragments by hard-hammer percussion (although his stone-flaking skills are not yet as well developed as those exhibited by the earliest known tool-making hominins) (Goodall, 1976; Sugiyama, 1994; Toth et al., 1993). Therefore it is not that members of *H. sapiens* are unique in showing cultural behavior but we are unique in the complexity and extent of the cultural behavior on which we depend for our survival. The adaptive key to human survival is that we have mastered what University of Michigan anthropologist C. Loring Brace (1995) refers to as our "cultural ecological niche."

The Evolution of Culture in Early Hominins

When did hominins begin using tools and what materials were these first tools made of? The use of simple unaltered objects found nearby, or **opportunistic tools**, presumably predated the actual physical alteration of an object for one or more specific uses, which is called tool making. It is difficult to make inferences about opportunistic tool use from artifacts found at fossil sites because many perishable objects, such as wood, may have been used long before permanent materials were. Even preserved objects such as stones and fossilized animal bone found in association with fossil hominins are sometimes difficult to assess as opportunistic tools; for example, bones may simply be the refuse of a meal and stones foreign to the site may have been deposited there through geological activity rather than through human intervention.

There is no evidence of tool use or tool making associated with any fossil hominoids in the Miocene, nor is it definite which, if any, australopith species made the stone tools found in the numerous Plio-Pleistocene archeological sites in eastern and southern Africa. This is because early species of *Homo* are also found in the same areas. However, it is probably safe to assume that in the Pliocene, about 5.0–2.5 mya, early hominins were using simple opportunistic tools such as sticks, bones, or stones as well as unaltered objects carried some distance before use, referred to as **manuports**, for collecting plant foods and insects and for scavenging and killing small animals.

The Oldowan Tradition

Several sites in the Shungura Formation at Omo, West Turkana, and the Middle Awash (Gona) indicate that stone-tools were being made by at least about 2.5 mya (Roche et al., 1999; Semaw et al., 1997). Since early *Homo* and *Australopithecus* are both represented at these sites, it is not certain which group(s) actually made the tools (Wood, 1997). However, there does seem to be technological stasis in these Oldowan tools types for nearly 1 million years (about 2.5–1.5 mya).

Several sites slightly younger than 2 million years at eastern Lake Turkana have also yielded stone tools. Here, again, the identity of the tool makers is uncertain. Some of these sites may have been butchery sites; all of them are distinguished by a low density of artifacts; a high frequency of flakes; and a rarity of larger, shaped core tools (Howell, 1978). **Cores** are simply lumps of stone from which flakes have been removed; sometimes a core is the by-product of tool making but it may also be shaped and modified to serve as a tool in its own right. Most of the early stone tools were made from quartz, quartzite, lava, and chert. The stone-tool industry from this time period is referred to as the **Oldowan tradition** named after Olduvai Gorge where it was first identified (Fig. 9.1).

Undoubtedly one of the finest archeological records for early hominins comes from Olduvai Gorge (Leakey, 1981). Dozens of occupational sites are found in Beds I and II containing artifacts of the Oldowan and the **Developed Oldowan tradition** (Fig. 9.2). The latter succeeds the former in lower Bed II and occurs thereafter in Beds II and IV. Oldowan and Developed Oldowan tools have also been found at several sites in North Africa (coastal Morocco and Tunisia), East Africa (Olduvai, Koobi Fora, Omo, Hadar), and South Africa (Swartkrans and Sterkfontein). After 2 mya these two traditions often overlap with each other and with later Stone Age industries.

The basic forms of stone tools that predominate from 2.0 to 1.5 mya in the Oldowan tradition include an assortment of choppers, usually made from cobblestones of quartz or quartzite; hammerstones made from pebbles or cobblestones; simple cores; polyhedrals, which are angular tools with three or more intersecting working edges; and flake scrapers (Toth, 1987). The Developed Oldowan tradition continues the flake-and-chopper industry seen in the Oldowan tradition. In addition, it includes proto-handaxes that are simple pointed choppers and crude bifacial forms (Fig. 9.2 a–d). Rarely present are more sophisticated bifacial forms, such as handaxes, which are bifacial cores with one end pointed for cutting and the other end rounded. These artifacts provide clear evidence of a rudimentary knowledge of working stone for the production of flakes and chipping edges. Some of these archeological occurrences suggest that the species making the tools may have established home bases at some of these sites.

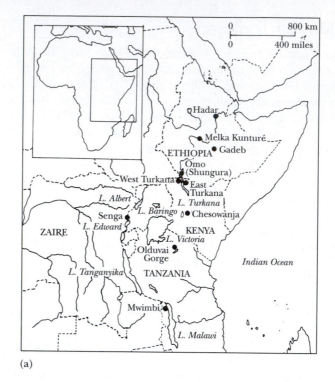

(a)

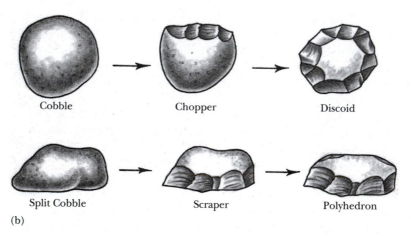

(b)

Fig. 9.1. (a) Sites in East Africa, all older than 1.4 mya, where Oldowan tools have been found. (b) Continuities among Oldowan artifact types. Removal of a few flakes transforms a cobble into a chopper and then, if more flakes are struck, into a discoid. Similarly, a split cobble, heavy-duty scraper, and polyhedron form a continuum. (c) The range of Oldowan tools and their traditional classification. (i) hammerstone, (ii) subspheroid, (iii) bifacial chopper, (iv) polyhedron, (v) discoid, (vi) flake scraper, (vii) flake, (viii) core scraper. (From Gowlett, 1992; Potts, 1993; Toth, 1985b.)

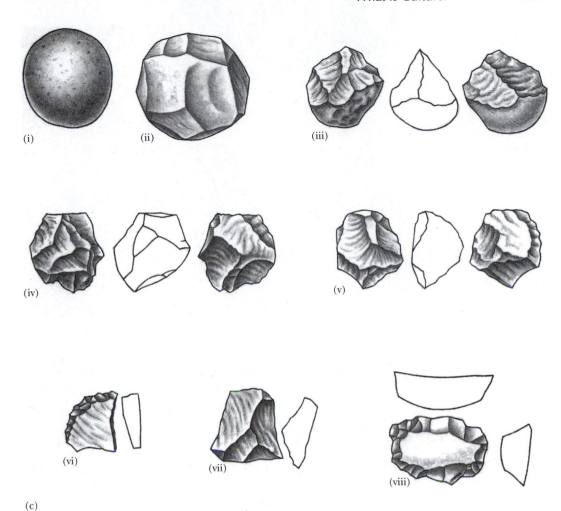

(i)   (ii)   (iii)

(iv)   (v)

(vi)   (vii)   (viii)

(c)

All the sites in eastern and southern Africa yielding Oldowan and Developed Oldowan stone tools also contain remains of *Homo* aff. *H. habilis*
and/or *Homo* aff. *H. erectus* (see later chapters). However, one cannot definitely conclude that *Homo* was the sole maker of these tools, since australopiths have also been found in association with these artifacts: *A. boisei* at
Lake Turkana (Koobi Fora), Omo, and Olduvai (Beds I and II) and *A. robustus* at Swartkrans (members 1–3) in southern Africa. However, in situ associations of *H. habilis* and Oldowan artifacts and bone assemblages have
been reported from the Western Lacustrine Plain of the Olduvai Basin
(Blumenschine et al., 1997).

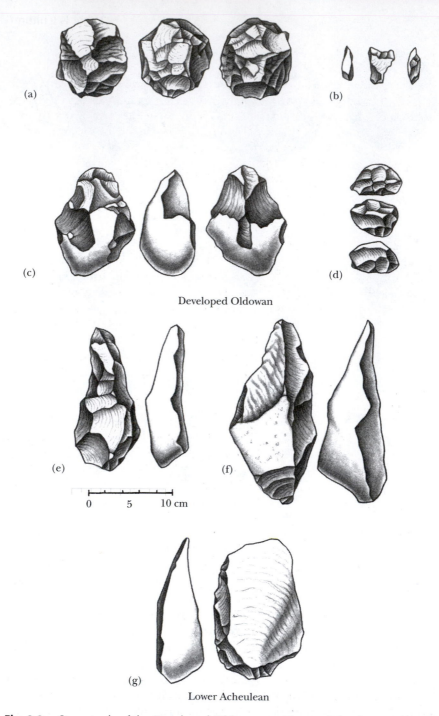

(a)

(b)

(c)

Developed Oldowan

(d)

(e)

(f)

0   5   10 cm

(g)

Lower Acheulean

Fig. 9.2. Stone tools of the Developed Oldowan and Lower Acheulean traditions. Developed Oldowan: (a) multifaceted polyhedral from North Africa, (b) small flake scraper from Olduvai, (c) core scraper from Olduvai, (d) proto-handaxe from Sterkfontein. Lower Acheulean: (e) handaxe from North Africa, (f) trihedral pick from North Africa, (g) cleaver from North Africa. (From Clark, 1970.)

The Acheulean Tradition

The most widespread and longest-lived cultural tradition on record is the **Acheulean industry**, a stone-tool tradition predominating in the late Early Stone Age. This tradition was named for St. Acheul, a site near Amiens, France, where artifacts of this style were first identified in the nineteenth century. Its earliest occurrence goes back to approximately 1.5 mya at Olduvai Gorge and Peninj (Tanzania) and Konso-Gardula (Ethiopia). It continues in some areas such as Kalambo Falls in northern Zambia to about 60 kya. More sophisticated than the Oldowan and Developed Oldowan traditions, it is sometimes found concurrently with the latter, as at Olduvai, where Acheulean tools have been recovered from the middle of Bed II up through Beds III and IV. The Acheulean tradition is characterized by large cutting tools like true handaxes, cleavers (the axe-like stone implements bearing a sharp, somewhat straight cutting edge on one end) and trihedrals (three-sided pick-like handaxes) (Fig. 9.2e–g). Perhaps it is surprising that archeologists still don't have any good idea as to what Acheulean handaxes were actually used for, although recent phytolith (microscopic plant residues) found on the cutting edges of about 1.5-million-year-old handaxes at Peninj suggest that they may have been used in woodworking activities, such as in making spears or other wooden tools (Dominguez-Rodrigo et al., 2001).

The Acheulean industry is often thought of as being associated with *H. erectus*; however, this association is sometimes tenuous. For example, although *H. erectus* is present at Lake Turkana from at least 1.6 to 1.2 mya, there is no trace of an Acheulean industry there. In southern Africa some early Acheulean artifacts have been found at Sterkfontein (member 5), which has yielded *Homo* aff. *H. habilis*. Both *H. erectus* and *A. boisei* fossils have been found at the Acheulean site of Konso-Gardula (Asfaw, 1995; Asfaw et al., 1992). We will discuss early *Homo* in later chapters (as mentioned earlier, some workers assign African *H. erectus* to the taxon *H. ergaster*).

The **Middle Stone Age** in Africa, which is generally dated from over 300 to 40 kya, is characterized by the use of carefully prepared stone cores for the production of flake tools. It is also the time in Africa when regional variation in stone-tool technologies becomes most evident. The **Late Stone Age** in Africa, which generally postdates 40 kya, is characterized by a predominance of blade tools and microliths, tiny geometrically shaped blades often set in handles made of bone or wood. The Middle and Late Stone ages are both associated exclusively with *H. sapiens* and will be discussed in more detail in later chapters.

In summary, we can say that deliberate stone tool making had evolved by about 2.5 mya but that the identity of the tool makers is inconclusive. Stone tools have not been found in direct association with either *A. afarensis* at Laetoli or Hadar or with *A. africanus* at Sterkfontein or Taung. Although these two species were presumably using some perishable tools, we have no evidence that they were actually making stone tools. The earliest stone tools of the Oldowan and Developed Oldowan traditions have been found at a number of sites yielding *A. robustus* and/or *A. boisei* and *Homo* aff. *H. habilis,* including Koobi Fora, Omo, and Olduvai. *Homo* aff. *H. habilis* is also associated with an early Acheulean industry in both eastern Africa (e.g., Olduvai) and southern Africa (Sterkfontein, member 5). The more developed Acheulean is generally associated with *H. erectus* and the Middle and Late Stone Age industries with *H. sapiens* (Table 9.1) (Potts, 1992).

No discussion of early hominin culture would be complete without some mention of the cultivation of fire. Evidence from China indicates that *H. erectus* had control over fire by about 500 kya years ago, and there is also some equivocal evidence that hominins may have been using and controlling fire about 1.4 mya at Chesowanja and Koobi Fora in Kenya (sites FxJj20E and FxJj50) (Gowlett et al., 1981; James, 1989). However, the best evidence for early control and use of fire is at about 1 mya at Swartkrans. The evidence consists of altered bones that laboratory analysis indicates were burned at temperatures consistent with campfires rather than natural conflagrations. These bones are found in member 3, dated at about 1.5–1.0 mya (Brain and Sillen, 1988). Although remains of *A. robustus* and *Homo* aff. *H. erectus* are found in members 1 and 2, only *A. robustus* is so far known from member 3; however, *Homo* is presumed to have been present as well. Tools of the Developed Oldowan tradition, usually associated with *Homo,* are found throughout the sequence. It is not clear, therefore, which hominin was using fire at Swartkrans.

OVERVIEW OF THE GENUS *HOMO*

Our own genus, *Homo,* first appears in the fossil record of Africa some 2.5–2.0 mya. Anthropologists traditionally divided the genus into three time-successive species, or **chronospecies,** *H. habilis, H. erectus,* and *H. sapiens,* reflecting the view that we represent a single anagenetic lineage—that is, one characterized by a gradual accumulation of changes from ancestor to descendant through time. But does this traditional view of human evolution actually underestimate, or overestimate, the number of species of *Homo* that existed at any one time during the Plio-Pleistocene (Conroy, 2002, 2003; Foley, 1991; Hunt, 2003; Tattersall, 1986)?

Over the past two decades an increasing number of fossils ascribed to early *Homo* have been discovered in both eastern and southern Africa, as well as in Eurasia (e.g., Republic of Georgia) (Fig. 9.3). However, until the recovery of a maxilla of *Homo* aff. *H. habilis* (AF 666-1) dated to about 2.3 mya found closely associated with Oldowan tools in the upper part of the Kada Hadar member of the Hadar Formation was reported, no fossil

Table 9.1   Inferences about Hominin Behavior and Ecology

Hominins and Time Periods (Years Ago)	Inference	Nature of the Evidence
Hominin ancestors (?8–5 million)	Equatorial African origin	Humans are genetically closest to African apes, which today are distributed across equatorial Africa; earliest hominid fossils are in eastern Africa
Earliest hominins (5–3 million)	Habitually bipedal on the ground; occasionally arboreal	Postcranial anatomy of fossils from Hadar in Ethiopia (but disagreements about similarity to modern human bipedalism and degree of arboreality)
	Inhabited a mosaic of grassland, woodland, and thick shrub	Faunas from Laetoli in Tanzania, Hada, and Makapansgat in South Africa
(3–2 million)	Occupation of open savannas	Fossil pollen and fauna
	Emphasis on a fibrous plant diet in robust australopiths	Microwear on teeth; large teeth and jaws
	First known manufacture of stone tools	Tools from Ethiopia, Kenya, Malawi, Zaire dated between 2.5 and 2.0 mya
Plio-Pleistocene hominins[a] (2.0–1.5 million)	Increased commitment to bipedalism on the ground	Postcranial anatomy associated with archaic *Homo* established
	Increased dexterity related to tool use and tool making, and possibly foraging	Anatomy of hand bones and characteristics of stone tools and cores
	Stones and animal bones carried repeatedly to specific sites	Earliest known complex sites with many stone artifacts and fossils
	Use of tools to procure and process food	Bone and stone tools with distinctive traces of use
	Dietary increase in protein and fat from large animals	Cut marks made by stone tools animal bones
	Scavenging and possible hunting of large animals; processing of animals at specific spots	Limb bones of animals concentrated at undisturbed archeological sites
	Increased cognitive capacities associated with making tools, foraging, social arrangements, and/or developing linguistic skills	Increase in brain size from about a third to a half that of modern humans
	Changes in maturation rate	Implied by brain size increase and possible changes in tooth development
	Increased mobility and predator defence	Large stature evident in skeletal remains of early *Homo erectus* from West Turkana in Kenya

[a] Stone technology and changes in diet, brain size, etc., are usually associated with *Homo*.
From Potts (1992).

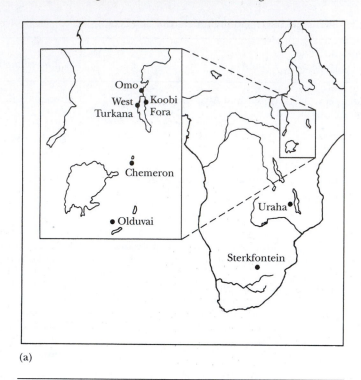

(a)

	Sites		
Mya	Olduvai (OH)	Koobi Fora (KNM-ER)	Omo
1.6	13		
	16		
1.7		3891	
1.8	7, 8, 62		
		1805	
	24		
1.9		1470, 1802, 1813, 3732, 3735	L894-1
2.0			

(b)

Fig. 9.3.   (a) Location of African sites where *H. habilis,* or similar forms, have been found. (b) Some of the better-known fossils often attributed to *H. habilis* arranged in approximate chronological order by site. (From Wood, 1992c.)

hominin attributed to the genus *Homo* unequivocally predated 2 mya (Kimbel et al., 1996, 1997).[1]

However, as the pace of discovery has quickened, so have the inevitable questions such discoveries raise: How can early *Homo* be distinguished from "gracile" australopiths, particularly *A. africanus* and/or *A. afarensis?* Is the range of morphological variation subsumed under the name *H. habilis* too great for a single species? If so, what other taxa are represented? Does the definition of *Homo* need to be modified, and if so, how? Is *H. habilis* really ancestral to *H. erectus?* These are just some of the interesting issues facing paleoanthropologists as they study the origins of the genus *Homo*.

The starting point for our discussion on the origin of *Homo* is the simple question: How does one define it? This is not as simple a question as it sounds. Our genus, which encompasses such diverse groups as modern humans, Neandertals, and *Homo erectus*, is notoriously difficult to define. To be sure, certain evolutionary "trends" are easy to visualize, such as increasing body and brain size and the lessening of sexual dimorphism, particularly during the *H. erectus* stage (Feldesman and Lundy, 1988; McHenry, 1992a, 1992b). And until quite recently most descriptions of the genus *Homo* were simply a litany of features, or general trends, characterizing the various species with little emphasis given to the possession of shared derived features that actually define them as members of a genus in the cladistic sense (Howell, 1978; Leakey et al., 1964; LeGros Clark, 1955). For example, Louis Leakey, Phillip Tobias, and John Napier, in their landmark 1964 paper describing the new species *H. habilis*, offered the following definition of the genus:

> A genus of the Hominidae with the following characters: the structure of the pelvic girdle and of the hind-limb skeleton is adapted to habitual erect posture and bipedal gait: the fore-limb is shorter than the hind-limb; the pollex is well developed and fully opposable and the hand is capable not only of a power grip but of, at the least, a simple and usually well developed precision grip; the cranial capacity is very variable but is, on the average, larger than the range of capacities of members of the genus *Australopithecus*, although the lower part of the range of capacities in the genus *Homo* overlaps with the upper part of the range in *Australopithecus;* the capacity is (on the average) large relative to body-size and ranges from about 600 c.c. in earlier forms to more than 1,600 c.c.; the muscular ridges on the cranium range from very strongly marked to virtually imperceptible, but the temporal crests or lines never reach the midline; the frontal region of the cranium is without undue post-orbital constriction (such as is common in members of the genus *Australopithecus*); the supra-orbital region of the frontal

---

[1]The *Homo*-like features of the maxilla include a relatively wide and deep palate (similar to other species of *Homo* and distinct from *Australopithecus*) with a parabolic dental arcade, a modest degree of subnasal prognathism, nasoalveolar clivus sharply angled to the roof of the palate and to the floor of the nasal cavity, shovel-shaped I^2 crown, large but symmetric canine, narrow M^1 crown, and rhomboidal M^2. Over 30 stone tools were recovered, most being typical Oldowan flakes made from basalt and chert. (Kimbel et al., 1996.)

bone is very variable, ranging from a massive and very salient supra-orbital torus to a complete lack of any supra-orbital projection and a smooth brow region; the facial skeleton varies from moderately prognathous to orthognathous, but it is not concave (or dished) as is common in members of the Australopithecinae; the anterior symphyseal contour varies from a marked retreat to a forward slope, while the bony chin may be entirely lacking, or may vary from a slight to a very strongly developed mental trigone; the dental arcade is evenly rounded with no diastema in most members of the genus; the first lower premolar is clearly bicuspid with a variably developed lingual cusp; the molar teeth are variable in size, but in general are small relative to the size of these teeth in the genus *Australopithecus;* the size of the last upper molar is highly variable, but it is generally smaller than the second upper molar and commonly also smaller than the first upper molar; the lower third molar is sometimes appreciably larger than the second; in relation to the position seen in the Hominoidea as a whole, the canines are small, with little or no overlapping after the initial stages of wear, but when compared with those of members of the genus *Australopithecus,* the incisors and canines are not very small relative to the molars and premolars; the teeth in general, and particularly the molars and premolars, are not enlarged buccolingually as they are in the genus *Australopithecus;* the first deciduous lower molar shows a variable degree of molarization.

Over the past few decades, a number of anthropologists have analyzed the genus *Homo* using cladistic techniques (Chamberlain and Wood, 1987; Skelton and McHenry, 1992; Stringer, 1986). One such analysis concluded that the *Homo* clade could be defined by only 8 character state changes out of a total of 90 cranial, mandibular, and dental characters investigated (Chamberlain and Wood, 1987; Wood, 1991, 1992c). These 8 are listed in Table 9.2.

THE DISCOVERY OF "HANDYMAN": *HOMO HABILIS*

In the summer of 1959, just a few weeks before the discovery of the "Zinj" cranium (*A. boisei*), a left mandibular fragment with M_3 and an isolated lower premolar were found about 8 feet above the basal lava at site MK, Bed I, Olduvi.[2] These teeth (OH 4) were small, narrow, and elongated. However, in the excitement over the discovery of the Zinj cranium just a few weeks later, a detailed analysis of the MK teeth was postponed.

The following year some fragmentary postcranial (tibia and fibula, OH 35) and craniodental (OH 6) remains of another small-toothed hominin were found at the same site (FLK)[3] that had yielded the massive-toothed type specimen of *A. boisei* (OH 5). The size and proportions of these

---

[2] *MK* stands for MacInnes Korongo.
[3] *FLK* stands for Frida Leakey Korongo.

Table 9.2   Morphological Features That Define the *Homo* Clade

---

The cladogram presented below is the most parsimonious generated from a set of
90 cranial, mandibular, and dental characters. The resulting *Homo* clade is
defined by the following character state changes at node A:

1. Increased cranial vault thickness
2. Reduced postorbital constriction
3. Increased contribution of the occipital bone to cranial sagittal arc length
4. Increased cranial vault height
5. More anteriorly situated foramen magnum
6. Reduced lower facial prognathism
7. Narrower tooth crowns, particularly mandibular premolars
8. Reduction in length of the molar row

The two species making up the original *H. habilis* hypodigm, *H. habilis* sensu
stricto and *H. rudolfensis*, share a hypothetical ancestor that neither shares with
any other taxon. That sister group is defined by the five character state changes
at node b:

1. Elongated anterior basicranium
2. Higher cranial vault
3–4. Mesiodistally elongated M_1 and M_2
5. Narrow mandibular fossa

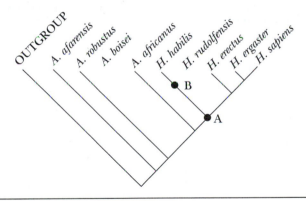

From Wood (1992c).

---

smaller teeth clearly ruled out the possibility that this was an example of
sexual dimorphism. Later that same year, Louis and Mary Leakey's eldest
son, Jonathan, discovered additional remains from a nearby occupational
site, or **living floor** (FLK NN). These consisted of the greater part of a juvenile mandible with teeth; an isolated upper molar; parts of two juvenile
parietal bones; and a number of wrist, hand, and finger bones. All of these
specimens were designated OH 7. At the same locality Mary Leakey found
at least a dozen foot bones (OH 8). All the dental remains clearly departed
from the australopith tendency toward dental enlargement (Tobias, 1991).

This "hominizing" trend was not confined to the teeth, however. Even though the parietals belonged to a juvenile, they were far bigger than any australopith parietals thus far described. Based on their size and shape, endocranial capacity was estimated at 642–723 cc in this individual, which is greater than in any australopith (Holloway, 1965; Tobias, 1964). Thus "the same creature which showed hominizing tendencies in its teeth also showed a more hominized brain-size" (Tobias, 1965a). Over the next few years several other specimens were found (e.g., OH 13 and 16), and in 1964 these became the basis for the description of a new species of *Homo*, which was formally named *H. habilis* (Table 9.3) (Leakey et al., 1964). The **type** of the new species, i.e., the specimen that serves as the standard for the taxon, became the OH 7 sample mentioned above. Other specimens attributed to *H. habilis* included the cranial fragments and teeth (OH 4 and 6), part of an adult foot (OH 8), an incomplete cranium of an adolescent (OH 13), a collection of juvenile cranial pieces (OH 14), and the fragmented cranial vault and

Table 9.3   Distinguishing Morphological Features of *H. habilis*

Cranial and mandibular

Maxilla and mandible smaller than in *Australopithecus* but equivalent in size to *H. erectus* and *H. sapiens*

Brain size greater than *Australopithecus* but smaller than *H. erectus*

Slight to strong muscular markings

Parietal bone curvature in the sagittal plane varying from slight (i.e., hominine) to moderate (i.e., australopithecine)

Relatively open-angled external sagittal curvature to occipital

Retreating chin, with a slight or absent mental trigone

Dental

Incisors large with respect to those of *Australopithecus* and *H. erectus*

Molar size overlaps the ranges for *Australopithecus* and *H. erectus*

Canines large relative to premolars

Premolars narrower than in *Australopithecus* and within the range of *H. erectus*

All teeth relatively narrow buccolingually and elongated mesiodistally, especially the mandibular molars and premolars

Postcranial

Clavicle resembles *H. sapiens*

Hand bones have broad terminal phalanges, capitate and metacarpophalangeal articulations resembling *H. sapiens*, but differ in respect of the scaphoid and trapezium, attachments of the superficial flexor tendons, and the robusticity and curvature of the phalanges

Foot bones resemble *H. sapiens* in the stout and adducted big toe, and well-marked foot arches, but differ in the shape of the trochlea surface of the talus and the relatively robust third metatarsal

From Leakey et al. (1964).

dentition (OH 16) of a young adult. The name *habilis* was suggested to Leakey, Tobias, and Napier by Raymond Dart and in Latin means "handy, skillful, able." The best-known specimens from Olduvai include OH 7 (known as "Jonny's Child," after its discoverer, Jonathan Leakey), OH 13 ("Cinderella"), OH 16 ("George"), and OH 24 ("Twiggy"). A possible *H. habilis* specimen from southern Africa, StW 53 from Sterkfontein, is a partial cranium that has been likened to OH 24 (Clarke, 1985a). At Sterkfontein, *Homo* aff. *H. habilis* is thus far known only from member 5, thus postdating the *A. africanus* specimens from member 4. Several specimens from Swartkrans (SK 847 and SK 45) have also been compared to *H. habilis* at one time or another (Clarke and Howell, 1972).

Some traditions die hard, and many anthropologists were not amused by the naming of a new species of *Homo*. While two of its describers proposed early on that *H. habilis* was both a phenetic and phyletic link between *Australopithecus* and *H. erectus* (Napier and Tobias, 1964; Tobias, 1966), this view was not universally shared (Howell, 1965; Robinson, 1965). Critics raised doubts on several fronts, reflecting both the prevailing paradigms and biases of the day (Tobias, 1965b, 1989a, 1989b):

- It was believed that the "morphological distance" between *A. africanus* and *H. erectus* was too slight to accommodate another species between them.
- Brain enlargement was accepted as a preeminent hallmark of *Homo*, thus hominins with brain sizes smaller than those of *H. erectus* could not be called *Homo*.
- The definition of the genus *Homo* was held to be immutable and sacrosanct, and some critics were uncomfortable that Leakey, Tobias, and Napier would broaden it to accommodate *habilis*.
- Behavioral considerations, such as stone-tool culture, were considered irrelevant to the definition and diagnoses of hominin species.

The senior author of the new species, Louis Leakey, took another tack altogether. He concluded that several features of cranial shape shared by *H. habilis* and *H. sapiens* were not found in *H. erectus;* therefore *H. habilis* should not be regarded as simply a stage between *A. africanus* and *H. erectus* but rather as a form directly ancestral to *H. sapiens* (Leakey, 1966).

By the end of the 1970s many anthropologists came to recognize the distinctiveness of *H. habilis* not only from Olduvai but also from other sites in East Africa, like Lake Turkana and Omo and possibly from locations in South Africa (Sterkfontein) as well (Fig. 9.3a) (Boaz and Howell, 1977; Clarke, 1985a; Clarke and Howell, 1972; Harris et al., 1988; Howell, 1978; Hughes and Tobias, 1977; Leakey et al., 1971).

As mentioned in the previous chapter, *H. habilis* and *Australopithecus* were contemporaries in East Africa for hundreds of thousands of years. The dates of some of the better-known *H. habilis* specimens from East Africa are shown in Figure 9.3b.

MORPHOLOGICAL FEATURES OF *HOMO HABILIS*

The basic morphological features of *H. habilis* are summarized in Table 9.3 and illustrated in Figure 9.4. In general, the cranium of *H. habilis* is more gracile than that of *Australopithecus*, particularly in its less well developed muscular crests. Cranial capacity averages about 650 cc and endocranial casts (arguably) reveal the first paleoneurological evidence for **Broca's area,** the speech area in the left cerebral cortex (Fig. 6.10) (Falk, 1980, 1983a, 1987a). This compares with average cranial capacities of 413 cc for *A. afarensis* and about 450 cc for both gracile (*A. africanus*) and robust australopiths (*A. robustus, A. boisei, A. aethiopicus*) (Falk et al., 2000). Facial heights and breadths are reduced relative to those in *Australopithecus*, and prominent anterior pillars are absent. In general, maxillas and mandibles are smaller than in *Australopithecus* and are within the size range of *H. erectus* and *H. sapiens*. The sagittal curvature of the parietal bone varies from slight (within the hominin range) to moderate (within the australopith range), and the curvature of the occipital bone is less than in *Australopithecus* or *H. erectus* and within the range of *H. sapiens.*

Regarding the dentition, the canines are proportionately large relative to the premolars. The premolars and molars are within or below the size range found in *A. africanus* while the incisors are relatively larger. There is a marked tendency toward buccolingual (side-to-side) narrowing and mesiodistal (front-to-back) elongation of most teeth, especially the lower premolars and molars.

H. habilis shows an interesting mosaic of australopith and *Homo*-like postcranial features. For example, while the foot is human-like in terms of metatarsal robustness and in having a well-marked longitudinal and transverse arch, other features, such as the shape of the talonavicular joint and the high talar neck angle, suggest the possibility of at least some divergence of the hallux (Kidd et al., 1996). The middle phalanges of the hand are somewhat ape-like in being robust and curved with well-marked insertions for powerful muscles of finger flexion; however, the overall length and morphology of the distal phalanges are similar to those of modern humans and, most important, the thumb joint, or **carpometacarpal joint**, is distinctly human-like (Trinkaus, 1989b). It would thus seem that *H. habilis* was bipedal but retained a hand capable of powerful grasping.

This view of *H. habilis* as essentially human in both form and function was seriously challenged in July 1986, when a partial skeleton (OH 62) was recovered from lower Bed I, Olduvai. The very fragmented remains included pieces of calvaria, maxilla, mandible, ulna, radius, humerus, femur, and tibia (Johanson et al., 1987). Unfortunately, none of the postcranial specimens, except the ulna, preserved any of their articular surfaces (Johanson, 1989). The palate and teeth were described as similar to other specimens attributed to *H. habilis*, especially StW 53 from Sterkfontein, OH 24 from Olduvai, and KNM-ER 1470 and 1813 from Koobi Fora, and for this reason OH 62 was referred by its discoverers to *H. habilis*. However, as we shall see below, some anthropologists now believe that these specimens (and others) are too morphologically diverse to be included in a single taxon called *H. habilis*. For example, most workers now consider KNM-ER 1470 to be the type of a different species, *H. rudolfensis*.

For the time being, if we assume that OH 62 is correctly identified as *H. habilis*, then it reveals details of body proportions and forelimb and hindlimb joint sizes that are totally unexpected for this species—namely, that some australopith species that predate it in time (e.g., *A. anamensis*) actually have more *Homo*-like limb proportions than this earliest species of the genus *Homo*! This raises difficult questions about the place of *H. habilis* in human evolution (McHenry and Berger, 1998a, 1998b). For example, the inferred high humerofemoral index (length of the humerus divided by the length of the femur multiplied by 100) of about 95 indicates that this individual had relatively long arms. This value is higher than in both modern humans (about 75) and *A. afarensis* (about 85) (Jungers and Stern, 1983). Moreover, this adult individual is as small, or smaller than, any other known fossil hominin, including the *A. afarensis* skeleton of Lucy (AL 288-1). This is particularly interesting in that OH 62 is also more similar to African apes in limb bone proportions than Lucy is, and yet Lucy is more than 1 million years *older* than OH 62 and is often considered to be ancestral to *H. habilis*.

This brings up an interesting problem. The juxtaposition in the fossil record of a relatively modern *H. erectus* skeleton (WT 15000) from West Lake Turkana dated to about 1.6 mya (see next chapter) and a postcranially primitive *H. habilis* skeleton (OH 62) dated to about 1.8 mya is perplexing: How could *H. habilis* have evolved so rapidly into *H. erectus* given that their skeletons were so completely different? It is just this type of problem that lends support to those who now view the entire known sample, or **hypodigm**, of *H. habilis* as too diverse to be sensibly encompassed within a single species. It also leads some to question whether or not *H. habilis* should be retained in the genus *Homo* (see below). If the hypodigm of *H. habilis* needs to be split, there are two interesting possibilities concerning OH 62: (1) OH 62 is not *H. habilis* and, on the basis of both its stratigraphic position and its limb proportions, it would not fit into an evolutionary lineage leading to *H. erectus* or (2) OH 62 does belong to *H. habilis* but, because of its skeletal features, it should be omitted from a role in later human evolution (Hartwig-Scherer and Martin, 1991). Whatever the final resolution of this problem, the place of OH 62 in human evolution is clearly puzzling.

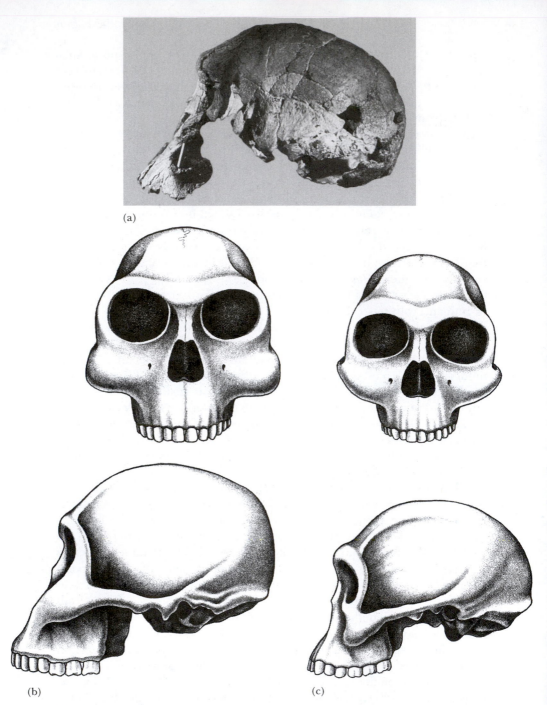

(a)

(b)   (c)

Fig. 9.4. Crania of *H. habilis* from Koobi Fora Formation (Eastern Lake Turkana). (a) Specimen ER 1470 (now considered the type of *H. rudolfensis*). (Courtesy of Alan Walker, © National Museums of Kenya.) (b) Reconstruction of ER 1470, presumably a male. (Redrawn from Howell, 1978.) (c) Reconstruction of specimen ER 1813, presumably a female. (Redrawn from Howell, 1978.) (d) Comparison of *H. habilis* to other early human fossils. (From Stringer, 1992.)

	Homo habilis (small)	Homo habilis (large)	Homo erectus	Archaic Homo sapiens	Neandertals	Early Modern Homo sapiens
Height (m) Physique	1 Relatively long arms	c 1.5 Robust but "human" skeleton	1.3–1.5 Robust but "human" skeleton	? Robust but "human" skeleton	1.5–1.7 As 'archaic H. sapiens,' but adapted for cold	1.6–1.85 Modern skeleton; ?adapted for warmth
Brain size (cc)	500–650	600–800	750–1,250	1,100–1,400	1,200–1,750	1,200–1,700
Skull form	Relatively small face; nose developed	Larger, flatter face	Flat, thick skull with large occipital and brow ridge	Higher skull; face less protruding	Reduced brow ridge; thinner skull; large nose; midface projection	Small or no brow ridge; shorter, high skull
Jaws/teeth	Thinner jaw; smaller, narrow molars	Robust jaw; large narrow molars	Robust jaw in larger individuals; smaller teeth than H. habilis	Similar to H. erectus but teeth may be smaller	Similar to 'archaic' H. sapiens; teeth smaller except for incisors; chin development in some	Shorter jaws than Neandertals; chin developed; teeth may be smaller
Distribution	Eastern (and southern?) Africa	Eastern Africa	Africa, Asia, and Indonesia (and Europe?)	Africa, Asia and Europe	Europe and western Asia	Africa and western Asia
Known date (years ago)	2–1.6 million	2.4–1.6 million	1.8–0.3 million	400,000–100,000	150,000–30,000	130,000–60,000

(d)

HOMO HABILIS: ONE SPECIES OR TWO?

Two questions that paleoanthropologists must constantly grapple with are: How different do two fossils have to be in order to be considered different species? and How similar must two fossils be in order to be attributed to the same species? Some have argued that paleoanthropologists probably err on the side of underestimating the amount of taxonomic diversity in the hominin fossil record (Tattersall, 1986, 1992), whereas others have argued just the opposite (Wolpoff et al., 1993). Perhaps in partial reaction to this, there has recently been renewed interest in reevaluating the taxonomic homogeneity of the early *Homo* hypodigm (Conroy, 2002, 2003; Grine et al., 1996; Rightmire, 1993).

Unfortunately, very few authors subdivide the hypodigm in the same way (Table 9.4). For example, of the two most recent monographic studies of early *Homo*, one concludes that all the Olduvai and Koobi Fora specimens can be attributed to *H. habilis* as a single **polytypic** species—that is, one comprising several geographical and/or morphological variants (Tobias, 1991), whereas the other concludes that while the Olduvai fossils can indeed be attributed to *H. habilis*, two different species are represented

Table 9.4   Multiple Taxon Solutions for Crania and Mandibles Attributed to *H. habilis*

| | Specimens | | |
Author(s)	OH	KNM-ER	Taxon Names
Robinson (1965)	7	—	*A.* aff. *A. africanus*
	13	—	*H.* aff. *H. erectus*
M. Leakey et al. (1971)	7, 16	—	*H. habilis*
	13, 24	—	*H. habilis/Homo* sp.
Groves (1989b)	7, 13, 16, 24	—	*H. habilis*
	—	1470, 1590, 1802	*H. rudolfensis*
	—	730, 820, 992, 1805,	*H. ergaster*
Stringer (1986)	7, 24	1470, 1590, 1802, 3732	*H. habilis* (group 1)
	13, 16	992, 1805, 1813	*H. habilis* (group 2) or *H. ergaster*
Wood (1991)	7, 13, 16, 24, 37, etc.	1478, 1501, 1805, 1813, 3735, etc.	*H. habilis*
	—	1470, 1482, 1590, 1802, 3732, etc.	*H. rudolfensis*

From Wood (1992c).

in the Koobi Fora sample—*H. habilis* and a new species, *H. rudolfensis* (Wood, 1991) (but see below concerning Wood's more current views on *H. rudolfensis*).

Our whole concept of the taxon *H. habilis* is really based on the fossil material from Beds I and II at Olduvai, and there seems to be a slowly growing consensus that most, if not all, of this material is reasonably encompassed within a single species, the more important specimens being OH 7 (the type), OH 13 (cranial parts and mandible), OH 16 (badly fragmented cranium and mandibular dentition), and OH 24 (crushed cranium) (Groves, 1989b; Leakey et al., 1971; Tobias, 1991; Wood, 1991, 1992c).[4] So in order to address the question of whether *H. habilis* is one species or two, we must turn our attention to the specimens from Koobi Fora, for that is where the problem lies.

Almost from the very beginning of fieldwork at Koobi Fora a number of late Pliocene–early Pleistocene hominins were found that could not be comfortably included within the existing hypodigms of either robust australopiths or *H. erectus.* Most, if not all, of them were either formally or informally allocated to an early species of *Homo* with similarities noted between them and *H. habilis* and/or *A. africanus* (R. Leakey, 1971, 1972, 1973, 1974; Leakey and Wood, 1973, 1974). Some of the better known examples within this group include KNM-ER 992 and 1802 (mandibles) and KNM-ER 1470, 1813, 1590, and 1805 (crania). The initial describers of this material were cautious in their taxonomic assessments. However, in 1975 the first serious proposal was put forward to formally subdivide this early *Homo* sample into two species, *H. habilis* and *H. ergaster*[5] (Groves and Mazak, 1975). Others followed suit and this early *Homo* sample was soon being divided in various and sundry ways (Stringer, 1986; Walker, 1981; Wood, 1992c). By the late 1980s it was proposed that *H. habilis* be split into two geographical subdivisions: (1) *H. habilis* sensu stricto (in the strict sense) from Olduvai and (2) *Homo* spp. (several species) from Koobi Fora and southern Africa (Chamberlain and Wood, 1987).

Further cladistic analyses of the variations within the cranial vault, face, and dentition of the *H. habilis* hypodigm reinforced the view that multiple taxa were being sampled and that the Koobi Fora and Olduvai early *Homo* samples could be sorted into three species: *H. habilis,* *H. rudolfensis,* and *H. ergaster* (Wood, 1992a). According to these studies,

---

[4]For differing views (Robinson, 1965; Stringer, 1986; Walker and Leakey, 1978).

[5]The mandible KNM-ER 992 was named the type specimen of the new species, *H. ergaster* (Groves and Mazak, 1975). "This taxon was inadvertently described under the impression that it was in the public domain, which it was probably not (an unintended breach of ethics); unfortunately, too, it was named before the description of such fossils as 1813 and 3733, with either of which the jaw 992 could perhaps be conspecific" (Groves, 1989b). An additional problem with using the nomen *H. ergaster* is that the type specimen, KNM-ER 992, has not been differentiated from *H. erectus* (Wood, 1992c).

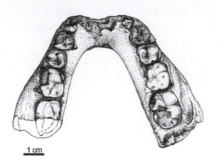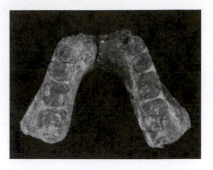

Fig. 9.5.   *Homo rudolfensis* from the Chiwondo Beds, Malawi.   (Photo courtesy of O. Kullmar.)

the hypodigm of *H. habilis* includes specimens from both Koobi Fora and Olduvai, whereas *H. rudolfensis* and *H. ergaster* are (thus far) restricted to the Turkana Basin. Recently, however, a new specimen attributed to *H. rudolfensis* has been recovered from deposits faunally dated to about 2.4 mya from the Chiwondo Beds of Uraha, Malawi (Fig. 9.5) (Bromage et al., 1995; Schrenk et al., 1993; Wood, 1993).

  H. rudolfensis is characterized by a large braincase, or **neurocranium,** and *Homo*-like endocranial morphology combined with facial and dental features that resemble, at least superficially, those of robust australopiths. These similarities between *H. rudolfensis* and robust australopiths are regarded as structural resemblances due to parallelisms or convergent evolution, or homoplasies, rather than to common ancestry. In this view the clade consisting of *H. habilis* and *H. rudolfensis* is united by five character state changes (Table 9.2) (Wood, 1992a; Chamberlain and Wood, 1987).

  In this taxonomic scheme, *H. habilis* from Olduvai is regarded as an early species of *Homo* that retains an essentially australopith postcranial skeleton and a more *Homo*-like masticatory complex, whereas *H. rudolfensis* combines a more *Homo*-like postcranial skeleton with a more robust australopith craniodental complex (Table 9.5).

  Two specimens from Koobi Fora, KNM-ER 1470 and 1813, are particularly instructive in illustrating the taxonomic difficulties involved in sorting out the *H. habilis* hypodigm (Fig. 9.6). Most researchers agree that both specimens belong to the genus *Homo*.[6] The question is whether or not both crania could be drawn from the same species of *Homo*, and if so, would this species be *H. habilis* as defined by the Olduvai fossils? Based mainly on differences in cranial size and shape, particularly in the supraorbital and cheek, or malar, region, and cranial capacity (about 510 cc for KNM-ER 1813 and about 770 cc for KNM-ER 1470), a number of researchers have concluded that these two crania (as well as others) show

[6]But see Walker (1981) for a different view.

Table 9.5   Evidence for and Features of *H. habilis* sensu stricto and *H. rudolfensis*

	H. habilis s.s.	H. rudolfensis
Skull and teeth		
Absolute brain size (cc)	$\overline{X} = 610$	$\overline{X} = 751$
Overall cranial vault morphology	Enlarged occipital contribution to the sagittal arc	Primitive condition
Endocranial morphology	Primitive sulcal pattern	Frontal lobe asymmetry
Suture pattern	Complex	Simple
Frontal	Incipient supraorbital torus	Torus absent
Parietal	Coronal > sagittal chord	Primitive condition
Face, overall	Upper face > midface breadth	Midface > upperface breadth: markedly orthognathic
Nose	Margins sharp and everted; evident nasal sill	Less everted margins; no nasal sill
Malar surface	Vertical, or near vertical	Anteriorly inclined
Palate	Foreshortened	Large
Upper teeth	Probably two-rooted premolars	Premolars three-rooted; absolutely and relatively large anterior teeth
Mandibular fossa	Relatively deep	Shallow
Foramen magnum	Orientation variable	Anteriorly inclined
Mandibular corpus	Moderate relief on external surface, rounded base	Marked relief on external surface, everted base
Lower teeth	Buccolingually narrowed postcanine crowns	Broad postcanine crowns
	Reduced talonid on P_4	Relatively large P_4 talonid
	M_3 reduction	No M_3 reduction
	Mostly single-rooted mandibular premolars	Twin, plate-like, P_4 roots, and bifid, or even twin, plate-like P_3 roots
Postcranium		
Limb proportions	Ape-like	?
Forelimb robusticity	Ape-like	?
Hand	Mosaic or ape-like and modern human-like features	?
Hindfoot	Retains climbing adaptations	Later *Homo*-like
Femur	Australopith-like	Later *Homo*-like

H. habilis sensu stricto and *H. rudolfensis* have been suggested as species components of the larger *H. habilis* hypodigm (Wood, 1991). Specimens allocated to the two taxa are as follows:

H. habilis sensu stricto
   Olduvai: OH 4, 6, 8, 10, 13–16, 21, 24, 27, 35, 37, 39–45, 48–50, 52, 62
   Koobi Fora: KNM-ER 1478, 1501 1502, 1805, 1813, 3735

H. rudolfensis
   Koobi Fora: KNM-ER 813, 819, 1470, 1472, 1481–1483, 1590, 1801, 1802, 3732, 3891
From Wood (1992c).

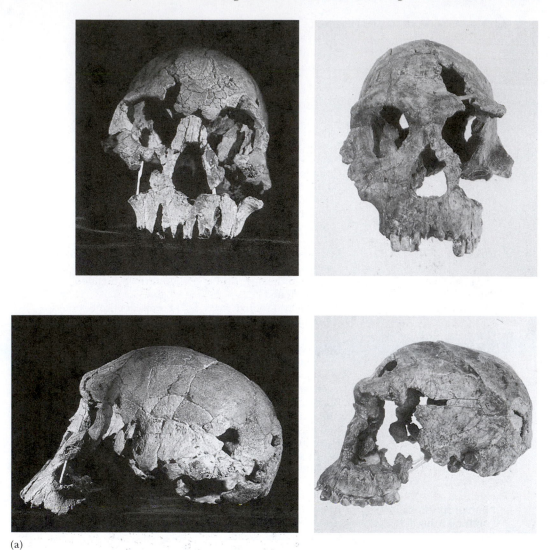

(a)

Fig. 9.6. (a) Two views of crania KNM-ER 1470 (left) and 1813 (right) (Wood, 1991) (Courtesy of B. Wood and the National Museums of Kenya.) (b) Some morphological differences between crania KNM-ER 1470 and 1813 (Stringer, 1992).

too much variation to be considered conspecific (Groves, 1989b; Kramer et al., 1995; Stringer, 1986; Wood, 1985, 1991; Walker and Leakey, 1978). For example, one cladistic analysis concluded that the "*H. habilis*" fossils represented by KNM-ER 1813 and the fossils from Olduvai Gorge are most likely the sister group of *H. erectus*, whereas the other taxon, *H. rudolfensis*, repre-

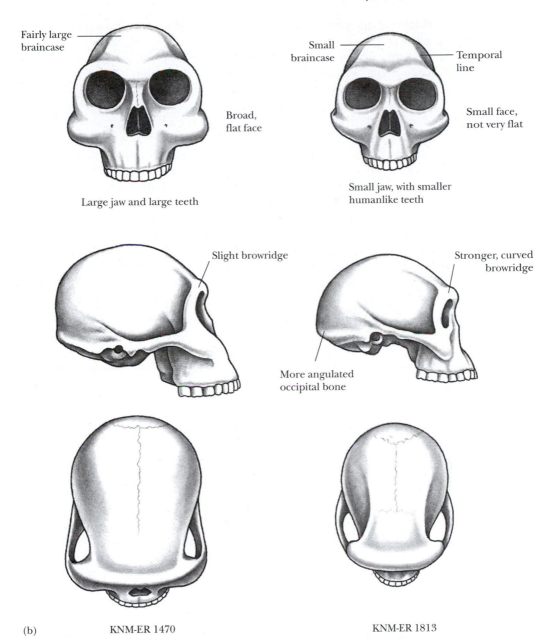

Fairly large braincase

Broad, flat face

Large jaw and large teeth

Small braincase

Temporal line

Small face, not very flat

Small jaw, with smaller humanlike teeth

Slight browridge

Stronger, curved browridge

More angulated occipital bone

(b)   KNM-ER 1470   KNM-ER 1813

sented by KNM-ER 1470 and other fossils from Lake Turkana, share many derived features with australopiths (Lieberman et al., 1996). However, another study concluded that perhaps two and possibly three separate species existed within the hypdigm of *H. habilis* and that all of these specimens were clearly distinct from *H. ergaster*, or early *H. erectus* (Grine et al., 1996).

This latter study also found that the magnitude of size and shape differences between early *Homo* from South Africa (e.g., SK 847 and StW 53) and East Africa would have a very low probability of being found in any modern human sample. This would be fine except that other analyses find few statistical reasons, at least based on craniofacial dimensions of other hominoids, to believe that more than one species of *Homo* is being sampled. For example, craniofacial variation in the four most complete *H. habilis* crania (KNM-ER 1470, 1813, OH 24, and Stw 53) were compared to similar measures in a large sample of gorillas. Multivariate analyses indicated a range of variation among the three smaller fossils (KNM-ER 1813, OH 24, and Stw 53), which some have regarded as representing two species, that is less than that seen in female gorillas. In addition, the differences between 1470 and the three smaller fossils was found to be comparable to that among male gorillas or that between average male and female gorillas, suggesting that multiple species proposals for this sample may not be warranted (Miller, 1991, 1994, 2000; J. Miller et al., 1997).

However, we must keep in mind two points when considering these confusing results: (1) many of these fossils were reconstructed from dozens of isolated pieces and, therefore, their overall shape may be suspect (e.g., KNM-ER 1470)[7] and (2) very large bodied, highly dimorphic extant primates like orangutans and gorillas may not be appropriate biological models with which to assess intraspecific variability in early *Homo*.

Some paleoanthropologists have also drawn a distinction between *H. erectus* as defined from the Far East and Koobi Fora specimens sometimes regarded as African versions of *H. erectus* (see next chapter). They attribute such *H. erectus*–like specimens from Koobi Fora—for example, KNM-ER 730, 992, 3733, and 3883—to a different species, *H. ergaster*. Cladistic analyses suggest that *H. ergaster* is the sister group of *H. sapiens* and can be distinguished from *H. erectus* by its retention of primitive features involving the form of the mandible and aspects of tooth crown and root morphology as well as by sharing with *H. sapiens* such derived cranial features as increased parietal breadth, longer occipital region, broader nasal bones and nasal aperture, shorter cranial base, more substantial basal component of the mandibular symphysis, and buccolingual narrowing of the mandibular canine and first molar (Wood, 1992a).

Bernard Wood has presented five hypotheses about early *Homo* that can be tested by the fossil record (Wood, 1991):

1. Fossils from Olduvai and the Turkana Basin sample a single species, *H. habilis* (the lack of temporal trends in this model is compatible with the idea of evolutionary stasis in early *Homo*, a view more consistent with punctuated equilibrium models than with gradualistic evolutionary models) (Fig. 9.7a.1).

---

[7]A point recently raised concerning the interpretation of *Kenyanthropus platyops* (White, 2003).

2. Early *Homo* consists of two time-successive species, the more recent being *H. habilis,* which evolved rapidly (Fig. 9.7a.2).

3. Early *Homo* consists of two time-successive species, the more recent being *H. habilis,* which evolved gradually (Fig. 9.7a.3).

4. Early *Homo* is represented by two **synchronic** (existing or occurring at the same time) and **sympatric** (occurring together in the same geographical area) species, one of which is *H. habilis* (Fig. 9.7a.4).

5. Early *Homo* consists of two synchronic, but allopatric (occurring in different geographical areas) species, *H. habilis* at Olduvai and a separate species in the Turkana Basin sites. This model implies that a speciation event took place before 2.5 mya (Fig. 9.7a.5).

The last four models suggest that variation in early *Homo* warrants recognizing more than one species. Wood's three most likely taxonomic schemes are shown in Figure 9.7b. The two likeliest schemes suggest *H. habilis* at Olduvai and two species in the Turkana Basin, *H. habilis* and *H. rudolfensis*.

HAVE THE LIMITS OF *HOMO* BEEN STRETCHED TOO FAR?

As we have seen in this chapter, early *Homo* has been subdivided into a number of species amid much controversy. As we will see in later chapters, the number of species included in the genus *Homo* increases even further. This state of affairs has spurred Bernard Wood and Mark Collard to ask the question posed above in the heading and to answer it in the affirmative (Collard and Wood, 2001; Wood and Collard, 1999a, 1999b). They have detailed six steps in the process of what they call "relaxing the criteria" for allocating species to *Homo:*

1. Naming the original Neandertal skeleton from Feldhofer as a new species of *Homo, H. neanderthalensis*

2. Naming the Mauer mandible from Germany as a new species of *Homo, H. heidelbergensis*

3. The recommendation that *Pithecanthropus erectus* should be transferred to the genus *Homo* as *H. erectus*

4. Designating the new gracile species from Olduvai as a new species of *Homo, H. habilis*

5. The allocation of KNM-ER 1470 to a new species of *Homo, H. rudolfensis*

6. Changing functional interpretations of *H. habilis* over time

As Wood and Collard point out, the various species now included in *Homo* run the morphological gamut from australopith-like postcranial morphology, limb proportions, and brain size seen in *H. habilis* to those same features in modern humans. They identify four criteria that have historically been used to place fossils in the genus *Homo*.

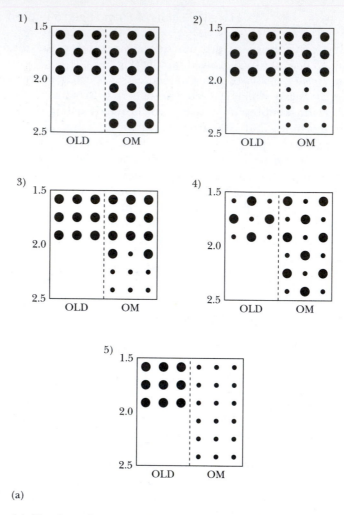

(a)

Fig. 9.7. (a) Five hypotheses put forward to explain the variation within East African samples of early *Homo*. Each box is divided into the two regional subsets of the fossil evidence: OLD (Olduvai) and OM (Omo Group; Shungura and Koobi Fora). The vertical axis represents millions of years (Wood, 1992c). Hypothesis 1 represents a single taxon solution; Hypotheses 2–5 all posit more than one early *Homo* taxon. Hypotheses 2 and 3 specify that the two taxa are time successive; Hypotheses 4 and 5 see them as synchronic. Hypotheses 4 and 5 differ in that the latter suggests that the two taxa are geographical variants (i.e., synchronic but allopatric). Note that in each case hominins do not appear in the Olduvai fossil record until slightly after 2.0 mya. (b) The three most likely taxonomic schemes for early *Homo* in order of descending likelihood. *Large dot, H. habilis; smaller dot,* a different early *Homo* species, perhaps *H. rudolfensis* (Wood, 1991.)

The first has to do with brain size. Going back to the early writings of Arthur Keith (1948), this "cerebral rubicon" for inclusion in *Homo* was put at about 750 cc. By the time Louis Leakey, Phillip Tobias, and John Napier (1964) described the new species *H. habilis*, this rubicon had been lowered to 600 cc.

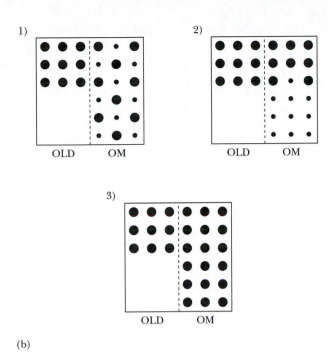

(b)

The second criterion was the possession of language. Based on his studies of hominin endocasts, Tobias (1991) has long championed the view that *H. habilis* had the ability to communicate using language. He believes that endocasts of *H. habilis* revealed cerebral prominences corresponding to two well-developed speech areas of the brain, Broca's and Wernicke's areas.

The third criterion was the ability to make stone tools. As we noted earlier, the name *habilis* (handyman) reflects this point of view concerning this species.

The final criterion is the possession of a human-like precision grip with a well-developed opposable pollex.

A strong case can be made that none of these criteria is satisfactory for a fossil species to be included in the genus *Homo*. The idea of a "cerebral rubicon" is meaningless because absolute brain size in and of itself is of limited biological interest without some reference to body size. Likewise, the idea that language ability can somehow be read off an endocast (paleophrenology?) is highly suspect (Gannon et al., 1998).[8] Linking *Homo* exclusively to tool use and manufacture is also problematic since it is certain that *Australopithecus* and *Homo* were both synchronous and sympatric during the earliest phases (at least) of stone tool manufacture and that both genera had hand grips compatible with this ability (Marzke, 1997; Semaw et al., 1997; Susman, 1983, 1998).

[8]Phrenology began to fall into disfavor when early phrenologists such as F. Gall found that the crania of homicidal felons often had larger areas for compassion than those of clerics (Lieberman, 2002)!

Given these problematic issues regarding the definition of the genus *Homo*, what are we to do? First of all, what is meant by the term *genus*? There are two, somewhat contradictory, definitions of the term. The first states that a genus is a species or group of species of common ancestry that share a unique "adaptive zone" different from that occupied by species of any other genus (an evolutionary systematics definition). By this definition, a genus could, in theory at least, be monophyletic or paraphyletic. The second is that a genus is a group of species that are more closely related to each other than to any species assigned to any other genus (a cladistic definition). A genus is always monophyletic in this definition. Wood and Collard (1999b) suggest a new approach—namely that the evolutionary systematic definition be modified so that paraphyletic taxa are inadmissible.

Here's how the idea would work. Numerous studies agree that later *Homo* species (e.g., *H. erectus, H. ergaster, H. heidelbergensis, H. neanderthalensis*) are more closely related to *H. sapiens* than they are to any australopith genera. In contrast, there is no such assurance that either *H. habilis* or *H. rudolfensis* are more closely related to *H. sapiens* than to other australopith genera. Of course, there is always the sobering study that showed that the types of morphology preserved in the hominin fossil record may not be a reliable source of information about phylogeny (e.g., phylogenies based on craniodental measurements could not, with any confidence, capture the "true" phylogeny" as determined by molecular means) (Collard and Wood, 2000). The conclusion seems evident: *H. habilis* and *H. rudolfensis* should be included as species in the genus *Australopithecus*, whereas the other *Homo* species should remain in *Homo*. However, even this proposal has been thrown into some doubt by the recent discovery of an early *Homo* specimen from Bed I Olduvai (OH 65) that bears a striking resemblance to KNM-ER 1470, the type of *H. rudolfensis*. Both specimens are said to differ little from the *H. habilis* holotpye (OH 7), thus casting some doubt on the recognition of *H. rudolfensis* as a biologically valid taxon in the first place (Blumenschine et al., 2003).

Leaving this added complication aside, the australopith group is unified by features such as: (1) relatively low body mass and brain size, (2) a postcranial skeleton suggesting a combination of terrestrial bipedalism with proficient climbing ability, (3) jaws and teeth reflecting heavy masticatory stresses, and (4) a life history (maturation) schedule more reminiscent of apes than of modern humans. The *Homo* group is unified by relatively larger body and brain size, a more modern postcranial skeleton, more gracile teeth and jaws, and a life history schedule more modern human-like. Collard and Wood (2000) conclude by noting "that if the genus *Homo* is to have any meaning, its lower boundary should mark a distinct shift in hominin adaptive strategy involving morphological and behavioral innovation. In other words, it should be a new adaptive type." Some authors have even taken all this one step further and consider all post-australopith species to be part of a single unbroken *H. sapiens* lineage leading directly to living humans (Hawks et al., 2000a).

EARLY HOMININ LIFESTYLES: TINKER, TAILER, SCAVENGER, HUNTER?

In order to reconstruct early human behavioral evolution, paleoanthropologists must develop models to organize and interpret an ever-expanding body of paleontological, archeological and primatological data. The goals of paleoanthropology should be (1) to explain as much as possible about human evolution in terms of animal analogs for the human traits we wish to understand and (2) to seek "common patterns of adaptations underlying those analogies" (Cartmill, 1990). Among the first, and most influential, researchers to apply this reasoning to the study of early hominin behavioral evolution were George Bartholomew and Joseph Birdsell (1953) who proposed that it "should be possible to extrapolate upward from ecological data on other mammals and suggest the biological attributes of the protohominins and to extrapolate downward from ethnological data on hunting and collecting peoples and suggest the minimal cultural attributes of the protohominins."

Today, most models of human behavioral evolution can be classified as either conceptual or referential (Moore, 1996; Stanford and Allen, 1991; Tooby and DeVore, 1987). **Conceptual models** reconstruct early hominin behavior using principles from behavioral ecology and evolutionary theory and information on the behavior of particular primate species, including humans. An example of this type is Lovejoy's (1981, 1993) model of human behavioral evolution based on pair bonding and ecological separation during foraging, which we discussed in the last chapter. In contrast, **referential models** use the social system of a particular nonhuman primate species to model early hominin behavioral evolution, examples being the savanna baboon model popular in the 1960s (DeVore and Washburn, 1963) and the pygmy chimpanzee model of the 1980s (Zihlman, 1983; Zihlman et al., 1978).

The savanna baboon model was predicated on the notion that, aside from humans, savanna-dwelling baboons were the most successful ground-living primates. Therefore, study of their adaptations should yield insights into some of the problems that confronted early hominins as they gradually left the trees for more terrestrial habitats on the African savannas. Thus this model attempted to reconstruct the evolution of human behavior by comparing the social behavior and ecology of baboons with that of living hunter-gatherer groups, including such aspects as troop size and structure, predator defense, home range size, dietary preferences, and (in particular) the roles of hunting and scavenging.

By contrast, the pygmy chimpanzee model was based more on the close genetic affinity between humans and African apes, and especially on the evidence (mostly molecular) that humans and chimpanzees share a relatively recent common ancestor (as noted earlier, humans and chimpanzees differ by only 1–5% of their DNA sequences) (Britten, 2002; Navarro and Barton, 2003). This model held that pygmy chimpanzees, therefore, were the most reliable source of morphological and behavioral data regarding protohominins. It is undoubtedly true that key behavioral innovations were involved in the divergence of the human line from the ape line and, as we have seen, many theories emphasize the shift from dense forests to more open habitats to "explain" human origins. It is interesting, however, that studies on the behavioral ecology of forest-dwelling chimpanzees of the Tai forest, Ivory Coast, demonstrate that many patterns of behavior once thought to favor a savanna-dwelling model for hominin origins now actually lead to the opposite conclusion. According to the savanna-dwelling model, human-like behaviors evolved only as a consequence of changes in the habitat of early hominins from forest to more open savanna woodland. However, studies of rain forest chimpanzees reveal behavioral trends at odds with the savanna model. Specifically, forest chimpanzees have been found to use more tools (including hammerstones to grind nuts), make them in more different ways, hunt more frequently and more often in groups, and show more frequent cooperation and food sharing than do savanna-adapted chimpanzees (Boesch-Achermann and Boesch, 1994; Mitani et al., 2002). Thus it seems that exploitation of the savanna habitat, in and of itself, is not sufficient to explain the evolution of such "human-like" behavioral traits as increased tool using, cooperative hunting, and/or food sharing.

The reconstruction of early hominin behavior is a challenging problem for anthropologists, and any number of conceptual and referential models have been put forward. A particularly important aspect of any such debate is the evolution of human hunting and what role, if any, scavenging and/or gathering played in the early evolution of this behavior (Hawkes, 1993; Hawkes et al., 1991; O'Connell et al., 2002). This question has led to a sometimes raucous debate among archeologists about the role of scavenging in early hominin behavior (Binford, 1985; Blumenschine, 1995).

THE DEBATE OVER "MAN THE HUNTER"

Until relatively recently, most models of human behavioral evolution in general, and the evolution of tool making in particular, revolved around the "Man the Hunter" paradigm (Washburn and Lancaster, 1968). The intensity of the debate about Man the Hunter sometimes made it seem as if the defining image of human nature were at stake (Cartmill, 1993). The traditional story goes something like this. A successful hunt put a premium on foresight, strategic planning, cooperation, communication skills, and dexterity, all of which in turn selected for larger brains, more efficient bipedalism, and nimbler hands. It envisions that these traits unleashed a technological revolution, raising the payoff for intelligence and augmenting the original selective pressure. In this scenario, hunting becomes the engine that drives a self-sustaining feedback loop of social and intellectual evolution (Blumenschine and Cavallo, 1992). In this hunter's paradise, early hominins lived in social groups characterized by a sexual division of labor in which Man the Hunter would return to his monogamously bonded Woman the Gatherer at a home base where he would altruistically share the product of his hunting prowess with other members of the social group.

At one time or another anthropologists have labored to correlate some or all of the following to a hunting way of life (Fedigan, 1982): (1) the reduction of canines and increased skill in the manufacture and use of tools and weapons; (2) bipedalism; (3) increasing brain size and human intelligence; (4) sharing of food; (5) sexual division of labor, with males providing sustenance and protection and females providing sexual and reproductive functions; (6) the human nuclear family; (7) continual sexual receptivity of the female, used to attract and hold a provider-male permanently; (8) the incest taboo, used to avoid disrupting nuclear families; (9) exogamy or the exchange of females; (10) cooperation replacing competition among males; (11) male bonding and prominence in social, especially political life; (12) language, in order to cooperatively stalk and hunt prey; (13) territoriality, larger home ranges, and increased mobility; (14) aesthetics, developed from the appreciation of beautiful tools; and (15) pleasure in killing.

Such testosterone-oriented hypotheses were once defended by appeals to both archeological and primatological observations. For example, behavioral studies on free-ranging chimpanzees at Gombe, Tanzania, showed that males spent significantly more time hunting than females; females, on the other hand, reportedly spent more time "gathering" ants and termites (Goodall, 1986). It was even suggested that one "function" of infanticide in chimpanzees might be to "correct" a mother's promiscuity by coercing her into more restrictive mating relationships with high-ranking adult males (Hamai et al., 1992). Likewise, interpretations of a number of early Pleistocene East African archeological sites reinforced beliefs that stone tools associated with animal bones unambiguously documented early human hunting and butchery practices (Fig. 9.8) (Isaac, 1971, 1978; Shipman, 1983).

But how valid is this Man the Hunter scenario? It is interesting that, as both primate field studies and archeological methods of analyses expand and mature over the years, the emerging picture is proving to be far more complex than previously thought (Hrdy, 1981). For example, it has been reported that chimpanzees living in the tropical rain forest at Tai National Park, Ivory Coast, use tree roots as anvils for cracking the hard nuts of kola and Panda trees with stone or wood hammers selected from the surrounding forest, some of which are carried up to 100 m for use in cracking nuts (Boesch et al., 1994). What is most interesting is that females engage in such tool use more frequently than males and that tools made and used by these chimpanzees are never used as hunting weapons. While it is true that females participate less often than males in hunting (4% at Gombe and 13% at Tai), they are more likely than males to share meat with other group members when they do hunt (Boesch and Boesch, 1984, 1989). Such recent disclosures about chimpanzee behavior have led to a much-needed rethinking about the evolution of early hominin behavior: "Th(ese) observation(s), combined with the suggestion that tool use may have been a predominantly female activity, (are) at odds with both early and more recent male-centered models of human social evolution" (Stanford and Allen, 1991).

In a review of hunting ecology of wild chimpanzees, Craig Stanford (1996) described some of the probable similarities in predation patterns between chimpanzees and early hominins: First, diets primarily consisted of plant foods, with meat contributing a relatively small percentage of the overall diet and with prey animals located opportunistically during the course of plant food foraging. Meat was likely eaten seasonally due to nutrient shortages and perhaps changes in prey availability owing to

(a)

Fig. 9.8. Cartoons illustrating various hypotheses purporting to explain why early hominins disarticulated animal carcasses: (a) to facilitate cooking, (b) for storage, (c) for transporting the carcass back to a camp or home base, and (d) for sharing meat with others . (From Shipman and Rose, 1983.)

(b)

(c)

(d)

329

birth seasons and prey ranging behavior. The hunting range was the home range of the group, and hunting frequency was correlated with patterns of home range use. Hunting was primarily a male activity, and hunting success was correlated with the number of male hunters involved. After a kill, meat was shared by members of the hunting party and with the females who were present. Bone marrow and the brain were the favored parts of the prey, suggesting that hunting was an important source of fat, particularly in the dry season. Finally, in chimpanzees the success of hunting is highly correlated with the number of estrous females within the group, suggesting that the capture, possession, and control of meat were used by males for their own political and reproductive benefits.

Scavenging opportunities available to early hominins would depend on two major factors: (1) the kinds of large carnivores in the area that would compete for the "kill" and (2) the ecological context in which the scavenging occurs. Based on analogies with scavenging opportunities existing today in the Serengeti and Ngorongoro Crater of East Africa, studies suggest that early hominins may have regularly encountered abandoned felid kills, particularly in riparian woodlands during the dry season (in a less dry and less seasonal savanna, scavenging opportunities are also available in open grasslands where lions dominate the landscape) (Tappen, 1995). Although most kills would have been of medium-size adult herbivores, it is unlikely that there would have been much flesh remaining on such carnivore kills, except for marrow bones and head contents, by the time hominin scavengers got to them. However, this last point might depend on the type of carnivore making the kill. For example, it is hypothesized that large quantities of scavengeable flesh may have remained if saber-tooth cats had made the kill, since these predators did not have the masticatory apparatus to crush bones and completely dismember carcasses the way that some modern felids do. In this regard, it is important to note that at least three large saber-tooth felids shared the African continent with early *Homo* in the Plio-Pleistocene (Blumenschine, 1987; Blumenschine and Cavallo, 1992; Lewis, 1995; Marean and Ehrhardt, 1995).

How did early hominins interact with such carnivore communities? One hypothesis is that saber-tooths may have concentrated their hunting activities in dense woodland and forest localities (closed habitats), while other, more modern felids may have been active in more open woodland and savanna habitats. In this scenario, *H. habilis*, with its inferred arboreal abilities, may have scavenged more effectively in forest habitats and may have been much less susceptible to predation and carcass competition than in more open habitats. The extinction of saber-tooths in sub-Saharan Africa coincides with a period of grassland expansion and forest retreat about 1.8–1.6 mya and perhaps this ecological shift forced *H. habilis* to increase its use of more open habitats in competition with modern felids.

It has been postulated that such high predation pressure and the need to switch to more confrontational scavenging and/or hunting strategies may have contributed to the rapid increase in body size from *H. habilis* to *H. erectus* and the closely coincident shift in stone-tool technology. The Acheulean tool kit makes its first appearance about 1.6–1.5 mya (Marean, 1989). However, some archeologists speculate that ecological overlap between hominins and large carnivores may have lessened in intensity by the Middle Pleistocene. For instance, the Lower Pleistocene sites at Olduvai Gorge dated to about 1.85–1.70 mya apparently demonstrate that hominins and carnivores exploited similar animal species, were attracted to the same body parts, overlapped spatially, and interacted directly on occasion.[9] For example, detailed studies of carcass processing by Plio-Pleistocene hominins and carnivores at Olduvai site FLK 22 (the *Zinjanthropus* site) indicate that long bones were processed in a three-stage carnivore–hominin–carnivore sequence of events: (1) long bones were first defleshed by carnivores, (2) hominins then processed the intact long bones for marrow, and (3) carnivores then processed the epiphyses for grease (Capaldo, 1997). However, the Middle Pleistocene sites of Lainyamok and Olorgesailie present a more complex picture. For example, at Lainyamok hominin activities were apparently rare, whereas the mammalian carnivores were diverse and common and hyenas were active collectors and chewers of bones. However at Olorgesailie, where hominin activity was high, carnivore fossils are very rare (Potts et al., 1988).

One other potential source of scavenged food for early hominins may have been tree-stored leopard kills of small bovids (Cavallo and Blumenschine, 1989).

The availability of scavenging opportunities to hominins in the past is a complex problem. For example, the greater number of carnivore species in both more open (e.g., the saber-tooth *Homotherium*) and more closed (e.g., the saber-tooth *Dinofelis* and *Megantereon*) habitats suggests that unless early hominins were near the top of the carnivore hierarchy, confrontational scavenging would have been difficult. In addition, different ecological pressures were operating on hominins in eastern and southern Africa with respect to dietary behavior. For example, hominins may have had better scavenging opportunities in eastern Africa because of the lack of bone-cracking abilities in saber-tooths (eastern Africa lacked the large bone-cracking *Pachycrocuta* found in southern Africa). Regardless of the scavenging versus hunting frequencies of early hominins, there can be little doubt that the extinction of both saber-tooth and large bone-cracking carnivores opened a variety of behavioral avenues to our early ancestors (Lewis, 1997).

Scavenging and/or hunting by early hominins also present another problem that is sometimes overlooked. Phylogenetic analyses of taeniid

---

[9]It is suggested that early hominins played a role in the accumulation of crocodile and turtle remains at sites in Olduvai Beds I and II. Aquatic reptiles would have provided predictably located and seasonally reliable sources of dietary fat for early hominins (West, 1997).

tapeworms indicate that the presence of these parasites in humans pre-dated the development of agriculture, animal husbandry, and domestica-tion of cattle or swine—that is, they colonized African hominins before the origin of modern humans (Hoberg et al., 2001). These parasitological data strongly suggest that, as early African hominins began scavenging and/or preying upon antelope and other bovids, they became exposed to colonization by *Taenia* tapeworms that had been using hyaenids, canids, and felids as definite hosts and bovids as intemerdiate ones.[10]

Archeological sites are also being reevaluated, and the view that early Pleistocene "living floors" represent home bases where meat was shared is coming under closer scrutiny (Sept, 1992).[11] Due in large part to the influ-ence of the late Glynn Isaac, home bases were traditionally interpreted as temporarily occupied camps or foci of activities to which mobile groups of hominins returned after foraging, prepared and ate food, and carried on family based social activities. Isaac argued that the use of home bases, sex-ual division of labor, and food sharing were important selective pressures that ultimately led to the development of language and the establishment of cultural rules in early hominin society. His home base hypothesis im-plied that early hominins had developed a pattern of land use and sociality that was more analogous to that of contemporary hunter-gatherers than to that of extant nonhuman primates.

Archeologists use several criteria for recognizing scavenged assem-blages in the archeological record: (1) a broad range of prey-animal sizes, (2) a low proportion of juveniles, (3) a broad range of prey-species habi-tats, and (4) a skew in the distribution of prey sizes toward the large end of the range (Shipman, 1983; Vrba, 1980b). In a study of the bones at Olduvai, one archeologist, at least, came to a conclusion about early ho-minin behavior that shares little with the Man the Hunter paradigm (Bin-ford, 1981): (1) hominins were scavenging animal kills after most of the other predator-scavengers had abandoned the carcass and scattered some of its parts; (2) the scavenged parts were mostly leg bones that already had most of the meat removed by other predators, or they were lower leg bones that had little meat on them; (3) the major, or in some cases the only, usable or edible parts consisted of bone marrow; (4) hominins were using hammerstones to break open the leg bones in order to expose the

[10]A recent molecular study of human body lice (*Pediculus humanus*), which feed on the human body but live in clothing, reaches the somewhat silly conclusion that human clothing originated only about 72,000 ± 42,000 years ago (Kittler et al., 2003). Neandertals living in glacial Europe must have been pretty thick-skinned!

[11]Three features thought to be common to archeological home bases are (1) the artifacts, or raw materials for tool making, were transported to the site from some distance and could not have accumulated at the site artificially; (2) the bones associated with the artifacts came from different species of animals and different individuals of the same species, suggesting that meat was transported to the site for food sharing; and (3) the sites were anomalous concentrations of debris, suggesting a spatial focus for hominin activity (Isaac, 1971).

marrow; (5) there is no evidence supporting the idea that hominins removed food to a base camp for consumption or that food was shared. These observations led Binford (1985) to conclude: "At the dawn of tool use the early hominins appear to have been scavenging carcasses largely for marginal foods and using tools to gain access to these tiny morsels, mainly bone marrow. That this can be taken as evidence for a 'scavenging' mode of adaptation is highly unlikely, since the tactics indicated must have contributed only slightly to the modal subsistence security of these creatures."

A rather different hypothesis concerning archeological sites at Olduvai was advanced by archeologist Richard Potts (1984, 1987, 1993) of the Smithsonian Institution, who argued that many of these localities were not home bases at all but rather stone caches where early hominins brought animal carcasses, or parts thereof, for processing. In order to minimize competition with other predators that would be attracted to both kill and processing sites, it was necessary for these early hominins to quickly dismember the carcasses and to abandon the sites as soon as possible. For this reason, they dispersed stone raw material and previously made tools at a number of "caches" within the foraging area. Because these processing sites were revisited over a period of time, numerous stone tools and bones from many different animals would be expected to accumulate. The notion that these sites were abandoned to carnivores helps explain the presence of both stone-tool cut marks and carnivore tooth marks on many of the bones.

A somewhat different model, called the resource-defense model, looks at living floors in a slightly different way. It emphasizes competition between conspecific groups for spatially fixed resource patches, such as fruiting trees, water, plant foods, shade, sleeping sites, tools, and raw material for tool making. According to this model, meat, whether hunted or scavenged, represented a movable high-quality resource patch that had to be defended from competitors, including other hominins as well as sympatric carnivores. For this reason, an efficient strategy would be to bring the carcasses (or parts thereof) to strategic areas of fixed resources where tools were cached and where the processing of the carcass could be carried out in a cooperative and safe manner. The model also suggests that carnivore competition would actually have favored, rather than prevented, the regular use of key defensible sites for these multiple home-base activities (Rose and Marshall, 1996).

But perhaps too much emphasis has been placed on the eating of meat and not enough on the eating of other foodstuffs that would have been available to early hominins. Both the scavenging and the hunting models still have as their central focus the procurement of meat by early hominins as a "high-quality" food. However, because there is an upper limit to the amount of plant or animal protein that a forager can safely consume for calories on a sustained basis, meat may actually have been a relatively minor source of sustenance for early hominins. This upper limit of about 50% of total calories means at least half of a forager's total energy needs must be obtained from nonprotein sources, either fat or carbohydrates (Speth, 1989).

If one considers the daily energy demands of primates in general, important insights may be gained about early hominin foraging ecology. Dietary quality is positively correlated with both day range and relative energy expenditure among living primates: more active species consume more energetically rich diets and have a greater territorial range. In contrast, species subsisting on poor-quality diets tend to have smaller ranges and lower total energy expenditure for their size. Based mainly on body size estimates of early hominins and the fact that resting metabolic rates in mammals scale to the three-quarters power of body weight, it would seem that daily energy needs must have increased substantially in early *Homo*, particularly *H. erectus*, compared to australopiths. Changing patterns of resource distribution associated with the expansion of African savannas between 2.5 and 1.5 mya likely would have made animal foods a particularly attractive energy resource to early hominins (Leonard and Robertson, 1997a, 1997b).

The procurement of meat as a high-quality food has become a central focus in a very intriguing hypothesis relating the coevolution of the brain and digestive system in human evolution—the so-called expensive-tissue hypothesis (Aiello and Wheeler, 1995). This hypothesis argues that an increase in the relative size of one (the brain) could only be accomplished by corresponding reduction in size of the other (the gut) since the brain and digestive systems are both metabolically expensive organs, but increases in basal metabolic rate do not seem to be correlated with increasing brain size in humans. As it turns out, the gut is the only metabolically expensive organ in the human body that is small relative to body size. In addition, gut size is highly correlated with diet, and a relatively small digestive tract is compatible only with high-quality, easy-to-digest food resources, animal products being one such important source.

It is also relevant in this regard to note that extant humans (and apes) are descended from a common plant-eating ancestor, which is reflected in their gut anatomy and digestive kinetics. It is usually the case in mammalian herbivores that body size increase is associated with a decrease in dietary quality. As body size in early hominins increased in the early *Homo* lineage, this ecological "dilemma" was circumvented by evolving mechanisms (i.e., hunting) enabling them to include more animal protein in their diet. They were thus able to reap the nutritional benefits enjoyed by carnivores, even though their gut anatomy retained many of its herbivorous characteristics (e.g., a simple acid stomach, a small intestine, a small cecum with a vermiform appendix, and a large, sacculated large intestine).

By using meat to supply essential amino acids and other nutrients, more space was freed up in the gut for selection of higher-quality plant foods (Milton, 1999).

Over the past decade or so, a number of anthropologists have questioned the central tenets of the hunting hypothesis—that is, that hunting arose early in human evolution and that meat was the primary food source of early hominins. Instead, these authors contend that a more significant early hominin adaptation was the *gathering* of plant foods in African savanna environments, which in turn led to the invention of tools for obtaining, transporting, and preparing such foods (Fedigan, 1986; Tanner, 1987; Zihlman and Tanner, 1978). Studies show that even today the diet of so-called hunter-gatherers consists mainly of vegetable foods gathered primarily by women (Bicchieri, 1972; Lee and DeVore, 1968).

The importance of plant food in early hominin diets in general, and the role of cooking such foods in particular, has recently inspired a novel theory: that the ability to cook tubers prompted the evolution of large brains, smaller teeth, modern limb proportions, and even male-female bonding—that is, almost everything that makes us human! Of course, this would mean that early hominins could control fire for cooking by approximately 1.6 mya when some of these features (for instance the modern limb proportions seen in *H. erectus*) are already evident from the fossil record. The argument goes something like this. Modern-day tropical hunter-gatherers do not rely heavily on meat, even though they have more sophisticated hunting weapons (e.g., bow and arrow) than any early hominin would. Even chimpanzees living in dry regions of the Congo today have been noted to dig down an arm's length to reach the roots of a particular vine, then chew on its moist root and carry it as a canteen for long trips. But, as the theory goes, cooking was the real trick that unlocked the nutrients of tubers for early hominins. Hard-to-digest carbohydrates turn into sweet, easy-to-absorb calories after cooking. It also turns out that a diet consisting of 60% cooked tubers and no meat (about the proportion of tubers used in modern native African diets) increases caloric intake by about 43% over that of a diet consisting of nuts, berries, and raw tubers. A 60% meat diet offers only a 20% advantage (Wrangham et al., 1999). Smaller teeth might result from such a diet, since cooked tubers have a lower fiber content than other plant foods. And what about the male-female bonding role of tubers? This is explained by the idea that such a valuable food source would be gathered by females, stored for later use, and the cache protected by the best male defenders who were lured to this role by the sexual attractiveness of females. Voilà! The evolution of human pair bonding! But it's only a theory.

We should bear in mind, however, that there are important distinctions between modern hunter-gatherers and early hominins (Shipman, 1983). For example, modern hunter-gatherers have bigger and more complex brains than early hominins and undoubtedly possess far greater intellectual and linguistic capabilities. All modern hunter-gatherers know how to use and control fire, whereas early hominins presumably did not. Fire can be used to keep predators from sleeping quarters and food remains and can also be used to cook or dry meat, thus forestalling spoilage. Modern hunter-gatherers live in ecologically marginal areas that are very different from the environments of early hominins. Furthermore, they possess tools, implements, and weapons far exceeding those known to early hominins. Modern hunter-gatherers are faced with fewer predator species (besides other humans) than their early Pleistocene ancestors. With these caveats in mind, modern archeological research reinforces the view that early hominins used animal carcasses in less systematic ways than modern hunter-gatherers do and that early humans were predominantly opportunistic meat scavengers and plant food foragers.

One last word of caution is in order about trying to "explain" human evolution as a response to some restricted dietary regime. It has been shown that humans, chimpanzees, and baboons eat a minimum of 333 different plant genera from eastern and southern Africa and that at least 28 of these plants are exploited by all three groups. At least six of these plant genera are recognized in the paleobotanical record: *Acacia* (pods), *Albizia* (flowers and leaves), *Cordia* (fruits), *Diospyros* (fruits), *Ficus* (fruits), and *Ziziphus* (fruits). In addition, woodland savanna nut-producing trees in Africa provide a nutritious mesocarp in addition to edible, oil-rich nut seeds that would have been available as a food resource to early hominins, particularly to those like *A. robustus* and/or *A. boisei,* that could crack the nuts with either a strong masticatory apparatus, or stone tools (Peters, 1987; Peters and O'Brien, 1981).

It is interesting to speculate that if the need for large social groups among early hominins became a necessity either for common defense and/or cooperative hunting, then this may have been one of the driving forces behind the evolution of language and increasing hominin encephalization (Aiello and Dunbar, 1993). The hypothesis is based on the close statistical relationship between relative brain size, groups size, and the amount of time devoted to social grooming among nonhuman primates and posits that at some point in early human evolution group size became so large that language would have been necessary in order to maintain social cohesion. According to this model, the necessity for both large group size and at least rudimentary language appeared early in the evolution of *Homo* and increased rapidly by the second half of the Middle Pleistocene and that language evolved as a form of bonding mechanism in order to use social time more efficiently.

We remarked earlier that two evident evolutionary trends within the genus *Homo* over the last 2 million years were an increase in mean body size and a reduction in the degree of sexual dimorphism. Let us conclude this chapter by looking at some recent theories that attempt to explain the adaptive advantages of such trends.

It has been suggested that increased terrestrial behavior by early *Homo* may have released a constraint on body size, since it is known that arboreal primate species are generally smaller than their more terrestrial relatives (Clutton-Brock and Harvey, 1977). Others have suggested that reproductive and social behaviors (e.g., greater longevity, longer gestation and prenatal periods, lower birth rates, increased sociality, and increased brain size) as well as a number of ecological parameters such as broader dietary niches and increased day and home ranges may all be consequences of increased body size (Foley, 1987).

THERMOREGULATION AND BIPEDALISM

Some researchers have sought more physiological explanations for *Homo* characteristics. One of the most intriguing is that increased body size (and alterations in body proportions) may have helped larger hominins exploit dispersed resources in savanna environments because (all else being equal) they would dehydrate less during the day than smaller individuals with similar levels of metabolic activity. According to this hypothesis, larger hominins would have been able to travel farther each day, forage at higher temperatures, and cover a greater home range from a single water source. In fact, three important human attributes—bipedalism, the loss of functional body hair, and increasing body size—all reduce thermal and water stress in open equatorial environments. For example, at normal levels of metabolic activity, a naked skin actually reduces the water requirements of bipedal hominins exposed to temperatures typical of the African savanna, whereas a naked skin confers no such advantage on a quadruped (Wheeler, 1991a, 1991b, 1992a, 1992b, 1993, 1994a, 1994b, 1996).[12]

The fossil record indicates that early hominins were bipedal by 4 mya. This locomotor development is widely considered to be a crucial first event in human evolution. There has been much speculation concerning which selection pressures might be responsible for the perfection of this type of unique locomotion in our evolutionary lineage.

A popular view has been that bipedalism liberated the hands to facilitate the use of tools and weapons, perhaps as part of an ecological shift toward hunting. However, bipedalism is now known to antedate by several million years both the occurrence of stone tools in the fossil record and evidence of the inclusion of significant quantities of meat in the diet. The oldest known stone tools in the fossil record are about 2.5 mya.

[12]But see Chaplin et al. (1994) for a different view.

It has also been suggested that a specialized grasping forelimb was necessary to hold infants or to transport food.

An alternative, although not mutually exclusive proposal, is that bipedalism might have evolved as a thermoregulatory response to the physiological challenges presented by the hot, dry, African savannas in which early hominins first evolved.

Hyperthermia, or overheating, caused by high levels of direct solar radiation is a major problem that any animal living on the open African savanna would have to face. Even if such an animal could theoretically dissipate this unwanted solar energy by evaporative cooling (e.g., sweating), the costs could be prohibitive in such arid environments because it would entail the loss of so much desperately needed water.

One possible adaptive strategy might be to seek shade during the hottest times of the day, although this would have the potential disadvantage of reducing foraging time for diurnal species (i.e., those that actively hunt and/or forage during the day).

Heat storage is an alternative strategy employed by many medium to large African mammals. Heat storage allows body temperatures to rise during the day as heat is retained in the animal's tissues until nightfall, when conditions are more favorable for its dissipation by nonevaporative means. However, there is a potential problem with this strategy since elevation of core body temperatures can be tolerated only if thermally sensitive tissues like the brain can be protected.

The normal functioning of the human brain becomes progressively impaired when core body temperatures rise above 37°C (98.6°F). In fact, temperatures as low as 40.5°C (105°F) can sometimes be fatal. Consequently, mammals utilizing such a heat storage strategy must possess some type of cooling mechanism in order to protect their brains from overheating. In many arid-adapted African mammals such cooling mechanisms utilize venous blood return in an ingenious way.

In such mammals, large amounts of venous blood are cooled by evaporation within the nasal cavity, and this cooler blood helps reduce the temperature of the arterial blood that enters the brain through the carotid arteries. The effectiveness of this process is greatly enhanced by the presence of a carotid rete, or meshwork of arteries and veins, near the base of the cranium. This is an example of a simple, but effective, countercurrent exchange mechanism in which the warmer arterial blood flowing toward the heat-sensitive brain actually gives up some of its heat to the cooler venous blood returning from the brain and nasal cavity as these blood vessels intertwine in the carotid rete.

Unfortunately for early hominins, the potential for achieving such localized brain cooling through this particular mechanism would have been extremely limited since their nasal chambers were relatively small (as are ours). In addition, the carotid rete is absent in all higher primates, including humans. Because of this, the heat storage capabilities of early hominins would have been much less than those of most other savanna-adapted mammals of similar size. Therefore, early hominins must have been more dependent on whole-body cooling to avoid damaging elevations of brain temperature.

It seems reasonable to suspect that strong selection pressures would have favored any adaptation in early hominins that either reduced the amount of heat gained from the environment and/or that facilitated the rapid removal of such heat from the body. It is interesting that the evolution of bipedal postures satisfies both conditions: (1) it greatly reduces the surface area of the body directly exposed to solar radiation and (2) bipedal posture places more of the body's surface area higher above ground level, within a microclimate where airflow and temperatures are actually more favorable for convective heat loss. How does this work?

Experiments confirm that windspeeds increase as one moves farther above ground level. In fact, due to frictional interactions the velocity of an airstream flowing over a solid surface decreases logarithmically as that surface is approached. In addition, during the day the absorption of solar radiation at ground level can raise ground temperature significantly above that of the air at higher elevations. Therefore, air temperatures increase closer to the hot ground surface (just the reverse of windspeed as noted above). Both higher windspeeds and lower temperatures increase the rate at which bipeds can dissipate heat. And as we noted earlier, experiments also show that bipedalism greatly reduces the amount of heat gained from the sun, since less body surface is directly presented to incoming solar radiation. In fact, calculations show that on a clear equatorial day at noon, bipedal posture reduces direct radiation by approximately 90 W (Wheeler, 1991b).

Bipedal postures result in a higher distribution of the skin surfaces above ground level. For example, if one looked at the distribution of the body surface of a quadrupedal chimpanzee compared to a bipedal *A. afarensis* (Lucy), the mean difference would be from about 43 to 63 cm above ground level. Thus there is a greater effective airflow over the biped than in the quadruped, which translates directly into differences in the rate of convective heat loss. Any convective advantage would have been particularly important to hominins since it would have reduced their reliance on evaporative cooling, and consequently on drinking water, which is a major consideration in arid savanna environments.

Despite the potential costs in terms of increased water loss, a higher maximum rate of cutaneous evaporative cooling would also be extremely advantageous to savanna-dwelling early hominins. It would have enabled them to cope with greater thermal loads, induced either by extremely high environmental temperatures or muscular activity. Since the rate at which water evaporates from the skin is also related to wind velocity (just like loss of heat by convection), the influence of windspeed over the biped and quadruped means heat dissipation by evaporation will be similar to that of convection loss (the higher the body surface above the ground, the greater the windspeed and the more efficient heat loss).

In summary, the higher distribution of body surfaces on a biped confers two distinct thermoregulatory advantages in savanna environments. First, it allows the animal to cope with higher maximum heat loads due to the increased potential for both evaporative and convective heat loss. Second, since more heat can be dissipated by convection before it becomes necessary to utilize cutaneous sweating, the total requirement of water for thermoregulation is reduced.

Clearly, the open, arid African savanna would have been a difficult habitat for early hominins to colonize, but bipedalism did confer certain thermoregulatory advantages. First, the lower environmental heat load experienced by early bipeds increased their independence from shade seeking, thereby allowing them to remain in the open for longer and at higher temperatures. This may have been a crucial ecological benefit when competing against other daytime predators. Second, the foraging range of early hominin bipeds was further extended by the lower energetic cost of locomotion, allowing them to maintain higher walking velocities without inducing hyperthermia. Studies have shown that bipedal walking is more energy efficient than quadrupedal walking over long distances. And, finally, bipedalism greatly reduces the amount of heat gained from the sun since less body surface is directly presented to incoming solar radiation.

These factors not only expanded the potential activity envelope of early hominins on the open savanna but also reduced the amounts of food and water required to sustain such foraging behavior, the latter advantage being particularly important in relatively arid environments. Studies predict that under the conditions of a 35/40°C day the maximum daily drinking water requirement of a 35 kg hominin would have been about 1.5 L, a value from which it is possible to make some tentative inferences about early hominin behavior. Access to surface water would have been a major influence not only on the daily activity patterns of early hominins but also on their distribution, since at these daily temperatures they would not normally be expected to be found much more than about half a days' travel from water.

Thus it is likely that bipedalism is an ideal mode of terrestrial locomotion for foraging on low-density, or scattered, resources on the African savanna, where neither food nor water is abundant. Not only does it significantly reduce the amount of heat gained from the environment but also facilitates its dissipation with less reliance on water for evaporative cooling (Wheeler, 1991b).

Humans are also unusual among mammals in that we have a functionally naked skin. This unusual human attribute may also have thermoregulatory consequences since there are some advantages of body hair loss to early hominins in a savanna setting.

First, the loss of functional body hair, or more specifically the loss of the insulating layer of air trapped by the hair, increases the thermal conductance of an animal, which in turn allows more heat to be dissipated by nonevaporative means through the skin. Second, the less-restricted airflow resulting from the absence of a trapped boundary layer of air under a hairy skin also increases the rate at which heat can be evaporated from the surface of the skin. Thus two distinct thermoregulatory advantages of body hair loss on early hominins could be that (1) greater maximum rates of sweat evaporation could increase the levels of environmental temperatures and muscular activity that could be tolerated without inducing hyperthermia and (2) higher potential rates of nonevaporative heat loss, together with more efficient sweating, could reduce the demand for drinking water (Wheeler, 1992a).

The evolution of body shape can also be analyzed in terms of climatic and thermoregulatory adaptations (Chaplin et al., 1994; Ruff, 1991, 1993, 1994). For example, in order to maintain a constant surface area to body mass ratio, absolute body breadth should remain constant, despite differences in body height (therefore, pelvic breadth relative to body height actually decreases as later hominins increase in stature). This relationship is illustrated by the fact that while modern human populations living in the tropics vary greatly in stature, they show little variation in body breadth. In contrast, populations living in colder climates have absolutely wider bodies, an adaptation to reduce heat loss by lowering the surface area to body mass ratio. All African early hominins have absolute body breadths within the range of modern human populations inhabiting tropical and subtropical climates. In addition, the taller, more linear body proportions of *Homo* (as opposed to the more "ape-like" proportions of *Australopithecus*) may have functioned to reduce daytime sweat losses by 20–30% in open equatorial environments, thereby reducing daily water requirements by 15–18% (Fig. 9.9).

As we have noted in this and earlier chapters, many dramatic morphological changes have occurred within the genus *Homo* over the last several million years. Such changes include large increases in absolute brain size accompanied by decreases in both postcanine dental size and skeletal robusticity. Recent detailed comparative studies have shown that body mass in Pleistocene *Homo* actually averaged about 10% larger than in living populations and that, relative to body mass, brain mass in late early *H. sapiens* (Neandertals) was actually slightly less than in early "anatomically modern" humans (mainly due to the fact that body mass in Neandertals was about 30% greater than in modern humans, thus slightly lowering their brain mass to body mass ratio compared to modern humans). Clearly the major increase in encephalization within *Homo* occurred during the Middle Pleistocene (600–150 kya) after a long period of stasis through much of the Early Pleistocene (Conroy et al., 2000). These data also reveal

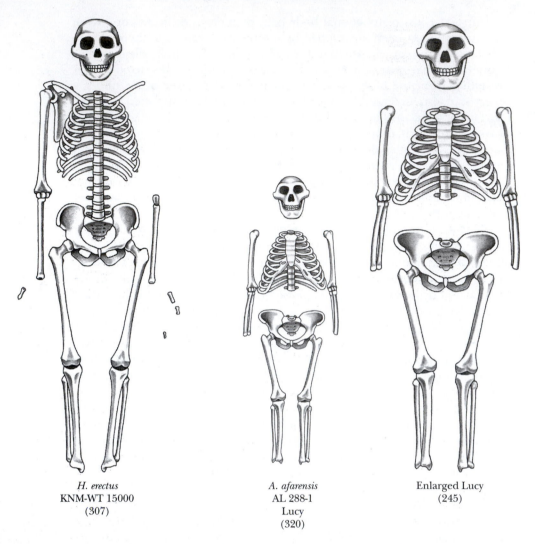

H. erectus
KNM-WT 15000
(307)

A. afarensis
AL 288-1
Lucy
(320)

Enlarged Lucy
(245)

Fig. 9.9. The skeletons of African *H. erectus* (KNM-WT 15000) and *A. afarensis* (Lucy). The outline of Lucy on the right is her shape if she were enlarged to the same height as *H. erectus.* Approximate ratios of surface area to body mass are given below each figure. The figures show that the evolution of *H. erectus* was accompanied by an increase in both body size and linearity of body form. That is, relative to their height, small australopiths had broad bodies, whereas early *H. erectus* had narrow ones. This is consistent with thermoregulatory constraints on body shape because in order to maintain the same ratio of body surface area to body mass any increase in height should be accompanied by no change in body breadth (Ruff, 1993).

a decrease in both average absolute brain size and body size over the past 35,000 years, clearly documenting a generalized overall size reduction in the human skeleton during the Upper Paleolithic (Ruff et al., 1997).

It is now time to leave these early hominins as they scavenge and hunt over the landscape of Africa and turn our attention to a more formidable and geographically widespread species, *Homo erectus*.

CHAPTER X

Quo Vadis *Homo erectus?*

INTRODUCTION

The eminent anthropologist W. W. Howells summed it up well (1981): "As Voltaire might have said, if *Homo erectus* did not exist it would be necessary to invent him. And, of course, a century ago Ernst Haeckel did just that . . . and named it *Pithecanthropus.*" But is *Homo erectus* simply an arbitrarily defined stage, or grade, of human evolution, temporally and morphologically sandwiched between Plio-Pleistocene *H. habilis* on the one hand and upper Middle Pleistocene early *H. sapiens* on the other? Or is it a "real" species with definable boundaries in time and space, a separate evolutionary lineage demarcated from other species of *Homo* by cladogenetic speciation events, and unique (autapomorphic) features? Did *H. erectus* exist only in the Far East or can it also be identified in Africa and/or Europe? Did *H. sapiens*-like morphology first evolve in Asia and then spread westward to Europe or was Asian *H. erectus* an evolutionary deadend, contributing little to modern human evolution? These are difficult questions to resolve, but ones that paleoanthropologists continually grapple with and ones to which we now turn our attention.

There are three mutually exclusive views about *H. erectus* prevalent among paleoanthropologists today: (1) that the entire known material, or hypodigm, of *H. erectus* represents a single, widespread species that originated in Africa, spread throughout the Old World in the early Pleistocene, and was broadly ancestral to later modern humans; (2) that the hypodigm should be split into several species, with the Far East group considered to have had no significant role in modern human ancestry; and (3) that the name *H. erectus* should be abolished altogether and all its fossils classified within an anatomically diverse, or polytypic, species—*H. sapiens.*

Our concept of *H. erectus* as an identifiable stage of human evolution derives from specimens first recovered in Asia toward the end of the nineteenth century. While there is currently debate about whether or not

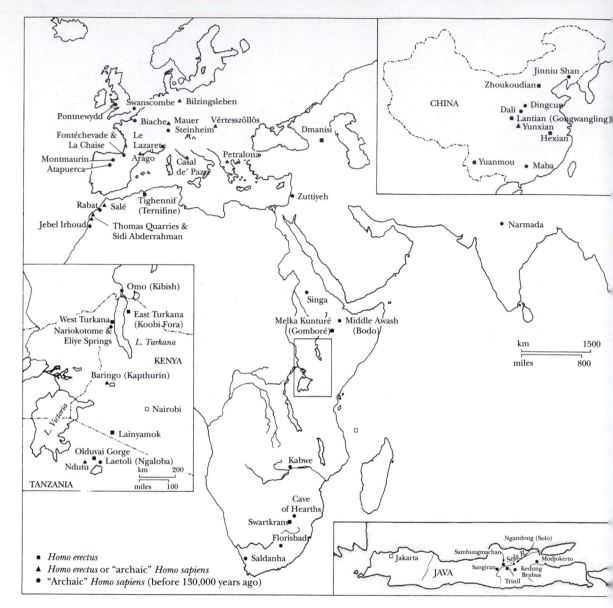

Fig. 10.1. Major *H. erectus* and early *H. sapiens* fossil sites. Some of the European sites may be early Neandertals. (Data from Rightmire, 1990; Stringer, 1992.)

H. erectus sensu stricto (in the strict sense of the term, i.e., pertaining to the original Javan hypodigm) ever existed in Africa and/or Europe, and about its place in the line of modern human ancestry, there is no doubt that the hypodigm includes a number of fossils from China (e.g., Zhoukoudian [formerly Choukoutien], Yunxian, Jianshi, Yuanmou, Lantian) and Java (including Sangiran, Trinil, Modjokerto, Ngandong) (Fig. 10.1; Table 10.1). In order to understand the arguments involved in these debates, we

Table 10.1a Listing of Principle Indonesian and Chinese Localities at Which Remains Attributed to *H. erectus* Have Been Recovered[a]

Fossil	Trinil	Sangiran	Sambungmachan	Ngangdong	Zhoukoudian	Hexian	Gongwangling
Whole crania		X					
Partial braincases	X	X	X	X	X	X	X
Mandibles		X			X	X	
Dentition		X			X	X	
Postcranial parts	X	?		X	X		

Table 10.1b Localities in Northwestern, Eastern, and Southern Africa That Have Yielded Remains Comparable to Asian *H. erectus*

Fossil	Ternifine	Sidi Abder-rahman	Thomas Quarries	Salé	Koobi Fora	Nario kotome	Baringo	Olduvai Gorge	Swartkrans
Whole crania					X	X			
Partial braincases	X		X	X	X			X	X
Mandibles	X	X	X		X	X	X	X	X
Dentition	X	X	X	X	X	X	X	X	X
Postcranial parts					X	X		X	

[a]Fossils are inventoried by body part represented rather than as individual specimens.
From Rightmire (1990).

first turn our attention to that part of the world where *H. erectus* was first discovered, defined, and named—the Far East. Then we will examine how the African fossils compare to the Asian *H. erectus* sample. Finally, we will consider the arguments, pro and con, about whether Asian *H. erectus* should be considered directly ancestral to modern humans.

HOMO ERECTUS FROM SOUTHEAST ASIA (CENTRAL AND EAST JAVA)

Ernst Haeckel was a German zoologist and philosopher and one of the earliest and most influential supporters of Darwin's theory of evolution. In 1866 he published the first formal phylogenetic tree depicting the course of human evolution, and in his treatise predicted the discovery of a "missing" phylogenetic link between humans and apes, to which he gave the name *Pithecanthropus*, meaning "ape man" (Fig. 10.2). Eugene Dubois had a passion for anatomy and natural history and an obsession with the idea of one day finding Haeckel's imaginary *Pithecanthropus*.[1] This obsession led him to seek out, and accept, a post as army surgeon in the Dutch East Indies (now Indonesia), a job he hoped would provide opportunities for fossil exploration in remote corners of Asia.

His first stop (in 1887) was Sumatra, but there he succeeded in finding only some fairly recent orangutan teeth. However, as soon as word reached him that part of a fossilized human cranium had been found by B. D. van Rietschoten at a place called Wajak (formerly Wadjak) in Java, he applied for permission to continue his own explorations on that island. The Wajak fossils turned out to be fairly recent—interesting, but no "missing link." By 1890, his searches had brought him to the Solo River in central Java where his workers soon found a fossilized lower jaw fragment of a juvenile hominin (Kedungbrubus 1)[2] (Fig. 10.1). Then the following year at Trinil, his workers made the discovery that would make him famous: a cranial cap, or calotte (Trinil 2), of a primate that was larger than a monkey but smaller than a modern human (Fig. 10.3a). Initially, Dubois thought that he had found a chimpanzee and thus named the new specimen (and an upper third molar found nearby) *Anthropopithecus*. However, by 1893 he concluded that he had actually discovered the missing link between apes and humans, and he renamed the specimen *Pithecanthropus erectus*. Luck continued to come his way. The following year he found a fossilized human femur (Trinil 3) only 35 feet from where the original calotte was found (five other femoral fragments that were found but never described were rediscovered decades later in the Leiden Museum, boxed up and collecting dust) (Fig. 10.3b). In 1894 he announced his discovery of the calotte and femur to an astonished world.[3] Haeckel's missing link had at last been found. Dubois christened it *P. erectus*, the "ape man" that walked erect.

The original calotte preserves much of the frontal bone, including a small portion of the left browridge (supraorbital torus), both parietals, and much of the upper part of the occipital bone. The area just above and behind the browridge, the **supratoral sulcus,** is eroded, exposing the air

---

[1]Today most anthropologists would include within the single taxon *H. erectus* virtually all the Javanese and Chinese specimens originally described by Dubois, Black, von Koenigswald, Weidenreich, and others as *Pithecanthropus erectus*. This would encompass specimens previously named *P. robustus, P. dubius, Homo modjokertensis, H. soloensis, Meganthropus palaeojavanicus, Sinanthropus pekinensis*, etc.

[2]This specimen, a lower jaw fragment preserving the canine alveolus and two premolars reportedly discovered at Kedung Brubus, was actually found at Kedung Lumbu (Tobias, 1993b).

[3]The *Dutch Government Mining Bulletin* carried a quarterly report by Dubois, and these reports actually carried the original accounts of his discoveries.

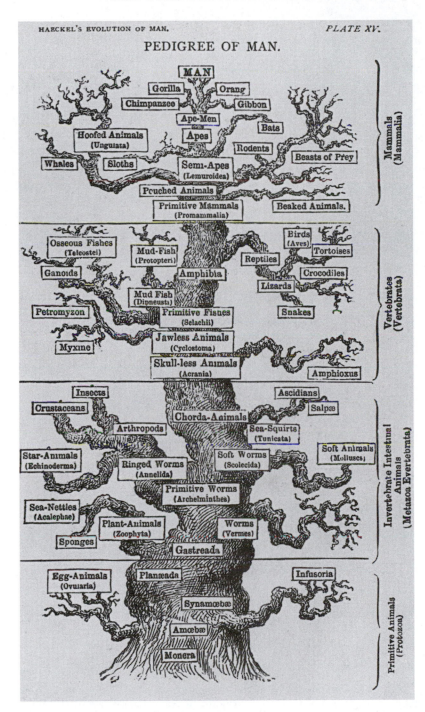

Fig. 10.2. Ernst Haeckel's "Pedigree of Man," as it appeared in his book *The Evolution of Man* (1896).

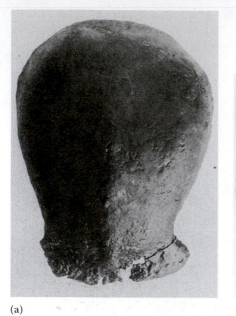

(a)

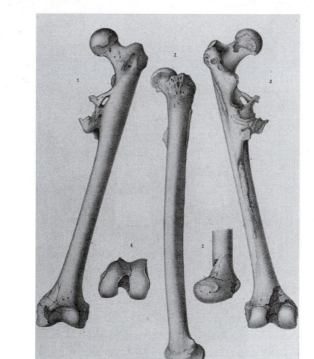

(b)

Fig. 10.3. First discoveries of *Pithecanthropus* from Java. (a) Eugene Dubois's original photographs of the Trinil 2 calotte (top and lateral views). (b) Dubois's original drawings of the Trinil 3 femur. (From Dubois, 1894.)

cavities within the frontal bone (frontal sinuses) on both sides. Unfortunately, the cranial base is missing. In overall shape, the calotte is long and narrow, or dolichocephalic. The **cephalic index,** the ratio of the greatest breadth of the cranium to its greatest length, multiplied by 100, is 70. Elongated or dolichocephalic crania have the smallest indices (below 75); short or **brachycephalic** crania have the largest indices (above 80); and **mesocephalic** crania have intermediate indices (from 75 to 80). Behind the supraorbital ridge, the forehead is very narrow and receding. The frontal bone also has a slight keel in the midline (sagittal keel). Based on the size of the calotte, brain size is estimated to be 850–950 cc (Rightmire, 1984).

There was never any doubt that the femur was from a bipedal animal, hence the name *P. erectus*. The only question was whether or not it was truly associated with the original *H. erectus* calotte, since its modern features seemed at variance with the primitive nature of the calotte. The proximal shaft, or **diaphysis,** of the femur has a well-developed **exostosis,** a benign bony growth projecting outward from the surface of a bone. This pathologic condition may have been caused either by myositis ossificans, an inflammatory disease of voluntary muscle characterized by aberrant bony deposits or ossification, or by diaphyseal aclasia, an autosomal dominant hereditary disease. Close inspection of the medial condyle shows clear evidence of osteoarthritis as well. Unfortunately, chemical (particularly flourine) analyses can only suggest, but not prove, that the calotte and femur are contemporary with the Trinil fauna (Day, 1984; Day and Molleson, 1973). After a thorough study of the Trinil femur, it was concluded that it could not be distinguished from that of modern *H. sapiens* and, therefore, neither its Middle Pleistocene antiquity nor its contemporaneity with the *H. erectus* calotte from Trinil could be confirmed.

It is sometimes said that prophets are seldom recognized in their own time or in their own country. So it was with Dubois. As might be imagined, his discovery caused a sensation, but it soon brought out the detractors as well (a fate that befell Raymond Dart three decades later). In what can be described only as an unfortunate conclusion to an inspired early career, Dubois slowly retreated from the verbal slings and arrows fired his way and retired to his home in Holland to become a scientific recluse. One story has it that Dubois took his *Pithecanthropus* and Wajak fossils out of scientific circulation and hid them under the floorboards of his dining room, apparently comforted in the knowledge that his precious fossils were safely hidden beneath his feet at meal time.[4] Although Dubois had discovered the Trinil calotte in 1891, it was 33 years before he published his first paper with photographs and a detailed description of the specimen (Dubois, 1924). Moreover, the Wajak fossils were handed over to Dubois by their

---

[4]The veracity of this story is suspect (Leakey and Lewin, 1992).

discoverer in 1890, but his publication dealing with them did not appear until 31 years later (Dubois, 1922).

In a final twist of irony, late in life Dubois became his own worst enemy by claiming that his original *Pithecanthropus* calotte was not that of a "missing link" after all, but rather that of an animal similar to a giant gibbon. Actually, Dubois believed that gibbons *were* the missing link based on the notion that the Trinil calotte was more gibbon-like than great ape–like and that gibbons were the only ape that habitually walked bipedally when on the ground. He also contended that most of the *H. erectus* crania found later in China (e.g., *Sinanthropus pekinensis*) and Java (including the *Pithecanthropus* crania II, III, IV, and the "Solo Man" crania) (see below) were all identical to "his" Wajak crania and thus were all *H. sapiens.*

For over 40 years after Dubois's original discoveries, no further *Pithecanthropus* fossils were unearthed in Java. Fortunately, however, paleontological interests there were rekindled in the 1930s by G. H. R. von Koenigswald, a young paleontologist working with the Dutch East Indies Geological Survey. His initial success came in 1936, when part of a 4- to 6-year-old child's braincase was discovered from the Pucangan Formation at Perning near Modjokerto (Fig. 10.1).[5] As we shall see later in the chapter, this cranium has recently become the focus of great interest because it may be one of the oldest *H. erectus* specimens ever found (Fig. 10.4) (Swisher et al., 1994). The child's cranial capacity was estimated to be 650 cc (Riscutia, 1975) and would have reached about 740–860 cc when an adult (Antón, 1997a). Von Koenigswald named the new specimen *H. modjokertensis* (later *P. modjokertensis*) and included within this taxon several other specimens from Sangiran, including a partial lower jaw discovered the same year (Sangiran 1b) and several cranial fragments with an associ-

[5]Professor Earnest Hooton (1946) of Harvard relates the following tale: "The janitor of the Peabody Museum has passed on to me a crumpled bit of paper that he picked up from the floor in front of the case in which the cast of the baby *Pithecanthropus* is on exhibition. He says that he noticed a frustrated-looking Radcliffe student gazing wistfully and prolongedly at this case and he thinks she may have written this pitiable effort:

> Ode to Homo Some-jerktensis
>
> Young Pithy from your Djetis bed
> You raise a scarcely human head,
> With all its soft spots ossified
> And sutures closed that should gape wide.
> Your marked postorbital constriction
> Would clearly justify prediction
> That had you lived to breed your kind,
> They would have had the childish mind
> That feeds upon the comic strips
> And reads with movements of the lips.
> They would have had no need for braces
> To warp their teeth into their places—
> Equipped for general mastication
> and not progressive education,
> In place of brows a bony torus,
> And no ideals with which to bore us."

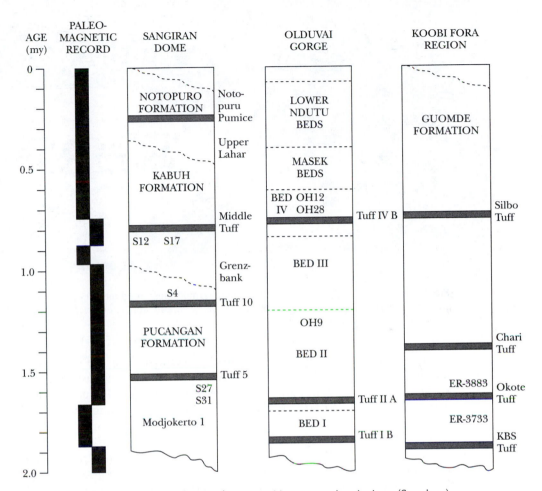

Fig. 10.4. Approximate correlations between *H. erectus* sites in Java (Sangiran), Olduvai Gorge, and Koobi Fora. Only some of the more important fossils attributed to *H. erectus* are shown. Recent ^{40}Ar-^{39}Ar dating suggests that the juvenile calvaria, Modjokerto 1, and two specimens from Sangiran, S27 and 31, may date to 1.8–1.6 mya. (Data from Rightmire, 1992; Swisher et al., 1994.)

ated upper jaw found a few years later (Sangiran 4ab). He identified a number of dental characters that he considered primitive, or ape-like, in this new species (Fig. 10.5): (1) the largest molar was the M_3, (2) the P^3 retained three roots, (3) the upper canine projected slightly beyond the level of the occlusal plane, and (4) the upper incisors were separated from the canine by a small diastema.

Von Koenigswald's efforts were further rewarded in 1937 with the discovery of a calvaria from the Kabuh Formation at Sangiran (Sangiran 2). Unfortunately, von Koenigswald had the habit of paying his fossil collectors by the quantity, not the quality, of the fossils they brought in to him, so

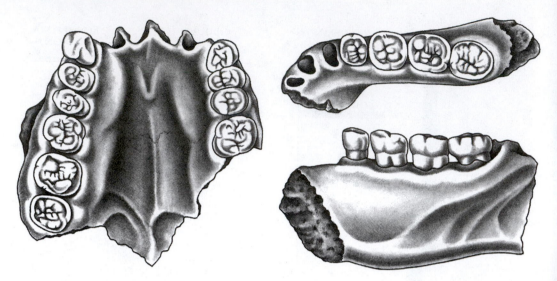

Fig. 10.5. Upper and lower jaw fragments originally described as *Pithecanthropus modjokertensis* by von Koenigswald but now generally attributed to *H. erectus.* (From von Koenigswald, 1971.)

perhaps he wasn't too surprised when they brought him the calvaria in about 40 small pieces! When the calvaria was finally reconstructed, it looked almost exactly like the one discovered by Dubois 40 years earlier, with a low cranial contour, sagittal keeling, and a strongly angled occipital bone (Fig. 10.3). It retained a good deal of the braincase, including the frontal; parietals; parts of both temporals and the occipital; part of the left supraorbital rim and browridge; and on the left, the zygomatic process, glenoid cavity, tympanic plate, and mastoid process. The endocranial capacity was estimated at a little more than 800 cc. However, as in Dubois's original *Pithecanthropus* calvaria, most of the cranial base was missing in this specimen. The fact that many of the Javanese crania were found without a cranial base (and, in most cases, facial remains as well) has led some anthropologists to suggest that *H. erectus* may have practiced cannibalism and extracted the brains of their victims through the cranial base (Roper, 1969).

It is interesting to note that the cranium of Sangiran 2 (as well as that of the Neandertals Gibralter 1 and Shanidar 5) shows evidence of a disease known as endocranial hyperostosis, findings that push the antiquity of this disease back 1.5 million years in the fossil record (the earliest occurrences were previously found in ancient populations from Egypt and Nubia). This disease produces an expansion of the endocranial surface of the cranium that can involve either the inner table alone or the inner table and diploe; the outer table is unaffected (Antón, 1997b).

When the elderly Dubois heard of the discovery of this more complete cranium of *Pithecanthropus*, which presumably should have delighted him

Table 10.2 Endocranial Volume Estimates for the More Complete
H. erectus Crania from Asia and Africa

Locality	Specimen Number[a]	Cranial Capacity (cc)
Ngandong	1	1172
Ngandong	6	1251
Ngandong	7	1013
Ngandong	11	1231
Ngandong	12	1090
Hexian		1025
Zhoukoudian	V	1140
Salé		880
Zhoukoudian	II	1030
Zhoukoudian	III	915
Zhoukoudian	VI	850[b]
Zhoukoudian	X	1225
Zhoukoudian	XI	1015
Zhoukoudian	XII	1030
Olduvai	12	727
Sangiran	10	855
Sangiran	12	1059
Sangiran	17	1004
Gongwangling		780
Trinil	2	940
Sangiran	2	813
Sangiran	4	908
Olduvai	9	1067
East Turkana	3883	804
West Turkana	15000	900
East Turkana	3733	848

[a]Specimens are listed in approximate chronological order.
[b]This value for Zhoukoudian VI is estimated.
From Rightmire (1990).

because it vindicated his original assessment of *Pithecanthropus* as a missing link, he declared that it was probably a fake. In fact, he died without ever bothering to see the new *Pithecanthropus* material (von Koenigswald, 1981).

The overall shape of the *H. erectus* cranium has been likened to that of a "fallen soufflé" (Howells, 1973). Adult cranial capacity ranges from about 700 to 1300 cc, with a mean value of about 883 cc (Table 10.2) (Holloway, 1981a). Taking body size into account, this is about 87% of the cranial capacity in modern humans. Since most of the *H. erectus* material from Indonesia (and China and Africa as well; see below) consists of crania or cranial fragments, it will be useful here to summarize the cranial features that characterize the species and how *H. erectus* differs from modern humans (Fig. 10.6; Table 10.3).

Table 10.3　General Cranial Features of *H. erectus*

- Cranium is long and low, with greatest cranial breadth situated toward the base
- Frontal bone is relatively flat and is characterized by pronounced, projecting browridges that are united medially by a distinct glabellar prominence; this whole structure is referred to as the supraorbital torus
- Boundary between the supraorbital torus and the frontal squama is typically marked by a trough-like depression called the supratoral sulcus
- There is a significant degree of postorbital constriction
- Frontal bone is characterized by a midline thickening of bone, referred to as a **frontal keel**
- Parietal bones are characterized by **parasagittal depressions** on either side of the midsagittal keel
- Occipital bone has short upper (occipital) and long lower (nuchal) portions that meet at a sharp angle to form a strongly developed **transverse occipital torus**
- Superior border of the temporal bone is generally straight and low compared to the highly arched border seen in modern humans
- Mandibular (**glenoid**) fossa is deep and narrow
- Mastoid process is relatively small, and the styloid process is not ossified to the cranial base
- Cranial vault bones are nearly twice as thick as in modern humans (averaging 9–10 mm)[a]
- Adult cranial capacity ranges from about 700 to 1300 cc, with a mean value of about 883 cc
- Orbits are deep and broad, and there is no lacrimal fossa
- Nasal bones are very broad, and the bridge of the nose is relatively flat
- There is a marked degree of alveolar prognathism
- Mandibles are relatively robust and are distinguished by their large bicondylar breadth, posteriorly inclined symphyseal region, absence of a chin, and broad ascending ramus
- Molars tend to have large pulp cavities (**taurodont**), and upper central incisors are typically shovel shaped

---

[a]It is interesting to note that cranial vault thickness at birth is apparently similar for all taxa of *Homo*, including *H. erectus*, Neandertals, early *H. sapiens*, and that most of the variance in cranial vault thickness among these groups most probably develops during later childhood under the influence of circulating growth hormones related to varying levels of exercise before skeletal maturity (Lieberman, 1996).

From Etler and Li (1994).

Fig. 10.6.　(a–b) Cranial comparisons between *H. erectus* and modern humans. Note in particular differences in the shape of the forehead, supraorbital tori, orientation of the occipital and nuchal planes, and chin. (Klein, 1989b.) (c–e) Several of the more complete *Homo erectus* crania from Java. (c) posterior views of Sangiran 2 (*top left*), Sangiran 4 (*top right*), Sangiran 10 (*bottom left*), and Sangiran 17 (*bottom right*). (d) Lateral views of Sangiran 4 (*top*) and Sangiran 10 (*bottom*). (e) Lateral views of Sangiran 2 (*top*) compared to East African *H. erectus* KNM-ER-3733 (*bottom*). (Photos c–e courtesy of G. P. Rightmire.)

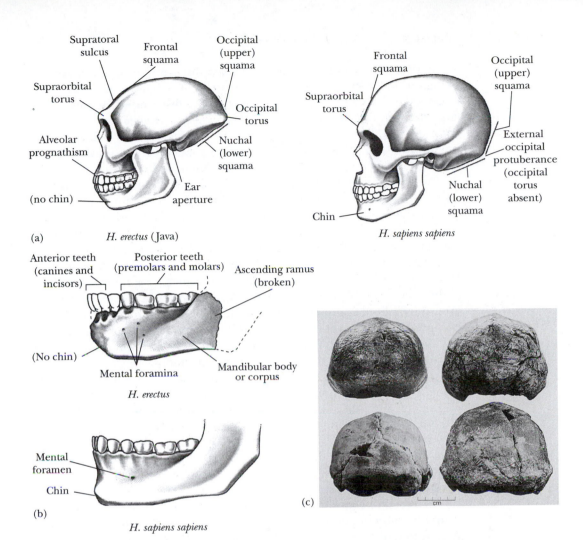

(a)

Supratoral sulcus

Supraorbital torus

Frontal squama

Occipital (upper) squama

Occipital torus

Alveolar prognathism

Nuchal (lower) squama

(no chin)

Ear aperture

H. erectus (Java)

Frontal squama

Supraorbital torus

Occipital (upper) squama

External occipital protuberance (occipital torus absent)

Nuchal (lower) squama

Chin

H. sapiens sapiens

(b)

Anterior teeth (canines and incisors)

Posterior teeth (premolars and molars)

Ascending ramus (broken)

(No chin)

Mental foramina

Mandibular body or corpus

H. erectus

Mental foramen

Chin

H. sapiens sapiens

(c)

cm

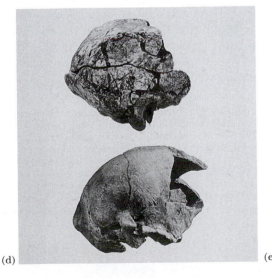

(d)

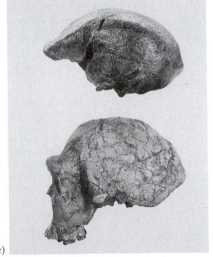

(e)

In 1941 von Koenigswald made his last discovery in Java, a lower jaw (Sangiran 6) from the Pucangan Formation of Sangiran that was much larger than any of the previous *Pithecanthropus* discoveries. Because of its large size, von Koenigswald named it *Meganthropus palaeojavanicus*. Both he and, later, J. T. Robinson of the Transvaal Museum in Pretoria initially considered it a "robust" australopith, a view not taken very seriously by most anthropologists today (see below). The original find consisted of a lower jaw fragment preserving P_3–M_1 and the alveolus for a small canine. In 1952 a second *Meganthropus* jaw fragment was found at Sangiran (Sangiran 8), but this one had only a displaced M_3 (von Koenigswald, 1971). One of the reasons von Koenigswald considered *Meganthropus* to be an australopith was that it came from the same layers as *H. modjokertensis* and it seemed unlikely to him that two different species of *Homo* would occur side by side.[6] More recently, chemical and mineralogical studies have shown that some of the specimens originally assigned to *M. palaeojavanicus* are more extensively mineralized compared to other Javan specimens attributed to *H. erectus*, presumably a reflection of their longer period of fossilization (Sighinolfie et al., 1993). We shall come back to the implications of this shortly when we discuss the dating of these specimens.

As alluded to above, a minority of anthropologists still hold that some of these Indonesian hominins represent robust australopiths. The five fossils usually mentioned in this regard include four mandibular fragments and one partial cranium from the Sangiran region of Java and all presumably dating to around 1 mya: (1) the original Meganthropus A mandible (Sangiran 6), (2) the Meganthropus B mandible (Sangiran 8), (3) the original *Pithecanthropus dubius* mandible (Sangiran 5), (4) a second *P. dubius* specimen (Sangiran 9), and (5) a distorted partial cranium (Sangiran 31).[7] However, a thorough phylogenetic analysis has shown that this view cannot be substantiated and that all these specimens are morphologically derived toward *H. erectus* and away from *Australopithecus* or even *H. habilis* (Kramer, 1994). Specifically, these Javan fossils differ from robust australopiths in a number of ways—for example, in showing no propensity toward molarized premolars, in having much thicker cranial bones (Gauld, 1996), and in having a cranial capacity estimated at 1000 cc (Sangiran 31), roughly double that of the latest australopiths.

[6]Similar arguments resurfaced several decades later (under the name of the single-species hypothesis), with the claim that only one tool-making hominin species could have lived at any one time in the Pleistocene of Africa: "Because of cultural adaptation, all hominin species occupy the same, extremely broad, adaptive niche. For this reason, allopatric hominin species would become sympatric . . . . The most likely outcome is the continued survival of only one hominin lineage" (Wolpoff, 1971a). This debate became a moot point, however, when it was conclusively shown that *Australopithecus* and *H. erectus* were contemporaries at Koobi Fora nearly 1.6 mya (Leakey and Walker, 1976).

[7]However, recent ^{40}Ar-^{39}Ar dating of Sangiran 31 suggests that it may be closer to 1.6 million years old (Swisher et al., 1994).

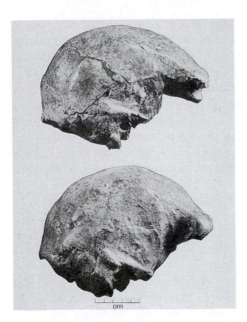

Fig. 10.7. Lateral view of two of the Solo crania: Ngandong 1 (*top*) and Ngandong 12 (*bottom*). (Photo courtesy of G. P. Rightmire.)

The Ngandong (Solo River) Sample

One of the most extensive samples of Javanese hominins was found between 1931 and 1933 when the Dutch Geological Survey discovered 11 hominin crania[8] and two shin (tibia) bones (collectively referred to as "Solo Man") from the upper terrace of the Solo River near Ngandong (Fig. 10.7). Initially some of these crania were excavated by untrained workers and were shipped back in boxes labeled "tiger crania" before their true identity was appreciated (Santa Luca, 1980; Weidenreich, 1951). Two partial hominin calvaria and hominin pelvic fragments were later recovered in excavations carried out between 1976 and 1980. Unfortunately, the geologic age of the Solo crania has never been satisfactorily determined, although preliminary uranium series (U-S; ^{230}Th-^{234}U) dating of vertebrate bone from the same area indicate ages between about 50 and 100 kya (Bartstra et al., 1988) although more recent electron spin resonance (ESR) and U-S dating techniques indicate ages as young as 27–53 kya (Swisher et al., 1996, 1997). If the younger age for these Ngandong hominins proves to be correct, and if they are unequivocally assigned to *H. erectus*,

---

[8] A fragment of a right parietal found during the preparation of Solo 3 probably does not belong to it and may indicate a 12th individual (Santa Luca, 1980).

then the obvious conclusion is that *H. erectus* overlapped in time with anatomically modern humans (*H. sapiens*) in Southeast Asia for a significant period of time. Unfortunately, both the dating and the taxonomic placement of the Solo hominin sample—that is, whether they belong to *H. erectus* or early *H. sapiens,* is still debated (Grün and Thorne, 1997).

Stone tools (mostly chalcedony cores and flakes) have also been found in the area, but there is no definite association of the Solo hominins with the tool industry. The Ngandong tool "industry," lacking handaxes, is distinct from the Acheulean tradition of both Europe and Africa. The absence of the characteristic unifacial and bifacial choppers and handaxes also excludes the Ngandong sample from the so-called chopper/chopping-tool complex of the Far East.

The crania were entrusted to von Koenigswald and moved with him first to the American Museum of Natural History in New York immediately after World War II, then to Utrecht in 1948, Frankfurt in 1968, and finally back to Indonesia in 1976.

There has never been unanimity of opinion on the taxonomy of the Ngandong crania. Some, like von Koenigswald, Henri Vallois in Paris, and C. Loring Brace of the University of Michigan, considered them "tropical" Neandertals, although in Brace's concept, this stage of evolution is really a link between *H. erectus* and modern humans. Others, like Dubois, argued that they were not Neandertals, but rather a primitive modern type or "proto-Australian." Franz Weidenreich initially considered the crania Neandertal-like, but ultimately concluded that they were more similar to the older Javanese and Peking *H. erectus.* Finally, in the most thorough study of these crania, A. P. Santa Luca (1980) concluded that:

> The entire set of Far Eastern *H. erectus*... presents a single morphological "bauplan": each cranium has the same basic shape, with group and individual variations overlaid on this plan. The Ngandong hominins share it with the Peking and Sangiran-Trinil 2 fossils. Absolutely no basis has been found for separating Ngandong as a different species from the latter groups.... In morphology, craniometry, and craniography, the Ngandong group agrees with the Far Eastern *H. erectus* specimens... and is clearly differentiated from other major hominin groups.

Many of the features of the Solo crania are similar to those found in *H. erectus* and differ from those characterizing modern humans. These include such features as: (1) the well-developed supraorbital tori united by a strong supranasal, or glabellar, torus; (2) the flat receding forehead; (3) marked postorbital constriction; (4) similar range of cranial capacity; (5) various characteristics of the cranial base; and (6) greatest cranial breadth located low down on the cranium (Antón, 1999; Durband, 1998; Jacob, 1981; Weidenreich, 1951; Santa Luca, 1980).

Since Indonesia's independence in 1945, anthropologists have continued working in the Sangiran area and have recovered many more crania, jaws, and teeth. The entire Indonesian *H. erectus* sample now represents parts of approximately 40 individuals. It is somewhat surprising, however, that even after all these years no further postcranial remains have been reported. It is also surprising that very few stone tools have been found in association with Javan *H. erectus* (Semah et al., 1992).

Finds announced in the summer of 1993 include an important new cranium from Sangiran (Pithecanthropus IX), which is one of the most complete yet found in Java. Initial reports describe the cranium as longer and narrower than other Javan *H. erectus* crania and as having well-developed and projecting supraorbital tori. The cranial vault bones are also very thick, and endocranial capacity has been estimated at 856 cc. What caused the greatest initial excitement about this discovery was the suggestion that it was the oldest hominin from Java, dating to some 1.4–1.0 mya. However, Sastrohamijoyo Sartono of the Institute of Technology, Bandung, Indonesia, concludes that the cranium may be from the Middle Pleistocene and only about 500,000–700,000 years old (Tobias, 1993b).

One of the most startling archeological discoveries to come out of East Asia is the recent claim that *H. erectus* had reached the Indonesian island of Flores by the Early/Middle Pleistocene, a journey requiring a sea crossing of at least 19 km even during periods of lowest sea levels during the last glacial maximum (Morwood et al., 1998). Paleomagnetism and zircon fission-track techniques both indicate that stone tools from the island site of Mata Menge date to approximately 800 kya and clearly suggest that east Asian *H. erectus* was capable of repeated water crossings using watercraft by this incredibly early date. Over a dozen stone tools made from volcanic rock and chert have been identified thus far and many show edge damage, striations, polishing, and residues consistent with use in the processing of plant material. It was previously thought that such water-crossing ability evolved only with later Pleistocene *H. sapiens*. The earliest widely accepted evidence for watercraft is generally considered to be the colonization of Australia by modern humans about 40–60 kya. If these claims hold up to further scrutiny, it will certainly suggest that cognitive abilities of Asian *H. erectus* were much greater than generally assumed.*

Taxonomic Issues of the Javan *Homo erectus* Sample

There has always been the temptation among taxonomic "splitters" to subdivide the Javanese hominin sample into different taxa and lineages, and von Koenigswald did not disappoint in this regard. He recognized no fewer than five hominin species from Java: *H. soloensis* (which he considered a Javanese Neandertal) from the Ngandong fauna; *P. erectus* from the Trinil fuana; and *P. modjokertensis* (Sangiran 1B, 4), *P. dubius* Sangiran 5, 9; so named because Weidenreich initially thought it might be an orangutan),

---

*A new dwarf species, *Homo floresiensis*, has recently been discovered from Late Pleistocene (~35–18 kya) deposits at Flores. Adult stature and brain size was about 1 m and 380 cc, respectively, similar to the smallest known australopithecines. Archeological evidence indicates these dwarf hominins were selectively hunting juvenile *Stegodon* (Brown *et al.*, 2004; Morwood *et al.*, 2004).

and *M palaeojavanicus* (Sangiran 6, which he regarded as an australopith from the Djetis fauna) (von Koenigswald, 1975).

This trend to split the Javanese hominins continues among some Indonesian anthropologists (Jacob, 1981; Sartono, 1975). For example, Teuku Jacob recognizes three distinct groups, or grades, of *H. erectus* from Indonesia (which he still refers to as *Pithecanthropus*): *P. modjokertensis* from the Lower Pleistocene of Sangiran and Perning; *P. erectus* from the Middle Pleistocene of Sangiran, Trinil, and Kedungbrubus; and *P. soloensis* from the Middle Pleistocene of Ngandong, Sambungmachan, and Sangiran.[9] Until recently it was thought that few, if any, of these Indonesian hominins were much older than about 1 million years (see below) (Pope, 1983, 1988; Pope and Cronin, 1984). Jacob (1980) considers *P. modjokertensis* and *P. soloensis* to be more robust than *P. erectus* in certain features—for example, in their larger cranial capacity (1000–1300 cc), thicker cranial vault bones, and more accentuated cranial muscular markings. *P. erectus*, on the other hand, has a cranial capacity of 750–1000 cc, a more rounded occipital torus, and no external occipital crest. Jacob rejects the idea that these taxonomic groupings simply reflect size differences due to sexual dimorphism. He argues that if this were so, only males would be preserved at Ngandong and only females (with one exception) at Sangiran (Kabuh Formation).

On the other hand, Sartono (1975) subdivides *H. erectus* into five subspecies: *H. e. dubius, H. e. modjokertensis, H. e. erectus, H. e. pekinensis,* and *H. e. soloensis.* Alternatively, he would subdivide the Javanese *H. erectus* sample into just two subspecies, a small-brained group and a larger-brained group that may have evolved from it. From analyses of cranial size and shape, he concludes that specimens referred to as *Sinanthropus pekinensis* (from China), *H. ngandongensis* (the Solo Man crania) and some *P. erectus* (e.g., *Pithecanthropus* VIII) can be accommodated within his "large-brained" subspecies of *H. erectus*, whereas some other *P. erectus* (e.g., *Pithecanthropus* I, II, III, VII), *P. modjokertensis* (*Pithecanthropus* IV), and *P. dubius* (*Pithecanthropus* C) can be accommodated within his "small-brained" subspecies of *H. erectus*.

As mentioned earlier, we now live in an age of taxonomic lumpers, and most anthropologists today tend to lump all these Javanese specimens within the single taxon *H. erectus*.

---

[9]Two stone tools (a chopper and a retouched flake) were also found at Sambungmachan, near the same site that yielded the hominin calotte (Jacob et al., 1978). More recently two other *H. erectus* calvaria from Sambungmacan (Sm 3 and Sm4) have been found. Sm 3 was "discovered" in a New York City natural history establishment. The calvaria differs from most other *H. erectus* samples in having a more vertically rising forehead and more globular vault. Notably absent are a number of other classic *H. erectus* characters such as a strongly expressed angular torus and continuous supratoral sulcus (Marquez et al., 2001). Sm 4 was discovered in 2001 and may represent a transitional form linking the Trinil/Sangiran and Ngandong hominins morphologically and temporally (Baba et al., 2003). The Sambungmachan hominins are most likely similar in age to the Ngandong sample (less than 50,000 years B.P.) (Antón et al., 2002; Swisher et al., 1996).

Age of Javan *Homo erectus*

Until recently, most investigations have concluded that most, if not all, of the fossils assigned to *H. erectus* in Asia, including Java, are probably younger than 1 million years of age (Pope, 1983, 1988; Pope and Cronin, 1984). For most of the twentieth century, age estimates of Indonesian *H. erectus* were based on three poorly defined biostratigraphic sequences: a Lower Pleistocene Djetis fauna (Pucangan Formation), a Middle Pleistocene Trinil fauna (Trinil and Kabuh Formations), and a late Pleistocene Ngandong fauna (Notopuro Formation) (Fig.10.4).

Some of these faunas, particularly the Trinil, are characterized by highly endemic groups and have few species in common with the Asiatic mainland (de Vos, 1985, 1994). In fact, such common Eurasian mammals as equids, giraffoids, and camelids are completely absent in the tropical and subtropical regions of Pleistocene Southeast Asia generally, thereby testifying to the presence of some biogeographical "filter" affecting mammalian, including human, dispersal. It is thought that these endemic species, and *H. erectus*, could have reached Java only during a period of low sea levels when the Sunda Shelf was exposed at about 3.0 mya, 1.25 mya, 0.9 mya, and/or 0.65–0.45 mya (Pope, 1988; Pope and Cronin, 1984; Pope and Keates, 1994). Because water along the Sunda Shelf is so shallow, lowering the sea level to the 40-m isobath would connect Java to Sumatra and Malaysia, thus creating a land bridge to the Asian mainland and to Borneo (Fig. 10.8). Accumulating evidence had suggested that the latter two dates were the most probable for the migration of *H. erectus* into Indonesia, and in fact, until recently there was little substantive evidence of hominin occupation in Java before about 1.3–1.0 mya. This view was based on a number of radiometric dates (mostly fission-track) indicating that both the Kabuh and the Notopuro Formations were younger than 700,000 years and on paleomagnetic data indicating that the stratigraphic zone of *Pithecanthropus* at Sangiran ranged from the lower boundary of the Jaramillo event to the Brunhes/Matuyama boundary and that the stratigraphic level of *H. modjokertensis* was at the lower border of Jaramillo event—that is, from about 0.73 to 0.97 mya for Sangiran and about 0.97 for Mojokerto (Hyodo et al., 1993). A widely cited earlier radiometric date of 1.9 ± 0.4 mya for some Javanese hominins (*Meganthropus* [Sangiran 8], or *H. modjokertensis*) was considered unreliable, since wherever proper excavations had been carried out on Java, hominins have been recovered only from Middle Pleistocene deposits.

This view has now been dramatically altered by the more recent age determination of several *H. erectus* specimens from Java (Huffman, 2001; Swisher, 1997; Swisher et al., 1994).[10] As noted above, the hominin-bearing portion of the Sangiran section had been considered to be between about

---

[10]But see Langbroek and Roebroeks (2000) for a different opinion.

0.7 and 1.0 mya (between the Jaramillo and Brunhes normal polarity intervals) and served as the primary basis for the argument that hominins arrived in Southeast Asia no earlier than about 1 million years ago. However, newer ^{40}Ar-^{39}Ar dates of volcanic horizons at Sangiran indicate the hominins may actually range from 1.7 to 1.0 mya. The new dates indicate that all of the hominins from Sangiran are older, not younger, than 1.0 mya, since no hominins have been reported from above these dated horizons at Sangiran. It is also reported, based on ^{40}Ar-^{39}Ar determinations, that the well-preserved juvenile calvaria known as the "Mojokerto child" (Perning 1) from the Pucangan deposits (see above) may be about 1.8 million years old and that several specimens from Sangiran (Sangiran 27 and 31) may be about 1.6 million years old (Fig. 10.4). If true, this has a number of important ramifications. For example, it would mean that the earliest known hominins from Java are approximately 0.6–0.8 million years older than the type of *H. erectus* from Trinil, at least 0.6 million years older than *H. erectus* from Olduvai Gorge (OH 9), and of comparable age to the oldest specimens of *H.* cf. *erectus* (= *H. ergaster*) from the Lake Turkana region of Kenya (see below). The obvious conclusion would be that *H. erectus* (or *H. erectus*–like hominins) migrated out of Africa into Asia far earlier than anyone had previously thought. As we shall see later in the chapter, there is still considerable debate as to whether or not *H. erectus* was a side branch of human evolution restricted to Asia, or whether it appeared in Africa as well.

This re-evaluation of the dates for the oldest *H. erectus* from Indonesia also affects the way anthropologists view the tempo and mode of Middle Pleistocene human evolution. For example, if the bulk of Javan *H. erectus* were really no older than about 1 million years, as previously thought, then the entire temporal range of *H. erectus* in Asia would not have spanned much more than about 700,000 years—that is, from about 1.0 to 0.3 mya, even if the Ngandong crania from Solo were assigned to *H. erectus*. This more restricted temporal range must be kept in mind when evaluating rival claims for "punctuational" or "gradual" models of human evolution and may be one reason why some workers discern little, if any, directed morphological change over time in the *H. erectus* sample from Asia (Rightmire, 1988) whereas others claim that gradual changes are easily decipherable in cranial capacity and other cranial and dental measures in the temporal sequence of Asian *H. erectus* in Java and China (Pope and Cronin, 1984; Wolpoff, 1984; Wu and Lin, 1983).

Thus let us turn to the other part of Asia that has produced a large *H. erectus* sample, China.

Fig. 10.8. Possible Pleistocene land connections between New Guinea and Australia and the Asian mainland during periods of lowered sea levels when the Sunda and Sahul land shelves were exposed. Arrows represent possible early hominin migration patterns; several important early hominin sites from these regions are also shown. (Stringer and Gamble, 1993.)

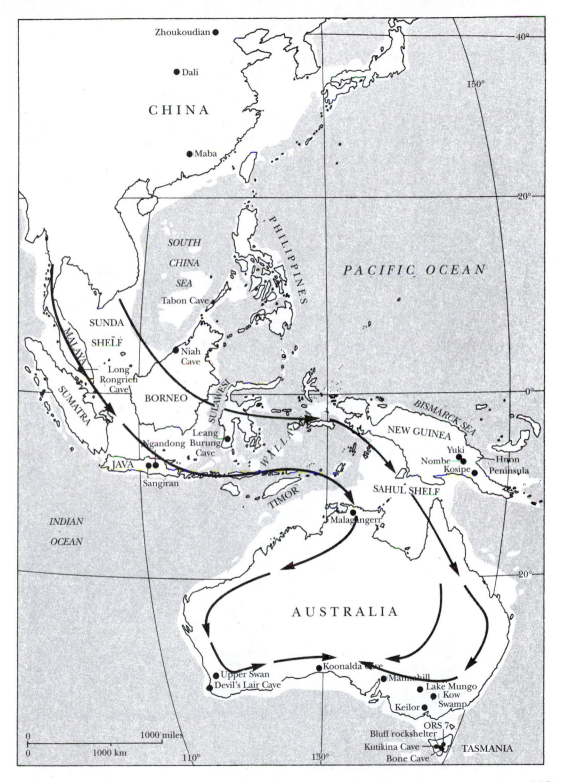

HOMO ERECTUS FROM EAST ASIA (CHINA)

In 1919, a relatively unknown Canadian anatomist, Davidson Black, arrived in China to take up his position as professor of neurology and embryology at the newly founded Peking (now Beijing) Union Medical College. Just 9 years later he found himself an academic celebrity lecturing in North America and Europe. During his lecture tour he wore a specially made gold receptacle tightly secured to his watch chain. In this gold receptacle there was a single fossil hominin tooth (Figs. 10.9 and 10.10).

Homo erectus from Zhoukoudian

Like Dubois before him, Black was inspired to take up a medical post in Asia because of his interest in human evolution and his belief that humankind first appeared in the Far East. And like Dubois, Black was lucky. Coincident with his arrival in Beijing, a Swedish paleontological expedition began excavations at a promising cave site called Choukoutien (now Zhoukoudian), only 30 miles from Beijing. The site had been discovered in 1918 by a Swedish geologist, J. Gunnar Andersson (1996). Paleontologist Otto Zdansky was placed in charge of the 1921 and 1923 excavations. Most of the fos-

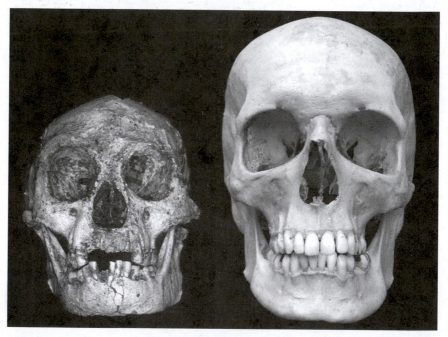

Fig. 10.9. A skull of the newly described Late Pleistocene dwarf species *Homo floresiensis* (left) from the island of Flores, Indonesia, compared to that of a modern human (right). (Credit: epa/AP/Wide World Photos)

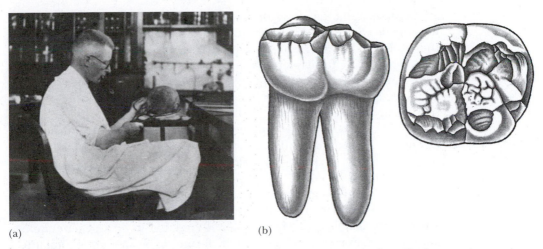

(a)   (b)

Fig. 10.10.   (a) In 1927 a relatively unknown Canadian anatomist, Davidson Black, named a new hominin genus from China, *Sinanthropus pekinensis*, which became popularly known as Peking Man. It is now generally referred to as *Homo erectus*. (Photo courtesy of the Bernard Becker Medical Library, Washington University.) (b) The first tooth of Peking Man, a lower first molar discovered by Birger Böhlin (von Koenigswald, 1981). Black used to carry this tooth in a gold receptacle secured to his watch chain.

sils discovered in these first excavations were shipped back to Sweden for study and curation. Fortunately, however, Zdansky recognized several human-like teeth from the sample (a right M^3 and a left P_3) and sent them to Black in Beijing for further study and identification. Then, on October 16, 1927, Birger Böhlin of the Swedish team found another hominin tooth, a left M_1, which he also turned over to Black for study. Black had no doubt that this tooth came from a previously unknown type of fossil hominin and considered it the oldest human-like fossil yet found on the Asian mainland. Within the year he had formally named it *Sinanthropus pekinensis* (Black, 1927). This was the single tooth tightly fastened to his watch chain.[11]

Many anthropologists were initially skeptical of Black's claims based on a single tooth, but Black's prescience was soon recognized when W. C. Pei (Pei Wenzhong) discovered the first *Sinanthropus* calotte at Zhoukoudian on December 2, 1929 (Shapiro, 1981) and shortly thereafter found indisputable evidence of stone tools in the same layers as the *Sinanthropus* fossils (Teilhard de Chardin and Pei, 1932). After Black's death in 1934, excavations continued at Zhoukoudian for 3 more years under the direction of Franz Weidenreich, until war with Japan made further work untenable.[12]

[11]As a historical note, this may not have been the first fossil hominin tooth described from China. In 1903, the German paleontologist Max Schlosser published descriptions of a number of fossil "dragon bones," including a human molar, that had been purchased from Chinese drugstores during the Boxer rebellion at the turn of the twentieth century (Schlosser, 1903; von Koenigswald, 1981).

[12]Elwyn Simons tells the story that Black was found dead at his desk early one morning with a *H. erectus* cranium firmly clutched in his hands.

Because of the Japanese threat to the Asian mainland, arrangements were made with U.S. Marines, who were evacuating north China, to ship the fossils to the American Museum of Natural History in New York for safekeeping. The fossils were packed and sent to the U.S. Marine base at Chinwangtao where they were stored in footlockers. However, before they could escape, all the Marines were taken prisoner and the fossils were not seen again after December 8, 1941 (Janus, 1975; Shapiro, 1974). Fortunately, Weidenreich had meticulously described and illustrated most of the Zhoukoudian material and had also made a number of excellent casts, which have been preserved in various institutions around the world (Fig. 10.11) (Mann, 1981).

In what can be regarded only as a fit of pique, Dubois never admitted any phylogenetic or taxonomic relationship between his *Pithecanthropus* and Black's *Sinanthropus*. He considered the latter to be a degenerate Neandertal and, as mentioned earlier, the former to be an animal similar to a giant gibbon.

After the upheavals of World War II and the Chinese Revolution, excavations at Zhoukoudian resumed in 1958 and have continued off and on since then under the overall direction of Wu Rukang.[13] In fact, a frontal and occipital bone found in 1966 actually turned out to be part of the same cranium (Cranium V) collected by Weidenreich in 1934! The inventory of fossil hominins collected from Zhoukoudian over the past half century now represents the remains of some 40–45 individuals (Table 10.4) (Etler and Li, 1994; Mann, 1981; Wu, 1985; Wu and Lin, 1983; Wu and Poirier, 1995; Wu and Yuerong, 1985).

The most famous of the Chinese *H. erectus* sites, the Zhoukoudian (Locality 1) cave ("Dragon-Bone Hill"), is only about 45 km southwest of central Beijing. Its deposits are more than 40 m thick (the bottom has not yet been reached) and are divided into a number of alternating layers of limestone breccia and nonbreccia consisting mainly of sand, silt, clay, travertine, and ash (Tables 10.4 and 10.5) (Etler and Li, 1994; Liu, 1983). The 45 or so fossil hominins derive from layers 3–11; although three-quarters of those are from layers 8–10, and the majority of the remaining hominins are from layers 3–4. Age estimates have varied for the Zhoukoudian *H. erectus* sample, but it is now generally held that most, if not all, of the specimens come from sediments well above the Matuyama/Brunhes boundary (from less than 780 kya) and are thus Middle Pleistocene in age (Fig. 10.12). The original Peking Man cranium found in 1929 was recovered from layer 11 and was originally dated by ESR to about 578 kya. Crania from layers 3–4 and 8–9 gave initial ESR ages of 282 kya and 418 kya, respectively (Huang et al., 1991). These ages were generally confirmed by

---

[13]Rukang, like Raymond Dart, was a product of my own anatomy department here at Washington University, where he got his Ph.D. under Mildred Trotter, the founding mother of the American Association of Physical Anthropology.

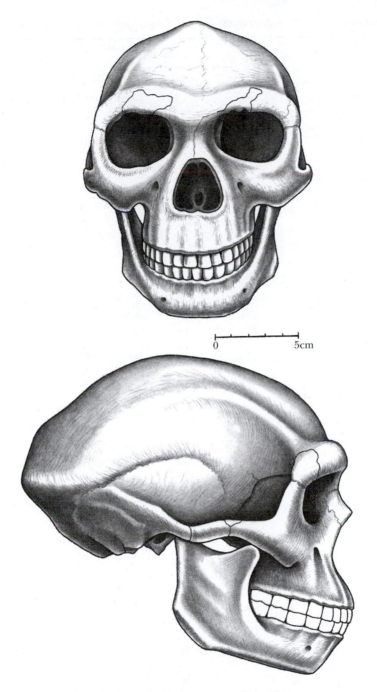

0   5cm

Fig. 10.11.   Skull of *H. erectus* from China.

Table 10.4   Archaic Human Remains from Zhoukoudian

Specimen Number[a]	Fossil Hominin Remains	Sex[b]	Age[b]	Locus	Layer	Individual[c]	Year of Discovery[d]
				Locality			
	Crania and cranial fragments						
I	fragmentary rt. parietal, lf. frontal	M	A	B	4	B II	1928
II	calvaria (lacking 2 temporals and occipital)	?	A	D	8–9	D I	1929
III	calvaria	M	J	E	11	E I	1929
IV	rt. parietal fragment	M	J	G	7	G II	1931
V	calvaria	M	A	H	3	H III	1934, 1934–36, 1966
VI	frontal fragment, lf. parietal fragment, rt. temporal fragment	F	A	I	89	I I	1936
VII	rt. parietal at mastoid angle	M	AD	I	8–9	III	1936
VIII	occipital fragment	F?	I	J	8–9	J I	1936
IX	frontal fragment, 4 small cranial fragments.	M	I	J	8–9	J IV?	1936
X	calvaria	M	A	L	8–9	L I	1936
XI	calvaria	F	A	L	8–9	L II	1936
XII	calvaria	M	A	L	8–9	L II	1936
XIII	lf. maxillary fragment (with I2, P3-M3)	M?	A	O	10	O I	1937
XIV	lf. maxillary fragment (with P3, M1-M3)	M	A	Upper Cave	—	UC?	1933
	Facial bones and facial bone fragments						
I	frontal process of lf. maxilla	M	A	L	8–9	Skull X	1936
II	left malar fragment	M	A	L	8–9	Skull X	1936
III	lf. maxillary fragment (with P3-M3)	F	A	L	8–9	Skull XI	1936
IV	rt. palate	F	A	L	8–9	Skull XI	1936
V	cf. Skull XIII						
VI	cf. Skull XIV						
	Adult mandibles						
I	part of rt. moiety	F	A	A	S	A II	1928
II	lf. condyle	M?	A	B	4	B II	1928–35
III	3 lf./rt. fragments	M	A	G	7	G I	1931
IV	symphysis and rt. corpus	F	A	H	3	H I	1934
V	symphysis fragment and lateral bodies	F?	A	H	3	K I	1936
VI	lf. corpus	M	A	K	8–9	K I	1936
VII	lf. fragment	M	A	M	8–9	M I	1937
VIII	lf. hemimandible	F	A	M	8–9	M II	1937
IX	lf./rt. fragments	F	A	—	10	—	1959

Specimen Number[a]	Fossil Hominin Remains	Sex[b]	Age[b]	Locality Locus	Layer	Individual[c]	Year of Discovery[d]
				Nonadult mandibles			
I	symphysis and rt. fragment	F	J	B	4	B I	1928
II	rt. fragment	M	J	B	4	B III	1932–38
III	rt. fragment	F	I	B	4	B IV	1932–35
IV	symphysis and rt. fragment	M	J	B	4	B V	1928–35
V	rt. ramus fragment	F	J	C	8–9	C I	1929
VI	rt. fragment	M	J	F	11	F I	1930
				Femurs			
I	proximal half lf. shaft	M	A	C	8–9	C III	1929–36
II	lf. midshaft	F	A	J	8–9	J II	1936–38
III	rt. proximal fragment	M	A	J	8–9	J III	1936–38
IV	near complete rt. shaft	M	A	M	8–9	M IV	1937–38
V	lf. proximal shaft	M	A	M	8–9	M IV	1937–38
VI	lf. midshaft (2 pieces)	M	A	M	8–9	M I	1937–38
				Assorted postcrania			
Tibia I	lf. shaft fragment	—	A	—	—	—	1951
Humeri I	lf. distal fragment	M	A	B	4	B II	1928–35
II	lf. shaft	M	A	J	8–9	J III	1936–38
III	rt. midshaft	M	A	—	—	—	1951
Clavicle I	lf. shaft	M	A	G	7	G II	1931
Lunate I	rt. lunate	M?	A	B	4	B II	1928
				Teeth			
	2 specimens; lower LP3, upper RM3						1921–23
1–147	64 isolated specimens; rest in upper and lower jaws; 52 upper, 82 lower, 13 deciduous						1927–37
	5 specimens; upper LI1, upper RP3, upper RP4, lower LMI, lower LM2						1949–50 1951–53
	lower RP4						1953
	lower LP3 (in jaw)						1959
	lower RP3						1966

[a]Specimen no. refers to the colloquial designation given to the Zhoukoudian remains by the original researchers.

[b]Sex and age were attributed by Weidenreich and other primary researchers.

[c]Individual refers to the locus from which individual human remains were recovered and the sequential number of the individual with which they are thought to be associated. Year of discovery refers to the year when individual specimens attributed to a single individual were found.

[d]*A*, adult; *J*, juvenile; *AD*, adolescent; *rt*, right; *lf*, left.

From Etler and Li (1994).

Table 10.5   Some Absolute Dates Obtained on the Zhoukoudian Deposits

Layer	Years		Dating Method
1–3	230,000 $+ 30,000$ $- 23,000$		Uranium-series
	256,000 $+ 62,000$ $- 40,000$		
4	290,000		Thermoluminescence
6–7	350,000		Uranium-series
7	370–400,000		Paleomagnetism
8–9	420,000 $+ > 180,000$ $- 100,000$	$; > 400,000$	Uranium-series
10	$462,000 \pm 45,000$		Fission-track
	520–620,000		Thermoluminescence
12	$> 500,000$		Uranium-series
13–17	$> 730,000$		Paleomagnetism

U-S dating methods, which dated layers 2 and 4 to 270 kya and 300 kya, respectively, and Cranium V from layer 3 to about 290 kya (Shen and Jin, 1991; Yuan et al., 1991). Fission-track analysis dates ashes, presumably left behind by *H. erectus* from layer 4, to 299 kya.[14] ESR dating on teeth collected from layers 3, 6/7 and 10 at Locality 1, Zhoukoudian, generally confirm an age range of 300–550 kya for the *H. erectus* sample (Grün et al., 1997).

However, more recent U-S dates seem to show that many of the hominins are actually older than this (Shen et al., 2001). For example, the age of Cranium V is now estimated at more than 400 kya, and the hominin fossils from lower strata may date to 600–800 kya. Thus it appears that *H. erectus* occupied the cave for about 350,000 years, from about 600 to 250 kya. This is an important consideration when trying to analyze morphological trends within the Zhoukoudian hominin sample. For example, Weidenreich (1937) thought that differences in tooth size within Zhoukoudian *H. erectus* simply reflected gender differences, with larger teeth belonging to males and smaller teeth to females. He therefore concluded that there was a long period of morphological stasis within the population

[14]Other dates for these layers are as follows: layers 1–3: 0.26–0.23 mya, based on U-S dating; layer 4: 0.32–0.29 mya, based on fission-track and thermoluminescence (TL) dating; layers 10–11: 0.610, 0.417–0.592, or 0.340 mya, based on TL and U-S dating (Pope, 1992). As for the Upper Cave at Zhoukoudian, radiocarbon dates on amino acids taken from bone give ages of ca. 23,000 and 10,000 years for the upper and lower boundaries of the Paleolithic culture and *H. sapiens* fossils found there (Chen et al., 1989). Many scholars believe that the strongest fossil evidence for Mongoloid origins derives from these fossils in the Upper Cave at Zhoukoudian (but see Kamminga and Wright, 1988).

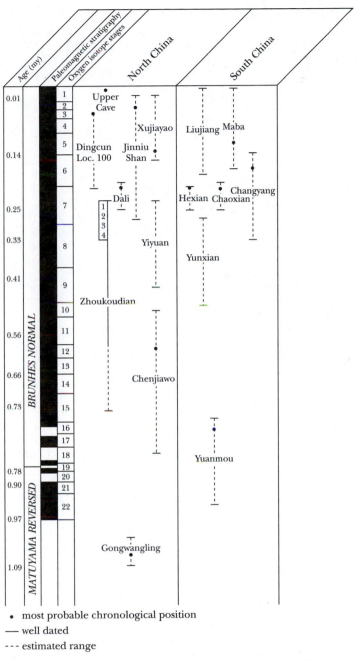

- most probable chronological position
— well dated
--- estimated range

(a)   *(Continued)*

Fig. 10.12.   (a) Chronostratigraphic distribution of important hominin sites in China (Pope, 1992).

▲ Late *Homo erectus*
■ Premodern (early *Homo sapiens*)
● Anatomically modern *Homo sapiens*

◫ Mean altitude = 4,000 m
◩ Mean altitude = 1,000–2,000 m
▢ Mean altitude < 1,000 m

(b)

Fig. 10.12. *(Continued)*   (b) Geographic distribution of important hominin sites in China (Pope, 1992).

through time. However, recent dental analyses comparing teeth from the upper and lower layers of the cave seem to show some temporal variation in that lower incisors tend to get larger while lower canines and postcanine teeth get smaller (P_3 less than P_4 and M_1 less than other molars), suggesting that the Zhoukoudian sample illustrates dental evolutionary change in the direction toward *H. sapiens* (Zhang, 1991). In addition, other Chinese

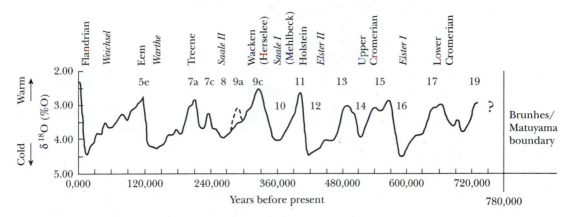

Fig. 10.13. Chinese geologists have attempted to correlate the various Zhouk-oudian layers to the ^{18}O stages of the deep-sea sediment record. For example, lay-ers 3–4 have been correlated to ^{18}O stage 8, layer 5 to stage 9, layers 6–7 to stage 10, layers 8–9 to stage 11, and layer 10 to stage 12. This signifies that *H. erectus* lived through at least three cold stages (stages 12, 10, 8) and two warm stages (11 and 9) during their occupation of the Zhoukoudian cave. In the ^{18}O record, even-numbered stages are cold periods and odd-numbered stages are warm periods. Names at the top of the figure correspond to European glacial stratigraphy. (Tattersall et al., 1988.)

anthropologists have suggested that cranial capacity increased through time in the Zhoukoudian sample, although this is open to debate (Pope, 1992; Wu and Lin, 1983). However, these conclusions may have to be mod-ified, or rejected, if more recent U-S dates of travertine in layers 1–2 are re-ally as old as about 414 kya (Shen et al., 1996).[15]

To interpret the paleoclimatological aspects of the site, Chinese geolo-gists have correlated the various Zhoukoudian layers to the ^{18}O stages of the deep-sea sediment record. For example, layers 3–4 have been corre-lated to ^{18}O stage 8, layer 5 to stage 9, layers 6–7 to stage 10, layers 8–9 to stage 11, and layer 10 to stage 12. If correct, this signifies that *H. erectus* lived through at least three cold stages (stages 12, 10, 8) and two warm stages (11 and 9) during their occupation of the Zhoukoudian cave (Fig. 10.13). The distribution of loess deposits also supports the view of alternat-ing cold and warm phases. **Loess**, a fine-grained, windblown deposit found downwind of glaciated areas, is generally considered a product of dry, cold climates and has been widespread in China since the early Pleistocene (Qi, 1990). In general, the loess distribution indicates a gradual trend during the Pleistocene toward drier and colder conditions in north China marked by many climatic fluctuations.

[15]Cranium V, one of the youngest *H. erectus* specimens at the site and originally thought to date to about 290 kya, was excavated just below these newly dated strata. It was largely based on this age assignment that hypotheses had been formulated concerning a possible coexistence of both *H. erectus* and *H. sapiens* and a possible slower evolution rate of Asian *H. erectus* compared with their African counterparts.

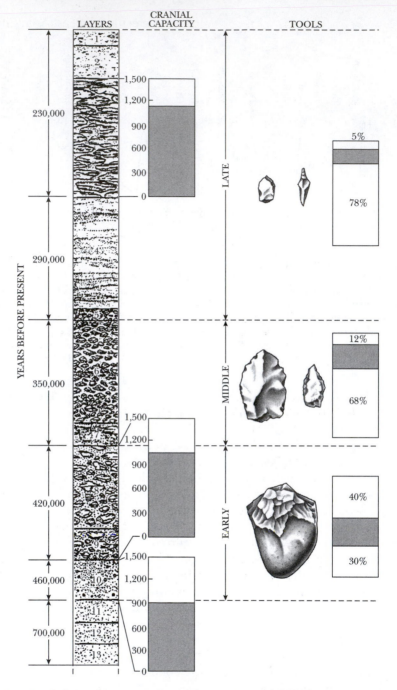

Fig. 10.14. Relationships among cranial capacity, tool manufacture, and time in the Zhoukoudian *H. erectus* sample. Cranial capacity increases from about 915 cc for the earliest cranium to about 1140 cc for the most recent cranium in the sample. Tools types were mainly larger choppers and scrapers in the lower levels. By later levels, the proportion of large and medium tools decreased whereas the proportion of small and more complex tools increased. (Wu and Lin, 1983.)

376

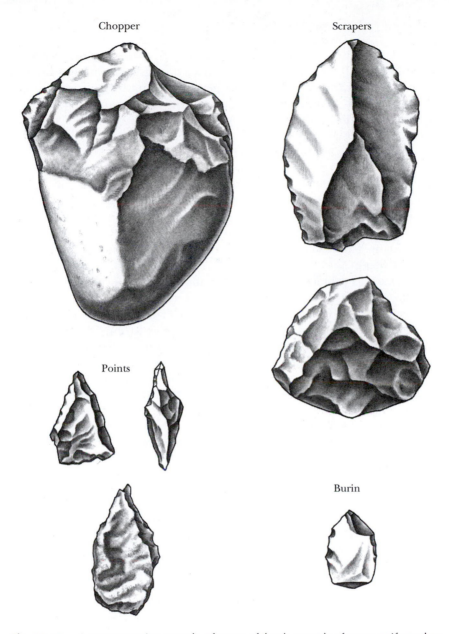

Chopper

Scrapers

Points

Burin

Fig. 10.15. A representative sample of some of the thousands of stone artifacts that have been found associated with *H. erectus* at Zhoukoudian.   The main tool types are choppers, scrapers, points, and burins. (Wu and Lin, 1983.)

Tens of thousands of stone artifacts have been found at Zhoukoudian, mostly made from quartz, flint, and sandstone. The main tool types are choppers, scrapers, points, and burins (Figs. 10.14, 10.15). While some of the flakes were apparently used as tools without further trimming many others were retouched to produce more specialized tools. Three different tool-making techniques were employed by the *H. erectus* tool makers: **anvil percussion,** in which a large flat stone placed on the ground was used as an anvil for breaking off flakes; **direct percussion,** in which a core flint was held and flakes were detached by striking it with a hammerstone; and **bipolar percussion,** in which an anvil was set on the ground, a piece of quartz held upright on it, and flakes chipped off both ends (bipolar flakes) by striking it with a hammerstone (Wu and Lin, 1983).

The stone tools found in the lowest layers of the cave (layers 8–11, dating to about 460–420 kya) are mainly large tools (less than 50 g in weight and 60 mm in length) and are made using all three tool-making techniques. In the middle layers of the cave, from about 370 to 350 kya, the anvil percussion technique is very rare and the bipolar percussion method is dominant. This results in a greater proportion of smaller tools (less than 20 g in weight and 40 mm in length). The last stage, dated to about 300–230 kya, is characterized by smaller tools of much better quality (Wu and Lin, 1983).

Over 50 years ago, Harvard archeologist Hallam Movius (1944) first noted a separation of stone-working technologies in the Old World: the Acheulean handaxe/cleaver complex of Africa and Europe, and the chopper/chopping-tool complex of Asia east of India (Fig. 10.16) (Clark, 1994; Schick, 1994).[16] The geographical division between the Acheulean industries and the chopper/chopping-tool industries[17] of Asia was thought by some prehistorians to correspond to the geographical barriers formed by the Caucasus, the Elburz, the Hindu Kush and the Himalayas: the so-called Movius Line. In fact, the archeological tool kit of the Far East was often defined more by what it lacked compared to many Western assemblages: the large tools characteristic of the Acheulean; the technique of tool making known as Levallois, in which the core is trimmed to control the form and size of the intended flake; and the patterned changes in standardized tool types seen over time. This led Movius and others to view the Far East as an area of "cultural retardation." It is now known that this characterization is misleading and that the Far East has diverse and rich Paleolithic tool traditions going back into at least the late Lower Pleistocene; nevertheless, there are distinct differences in the tool complexes of East and West (Clark, 1994; Movius, 1944; Pope and Keates, 1994; Schick, 1994).

Recently, stone artifacts have been recovered from the Bose basin in southern China dated to about 800 kya. These represent the oldest known large cutting tools from East Asia and are quite similar to Mode 2 Acheulean stone tools from Africa. This discovery of Acheulean tools in the early Middle Pleistocene of China demonstrates that technical ad-

---

[16]Handaxes and cleavers identified as late Acheulean have been found in association with the *H. erectus* /early *H. sapiens* cranium from the late Middle Pleistocene of Narmada, India (Kennedy, 1999; Kennedy et al., 1991).

[17]Technically, choppers are unifacially flaked and chopping tools are bifacially flaked tools.

- • Acheulean sites (with handaxes)
- × Non-handaxe sites

Swanscombe & Hoxne

Clacton
Boxgrove
Bilzingsleben
St. Acheul
Terra Amata
Vértesszöllös

Torralba & Ambrona
Isernia

Aïn Hanech
Tighennif
Thomas Quarries & Sidi Abderrahman
Tihodaine

Ubeidiye

Zhoukoudian ×   × Chongokni
Xihoudou ×

Non-handaxe industries

Hunsgi

Middle Awash (Bodo)
Baringo (Kapthurin)
Kilombe
Olorgesailie
Peninj
Olduvai Gorge
Isimila

Kalambo Falls

Sterkfontein & Swartkrans

Saldanha   Amanzi

St. Acheul
(France)   Tihodaine
(Algeria)   Hunsgi
(India)

Fig. 10.16. Geographical distribution of the Acheulean handaxe industry and the nonhandaxe industries of East Asia. The geographical division between the Acheulean industries and the chopper/chopping-tool industries of East Asia was thought by some prehistorians to correspond to the geographical barriers formed by the Caucasus, the Elburz, the Hindu Kush, and the Himalayas: the so-called Movius Line. Three representative Acheulean tools are shown (*left to right*): a handaxe, a cleaver, and another handaxe. (Gowlett, 1992.)

vances were manifested in East Asia contemporaneously with handaxe technology in Africa and western Europe (Yamei et al., 2000).

Many hypotheses have sought to explain this archeological phenomenon, focusing on different tool requirements of hominin populations in the two regions, the absence of proper stone raw materials, the presence of nonlithic materials for tools, and cultural interruptions during migration. For example, it has been proposed that Asian *H. erectus* may have relied heavily on bamboo in place of stone as a specific adaptation to the heavily forested and cave-filled, or karstic, areas of Southeast Asia (Pope, 1983; Schick and Zhuan, 1993). However, there is another intriguing possibility. We noted earlier that new evidence suggests that *H. erectus* may have first appeared in eastern Asia as early as 1.8 mya.[18] The Acheulean tool kit first appears in Africa about 1.5 mya, some 0.3–0.4 million years after *H. erectus* left Africa for Asia (Asfaw et al., 1992). According to this scenario, the reason the Acheulean does not appear in Asia is that *H. erectus* left Africa *before* Acheulean tools were even developed.

In China, proto-handaxes are made of pebbles and thick flakes but are not similar to Acheulean handaxes from Europe and Africa. They are large in size; are usually irregular in shape; and can be classified as bifaces, unifaces, and artifacts with a triangular cross section. They are associated with bolas and other artifacts and together constitute assemblages of large stone implements. Chinese archeologists have described two cultural traditions in the early Paleolithic of China: one is the pebble industry, represented by proto-handaxes, and the other is the flake industry, represented by Zhoukoudian culture (An, 1990). It is possible, however, that these different "cultural traditions" simply represent different activity facies or environmental or geographical contexts.

The four thick layers of ash in the cave, the thickest one being over 6 m deep in some places, suggest to some archeologists that the Zhoukoudian hominins had mastered the use of fire even at the earliest occupation levels and that they had the ability to control fire and to keep it burning in the cave over prolonged periods of time.

A number of plant and animal remains found at Zhoukoudian provide clues to the dietary habits of *H. erectus*. For example, seeds and pollen from Chinese hackberry, walnut, hazelnut, pine, elm, and rambler rose suggest that the fruit and/or seeds of these species may have been part of the *H. erectus* diet. Animal bones—including those of boar, horse, buffalo, and rhinoceros—have also been found, indicating that *H. erectus* was capable of hunting both small and large game. The remains of over 3000 individual deer attest to a certain taste for venison!

This conventional view of Zhoukoudian archeology has been challenged by archeologist Lewis Binford and co-workers (Binford and Ho, 1985; Binford and Stone, 1986). Their arguments include the following points: (1) Since hominins, artifacts, and ash layers are not consistently associated in the cave, they should not be considered unequivocal evidence of hominin occupation. (2) The ash layers are too thick to be "hearths" and may be the remains of naturally occurring fires that were concentrated in the cave by geological agencies (alternatively, the ash may have resulted from the spontaneous combustion of guano). (3) The vertebrate

---

[18]Early hominins were certainly in East Asia (Ubeidiya in Israel) by 1.4 mya.

fossils are not necessarily indicative of hominin diets because *H. erectus* may have been just another prey item for animal carnivores responsible for all the fossilized remains.

It is fair to say, however, that these arguments have been challenged by other paleoanthropologists who claim that the results were based on questionable statistical techniques that utilized only a small fraction of the total faunal evidence; hence most archeologists believe that the Zhoukoudian Locality 1 assemblage results from, for the most part, repeated hominin occupations (Pope, 1988, 1992).

One of these challenges concerning evidence for the controlled use of fire has recently been supported by the finding that no ash or charcoal remnants can be detected in layer 10, where stone tools are associated with burned and unburned bones. Although the sediments of layer 10 have often been described as containing ash, this apparently is not the case. Instead, these so-called hearths are laminated, water-lain silts and organic matter, all of which have been transported into the site (Goldberg et al., 2001). Fresh wood ash is composed mainly of fine-grained calcite and a minor amount of a substance called siliceous aggregates. The absence of the latter substance indicates that there is no unequivocal evidence for wood ash in these sediments. The absence of wood ash is peculiar given that the strongest evidence for fire associated with layer 10 is the presence of burned bones. Since most of the fine-grained sediments are not in their primary context, but rather water lain, it is not possible to determine their original source (Weiner et al., 1998).

Other *Homo erectus* Sites from China: Lantian, Yuanmou, Jian Shi, Hexian, Yiyuan, Yunxian

While Zhoukoudian is unquestionably the most famous of the Chinese *H. erectus* sites, similar fossils have now been recovered from numerous other Lower to Middle Pleistocene sites in both northern and southern China (Fig. 10.12b) (Pope, 1992; Schick and Zhuan, 1993; Wu and Poirier, 1995).

The *H. erectus* material discovered in the mid-1960s from loess deposits at Lantian, Shensi Province, includes an adult mandible with shovel-shaped incisors and congenital absence of the M_3s from Chenjiawo and a partial cranium from Gongwangling (Woo, 1964, 1966). The two specimens are from deposits about 25 km apart, which appear to straddle the Matuyama/Brunhes paleomagnetic boundary (780 kya), although there is still some debate about this. For example, the cranium is found in reversed polarity sediments (Matuyama) that may be as old as 1 million years and, if true, would make this the oldest hominin from China (Fig. 10.12a) (but see below). The Chenjiawo mandible is from overlying normal polarity sediments (Brunhes) dated to about 650 kya (An et al., 1990).

The Gongwangling cranium includes the frontal and parietal bones, right temporal bone, most of the orbits, partial remains of the nasal bones, and most of the right maxilla with two teeth. The cranial vault bones are exceedingly thick, supraorbital tori are massive and continuous, the frontal squama is low, and postorbital constriction is well marked. Endocranial volume is estimated at 775–783 cc. The overall impression is of a cranium even more primitive in morphology than any of those from Zhoukoudian or Indonesia (Howells, 1980; Woo, 1966). The Gongwangling fauna at Lantian is considered the earliest mammalian fauna associated with *H. erectus* in northern China and suggests that forest environments and warm subtropic conditions existed at the time. This characteristic giant panda–primitive elephant (*Ailuropoda–Stegodon*) fauna slowly gave way to more temperate faunas about 700 kya at Chenjiawo. A small number of chopper/chopping tools have also been found at Lantian, but their association with the hominin layers is problematic (Keates, 1996).

Dental remains from Yuanmou have assumed some importance, not because of the fossils themselves, which consist only of two central incisor teeth (and several stone tools), but because of the date of about 1.7 mya that Chinese anthropologists have given to them. This older age was bolstered by a preliminary amino acid racemization date of 1.54 mya on wild boar (*Sus*) and red deer (*Cervus*) teeth from the site and ESR and fission-track dates of about 1.3 mya (Wu and Poirier, 1995). However, a different interpretation of the paleomagnetic profile of the site suggests that the hominin-bearing sediments may actually be younger than about 900 kya and possibly closer to 500–600 kya (Fig. 10.12a) (Schick and Zhuan, 1993; Wu, 1985; Wu and Qian, 1991). The incisors are fairly robust, clearly shovel shaped, and in general similar to central incisors from Zhoukoudian in having these features as well as a swollen basal part of the crown and a strong prominence of the basal tubercle (Howells, 1980).

However, it has been reported that ESR dates combined with a paleomagnetic sequence suggest an age of about 1.7–1.9 million years for a small early *Homo* sample (fragmentary left mandible with P_4 and M_1 and an upper incisor) and associated stone tools from Longgupo Cave, Sichuan, China (Fig. 10.17) (Wanpo et al., 1995). If this date is correct, these would be the oldest hominins and tools from China and would be roughly contemporaneous with the earliest *Homo* from Java, mentioned earlier. The Longgupo teeth are said to bear more resemblance to early Pleistocene hominins from East Africa such as *H. habilis* and *H. ergaster* than to Asian *H. erectus*, leaving open the possibility that a pre-*erectus* hominin may have entered Asia before 2 mya, coincident with the earliest diversification of the genus *Homo* in Africa. The crowns of P_4 in *H. erectus* are generally simple and single rooted, as in modern humans. By contrast, the Longgupo P_4 root is bifid for most of its length. The M_1 in *H. erectus* usually has six cusps and somewhat thickened and wrinkled enamel. The Longgupo molar, in contrast, has five cusps, and thin, smooth enamel.[19]

Three hominin molars from Jianshi, variously identified as either *H. erectus* or early *H. sapiens*, are interesting in that they represent one of only three known associations of Middle Pleistocene hominins and *Gigantopithecus* yet found in East Asia (Pope, 1988).[20] These molars have been dated by U-S to about 300–200 kya.

In 1980–1981, *H. erectus* remains representing several individuals were found at Lontandong (Dragon Pool) Cave, Hexian County (Figs. 10.12 and 10.18). The initial Hexian discoveries included a calvaria of a young adult lacking most of the cranial base, a partial left mandibular fragment preserving M_2 and M_3, and five isolated teeth. The next year a weathered frontal fragment preserving the right supraorbital region and a small part of the squama, a right parietal fragment, and five additional isolated teeth were recovered. These fossils belong to at least three individuals and are particularly significant because they may represent the last known occurrence of *H. erectus* from the Far East. Paleomagnetic stratigraphy suggests that the Hexian fossils are younger than 700 kya and may be as young as 250–280 kya, if the correlation of the Hexian fauna to ^{18}O stage 8 is correct (Fig. 10.12) (Liu, 1983; Xu and You, 1984). These younger ages seem to be confirmed by various other dating techniques, including TL dates that bracket the calvaria between 195 and 184 kya, a U-S date of 150 kya, and an amino acid racemization date of 300–200 kya. These young dates raise the intriguing possibility that *H. erectus* and early *H. sapiens* were contemporaries; a situation, if true, that would thus far be unique to China (Day, 1984).

However, these earlier age estimates have recently been superceded by new combined ESR and U-S age determinations, giving an average age of 412 ± 25 kya, or about the transition between ^{18}O stages 12 and 11 (Grün et al., 1998). This age implies that the more-advanced Hexian *H. erectus* occurred at a similar time as the less-advanced *H. erectus* specimens from Locality 1 at Zhoukoudian.

The Hexian cranium is the first Asian *H. erectus* cranium discovered outside the northern temperate zone of China. Like most *H. erectus* crania, the vault is low and thick and the supraorbital torus is both thick and continuous. However, both the supratoral sulcus and postorbital constriction are less developed than in the Zhoukoudian *H. erectus* sample. The flattened frontal bone has a sagittal keel. The mastoid process is small and maximum cranial breadth is low down on the side of the cranium at the

---

[19]Other workers have suggested that the Longgupo "hominin" sample is not hominin at all, but rather morphologically and metrically similar to the Mio-Pliocene fossil ape *Lufengpithecus* from Lufeng and Yuanmou in Yunnan, China (Etler and Guoxing, 1998).

[20]The others being one Pleistocene locality in Vietnam, Tham Om in western Nghe Tinh province, dated to about 500,000 years ago, and Longgupo in China (Olsen and Ciochon, 1990).

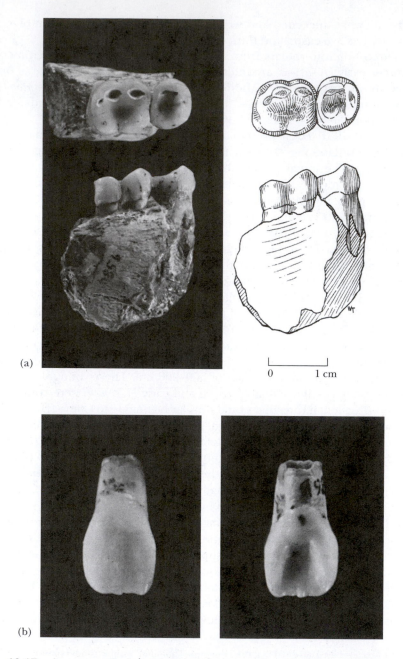

0   1 cm

Fig. 10.17.   Longgupo Cave hominins and stone tools.   These may represent the earliest hominins and stone tools from China. (a) Left mandibular fragment with P_4 and M_1. (b) (Labial view (*left*) and lingual view (*right*) of a right I^2. (c) (*top*) Elongated, spherical cobble with three relatively discrete areas showing crushing and pitting, suggesting repeated battering; (*bottom*) lenticular-shaped flake tool. (Photos courtesy of R. L. Ciochon, University of Iowa.)

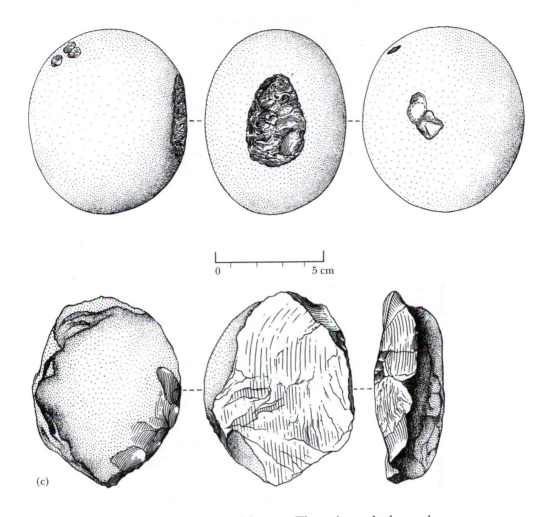

0   5 cm

(c)

level of the well-developed supramastoid crest. There is marked angulation of the occipital bone. Cranial capacity is about 1000 cc (cranial capacity averages about 1050 cc for the Zhoukoudian sample and about 1100 cc for the Ngandong sample). The body of the mandible is massive, and the incisors are characteristically shovel shaped with well-developed basal tubercles and are morphologically similar to similar teeth from Zhoukoudian and Krapina (Wu, 1983, 1985; Wu and Dong, 1982). Overall, the Hexian material is most similar to Zhoukoudian V. One of the important lessons from this material is that, taken in conjunction with the Zhoukoudian sample, there is no simple continuous decrease in cranial robusticity through time in the Chinese *H. erectus* sample.

Several hominin fragments, including a left and right parietal, frontal and occipital fragments, and seven isolated teeth from at least two individuals, have been recovered from Yiyuan. In general overall morphology, the

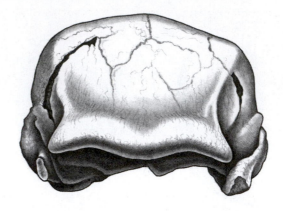

Hexian

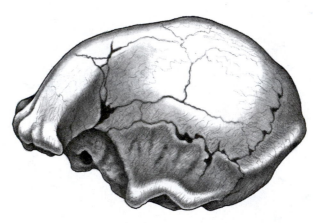

Fig. 10.18. *H. erectus* calvaria from Lontandong (Dragon Pool) Cave, Hexian County.

specimens are similar to those from Zhoukoudian and, along with the Hexian material, could record one of the latest occurrences of *H. erectus* in China (Etler and Li, 1994; Pope, 1992).

Undoubtedly the most significant Middle Pleistocene *H. erectus* fossils to come out of China in many years are two relatively complete crania and artifacts from Yunxian, provisionally dated to about 350 kya (Fig. 10.19). However, more recent ESR dates on several fossil mammal teeth stratigraphically associated with the hominin crania yield an average age of 581 ± 93 kya (Chen et al., 1996). Even though it is distorted, the Yunxian II cranium is clearly the largest *H. erectus* cranium ever recovered in China. While they share many of the "typical" *H. erectus*–like cranial features noted earlier, it is interesting that other "typical" *H. erectus* traits, like well-

(a)

(b)

Fig. 10.19. (a) Frontal view of EV 9002 and (b) lateral view of EV 9001, two of the most complete Middle Pleistocene *H. erectus* crania from China. Both were discovered at Yunxian and are provisionally dated to about 350 kya. Even though distorted, EV 9002 is the largest *H. erectus* cranium ever recovered from China. (Photos courtesy of L. Tianyuan.)

developed cranial buttressing and the form of the supraorbital tori, are not well expressed in the Yunxian crania, suggesting that such characters are polymorphic within Middle Pleistocene hominins.

What is perhaps more noteworthy is that these two *H. erectus* crania have a number of midfacial features that are often seen in (non-Neandertal) early modern *H. sapiens* (Etler and Li, 1994; Li and Etler, 1992): (1) a more flattened, or orthognathic face with only moderate alveolar prognathism; (2) a distinct maxillary canine fossa; (3) the lateral part of the maxilla oriented coronally and highly angled to the zygomatic; (4) a high origin of the zygomatic root; and (5) a horizontal inferior zygomaxillary border with a pronounced malar notch, or incisure.

By way of contrast, many Middle Pleistocene hominins from Europe and/or Africa often classified as *H. erectus* have a different midfacial pattern that is more reminiscent of later-occurring Neandertals, such as a pneumatized, obliquely set midface and a low origin of the zygomatic root. If this assessment is correct, it implies that facial structures characteristic of (non-Neandertal) early modern *H. sapiens* were widespread in East Asia at a time when European and African hominins still possessed a morphological pattern distinct from the modern human condition (Pope, 1991). This would have important implications in the debate about the geography of modern human origins (Li and Etler, 1992):

> Given the common occurrence of a mid-facial anatomy characteristic of Late Pleistocene non-Neandertal *H. sapiens* in Middle Pleistocene hominin crania . . . from east Asia and its less frequent . . . occurrence in Middle Pleistocene Eurafrican hominins, it can be argued that this morphology appears first in Asia and subsequently spread westward.

This view has not gone unchallenged. Several anthropologists have tried to decouple Asian *H. erectus* from any direct role in modern human ancestry by claiming that the "modern" features described for the Yunxian crania also appear in African fossils of equivalent age, the implication being that these features are, therefore, primitive ones and not indicative of any special phylogenetic relationship. We will come back to this issue in the next section when we address the question of whether or not *H. erectus* can be identified in Africa.

HOMO ERECTUS IN AFRICA?

At the beginning of the chapter we posed the question of whether or not *H. erectus* was a "real" species with definable boundaries in time and space and, if so, whether it could also be identified in the Lower to Middle Pleistocene of Africa and/or Europe. Most anthropologists would answer a definite yes to the first question and a definite maybe to the second. Let us first review the specimens that have been most consistently classified as *H. erectus* from Africa (we will look at Middle Pleistocene early hominins from Europe in the next chapter) and then discuss some of the current contro-

versial issues surrounding *H. erectus*. As we will see later, some workers describe this African *H. erectus* sample as a distinct species, *H. ergaster*.

A number of fossils from North, East, and South Africa have been described as *H. erectus* over the last half century (Fig. 10.1). For many years it
has been thought that *H. erectus* was present in Africa perhaps as much as 1
million years before its occurrence in the Far East. However, as mentioned
above, if the date for Javan *H. erectus* at 1.8 mya is correct, then the earliest
known hominins from Java are of comparable age to the oldest specimens
of *H.* cf. *erectus* (= *H. ergaster*) from Africa.

Possible *Homo erectus* from North Africa

The first discoveries of *H. erectus* in Africa were from several poorly dated
sites in Algeria and Morocco in northwestern Africa associated with variants of the Acheulean tool tradition (Fig. 10.1) (Hublin, 1985; McBurney,
1958).

The initial discovery in 1933 included part of a cranial vault, the left
maxilla, and the lower jaw of a subadult found near Rabat, Morocco. However, because the mandible has a bony chin and the occipital bone lacks a
transverse torus, some workers consider the Rabat hominin an early form
of *H. sapiens* (Howell, 1978; Rightmire, 1990). Other more "archaic" looking hominins from Morocco include two fragmentary jaws and teeth
found in 1955 at Sidi Abderrahman, near Casablanca; a mandible and cranial pieces found between 1969 and 1972 at Thomas Quarries; and a damaged cranial vault, natural sandstone braincast, and part of the left maxilla
with I^2–M^2 and lower face found in 1971 at Salé.

The Salé cranium is thick walled, and the endocranial volume is estimated at 880 cc (Holloway, 1981c). It has other typical *H. erectus* features,
including pronounced postorbital constriction, frontal keeling, lack of articular tubercle, and greatest cranial breadth across the prominent supramastoid crests (Hublin, 1985; Rightmire, 1990). However, it does have
some "advanced" *H. erectus* features, such as the development of parietal
eminences and a more rounded occipital contour, although the pathological nature of the nuchal area makes measurements of this area suspect.

Between 1954 and 1956, three jaws, a parietal bone, and several teeth
were discovered at Ternifine (now Tighenif), Algeria (Fig. 10.20). A number of stone artifacts were recovered as well, consisting mainly of pebble
tools, bifaces, and cleavers. Also recovered from the site was a bone tool (a
zebra distal metacarpal), the earliest found from this part of Africa (Geraads et al., 1986). The Ternifine jaws are described as quite similar in overall morphology and robustness to *H. erectus* jaws from the Far East and
from Olduvai (e.g., OH 22, OH 23, OH 51) and differ from the Rabat
specimen in showing little, if any, development of a bony chin (Rightmire,
1990). The Ternifine fossils were found in sediments of normal polarity,

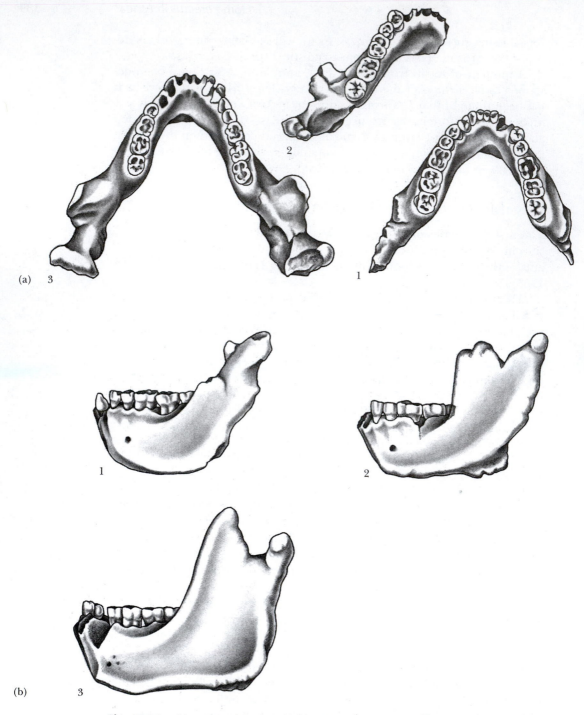

(a)

(b)

Fig. 10.20. *H. erectus* lower jaws from Ternifine. (*top*) Occlusal views; (*bottom*) lateral views. (Rightmire, 1990.)

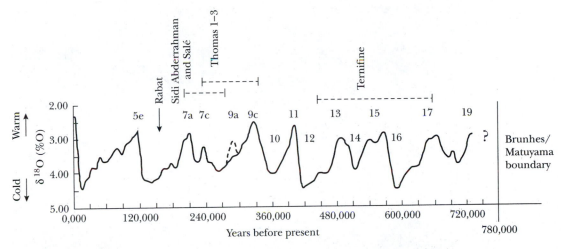

Fig. 10.21. Tentative correlations between fossil hominin sites in North Africa (Rabat, Sidi Aberrhaman, Salé, Thomas Quarry, Ternifine) and the oxygen isotope record. (Jaeger, 1981.)

presumably from within the Brunhes normal epoch less than 780 kya. Tentative correlations of these North African sites with the ^{18}O marine stratigraphic record are given in Figure 10.21.

Possible *Homo erectus* from East Africa

By far the most abundant and informative *H. erectus* material from Africa comes from Olduvai Gorge, Tanzania, Lake Turkana, Kenya, and the Middle Awash site of Bouri.

The first *H. erectus* from Olduvai Gorge was found by Louis Leakey in 1960 at site LLK, upper Bed II (Figs. 10.4 and 10.22). The specimen, Olduvai Hominin (OH 9), is dated to about 1.2 mya and consists of a partial braincase that includes the supraorbital region, occiput, and much of the cranial base.[21] Unfortunately, the face is missing. It shares many of the cranial features that we have already noted for Asian *H. erectus*: (1) a shelf-like and robust supraorbital torus that is especially thick above the nose, (2) a low lateral cranial profile with a receding frontal bone (however, unlike many Asian *H. erectus*, the frontal lacks a midsagittal keel, (3) greatest cranial breadth low near the mastoid crests, and (4) a reduced degree of basicranial flexion. Endocranial capacity has been estimated at 1060–1070 cc (Holloway, 1981b). In a plane of cranial orientation passing through the

---

[21]Since the bottom of Olduvai Bed III is dated to 1.25–1.47 mya, the Bed II OH 9 cranium may actually be somewhat older than 1.47 mya (Antón, 2003).

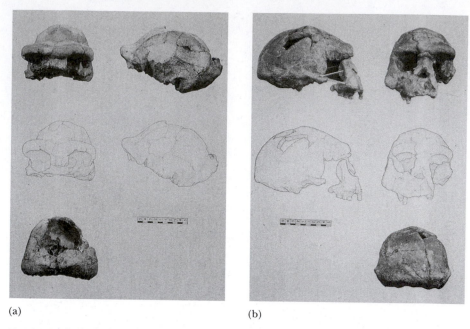

(a)   (b)

Fig. 10.22.   The first *H. erectus* discovered at Olduvai Gorge (OH 9) (a) compared to Sangiran 17(b). OH 9 is dated to about 1.2 mya and consists of a partial brain-case that includes the supraorbital region, occiput, and much of the cranial base. Note the shelf-like and robust supraorbital torus that is especially thick above the nose (glabellar prominence) and the low lateral cranium profile with a receding frontal bone. Endocranial capacity has been estimated at 1060 cc. (Photos courtesy of G. P. Rightmire.)

top of the external auditory meatus and the bottom of the orbit, called the **Frankfurt Horizontal** (FH) plane, it can be appreciated that the rather flattened cranial base contributes to the high position of the occipital condyles, the shallow posterior cranial fossae, and the relatively high position of the occipital protuberance (Fig. 10.23) (Maier and Nkini, 1984). In overall size, shape, and robustness OH 9 is most similar to *H. erectus* from Java, particularly to Sangiran crania 4, 12, and 17 (Rightmire, 1981a, 1984).

Several quartz flakes and other tools were recovered from excavations at the site but are not considered diagnostic and OH 9 is not directly associated with them.

A second *H. erectus* cranium from Olduvai, OH 12, was found in a number of pieces scattered over the surface of site VEK, Bed IV. Upper and lower age estimates for Bed IV are between 620 and 830 kya. Some of the facial skeleton is also preserved, including part of the left maxillary alveolar process with tooth roots and a frontal fragment preserving some of the superior rim of the right orbit (Rightmire, 1981a, 1984). Brain capacity is

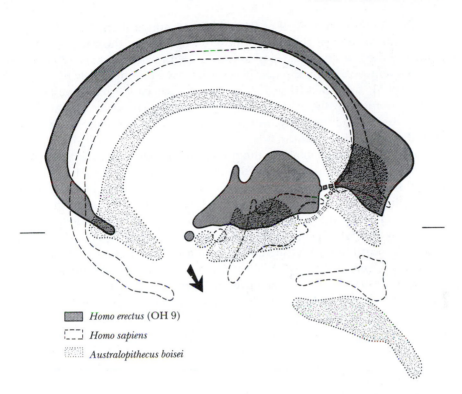

Homo erectus (OH 9)

Homo sapiens

Australopithecus boisei

Fig. 10.23. When OH 9 is oriented in the Frankfurt Horizontal plane, it can be appreciated that the rather flattened cranial base contributes to the high position of the occipital condyles, the shallow posterior cranial fossae, and the relatively high position of the occipital protuberance compared to *H. sapiens* and *A. boisei*. *Arrow* designates location of the foramen magnum (Maier and Nkini, 1984).

estimated at 700–800 cc (Holloway, 1975). In many features the cranium is more gracile than OH 9 or any of the Indonesian *H. erectus*. For example, a true occipital torus is not well developed, the cranial vault appears more rounded in posterior view, there is no sagittal keel or parasagittal flattening along the parietals (but there may be traces of slight keeling in the frontal bone), and the temporal lines marking the origin of the temporalis muscle are faint. In addition, the supraorbital torus is lightly constructed (only about 10 mm thick) but there is a distinct supratoral sulcus similar to that seen, for instance, in KNM-ER 3883.

There are no stone tools directly associated with OH 12, although other skeletal remains attributable to *H. erectus* from upper Bed IV have been found with Acheulean tools (M. Leakey, 1971).

Three mandibular fragments from Olduvai have usually been assigned to *H. erectus* (OH 22, 23, 51) (Rightmire, 1990). The most complete of the three is OH 22, a nearly complete right mandible preserving P_3–M_2. It probably comes from Bed III or IV and is not younger than about 620 kya. Its mandibular body is thick and robust, particularly in the symphyseal region, and there is no evidence of any bony chin formation. OH 23 is a left jaw fragment preserving the heavily worn P_4–M_2 from the overlying Masek Beds. OH 51, from Bed III or IV, consists of a partial left mandibular corpus preserving only the worn crowns of P_4 and M_1. The latter two jaw fragments are not too informative but generally conform to OH 22 in terms of overall shape and robustness.

The first information about the postcranial skeleton of African *H. erectus* also came from Olduvai. In 1970 a hip bone and femoral shaft (OH 28) were discovered at site WK, Bed IV, in association with Acheulean tools (mainly handaxes, cleavers, scrapers) (M. Leakey, 1971). These postcranial fossils, combined with those from Koobi Fora (see below) and those described by Weidenreich from Zhoukoudian, identify a unique *H. erectus* hindlimb morphology that includes: (1) a large acetabulum; (2) a robust vertical iliac pillar; (3) a small auricular surface for articulation with the sacrum; and (4) a femur characterized by a large femoral head, anteroposteriorly flattened, or **platymeric,** femoral shaft characterized by thickened cortical bone, narrow medullary cavity, and heavy muscular markings. In terms of function, there is little doubt that this pelvic–femoral complex is that of a habitual upright biped (Day, 1971, 1984; Kennedy, 1983). Judging from the size of the femur and hip, a body size of 50 kg for this individual has been estimated (Rightmire, 1990).

A number of beautifully preserved specimens from Koobi Fora have been assigned to *H. erectus.* Two of the best preserved crania, KNM-ER 3733 and KNM-ER 3883, are from the upper member of the Koobi Fora Formation (Figs. 10.4 and 10.24). KNM-ER 3733 is from sediments just below, and KNM-ER 3883 from sediments just above, the Okote Tuff complex dated to approximately 1.6 mya.

KNM-ER 3733 is a relatively complete cranium that includes a partially preserved facial skeleton. The nasal bridge and both zygomatic bones are present, but the maxilla is eroded and all the anterior teeth are missing. KNM-ER 3883 also includes part of a face and braincase (Fig. 10.24b). While the cranial vault is largely complete, only the supraorbital region and right zygomatic bone of the face are preserved. Both specimens have an estimated cranial capacity of 800–850 cc and are somewhat smaller than the heavily built OH 9 braincase from upper Bed II, Olduvai (Rightmire, 1984).

In lateral view, both KNM-ER 3733 and 3883 exhibit the low cranial profile typical of *H. erectus.* The crania are broad with maximum breadth low on the temporal bones rather than higher up on the parietal vault as in *H. sapiens.* No strong angular process is present, and the mastoid process is small. Occipital bones of both East African and Indonesian *H. erectus* are highly angled (between about 100° and 110°) rather than having the more rounded contour of modern humans (Fig. 10.6, Fig. 10.24). This

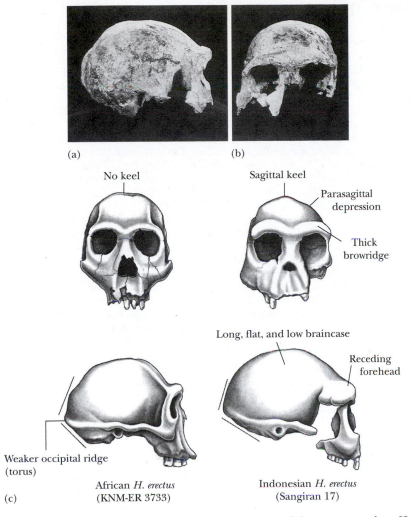

Fig. 10.24. (a) Lateral and (b) frontal views of one of the most complete *H. erectus* crania, KNM-ER 3883, from the upper member of the Koobi Fora Formation, dated to approximately 1.6 mya. Estimated cranial capacity is 800–850 cc, somewhat smaller than the heavily built OH 9 braincase from upper Bed II, Olduvai. In lateral view, KNM-ER 3883 exhibits the low cranial profile typical of *H. erectus*. The cranium is broad with maximum breadth low on the temporal bones rather than higher up on the parietal vault as in *H. sapiens*. (c) Some of the differences between a similar *H. erectus* cranium from Kenya, KNM-ER 3733, and Javan *H. erectus* are highlighted. (Photos courtesy G. P. Rightmire.)

occipital angulation is associated with the formation of a transverse torus (less developed in KNM-ER 3883). In KNM-ER 3733 the length of the upper portion of the occipital squama exceeds that of the nuchal plane, but in KNM-ER 3883 the upper portion is shorter, which is the usual condition for *H. erectus*.

Box 10.1   Skeletal Pathology in *Homo erectus*

A partial *H. erectus* skeleton (KNM-ER 1808) was recovered in the 1970s from the upper member of the Koobi Fora Formation. Unfortunately, most of the bones are pathologically altered, encrusted with a coarse woven bone that is possibly the result of chronic hypervitaminosis A. One possible cause of this pathology is an excessively high dietary intake of animal liver, particularly carnivore liver, by this individual. Such a condition has been documented in early Arctic explorers after ingestion of polar bear, seal, or husky dog liver. Does the ingestion of toxic amounts of carnivore liver reflect a major dietary shift in early human populations marked by increased meat-eating behaviors? In this regard, it may be significant that the first association of stone artifacts and animal bones at Koobi Fora antedates KNM-ER 1808 by only some 200,000 years (Walker et al., 1982).

A second interesting hypothesis to explain this skeletal pathology is that increased ingestion of bee brood (eggs, pupae, larvae) and other immature insects may have resulted in a new foraging strategy in early *H. erectus* (Skinner, 1991). Bee broods have a high concentration of vitamin A and protracted ingestion of honey and insect larvae could produce the skeletal pathology seen in KNM-ER 1808. The density of nests of the East African bee, *Apis mellifera*, within the foraging area of early *H. erectus* would provide an ample and reliable energy source that could contribute substantially to early hominin nutritional requirements. The human brain is a voracious energy consumer and was expanding rapidly during this phase of human evolution. Even though the brain constitutes only about 2% of body weight, it requires about 17% of the normal cardiac output and consumes about 20% of the oxygen utilized by the entire body. Perhaps a new foraging strategy to secure one of the necessary energy sources, honey, led inadvertently to isolated cases of hypervitaminosis A in early *H. erectus*.

The Turkana *H. erectus* crania vary in the size and shape of their supraorbital region. The torus in KNM-ER 3733 is especially gracile, with only moderate expression of a supratoral sulcus. On the other hand, KNM-ER 3883 has a much larger torus with a more massive glabella region. In this it more closely resembles OH 9, even though the overall cranium is smaller. These Turkana crania have frontal bones that show the typical *H. erectus* pattern of postorbital constriction (Rightmire, 1984).

Several other cranial fragments from Koobi Fora are generally similar to comparable parts of KNM-ER 3733 and/or 3883 and are tentatively referred to *H. erectus* as well, or to *H. ergaster* (e.g., KNM-ER 730). The problem in sorting much of this material is due to the fact that both *Homo* and *Australopithecus* occur in deposits above the KBS tuff, so taxonomic assignments of such isolated and unassociated material are often difficult.

Perhaps the most extraordinary and unique information about *H. erectus* discovered at Lake Turkana pertains to postcranial adaptation. Several partial *H. erectus* skeletons and isolated postcrania from Koobi Fora have been described, including one nearly complete left femur (KNM-ER 1481a) from sediments stratigraphically below the KBS tuff (Kennedy, 1983). If the taxonomic assessment of this femur is correct, it would be the oldest *H. erectus* postcranial specimen known.

A more complete and nonpathological *H. erectus* skeleton (WT-15000) was discovered in 1984 on the west side of Lake Turkana (Fig. 10.25) (Walker and Leakey, 1993). The specimen derives from sediments that immediately overlie a tuff identified as part of the Okote Tuff complex dated to approximately 1.65 mya. Much of the cranium and dentition were also recovered, and the teeth are similar in size to the Zhoukoudian *H. erectus*

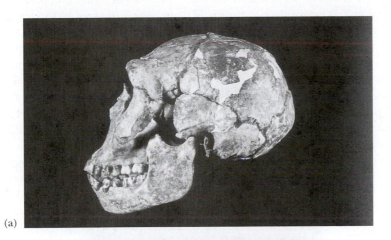

(a)

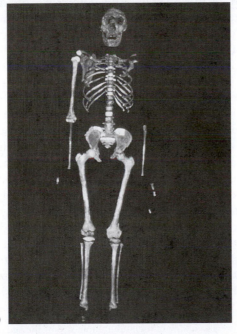

(b)

Fig. 10.25.   The most complete *H. erectus* skeleton ever found, KNM-WT 15000 from Nariokotome, Kenya.   (a) Lateral view of cranium, (b) The skeleton. (Photos courtesy of A. Walker and National Museums of Kenya.)

sample. The physiological age of this individual has been assessed using three different age estimators: dental maturity (10.5–11.3 years), epiphyseal closure (13.0–13.5 years), and stature (about 15 years). Based on standards of modern human dental development, the individual was about 10–12 years old at the time of death (Clegg and Aiello, 1999; Smith, 1993; B. Smith et al., 1995). Both the central and the lateral upper incisors are shovel shaped, a feature often associated with Far Eastern *H. erectus* and modern Chinese populations (Walker, 1993). The cranial capacity is estimated at 880 cc and would probably have been just over 900 cc if the individual had lived to maturity (Begun and Walker, 1993).[22]

Cranial morphology suggests that East African *H. erectus* may have been quite sexually dimorphic. For example, the WT-15000 cranium does not show the exaggerated ectocranial buttressing typical of Asian *H. erectus*, although this may be solely a reflection of its young age at the time of death. In spite of its young age, however, the supraorbital tori are thicker, the palate broader, and the facial skeleton more robust than in KNM-ER 3733 (Brown et al., 1985a).

Probably more informative than the teeth and cranial parts, however, is the extraordinarily complete postcranial skeleton. As noted above, postcranial remains of *H. erectus* are few and far between and before the discovery of WT-15000, *H. erectus* postcrania were either fragmentary, not definitely associated with crania or teeth, disputed as to species identification, or diseased (as in KNM-ER 1808). Therefore, the discovery of a virtually complete cranium and nonpathological skeleton was unprecedented.

The height of this individual is estimated to be about 5 feet 3 inches (160 cm), and if he had reached maturity would probably have stood over 6 feet (182 cm) (Feldesman and Lundy, 1988; Ruff and Walker, 1993). Overall body proportions are similar to those found in equatorial modern people. The vertebral column, while showing a human-like thoracic and lumbar curvature, differs from modern human vertebral columns in several features, not the least of which is the possible presence of six lumbar vertebrae—but as we have seen, this is debatable both for australopiths and for *H. erectus* (Haeusler et al., 2002). Modern humans normally have five lumbar vertebrae and African great apes three or four. In addition, the spinous processes are relatively longer and less inferiorly inclined and the laminae are not as broad. This means that the roof-tile-like layering effect of adjacent vertebrae typical of modern humans is not so evident in *H. erectus*. Also, the vertebral (neural) canal for passage of the spinal cord in the cervical and thoracic regions is relatively smaller than in modern humans, and the orientation of some of the articular facets differs as well (Latimer and Ward, 1993; MacLarnon, 1993; Walker, 1993).[23]

---

[22]Modern humans have about 95% of their adult brain size by the age of 10 years.

[23]However, vertebral canal dimensions in KNM-WT 15000 fall within the human range when controlled for cranial capacity (Hunley, 1998).

Important differences from modern humans are also seen in the pelvis and femur. For example, the ilium is strongly flared laterally but lacks a well-developed iliac pillar (unlike OH 28; see above). This lateral iliac flare, and accompanying large biacetabular width, is associated with an extremely long femoral neck (85 mm) that is more than 3 standard deviations (SD) from the average value in modern humans. Moreover, the angle between the femoral neck and shaft is very small (110°) and is 5 SD from the average value for modern *H. sapiens*. The obstetrical conclusions from this (and other early *Homo* specimens) is that birth canal diameters in early *H. erectus* would have been quite narrow from front to back and broad from side to side, similar to lower pelvic shape in australopiths. Furthermore, this suggests that nonrotational birth, in which the newborn's head is oriented transversely through the pelvic outlet, characterized early *Homo* as well as australopiths and that passage of a modern human-size, full-term fetus would have been difficult if not impossible even in *Homo erectus*. This implies that at least some growth patterns characteristic of modern humans, such as a continuation of fetal growth rates into the neonatal period resulting in relatively helpless infants and increased infant dependency, must have already evolved in *H. erectus* by 1.6 mya (Brown et al., 1985a; Martin, 1983; Ruff, 1995; Walker and Leakey, 1993).

It is interesting to speculate on the functional reasons for the marked postcranial differences in overall size and shape between *Australopithecus* and *H. erectus*. As we have seen, early australopiths were characterized by relatively short hindlimbs and long forelimbs, a long and bulky trunk (possibly) having six lumbar vertebrae, and long and curved fingers and toes—all features pointing to retention of some arboreal activity (or to retention of at least this phylogenetic "baggage" from a previous arboreal ancestry). On the other hand, *H. erectus* exhibits postcranial features more conducive to walking long distances, such as relatively long hindlimbs and shortened toes (Schmid, 1991; Preuschoft and Witte, 1991).

Probably the two oldest *H. erectus* specimens from Koobi Fora (and indeed from Africa) are the KNM-ER 3228 innominate and the KNM-ER 2598 occipital bone dated to approximately 1.89 and 1.95 mya, respectively (Rose, 1984; Wood, 1991). The occiput is thick, broad, and vertically tall with a thickened nuchal torus reminiscent of *H. erectus* and quite different from the same bone in australopiths. The innominate is also large and differs from australopith innominates in possessing a large acetabulum and strongly developed iliac pillar.

Several specimens assigned to *H. erectus* have been recovered from the Lake Baringo area and from the Ethiopian Rift. The Baringo specimens include two mandibles and some postcranial fragments, such as a well-preserved ulna, and date to between 700 and 230 kya (Leakey et al., 1969; Solan and Day, 1992; Tallon, 1978; Wood and Van Noten, 1986). The ulna is more gracile than the "robust" australopith ulna from Omo (Omo L.40-19) and Neandertal ulnae (Feldesman, 1979). One bifacial core tool and

14 flakes were recovered in situ with the hominins, although artifacts are common over the surface near the fossil locality.

A well-preserved *H. erectus* mandible preserving P_4–M_3 (and an isolated M^3) was discovered in direct association with Acheulean tools (mostly roughly made bifaces and trihedral picks) at the Middle Awash site of Konso-Gardula (Asfaw et al., 1992). The site is dated to 1.9–1.3 mya. It is interesting that grooves between the mandibular teeth indicate that these early hominins were using some type of wood, bone, and/or sinew for toothpicks. Overall, the tools are most similar to those found from middle Bed II, Olduvai. It seems clear from the cut marks on some of the animal bones that early hominins were using stone tools to "process" them (perhaps cutting off pieces of meat, or breaking bones for marrow). A total of 11 hominins have been found at the site since 1991, and field research indicates the presence of both *Homo* and *A. boisei* (Asfaw et al., 1992; Suwa et al., 1997).

The discovery at Konso-Gardula is particularly informative in showing that the Acheulean appears abruptly in East Africa about 1.4 mya, following about 1 million years of exclusive Oldowan tool manufacture. The first African appearance of *H. erectus* and Acheulean tools date to about 1.7 and 1.4 million years ago, respectively, thus calling into question the view that "changes to open and arid conditions may have triggered the origin of *H. erectus* and of his characteristic tool kit" (Vrba, 1985a), since both these appearances substantially postdate the marked period of global cooling dated to about 2.8–2.4 mya (Prentice and Denton, 1988).

A hominin calvaria, three femora, and a proximal tibia referred to *H. erectus* have recently been reported from the Dakaniylo ("Daka") member of the Bouri Formation, Middle Awash (Asfaw et al., 2002; Gilbert et al., 2003). The postcrania are not associated with the calvaria, but the marked platymeria and thickened midshaft cortex of the femora are typical of *H. erectus* . The site also contains an abundance of Acheulean tools and an associated fauna dominated by alcelaphine bovids indicative of savanna environments.

The calvaria (BOU-VP 2/66) is very well preserved with only minimal distortion. Endocranial capacity is estimated at 995 cc. The supraorbital tori are thick and strongly arched, with marked depressions at the glabellar and supraglabellar regions. As in many *H. erectus* calvaria, there is some sagittal keeling along the frontal and parietals. In posterior view, the parietal walls are vertical. The calvaria is smaller and shorter than OH 9 and is most similar to the Buia cranium from Eritrea (see below). The cranial metrics overlap with both Asian and African sample ranges and fail to distinguish the fossil consistently from either sample. Using 22 cranial characters for a cladistic analysis, Asfaw et al. (2002) were unable to demonstrate a deep cladogenic split between African and Asian *H. erectus* samples, thus throwing into question the view that *H. erectus* should be split into an Asian species conspecific with the Trinil holotype (*H. erectus*) and an African version (*H. ergaster*). They conclude that geographic subdivision of early

H. erectus into separate species lineages is biologically misleading and artificially inflates early Pleistocene species diversity. This conclusion is also reinforced by the recent study showing that extant mammalian genera in the body range of early *Homo* are not very speciose (one to three species being the norm), thus making it very unlikely that early *Homo* would have comprised a half dozen or more species, as extreme taxonomic splitters have suggested (Conroy, 2002).

A very interesting cranium with a mixture of *H. erectus–H. sapiens* characteristics has been recovered from 1-million-year-old sediments near Buia, Eritrea, along with two hominin incisors and two pelvic fragments (Abbate et al., 1998). The hominins were recovered in association with a rich African savanna fauna, indicating an age interval from Early to early Middle Pleistocene. Magnetostratigraphic profiles from the site are consistent with this age assessment. The cranium is a nearly complete braincase (missing the basicranium) including part of the facial skeleton. Its most distinguishing feature is its low, long, narrow shape (anteroposterior length is 204 mm, maximum cranial breadth is 130 mm). Endocranial capacity is estimated at 750–800 cc. Overall, the face is narrow and short with a slightly concave upper middle region and a quite prognathic subnasal region. The forwardly projecting supraorbital tori are massive and arched. Although the greatest cranial breadth is located at the level of the supramastoid crests, maximum biparietal breadth is actually located quite high across the parietal region. The specimen resembles other African specimens referred to *H. erectus/ergaster* in having a long ovoid braincase with low endocranial capacity, greatest cranial breadth across the supramastoid crests, and massive supraorbital tori. However, the high position of greatest biparietal breadth is a more *sapiens*-like feature, suggesting that at least some *sapiens*-like features had begun to evolve in Africa by about 1.0 mya.

The most recent *H. erectus* discovery from East Africa comes from Olorgesailie, Kenya (Potts et al., 2004). As mentioned earlier, virtually all Middle Pleistocene *H. erectus* and archaic hominins are associated with one form or another of the Developed Oldowan/Acheulean and/or prepared core (e.g., Levallois) technocomplexes. One of the richest examples of the Developed Oldowan/Acheulean is found at the lake margin site of Olorgesailie, Kenya. For well over 1 million years (about 1.4–0.2 mya), the type of Acheulean technology seen at Olorgesailie was the dominant component of hominin culture throughout much of the Old World. In fact, while a date of 400–500 kya has usually been given for the Acheulean occurrences at Olorgesailie, more recent ^{40}Ar-^{39}Ar results indicate that the Olorgesailie Formation may span much of the entire Pleistocene (Potts, 1989a). Many of these Acheulean sites have been interpreted as occupation sites, or home bases, of early hominin hunter-gatherer populations— for example, the numerous remains of extinct gelada baboons at one Olorgesailie location (DE/89B) are thought to be the result of systematic hunting and butchery by early hominins (Shipman et al., 1981a). Analyses of the stone flakes associated with elephant butchery sites at Olorgesailie have led to an interesting hypothesis regarding the use of handaxes. It seems that the flakes were derived from large handaxes, suggesting that one function of handaxes may have been as "blade tool dispensers" that were carried around by early hominins but seldom discarded while foraging. On the other hand, the used and unused flakes made from them were simply left behind at the butchery sites (Potts, 1989b; Potts, 1993). The recently discovered partial hominin cranium consists of the frontal and left temporal and nine other cranial fragments and was found stratigraphically associated with the Acheulean handaxes. The cranium represents one of the smallest adult specimens assigned to *H. erectus* (cranial capacity estimated at less than 800 cc) and seems quite similar in overall size to the much older Dmanisi crania discussed in the next chapter. The partial cranium is securely dated to about 950 kya and is one of the few hominin fossils known from Africa during this time period.

Possible *Homo erectus* in Southern Africa

Only one site in southern Africa has yielded hominin fossils that may be attributed to *Homo* aff. *H. erectus*. In 1949, Robinson discovered a mandible (SK 15) at Swartkrans, South Africa, that he and Broom thought to be an early hominin distinct from *Australopithecus*, which they named *Telanthropus capensis* (Broom and Robinson, 1949; Robinson 1950). Another mandibular fragment (SK 45), maxillary fragment (SK 80), proximal radius (SK 18b), and P_3 (SK 18a) were subsequently found and all were eventually included within the same genus. By the 1960s, however, Robinson (1961) had formally sunk *Telanthropus capensis* into *H. erectus*. In 1969, Ron Clarke of the University of the Witwatersrand recognized that the facial part of a different specimen, SK 847 (originally cataloged as *Paranthropus*), articulated perfectly with the SK 80 maxilla and that they were, in fact, from the same individual. The composite SK 847 cranium and several mandibular pieces (SK 15 and SK 45) are now generally included within the genus *Homo* (Clarke, 1994c; Clarke and Howell, 1972; Clarke et al., 1970; Olson, 1978) (Fig. 10.26).

One statistical study of SK 847 has cast doubt on its affinities to *H. erectus*, however, by demonstrating that morphological differences between it and two other crania often attributed to *H. erectus*, KNM-ER 3733 and KNM-WT 15000, are greater than would be expected in a single modern human population drawn from eastern and southern Africa (Grine et al., 1993). Instead, these authors see more similarities to specimens often regarded as *H. habilis* such as KNM-ER 1813 or Stw 53. The supraorbital torus of SK 847 is pronounced and thickened, but not nearly as much as in other African specimens, and there is a distinct supratoral sulcus separating the torus from the rather steep frontal squama. The specimen lacks the marked postorbital constriction characteristic of Asian *H. erectus* (Clarke, 1985a).

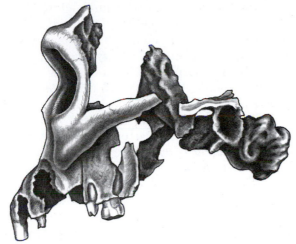

Fig. 10.26. Lateral view of the composite SK 847 cranium. The cranium and several mandibular pieces (SK 15 and SK 45) from Swartkrans are now generally included within the genus *Homo*. The supraorbital torus of SK 847 is pronounced and thickened but not nearly as much as in other African specimens, and there is a distinct supratoral sulcus separating the torus from the rather steep frontal squama. The specimen lacks the marked postorbital constriction characteristic of Asian *H. erectus*. (Photo by D. Panagos, courtesy of the Transvaal Museum, Pretoria.)

CURRENT ISSUES AND DEBATES

In this chapter we have reviewed the *H. erectus* sample from Asia and Africa. The Middle Pleistocene hominin record of Europe will be the subject matter of the next chapter. With this information as background, we can now begin to discuss some of the interesting and vexing questions about *H. erectus* that were posed at the beginning of this chapter.

As noted earlier, several anthropologists have questioned whether any of the African and European specimens traditionally classified as *H. erectus* should in fact be classified in the same species as Asian *H. erectus*. Indeed, some have even questioned whether Asian *H. erectus* is a valid species and whether it was in the mainstream of modern human evolution (Andrews, 1984; Clarke, 1990; Kennedy, 1991; Stringer, 1984, 1985; Wood, 1984).

But before deciding on what *H. erectus* is *not*, it is first necessary to decide what it *is*. One problem in defining *H. erectus* is that it may well represent a grade, rather than a clade, of human evolution. Differences of interpretation generally relate to different philosophies of systematics. As my colleague D. T. Rasmussen of Washington University in St. Louis notes, throwing out the notion of grades essentially leads to throwing out anagenesis, which in turn automatically leaves nothing but typological species definitions and the impossibility of studying gradual change. Over the past decade or so a number of workers have begun to address this problem by redefining *H. erectus* using cladistic analyses that distinguish those features found in hominoids generally (plesiomorphies) from those restricted to various groups within the genus *Homo* (synapomorphies) and those unique to *H. erectus* (autapomorphies).

Starting from the premise that *H. sapiens*, *H. habilis*, and *H. erectus* are more closely related to one another than to any other species, Bernard Wood (1984) of George Washington University considers how these species differ from their hypothetical common ancestor, the possible cladistic relationships among them, and the autapomorphic features of *H. erectus* (Fig. 10.27). As he points out, however, most previous analyses concentrated on the morphological features that distinguish *H. erectus* from *H. sapiens* and have placed much less emphasis on whether such features distinguish *H. erectus* from *H. habilis* as well. For example, while various morphological indices have been used to highlight cranial shape differences between *H. erectus* and *H. sapiens* (e.g., the long, low vault and postorbitally constricted frontal region), these same indices show little difference between *H. erectus* and *H. habilis* crania. Further difficulties depend on which specimens are included in the hypodigm of *H. erectus*. For instance, if massive crania like Bodo, Broken Hill, and Petralona (see following chapters) are classified in *H. sapiens*, then even some of the characteristic *H. erectus* features, like thick cranial vault bones and robust supraorbital tori, cannot, by definition, be *H. erectus* autapomorphies. Conversely, African *H. erectus* crania like KNM-ER 3733 and 3883 have supraorbital tori that are much smaller than those in Asian *H. erectus* and cranial bones that are no thicker than those found in some anatomically modern human populations. The question then becomes, should the "definition" of *H. erectus* be amended to include these specimens or should these specimens be removed from *H. erectus*? Note, however, that Wood now believes that *H. habilis* should be transferred to the genus *Australopithecus* (Wood and Collard, 1999a, b).

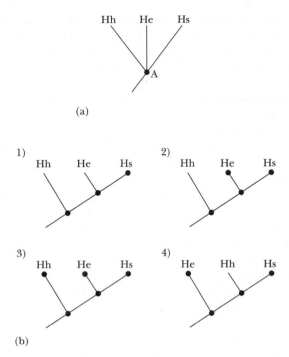

Fig. 10.27.   (a) Simplest relationship between the three taxa, *H. habilis, H. erectus,* and *H. sapiens,* and a hypothetical common ancestor. Examples of possible character states of the common ancestor (*A*). *Primitive* (inherited from a common ancestor with *Australopithecus*): (1) absolute brain size greater than 500 cc, (2) emphasis of ectocranial cresting shifted anteriorly with respect to apes, (3) foramen magnum more centrally placed than in the apes, and (4) thin cranial vault bones. *Derived* (with respect to *Australopithecus*): (1) reduced facial prognathism, (2) more discrete mastoid process associated with a reduction in supramastoid breadth, (3) absolute and relative reduction in tooth size, and (4) tendency to extra lingual rather than distal cusps on the lower molars. (b) Cladograms depicting possible relationships between the three *Homo* species. *Solid circles* at the end of a branch indicate the presence of autapomorphic features. (Wood, 1984.) As we noted earlier, Wood now includes *H. habilis* in the genus *Australopithecus* (Wood and Collard, 1999a, b).

Wood (1984) offers a philosophy to deal with this conundrum:

It is axiomatic that the definition of a taxon should include all its autapomorphies, but a definition is not limited to such features. For, while symplesiomorph and shared-derived characters are (by definition) not unique to a taxon, what may be unique is a particular combination of such character states. For example, although individual members of early hominins may have prominent supraorbital tori and a thick vault, and *H. habilis* a relatively long and low cranium and cranial capacity of around 800 cc, it is only in *H. erectus* that these four features are found in combination. Thus, while as individual characters they have no validity within the definition of *H. erectus*, they are potentially significant in combination.

Wood rejects the strict cladistic logic stipulating that if a cranium shares even a single autapomorphic feature with *H. erectus*, it must be classified as such. Instead, he prefers the definition emphasizing *combinations* of primitive and shared derived characters (Fig 10.27a)—and using such a definition he feels that KNM-ER 3733 and 3883 should not be automatically placed in *H. erectus*, at least as presently defined (Turner and Chamberlain, 1989; Wood, 1984).

Christopher Stringer (1984) of the Natural History Museum, London, has also tried to define *H. erectus* in terms of autapomorphic features, and like Wood, he does not intend that any one or two of these characters be used in isolation to identify the species because "such a typological approach takes no account of individual variation." Instead, he describes a range of characters, most of which would be expected to be present in any member of the species. Like Wood, he also queries the inclusion of the African forms in *H. erectus* but concludes that they might be considered early representatives of a *H. erectus* grade. If true, their morphological differences from Asian *H. erectus* would call into question the claim for stasis in the *H. erectus* grade through time.[24]

A much more ideologically extreme cladistic judgment of *H. erectus* is rendered by Stringer's Natural History Museum colleague Peter Andrews (1984), who argues that "On balance . . . the African crania formerly attributed to *erectus* would have been close to the line leading to *sapiens* and that the Asian *erectus* was some way removed from this lineage." Furthermore, he adds that if cladistic analysis confirms that *H. sapiens* is more closely related to *H. habilis* than to *H. erectus*, then the "scenario arising from this is that human evolution bypassed *erectus* in Asia, with a sequence of change from *habilis* through ER 3733 and 3883 and OH 9 and 12, giving rise to a Middle Pleistocene early *sapiens*." Not surprisingly, these conclusions do not sit well with some, particularly Chinese, anthropologists. How well do they stand up to further analysis?

Andrews's conclusions are based on his interpretation that most of the features used to define *H. erectus* are in fact primitive retentions from a common hominoid and/or hominin ancestor (i.e., plesiomorphies) that are not valid for a species definition. To a strict cladist, if any plesiomorphic character used to define *H. erectus* (e.g., maximum cranium breadth across the supramastoid crests or marked postorbital constriction) is found in great apes and/or other catarrhines generally then it cannot be used to define *H. erectus*. Such characters in *H. erectus* should instead be considered assemblages of primitive features. Andrews believes that the only features linking Asian and African forms are primitive features. In contrast, he believes that a number of derived features separate the hominin fossils of the two continents.

For example, the seven autapomorphic features described by Andrews as unique to Asian *H. erectus*, and, by definition, not found in European or African Lower to Middle Pleistocene hominins, are (1) presence of a

[24]Compare, for example, Rightmire (1981b) and Wolpoff (1984).

frontal keel, (2) thick cranial vault bones, (3) presence of a parietal keel, (4) angular torus on parietal, (5) inion well separated from endinion, (6) mastoid fissure developed, and (7) the presence of a recess between the entoglenoid and the tympanic plate.

Probably the most persistent (and persuasive) critic of this strict cladistic approach has been Günter Bräuer from the Universität Hamburg, Germany. He has challenged these conclusions after examining European and African hominins for each of the seven supposedly autapomorphic characters of Asian *H. erectus* (Bräuer, 1990, 1994; Bräuer and Mbua, 1992; Wu and Bräuer, 1993):

1. A frontal keel accompanied by parasagittal flattening is generally present in *H. erectus* crania from Zhoukoudian and Hexian and on some, but not all, of the Indonesian crania. However, the trait is also found in some African hominins usually assigned to *H. erectus* (KNM-ER 3733, OH 12), *H. habilis* (StW 53), *A. africanus* (Sts 5), early *H. sapiens* (Bodo, Omo 2, Broken Hill, Eliye Springs, Laetoli 18), and in some European specimens like Salé and Arago 21.

2. Cranial vault thickness is variable, and these measures do not differ significantly between East African and East Asian specimens. Some early African and European *H. sapiens* have crania as thick, or thicker, than Zhoukoudian *H. erectus*.

3. The midsagittal keel on the parietal is highly variable among East Asian *H. erectus* specimens. In Zhoukoudian Cranium XII, it is well developed anteriorly and in others (for example, Cranium X and Sangiran 2) it is situated nearer to bregma. KNM-ER 3883 exhibits a slight keel with some parasagittal flatness (the fragmentary bregmatic region of KNM-ER 3733 cannot be evaluated). Slight keeling or midsagittal protuberances also appear in specimens from Ternifine, Omo 2, Petralona, KNM-ER 3883, Ternifine, Bodo, Eliye Springs, and Salé.

4. A tuber-like swelling at the mastoid angle is more or less strongly developed on all Zhoukoudian parietals but is more variable among Indonesian hominins (e.g., absent in Sangiran 2 and 10, slight in Sangiran 4, strong in Sangiran 31). This feature is variable in the African fossils as well. Some swelling in this region occurs in OH 9, OH 12, Ternifine, and Broken Hill. A clear angular torus is present in the Bodo cranium, and the Arago parietal shows swelling in this region as well.

5. At least three African hominins, KNM-ER 3733, OH 9, and KNM-ER 1805, exhibit values within the range of East Asian *H. erectus* for this feature.

6. This is a fissure between the petrosal crest of the tympanic and the mastoid process. In both KNM-ER 1813 and OH 12 the petrosal crest is not fused to the mastoid process. Variants of a mastoid fissure are also found in KNM-ER 3884 and OH 24.

7. This is the recess between the convex entoglenoid process and the tympanic plate. A cleft-like morphology occurs in KNM-ER 3883 and

possibly in KNM-ER 1813. It is interesting to note that this morphology is quite different on each side of Zhoukoudian Cranium III, thus making its diagnostic value somewhat suspect in any event.

It appears that some of the "autapomorphic" features of Asian *H. erectus* are even found in crania identified as Asian *H. sapiens*. Take, for example, the thick cranial vault bones. The average thickness for some cranial bones of early *H. sapiens*, like the crania from Dali and Xujiayao, are similar to those of Zhoukoudian *H. erectus* and some bones, like the parietals, are even thicker. Pronounced postorbital constriction is more strongly developed in the early *H. sapiens* Mapa cranium than in Hexian *H. erectus*, and frontal keeling is also present in early *H. sapiens* crania from Dali, Yinkou, and Maba. A sharply angulated occipital appears on Dali and Yinkou crania and a prominent angular torus appears on the Dali cranium (these early *H. sapiens* specimens will be more fully discussed in the following chapter).

Thus, if such assessments of *H. erectus* morphology are correct, it would seem that many, if not all, of the "autapomorphies" of Asian *H. erectus* actually occur in other crania from Europe, Africa, and China variably classified as *H. habilis*, *H. erectus*, and/or early *H. sapiens*. In some cases, the character in question is present in East African *H. erectus* hundreds of thousands of years before it appears in Asian *H. erectus*. For this reason, most, if not all, of these characters could just as easily be interpreted as primitive rather than as autapomorphies of Asian *H. erectus*. The hypothesis that Asian *H. erectus* is a highly specialized species on a side branch of human evolution is even more questionable, given that it apparently shares many features with later Asian early *H. sapiens* (Bräuer, 1990; Bräuer and Mbua, 1992). Thus to dismiss Asian *H. erectus* from the mainstream of modern human ancestry based on this type of strict cladistic analysis seems premature at the very least (Pope, 1992). To paraphrase Mark Twain, reports of the death of *Homo erectus* are greatly exaggerated.

Other criticisms of an "anywhere but Asia" philosophy of modern human origins have also been offered. For instance, it has been argued that of the seven autapomorphies listed by Andrews, few, if any, are genetically independent and functionally meaningful. For instance, features 1 and 3 may be combined as can features 6 and 7. Even if the function(s) of characters 2, 3, 4, and 5 were known—which they aren't—they may simply reflect the general robustness of the cranium.

If Asian *H. erectus* is not ancestral to modern *H. sapiens*, then it would be necessary to invoke a number of parallelisms and convergences between the two taxa in order to account for such similarities as progressively increasing brain size, more vertical foreheads, thinning of cranial vault bones, and decreasing postorbital constriction. As we shall see in following chapters, those who support a phylogenetic relationship between *H. erectus* and *H. sapiens* in Asia point to the presence in the Far East of temporally and morphologically intermediate specimens such as those from Dali, Ngandong, Narmada, Yunxian, and Jinniu Shan (Pope, 1988, 1992).

As the hominin fossil record of the Far East improves, it seems apparent that facial morphology of Middle Pleistocene Asian hominins was quite distinct from their European and African contemporaries, with many of these features presaging those found today in modern Asian populations. Such distinguishing facial characteristics include much smaller upper and lower midfacial regions, more horizontally oriented zygomatic bones, pronounced and more medially situated malar tubercles bearing a distinct incisura malaris, more acute and inferiorly situated zygomaticomaxillary angles, and a vertically shorter maxilla.

Conversely, European fossil hominins are generally characterized by larger upper and lower facial areas, obliquely oriented zygomatic bones, vertically taller maxillas, and zygomatic bones lacking a malar tubercle and incisura malaris.

It is interesting that some morphological traits characteristic of Far Eastern Middle Pleistocene hominins are now found in all modern human populations (although their frequency is still higher in Asian groups), leading some to conclude that "the world-wide dissemination of morphological traits which first appeared in the Asian fossil record suggests that at least some of the facial traits associated with the emergence of modern humans, resulted not from a single African origin, but from admixture and gene flow between different regions of the Old World" (Pope, 1991).

Other authors (Wu, 1990) have emphasized a mosaic of morphological similarities between Middle Pleistocene *H. erectus* and Late Pleistocene *H. sapiens* from the Far East (e.g., the anteriorly oriented anterolateral surface of the fronto-sphenoidal process of the zygomatic bone, the contour of the lower margin of the zygomatic process of the maxilla and the rounded inferolateral margin of the orbits, the flat nasal region and lower face, sagittal keeling, and the presence of shovel-shaped upper incisors) and use this as evidence that Asian populations of *H. sapiens* evolved directly from Asian populations of *H. erectus*. We will have much more to say on this subject when we discuss the various models of modern human origins in the last chapters.

Earlier mention was made of the two *H. erectus* crania from Yunxian that apparently have a number of midfacial features usually associated with (non-Neandertal) early modern *H. sapiens*. By way of contrast, some of the European and African Middle Pleistocene hominins classified as *H. erectus* and/or early *H. sapiens* have a midfacial pattern more reminiscent of later-occurring Neandertals in Europe. If this assessment is correct, it implies that facial architecture characteristic of early modern *H. sapiens* was evident in the Far East far earlier than in Europe or Africa and that *H. sapiens*–like morphology appeared first in Asia and then spread secondarily to the Near East and Europe (Li and Etler, 1992).

This view is diametrically opposed to that which considers Africa the birthplace of anatomically modern humans. Before the evidence from Yunxian was available, supporters of this model could point to the absence of "*sapiens*–like" features in Middle Pleistocene Asian hominins in arguing that modern humans were derived from a non-Asian stock. However, the Yunxian evidence indicates that Middle Pleistocene hominins were highly variable and regionally differentiated and it now seems reasonable to conclude that *H. sapiens*–like facial morphology appeared at different times in regionally disparate hominin populations—a fine example of what anthropologists call **mosaic evolution**. One might reasonably argue that these are regionally disparate only because of the vagaries of the fossil record. However, if specimens were known from each 100-km interval from Swartkrans to Beijing in 10,000-year intervals, probably most variation would prove to be clinal in space and anagenetic in time.

No one would deny that there are a number of differences between Asian and East African *H. erectus* samples, in particular the less obvious midline keeling and parasagittal flatness along the parietal bone in the East African specimens. But given the fact that fossils attributed to *H. erectus* cover such an enormous geographic and temporal range, such morphological variation seems surprisingly minor. Over 20 features common to African and Asian *H. erectus* samples that may be used to define *H. erectus* as a real taxon have been identified and "while there are obvious differences of size within both Asian and African assemblages, it is apparent that the better preserved crania from these regions are remarkably similar" (Rightmire, 1990). Some of these features are undoubtedly primitive retentions, whereas others are not. But again, it is important to emphasize the distinctive *combination* of features that together unite these assemblages from China, Java, and Africa.

There is another interesting way to view this problem. If the *H. erectus* sample truly represents a number of different species in Asia and Africa, then human taxonomic diversity must have been significantly pruned since the Middle Pleistocene, since only one hominin species, *H. sapiens*, is extant today (Conroy, 2002). And indeed, if this is the case, what agent could possibly have accomplished such drastic pruning? In order to test whether human taxonomic diversity has been significantly pruned over the last several hundred thousand years or whether the number of Lower to Middle Pleistocene hominin taxa have been overestimated by some paleoanthropologists, cranial variation in mixed samples of early fossil hominins, modern humans, and fossils attributed to *H. erectus* must be compared. The results of one such study indicate that the pattern and degree of cranial variation found in *H. erectus* closely approximates that found in the single species, *H. sapiens* and implies that there is no statistical justification for subdividing the *H. erectus* sample into multiple species (Kramer, 1993).

Finally, a number of generalizations emerge about this stage of human evolution that can be summarized as follows: (1) the appearance of *H. erectus* at about 1.8–1.7 mya in East Africa seems to coincide with the expansion of savanna grassland; (2) analysis of KNM-WT 15000 (Turkana boy) demonstrates increasing body size and essentially modern skeletal adaptations for arid, open-country environments (e.g., pronounced ectomorphy, relative length of limb segments, narrow bi-iliac breadth); (3) the density of the archeological record also increases about this same time, which might signify niche expansion associated with a greater reliance on vertebrate meat, fat, and marrow (hunting as opposed to scavenging?); (4) archeological sites document hominin penetration of arid habitats and higher elevations by 1.4 mya in East Africa and by 1.0 mya in Eurasia; (5) hominin penetration of higher latitudes and the associated reduction of competition from sympatric hominin species might have resulted in character release, which may help explain the amount of morphological variation in *H. erectus*; and (6) *H. erectus* emerged as a "weed" taxon in tropical Africa, where habitats were disrupted by Pleistocene climatic perturbations, tectonic movements and volcanism (Cachel and Harris, 1995).

Taken all together, then, the fossil record of *H. erectus* encourages us to view all Middle Pleistocene hominins as essential parts of an evolving lineage that ultimately led to modern humans. This journey continues in the next chapter.

CHAPTER XI

Almost There—But Not Quite: "Archaic" Hominins of the Middle Pleistocene

412

INTRODUCTION

By some 800 kya, *H. erectus* (or *H. ergaster*) populations throughout Africa were being supplanted by, or evolving into, a highly varied group of hominins that began spreading into almost all of Africa's ecological niches, except perhaps for the evergreen tropical forest (Fig. 10.1). Like many other "intermediate" or "transitional" fossil groups, these hominin populations have been difficult to classify to everyone's satisfaction.[1] For this reason, they were often unceremoniously lumped together under the informal and unflattering designation of "archaic *H. sapiens*" because they had not yet evolved morphological features that could be considered typical of anatomically modern humans.

There is simply no point in being dogmatic about the taxonomic and/or phylogenetic positioning of all these early hominins of the Middle Pleistocene. In the immortal words of Clint Eastwood's Dirty Harry: "Opinions are like _____, everyone has one," and that has certainly been true regarding this group of hominins. While some think that paleoanthropologists have seriously *underrepresented* the number of Middle Pleistocene hominin taxa (Tattersall and Schwartz, 2000) others think that paleoanthropologists have seriously *overestimated* the number of hominin taxa (Hawks et al., 2000a; Wolpoff et al., 1993). For example, some regard the early Middle Pleistocene hominins from Gran Dolina, other parts of Europe, and Africa all as separate species—*H. antecessor, H. heidelbergensis,* and *H. rhodesiensis,* respectively—whereas others regard this whole hominin

---

[1]Of course, every fossil group that doesn't become extinct is, by definition, "transitional" between the species it evolves from and the one it evolves into!

413

sample as simply reflective of the large temporal and geographic variation found within a single, widespread, Old World species—*H. erectus*. And there are even those who regard this entire assortment of post-australopith hominins as members of a single evolving lineage of *H. sapiens*.

For ease of communication, we shall use the informal designation "archaic hominins" when referring to this Middle Pleistocene hominin sample as a whole and will use more specific taxonomic labels (e.g., *H. antecessor, H. heidelbergensis*) when talking about specific hominin samples within this broader group of early hominins. The Neandertals, whom many regard as members of this group, will be discussed separately in a later chapter.

Throughout the Old World these archaic hominins are usually associated with some form of the Developed Oldowan/Acheulean and/or prepared-core (e.g., Levallois) tool complexes and are known from such geographically diverse areas as East Africa (e.g., Bodo, Ndutu, Kabwe), Europe (e.g., Mauer, Steinheim, Arago), the Near East (e.g., Zuttiyeh), India (e.g., Narmada), Java (e.g., Ngandong, Sambungmachan), and China (e.g., Dali, Maba, Jinniu Shan, Xujiayao, Yunxian) (Fig. 11.1) (Clark, 1992; Kennedy et al., 1991). As we saw in the previous chapter, in eastern Asia

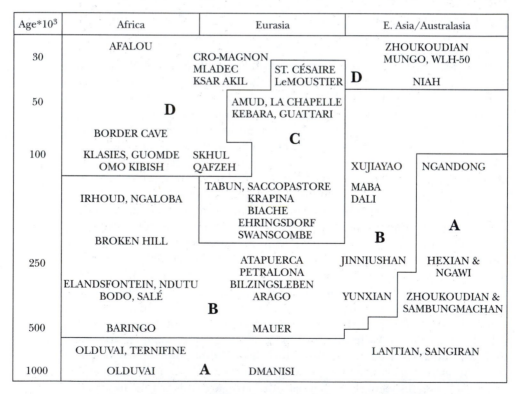

Fig. 11.1. Fossil hominin sites over the last million years are geographically widespread. This is one possible classification of fossil hominins during this time period. *A, H. erectus; D, H. sapiens; B* and *C,* hominins often considered archaic *H. sapiens* (classified by some as *H. heidelbergensis* or *H. neanderthalensis*). (Stringer, 1993a.)

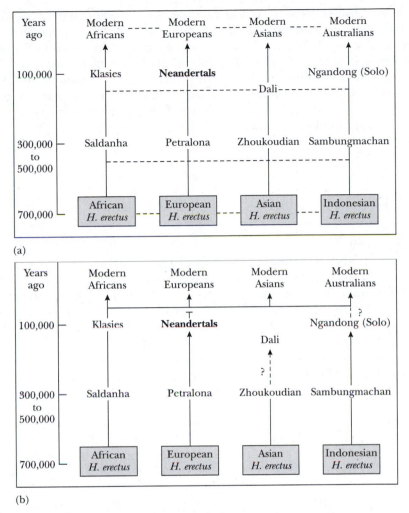

Fig. 11.2. Two hypotheses concerning modern human origins. Important fossils in different regions are shown at their approximate time levels, starting from *H. erectus*. (a) In this model, each line evolves locally to populations found in the region today; similarity among various geographic populations is explained by gene exchange at all time levels (implied by the *horizontal dashed lines*). Regional continuity is demonstrated by perceived morphological similarities through time within the same geographical regions. (b) In this model, similarity among modern humans is explained by the late expansion of a single modern human population out of Africa that then replaced the local populations existing in other parts of the world. (Howells, 1992.)

characteristic Acheulean bifaces are not seen; instead there is a core/chopper and flake tradition. While many of these fossils are poorly dated, they probably all fall within a time range of approximately 800–200 kya.

An important, and still contentious, issue is whether there was an in situ evolutionary continuum from *H. erectus* through these archaic hominins to anatomically modern *H. sapiens* in these various geographical regions (**Multiregional Continuity Model**) or whether anatomically modern *H. sapiens* first evolved in Africa and then migrated from Africa to Eurasia sometime in the Middle/Late Pleistocene, replacing all *H. erectus* and/or other archaic hominins in their path (**Out of Africa Model,** Noah's Ark Model, or Garden of Eden Model) (Fig. 11.2). This is a debate we shall come back to in the last two chapters when we consider the emergence of anatomically modern *H. sapiens*.

THE FIRST ARCHAIC HOMININS OUT OF AFRICA

Although modern Europeans may find it unpalatable, western Europe (in a paleoanthropological, not necessarily political, sense) is essentially just a peripheral peninsula on the Asian landmass that was (for the most part) uninhabited for much of the Lower Pleistocene, until several hundreds of thousands of years after hominins first appeared in eastern Asia and the Caucasus region. As we have seen, some evidence suggests that hominins (*H. erectus*) may have been present in eastern Asia (Java) by about 1.8 mya (although these dates are still controversial), but until recently no hominin fossils or securely dated archeological evidence was known for western Europe to suggest permanent occupation there before about 500 mya (although it is suggested that some archeological occurrences predated that age, such as at Le Vallonet in France, Kärlich A in Germany, and the Guadix-Baza Basin and Bertic Range of southern Spain) (Oms et al., 2000; Roebroeks, 1994, 2001; Roebroeks and Kolfschoten, 1994).[2] In fact, there is still little solid evidence for permanent human occupation of some parts of Europe, such as western-central Europe, much before the Cromer IV interglacial (oxygen isotope state 11–13) between about 362 and 524 kya (e.g., Kärlich G, Meisenheim I, and Mauer). In northwestern Europe, the earliest sites are Boxgrove (see below) and some of the sites in the Somme Valley of northern France (Roebroeks and Kolfschoten, 1994).

However, dramatic new finds, particularly those at Dmanisi (Republic of Georgia) and Gran Dolina, Spain, have drastically altered views about when hominins first migrated into Eurasia and western Europe, respectively.

---

[2]It has been reported that archeologist Yuri Mochanov of the Russian Academy of Science has found stone tools in Siberia, which he claims could be as much as 3.4 million years old, which, if true, would overturn virtually every current scenario of human origins, to say the least (Morell 1994, 1995).

DMANISI (REPUBLIC OF GEORGIA)

The site of Dmanisi is located about 85 km southwest of Tbilisi. The hominin fossils lie stratigraphically above an erosional spur of the Masavera Basalt dated by ^{40}Ar-^{39}Ar to about 1.78–1.95 mya. This date is further supported by geomagnetic polarity studies indicating an Oludvai Subchron age for the majority of the fossils. A number of hominin fossils have been found, including several crania, as well as thousands of stone tools (Fig. 11.3). The abundance of carnivore fossils, combined with the absence of cut marks or any other indications of hominin bone modification, suggest that carnivores may have been responsible for much of the bone accumulation. Associated faunal and floral remains indicate a mixed woodland environment somewhat warmer and drier than that of today.

The Dmanisi stone tools are similar to the Oldowan core and flake industry of East Africa. The majority of the artifacts are flakes with some slight retouch. Most of the core tools are unifacially worked, although some bifacial manufacture is present. There are no handaxes, spheroids, or cleavers. All tools were produced from local raw materials, particularly from finer-grained stone like quartzite.

Hominin discoveries include the remains of at least three crania (more crania have reportedly been discovered), several mandibles, and a metatarsal. Even though brain size in each cranium is under 800 cc (brain size in one cranium, D2700, is estimated at only about 600 cc) other morphological details of the crania and mandibles clearly align them with early African *H. erectus/ergaster* (such as the Turkana boy; KNM-WT 15000) rather than with *H. habilis* or *H. rudolfensis*. This is evidenced by the presence of single-rooted upper premolars, thin but well-developed supraorbital tori, angulated cranial vaults, large orbital areas, and overall midfacial profiles. It is interesting that the Dmanisi hominins are said to resemble African *H. erectus/ergaster* far more than Asian *H. erectus* in possessing more moderate-size supraorbital tori, relatively taller and thinner-walled cranial vaults, smaller cranial capacity, and certain aspects of the lower dentition (such as the buccolingually narrow anterior teeth and detailed occlusal morphology of the molars). Details of the face are also more similar to African *H. erectus* than to Asian *H. erectus*—for example, the presence of nasal pillars; the long, narrow dental arcade shape (rather than parabolic); and the lack of a sagittal keel.

The Dmanisi finds are important because they document the first unequivocal evidence for dispersal of hominins out of Africa and into Eurasia. This dispersal event, which must predate about 1.7 mya, if the Dmanisi dates are sustained, occurred very soon after the first appearance of *H. erectus/ergaster* in Africa and apparently preceded the development of the Acheulean tool-making tradition. The Dmanisi hominins are among the most primitive fossils currently assigned to *H. erectus/ergaster*. They clearly

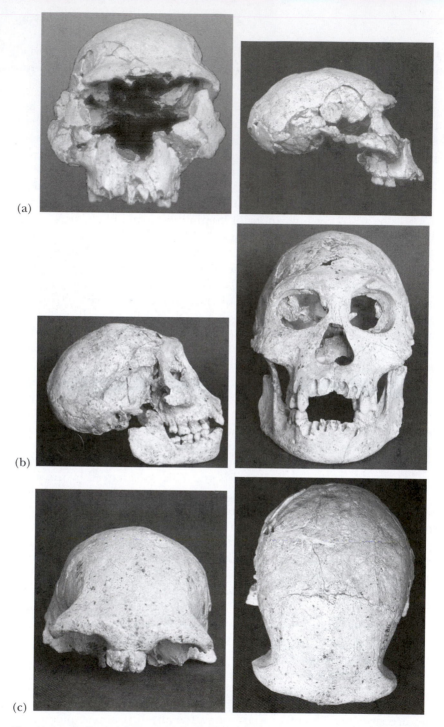

Fig. 11.3. Early Eurasian representatives of *Homo* cf. *ergaster* from Dmanisi (Republic of Georgia). These specimens have been dated to about 1.8 mya. (a) Front and lateral views of DM 2282. (b) Front and lateral views of DM 2700. (c) Front and top views of DM 2280. (d) Mandible (DM 211). (Photos courtesy of D. Lordkipanidze.)

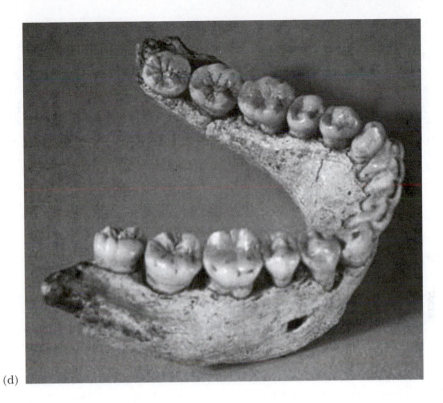

(d)

show that hominins with brain sizes within the *H. habilis* size range were fully capable of migrating from Africa northward into Asia presumably through the Levantine corridor (Bräuer and Schultz, 1996; Gabunia and Vekua, 1995; Gabunia et al., 2000; Vekua et al., 2002).

THE OLDER ARCHAIC HOMININ GROUP

A number of Middle Pleistocene sites in Europe have yielded fossil hominins that have at one time or another been classified as *H. erectus*, early *H. sapiens*, and/or Neandertals. However, the precise number of fossil sites is misleading, as it belies the paucity of good specimens and reliable dates that are actually available from Europe. Some of the better-known localities, with approximate age correlations, are shown in Figure 11.1.

For heuristic purposes it is best to distinguish two archaic Middle Pleistocene hominin groups in Europe. The first is sometimes referred to as the older archaic group (e.g., Gran Dolina, Boxgrove, Mauer, Vértesszöllös, Bilzingsleben, Arago, Petralona) and the second as the younger archaic group (e.g., Reilingen, Steinheim, Swanscombe, Pontnewydd, Ehringsdorf,

Biache, La Chaise, Fontéchevade, Montmaurin, Atapuerca (Sima de los Huesos). Because members of the older group show few, if any, synapomorphic features with later Neandertals and/or modern humans, some regard them as suitable morphological types for the common ancestor of both Neandertals and modern humans (e.g., *H. antecessor* from Gran Dolina). We have already introduced the controversy in the last chapter over whether or not *H. erectus* really existed in Europe at all. For those who argue for its presence, the most often cited, if not totally convincing, *H. erectus*–like specimens from Europe are members of this older Middle Pleistocene group. By contrast, members of the younger group share a number of morphological features that presage those seen in later Neandertals and it is for this reason that some paleoanthropologists refer to them collectively as "anteneandertals" (Stringer, 1984, 1985).

Gran Dolina (Atapuerca), Spain

New Iberian finds at Atapuerca dramatically change the view that western Europe was not permanently occupied until around 500 kya. The oldest human fossils and artifacts thus far reported from western Europe are the specimens from Gran Dolina, Atapuerca, Spain, now generally classified as *H. antecessor*.[3] Faunal, paleomagnetic, electron spin resonance (ESR) and uranium series (U-S) dating methods all converge on an age of about 800 kya—that is, just below the Matuyama/Brunhes boundary (Carbonell et al., 1995, 1999a, 1999b; Falguères et al., 1999; Parés and Perez-Gonzalez, 1995, 1999).

The hominin sample consists of over 100 cranial, mandibular, dental, and postcranial fragments, representing at least six individuals ranging in age from about 3 to 20 years old (de Castro et al., 2004). The largest fossil fragment is a piece of frontal bone that is larger than the equivalent bone in early *Homo* or *H. erectus* crania having cranial capacities less than 1000 cc, such as ER 3733, ER 3883, and OH 9 from Kenya, Sangiran 2 and Trinil from Java, or the Zhoukoudian sample from China. The frontal bone is relatively thin and has a double-arched supraorbital torus rather than the straight, or horizontal, supraorbital shelf characteristic of Asian *H. erectus* and OH 9. Somewhat surprising for such an ancient hominin, the partial face of a juvenile (ATD 6-69) shows a completely modern midfacial morphology (Arsuaga et al., 1999b). Modern human-like features include the slightly backward and inferiorly sloping midface, which produces a marked depression (canine fossa); the somewhat prognathic (not flat)

---

[3]Other claimants for similarly aged hominins and/or artifacts include fragments of a *Homo erectus*–like cranium discovered near Ceprano, Italy, indirectly dated to over 700,000 years ago (Ascenzi et al., 1996); archeological material from Kuldara (Republic of Tajikistan) said to date to 850,000, which if true, is the earliest evidence of human occupation in Central Asia (Ranov et al., 1995); Acheulean artifacts from India (Bori) said to date to 670,000 years ago (Mishra et al., 1995).

midface; the horizontal zygomaxillary border; and the sharp lower nasal margin. Such a modern midfacial region had not previously been found in hominins older than about 100 kya—for example, Djebel Irhoud 1, Skhul, Qafzeh, and Laetoli 18.

Over 45 postcranial elements (including hand and foot bones, vertebrae, ribs, clavicles, femoral fragments) representing at least four individuals have been recovered (Carretero et al., 1999; Lorenzo et al., 1999). The atlas vertebra, although quite small, does not differ from the same bone in modern humans, at least in terms of absolute or relative size measures. The long, slender clavicle is, however, most similar to that of Neandertals. The predicted stature of one *H. antecessor* individual is estimated between 162 and 186 cm using formulas derived from the clavicle and radius.

Cut marks, percussion marks, and fractures on some of the bones provide evidence of animal butchery among these Gran Dolina hominins. In addition, some of the human bones also show clear evidence of butchering, bone marrow extraction, and peeling fractures, suggestive of some level of cannibalism at the site (Fernández-Jalvo et al., 1999).

Nearly 200 stone tools have been found in association with the hominins. They mainly consist of cores, pebble tools, and choppers similar to African Oldowan tool assemblages. The absence of handaxes, cleavers, picks, and blades is indicative of a pre-Acheulean level of stone-tool technology. Many of the tools bear traces of butchery and woodworking activities (Carbonell et al., 1999b).

Most of those who have studied the original fossils conclude that the combination of primitive and modern features, particularly the modern-looking midfacial region, warrant a new species designation for these Gran Dolina hominins, *H. antecessor,* which they regard as a common ancestral form to later *H. sapiens* and *H. neanderthalensis* (the latter having evolved from *H. heidelbergensis*) (de Castro et al., 1997a, 1999a).

If Iberia were occupied substantially earlier than northern and central Europe, where did these hominins come from? Three obvious possibilities are from North Africa across the Strait of Gibraltar, from Asia across the Strait of the Bosphorus, or from north of the Black Sea into eastern Europe. At first glance, the first option seems attractive because the Strait of Gibraltar is only about 12 km wide at times of low sea levels. However, North Africa has no hominin record earlier than about 1 mya, so the ancestral population is either not there or at least has not been found yet. In favor of the second option is the evidence at Ubeidiya, Israel, which indicates the presence of hominins in western Asia in the Lower Pleistocene at least by 1.4 mya. If hominins did enter Europe via the Strait of Bosphorus we should expect to find the earliest European hominins in Greece and Turkey (Dennell and Roebroeks, 1996). Evidence for the final option might be the site at Dmansi dated to about 1.8 mya. Only further discoveries will provide the answer.

Boxgrove

Another archaic hominin from western Europe is a tibia discovered in an archeological excavation at Boxgrove, Sussex, southern England.[4] The "Boxgrove man" discovery was initially dated to about 500 kya, although some amino acid racemization dates on fossil marine gastropods that underlie the strata in which the tibia was found suggest an age closer to 362–423 kya. The tibia is associated with early Acheulean tools (Bowen and Sykes, 1994; Roberts, 1994; Roberts et al., 1994; Stringer et al., 1998). It is a remarkably robust tibia, indicating exceptional strength and/or cold-adapted body proportions similar to those seen in Neandertals (Trinkaus et al., 1999). Histomorphologic studies suggest the individual lived into his 40s, thus making him one of the older Middle Pleistocene individuals known (Streeter et al., 2001).

Mauer

In 1907 the lower jaw of an archaic hominin was recovered from fluvial beds near the village of Mauer, just south of Heidelberg, Germany (Fig. 11.4). Its discoverer, Otto Schoetensack, professor of paleontology at the University of Heidelberg, described the jaw in 1908 as an early member of the genus *Homo,* thus making Schoetensack the second scientist to ever include such an ancient hominin fossil within *Homo.*[5] The mandible was virtually complete when discovered, but some of the teeth were lost in 1945. As with most of the fossils in the older archaic group, the Mauer mandible has a mosaic of features intermediate between *H. erectus* and *H. sapiens.* For example, although the mandible has the robust body and wide, relatively low ascending ramus and receding chin typical of *H. erectus,* it also has relatively small molars, within the size range of modern humans and at the lower end of the size range for the Zhoukoudian *H. erectus* sample (Schwartz and Tattersall, 2000; Stringer et al., 1984).

There are some faint indications of periodontal disease and incipient osteoporosis in the mandible and the presence of a well-healed fracture near the mandibular condyle (Czarnetzki et al., 2003). Despite the fact that over 5000 bones, teeth, horns, and antlers of a Middle Pleistocene tropical fauna were recovered from the site before it was closed in 1962, only the single hominin mandible and about 20 bone and pebble fragments that may have been used or altered by hominins were ever found at the site (Kraatz, 1985). With the possible exceptions of the more recently described hominin specimens from Atapuerca (Spain), Boxgrove (England), and Ceprano (Italy), this is probably one of the oldest of the early

---

[4]For a wonderfully irreverent essay on why the public was served such "codswallop" by the English press about this rather pitiful tibia, see Dennell (1994).

[5]The first to do so was William King (1864), who named the original Feldhofer Neandertal specimens *Homo neanderthalensis.*

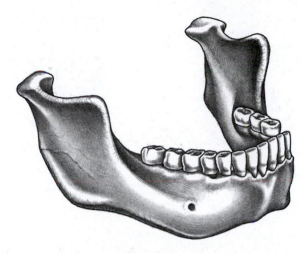

Fig. 11.4. In 1907 the lower jaw of an archaic hominin was recovered near the village of Mauer, just south of Heidelberg, Germany. The Mauer mandible has a mosaic of features intermediate between *H. erectus* and *H. sapiens*. For example, although the mandible has the robust body and wide, relatively low ascending ramus and receding chin typical of *H. erectus*, it also has relatively small molars, within the size range of modern humans and at the lower end of the size range for the Zhoukoudian *H. erectus* sample.

European Middle Pleistocene hominins, as it dates to an early Middle Pleistocene interglacial, possibly around 500 kya.

This specimen is now generally referred to *H. heidelbergensis* (as are most of the archaic European hominins discussed in this chapter) and serves as the type specimen of this species.

Vértesszöllös

Archaic hominin remains of two individuals were recovered in 1965 from Middle Pleistocene (inter-Mindel) deposits at Vértesszöllös, Hungary, about 50 km west of Budapest. The hominins were found in association with a pebble/chopper-tool industry said to be similar to that from Zhoukoudian, China. The large mammal fauna from the site suggests a temperate woodland environment. U-S dates give inconsistent ages of about 250–475 kya for the archeological/hominin levels (Gamble, 1986; Kretzoi and Vertes, 1965; Oakley, 1966).

The first individual is known from only the crowns of a lower left deciduous canine and fragmentary lower left deciduous molar and the second individual from an adult occipital bone reconstructed from two articulating pieces. The occipital bone has some of the *H. erectus*–like features we have previously identified: A very high and strongly built occipital torus; small cerebellar fossae compared to cerebral fossae; and large nuchal plane relative to occipital plane (Fig. 11.5). On the other hand, the some-

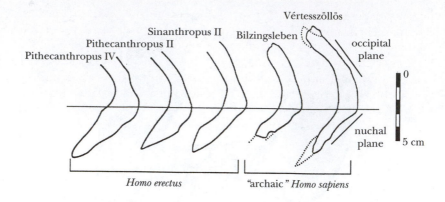

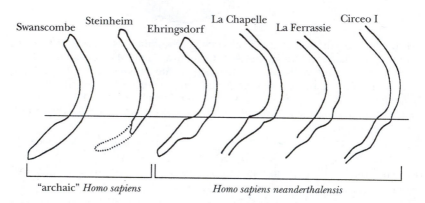

Fig. 11.5. Comparison of the midline profile of the Vértesszöllös occipital bone with those of other Middle Pleistocene hominins from Asia and Europe. Note the sharp angulation between the nuchal and occipital planes in the Vértesszöllös specimen. (Klein, 1989b.)

what thinner cranial bones and the estimated cranial capacity of around 1300 cc are considered more advanced features than typically found in *H. erectus* crania. Needless to say, opinions have been divided over the taxonomic and phylogenetic significance of these mosaic features (Thoma, 1978, 1981; Wolpoff, 1971b, 1980). It is also now generally included in *H. heidelbergensis*.

Bilzingsleben

About the same time the first *H. erectus* molars were being discovered from Zhoukoudian, a private naturalist, Adolf Spengler, discovered an equally primitive-looking human molar among the stone tools and animal bones in travertine quarries near the small village of Bilzingsleben, Germany. Unfortunately, the mine quarry closed soon after his 1927 discovery, and the human tooth was subsequently lost. However, the site was reopened in 1969 and, as luck would have it, further hominin fossils were discovered there between 1974 and 1977. Radiometric dates have been published for the site, including a date of about 230 kya based on ^{230}Th-^{234}U analysis of associated travertine and an amino acid racemization date of about 340 kya (Harmon et al., 1980; Howell, 1981; Mania and Vlcek, 1981). However, it is now felt that these ages might be on the young side. The age of Bilzingsleben is now estimated to be between about 414 and 300 kya (in an interglacial somewhere between ^{18}O stages 9 and 11). Excavations reveal some distinctive patterning of activity areas, including apparent dwelling sites. The hominin sample includes 25 cranial fragments and seven molars as well as over 100,000 artifacts, such as polished ivory points, wooden staffs, and a series of incised objects (Bednarik, 1995; Schwarcz et al., 1988a).

The most diagnostic of the Bilzingsleben hominin material consists of two connecting occipital fragments, two frontal bone fragments, and one parietal fragment. The occipital bone is broad and low with a well-developed occipital torus. In overall size and shape, the Bilzingsleben occipital is more reminiscent of the same bone in *Sinanthropus* III, *Pithecanthropus* VIII (Sangiran 17), OH 9, Vértesszöllös, and Petralona than it is to such younger European hominins as Swanscombe, Steinheim, and Ehringsdorf (Fig. 11.5). These latter crania have smaller occipital tori with curved, rather than highly angled, occipital contours. The frontal bone is described as having a rather "flattish" forehead region and strong supraorbital tori with a broad and smooth glabellar depression between them. The cranial bones are quite thick, averaging about 9 mm in thickness. The Bilzingsleben forehead region is also more similar to such specimens as *Pithecanthropus* VIII and OH 9 than it is to younger archaic hominins like Steinheim and Ehringsdorf.

Abundant fauna and flora recovered from Bilzingsleben include macaques, forest elephants, steppe and forest rhinoceros, bison, deer, large horses, wild oxen, bears, and beavers. Larger carnivores such as the lion, wolf, panther and wild cat are rare. Plant remains are indicative of deciduous mixed forest habitats more similar to those found today in the Mediterranean region than to those currently in northern Europe. These plants, along with the remains of Mediterranean-dwelling mollusks, indicate warmer climates than those existing today in the region and are consistent with an interglacial age for this site (Roebroeks et al., 1992).

A large number of stone, bone, and antler tools have also been recovered (Fig. 11.6). Animal bones were fashioned into straight and bowed scrapers, knife-like cutting tools, chisels with splintered ends, shaver-like tools, and needle and awl-like tools. Antlers were manufactured into picks and clubs. Most of the smaller stone tools are made from flint and are mainly broken cores and flakes; larger and cruder quartzite tools are also known. The numerous holes and cracks found on many of the long bones

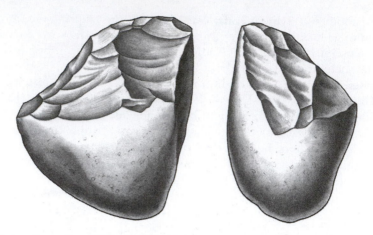

Fig. 11.6.   Quartzite pebble tool from Bilzingsleben. (Mania and Vlcek, 1981.)

have been interpreted to mean that hominins intentionally split them with the aid of small wedges and hammer-like instruments. Burned flint tools and some traces of charcoal suggest the use of fire (Mania and Vlcek, 1981).

Petralona

In 1960 a massive cranium covered in stalagmite was found in a complex cave system near Petralona, Greece (Fig. 11.7). Unfortunately, there have been conflicting views on the dating of the Petralona cranium, ranging from more than 700 kya to less than 100 kya (Kurten and Poulianos, 1977; Poulianos, 1978). ESR age determinations from calcite encrustations and from small bone fragments removed from the cranium yield bracketing ages of about 150–250 kya for the cranium (Grün, 1996). This is more or less consistent with a U-S determination of around 160–200 kya (Hennig et al., 1981).

The cranium is well preserved and virtually complete, lacking only the incisors and right canine crown. The cranium was encased in a pink stalagmitic matrix when discovered, which has since been removed. As with the other older European archaic hominins, the Petralona cranium displays a mosaic of *H. erectus* and early *H. sapiens* features. For example, the cranial vault is low with a receding forehead, and some of the occipital features and cranial thickness values are more characteristic of *H. erectus*. However, the large cranial capacity of approximately 1200 cc is in the *H. sapiens* range. In addition, while the supraorbitals are massive they follow the orbital contours as in early *H. sapiens* rather than being straight shelf-like structures as in *H. erectus*. The face is large and the maxilla has a "puffed out" appearance, presumably due to an expanded maxillary

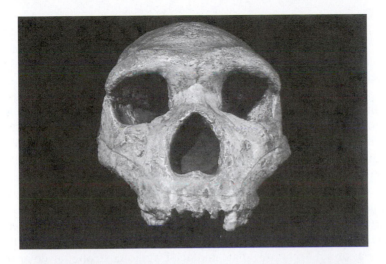

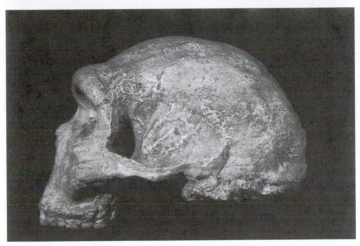

Fig. 11.7. In 1960 a massive cranium covered in stalagmite was found in a complex cave system near Petralona, Greece. The Petralona cranium displays a mosaic of *H. erectus* and early *H. sapiens* features, including a low cranial vault with a receding forehead in combination with a large cranial capacity of about 1200 cc. (Photos courtesy of E. Delson.)

sinus (reminiscent of the Neandertal condition) (Stringer, 1984; Wolpoff, 1980). In fact, several other cranial bones, including the frontal, mastoid, and temporal bones, also show remarkable degrees of pneumatization. In terms of overall size, the Petralona specimen is larger than any *H. erectus* cranium, although Sangiran 17, Ngandong 6 (Cranium V), and Olduvai 9 match or exceed it in certain cranial dimensions (Stringer et al., 1979).

Arago

Some of the most informative archaic hominins are the remains recovered from cave deposits at Arago, France, dated to approximately 320–470 kya.

Cranial and postcranial remains of at least four adults and three children are known from this site. The most important specimens are two mandibles (Arago 2 and 13), a distorted face with associated cranial bones (Arago 21 and 47), and part of a left pelvis (Arago 44) (Fig. 11.8). The mandibles show considerable variability in size and robustness, probably indicative of marked sexual dimorphism in this Middle Pleistocene archaic hominin population (see below). They have typical archaic features, such as a receding chin, mandibular bodies that are long and low, and ascending rami that are high and broad (in Arago at least).[6] The ruggedly built cranium is characterized by thick supraorbital tori separated from the long, flattish frontal bone by a deep supratoral sulcus; low and rectangular orbits; a broad, relatively flat midfacial region; strong alveolar prognathism; and the absence of a canine fossa. Cranial capacity is estimated at 1100 cc (de Lumley, 1975). Cranial thickness values are similar to Petralona; however, unlike Petralona, the Arago occipital does have a true angular torus. The pelvis and femoral fragments resemble those of *H. erectus* from Olduvai, Zhoukoutien, and Broken Hill (Day, 1988).

Some of the similarities between the Petralona and Arago crania, such as the shape of the supraorbital torus and the narrowness of the frontal bone, are probably primitive or plesiomorphic features shared with *H. erectus*. As we will see later, other features, such as the absence of a canine fossa, may be regarded as synapomorphies with Neandertals (de Bonis and Melentis, 1982).

Arago shares several tool-making similarities with other archaic hominin sites, such as Bilzingsleben and Vértesszöllös, including production of small artifacts, usually without preliminary core preparation; secondary modification by retouch; and a supplementary role for heavy-duty stone artifacts and bone, antler, and wooden tools (Svoboda, 1987a).

Ceprano

In 1994 a fragmented archaic hominin calvaria was recovered from a highway cut near Ceprano, Italy (Ascenzi et al., 1996; Mallegni et al., 2003; Manzi et al., 2001). The fossil comes from a clay layer below gravels dated by potassium-argon (K-Ar) to approximately 0.8–0.9 mya. The main features of the specimen are said to be broadly comparable to those of the Broken Hill cranium (see below): a low cranial vault with a flattened, retreating forehead; massive, shelf-like supraorbital ridges; and a prominent

---

[6]However, the ascending ramus is high and narrow in Arago 13 (E. Trinkaus, personal communication).

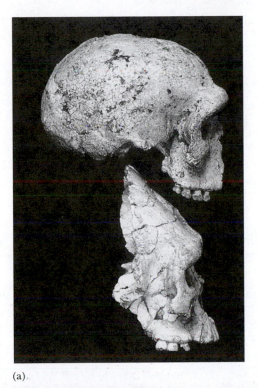

(a)

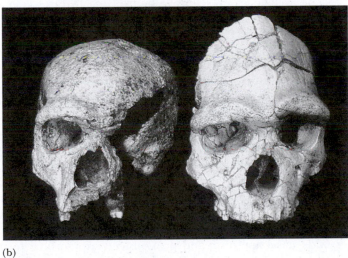

(b)

Fig. 11.8. (a) Lateral views of the Steinheim (*top*) and Arago 21 (*bottom*) crania. (b) Frontal views of the Steinheim (*left*) and Arago 21 (*right*) crania. (Photos by C. Tarka, courtesy of E. Delson and Institut de Paleontologie Humaine, Paris, and Staatliches Museum fur Naturkunde, Stuttgart.)

angle between the occipital and nuchal planes. One of the most notice-able features of the cranium is its relatively large breadth compared to its length. Endocranial capacity is estimated at about 1185 cc, larger than any Asian *H. erectus*.

The Ceprano calvaria differs from both *H. ergaster* and *H. erectus* in having a shorter cranial vault, thicker cranial bones, more massive supraorbital torus, and larger endocranial capacity. It differs specifically from *H. erectus* in having the widest portion of the calvaria near the temporal squama, not low across the supramastoid region. The presence of a double-arched supraorbital torus and the lack of any frontal keeling also differentiate the specimen from *H. erectus* (Manzi, 2004).

THE YOUNGER ARCHAIC HOMININ GROUP

As mentioned above, hominins representing a younger archaic group have been recovered from a number of sites in Europe, some of the better known being Steinheim, Swanscombe, Reilingen, Pontnewydd, Ehringsdorf, Biache, La Chaise, Fontéchevade, Montmaurin, and Atapuerca (Sima de los Huesos). Whereas members of the older archaic group we have been discussing show many *H. erectus*–like features, this younger Middle Pleistocene archaic group seems to be evolving features later seen in more exaggerated form in European Neandertals—hence the designation anteneandertals (Stringer, 1984, 1985).

Steinheim

Two of the most famous of these anteneandertals are the crania from Steinheim, Germany, and Swanscombe, England. These were, in fact, the first of the European archaic *Homo* crania to be discovered. Dating of both specimens remains problematic, but both clearly seem to be Middle Pleistocene in age. The Steinheim cranium (Fig. 11.8) was found in 1933 by Karl Sigrist in his father's gravel pit. It is distorted but nearly complete, lacking the anterior maxillary region and teeth and parts of the left side and base (Adam, 1985). Some of its more archaic features include an overall shape that is long, narrow, and moderately flattened; small mastoid processes; wide nasal aperture; and pronounced supraorbital torus separated from the frontal squama by a broad supraorbital sulcus. Endocranial capacity is estimated at 1140 cc based on three-dimensional computed tomography (3D-CT) reconstructions (Prossinger et al., 2003). More modern features are the gracile nature of the cranial vault, the absence of occipital bunning, the well-developed canine fossa, and greatest cranial breadth located high up across the parietals. Because of the mosaic of primitive and advanced features, this cranium, and others like it, are often thought of as transitional forms between *H. erectus* and *H. sapiens*. Some unique specializations of the nasal cavity that show up in later Neandertals appear in incipient form in the Steinheim cranium (Schwartz and Tattersall, 1996). Unfortunately, no other hominin bones or tools have been recovered from the site.

Swanscombe

The Swanscombe cranium consists of an occipital and left and right parietal bones that fit together (Fig. 11.9). It is interesting that the occipital was found in 1935, the left parietal in 1936, and the right parietal in 1955. Since the sutures are clearly open, the cranium probably belongs to a young adult. As in the Steinheim cranium, the occipital is somewhat rounded and lacks the marked angulation between occipital and nuchal planes seen in many *H. erectus* crania. However, the parietal bones are quite thick, and there is a midline depression on the occipital bone, known as a **suprainiac fossa,** a distinctive Neandertal-like feature (Santa Luca, 1978). Cranial capacity is estimated at about 1300 cc.

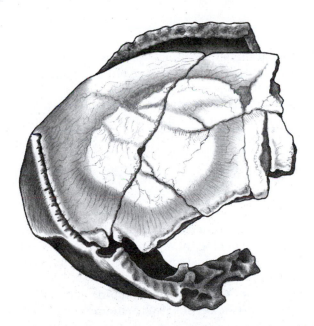

Fig. 11.9. The Swanscombe cranium consists of an occipital, and left and right parietal bones that fit together. Since the sutures are clearly open, the cranium probably belongs to a young adult. As in the Steinheim cranium, the occipital is somewhat rounded and lacks the marked angulation between occipital and nuchal planes seen in many *H. erectus* crania.

The cranial bones were found in association with Acheulean handaxes and a Middle Pleistocene mammalian fauna of Hoxnian interglacial affinities. Based on geomorphological evidence, the Swanscombe fossils most probably date to ^{18}O stage 11, or about 400 kya (Stringer and Hublin, 1999). If this age is correct, then the Swanscombe hominins are some of the oldest to show at least some Neandertal affinities in the cranial vault (e.g., central suprainiac depression of the occipital). This would support recent DNA evidence (see Chapter 12) that the Neandertal lineage was already separate from the modern human lineage by this time.

Reilingen

A well-preserved cranium was found near Reilingen, Germany, in 1978. The specimen consists of both parietals, most of the right temporal, and much of the occipital. Features such as maximum cranial breadth at the supramastoid crests, presence of an angular torus, a shortened squamous temporal, and strong mastoid, are all archaic hominin features. Other features are reminiscent of Neandertal crania—for instance, the presence of a suprainiac fossa, protuberant occipital torus, and lambdoid flattening. The accompanying fauna indicates a Holstein (Mindel/Riss or ^{18}O stage 11–9) interglacial age for the hominin (Dean et al., 1998; Ziegler and Dean, 1998).

Biache

In the 1970s the back half of a cranial vault was found at the site of Biache, France, associated with a maxillary fragment containing the molar teeth and five isolated teeth. The cranium is described as small and gracile (cranial capacity of about 1200 cc) but rather Neandertal-like in overall shape. The occipital bunning, lambdoid flattening, and oval profile (seen in posterior view) with maximum breadth low on the parietals are more reminiscent of features seen in later Neandertals than in the Swanscombe cranium (Cook et al., 1982).

Ehringsdorf

Fossils have been known from the quarries at Ehringsdorf, Germany, since 1780. A number of archeological horizons associated with the remains of at least nine hominin individuals are represented in the sample. The geology, fauna, and flora have generally been considered to indicate a last interglacial age (possibly ^{18}O stage 7). Radiometric dates give an average age of about 186–245 kya (Cook et al., 1982; Schwarcz et al., 1988a).

Montmaurin

Several specimens are known from two sites and from several levels at Montmaurin, France, including a mandible, several isolated teeth, the mandibular symphysis of a child, an adult maxilla, and a single vertebra.

The most important of these, the mandible found in 1949, is similar to other archaic mandibles in that it is robust with a relatively high and broad ascending ramus and chinless. As with virtually all of the European Middle Pleistocene sites, the age of the Montmaurin hominins is in dispute (Vallois, 1956).

As noted earlier, there is no shortage of opinions among paleoanthropologists regarding the taxonomy and phylogenetic relationships among these (and other) European Middle Pleistocene archaic hominins. For convenience, these are summarized in Table 11.1 (Stringer, 1993b). Let us now take a closer look at the reasoning behind some of these proposals.

In an influential analysis of European Middle Pleistocene hominin crania, Milford Wolpoff (1980) of the University of Michigan suggested that most cranial variation in Middle Pleistocene European hominins could be explained by "time, sex and idiosyncrasy." Specifically, he surmised that much of the cranial variation seen in Middle Pleistocene European hominins could be a reflection of marked sexual dimorphism in an evolving lineage rather than being indicative of multiple hominin taxa in the sample. He reckoned that where these early hominins differed from

Table 11.1   Four Interpretations of the European Hominin Sequence[a]

Age (ky)	Fossil Hominins	A	B	C	D
30	Early modern	*H. sapiens sapiens*	Modern *H. sapiens*	*H. sapiens*	*H. sapiens*
50	Late Neandertals	*H. sapiens neanderthalensis*			
120	Saccopastore Biache			*H. neanderthalensis*	
220	Ehringsdorf Pontnewydd Reilingen? Swanscombe? Steinheim?	*H. sapiens steinheimensis*	Archaic *H. sapiens*		*H. neanderthalensis*
300	Atapuerca Petralona? Bilzingsleben Vértesszöllös? Arago?	*H. erectus*		*H. heidelbergensis*	
500	Mauer?				
800	Gran Dolina			*H. antecessor*	

[a]Scheme *A* recognizes two species (*sapiens*, represented by three subspecies, and *erectus*), *B* only one (*sapiens*, in "modern" and "archaic" forms), *C* four (*sapiens*, *neanderthalensis*, *heidelbergensis*, and *antecessor*), and *D* two (*sapiens* and *neanderthalensis*).

Neandertals, it was generally in the direction of being more *H. erectus–*like, with the more robust specimens, presumably the males (e.g., Petralona, Bilzingsleben, Vértesszöllös), having a greater expression of such features than the smaller, more gracile, and presumably female specimens (e.g., Steinheim, Swanscombe, La Chaise, Biache, Arago 21). Critical to this argument is the contention that these "robust" and "gracile" Middle Pleistocene hominins differ from one another "mainly in metric and morphological features that distinguish males from females in both living populations and in Neandertals." This implies that the group we have referred to as the older archaic hominins comprises only the males of this evolving Middle Pleistocene *Homo* lineage and the younger archaic group comprises only the females.

However, others have argued that the size differences between some of the large specimens (e.g., Petralona) and the small specimens (e.g., Steinheim) are too great to be males and females of one sexually dimorphic taxon and, therefore, require some degree of taxonomic separation (Stringer, 1985). In this scenario, as we noted above, the Petralona-like group is regarded as a suitable morphotype for the common ancestor of both Neandertals and modern humans, whereas the Steinheim-like group is regarded as anteneandertals.

What sort of paleontological evidence would help resolve these contradictory viewpoints? Ideally, what is needed to test hypotheses about the degree of sexual dimorphism in Middle Pleistocene hominin populations is a reasonably complete hominin sample from a single site. If such a site could be found, would the hominins from this single population be more, or less, sexually dimorphic than the hominins found at sites like Petralona and Steinheim?

Atapuerca (Sima de los Huesos)

Incredibly, it appears that just such evidence has been uncovered in a cave in the Sierra de Atapuerca, northern Spain. Over the past decade or so the remains of at least 28 Middle Pleistocene hominin individuals have been recovered from Sima de los Huesos (Pit of the Bones), which represent the most complete Middle Pleistocene hominin sample yet found at a single site anywhere in the world (Arsuaga et al., 1991, 1993, 1997a, 1997b, 1997c, 1999a; de Castro et al., 2004). As remarked on earlier, there is a growing consensus that these, and other similar early *Homo* specimens (e.g., Mauer) should be classified as a separate species, *H. heidelbergensis*. This sample now includes portions of at least 13 crania (2 of which are more or less complete adult individuals, and 1 a more fragmentary cranium of an immature individual), over 450 permanent and deciduous teeth, 5 mandibular fragments, and assorted postcranial remains (Fig. 11.10). It is interesting that the extensive amount of interproximal grooving on many of the posterior teeth suggests the use of dental probes (toothpicks) and/or use of the teeth for fiber and sinew processing (Arsuaga et al., 1997c; de Castro et al., 1997b).

The absence of herbivore bones and the paucity of stone tools (one finely made handaxe has been found) suggest that the site was neither a human occupation site nor a product of carnivore activity. It is quite possible that the hominin accumulation was the product of perimortem hominin mortuary practices (Andrews and Jalvo, 1997; Arsuaga et al., 1997b). Combined U-S and ESR dating on both speleothems and hominin bones in the cave indicate a minimum age of about 200 kya and an actual age probably closer to 400–600 kya (Bischoff and Shamp, 2003; Bischoff et al., 1997). Paleomagnetic age estimates range from about 205 to 325 kya for the hominin fossils (Parés et al., 2000).

In answer to the question of variability posed above, it seems that the Sima de los Huesos hominin sample lends support to the view that extensive variation (presumably due in large part to sexual dimorphism) does indeed characterize Middle Pleistocene hominins (e.g., in certain mandibular dimensions), although this level of size variation is not always greater than that found in either Neandertal and/or modern human samples (Arsuaga et al., 1997a; Rosas et al., 2002). For example, the largest cranium (Cranium 4) has a cranial capacity of 1390 cc, whereas the smallest cranium (Cranium 5) has a cranial capacity of only 1125 cc.[7] Therefore, in this feature, Cranium 5 is similar in size to some of the smaller Middle Pleistocene hominins (e.g., Steinheim, Ndutu), whereas Cranium 4 has one of the largest cranial capacities of any Middle Pleistocene hominin. It is somewhat surprising that facial architecture in the smaller cranium (Atapuerca 5) shows some resemblances to the Petralona cranium, whereas another facial fragment (AT 404) is more similar to the same region in the Steinheim cranium. Thus some of those who once argued that Middle Pleistocene hominin variation reflected taxonomic distinctions now concede that it is indeed possible that two crania as different as Petralona and Steinheim could be encompassed within the variation seen in the Sima de los Huesos sample.

A complete pelvis has also been found and is associated with two fragmentary femora. The pelvis is robust and very broad with a very long superior pubic ramus and marked iliac flare. The femora have long femoral necks (Arsuaga et al., 1999a). Body mass of this individual is estimated at 95 kg. Estimated encephalization quotient (EQ) values for this hominin sample is about 3.7–3.8, using a cranial capacity value of 1390 cc and a body weight of about 95 kg. This figure is well below that for both modern humans (about 5.3) and Neandertals (about 5.0).

---

[7]The estimated cranial capacity of the immature individual is 1100 cc.

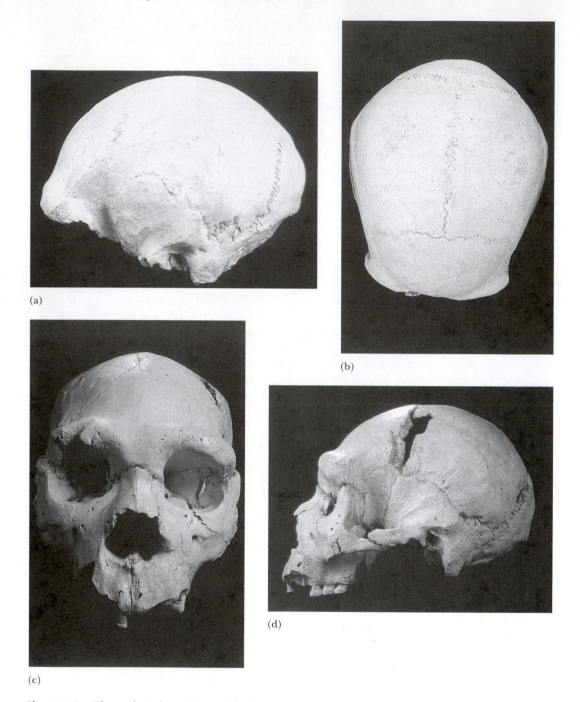

Fig. 11.10.   The archaic hominin sample from Atapuerca (Sima de los Huesos), Spain.   (a) Lateral and (b) superior views of Cranium 4. (c) Facial, (d) Lateral, and (e) Posterior views of Cranium 5. (f) Lateral view of Cranium 6. (Photos courtesy of Madrid Scientific Films.)

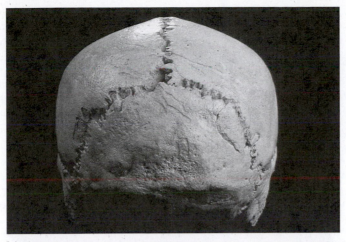

(e)

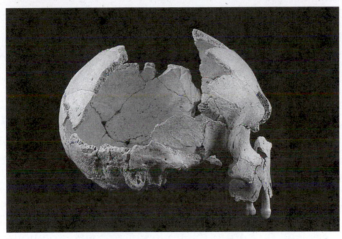

(f)

The mosaic nature of both the cranial and the postcranial Sima de los Huesos sample is quite remarkable: Some features are typical of *H. erectus,* others of Neandertals, and still others of modern *H. sapiens* (Carretero et al., 1997; Rosas, 1997). It seems clear from Table 11.2, however, that more features are shared in common with Neandertals than with the other two taxa (e.g., position of the mental foramen, appearance of a retromolar space); and for this reason the Sima de los Huesos sample reinforces the hypothesis expressed earlier that some of these Middle Pleistocene archaic hominins do indeed document an early stage of Neandertal evolution (Rosas, 2001). If, in fact, it turns out that the Neandertal lineage was distinct from our own back into the Middle Pleistocene, then this would, of

Table 11.2   Some Character Distributions in the Atapuerca Sample

Feature	H. erectus	Neandertal	H. sapiens
Vault broadest near base	X		
High total prognathism	X		
Laterally thick supraorbital torus	X		
Mandibular morphology	X	X	
Lower limb robusticity	X	X	
Cranial capacity range	X	X	X
Shape of supraorbital torus		X	
Incipient suprainiac fossa		X	
Midfacial projection		X	
Lateral occipital profile		X	X
Tympanic morphology		X	X
High cranial vault		X	X
Shape of temporal squama		X	X
Rear parietal profile	X		X
Adult occipitomastoid morphology			X

From Stringer (1993b).

course, also imply an ancient date for the origin of the modern *H. sapiens* clade. Furthermore, if the more fragmentary fossils from Vértesszöllös and Bilzingsleben, which are the most likely candidates for *H. erectus* status in Europe, can be morphologically linked to the Sima de los Huesos sample, then the claims for the presence of *H. erectus* in Europe would likewise be diminished (Stringer, 1993b).

Thus both cranial and dental morphology of the Sima de los Huesos material may lend support to the notion of regional evolutionary continuity between Middle Pleistocene archaic hominins and Upper Pleistocene Neandertals in western Europe (de Castro, 1988; de Castro and Rosas, 1992; Rosas, 1987, 1997). In other words, these claims suggest the possibility of hominin "grades" in Europe throughout the Middle Pleistocene: the earliest material being *H. erectus,* or *H. erectus*–like (e.g., *H. antecessor*); leading to the more transitional, archaic hominins (anteneandertals or *H. heidelbergensis*); resulting finally in the classic Neandertals of Europe. Such a view, however, would lead to the exclusion of all early Middle Pleistocene European hominins from the origins of anatomically modern *H. sapiens* if one also believes that the Neandertals were evolutionary dead ends (or that their contribution to the modern human gene pool was minimal). We shall have more to say about Neandertals in Chapter 13.

SOME DENTAL TRENDS IN MIDDLE PLEISTOCENE ARCHAIC HOMININS

Middle Pleistocene archaic hominins were characterized by a number of dental trends that are important to note. For example, there was enlargement of the anterior dentition combined with reduction of the postcanine dentition relative to earlier hominins. Levels of dental sexual dimorphism, particularly of the canines, exceeded those of modern human populations (de Castro et al., 1993, 2001; Wolpoff, 1980). This postcanine size reduction affected a number of dental features, including a simplification of the molar crowns that involved a reduction and eventual disappearance of the distal major cusps, modification of the so-called Y-5 occlusal pattern of fissures and cusps on the lower molars (the "arms" of the Y embrace the hypoconid, and the 5 refers to the number of well-developed cusps), disappearance of the cingulum, and some reduction of the swelling of the lingual and buccal faces of the crown. In addition to these general dental modifications, archaic hominins from northwest Africa, the Far East, and Western Europe all share a number of detailed morphological traits in the permanent postcanine teeth such as the presence of a tuberculum molare in P^3, an asymmetric P_3, a strong development of the hypocone in M^1, and enlarged pulp chambers (taurodontism).

However, the Asian and African archaic groups did retain some plesiomorphic dental traits that differentiated them from other European Middle and early Upper Pleistocene hominins, such as the presence of a

Table 11.3   Dental Traits Shared by the Eastern Asia and Northwest African Mid-Pleistocene Hominins[a]

(A) Buccal cingulum	Upper and lower canines, premolars and molars
(A) Strong molarization	Lower fourth premolar
(A) Two roots[b]	Lower premolars
(B) Invariable presence of hypoconulid and a Y fissure pattern	Lower molars
(C) Secondary crenulation and fissuration	Upper and lower premolars and molars

[a]A, traits are not present in the European Mid-Pleistocene hominins; B, traits are frequently absent in the European Mid-Pleistocene hominins; C, traits are sometimes present, but usually less marked, in the European Mid-Pleistocene hominins.
[b]It is possible that this trait has a very low frequency in the European Mid-Pleistocene hominins, since it is present, although rarely, in the European Neandertals.
From de Castro (1988).

buccal cingulum, double-rooted lower premolars, strong molarization of the P_4, invariable presence of a hypoconulid in the lower molars, and secondary crenulation or enamel wrinkling that in the Zhoukoudian teeth reached great complexity (de Castro, 1988). These dental similarities between Middle Pleistocene populations of northwest Africa and eastern Asia have been pointed out by a number of authors and have been used to support the notion of two hominin lineages existing in the Middle Pleistocene, one represented by eastern Asian and northwest African populations and the other by western European populations (Table 11.3).

ARCHAIC HOMININS FROM CHINA

There are a number of fossil sites in China that also yield Middle Pleistocene archaic hominins, and it is to these sites that we next turn (Fig. 11.11).

The hominin fossils from Chaoxian, consisting of a partial occipital, right maxilla with P^3–M^1, and three isolated teeth, were recovered in 1982–1983. A U-S date of about 167 kya has been reported from the hominin levels. The relatively thin occipital bone, lack of well-developed ectocranial markings, less pronounced subnasal prognathism, and relatively thin supraorbital tori are all differences from conditions found in *H. erectus*. For this reason most regard the fossils as early *H. sapiens*.

In 1956 a partial maxilla and isolated teeth were recovered from Changyang, dated to about 195 kya based on U-S methods. Several features of the maxilla suggest affinities to *H. sapiens*, including the anterior position of the incisive foramen, the large maxillary sinus, and the very orthognathic subnasal plane.

Several small isolated teeth from the site of Dingcun provisionally dated to 210–160 kya provide some of the earliest evidence of dental reduction in Far Eastern archaic hominins.

The largest archaic Far Eastern hominin sample to bridge both the temporal and morphological gap between *H. erectus* and *H. sapiens* comes from Xujiayao. At least 11 individuals are represented at the site by fragmentary cranial bones and isolated teeth. In both size and shape, the cranial bones are described as intermediate between Zhoukoudian and modern humans. As is usual for the Far Eastern sites, dating is problematic, but two U-S dates give ages in excess of 100 kya and 104–125 kya, respectively. Thousands of stone artifacts have also been recovered. These are sometimes taken as evidence of a kill/butchery or occupation site. The Xujiayo hominins exhibit features similar not only to Chinese *H. erectus* but also to populations occupying the same region today, and, as we shall see in the next chapter, is one line of fossil evidence used in support of the Multiregional Continuity Model of modern human origins (Pope, 1992).

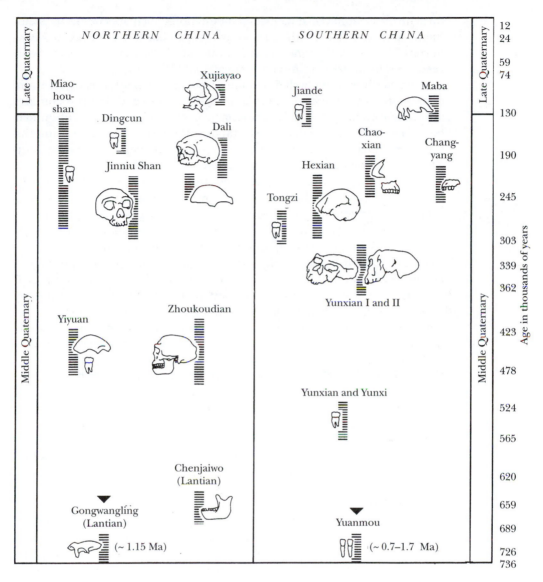

Fig. 11.11. Temporal distribution of some important fossil hominin sites from China (Etler and Li, 1994).

One of the better known Chinese specimens, the Dali cranium, also shows a number of features transitional between Asian *H. erectus* and living Asians. The cranium has been insecurely dated by U-S to about 200 kya and correlated to ^{18}O stages 6–7. Cranial capacity is about 1200 cc. The face is described as broad and short (possibly due to crushing), with a very broad, bell-shaped nasal aperture and massively developed supraorbital tori. In most midfacial dimensions it resembles such specimens as Steinheim, Arago, and Jebel Irhoud and has few similarities to Eurasian Neandertals. Nearly 200 stone tools, mostly cores and flakes, have been recovered from the hominin layer (Keates, 1996).

Another important archaic hominin specimen from the Far East is the cranium from Jinniu Shan unearthed in 1984. Associated with this cranium are some vertebrae, ribs, pelvis, patella, and limb bones. The cranium may have the largest cranial capacity (about 1300 cc) associated with the thinnest cranial bones of any archaic hominin specimen from the Far East. The cranium dates to about 200 kya based on ESR and U-S dating (Chen et al., 1993). The significance of this date is that it raises the possibility that *H. sapiens* (if that is what the Jinniu Shan cranium actually represents) coexisted in China with *H. erectus* as represented by Cranium V in the upper layer at Zhoukoudian and the Hexian cranium.[8] In addition, Chinese paleoanthropologists believe that some features in the Jinniu Shan cranium such as the broad nasal bridge, shovel shaped incisors, and prominent cheekbones, differentiate early Chinese *H. sapiens* from its counterparts in Europe and Africa and, therefore, best fit the Multiregional Continuity Model of human evolution, which we will discuss more fully in the following chapters (Tiemei et al., 1994). About a dozen artifacts consisting mainly of small quartz flakes have also been recovered from the site. It has also been claimed that circular-shaped ash concentrations containing charcoal, burned bones, and charred stones may represent ancient hearths.

As noted above, the Jinniu Shan site preserves not only a complete cranium but parts of the pelvis as well. The size and shape of both the cranium and the pelvis suggest this individual was a female. The pubic bone is interesting in that it has several Neandertal-like features, including its length and extremely thin cross-sectional shape. However, although elongated, the pubis is still within the expected range for a female of its body size, a pattern also seen among Neandertals (e.g., Tabun, Krapina) in which pubic elongation is more evident in males than in females and therefore must be viewed as an adaptive response to something other than simply obstetric considerations. An extremely thin pubis is seen in both male and female Neandertals, and its presence in the Jinniu Shan pelvis indicates that this peculiar trait is not necessarily a derived feature unique to Neandertals (Rosenberg and Lu, 1997).

One Chinese specimen that does seem to show some similarities to "classic" Eurasian Neandertals is the Maba cranium dated by U-S to about 169–129 kya. Similarities to Neandertals include the shape of the supraorbital tori that are thickest in their medial third and the distinctly rounded orbits lacking supraorbital notches.

---

[8]As we noted in the previous chapter, a similar argument has been made for the Ngandong (Solo) hominin sample from Java. Also, as noted earlier, new dates of Cranium V from Zhoukoudian suggest that it may be much older than previously thought (Shen et al., 1996).

ARCHAIC HOMININS FROM AFRICA

By at least 200 kya, a crucial change took place in the archeological record of Africa that may relate to a major technological breakthrough—the invention of tools with handles by which they could be attached, or hafted, to pieces of wood for use as spears or knives. This is reflected in the disappearance of large bifaces in Acheulean assemblages and their replacement by assemblages of smaller bifaces and Middle Paleolithic flake technology. This foreshadowing of Middle Paleolithic technology in Late Acheulean assemblages indicates that the Middle Stone Age (MSA) of Africa evolved directly out of the terminal Acheulean (called the Fauresmith industry in southern Africa) (Clark, 1992).

Documenting an African transition from archaic to anatomically modern humans depends on the identification of African fossils that are both morphologically and chronologically intermediate between archaic specimens like Broken Hill (Kabwe), Bodo, or Ndutu and modern Africans. Several African fossils often considered for this role include those from Jebel Irhoud (Morocco), Eliye Springs (Kenya), Florisbad (South Africa), Ngaloba (Tanzania), and Omo (Ethiopia) (Fig. 11.1). However, there are a number of formidable problems with this sample (Smith, 1992): (1) the sites are few and far between (extending from South to North Africa), and thus preclude any information about regional variation and/or sexual dimorphism in this "transitional" group; (2) the material is incomplete and fragmentary—for example, the only postcranial specimen for the entire sample is one humerus from Jebel Irhoud (the only mandible, Jebel Irhoud mandible 3, also comes from this site); and (3) problems of dating exist at four of the five sites.

Two of the more complete African Middle Pleistocene archaic crania are those from Kabwe (Broken Hill), Zambia, and Bodo, Ethiopia.

Kabwe (Broken Hill) and Saldanha (Hopefield) Crania

The Kabwe cranium, discovered in 1921 in the Broken Hill mine of what was then northern Rhodesia, became known in anthropological circles as "Rhodesian Man" (Fig. 11.12). The cranium was found with several postcranial bones, including several femoral fragments, tibia (the only postcranial element associated with the cranium), sacrum, two iliac fragments and a small number of Sangoan-type tools, a terminal Early Stone Age industry (Clark, 1970; Clark et al., 1968; Pearson, 2000). Opinion has varied over the years about this cranium—some considered it an African Neandertal variant, whereas others, particularly Franz Weidenreich, considered it an enlarged version of Solo Man from Java. Indeed, Weidenreich (1943) was

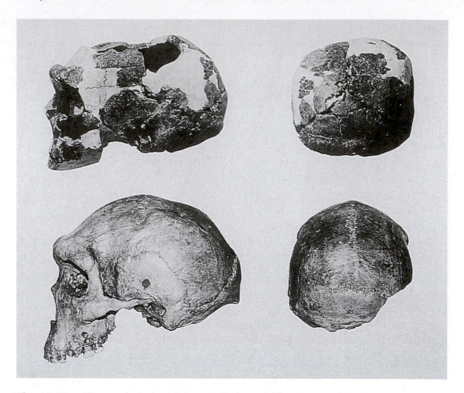

Fig. 11.12.   Two archaic hominin crania from Africa.   (*top*) The Ndutu cranium, dated to about 400–200 kya, was found in association with a number of stone tool types, including spheroids, hammerstones, flakes, cores, and handaxes. It has many of the features found in "typical" Asian *H. erectus,* including the overall form and contour of the occipital with a thickened nuchal torus, the size and shape of the mastoid region, the (inferred) size of the supraorbital torus, and the great thickness of the cranial bones. However, similarities to *H. sapiens* include the presence of pronounced parietal bosses, the more vertical sides of the cranial vault, and the apparent absence of a sagittal keel. Cranial capacity is estimated to be about 1100 cc. (*bottom*) The Kabwe cranium, discovered in 1921 in the Broken Hill mine of what was then northern Rhodesia. The cranium is characterized by heavy browridges and a slightly keeled and constricted frontal bone. (Photos courtesy of G. P. Rightmire.)

moved to write: "There is small doubt that the type of Rhodesian man is closer to that of *Homo soloensis* and, consequently, also to his descendants, the Australians, than he is to the European Neanderthal forms and their descendants."

The cranium is characterized by heavy browridges, a slightly keeled and constricted frontal bone, short parietals that show little bossing, acutely flexed occiput with prominent occipital torus, lateral expansion of mastoid and supramastoid regions, and extensive paranasal sinus development (Singer, 1958; Spoor and Zonneveld, 1999). Endocranial volume is estimated at about 1280 cc. Two of the more intriguing features of the cranium are the severe dental decay, which may have been caused by chronic lead poisoning (Bartsiokas and Day, 1993), and several pathological lesions in the left temporal bone, possibly caused by dermoid cysts (Montgomery et al., 1994).

The Kabwe femoral fragments lack the elongated femoral neck seen in *H. ergaster* but are similar to the latter in retaining thickened cortical bone (Pearson, 2000). The iliac blade also has greatly thickened cortical bone on its lateral side, which differs from the condition present in modern humans. The tibia shares several features with that of early *Homo,* including a rounded anterior crest and rounded posteromedial and posterlateral angles. Otherwise, the Kabwe postcranial material is similar to that of anatomically modern humans.

Dating the cranium has been difficult. Relative chemical dating techniques using fluorine, nitrogen, and uranium initially indicated that it was contemporary with the other human and animal bones at the site, probably of Upper Pleistocene age (Oakley, 1958a). Latter studies, using a combination of archeological and paleontological evidence, suggested that both Broken Hill and Saldanha (see below) probably dated from the later part of the Middle Pleistocene, more than 125 kya (Klein, 1973). The revised older dates for both these specimens have important implications because some anthropologists had previously argued that human evolution was somehow "retarded" in sub-Saharan Africa using the "evidence" that primitive-looking hominins like Kabwe and Saldhana dated to only 30–40 kya (Coon, 1962).

In the 1950s, another important hominin was discovered at Saldanha Bay (near Hopefield), South Africa (Singer, 1958). A diverse fauna and a great number of artifacts have been recovered from the site, initially described as final Acheulean (Fauresmith) and MSA (Stillbay). The Saldanha cranium was originally found in about 30 pieces that, when reconstructed, bore a certain resemblance to the Kabwe cranium in its low, receding forehead separated from large supraorbital tori by a distinct supratoral groove, thickened cranial bones, and prominent occipital crest. A mandible from the same site (but 460 m away) shows a broad ramus much like that seen in the Mauer jaw.

Another southern African Middle Stone Age archeological and faunal site has been reported from Saldanha Bay (Hoedjiespunt). U-S dating suggests the fauna and tools are older than 74 kya and may be closer to 300 kya. Thus far, only two upper hominin molars have been recovered from the site. They are said to be large in comparison to modern humans but smaller than the known upper dentitions of southern African archaic hominins (Berger and Parkington, 1995).

Bodo

One of the most beautifully preserved Middle Pleistocene hominins is the cranium from Bodo, Ethiopia (Fig. 11.13) (Conroy, 1980; Conroy et al., 1978). The cranium was found in 1976 during paleontological, archeological, and geological surveys conducted by the Rift Valley Research Mission in Ethiopia (Kalb, 1993, 1995; Kalb et al., 1982a, 1982b, 1984; Kalb and Mebrate, 1993). A

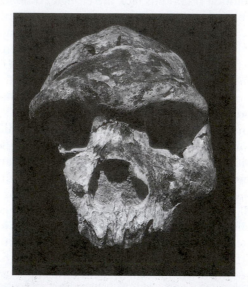

Fig. 11.13. The Bodo cranium. One of the most striking features of the face is the great width and overall robustness. A particularly interesting aspect of the Bodo cranium is the identification of cut marks that closely resemble those caused by cutting fresh bone with stone tools. This may be the first documented evidence of intentional postmortem defleshing of bone in the hominin fossil record. (Photos courtesy of T. White.)

second hominin parietal bone was found in 1981, and a distal humerus fragment was recovered in 1990. While the Bodo cranium and the isolated parietal bone come from very robust individuals, the humerus is appreciably smaller than many modern human humeri. This suggests that the Bodo hominins may have been quite sexually dimorphic in overall body size (Clark et al., 1994).

Paleontological and radiometric dating evidence confirms that the Bodo hominins are Middle Pleistocene in age and date to about 600 kya. The hominins are associated with a number of Acheulean artifacts, including relatively well-made bifacial handaxes and cleavers. It is interesting to note that a local shift from Oldowan to Acheulean tools occurred within this Middle Awash sequence about this time. While such a shift in tool types occurred elsewhere in Africa by at least 1.5 mya, its occurrence here was much later in time (Kalb et al., 1982a; Clark et al., 1984; Clark et al., 1994).

The Bodo cranium consists of an almost complete face and partial neurocranium, as well as part of the basicranium anterior to the midline point on the anterior margin of the foramen magnum, known as **basion.** Unfortunately, no tooth crowns are present, but the roots and/or alveoli for many of the teeth are preserved. The cranium is large and robust, and the cranial vault is exceedingly thick. The nasal root is broad, and the supraorbital ridges are thick, arched, and separated by a prominent glabellar region rather than forming a continuous bony shelf. One of the most striking features of the face is the great depth, width, and robustness of the zygomatic bone, far exceeding that of the Broken Hill or the classic Neandertal of La Chapelle-aux-Saints. As in the Broken Hill cranium, the zygomatic flares more directly laterally than is characteristic of many classic Neandertal crania. As in most *H. erectus* and archaic *H. sapiens,* a true canine fossa is absent, perhaps due to the extremely large maxillary sinus development. However, unlike most *H. erectus* (including OH 9), the mandibular fossa is not notably deep or narrow, resembling instead that of Broken Hill.

In side view the cranium is long and low, with a low receding forehead. Postorbital constriction is less pronounced than in *H. erectus.* As in most *H. erectus* and archaic hominins, there is a slight but distinct keeling of bone along the midsagittal line, especially in the region around bregma. Cranial capacity is estimated at about 1250 cc (Conroy et al., 2000).

In overall appearance, the Bodo cranium is most similar to other archaic Middle Pleistocene crania, like those from Broken Hill, Petralona, and Arago 21, and is certainly more archaic looking than the undoubted *H. sapiens* crania from the Kibish Formation in Ethiopia. This conclusion is reinforced by the 1981 discovery of a *H. erectus*–like parietal bone from a second individual at Bodo (Asfaw, 1983). Resemblances to later Middle Pleistocene hominins include the large cranial capacity associated with a broadened braincase located across the parietal region, the shallow glenoid cavity, and the vertical border of the nasal aperature (seen in side view).

This is not to imply, however, that the Bodo cranium does not share a number of interesting craniofacial similarities to *H. erectus.* For example, the low braincase (particularly the frontal profile); overall craniofacial shape, particularly the broad and robust facial skeleton; thickened cranial bones; projecting and heavily constructed supraorbital tori; and midline keeling of the frontal bone extending to bregma are all features shared with *H. erectus* (Rightmire, 1996).

A particularly interesting aspect of the Bodo cranium is the identification of cut marks that closely resemble those caused by cutting fresh bone with stone tools. This may be the first documented evidence of intentional postmortem defleshing of bone in the hominin fossil record (White, 1985, 1986b).

Ndutu

Another archaic hominin from East Africa is the cranium found in 1973 at Lake Ndutu, a seasonal soda lake at the western end of Olduvai Gorge, Tanzania (Fig. 11.12) (Clarke, 1976, 1990; Mturi, 1976; Rightmire, 1983). The Ndutu cranium, dated to about 400–200 kya, was found in association with a number of stone tool types, including spheroids, hammerstones, flakes, cores, and handaxes. Ron Clarke of the University of the Witwatersrand has meticulously reconstructed the cranium and now classifies it as an East African early *H. sapiens,* rather than *H. erectus,* mainly because its greatest cranial breadth is high up on the parietal region rather than low down by the mastoids as in typical *H. erectus.* Clarke (1994c) argues that *H. sapiens* evolved in Africa about 1.5 mya from *H. habilis* through an intermediary species he calls *H. leakeyi.* For him, *H. erectus* is strictly an Asian species that arose in, and was confined to, Asia and thus was not ancestral to modern humans.

To be sure, the Ndutu cranium has many of the features found in typical Asian *H. erectus,* including the overall form and contour of the occipital with a thickened nuchal torus, the size and shape of the mastoid region, the inferred size of the supraorbital torus, and the great thickness of the cranial bones. It also shows similarity to the Salé cranium from Morocco dated to around 400 kya and possibly to SK 847 from Swartkrans and KNM-ER 3733 from Lake Turkana. However, the similarities to *H. sapiens* include the presence of pronounced parietal bosses, the more vertical sides of the cranial vault, the presence of an ossified styloid process, the apparent absence of a sagittal keel, the weak development of the supramastoid crest, and the presence of a raised articular tubercle. Cranial capacity is estimated to be about 1100 cc.

Eyasi

Many years ago, hominin specimens discovered from Lake Eyasi, Tanzania, were initially assigned to *H. erectus* (Leakey, 1936; Weinert, 1937). These fossils were found by members of the German Ludwig Kohl-Larsen Expedition to East Africa between 1934 and 1940. Lake Eyasi is situated about 50 km south of Olduvai Gorge, and the fossils were found in surface or subsurface layers located within 30–100 m of the lake shore. The Eyasi hominins consist of over 250 small pieces, few of which actually fit together. Thus it is not surprising that various attempts to reconstruct the cranium have not met with great success. The fossils were taken to Germany and stored in a farmhouse for protection during World War II. It was thought that they were lost or destroyed during the war, but in the late 1960s they were located at Tübingen.

More recent analysis has concluded that the Eyasi specimens probably belong to an early form of *H. sapiens,* not *H. erectus.* In overall morphology the reconstructed Eyasi cranium is more similar to the Saldanha (Hopefield) and Broken Hill crania and is quite dissimilar to *H. erectus* crania like OH 9. For example, it lacks such typical *H. erectus*–like features as a continuous occipital torus, a heavy supraorbital torus, and extensive postorbital constriction. In addition, maximum cranial breadth seems high on the parietals, rather than low across the mastoids. The thickness of the cranial bones is within modern limits as is its cranial capacity (estimated at 1200–1250 cc). One amino acid racemization study concludes that the specimen may date to only about 35 kya (Protsch, 1981).

Turkana Region

Hominin specimens that may represent two of Africa's older near-modern hominins come from the Ileret region of Lake Turkana. New U-S dates for the cranium (KNM-ER 3884) and femur (KNM-ER 999) give ages of around 270 kya and 300 kya, respectively.

Both specimens are from the Chari member of the Koobi Fora Formation near the base of the Pleistocene/Holocene Galana Boi Formation. The cranium belongs to an adult individual and includes much of the posterior part of the cranial vault, including occipital, parietals, and temporals; a nearly complete supraorbital region; and a maxilla with teeth. Cranial capacity is estimated at 1400 cc. The posterior vault has thin walls and lacks any clear archaic features. In contrast, the torus-like supraorbital region differs from modern humans and is closer to late archaic specimens like Florisbad and Laetoli 18. The femur is robust and shows some modern features common among the earliest modern humans from Qafzeh and Skhul. The revised dating of these fossils suggests that the transition from early archaic to late archaic hominins occurred around 350–250 kya (Bräuer et al., 1997).

None of these sub-Saharan Middle Pleistocene "transitional" crania that we have been discussing resembles European Neandertals in any meaningful way. As we shall see, this observation has most interesting implications—namely that the emergence of more modern-looking humans in both sub-Saharan Africa and in the Near East over 100 kya took place much earlier than in western Europe, where such modern-looking populations do not occur until about 40 kya.

The origin of these anatomically modern hominins is the subject of the last two chapters.

CHAPTER XII

Between Apes and Humanity: "Modern" Human Origins

INTRODUCTION

Our own species name, *sapiens*, which in Latin means "wise," was coined by Swedish naturalist Carolus Linnaeus (1758) in the eighteenth century, and for many years the taxonomic designation *Homo sapiens* was the first, and only, hominin listed in primate classifications.

Fossils of early modern *H. sapiens* have been recovered from a number of sites throughout Europe, Africa, and Asia (Figs. 12.1 and 12.2), but it is still hotly debated just when and where the first modern representatives of our species evolved, a point we shall consider in more detail later in the chapter.

What kind of mental image is conjured up by the term modern *H. sapiens*? More to the point, what do paleoanthropologists mean by the term *anatomically modern human*? This is not as straightforward a question as it sounds because, surprisingly enough, there is no inclusive definition of our own polytypic species, *H. sapiens* (Howell, 1978). Indeed, the taxon *Homo sapiens* does not even have a type specimen! However, virtually all anthropologists agree that, from the neck up, any anatomical definition of modern humans would include (but not necessarily be limited to) the features listed in Table 12.1.

The modern human form can be thought of as a reduced version of our Pleistocene antecedents, particularly in those specific instances in which cultural ingenuity has reduced the necessity of having the once-mandatory degrees of robustness (e.g., cooked foods lead to dental reduction), a result of what C. Loring Brace (1995) refers to as the probable mutation effect.

From the neck down, modern humans are characterized by hip and lower limb structures fully adapted to a striding bipedal gait and by upper

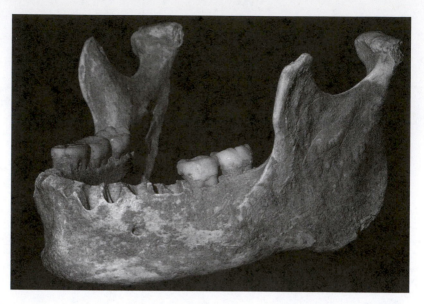

Fig. 12.1. Oldest directly dated anatomically modern *Homo sapiens* (about 35 kya) from Pestera cu Oase, Romania. (Photo courtesy of E. Trinkaus and Institutul de Speologie "Emil Racovita," Cluj-Napoca.)

limbs capable of very fine movements of the hand and thumb. The transition from archaic to modern humans saw a pronounced overall reduction in upper limb muscularity, perhaps correlated with these more precise hand movements (Pearson, 2000). This may account, in part, for the increasing numbers of blades relative to flakes and endscrapers relative to sidescrapers found in Upper versus Middle Paleolithic assemblages and for the development of polished bone technology, all of which demonstrate a shift toward elongated tools having greater mechanical advantages than shorter ones (Trinkaus, 1989c).

In addition to these anatomical details, we should also note that modern humans have an unusually prolonged life span, a protracted period of childhood dependency, and a pronounced adolescent growth spurt. Perhaps the most distinguishing feature of all, however, is our complete reliance on tools and other forms of material culture for survival.

Now that we have a better sense of what paleoanthropologists mean by the term *anatomically modern,* what do archeologists mean by the term *behaviorally modern?*

Fig. 12.2. Some of the important sites in (a) Africa and (b) Eurasia where Neandertal-like and/or early modern *H. sapiens* have been discovered. (c) Possible classification of some of the fossil hominins of the later Pleistocene. (Stringer and Gamble, 1993.)

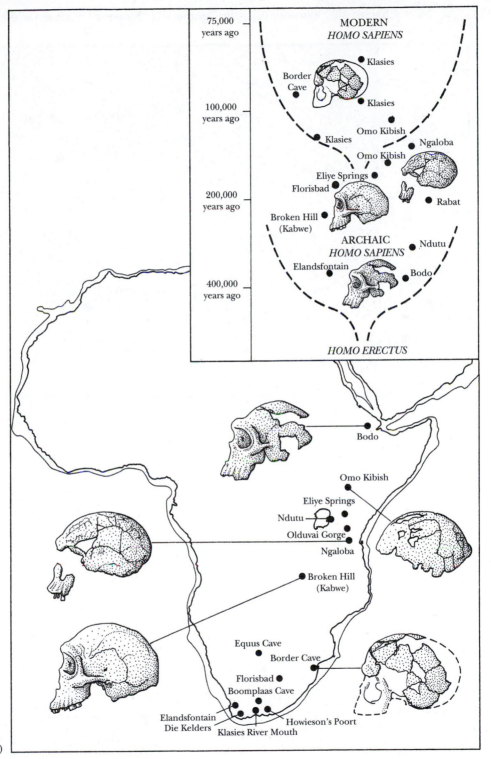

75,000 years ago

MODERN
HOMO SAPIENS

Klasies

Border Cave

Klasies

100,000 years ago

Omo Kibish

Klasies

Ngaloba

Omo Kibish

Eliye Springs

Florisbad

Rabat

200,000 years ago

Broken Hill (Kabwe)

Ndutu

ARCHAIC
HOMO SAPIENS

Elandsfontain

Bodo

400,000 years ago

HOMO ERECTUS

Bodo

Omo Kibish

Eliye Springs

Ndutu

Olduvai Gorge

Ngaloba

Broken Hill (Kabwe)

Equus Cave

Border Cave

Florisbad

Boomplaas Cave

Elandsfontain

Die Kelders

Howieson's Poort

Klasies River Mouth

(a)

(Continued)

Fig. 12.2.   *(Continued)*

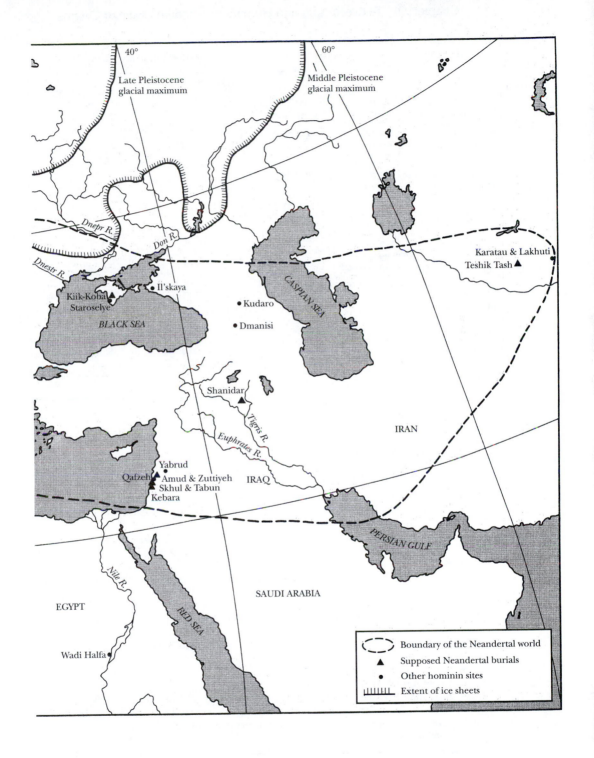

Late Pleistocene
glacial maximum

Middle Pleistocene
glacial maximum

40°   60°

Dnepr R.

Don R.

Dnestr R.

Kiik-Koba ▲   • Il'skaya
Staroselye

BLACK SEA

• Kudaro

• Dmanisi

CASPIAN SEA

Karatau & Lakhuti
Teshik Tash ▲

Shanidar ▲

Tigris R.

Euphrates R.

IRAN

Yabrud
Qafzeh ▲
Amud & Zuttiyeh
Skhul & Tabun
Kebara

IRAQ

PERSIAN GULF

Nile R.

RED SEA

SAUDI ARABIA

EGYPT

Wadi Halfa •

- - -   Boundary of the Neandertal world
▲   Supposed Neandertal burials
•   Other hominin sites
⊔⊔⊔⊔   Extent of ice sheets

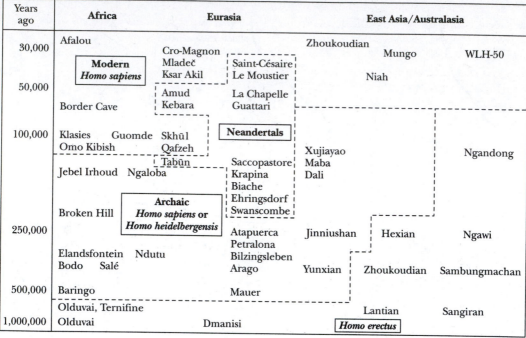

(c)

Fig. 12.2.   *(Continued)*

Table 12.1   Important Cranial Features of Modern *Homo sapiens*

- Cranial vault enlarged and elevated especially in the frontal and parietal regions; cranial bones reduced in thickness
- Biparietal breadth greater than, or equal to, biauricular breadth (i.e., breadth across the ear region)
- Occipital region rounded; reduced angulation and reduction of the nuchal (neck) musculature
- Reduction and/or loss of sagittal keeling and parasagittal flattening
- Reduction of supraorbital tori into glabellar and supraciliary elements with development of crest-like superior orbital margins
- Shortened cranial base with increased flexion of basicranial axis
- Reduction of both facial prognathism and height with progressive facial shortening; development of a canine fossa
- Reduction of alveolar processes of maxilla and mandible associated with reduction in tooth crown and root size
- Reduction of mandibular robusticity
- Development of a bony chin
- Brain size averages around 1300 cc but varies from about 1000 to 2000 cc
- Brain and vocal tract fully adapted for speech, including the presence of cerebral asymmetry with language centers predominantly in the left cerebral hemisphere

When archeologists talk about the evolution of modern behavior, they are usually referring to the transition from Middle to Upper Paleolithic cultures. In western Europe, this cultural transition appears about 45–40 kya and is associated with the first appearance of what paleoanthropologists refer to as anatomically modern humans (Fig. 12.3). However, this is *not* the case in other areas of the Old World, such as western Asia or sub-Saharan Africa, where the first appearance of anatomically modern humans in excess of 100 kya is associated with Middle Paleolithic or Middle Stone Age assemblages, respectively. In particular, the higher frequencies of blades and bone tools in sub-Saharan MSA (Middle Stone Age) industries give them more of an Upper Paleolithic feel than European Middle Paleolithic industries, an observation of particular interest given the early appearance of anatomically modern humans in various MSA sites of southern and eastern Africa (d'Errico, 2003; McBrearty and Brooks, 2000). In western Asia, the cultural transition from Middle to Upper Paleolithic appears slightly earlier than in western Europe, and in sub-Saharan Africa the transition appears variably about 40–18 kya.[1] However, as noted above, in both these regions anatomically modern humans first appear well over 100 kya (White et al., 2003).

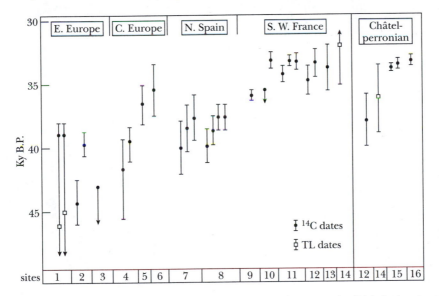

Fig. 12.3.   Age determinations for first appearance of Upper Paleolithic industries in Europe (Aurignacian in eastern, central, and western Europe and Châtelperronian in France).   Note the general east to west time gradient. Sites: *1,* Temnata (Bulgaria); *2,* Istallosko (Hungary); *3,* Bacho Kiro (Bulgaria); *4,* Willendorf (Austria); *5,* Geissenklosterle (Germany); *6,* Krems (Austria); *7,* Castillo (Spain); *8,* L'Arbreda (Spain); *9,* La Rochette (France); *10,* La Ferrassie (France); *11,* Abri Pataud (France); *12,* Roc de Combe (France); *13,* Le Flageolet (France); *14,* Saint-Césaire (France); *15,* Arcy-sur-Cure (France); *16,* Les Cottes (France). (Mellars, 1992.)

[1]In sub-Saharan Africa this transition is from the Middle Stone Age to the Late Stone Age.

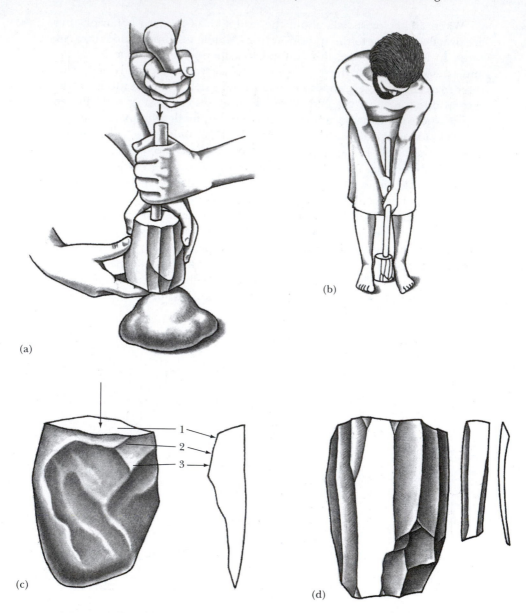

Fig. 12.4. (a–d)Techniques used by Upper Paleolithic toolmakers. (a) Cores could be placed on a large stone and then a flake detached with a hammer and punch—the indirect percussion or punch technique. (b) Blades could be detached by exerting pressure on the core with a pointed tool. (c) Characteristic markings of a flake tool. *1,* Striking platform; *2,* percussion cone; *3,* small conchoidal bulb of percussion. (d) Appearance of prepared core with flake removed. (e–i) Characteristic Upper Paleolithic tools. (e) Aurignacian blade. (f) Gravettian point. (g) Gravettian endscraper. (h) Solutrean point. (i) Magdalenian burin. (Gowlett, 1992.)

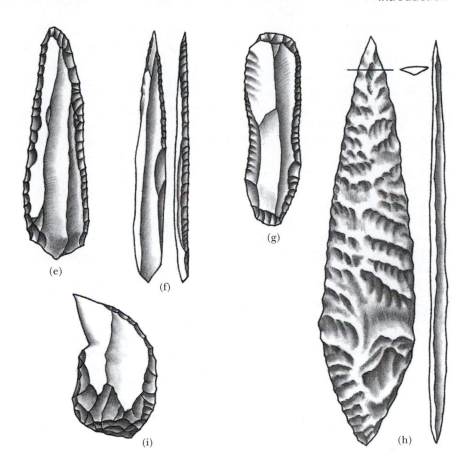

(e)

(f)

(g)

(h)

(i)

The period of the Middle/Upper Paleolithic transition also witnessed the first human migrations into previously uninhabited areas of the Old World, such as Japan and Australia (which imply significant boatbuilding and navigational skills), and ended with the first human migrations into the New World via Beringia well before 12 kya (Hoffecker et al., 1993; Kunz and Reaniert, 1994; Reynolds, 1991; Roosevelt et al., 1996).

So what kinds of archeological evidence might provide clues to this behavioral revolution from Middle to Late Paleolithic cultures? A partial list would certainly include the following (Fig. 12.4) (Chazan, 1995b; Klein, 1992; McBrearty and Brooks, 2000):

- Upper Paleolithic assemblages are dominated by blades, particularly ones that are well designed for hafting, whereas Middle Paleolithic assemblages are dominated by flakes.
- Upper Paleolithic tool kits consist mainly of endscrapers, burins (gravers), and points, whereas Middle Paleolithic tool kits consist mainly of sidescrapers and denticulates.

- Upper Paleolithic tool types exhibit more regional and temporal distinctiveness compared to the more static tool assemblages of the Middle Paleolithic.
- Upper Paleolithic assemblages include more bone, antler, and ivory tools as well as more objects of personal adornment and "art."[2]
- Upper Paleolithic archeological sites are more complex—that is, shelters are more elaborate and substantial.
- Upper Paleolithic tool kits include more sophisticated weapons, such as the bow and arrow and the spear thrower (earlier than 20 kya).
- Upper Paleolithic sites show more evidence of economic specialization—for example, the hunting of such particular game species as birds, fish, and sea mammals (e.g., seals).
- Upper Paleolithic populations show more evidence of economic exchange and mobility over large distances, including over water.
- Upper Paleolithic graves are more elaborate, suggesting burial rituals or ceremony.
- Upper Paleolithic knapping included soft hammer techniques (no evidence of soft hammer technique appears in the Middle Paleolithic).

The debate over the biological and behavioral origins of modern humans remains one of the most contentious, and exciting, issues in contemporary paleoanthropology. Virtually all anthropologists agree that sometime during the Middle/Upper Pleistocene transition, important biological and cultural changes were taking place in human evolution between populations of (what are best called) archaic hominins and early modern humans (Fig. 12.5). During the Late Middle Pleistocene (approximately 150 kya), only archaic hominins are present in the fossil record of Eurasia—and these are all associated with what archeologists term Middle Paleolithic assemblages (or Middle Stone Age assemblages in sub-Saharan Africa). But in Africa (and possibly the Levant) at this time there were hominins that looked far more like anatomically modern humans (White et al., 2003) (see below). However, by about 30–40 kya, modern humans are present throughout much of the Old World and are associated with distinctive Upper Paleolithic assemblages (Mellars et al., 1992; Trinkaus, 1989c; Trinkaus et al., 2003a, 2003b). Some genetic evidence, specifically mitochondrial DNA studies, also hint that the

---

[2]For example, during the Aurignacian, Cro-Magnons devised various techniques for working ivory, including the preparation and use of metallic abrasives (notably powdered hematite) for polishing. In France, beads were crafted by first forming pencil-like rods of ivory or soapstone and then circumferentially inscribing them at intervals of 0.5–0.75 inch. The beads were then snapped off as cylindrical blanks, thinned, and perforated by gouging from each side (rather than drilling), and then ground and polished into their final form using hematite as an abrasive. Ornaments were also made from fossil coral and belemnites, the fossilized, cigar-shaped shells of extinct squids (e.g., at the 36,000-year-old site of Kostenki 17 in the Don Valley of Russia). A flute from the site of Isturitz in southwestern France was made of bird bone, which is naturally hollow, and had at least three finger holes. The first fired ceramics and female figurines are found in the Gravettian of central and eastern Europe about 26,000 years ago (White, 1993).

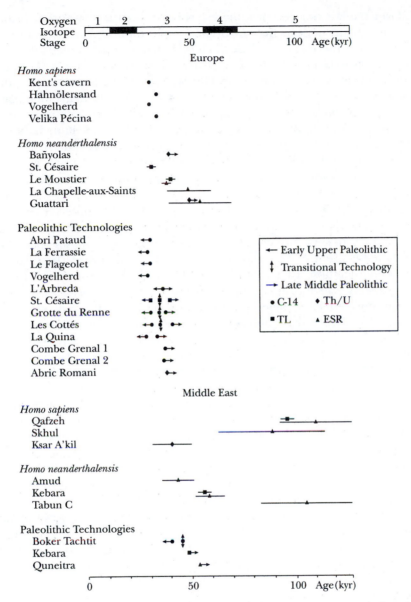

Fig. 12.5. Age estimations for Neandertal and early modern *H. sapiens* and various Paleolithic tool technologies. *kyr*, 1000 years; *c-14*, carbon-14; *Th/U*, thorium/uranium; *TL*, thermoluminescence; *ESR*, electron spin resonance.   (Stringer and Grün, 1991.)

Middle/Upper Pleistocene transition may be a time of major human population expansion throughout the Old World (Alsonso and Armour, 2001; Rogers, 1995). This is about the extent of the agreement, however. What is not agreed upon is exactly where, when, and how these modern humans first arose.

Over the last two decades, there has been a virtual revolution in our thinking about modern human origins. Until then, it had usually been assumed that the emergence of modern humans and Upper Paleolithic assemblages were causally related, virtually synchronous events. Accumulating evidence from a number of Old World sites now undermines this view and suggests that the emergence of early modern humans took place mainly within a Middle, not Upper, Paleolithic cultural context (e.g., Klasies River Mouth, Border Cave in South Africa; Dar-es-Soltane in North Africa; Qafzeh and Skhul in the Near East; Krapina A in central Europe; and Middle Awash in Ethiopia) (Rigaud, 1989; Thackeray, 1992; White et al., 2003) (see below).[3] Ironically, only in western Europe do we find a situation in which both archaic and early modern humans are associated with Upper Paleolithic industries, as for example in the Neandertal remains found in an Upper Paleolithic context at Saint-Césaire, France. Given its association with early Upper Paleolithic technology, one might expect that the Saint-Césaire 1 Neandertal should contrast with earlier (last glacial) Neandertals in those aspects of upper and lower limb robusticity related to manipulatory and locomotor biomechanical loading, as well as in body proportions reflecting degrees of technological thermal buffering and should, therefore, more closely approximate early modern humans. However, there seems to be little postcranial difference between Saint-Césaire 1 and last glacial Neandertals, indicating that the technological changes in the Châtelperronian appear to have had little effect on these aspects of human biology (Trinkaus et al., 1997).

We can frame some important questions about the tempo and mode of human evolution around this important transitional period (Trinkaus, 1989a). For example, were the dramatic changes in human behavior inferred from the archeological record causally related to changes in morphology, as identified in the human paleontological record? To what extent was the biocultural emergence of modern humans an evolutionary "revolution," or punctuational event, as opposed to a more gradual continuation of previously existing tempos of evolutionary change? Was the biocultural transition from archaic hominins to early modern humans restricted in time and space or was it a more universal Old World phenomenon? What were the selective advantages of the biocultural changes in the Upper Paleolithic that allowed early modern humans to become dominant in such a relatively short time span?

There are no easy answers to these questions, but anthropologists have gained valuable insights by amalgamating evidence from a number of separate, but interrelated, disciplines including paleoanthropology, archeology, geology, and molecular genetics. In fact, one of the most at-

---

[3]However, for the view that there is little evidence for symbolic behavior by either archaic *H. sapiens* or morphologically modern humans before the Upper Paleolithic, see Lindly and Clark (1990).

tractive and rewarding aspects of anthropology is its ability to synthesize data from numerous subdisciplines within the biological and behavioral sciences.

CURRENT ISSUES AND DEBATES OVER MODERN HUMAN ORIGINS: OUT OF AFRICA OR MULTIREGIONAL CONTINUITY?

At present, there are two main competing models concerning the evolution of modern *H. sapiens:* the Multiregional Continuity Model and the Out of Africa Model (also sometimes known as the Noah's Ark or Garden of Eden Model). In the Multiregional Continuity Model, recent human variation is seen as the product of an Early to Middle Pleistocene radiation of *H. erectus/ergaster* (or archaic *H. sapiens,* as some of its advocates would argue) out of Africa and into different regions of the Old World. There these regional populations gradually evolved into the modern populations found in those same regions today via a process of genetic exchange between evolving populations that continually divided and reticulated. Genetic contacts between these expanding African and "indigenous" non-African *H. erectus/ergaster* populations were maintained, although restricted, through isolation by distance. This allowed local populations to become differentiated from one another, while at the same time the limited gene flow between populations prevented any long-term independent evolution of each population. The end result of such a process was that archaic hominins slowly evolved into modern hominins as a single evolutionary lineage throughout the entire Old World. Obviously, gene flow between these regional populations must have been sufficient to maintain overall "grade" similarities among the various groups (i.e., all these regional archaic populations were evolving into *H. sapiens*) while at the same time allowing regional morphological characteristics to develop and persist (Frayer et al., 1993; Wolpoff, 1989a; Wolpoff et al., 1984).

Despite statements to the contrary by many of its detractors, the Multiregional Continuity Model does *not* advocate "independent multiple origins, ancient divergence of modern populations, simultaneous appearance of adaptive characters in different regions, or parallel evolution" (Wolpoff et al., 2000). In fact, one of the major misconceptions about the multiregional model is the assumption that the primary genetic input into a region of modern humans came from the same geographic region—for example, the prediction that modern Europeans will be, on average, more similar to archaic Europeans (Neandertals) than to archaic populations elsewhere (Waddle, 1994). As we will see below, this assumption is incorrect.

The Out of Africa Model is diametrically opposed to the Multiregional Continuity Model. It assumes that there was a relatively recent common ancestral population of *H. sapiens* in Africa that had already evolved most of the anatomical features typical of modern humans. This population differentiated regionally in Africa and then expanded beyond that continent about 100 kya to *completely replace all other populations* of archaic hominins in the Old World over a relatively short period of time. In its strict form, this model demands the genetic extinction of all non-African archaic hominins from the Old World by these expanding populations of anatomically modern humans from Africa. As we shall see, these two models lead to different predictions concerning the evolution of *H. sapiens* that can be tested in the fossil record (Table 12.2).

Actually, many paleoanthropologists now adhere to various intermediate versions of the above two models with either a single origin and major admixture with expansion or a continuity in many but not all geographical regions, with especially the Neandertal regions experiencing replacement through genetic swamping. Two of the most popular versions are the African Hybridization Model (Bräuer, 1989) and the Assimilation Model (Smith et al., 1989), both of which envision some Neandertal and anatomi-

Table 12.2   Predictions from Models of *H. sapiens* Evolution

Aspect	Multiregional Model	Single-Origin Model
Geographic patterning of human evolution	Continuity of pattern from middle Pleistocene to present	Continuity of pattern only from late Pleistocene appearance of *H. sapiens* to present
	Interpopulation differences high; greatest between each peripheral area	Interpopulation differences relatively low; greatest between African and non-African populations
	Intrapopulation variation greatest at center of human range	Intrapopulation variation greatest in African populations
Regional continuity and establishment of *H. sapiens*	Transitional fossils widespread	Transitional fossils restricted to Africa, population replacement elsewhere
	Modern regional characters of high antiquity at peripheries	Modern regional characters of low antiquity at peripheries (except Africa)
	No consistent temporal patterns of appearance of *H. sapiens* characters between areas	Phased establishment of *H. sapiens* suite of characters: (1) Africa, (2) southwestern Asia, (3) other areas
Selective and behavioral factors involved in the origin of *H. sapiens*	Factors varied and widespread, perhaps related to technology; local behavioral continuity expected	Factors special and localized in Africa; behavioral discontinuites expected outside Africa

From Stringer and Andrews (1988).

cally modern human contributions to the later Pleistocene human gene pool. Although these alternative models are often characterized as modifications of the Out of Africa Model they are, in fact, more logically considered modifications of the Multiregional Continuity Model, since they envision at least *some* genetic contribution of archaic hominins to modern human populations, not the complete replacement by expanding anatomically modern humans from Africa demanded by the Out of Africa Model.

The main characteristic of all these models is that they present reasonably falsifiable expectations given existing fossil and biochemical evidence. This is the evidence we turn to next.

WHAT DO THE MOLECULES SAY?

All about "Eve"

Based on the initial mitochondrial DNA (mtDNA) comparisons of modern human populations, some geneticists concluded that the mtDNA of all modern humans was derived from a single African (woman) ancestor who lived approximately 290–140 kya (Cann et al., 1987; Stoneking et al., 1992; Vigilant et al., 1991). In popular parlance, this "woman" became known as "Mitochondrial Eve." If her story were true as stated, then the Multiregional Continuity Model would be dead and the Out of Africa Model alive and well. But how true is it?

Mitochondria are organelles in the cell's cytoplasm containing circular strands of DNA, each having their own genetic coding system. Mitochondrial DNA has a couple of characteristics that make it a potentially powerful tool for human evolutionary studies: (1) unlike nuclear DNA, mtDNA has a clonal mode of inheritance that is passed down only through the maternal lines, thereby avoiding some of the complexities caused by recombination during sexual reproduction;[4] (2) mtDNA evolves about 5–10 times faster than nuclear DNA, thus allowing more molecular changes to accumulate in less time so that more recent evolutionary events can be studied. The importance of this mode of inheritance to anthropological studies is that a pair of breeding individuals can transmit only one type of mtDNA to their offspring, and this is solely through the maternal line (Weiss, 1987).

It seems well established that mtDNA variability in modern human populations is relatively low compared to other primates; for instance, variability is less than 10% of that found in five orangutans and two crab-eating macaques, only about 33% of that found in 10 common and two pygmy

---

[4]It is now suspected that this may not be strictly true and that some recombination may take place (Awadalla et al., 1999). As molecular biologist Svante Paabo is quoted as saying about Mitochondrial Eve: "There was no such woman if there was recombination" (*Science*, 283: 1438, 1999).

chimpanzees, and only about 65% of that found in four lowland gorillas sampled from one small area of Africa (Cann et al., 1987). In fact, several chimpanzee and bonobo (pygmy chimpanzee) clades, and even some single social groups, retain substantially more mtDNA variation than is seen in the entire human species (Gagneux et al., 1999). In addition, it has been reported that mtDNA haplotypes, or the unique sequence of alleles in the mtDNA, are fairly homogeneous among most (nonaboriginal) human populations: about 94% of human mtDNA diversity can be found within any one major geographical population, whereas only about 6% distinguishes most human populations from one another (Melnick and Hoelzer, 1993). These types of genetic data were immediately seized upon by Out of Africa enthusiasts to support the claim of a recent common ancestry of modern *H. sapiens* compared to other primate groups.

As mentioned, it was originally claimed that all modern human mtDNA could be traced back to a single common female ancestor (Cann et al., 1987; Stoneking, 1993; Stoneking and Cann, 1989; Stoneking et al., 1986). Why was this proposal so startling? After all, it is hardly surprising that all mtDNA sequences could be traced back to one woman. As Washington University population biologist Alan Templeton (1993) wrote:

> All homologous DNA copies in a population must ultimately be traceable to a common ancestor under the theory of evolution (and) since mtDNA is maternally inherited in primates, this implies that all copies of human mitochondrial DNA must trace backward to a common female ancestor. The same is true for any species in which mtDNA is maternally inherited, so all such species have a mitochondrial "Eve."

What was startling was the second part of the claim, that molecular biologist could pinpoint this Mitochondrial Eve in both time and space. This claim led to a number of secondary hypotheses, dubbed by the press "The African Eve Hypothesis": (1) this common female ancestor lived in Africa around 200 kya (with a range of 290–140 kya using mtDNA restriction-site data or a narrower range of 249–166 kya using mtDNA sequence data); (2) the mtDNA phylogeny determined by molecular biologists was also a population phylogeny, meaning not only that all mtDNAs in modern humans trace back to this common female ancestor but also that all modern humans were derived from the same geographical portion of Africa in which this common female ancestor lived; and (3) anatomically modern humans first evolved in Africa and then spread throughout the Old World about 100 kya, driving all other earlier *Homo* populations to extinction without any genetic intermingling (i.e., a complete genetic holocaust).

These hypotheses were originally based on an analysis of mtDNA restriction-site maps (representing about 9% of the human mtDNA genome) drawn from a sample of 148 humans from five major geographical areas: 20 Africans (18 of whom were African-Americans), 34 Asians, 21 aboriginal Australians, 26 aboriginal New Guineans, and 46 whites (Cann et al., 1987). From these individuals, 134 distinct mtDNA types were identified. The mtDNA differences within and between each of these five "populations" showed that, in general, variability within a population was greater than variability between populations (suggesting that human "races" had only recently diverged) and that the particular mtDNA variation *within* the African population (0.47% sequence divergence) was greater than that *between* Africans and any other geographical group (Fig. 12.6a). From these data, a genealogical tree of the different mtDNA types was constructed using the parsimony analysis computer program *PAUP* (Phylogenetic Analysis Using Parsimony) (Fig. 12.6b) (Swofford, 1991). Two (apparent) features of the resulting tree were particularly noteworthy: (1) there were two primary branches, one leading exclusively to African mtDNA types (mtDNA types 1–7) and the other to all other mtDNA types (mtDNA types 8–134), and (2) the data suggested multiple colonization events, since each "population" stemmed from multiple lineages connected to the tree at widely separated positions (e.g., mtDNA type 49 from New Guinea was more closely aligned to mtDNA type 50 from Asia than to the other New Guinea mtDNA types 26–29). It was also concluded that Africa was the likely source of the entire modern human mtDNA gene pool because one of the two primary branches led exclusively to African mtDNAs while the other included African mtDNAs as well. Moreover, if the common ancestral mtDNA was considered to be African, then the number of intercontinental migrations needed to account for the geographic distribution of the mtDNA types would be minimized (Cant, 1987; Stoneking and Cann, 1989).

A time scale was affixed to this mtDNA tree by assuming that mtDNA sequence divergences accumulated at a constant rate within lineages and that the main source of mtDNA variation was through neutral mutations. Since mtDNA mutations were considered to be largely neutral, with alternative alleles conferring no differential fitness effects on their bearers, their accumulation was considered to be mostly a function of time. However, it is now strongly suspected that selection may actually influence the distribution of both mtDNA and Y chromosome variation in humans, thus violating one of the central assumptions of this model (Hawks et al., 2000a; Thomson et al., 2000). For example, it is now known that mtDNA rearrangements and point mutations are directly linked to more than 100 neurological disorders, thus suggesting that mtDNA is actually under intense natural selection (Curnoe and Thorne, 2003).

This concept, known as "coalescence theory," holds that all genes (alleles) in any extant population descend from a single gene to which they coalesce sometime in the past.[5] If this were the case, it is postulated that

---

[5] In a random mating population at equilibrium, the mean coalesence time (T) is determined by the equation $T = 4N \times [1 - (1/i)]$, where T is the number of generations to coalescence, N is the effective population size, and i is the number of genes under consideration. For example, for any two genes ($i = 2$), T reduces to $2N$ generations; for a large number of genes, T reduces to approximately $4N$. Thus genes in a population with N equal to 1 million individuals would be expected to coalesce to their one common ancestor 4 million generations earlier.

populations having the most variable mtDNA would, by definition, be the oldest, since more time had elapsed for mutations to accumulate within them (it has subsequently been shown that other factors, such as population size, can influence mtDNA variation within populations). However, these calculations neglected one important aspect of strict neutrality theory: that molecular variability is a function of both the neutral mutation rate and the *evolutionary effective population size* (see below) (Avise, 1994).[6] Since the African (African-American) "population" in the original study showed the most mtDNA variability, they were considered to be the oldest. However, even if this were true, it would *not* necessarily follow that the various biological and cultural traits by which we define "modern" humans had an African origin, only that modern mtDNA types had an African origin.

The mtDNA mutation rate was then calculated from what were claimed to be "known" dates of past human migrations into restricted geographical areas: 30 kya for the peopling of New Guinea, 40 kya for Australia, and 12 kya for the New World. By using these dates, the mean rate of mtDNA divergence within humans was determined to be 2–4% per million years (but as we shall see below, these estimates are highly suspect). No reason was given to explain why a narrow 2–4% range was used in the original study given that the true range was reported to be 1.8–9.4% (Stoneking et al., 1986).

Using a figure of 0.57% for the average sequence divergence that has accumulated since the common human mtDNA ancestor and a rate of 2–4% change per million years, it was determined that all surviving mtDNA types "coalesced" to a common ancestor some 290–140 kya (these dates were later stretched to 500–50 kya) (Stoneking and Cann, 1989). Similarly, it was also calculated that the first migrations out of Africa carrying modern mtDNA types occurred 180–90 kya, or even possibly as recently as 105–23 kya.

Fig. 12.6. (a) Intrapopulational vs. interpopulational mtDNA divergences in five modern human populations. Values of mean pairwise sequence divergence between individuals within populations are on the diagonal; values below the diagonal are the mean pairwise sequence divergences between individuals belonging to two different populations. For example, mean sequence divergence within African populations is 0.47% (on the diagonal); mean sequence divergence between Australian and African individuals is 0.40% (below the diagonal). (b) Genealogy of 134 mtDNA types among 148 people in five different geographic regions. Two (apparent) features of this tree are noteworthy: (1) there are two primary branches, one leading exclusively to African mtDNA types (mtDNA types 1–7) and the other to all other mtDNA types (mtDNA types 8–134), and (2) the data suggest multiple colonization events since each "population" stems from multiple lineages connected to the tree at widely separated positions (e.g., mtDNA type 49 from New Guinea was more closely aligned to mtDNA type 50 from Asia than to the other New Guinea mtDNA types 26–29). (Stoneking and Cann, 1989.)

---

[6]Effective population size (N_e) is the number of individuals in an ideally behaving, random-mating population that has the same magnitude of genetic drift as the actual population of interest. Its calculation always assumes that the genes concerned are neutral and unlinked to genes that may be perturbed by selection.

MtDNA Divergence within and between Five Human Populations

Population	% Sequence Divergence				
	1	2	3	4	5
1. African	0.47				
2. Asian	0.45	0.35			
3. Australian	0.40	0.31	0.25		
4. Caucasian	0.40	0.31	0.27	0.23	
5. New Guinean	0.42	0.34	0.29	0.29	0.25

(a)

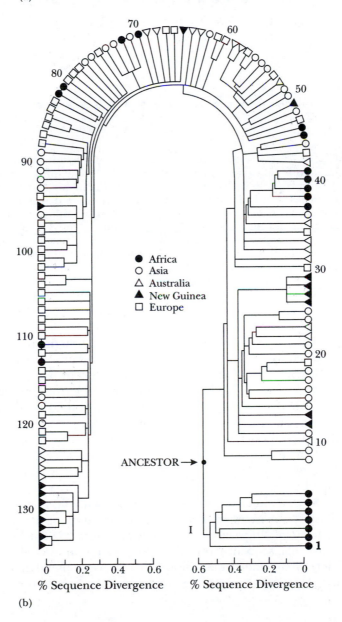

(b)

469

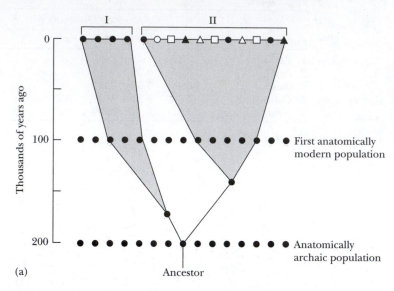

Fig. 12.7. (a) Scenario relating mtDNA results to an African origin for modern humans. Solid circles represent African mtDNA, and other symbols represent non-African DNA, as in Figure 12.6. The shaded branches I and II represent the two branches seen in Figure 12.6b and encompass the descendants of the common mtDNA ancestor. (b) Expected genealogical relationship of human mtDNA if resident populations in Asia and Europe contributed mtDNA to modern populations. The shaded group to the right (*Not Observed*) shows that if the resident non-African population had contributed mtDNA to modern human populations, then we would expect to observe a third group of non-African mtDNA types approximately five times more divergent than any types observed. (Stoneking and Cann, 1989.)

The mitochondrial data also implied that there would have been no interbreeding between African Eve's descendants and the indigenous archaic *Homo* populations they encountered throughout the Old World because it was thought that only the mtDNA types traceable to Eve were currently present throughout the Old World. If interbreeding had occurred, the mtDNA lineages of the non-African archaic resident populations would have been mixed into the gene pools of the invaders (Fig. 12.7). The unavoidable conclusion seemed to be that all Old World *H. erectus* and other archaic hominins not ancestral to this African Eve were wiped out without interbreeding.

Several other studies based on analyses of nuclear DNA polymorphisms—for example, DNA sequence variation at the β-globin locus and patterns of single nucleotide polymorphism (SNPs)—also purported to show that sequence diversity was greatest in African populations and thereby concluded that European and Asian populations (including Native Americans and Aboriginal Australians) were more closely related to

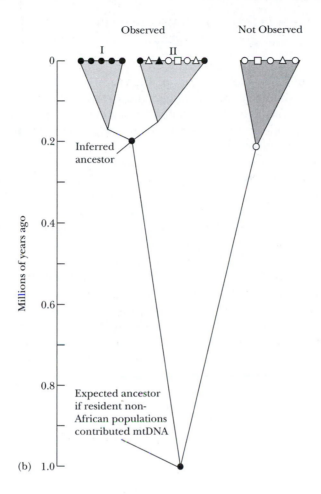

each other than any were to sub-Saharan African populations (Cavalli-Sforza et al., 1993; Fullerton et al., 1995; Mountain et al., 1992; Rouhani, 1989; Wainscoat et al., 1989; Yu et al., 2002).

However, one study simultaneously scored both nuclear DNA polymorphisms and mtDNA polymorphisms from the same individuals, thereby performing the *first direct test* of concordance of the mtDNA with the nuclear DNA that would be expected under the Out of Africa replacement hypothesis but not necessarily under a model with some gene flow. The results of this direct test of concordance were quite clear: The two data sets were discordant at the population level (Jorde et al., 1995).

So, has molecular biology really solved the question of modern human origins? How "solid" are these conclusions drawn from the molecular data? There are some problems.

CRITICISMS OF THE OUT OF AFRICA MODEL

Two of the most outspoken critics of the Out of Africa Model have been University of Michigan anthropologist Milford Wolpoff and Australian anthropologist Alan Thorne (Wolpoff, 1989a,1989b; Wolpoff et al., 2001). How do they, and others, parry what seems to be the open and shut case presented by the molecular biologists?

First, they argue that the dates of the first human migrations into New Guinea, Australia, and the New World used by molecular biologist to "calibrate" the molecular mtDNA clock may seriously underestimate the appearance of modern humans in these regions. Moreover, other mtDNA studies suggest that mtDNA mutation rates, and therefore dates of coalescence, may not be as constant as presented by proponents of the Out of Africa Model (Avise, 1994; Hawks et al., 2000a; Wallace et al., 1985). If modern humans arrived in New Guinea, Australia, and the New World much earlier than the assumed 40–12 kya, and/or mtDNA mutation rates are proven to be more variable than proponents of the Out of Africa Model suppose, then this could seriously affect the calculation of mean mtDNA mutation rates for assessing times of divergence. Thus a more accurate estimate of mean rate of mtDNA divergence within humans may be very different from the 2–4% per million years used by proponents of the Out of Africa Model.

Ultimately, however, their arguments have to explain why there is apparently so little mtDNA variation in non-African populations if these populations had been evolving in situ for hundreds of thousands of years or more. Several possibilities can be entertained. First, such diversity may actually exist but has not yet been discovered. Second, it is possible that indigenous non-Africans did contribute mtDNA types to the dispersing African populations, but they were subsequently lost by either selective or random mechanisms. For example, mtDNA types can be lost through drift (differential mtDNA lineage survival) in which one type slowly replaces all others or through population bottlenecks that reduce the population down to small size and limit genetic diversity (Rouhani, 1989). Finally, extremely divergent non-African mtDNA types are not found in modern human populations because they were never contributed by the resident population, leading inevitably to the rather staggering conclusion that the dispersing African populations actually did replace the non-African resident archaic populations without any interbreeding—in other words, the complete genetic holocaust noted earlier.

Wolpoff (1989a) has argued that genealogical "trees" such as those produced by the mtDNA analyses do not necessarily reflect relationships among human populations or their history. This is because tree diagrams assume that population differences arose through population splitting (cladogenesis) and subsequent isolation. Interpretations of such trees assume that the observed differences are the consequence of constantly accumulating random mutations and drift and that gene flow did not occur. He argues, however, that even minimal gene flow between two populations will greatly reduce the observed magnitude of population differences, thus potentially underestimating the time since population splitting. Because everything we know about recent human migrations and invasions indicate significant amounts of gene flow during and after these events, all populations may appear genetically and morphologically more closely related than they really are. In other words, the date of first arrival is not necessarily reflected in the amount of genetic divergence actually seen under the hypothesis of no gene flow with outside populations after the first arrival. Because of gene flow, the divergence is less than expected under the isolation hypothesis, and this creates difficulties in using such dates to calibrate the molecular clock.

Another point that casts some doubts on the accuracy of mtDNA data for interpreting splitting events are the apparent contradictions among geneticists in dating the human/chimpanzee split. If one assumes a constant rate of divergence of mtDNA at 2–4% (an assumption of dubious validity, as we have seen), one would conclude that humans and chimpanzees diverged about 2 mya, a figure that is clearly at odds with the hominin fossil record. However, by using a rate of 0.71% (Nei, 1987), the human/chimpanzee split is calibrated at about 6.6 mya, which is more in line with present paleontological evidence. This same rate gives a divergence time for modern human populations of about 850 kya, a time period that is not incompatible with the human fossil record, for by that time *H. erectus/ergaster* populations had already emigrated from Africa to Eurasia (Gabunia et al., 2001; Swisher et al., 1994). Thus changing the "constant" mtDNA divergence rates by only a small amount makes the mtDNA data more compatible with the Multiregional Continuity Model.

More recently, doubts about the Out of Africa Model have begun to surface even among molecular biologists and systematists as well. As mentioned previously, the original Out of Africa Model was based on a *PAUP* analysis, a computer algorithm designed to find minimum length trees that can account for the observed differences in the mtDNA sequences. One problem, however, is that for large human mtDNA data sets the computer programs cannot possibly find all the possible trees because there are simply too many[7] (Box 12.1). Thus there is no guarantee that the parsimony analysis would, or even could, find the "best" tree. For this reason, it did not take long before others started coming up with even shorter "best fit" trees using the *same* mtDNA data set—in fact one such study found 10,000 shorter trees, most of which did not even require an African origin (Maddison, 1991).

---

[7]For example, the number of unrooted, binary, terminally labeled trees that can be generated for 5 taxa is 15, for 10 taxa is 2×10^6, and for 20 taxa is 2×10^{20} (Swofford, 1991)!

Box 12.1   Selecting "Parsimonious" Trees

A central problem in the Mitochrondrial Eve debate is how to interpret nucleotide sequences in human mtDNA so as to construct a tree that reveals human origins. In parsimony analysis, the DNA sequences are sequentially arranged to build the most "parsimonious" tree—that is, the one that considers all the observed sequences and then determines which requires the fewest mutations over the course of evolution. In this example, five DNA sequences, each five nucleotides long, are shown. In the third position, two people have an A nucleotide and three have a G. If comparison to an ancient sequence such as that of a chimpanzee suggests G was originally at that position, then it follows that a mutation must have given rise to the A. Of the two trees shown, the upper tree arranges the sequences in a way that requires only one mutation; therefore, it would be considered a more parsimonious tree than the lower one, which requires two mutations.

The situation can become much more complex. For example, when we consider the fifth position it suggests that individuals I and II are more closely related than I and III (which was the conclusion when we looked at only the third position). With this new information a computer running the *PAUP* program could create a different tree that is just as parsimonious as the upper tree. Conflicts like these cause the number of equally parsimonious trees to grow exponentially. With large sample sizes the number of equally parsimonious trees may be in the millions. *PAUP* goes about the process of finding the best solution by adding sequences to the tree one at a time and then swapping branches around to find better trees. The trees it finds on any one run are necessarily related to the starting tree, and the shape of that tree is influenced by the order in which the samples were added. To get the best range of possible trees, one needs to sample trees from many runs with samples added in different random orders.

This one study alone demonstrated that the Out of Africa Model as originally presented was invalid (this, in and of itself, doesn't necessarily disprove an African origin, only that the parsimony test does not resolve the issue). In fact, this study pointed out that an ancient migration *into* Africa would be just as parsimonious an explanation of the mtDNA data as a migration out of Africa would be.

Because of these types of criticisms, further mtDNA studies were undertaken, but this time the mtDNA genealogical tree was rooted by using mtDNA data from a chimpanzee as an outgroup comparison.[8] The molecular biologists once again concluded that the most parsimonious tree indicated a relatively recent African origin for modern humans (Hasegawa and Horai, 1991; Stoneking et al., 1992; Vigilant et al., 1991). The issue now seemed resolved once and for all.

Once again, however, other researchers showed that these studies were still seriously flawed, or at the very least, too simplistic (Goldman and Barton, 1992; Hedges et al., 1991; Maddison et al., 1992; Templeton, 1991, 1993). For example, (1) more parsimonious trees could still be generated from the human mtDNA data and furthermore, some of these "more parsimonious" trees still had non-African roots. (2) The divergence between chimpanzee and human mtDNA was so much greater than that within humans that there was little statistical confidence in the placement of the chimpanzee sequence within the human part of the mitochondrial tree. (3) To a significant degree, the genealogical tree determined from the mtDNA data was an artifact of the *order* in which the data had been entered into the *PAUP* program.

Finally, and perhaps most disturbingly, is the revelation that direct measures of mtDNA substitution rates in some modern humans are roughly 24 times higher than estimates derived from phylogenetic studies (Parsons et al., 1997).[9] These newer data indicate a remarkably high substitution rate of approximately 1 change per 33 generations. Assuming a generation time of 20 years, this extrapolates to a substitution rate of 2.5 changes/site/million years, nowhere near the rate of approximately 0.025–0.261 changes/site/million years derived from phylogenetic studies. If one calibrated the mtDNA molecular clock using these newer, empirically derived mutation rates rather than those based on "known" dates from the fossil record, one would conclude that Mitochondrial Eve existed only about 6500 years ago!

Clearly something is very wrong here, but for the moment it is not certain just why empirically determined mtDNA mutation rates differ so greatly from those deduced from phylogenetic studies.

---

[8]One confounding factor in using the chimpanzee as an outgroup is that the control region of their mtDNA is so divergent from humans that multiple substitutions may make it suboptimal as an outgroup (Zischler et al., 1995).

[9]Among other things, this raises the possibility that maternal relatives may actually differ from one another at one or more base positions (heteroplasmy), as was found in the case of Czar Nicholas II, who actually inherited two *different* mtDNA sequences from his mother!

Where does all this leave the Out of Africa Model? One critic of these earlier mtDNA studies concluded that (Templeton, 1993, 1994):

- The mtDNA data do *not* resolve the geographical origin of the human mitochondrial common ancestor.

- The possible time range within which this common ancestor existed is considerably wider than the 290–140 kya commonly cited by the Out of Africa supporters. For example, using the full 1.8–9.4% mtDNA divergence rates, and even assuming a perfect molecular clock, the lower bounds of the 95% confidence intervals of the mtDNA ancestor would be as low as 32 kya (using the 9.4% rate) and as high as 524 kya (using the 1.8% rate). In fact, more recent analyses of all the mtDNA data concludes that there is a 95% probability that the Mitochondrial Eve lived between 481 and 336 kya, assuming a chimpanzee/human split of 4 mya, or between 889 and 622 kya, assuming a human/chimpanzee split of 7.4 mya (Wills, 1995).

- The mtDNA haplotype tree provides evidence for only very recent and geographically limited expansions of human populations; and other than that, the mtDNA haplotype tree reflects restricted gene flow through isolation by distance throughout the entire time period tracking back to the common mitochondrial ancestor.

- The mtDNA and nuclear DNA data are not inconsistent with a Multiregional Continuity Model.

- The claim that Africans have higher levels of mtDNA diversity is lacking in statistical rigor, even though the amount of mtDNA sequence diversity among Africans is apparently more than twice that among non-Africans (Ingman et al., 2000).[10]

- mtDNA divergence measures may be more indicative of effective population size than they are of population ages (see below).

Some of these points are best summed up this way by Templeton (1994):

Because there is no recombination for mtDNA, even a single selected mutation arising in a human population can have a major impact on overall diversity. . . . Diversity measures in DNA regions with little or no recombination often display unusual patterns of diversity relative to the remainder of the genome and/or to interspecific divergence patterns, and these inconsistencies are explained simply by these selective hitchhiking effects. . . . Hence, diversity levels in DNA regions with little to no recombination are unreliable indicators of age. Second, the diversity level in a geographic area can be greatly influenced by current and past

---

[10]However, microsatellite data do show a statistically significant increase in African diversity (Jorde et al., 1997). Some studies do show, however, that the African mtDNA haplogroup is the most divergent among all continent-specific haplogroups and that the ages estimated for each of the continent-specific haplogroups are congruent with the hypothesis that all modern human populations have a common and recent origin from an ancestral *H. sapiens* population in Africa. The sequence divergence of all African mtDNAs is calculated at 0.292%. Using a constant mtDNA evolution rate of 2.2–2.9% per million years, this results in a maximum age for African mtDNAs of 101,000–133,000 years (Chen et al., 1995).

gene flow. These human populations are not isolated; hence, diversity is not a reliable indicator of age. . . . Thus, relative to testing the hypothesis of an African versus non-African origin, diversity measures are irrelevant.

Templeton also notes that when geographical data are overlaid on the mtDNA haplotype tree, a pattern of continental distributions is observed that could have arisen from low levels of recurrent gene flow (isolation by distance) rather than from a single episode of range expansion, such as an Out of Africa replacement. If an African/non-African split had occurred as recently as about 150 kya, genetic distances should reflect the time since that split or, alternatively, should reflect a pattern of recurrent but restricted gene flow among human populations throughout recent human history with lower amounts of gene flow leading to larger genetic distances. One such mechanism for restricted gene flow, isolation by distance, predicts that the most geographically distant populations would have the lowest amount of effective gene flow. A split between Africans and non-Africans would imply that Asians and other non-Africans would be equally distant genetically from Africans, and Asians and Europeans should be equidistant from their common ancestral node. In contrast, the restricted gene flow hypothesis with isolation by distance predicts that Asians should be the most distant genetically from Africans, with Europeans in between. This is exactly what the nuclear data sets support as opposed to the African/non-African split and suggests that all humans constitute a single evolutionary lineage with populations showing regional genetic differentiation because of restricted, but recurrent, gene flow along with some recent regional range expansion.

According to this model, different modern traits could have evolved in different geographical regions and then spread throughout all of humanity by the combined effects of gene flow and selection. Alternatively, modern traits could have arisen first in a single geographical location within the range of ancient humans, which includes Africa, and then spread throughout all of humanity through the combined effects of gene flow and selection. Because gene flow was restricted, regional genetic differentiation among human populations would be expected and could persist even as the genes for anatomically modern traits were spreading. Much of the Out of Africa/Multiregional Continuity Model debate still centers on the myth that replacement of one physical feature with another in a series of fossils can be created only by one population replacing another (by extermination). However, such fossil patterns could simply be a reflection of one genotype replacing another through gene flow and natural selection. The lesson here is that *when dealing with populations that can interbreed, morphological replacement should not be equated with population replacement* (Templeton, 1996).

One last point is in order. There is no logical connection between the date of coalesence of mtDNA (or any other gene) and any particular speciation event—particularly one signaling the emergence of anatomically modern *H. sapiens* (Jorde et al., 1998). As I wrote on another occasion (Conroy, 1998):

> And speaking of coalesence time, why do some writers keep equating modern human mtDNA coalescence time with the origins of "anatomically modern humans?" Why couldn't human mtDNA coalesce back to early *H. sapiens, H. erectus, Otavipithecus* (my personal choice), or sea cucumbers? Why should the two necessarily have anything to do with one another? Answer: they don't!

The Limitations of mtDNA

A partial explanation for the conflicting results of various mtDNA studies may be that, until fairly recently, the limitations of this molecule for evolutionary studies have not been clearly presented.

First, the mitochondrial genome is a small fraction of the total genetic makeup of any organism, including humans, and thus may present a deceptively simple picture of overall genetic similarities or differences within and among populations, particularly in regard to their social structure. For example, in cases in which virtually all males leave the social group into which they are born and all females remain throughout their lives (female philopatry), one would expect nuclear genomic variation (which is transmitted by both sexes and recombined in each succeeding generation) to be spread fairly homogeneously by male migration. Conversely, in such groups mitochondrial genomic diversity, which is transmitted exclusively by the female parent to the offspring, would be expected to be geographically restricted and to exhibit large differences between localities. Both of these expectations are borne out in mtDNA analyses of rhesus macaques (Fig. 12.8) (Melnick and Hoelzer, 1993).

Second, when considerable intraspecific mtDNA variation exists, failure to consider this variation may lead to inaccurate estimates of differences among taxa (Deinard and Kidd, 1999). It must be remembered that a phylogenetic tree generated from mtDNA data is first and foremost a "gene tree"—and there is no a priori reason why it must reflect the underlying "species tree" given that genes will sort randomly during speciation events (Fig. 12.9) (Bailey, 1993).

Third, the notion of a mtDNA molecular clock rests on several assumptions, none of which may be valid: (1) that genetic variation within a taxon is negligible as compared to the differences among taxa and that therefore there are virtually no molecular differences between "parent" and "daughter" species at the time of reproductive isolation; (2) that the rate of nucleotide substitutions must be calibrated by independent estimates of divergence and must be approximately the same in all populations or species (so-called rate constancy); and (3) that the mtDNA mutations are selectively neutral. The first assumption is belied by the known fact that in-

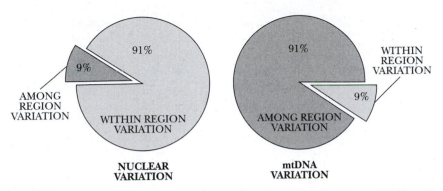

Fig. 12.8. A partial explanation for the conflicting results of various mtDNA studies. The mitochondrial genome is a small fraction of the total genetic makeup of an organism and thus may present a deceptively simple picture of overall genetic similarities or differences within and among populations, depending on their social structure. For example, in social groups in which virtually all males leave the social group into which they are born and all females remain in their natal groups throughout their lives, one would expect nuclear genomic variation (which is transmitted by both sexes and recombined in each succeeding generation) to be spread fairly homogeneously by such extensive male migration. Conversely, in such groups mitochondrial genomic diversity, which is transmitted exclusively by the female parent to the offspring, would be expected to be geographically restricted and to exhibit large differences between localities. In this figure the portions of total rhesus monkey species diversity in the nuclear and mitochondrial genomes that can be attributed to variation within a geographic region (*shaded*) and to differences among regions (*black*) are shown. Note that the distributions are mirror images of one another, in large measure due to the male-biased dispersal pattern of this species. (Melnick and Hoelzer, 1993; Melosh et al., 1990.)

traspecific mtDNA variability is significant in a number of primates (e.g., as high as 8.4% in populations of the pigtailed macaque, *Macaca nemistrina*) (Gagneux et al., 1999; Melnick and Hoelzer, 1993; Ruano et al., 1992). Therefore, at the time of separation, two incipient species may already have a considerable level of mtDNA divergence, the result being that some clock estimates will include significant errors if they assume intraspecific homogeneity at the time of divergence. The second assumption is belied by the fact that several studies have documented differential rates of amino acid and nucleotide sequence evolution in nuclear genes, and recent research also casts doubt on the assumption of rate constancy in mtDNA sequences as well. For example, mtDNA genomes of macaque populations from the Malaysian Peninsula and Sumatra are about 30 times more different than would be expected on the basis of the standard molecular clock. The third assumption is also doubtful, as we will see below. Thus "the use of mtDNA to date past evolutionary events should be regarded as an extremely crude method—a sundial rather than a chronometer" (Melnick and Hoelzer, 1993).

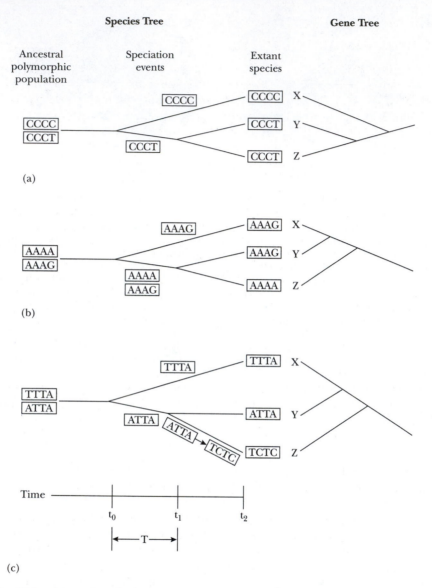

Fig. 12.9.   Means by which a species tree may differ from a gene tree.   Note how alleles may randomly assort during two speciation events (t_0, t_1) involving three lineages from a common ancestral population. T is the time between the two speciation events, measured in generations. (a) The gene tree reflects the true species relationships. This is because the ancestral alleles, represented by a four-base-pair site, segregated into two subpopulations, one of which became fixed along the descent of the species that are most closely related (in this case Y and Z). (b–c) Two situations in which the gene tree could differ from the species tree, depending on how the alleles sort at various speciation events. (Bailey, 1993.)

Of Molecules and Men: Tales from the Y Chromosome

While the mtDNA story tells us something about our maternal genealogy, are there any genetic data that tell us something about our paternal roots? Ideally, for this we need some information from the nonrecombining part of the Y chromosome whose DNA is inherited paternally. Some clues are emerging.

For example, a 729-base-pair **intron** (a part of a gene that is not translated into a protein, as opposed to an exon, which is) at the ZFY locus on the human Y chromosome was sequenced in a worldwide sample of 38 human males (Whitfield et al., 1995). Unlike the situation in other nonhuman primates in which phylogenetically informative sequence variability is found in this intron, no sequence variation at all was found in the human sample (however, five nucleotide differences were found between humans and chimpanzees). Based on the absence of genetic variability at the ZFY locus in a small human sample as compared to that in nonhuman primates, the expected time to coalescence of this gene in the ancestral human male lineage was calculated to be about 270 kya, with 95% confidence limits falling between 0 and 800 kya (Dorit et al., 1995, 1996).[11] Several other studies of Y chromosome polymorphisms also tend to coalesce around 200 kya (some as recent as 50 kya), but with wide confidence intervals that cannot rule out gene flow between regions before the suggested origin of modern humans (Hammer, 1995; Thomson et al., 2000; Underhill et al., 1997). Thus these genetic data seem to weakly reinforce the side of the argument that opts for a single, as opposed to a multiregional, recent origin of modern human origins, although the geographical location of this ancestral Y lineage cannot be determined as yet from these data (Relethford, 2001c).[12]

How can the lack of intraspecific nuclear DNA, mtDNA and/or Y chromosome variation in modern humans, as compared, say, to chimpanzees be explained (Gagneux et al., 1999; Kaessmann et al., 1999; Thomson et al., 2000)?

There are several considerations. First, nucleotide diversity in species is directly proportional to a quantity that population geneticists refer to as effective population size (N_e). All genetic systems seem to agree that the long-term average N_e for the human species through much of the Pleistocene was on the order of 10^4–10^5 (this is not to be confused with the N_c, or total population census size during this time).[13] In other words, all else being equal, a

---

[11]In other words, these researchers are telling us that it could take anywhere from 0 to 800,000 years for *no genetic variability to occur*, a rather odd way of looking at things!

[12]A combined data set derived from three distinct loci linked to the Y chromosome—RPS4Y, SRY, and ZFY—also fails to provide unequivocal support for any single, dichotomously branching species tree linking *Homo, Pan,* and *Gorilla* (Samollow et al., 1996).

[13]One shouldn't be alarmed by this seemingly small effective population size. No large mammalian species has an N_e greater than 10^5 and even species of *Drosophila* with census population sizes on the order of 10^{11}–10^{14} do not have N_e exceeding 10^6 (Kaplan et al., 1989).

smaller population will contain less nucleotide diversity than a larger population. There are several ways in which effective population size can be reduced—for example, during population bottlenecks and/or speciation events. Another way to potentially reduce intraspecific variation at a specific genetic locus is if one genetic variant at the locus becomes favored by selection, thereby causing it to sweep through the population carrying along with it all linked nucleotide sequences on the same chromosome (Hammer, 1995; Hammer and Zegura, 1996).[14] Since much of the Y chromosome does not recombine, it could be particularly vulnerable to such selective sweeps. However, it should also be noted that, like humans, there seems to be very little intraspecific variation in the ZFY gene in *any* of the great apes (gorillas, chimpanzees, orangutans) (Burrows and Ryder, 1997). Hence, inferences based on diversity levels for Y chromosomes and mtDNA may be unreliable, as has been documented for *Drosophila,* in contrasts between regions with and without recombination (A. Templeton, personal communication).

As noted above, the paternally transmitted Y chromosome provides a complement to maternally inherited mtDNA in phylogenetic analyses. The absence of intraspecific variability in human Y-linked loci is usually attributed to a relatively recent common ancestor, a small effective number of males in the population, or selective sweeps that fix the sequences of linked genes on the nonrecombining portion of the Y chromosome. However, as noted above, it has now been determined that there is complete lack of variation in the sex-determination gene ZFY within species of great apes as well as in humans, a situation that contrasts sharply with the high levels of polymorphism found in mtDNA sequences. The clear implication is that there are as yet unknown factors that must limit levels of intraspecific polymorphism in this region of the Y chromosome that render these data problematical in trying to establish Y chromosome divergence times in both great apes and humans (Burrows and Ryder, 1997).

It is also evident that calculating the age of a common ancestor of human DNA sequences highly depends on which models of human demography are used (e.g., models of constant population size versus those of increasing population size) and on differing estimates of effective population size (Brookfield, 1997; Hawks et al., 2000a). As noted above, the original study on the ZFY intron yielded an expected time to coalesence of about 270 kya. Other calculations, however, give age estimates that vary 40-fold, ranging from 17 kya to over 700 kya, depending on the population model and effective population size used in the calculations (Donnelly et al., 1996; Dorit et al., 1996; Fu and Li, 1996; Weiss and von Haeseler, 1996).

---

[14]It must be remembered that in all such analyses one should distinguish between the time to the last common ancestor of the particular human sample analyzed and that to the last common ancestor of all Y chromosomes (Hammer and Zegura, 1996). They may not necessarily be the same thing.

Other data on nuclear DNA are used to bolster the Out of Africa hypothesis (Tishkoff et al., 1996). The DNA in question is a piece of chromosome 12 (CDS4 locus). This locus has a variety of haplotypes in sub-Saharan African populations, seems to lose many of these patterns in northeast African populations, and appears to be dominated by a single pattern in the rest of the world. One interpretation of these data is that they track a series of small populations moving through population bottlenecks as they travel from sub-Saharan Africa through northeast Africa and ultimately to Eurasia, losing DNA variability along the way. Assuming constant rates of nuclear DNA mutation, this study suggests that the migration out of Africa occurred within the last 100,000 years or so.

However, as was the case with mtDNA, other interpretations are possible. For example, genetic diversity in a population is not necessarily a reflection of when it originated. As supporters of the Multiregional Continuity Model have noted, a small, ancient population existing outside of Africa could create a similar genetic picture since small populations also tend to lose genetic diversity. Furthermore, estimates of population divergences based on such a single mutating locus (in this case, estimating the relative ages of the *Alu* deletion in African and non-African populations at the CDS4 locus) should be viewed with caution, since changing some of the assumptions in the calculations lead to migration times out of Africa that are as much as sevenfold times greater than this study indicates (Pritchard and Feldman, 1996).

Other studies on nuclear DNA give similar results—that is, genetic variation seems minimal in human populations but interpretations of coalescence times vary widely. For example, over 55 kilobases from three autosomal loci encompassing *Alu* repeats have been sequenced from diverse human populations, and the nucleotide diversity was found to be very low. In fact, most individuals and populations were identical. These results were not considered compatible with the view that alleles from divergent archaic populations were maintained through multiregional continuity. Instead they were regarded as a signature of a recent single origin for modern humans, with general replacement of archaic populations within the last 50,000 years or so (Knight et al., 1996).

This evidence of a young time of coalescence for nuclear DNA would be compelling, except that reanalysis of these same DNA data again show how dependent these coalescence ages are on assumptions about effective population size and various estimates of DNA mutation rates. For example, the 95% confidence limits on age of coalescence using an effective population size of 5,000 individuals is 116–674 kya (mean = 308 kya), while using an effective population size of 15,000 gives ages of coalescence ranging from 0.246 to 1.134 mya (mean = 574 kya) (Fu and Li, 1997). Obviously, these ages are far in excess of the 50,000 years or so originally reported as supporting an Out of Africa model.

A Rush to Judgment?

Before leaving this section about what the molecules say, we should ask a simple question: Shouldn't studies of mtDNA and nuclear DNA be telling us the same demographic story about modern human origins? Do they? Evidently not.

Genetic evidence, mainly from variability studies of mtDNA, have been used to support the theory that modern human populations passed through a bottleneck (or episodic reduction in size) sometime in the early Late Pleistocene, followed soon thereafter by a large, rapid population expansion. As we have noted, the amount of DNA sequence variation in any region of interest is expected to be proportional both to effective population size and to elapsed time since coalescence, *assuming the DNA sequence variation is selectively neutral.*

One way such nucleotide variation can be described is by constructing a frequency distribution of polymorphic sites within the genomic region of interest. This is done by counting the occurrence of the least frequent base at any one nucleotide site. For example, a mutation present in a single sequence is referred to as a low frequency mutation (frequency class 1). On the other hand, mutations appearing in half the sequences represent intermediate frequency mutations. The frequency distribution of polymorphic sites in mtDNA control regions I and II show an abundance of low frequency polymorphisms and a much smaller percentage of intermediate frequency polymorphisms. What is interesting is that this pattern is not expected when sequences have evolved neutrally and when population sizes have remained stable. Thus the mtDNA data are compatible with either one of two scenarios (or possibly both in humans to at least some extent; i.e., population growth and selection): (1) an initially small population that recently underwent a dramatic size increase; or (2) the mitochondria are under intense natural selection (i.e., they are not selectively neutral). If the mtDNA is telling us the actual demographic history of modern humans, then the nuclear DNA studies should reflect the same "fact."

However, when one compares similar frequency distribution patterns for polymorphic nuclear genomic sites (e.g., lipoprotein lipase, several X-linked genes such as those for PDHA1, dystrophin, myelin proteolipid protein, glycerol kinase) something quite different emerges—an abundance of intermediate frequency polymorphisms (Harris and Hey, 1999a). Unlike the mtDNA pattern, the nuclear gene pattern is more consistent with a scenario in which mutations were occurring on deep (or old) branches of a population's genealogical tree and within a population whose size has remained somewhat constant. For example, in the case of the dystrophin gene it appears that African chromosomes derive from at least two separately evolving lineages, one of which underwent range expansion on different continents as well as in Africa where it subsequently mixed with another local lineage represented today by a large fraction of African-specific haplotypes. Such genetic admixture may help explain some of the greater genetic diversity found in sub-Saharan populations (Labuda et al., 2000). Thus it appears that the nuclear genes and the mitochondrial genes may not be telling the same demographic history of modern humans.

The case of the X-chromosome gene for PDHA1 is instructive in this regard (Harris and Hey, 1996b). Analyses of this gene, which codes for a key enzyme in sugar metabolism, suggests that one archaic hominin population subdivided into two geographically separate populations at least 200 kya, one of whom gave rise to modern Africans and the other to all non-Africans. These two populations have retained a fixed genetic difference between them—all the Africans having one particular base in the PDHA1 gene sequence and all non-Africans a different one. This is the first study to show a fixed regional difference in human genes and is strong evidence of the historical subdivision of an ancestral population. These data show no evidence of an expanding human population and thus are in conflict with mtDNA patterns on this point. The implication of this study for the Out of Africa vs. the Multiregional Continuity Model is obvious: since these two populations (African vs. non-African) were already in existence before the known appearance of anatomically modern *H. sapiens,* the transformation from archaic hominins to anatomically modern *H. sapiens* must have occurred in geographically subdivided ancestral populations (i.e., Multiregional Continuity Model).[15]

So we come back to the same dilemma—what might explain the low variation found in modern human mtDNA? One possibility is that mitochondrial genes form a single linkage group that may be susceptible to natural selection. Selection for a favorable mtDNA may have spread rapidly through the population (selective sweep), thereby producing the pattern of low variation seen today. In a sense, then, maybe it was just the mtDNA that underwent a bottleneck and subsequent expansion, not the rest of the genome.

Given all these uncertainties, perhaps an alternative model is called for—one that combines elements of both the Multiregional Continuity and Out of Africa Models.

A Third Choice: The "Weak Garden of Eden" Hypothesis

As we have discussed, there are four general lines of genetic evidence that have been used to support a recent African origin model: (1) the

---

[15]See Disotell (1999) for a critique of this study.

relatively low degree of among-group variation in modern humans, (2) the generally higher levels of within-group variation in sub-Saharan African populations, (3) the (apparent) higher levels of genetic diversity in sub-Saharan African populations, and (4) the very small estimated average effective population size of the human species over the past 100,000–200,000 years.

Approximately 10% of modern human genetic variation can be accounted for among groups, whereas 90% of the variation occurs within groups. While this could be taken to support the Out of Africa model of a relatively recent common origin for modern human groups, the same pattern of genetic variation could simply be a consequence of relatively high migration rates between modern groups, a notion compatible with either the Multiregional or Out of Africa model.

One problem with using levels of within-group variation to assess a population's relative age is that it requires a critical assumption that is sometimes overlooked. For this method to work, a newly formed daughter population (such as non-Africans) must experience a genetic bottleneck to reduce its level of within-group variation; if it were not for this genetic "reset button" the new daughter population would be expected to have the same within-group variation as its parent population. Indeed, if 93–95% of genetic variation is due to genetic differences among individuals of the same population and only 7–5% of genetic variation to differences among major population groups (King and Motulsky, 2002; Rosenberg et al., 2002), it stands to reason that any new species that arises by the eventual genetic isolation of one population will still have a great deal of genetic diversity, *unless* it has gone through some type of severe population bottleneck during the speciation process. Obviously, the overall effect of any bottleneck would be a function of both parental and daughter population sizes, the duration of the bottleneck, the population size after the bottleneck, and the length of the recovery period (Relethford, 1995). Thus levels of within-group variation more likely reflect past population bottlenecks than relative age.

There are several possible explanations for the (apparent) higher levels of genetic diversity in sub-Saharan African populations including higher levels of gene flow into Africa, a larger African population, or both. Naturally, one would expect to find greater genetic diversity in African populations if that population were substantially larger than populations in other parts of the world (which is almost certainly the case for most of human history). In fact, any significant genetic variances between Africa and any other region in the Old World would be essentially nullified if the effective population size of Africa were as little as three times that of any of those other regions (Relethford and Harpending, 1994, 1995; Relethford and Jorde, 1999). Given that human occupation of Europe was a relatively late event (at least compared to Africa) and that much of at least northern Eurasia was probably uninhabitable for much of the Pleistocene because of climatic extremes, this seems like a very safe inference.

Let's consider another approach, this time by comparing fossil samples instead of genes across time. Several studies have claimed that more recent fossil hominins tend to be more similar to earlier samples from Africa and the Middle East than they are to earlier samples from within their own geographic region—although as we will see later, this does not seem to be true of some hominins on the "periphery" of the human geographic range, such as Australia (Wolpoff et al., 2001). Supporters of the Out of Africa Model take this as support for their position, arguing that if the Multiregional Continuity Model were true, fossil samples from any single geographic area would be expected to be more similar to one another than to African fossils through time. In other words, this is the pattern the Out of Africa model would predict if all recent modern humans came from Africa within the last 100,000 years or so.

This seems like a reasonable assumption, that most genes in modern European populations would derive from European ancestors, most genes from modern Asian populations would derive from Asian ancestors, and so on. But this may not be a correct assumption. Using a simple population genetics model of gene flow, John Relethford (1999), from the State University of New York, explains why.

Let us assume two populations of constant size over time. Population A consists of 4000 reproductive adults and population B consists of 1000 reproductive adults. Assume that each population exchanges only 10 mates per generation. Using a simple migration matrix of probabilities, the probability of a gene in population A coming from population A (endogamy) is 0.9975, while the probability of a gene in A coming from population B (exogamy) is only 0.0025. Both populations are highly endogamous, but over time the total accumulated ancestry in each population will change. For example, after 100 generations, even at this low level of gene flow, population A will have derived roughly 14% of its genes from population B, and population B would have derived roughly 57% of its genes from population A. After 200 generations, both populations will have derived the majority of their ancestry from population A. The matrix will continue to change until an equilibrium is reached, at which time both populations would reflect 80% ancestry from population A and 20% from population B.

What this simple exercise means for the Out of Africa versus the Multiregional Continuity Model debate is that, given enough time, the accumulated ancestry of any population will be dominated by the largest population. The larger the population (i.e., Africa), the greater the proportion of its genes are contributed to later generations. Thus the finding that some later European fossils may show certain similarities to earlier African fossils rather than to earlier European ones does not necessarily support the Out of Africa Model to the exclusion of the Multiregional Continuity Model, given that African populations were much larger than European ones through most of human history (Relethford, 1999, 2001a, 2001b, 2001c).

One other possibility can be considered. It seems that in large mammals there is some genetic evidence to suggest that species inhabiting glaciated regions tend to have lower genetic variability than their close relatives living in temperate and/or tropical regions. This is purportedly due to population bottlenecks accompanying serial recolonization of northern latitudes following retreats of the Pleistocene glaciers (Sage and Wolff, 1986).

A further problem with dendrograms of genetic distances between different geographic groups is that the genetic distances are assumed to reflect primarily a branching process, when in fact these distances may reflect overall dissimilarity resulting from a variety of causes, including various migration models. For example, the genetic distinctiveness of Africans could have resulted from small numbers of migrants between each region combined with a larger African population.

The implications of all these scenarios suggest a third model of modern human origins, one that incorporates aspects of both the Multiregional Continuity and the Out of Africa Models. The **Weak Garden of Eden Model** proposes that modern humans originated in a small local region, as postulated by the recent African origin model, and that this population underwent a genetic bottleneck sometime in the last 100,000 years or so. The age of the coalescent mtDNA reflects population size in the past, in this case suggesting that the effective population size in the late Middle Pleistocene (i.e., 200 kya) was on the order of 1,000–10,000 (Harpending et al., 1993). Such a small estimated pre-expansion effective population size argues against the multiregional model in that it seems unlikely that such a small population could be spread over three continents and remain connected by gene flow for a long time. However, evidence of a dramatic population expansion after the bottleneck also rules out the classic Out of Africa replacement model, which holds that modern humans arose in Africa and replaced other human populations while expanding.

According to the Weak Garden of Eden Model, genetic evidence indicates that population divergence occurred before population expansion: Modern humans arose in Africa and, starting about 100 kya, separated into small regional populations that were weakly connected by gene flow. These groups experienced population growth or recovery from the bottleneck several tens of thousands of years after regional divergence

(Harpending et al., 1993). More specifically, these results suggest that modern human populations divided from separate ancestral populations that were relatively isolated from each other sometime before 50 kya. Major population expansion then took place between about 80 and 30 kya in Africa and later, perhaps about 40 kya among ancestors of Europeans during the Upper Paleolithic (Marth et al., 2003). The ancient effective population size of our ancestral species was perhaps on the order of 1,000–10,000 females.

An alternate scenario, and one still compatible with the genetic data, is that the low estimated population size reflected a bottleneck that reduced the size of the human population at some time before population expansion; however, this pre-bottleneck population may still have been large enough to accommodate the multiregional model. In this scenario, some environmental catastrophe could have caused a specieswide bottleneck (such as the supereruption of Mount Toba in Sumatra about 71 kya, which could have produced a volcanic winter in Eurasia) (Rampino and Self, 1992), followed by a population explosion in the late Pleistocene (Ambrose, 1998, 2003; Gathorne-Hardy and Harcourt-Smith, 2003).

The multiregional model holds that humans expanded throughout the world over 800 kya and have remained united by gene flow ever since. Proponents of the Weak Garden of Eden Model argue that it seems unlikely that a small number of females (say 1,000–10,000) spread across three continents could have remained strongly connected by gene flow. Conversely, the Out of Africa hypothesis holds that modern humans originated in Africa around 100 kya and then spread rapidly throughout the world, replacing earlier populations. This implies that the expansion of the modern human population occurred along with the initial separation of regional populations (races) and is also inconsistent with predictions of the Weak Garden of Eden hypothesis, which holds that racial populations separated about 100 kya and then underwent population expansion about 30,000 years later. But could several widely separated populations experience roughly simultaneous bottlenecks? Perhaps, if such bottlenecks were caused by cultural innovation that swept across the entire species, by a change in climate, or by the Toba volcano about 71 kya. In the latter two cases, the disruption should have affected other species as well, although this has not been demonstrated to everyone's satisfaction (Ambrose, 1998, 2003; Gathorne-Hardy and Harcourt-Smith, 2003).

Thus this model concludes that the ancestral modern human population separated from a small initial population roughly 100 kya and that most of these separate populations experienced a bottleneck, or an episode or growth, several tens of thousands of years later (Rogers and Jorde, 1995).

We can now summarize the salient features of the three main models of modern human origins as follows:

- *Out of Africa Model:* posits that modern humans appeared in a subpopulation of archaic hominins fairly recently, perhaps as a new species, and spread continuously and rapidly over much of the Old World, replacing all other archaic *Homo* populations in their wake.

- *Weak Garden of Eden Model:* posits that modern humans appeared in a subpopulation and spread slowly over several tens of thousands of years, then later expanded from separated daughter populations bearing modern technologies, such as those of the African Late Stone Age or the European Upper Paleolithic.

- *Multiregional Continuity Model:* posits that the entire (or at least widely dispersed components) archaic hominin gene pool contributed to the gene pool of modern humans and that "racial" or geographic distinctions were maintained through isolation by distance.

CONCLUSIONS: A "MOSTLY" OUT OF AFRICA MODEL

Even though molecular evidence indicates that mtDNA sequences in modern humans coalesce to one ancestral sequence (probably from Africa), it would be incorrect to conclude (as has much of the press and lay public) that this so-called Mitochondrial Eve was the one mother from whom all humans descended. Instead, Mitochondrial Eve should be regarded as a mtDNA molecule (or the woman who carried that molecule) from which all modern mtDNA molecules descended. This is a big difference. As University of California biologist Francisco Ayala (1995) points out, the notion, popularized in the press, that all humans descend from only one African woman about 200 kya is based on a confusion between gene genealogies and individual genealogies. Whereas gene genealogies do coalesce toward single ancestral DNA lineages, individual genealogies do not, increasing by a factor of two each generation—that is, each of us has two parents, four grandparents, eight great-grandparents, and so on. Therefore, the fact that any one gene coalesces back in time to an ancestral DNA lineage does not negate the fact that many other ancestors existed at the same time from whom other genes were inherited. As Ayala (1995) notes:

> A person inherits the mtDNA from the great-grandmother in the maternal line, but also inherits other genes from the three other great-grandmothers and the four great-grandfathers (about one-eighth of the total DNA from each great-grandparent). The mtDNA that we have inherited from the mitochondrial Eve

represents a four-hundred-thousandth part of the DNA present in any modern human. The rest of the DNA, 400,000 times the amount of mtDNA, was inherited from other contemporaries of the mitochondrial Eve.

The same conclusion holds for the ZFY gene inherited along paternal lines. While this "ZFY Adam" is the individual from whom all humans have inherited this particular gene, he is not our only ancestor in his generation. We have inherited thousands of other genes from many of this Adam's contemporaries.

So where does all this somewhat confusing and contradictory molecular evidence leave us? Part of the problem is that many molecular biologists continue to make the same kinds of mistakes that many paleoanthropologists have been guilty of—namely, overreaching the limitations of their data. In the case of molecular biologists it is by making far-reaching claims based on analyses of often miniscule parts of the genome, whether from mtDNA, Y chromosomal regions, X-linked DNA regions, or autosomal DNA regions. In the case of paleoanthropologists it has been by the "atomization" of traits without due regard for the developmental and/or functional integration of those traits. Throughout this text we have seen numerous examples of how paleoanthropologists are now addressing these issues. With few exceptions, the same cannot be said as yet for molecular anthropology.

One major exception is the recent study in which haplotype trees for mtDNA, Y chromosomal DNA regions, X-linked DNA regions, and several autosomal DNA regions have been analyzed and combined into a single picture of hominin evolution that is internally consistent with *all* these data (Fig. 12.10) (Templeton, 2002). In this model, the hominin lineage started in Africa and initially spread out of Africa about 1.7 mya. This is based on the fossil data from Dmanisi (Republic of Georgia) and Java discussed earlier. The evidence for gene flow with isolation by distance among Old World populations is increasingly evident and indicates that recurrent gene flow occurred among Old World hominin populations from the present back to at least 600 kya and probably further. Both the mtDNA and Y chromosome DNA data and the autosomal DNA data suggest a minimum of at least two Out of Africa expansion events, the older one being between about 420 and 840 kya and the younger between about 80 and 150 kya. *Most important, these data show that the most recent Out of Africa event represented a major movement of peoples characterized by interbreeding, not replacement.* This is also the most likely scenario for the earlier Out of Africa event as well. The conclusion that there were at least two major Out of Africa expansions after the initial expansion of *H. erectus/ergaster* is also consistent with the archeological record documenting the expansion of Acheulean tool-making traditions in the Middle Pleistocene.

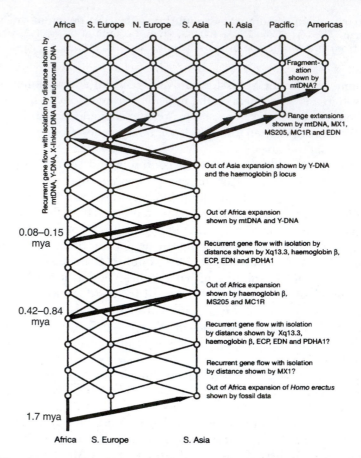

Fig. 12.10. A new model of human evolution.   Major expansions of human populations are indicated by *heavy arrows.* Genetic descent is indicated by *vertical lines,* and gene flow by *diagonal lines.* The timing of inferences lacking resolution at the 5% level and/or not validated by more than one gene locus are indicated by *question marks.* (From Templeton, 2002.)

Thus the reason that Africa has such a large genetic effect on modern humans is that at least three major population expansions originated from there, although the genetic impact is not as complete as it would have been under a total replacement Out of Africa Model. These results are more compatible with various models that envision population expansion coupled with gene flow, not replacement (i.e., Multiregional Continuity, Assimilation, and Mostly Out of Africa Models) (Relethford, 2001c; Smith et al., 1989; Wolpoff et al., 2000), and show the importance of examining many DNA regions, not just one locus or DNA region, when making phylogenetic inferences.

Having reviewed some of the arguments for and against the Out of Africa Model put forward by molecular biologists, we turn, in the final chapter, to what the fossil evidence has to say on the subject—for the fossil record is the ultimate reality check of what actually did happen in human evolution. We begin with the fossil evidence from Africa and then conclude with the evidence from Eurasia.

CHAPTER XIII

What the Fossils Say About "Modern" Human Origins: A Reality Check

INTRODUCTION

How do the molecular data discussed in the last chapter fit the fossil data concerning the origins of "modern" *H. sapiens* populations? As we have seen, mtDNA comparisons have mainly been used with varying success to support the Out of Africa Model—namely, that *H. sapiens* emerged in Africa about 140–100 kya and that all present-day humans are descendants of that African population. Proponents of this model argue that the alternative Multiregional Continuity Model, which posits that *Homo* has been present in Eurasia for much of the Pleistocene and that the transition from "archaic" to modern humans took place in parallel in different parts of the world, is refuted by the mtDNA data. If the Multiregional Continuity Model is correct, they argue, one would expect to see a great deal of mtDNA variation in modern Eurasian populations, which, as we have seen, is apparently not the case. Their conclusion, then, is that early Eurasian populations of *H. erectus* and/or other archaic hominins contributed no surviving mtDNA lineages to the gene pool. In the last chapter we reviewed some of the problems with this strict interpretation.

We also noted some of the different variations of the Out of Africa Model. For example, various multiple dispersal models also posit a single origin for modern humans in Africa, the essential difference between the two is that the former emphasizes dispersal and differentiation beyond Africa whereas the latter emphasizes dispersal and differentiation within Africa as well. Such dispersal and divergence within Africa would lead to variable populations leaving Africa at different times and possibly by different routes,

Table 13.1   Inferences about Hominin Behavior and Ecology

Hominins and Time Periods (Years Ago)	Inference	Nature of the Evidence
Early Pleistocene hominins (1.5–0.1 million)	Occupation of new habitats and geographic zones	Sites in previously unoccupied areas of eastern Africa; first appearance of hominins outside Africa
	Definite preconception of tool form	Biface handaxes of consistent shape made from rocks of varying original shape
	Manipulation of fire	Indications of fire differentially associated with archeological sites
	Increased levels of activity and stress on skeletons	Massive development of postcranial and cranial bones
Late Pleistocene hominins (100,000–35,000)[a]	Increased sophistication of tool kit and technology; still slow rate of change to tool assemblages	Larger number of stone-tool types than before; complex preparation of cores
	Intentional burial of dead and suggestion of ritual	Preservation of skeletons; some with objects
	Maintenance of high activity levels (locomotor endurance; powerful arms) and high levels of skeletal stress (e.g., teeth used as tools)	Robust skeletons, especially thick leg bones and large areas for muscle attachment on arm bones; prominent wear patterns on incisor teeth
(35,000–10,000)[b]	Decreased levels of activity and stress on skeleton	Decrease in skeletal robusticity (also seen in early modern humans before 35,000 years ago)
	Enhanced technological efficiency	Innovations in stone- and bone-tool production (e.g., blades and bone points)
	Innovations in hunting and other foraging activities, including systematic exploitation of particular animal species	Evidence of spearthrower and harpoon, and trapping netting of animals; animal remains in archeological middens
	Colonization of previously uninhabited zones	For example, sites in tundra in Europe and Asia; colonization of the Americas (Australasia was probably first inhabited around 50,000 years ago)
	Elaboration of artistic symbolic expression and notation	Engraving, sculpting, and painting of walls and figure repetitive marks on bones; jewelry
	Surge of technological and cultural differentiation and change	Variations in tool kits over space and time
	Harvesting and first cultivation of grains; first domestication of animals	Evidence of seeds and fauna from sites dating to the end of the Pleistocene

From Potts (1992).

[a]Neandertals.

[b]Fully modern *H. sapiens*.

one through northeastern Africa to the Middle East and the other through the Horn of Africa toward the Arabian peninsula. These migrations would then be followed by population expansions and dispersals from these secondary geographical areas occurring at different rates in different regions, depending on levels of gene flow and demographic pressures, thereby accounting for the regional variation found among Upper Pleistocene hominins (Lahr and Foley, 1994).

Models like these, and others, are fine, but ultimately their veracity needs to be gauged by how well, or how poorly, their predictions fare against a reality check—the fossil record. As we emphasized before, models tell us what *may* have happened in human evolution but only the fossil record can tell what actually *did* happen. So we conclude our story of human evolution with such a reality check by reviewing what the fossils themselves say (and sometimes do not say) about modern human origins. Table 13.1 provides a summary of the behavioral and ecological inferences that can be drawn from the fossil and archeological record of this latest phase of human evolution (Potts, 1992).

FOSSIL EVIDENCE FROM AFRICA

South Africa

Some of the most important fossil and archeological sites relevant to the question of modern human origins are in southern Africa (e.g., Die Kelders Cave, Equus Cave, Border Cave, Klasies River mouth, and possibly Florisbad) (Fig. 13.1. Of these, the only one to yield a clearly archaic-looking *Homo* fossil is the late Middle Pleistocene site at Florisbad where a hyena-gnawed partial cranium, morphologically similar to such East African specimens as Ngaloba and Omo II dated to about 130–120 kya (see below), was recovered. The other South African sites mentioned above contain more modern-looking hominins and date to the earlier part of the Late Pleistocene, some 130–60 kya (Deacon, 1992; Thackeray, 1992).

Die Kelders   Die Kelders consists of two contiguous caves situated on the southwestern coast of South Africa. The site contains both Middle Stone Age (MSA) and Late Stone Age (LSA) layers separated by a long hiatus of archeologically sterile strata. The LSA layers contain several fully modern adult human bones and a child's partial skeleton dating to about 1.5–2 kya. Excavations in the MSA layers have produced a number of small quartzite artifacts (mainly elongated flakes) and 27 hominin specimens (24 isolated teeth, a mandibular fragment, and two manual middle phalanges) (Grine, 2000). These levels are tentatively correlated by luminescence and electron spin resonance (ESR) dating to ^{18}O stage 4 at the beginning of the last

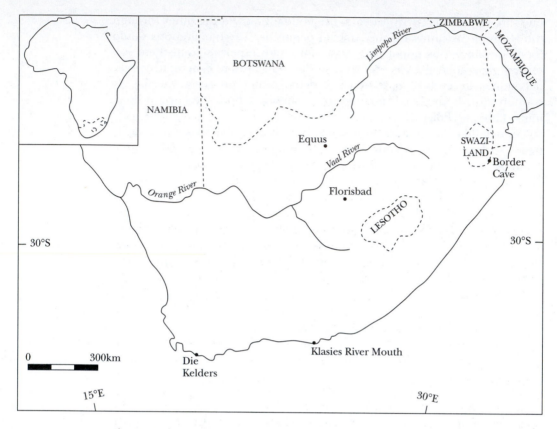

Fig. 13.1. Several of the more important fossil and archeological sites relevant to the question of modern human origins in South Africa (Die Kelders Cave, Equus Cave, Border Cave, Klasies River mouth, and Florisbad).   (Thackeray, 1992.)

glaciation, around 71–57 kya (Feathers and Bush, 2000; Schwarcz and Rink, 2000; Thackery, 2002). Micromammals are abundant in the cave fauna and were probably deposited by roosting owls. That these MSA people exploited animal resources less broadly or effectively than did their LSA successors is suggested by the nature of the fauna, particularly the predominance of less dangerous wild game (such as eland relative to wild pigs and Cape buffalo), the dominance of penguins over flying birds, and the absence of fish. This has important implications for reconstructing the evolution of early modern human behavior in the Upper Paleolithic (Klein and Cruz-Uribe, 2000). The hominin remains from the MSA levels represent a minimum of 10 individuals and provide some sketchy evidence for the anatomical modernity of the MSA inhabitants of southern Africa. Although the teeth are as large as some Neandertal teeth, they are both morphologically and metrically within the range of modern Africans (Grine et al., 1991; Klein, 1987).

Equus Cave   Equus Cave, located only 500 m from the australopith-bearing cave at Taung, has yielded an extensive late Pleistocene fauna that was probably accumulated by hyenas. Both MSA and LSA tools are present. The LSA level, known as layer 1A, is clearly Holocene in age (less than 10,000 years old). Circumstantial geological evidence suggests that layers 1B, 2A, and 2B were deposited between about 103 and 33 kya.[1] Thirteen hominin specimens, including 12 isolated teeth and one fragmentary left mandibular corpus containing two molars, have been recovered from these four layers. Unfortunately, their exact age is uncertain, since none of the hominin teeth was recovered with in situ MSA artifacts. These hominin remains are all modern in appearance (Grine and Klein, 1985; Klein et al., 1991; Morris, 1991).

Border Cave   The hominin fossils from Border Cave in Natal include a partial adult cranial vault, two mandibles (one partial and one nearly complete), a largely complete skeleton of a 4- to 6-month-old infant, and some postcranial fragments. The deposits are over 4 m thick. At least four of the specimens come from MSA levels. Specimens BC 1 and BC 2, a cranium and a mandible, respectively, were recovered from a guano pit and are of unknown stratigraphic provenance (however, BC 1 cannot be younger than 33 kya, the age of the youngest Stone Age horizon). New ESR dates suggest that the partial cranium BC 1 may date to over 175 kya; however, both BC 1 and BC 2 may date to only about 82 kya. Chemical analyses associate both specimens with an infant skeleton (BC 3), reportedly a burial that was excavated from below the third white ash layer (3WA). The BC 3 infant's skeleton and another mandible (BC 5), if in situ, are dated on the basis of ESR to about 76 kya (Grün and Beaumont, 2001; Grün et al., 2003). The infant skeleton was also associated with a perforated *Conus* shell, which must have originated from the seacoast at least 80 km to the east. This is one of the only ornaments or ritual objects, and the only grave, known within a South African MSA context (Thackeray, 1992).

The white ash layer is an important marker bed since it contains the distinctive **Howiesons Poort** artifact assemblage, comprising many replaceable bits or inserts specifically designed for hafting in composite tools. Howiesons Poort assemblages are too old to be accurately dated by radiocarbon methods, but an age of 45–75 kya is the best estimate (Fig. 13.2). The production of such stone inserts for composite tools is significant at such an early date, since in a European context these are the kinds of artifacts that one finds in much more recent Upper Paleolithic industries associated with anatomically modern populations. ESR dates on bovid enamel from the site give ages of between 50 and 90 kya for the human remains and a date of about 70 kya for a mandibular fragment (BC 5) from layer 3WA (the other remains may be of similar age) (Grün and Stringer, 1991; Grün et al., 1990a).

---

[1]These dates are uncertain given that radiocarbon dates on organic residues from bones in layer 2B give ages of only about 16,000 years (Klein et al., 1991).

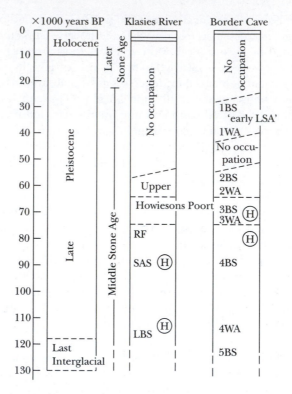

Fig. 13.2. Dating and stratigraphy of Border Cave and Klasies River. *H*, hominin fossils. (From Deacon, 1992.)

Although the Border Cave hominin sample is often described as "anatomically modern," this is by no means uncontested. For example, multivariate statistical tests show that BC 1 falls outside the morphometric envelope of modern Africans and is almost four times as dissimilar from living Africans as the average dispersion within these diverse populations (Corruccini, 1992, 1994). In addition, a fragmentary humerus from the site is more similar to that of early *Homo* than it is to anatomically modern humans (Pfeiffer and Zehr, 1996). Furthermore, the excellent state of preservation of an infant skeleton (BC 3) and a nearly complete adult mandible (BC 5) warrants caution when assuming great antiquity for some of the Border Cave hominins (Sillen and Morris, 1996).

Klasies River   The best evidence for anatomically modern humans in early Late Pleistocene populations of southern Africa comes from the caves at Klasies River mouth situated on the Tsitsikama coast of South Africa (Figs. 13.1–13.3) (Deacon, 1992; Deacon and Geleijnse, 1988; Deacon and Shuurman, 1992; Grine et al., 1998; Rightmire and Deacon, 2001). The cave

Description	Location in Chamber Complex	Stratigraphic Level	KRM Designation (1967–68 excavations)
Right mandibular corpus with P_4 to M_2. Three loose teeth probably belong with this individual.	cave 1	SAS member	13400. Also 14691, 14693 14694?
Anterior part of mandibular corpus including symphysis. One loose tooth may belong with this individual.	cave 1	SAS member	14695. Also 14696?
Right mandibular corpus with M_1 to M_3.	cave 1	SAS member	16424
Left mandibular corpus.	cave 1	SAS member	21776
Damaged mandible with M_1 and M_2, right P_4 and M_1.	cave 1B	Base of SAS member	41815
Fragment of left maxilla with alveoli and part of palate.	cave 1A	LBS member	—
Fragment of left maxilla with M^1.	cave 1A	LBS member	—
Frontal fragment, with nasal bones attached.	cave 1	SAS member	16425
Left zygomatic bone.	cave 1	SAS member	16651
Vault fragment, including parts of right parietal and frontal squama.	cave 1A	SAS member	41658
Left clavicle, broken at sternal end.	cave 1	SAS member	26076
Proximal end of left radius.	cave 1	SAS member	27889
Left first metatarsal.	cave 1	SAS member	—
Lumbar vertebra.	cave 1	SAS member	—
Proximal portion of right ulna.	cave 1A	SAS member	—

(a)

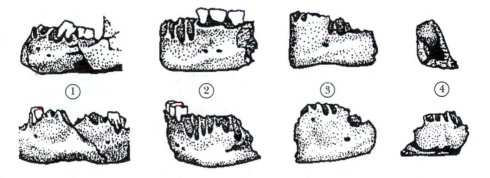

(b)

Fig. 13.3. (a) Some of the more complete hominin specimens from Klasies River. (From Rightmire and Deacon, 1991.) (b) Lateral and anterior profiles of four Klasies River mandibles. *1*, 41815; *2*, 13400 (reversed); *3*, 21776; *4*, 14695. (From Frayer et al., 1993.)

deposits consist of a 20-m-thick cone of sediment resting against the cliff face and filling side caverns within the cliff face. Geological evidence shows that the deposits began to accumulate at the end of the last interglacial, about 130–118 kya as sea levels dropped to near their present levels from their maximum interglacial height. Quantities of hearth ash, shell, animal bones, and human remains have been recovered in association with an MSA industry. The culture/stratigraphy at Klasies River mouth is recognized from the base upward as MSA I, MSA II, Howiesons Poort, and MSA III (Singer and Wymer, 1982).

It is well established that the site was first inhabited by humans during the last interglacial, about 120 kya, and was apparently abandoned about 60 kya. This may be due to increased periods of aridification in southern Africa because the last interglacial period saw peaks of arid dune building at approximately 95–115 kya, 41–46 kya, 20–26 kya, and 9–16 kya (Stokes et al., 1997). The bulk of the human fossils come from two strata: the Light Brown Sand (LBS) member and the overlying Sands-Ash-Shell (SAS) member. Two maxillary fragments were recovered from the LBS member, and these are the oldest hominins from the site. A last interglacial date of approximately 120 kya for these specimens is supported by oxygen isotope measurements on shell, aspartic acid dating, and uranium-thorium (U-Th) dating (Deacon et al., 1988). These oldest Klasies River hominins are more similar to anatomically modern individuals than they are to such late early hominins as LH 18, ER 3884, and Jebel Irhoud I (Bräuer et al., 1992) (see below).

Most of the hominin fossils come from the overlying SAS member, for which ESR analysis of associated bovid enamel gives dates in excess of 90 kya (equivalent to ^{18}O stage 5c) (Grün and Stringer, 1991; Grün et al., 1990b). The human fossil material is fragmentary and consists mainly of upper and lower jaws, isolated teeth, a frontal bone, partial temporal bone, and other cranial pieces. Postcranial remains are limited to portions of ulna, radius, lumbar and atlas vertebrae, metatarsal, and clavicle. As many as 10 individuals are represented at the site. The hominin sample shows a degree of robusticity and strong sexual dimorphism that is coupled to a modern facial and dental morphology. There is little resemblance to Neandertal morphology or to that of more archaic *Homo*. For example, mandibular bodies tend to be deeper anteriorly than posteriorly, a chin eminence is variably present, and there is no retromolar space (Lam et al., 1996). In addition, none of the jaws exhibits the type of internal symphyseal buttressing common to Neandertals. The few postcranial elements are fully modern and, with the exception of the archaic-looking ulna, none shows any distinctive Neandertal features (Churchill et al., 1996; Grine et al., 1998; Rightmire and Deacon, 1991).[2]

[2]See Smith (1992) for a cautionary view.

One interesting question that emerges from this fossil material is what constitutes a late archaic from an early modern African face? For example, some late archaics like Florisbad, Ngaloba, and Irhoud I (see below) all have very small faces that would easily fit several of the mandibles/maxillas from Klasies River. Only the Klasies River frontal shows a real contrast with known regions of late Middle Pleistocene African archaics.

There are few artifacts in the overlying Rockfall (RF) member. However, the upper member contains numerous Howiesons Poort and MSA III artifacts and hearths in association with several isolated human teeth and two parietal fragments, which are correlated to ^{18}O stages 4–5a (an age in excess of 60 kya) (Rightmire and Deacon, 1991). The MSA people of Klasies ate shellfish, the meat of various sea and land mammals, and plant materials having underground bulbs (**geophytes**).[3]

The fossils are broken and burnt and show cut marks and impact fractures, perhaps reflecting cannibalism at the site (White, 1987). None of the hominins is from deliberate burials.

As mentioned, the individuals also show a marked degree of morphological variation and sexual dimorphism. For example, some specimens are quite robust (presumably males) and others quite gracile (presumably females), and two of the four mandibles lack a chin. Because of this, some anthropologists have suggested that designating the Klasies River hominins as anatomically modern *H. sapiens* may be misleading, unless the phrase is broadened to include a wider morphological range than recent or extant populations would suggest (Caspari and Wolpoff, 1990; Frayer et al., 1993; Wolpoff and Caspari, 1990). However, even with that caveat in mind, the most important thing about Klasies River is that it securely documents the association of certain morphological "trends" characteristic of modern humans with MSA assemblages as early as about 100 kya in southern Africa. As we will see below, new dates from sites in southwestern Asia, particularly Qafzeh and Skhul in Israel, also show that anatomically modern humans were present in that area around 100 kya—and new discoveries in Ethiopia show that they were in East Africa even earlier. It is ironic, as we shall see later in the chapter, that only Neandertals were present during this same period in western Europe.

Florisbad   One other pertinent discovery from South Africa is the Florisbad cranium recovered from the depths of a warm lithium spring deposit in South Africa's Orange Free State in 1932. The cranium consists of frontal and parietal pieces and the incomplete right side of the face. Its major features include a low, broad, prognathous face; rectangular orbital margins separated by a wide, flattened nasal bridge; and rounded some-

[3]The discovery of early Middle Stone Age artifacts in an emerged reef terrace on the Red Sea Coast of Eritrea indicates that hominins were exploiting marine food resources about the same time in East Africa as well (Walter et al., 2000).

what projecting browridges. The forehead is very broad and rounded, not like the flatter and narrower frontal region of the Kabwe and Saldanha crania (Singer, 1958). A recent reconstruction of the specimen shows it to be intermediate in morphology between the more archaic Kabwe (Broken Hill) and Saldanha specimens and the more premodern Middle/Late Pleistocene crania from Jebel Irhoud I of North Africa (Morocco), and Eliye Springs, Ngaloba (Laetoli 18), and Omo 2 from East Africa (Clarke, 1985b).[4] This latter African group makes a plausible ancestral form for the transitional or early modern populations at Klasies River, Irhoud 2, Omo 1, Dar-es-Soltane 5, and Border Cave, all dated to 120–50 kya and associated with Middle Paleolithic industries (Stringer, 1989). The Florisbad cranium is beyond the range of radiocarbon dating, and may date to 250 kya based on new ESR dating techniques (Grün et al., 1996).

East Africa

Ethiopia: Middle Awash (Herto, Aduma), Omo   The most convincing, as well as the earliest dated, fossils representing early anatomically modern humans are three recently described crania from Herto, Ethiopia. The two adult and one immature hominin crania, along with associated stone tools and fauna, were discovered in the Herto member of the Bouri Formation (Middle Awash) and are dated by ^{40}Ar-^{39}Ar to between 160 and 154 kya (Clark et al., 2003; White et al., 2003)—although there is some question as to the reliability of the minimum age (Faupl et al., 2004). No hominin postcrania have yet been reported. Cranial remains representing four adult anatomically modern hominins have also been reported from somewhat younger deposits at Aduma (about 105–79 kya) (Haile-Selassie et al., 2004a).

The most complete Herto cranium (BOU-VP 16/1) is large and robust and has an endocranial volume of about 1450 cc, at the high end of the modern human range. The overall impression is of a very long and high cranium. The great height of the cranium is reflected in the fact that the distance between the articular eminence and the occlusal plane exceeds that found in a comparative sample of 2000 modern human crania. The length of the cranium exceeds that found in most other fossil hominins as well as in a comparative sample of over 3000 modern humans (glabella to occipital length is about 220 mm). The occipital bone has a prominent external occipital protuberance and is strongly flexed. Its occipital angle (103°) is more acute than typically seen in most modern crania but unlike the Neandertal occipital there is no occipital bun or suprainiac fossa. The mastoid process is large and projecting, more so than in Neandertals or

---

[4]The Singa (Sudan) calvaria has a mixture of modern and early characteristics and may actually be a rare example of an early *H. sapiens* African population, as new uranium series (U-S) and ESR dates suggest an age of at least 133,000 years (^{18}O stage 6) (McDermott et al., 1996).

even modern humans. The infraorbital plate is flattish (oriented paracoro-
nally) with a distinct canine fossa. The face is broad with only moderate
alveolar prognathism, a condition very different from the drawn out midfacial region typical of Neandertals. As in all modern humans, the greatest
interparietal breadth is high up on the cranial vault.

The second adult specimen (BOU-VP 16/2) is even larger in comparable parts. The immature cranium (BOU-VP 16/5) was restored from over
180 fragments. Based on modern dental standards, the individual was
probably around 6–7 years old at the time of death.

All three Herto crania show evidence of postmortem cultural modification (i.e., defleshing cut marks) probably made by hominins using very
sharp obsidian flake edges. Comparative ethnographic studies suggest that
these types of cut marks are probably indicative of some sort of mortuary
practice (Clark et al., 2003; White, 1992).[5]

The cranial morphology of both the adult and the immature Herto
crania clearly show that these hominins were not Neandertal-like. Instead,
their overall size and morphology are much more reminiscent of crania
seen in anatomically modern *Homo sapiens*. This is particularly evident in
the high cranial vault and relatively large frontal and parietal sagittal dimensions. However, they are not completely modern in all aspects. As
their describers state: "They sample a population that [was] on the verge
of anatomical modernity but not yet fully modern" (White et al., 2003).

There is apparently little similarity of the Herto crania to any particular
modern African population. In fact, in terms of such features as overall
size, morphology, and facial robusticity, some Australian and Oceanic individuals would actually be more similar. Overall, however, the Herto hominins provide an excellent morphological and temporal link between
earlier, more primitive, African hominins such as Bodo and Kabwe and
later, more derived, anatomically modern hominins such as found at
Klasies and Qafzeh (White et al., 2003).

The associated stone tools are of particular interest (Clark et al., 2003).
The stone-tool kit includes both Acheulean (e.g. cleavers and bifaces) and
Middle Stone Age (e.g., Levallois cores and flakes) elements. Other East
African sites such as Gaddemota (Ethiopia) and Kapthurin (Kenya) indicate that some Acheulean assemblages had already incorporated new elements typical of the MSA by about 280 kya. These sites, and the new Herto
tool assemblage, reinforce the view discussed earlier that this transition
probably occurred much earlier in Africa than in other parts of the Old
World (McBrearty and Brooks, 2000). There is strong evidence at Herto
that the hominins were butchering large mammals, including both adult
and newborn hippopotamids and various bovines.

---

[5]The earliest evidence of cultural modification of hominin remains is the cutmarks present
on the early *Homo* StW 53 from Sterkfontein. The earliest record of hominin defleshing is
found on the Bodo cranium (Pickering et al., 2000; White, 2000).

The more complete cranium from the site of Aduma (ADU-VP 1/3) consists of most of the parietal, occipital, and part of the frontal. The cranium shows a mosaic of features shared with such specimens as Omo, Skhul, and Qafzeh (see below) and anatomically modern *Homo sapiens,* including its high vault profile, rounded occipital, well-curved parietals, and overall size. Its lacks any diagnostic features that would align it with Neandertals (Haile-Selassie et al., 2004a).

With the discovery of anatomically modern humans at Herto and Aduma, the Middle Awash has now provided fossil evidence of every major grade of hominin evolution spanning the last 5–6 million years: the australopith grade by a number of taxa (e.g., *Ar. kadabba, Ar. ramidus, A. afarensi, A. garhi*), the *H. erectus* grade by the 1.0-million-year-old Daka material, the archaic hominin grade by the 600,000-year-old Bodo material, and the anatomically modern human grade by the 160,000-year-old Herto material.

Other fossil material relevant to modern human origins has been recovered from Ethiopia's Omo region. Omo I, consisting of cranial and postcranial fragments, was recovered from the base of member 1 of Omo's Kibish Formation and is dated to about 130 kya. The cranium is said to exhibit some modern-looking features, such as its more rounded occipital region and moderately developed browridges (Leakey, 1969). A second calvaria, Omo 2, is thought to be about the same age, although this is uncertain because it was a surface find (Fig. 13.4). Unlike Omo 1, its braincase is long and low and the occipital region is strongly curved, as in the more archaic-looking Kabwe (Broken Hill) cranium. The frontal bone is

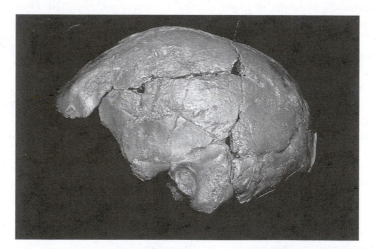

Fig. 13.4.   Lateral view of the Omo 2 cranium.   Its braincase is long and low and the occipital region is strongly curved as in the more archaic-looking Kabwe (Broken Hill) cranium. The frontal bone is relatively broad and flattened, but the supraorbital tori are appreciably less thickened than in other specimens of archaic *H. sapiens.* (Photo courtesy of F. Smith.)

relatively broad and flattened, but the supraorbital tori are appreciably less thickened than in other specimens of archaic hominins. A third hominin specimen, Omo 3, consists of only frontal and parietal fragments and is dated to about 30 kya.

Given the anatomical variability expressed in this Omo sample, some anthropologists have suggested that Omo 1 and 2 may represent different populations, with Omo 1 being from a more anatomically modern population and Omo 2 from a more archaic one (Rightmire, 1989; Stringer, 1989). Whatever the correct interpretation, the important point is that none of these crania shows any significant similarities to the European Neandertals, all being more modern in appearance.

Tanzania, Kenya (Ngaloba, Eliye Springs)   The cranium from the Ngaloba Beds at Laetoli, Tanzania (LH 18), found in 1976, is about the same age as the older Omo Kibish specimens (Day et al., 1980) and was excavated in direct association with MSA artifacts and fauna (Fig. 13.5). Two U-S ages for the site are about 129 kya and 108 kya; a date of 120 kya is based on geological correlations to the Ndutu Beds at Olduvai. In some morphological features LH 18 is reminiscent of the Kabwe cranium, but these similarities should not be overemphasized because LH 18 has a number of more modern-looking features as well. These include considerable facial and nasal

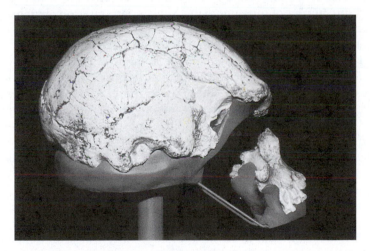

Fig. 13.5.   The cranium from the Ngaloba Beds at Laetoli (LH 18).   In some morphological features LH 18 is reminiscent of the Kabwe cranium, but these similarities should not be overemphasized because the cranium has a number of more modern-looking features as well, including considerable facial size reduction, slight postorbital constriction, a canine fossa, moderately thickened (although continuous) browridges, and greatest cranium breadth situated higher on the parietal bones rather than lower down on the side of the cranium near the supramastoid crests. (Photo courtesy of E. Delson and Department of Antiquities, Dar-es-Salaam, Tanzania.)

size reduction, slight postorbital constriction, a canine fossa, moderately thickened (although continuous) browridges, and greatest cranial breadth high up between the parietal bones rather than lower down near the supra-mastoid crests (Cohen, 1996; Rightmire, 1989; Smith, 1992).

Another, probably similarly aged, hominin cranium is from Eliye Springs on the west shore of Lake Turkana, Kenya. Overall, it shares many of the archaic and modern features noted above for the LH 18 cranium. For example, while both the low cranial vault and the broad cranial base recall archaic *Homo* morphology, the size and shape of the frontal, parietal, and occipital bones align it more with *H. sapiens* (Bräuer and Leakey, 1980; Bräuer et al., 2004).

North Africa

Mugharet el Aliya, Rabat, Dar-es-Soltane, Zouhra   The first anatomically modern humans from North Africa were discovered in 1939 by Carleton Coon at the site of Mugharet el Aliya (Tangier). The finds consisted of an isolated M^2, a left maxillary fragment containing two unerupted premolars, and an unerupted canine. They were associated with the **Aterian** stone-tool industry, a North African tool tradition marked by the predominance of tanged artifacts that have narrow projections from their base for securing them to hafts and endscrapers. The Aterian seems to have evolved directly out of the underlying Mousterian tradition (Hublin, 1992; Minugh-Purvis, 1993).

In 1959 a more complete mandible from Rabat (Temara) was discovered. The Temara mandible was initially thought to be associated with an Acheulean industry but later excavations indicate an Aterian level for this fossil as well. In 1975 a partial cranium was found at the same site, which included the occipital, part of the parietals, and the left supraorbital portion of the frontal. The Temara occipital and supraorbital have been described as essentially modern in appearance.

That same year human fossils were found in a cave at Dar-es-Soltane II. Three individuals were represented: a partial cranium preserving part of the upper face and an associated hemi-mandible (Dar-es-Soltane 5), an adolescent mandible, and a juvenile calvaria. The Dar-es-Soltane 5 cranium is more robust than the Temara specimen, particularly in facial breadth dimensions and in its well-developed browridge and glabella region. However, more modern-looking features are apparent in the lateral view, in which it can be seen that the face is flattened with only moderate alveolar prognathism and the cranial vault is high. In terms of overall cranial morphology, however, these Aterian people are characterized by an enlarged masticatory apparatus (and associated structures) and pronounced postcanine megadonty.

In 1977–78 a mandible and canine, also associated with an Aterian industry, were discovered at Zouhra cave.

Accurate dating of these hominins is still somewhat problematic since all seem to lie beyond the limits of radiocarbon dating. One thermal luminescence (TL) date of about 41 kya has been obtained from the cave at Zouhra. Currently, the best age estimates for most of these fossils are between about 20 and 40 kya (Hublin, 1992).

Jebel Irhoud   The only North African site that has yielded a reasonable sample of older Mousterian hominins is the cave at Jebel Irhoud, Morocco, where four hominins were recovered between 1961 and 1969: Irhoud 1, a fairly complete adult cranium; Irhoud 2, an adult calvaria; Irhoud 3, a child's mandible; and Irhoud 4, a child's humerus. It is significant that the associated stone tools, with sidescrapers predominating, were manufactured using the Levallois technique, hinting that the Jebel Irhoud specimens may be older than the fossils from North Africa discussed above. Aterian endscrapers and tanged artifacts are absent from the Irhoud deposits.

The first hominin from the site, the Irhoud 1 cranium, was discovered in 1961 and, once again, shows a combination of archaic and modern features (Fig. 13.6). Its cranium is long and wide, and the vault is relatively low, within the range of variation seen in Neandertals or other archaic *Homo*. However, the convexity of the frontal bone is more vertical than in Neandertal crania and lies within the modern range. In addition, the occipital bone lacks the protruding occipital torus so typical of Neandertals. Irhoud 1 differs from *H. erectus* crania in that the lateral sides of the cranium are nearly parallel and the parietal swellings are superiorly positioned. The supraorbital tori are moderately developed and the face is broad, but midfacial prognathism does not exceed the modern range. Cranial capacity has been estimated at 1305–1480 cc. A second calvaria (Irhoud 2) was discovered in 1962 and is similar to Irhoud 1.

A juvenile mandible (Irhoud 3) was recovered in 1968, and a juvenile robust humeral shaft was recovered in 1969. While the Irhoud 3 mandible is robust, it does not show any unequivocal Neandertal derived characters, or **apomorphies** (Hublin and Tillier, 1981). Its combination of a modern-like chin associated with especially large cheek teeth is reminiscent of the Qafzeh-Skhul hominin sample from the Near East, therefore excluding the Irhoud population from the Neandertal clade and aligning it more with the first modern humans of the Near East.

The Irhoud cave may correlate to ^{18}O stage 5e; if so, the Irhoud hominins predate the classic Neandertals of western Europe. Several ESR dates have been run on horse teeth from the site and give ages of 90–125 kya and perhaps even much older (some dates correlate with ^{18}O stage 6 at 190–130 kya) (Grün and Stringer, 1991). Studies of associated fauna suggest steppe and desert conditions.

In the earlier anthropological literature, the Irhoud hominins were often treated as North African Neandertals, or at least Neandertal-like, but this view is changing. It now appears that while there was a steady evolution

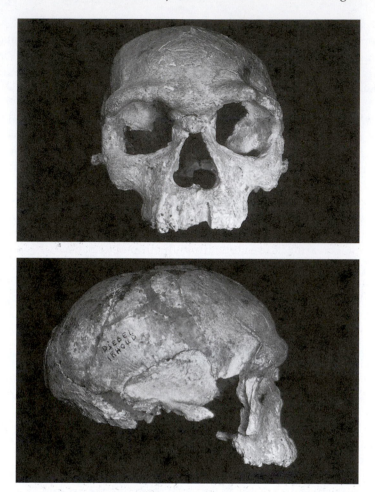

Fig. 13.6. The hominin cranium Jebel Irhoud 1. The cranium is long and wide, and the vault is relatively low, within the range of variation seen in Neandertals or other archaic *Homo*. (Photo courtesy of R. Klein.)

of Neandertal-like features in western European hominins through the Middle to Upper Pleistocene (e.g., at Atapuerca), this trend was not so apparent in the North African hominin sample. As a result, some paleoanthropologists believe that by the beginning of the Upper Pleistocene there may have been two very different hominin populations on either side of the Strait of Gibraltar, implying that the Mediterranean was a substantial barrier to population migration during this time period. Thus, if the Irhoud population is considered a hominin grade immediately preceding the first modern humans and if Africa is the "cradle" of modern humans, then this cradle was large enough to encompass early modern populations stretching all the way from South Africa to North Africa.

As we have now seen, fossil evidence that helps document the evolutionary sequence from late archaic hominins to early modern *H. sapiens* in Africa continues to accumulate. How do they affect the Out of Africa or Multiregional Continuity Models? Proponents of the Out of Africa Model maintain that at least some of these specimens (e.g., Eliye Springs, Omo 1, Dar-es-Soltane 5) show more similarities to Upper Paleolithic modern Europeans (e.g., Cro-Magnon 1) than western European Neandertals do and, therefore, are more suitable ancestors for modern European populations. Their assumption is that modern humans first evolved in Africa, then spread into the Near East and then to Europe, where they ultimately replaced the local Neandertal populations (Bräuer and Rimbach, 1990). However, while this simple replacement theory may explain the situation in western Europe, events in central Europe and the Near East are far more complex, as we shall see.

So, for example, does the discovery of 160,000-year-old anatomically modern humans (like those from Herto) that predate classic Neandertals by about 100,000 years effectively rule out Neandertals from any genetic role in the ancestry of modern humans? Does it finally kill off the Multiregional Continuity Model? It really depends on how one reads the fossil "tea leaves" and the logical deductions that follow from them. Here are just a few questions to ponder.

First, should we be surprised to learn that hominins living in Africa about 160 kya do not look like classic Neandertals? Not really. If classic Neandertal skeletal biology and associated physiology reflect adaptations perfected over tens of thousands of years in the Pleistocene to life in the cold higher latitudes of glacial Eurasia (as all evidence suggests), then one might argue that *no* hominin evolving in the tropics of Africa would ever be expected to share such classical Neandertal morphology.

Second, far from disproving the Multiregional Continuity Model, one might argue that the fossil hominin grade sequence now known from the Middle Awash actually *demonstrates* it unfolding through the Plio-Pleistocene of eastern Africa. Unfortunately, there is no comparable fossil hominin sequence in the world to compare with that of the Middle Awash, but certainly supporters of the Multiregional Continuity model would strongly argue that at least the sequence of *H. erectus* grade, through archaic hominin grade, to anatomically modern human grade is as demonstrable in various geographical regions of both Europe and Asia as it is in the Middle Awash.

Third, the discovery of *any* African hominin may actually have relatively little relevance to the specific question of whether or not Neandertals contributed genetically to modern human populations. One might argue that the question can ultimately be answered only by relevant in situ fossil, archeological, and/or genetic data (e.g., Neandertal DNA) from Eurasian sites that can demonstrate either Neandertal extinction or genetic assimilation into later Eurasian populations.

Fourth, one might argue that there is still no behavioral (i.e., archeological) clue as to what would make Herto-like hominins so superior to contemporary, or even later, Neandertal populations thereby causing the latter's complete replacement. As far as we know, Middle Palelithic tool assemblages did not differ significantly between Neandertal and anatomically modern populations for tens of thousands of years (e.g., Tabun and Skhul).

And finally, one might argue that any modification of a strict Out of Africa scenario (i.e., complete replacement model) that envisions both Neandertal and anatomically modern human contributions to the modern human gene pool, no matter how limited the Neandertal contribution may actually turn out to be (e.g., African hybridization model [Bräuer, 1989], the assimilation model [Smith et al., 1989], or various multiple dispersal models [Lahr and Foley, 1994]), should more logically be considered modifications of a Multiregional Continuity Model of hominin evolution, not modifications of an Out of Africa Model.

Perhaps it is now time to finally come to grapple with the Neandertals in more detail.

FOSSIL EVIDENCE FROM EUROPE: THE NEANDERTAL QUESTION

Although Cormac McCarthy was not describing the Neandertals when he wrote (1993): "They are gone now. Fled, banished in death or exile, lost, undone. Over the land sun and wind still move to burn and sway the trees, the grasses. No avatar, no scion, no vestige of that people remains. On the lips of the strange race that now dwells there their names are myth, legend, dust"—he may just as well have been.

As we have seen, from about 300 to 35 kya, the fossil record appears to demonstrate the relatively gradual development and establishment of the Neandertal morphotype in Europe. The time of transition from Neandertal to modern *H. sapiens* in Europe appears to have an east to west gradient, occurring at about 34 kya in eastern Europe but several thousand years later (about 30–28 kya) in western Europe. Remarkably, Neandertals evolved gradually in Europe for over several hundred thousand years but then abruptly disappeared over a relatively short time span (Klein, 2003; Stringer, 1989; Zeuner, 1958).

In Europe, the transition from Middle to Upper Paleolithic assemblages occurred about 45–35 kya, much later than in either Africa or western Asia (Near East). Archeological evidence suggests that this transition was associated with the arrival of anatomically modern populations in Europe who were equipped with new technologies, the Aurignacian, named for the assemblage first unearthed at L'Aurignac in France. In some instances, there is evidence for a significant period of coexistence between these new populations and final Neandertal populations (Hublin et al., 1996; Mellars, 1992; Reynolds, 1991; Straus, 1995). For example, in western Europe the youngest Neandertal remains, like those from Arcy-sur-Cure, France, and Zafarraya, Spain, date to about 34 kya and are associated with a Châtelperronian tool industry, whereas Aurignacian industries associated with anatomically modern humans occur as early as 40 kya—for example, in a number of sites in the Swabian Jura of southwestern Germany (e.g., Vogelherd) (Conard and Bolus, 2003). As we have previously noted, in both Africa and the Near East, modern human populations first appear in association with Middle Paleolithic (Middle Stone Age) industries.

In a thorough review of the Middle to Upper Paleolithic transitional period, anthropologists Steve Churchill and Fred Smith (2000) note the following:

- The Middle Paleolithic industries of Europe appear to have been made exclusively by Neandertals.
- Initial Upper Paleolithic industries most likely have their roots in the late Middle Paleolithic industries of their respective geographical regions.
- All of the human fossils presently known from initial Upper Paleolithic contexts are most similar to Neandertals and not early modern humans.
- Modern humans were present in Europe by about 32 kya, and possibly by about 36 kya. Claims for an appearance of modern humans before 36 kya cannot be substantiated at present.
- The hypothesis that modern humans are uniquely associated with the Aurignacian cannot yet be refuted. Aurignacian-associated human fossils are more similar to early modern Europeans and not Neandertals, except possibly for the presence of Neandertal fossils and the Aurignacian-like site of Vindija Cave (Croatia) (see below).
- Neandertals and moderns humans co-existed in Europe for at least 2,000–4,000 years, and perhaps for 8,000–10,000 years or longer.

The classic Neandertals of Europe and Western Asia are one group of Middle/Upper Pleistocene early hominins that have received special attention in discussions of modern human origins. Perhaps these early humans, once defined by Ales Hrdlicka (1927) as simply "the man . . . of the Mousterian culture," initially received this special notoriety because the discoveries of their fossilized remains were sympatric (if not synchronous!) with the lives of many influential European students of human evolution in the late nineteenth and early twentieth centuries. As Hrdlicka (1927) wrote:

Since Huxley, the Neanderthal cranium and Neanderthal man have been written about extensively, but often with but little originality. New finds belonging to the period have become numerous—almost more numerous than legitimate new thoughts. . . . The distressing part is, that the more there is the less we seem to know what to do with it. Speculation there has been indeed enough, but the bulk of it so far has not led into the sunlight, but rather into a dark, blind alley from which there appears no exit.

In Europe, Middle Paleolithic (Mousterian) assemblages are almost invariably associated with Neandertals, whereas Upper Paleolithic (early Aurignacian) industries are almost always associated with anatomically modern humans. Thus far, the only exceptions to these observations come from two sites in France, Arcy-sur-Cure and Saint-Césaire (dated to about 36 kya), where an Upper Paleolithic (Châtelperronian) industry, including about three dozen personal ornaments of different kinds made from animal teeth, ivory beads, and bone, is associated with a Neandertal skeletal morphology (d'Errico et al., 1998; Hublin et al., 1996; Klein, 1992).[6] The other exception is the recent report of a direct association between Neandertal fossils and Aurignacian-like tools dated to about 29 kya from Vindija Cave (Croatia) (Ahern et al., 2004; Churchill and Smith, 2000). It does appear, however, that in certain parts of Europe (e.g., the southern part of the Spanish peninsula) local Neandertal populations survived for 5,000–10,000 years *after* the arrival of more modern-looking people. For example, the Neandertal lower jaw from Zafarraya (southern Spain) is dated to about 30 kya whereas Aurignacian industries most likely produced by anatomically modern humans have been dated to about 38–40 kya in northern Spain.

The "Neandertal Question" is probably paleoanthropology's longest running headache, confounding anthropologists ever since fossil Neandertals were first discovered and Thomas Huxley's successful 1863 challenge to Rudolf Virchow's contention that they were just the remains of modern pathological idiots.

The first Neandertal ever discovered was actually from Engis Cave, Belgium, in 1829–30. There the Belgian physician and anatomist Phillipe-Charles Schmerling recovered the cranial remains of at least three individuals who were associated with extinct animals. One of the crania soon deteriorated and was lost to science and another was that of a rather robust, essentially modern male dating to only about 8 kya. However, the third specimen turned out to be a partial cranium of a 2- to 3-year-old Neandertal child, although it was not recognized as such at the time.

The second Neandertal ever discovered was unearthed in 1848 at Forbes' Quarry, Gibraltar, during construction of British military fortifications there. Like the Engis specimen, the Gibraltar cranium was not recognized as a Neandertal until decades later. The name "Neandertal" traces back to the 1856 discovery of a Neandertal skullcap, or calotte,

---

[6]A juvenile temporal bone was found at Arcy-sur-Cure and a skeleton from Saint-Césaire. The Châtelperronian is a tool assemblage that probably developed directly out of the preceding Mousterian of Acheulean tradition, a tool tradition that is normally associated with Neandertals. Other Mousterian/Upper Paleolithic mixes occur in the Uluzzian of Italy and the Szeletian/Jerzmanovician of Central Europe (Klein, 1992).

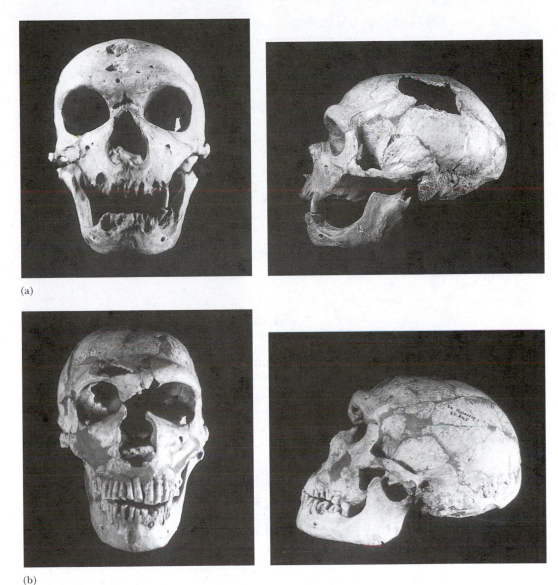

(a)

(b)

Fig. 13.7. Classic Neandertal crania. (a) Front and lateral views of a La Chapelle-aux-Saints specimen. (b) Front and lateral views of La Ferrassie 1. (Photos courtesy of R. Klein.)

and some postcranial bones from the Feldhofer Cave in the Neander Valley, Germany (Fig. 13.7) (Smith, 2002; Trinkaus and Shipman, 1993). A summary of some of the early, and still most important, Neandertal discoveries is given in Table 13.2, and some of the major sites are shown in Figure 12.1b.

Table 13.2   The First Major Discoveries of Neandertal Remains

First Phase, 1914 and Before		Second Phase, 1920–39	
Belgium		Crimea	
Engis	1830	Kiik Koba	1924–26
Gibraltar		Israel	
Forbes' Quarry	1848	Mount Carmel, Tabun Cave	1929
Germany		Italy	
Neander Valley	1856	Saccopastore	1929–35
		Guattari	1939
Belgium			
Spy Caves	1886	Central Asia	
		Teshik Tash	1938
Croatia			
Krapina	1899–1906		
Germany			
Ehringsdorf	1908		
France			
Le Moustier 1	1908		
La Chapelle-aux-Saints	1908		
La Ferrassie 1	1909		
La Ferrassie 2	1910		
La Quina	1911		
La Ferrassie 3 & 4	1912		
Le Moustier 2	1914		

From Stringer and Gamble (1993).

Since Neandertals are now generally regarded as geographic variants restricted to the Middle/Upper Pleistocene of Europe and western Asia, the Neandertal Question, simply put, is this: "What is their relationship to the succeeding modern European populations" (Wolpoff, 1989b)? In other words, were European Neandertals totally replaced by anatomically modern "invaders" from the East, or was there evolutionary continuity between Neandertals and modern human populations in Europe? As we have seen, conflicting opinions on the subject still bubble to the surface today.[7] To put the question into some perspective, let's briefly outline three of the more historically influential hypotheses on Neandertal phylogeny proposed over the past several decades:

[7]It is hard for me to understand why this has been such a vexing and contentious issue in paleoanthropology. To put the question into a more modern context, it would be like asking, "What is the relationship of Australian aborigines to the contemporary population of Australia? Were they totally replaced by English convicts (analogous to the Out of Africa Model) or was there some evolutionary continuity (i.e., interbreeding) between them (analogous to the Multiregional Continuity Model)?" Anyone who favors the former model probably underestimates the randiness of English convicts.

- The first hypothesis proposes that since Neandertal morphology diverges from that of modern Europeans, Neandertals are peripheral to mainstream human evolution. In this view, they were genetically isolated from the more anatomically modern human populations evolving in the Near East (e.g., Qafzeh and Skhul) by Würmian glaciers in western Europe. The ancestry of these classic Neandertals were seen to trace back through European pre-Neandertals, like those from Ehringsdorf, Krapina, and Saccopastore (Howell, 1951, 1958, 1958).[8]

- The second proposes that not only is there evolutionary continuity between Neandertals and modern humans in Europe but that human evolution as a whole went through a worldwide Neandertal stage or phase (Brace, 1967; Brose and Wolpoff, 1971; Frayer, 1992; Hrdlicka, 1927).

- The third, known as the "Praesapiens Theory," holds that Neandertals are an archaic group that went extinct without issue. Therefore, modern *H. sapiens* cannot be descended from Neandertals, nor can they have passed through a Neandertal stage. Instead, modern humans are envisioned as descending from a praesapiens type of early human, contemporary with, but distinct from, Neandertals. Two arguments are usually put forward to defend this view: (1) the perceived impossibility of deriving Aurignacian Upper Paleolithic Europeans from the underlying early Mousterian Neandertals in so short a time span and (2) discoveries of more modern-looking fossils in Europe that are contemporary with, or even antecedent to, classic Neandertals (e.g., Swanscombe and Fontéchevade) (Boule, 1923; Vallois, 1954).

Today, the Neandertal Question is generally framed in terms of the degree (zero, low, high) of continuity between Neandertals and early modern Europeans in the context of a worldwide process of modern human origins.

Now that we have outlined some of the competing hypotheses about the fate of Neandertals, let's examine what they actually looked like.

Neandertal Morphology

Virtually all paleoanthropologists agree that classic Neandertals are morphologically unique and that this distinctive morphology is best displayed in the western European sample.[9] We will explore some of the functional

---

[8]Some European Neandertals probably date to the pre-Würm, or end of the Riss-Würm interglacial (e.g., Krapina level 5 and below and Saccopastore), the Würm (e.g., Ganovce, Ochoz), and the Riss (e.g., Fontéchevade, Ehringsdorf).

[9]Some of the more famous classic Neandertal sites include Germany (Neandertal), Belgium (Bay-Bonnet, Engis, La Naulette, Spy), Channel Islands (St. Brelade), France (Malarnaud, La Chaise, La Quina, Petit-Puymoyen, La Chapelle-aux-Saints, Genay, Combe-Grenal, La Ferrassie, Le Moustier, Pech de l'Aze, Monsempron, Arcy-sur-Cure), Spain (Banolas, Cova Negra, Gibraltar, Pinar), and Italy (Monte Circeo, Santa Croce di Bisceglie).

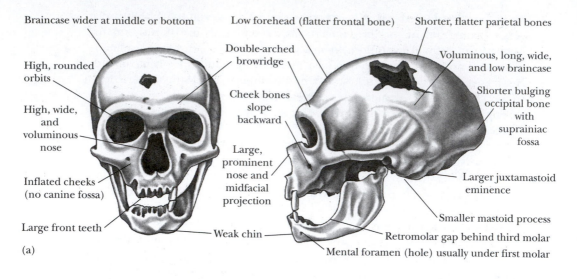

Braincase wider at middle or bottom

Low forehead (flatter frontal bone)

Shorter, flatter parietal bones

High, rounded orbits

Double-arched browridge

Voluminous, long, wide, and low braincase

High, wide, and voluminous nose

Cheek bones slope backward

Shorter bulging occipital bone with suprainiac fossa

Inflated cheeks (no canine fossa)

Large, prominent nose and midfacial projection

Larger juxtamastoid eminence

Large front teeth

Smaller mastoid process

Weak chin

Retromolar gap behind third molar

(a)

Mental foramen (hole) usually under first molar

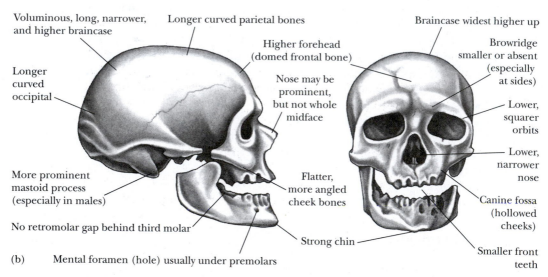

Voluminous, long, narrower, and higher braincase

Longer curved parietal bones

Braincase widest higher up

Longer curved occipital

Higher forehead (domed frontal bone)

Browridge smaller or absent (especially at sides)

Nose may be prominent, but not whole midface

Lower, squarer orbits

Lower, narrower nose

More prominent mastoid process (especially in males)

Flatter, more angled cheek bones

Canine fossa (hollowed cheeks)

No retromolar gap behind third molar

Strong chin

Smaller front teeth

(b)   Mental foramen (hole) usually under premolars

Fig. 13.8.   Some distinguishing features of the Neandertal skull.   (a) The Chapelle-aux-Saints skull, with Neandertal features highlighted. (b) The anatomically modern skull of Cro-Magnon 1, with features of *H. sapiens* highlighted. (Stringer and Gamble, 1993.)

aspects of this morphology later, but first let's look at some of the striking anatomical features that characterize most, if not all, Neandertal crania (Figs. 13.7 and 13.8).

- Cranial vault long, low (platycephalic), and wide; cranial base relatively flat
- Massive facial skeleton, prognathic midfacial region, large nasal aperture, absence of canine fossa
- Supraorbital tori well developed and semicircular in shape (i.e., not a continuous bar or shelf-like structure)
- Occipital bone angulated and characterized by occipital ridges, occipital bunning, and presence of a suprainiac fossa
- Smaller radii of curvature of the anterior and posterior semicircular canals of the inner ear, and a posterior semicircular canal placed inferiorly relative to the plane of the lateral canal[10]
- Molars characterized by enlarged pulp chambers (taurodontism)
- Incisors large relative to postcanine teeth, often shovel shaped, and showing peculiar wear patterns, indicating their use as vise-like tools
- Mandible characterized by distinct retromolar spaces, an absence of a true chin, and posteriorly positioned mental foramina

Many of the distinctive Neandertal cranial features, such as the elongated vertical facial dimensions, the lack of canine fossae, the large nasal apertures, and the pronounced midfacial prognathism, relate to structures of the midfacial region. Other cranial features, such as those of the inner ear (e.g., size, shape, and disposition of the semicircular canals), probably relate to the shape of the petrous pyramid of the temporal bone which, in turn, has been sculpted by the shape of the developing cerebellum in the posterior cranial fossa (Spoor et al., 2003).

Many of the diagnostic Neandertal mandibular features relate to this unique facial profile as well. There have been a number of hypotheses put forward to explain Neandertal facial prognathism: (1) as an adaptation to cold, (2) as a passive result of enlarged paranasal sinus development, (3) as a result of accelerated growth in cartilaginous precursors of cranial bones, and/or (4) as a response to increased anterior dental loads (Churchill, 1998; Green and Smith, 1991). All of these factors undoubtedly came into play in subtle and interrelated ways. For example, while some facial features, notably nasal morphology, can plausibly be regarded as skeletal/physiological adaptations to high-activity levels in extremely cold and arid Middle/Upper Pleistocene glacial climates (Trinkaus, 1989c), many other facial features undoubtedly relate to increased loads placed on the anterior dentition by using these teeth as vise-like tools. The precanine and postcanine teeth have followed somewhat different evolutionary trajectories during the Middle/Upper Pleistocene—the posterior dentition became somewhat reduced while the anterior dentition remained relatively large (Antón, 1994;

[10]However, the configuration of the semicircular canals in at least one Neandertal, Le Moustier 1, seems to fall within the modern human range (Ponce de León and Zollikofer, 1999).

Brace, 1979; Frayer, 1978). Clearly, Neandertal anterior teeth were responding to different selection pressures than were the posterior teeth.[11]

Recent research suggests that many of the craniofacial features by which anatomically modern humans differ from Neandertals and early *Homo,* such as more globular braincase, more vertical forehead, smaller browridges, presence of a canine fossa and chin, may all be explained by a relatively simple developmental feature, the shortening of the sphenoid bone during early ontogeny. Anterior sphenoidal shortening results in the reduction of facial projection by positioning the posterior margin of the face closer to the middle cranial fossa. The effect of such a developmental shift may help explain how modern human craniofacial shape could have evolved fairly rapidly from more early forms. This developmental shift suggests to some that more primitive forms like Neandertals and early *Homo* should be a separate species from *Homo sapiens* (Lieberman, 1998; Lieberman et al., 2002).[12]

What may have been the adaptive value of such a developmental change in the sphenoid bone in the modern human lineage? One suggestion is that the shorter sphenoid is an adaptation for speech, since it changes the dimensions of the oropharynx so that the horizontal length of the vocal tract becomes approximately equal to its vertical length rather than being markedly longer as in other primates. This configuration improves the ability of the supralaryngeal vocal tract to produce acoustically distinct sounds and so may have been selected for as an adaptation for language production. We will come back to the issue of language a bit later.

One other developmental quirk may help explain the prognathic Neandertal midface. It seems that synostosis of the premaxillary suture occurs relatively late in Neandertal children compared to modern human children. The persistence of such an open premaxillary suture during Neandertal ontogeny would allow for an extended period of growth in the Neandertal midface, eventually leading to the facial configuration seen in adults (Maureille and Bar, 1999).

---

[11]Note that it has been demonstrated that wear striations on the buccal surfaces of the anterior teeth were produced when Neandertals held meat or other matter between their anterior teeth and then cut it with a sharp tool held in the right hand (de Castro et al., 1988; Frayer and Fox, 1998). Similar buccal wear striations have been found in several other Middle and early Upper Pleistocene hominins (e.g., Atapuerca/Ibeas, Cova Negra, La Quina). This reinforces an earlier observation that tool-making techniques from Lower Pleistocene (e.g., Koobi Fora) and Middle Pleistocene (e.g., Ambrona) sites reflect a preferential use of the right hand in early hominins (Toth, 1985a; Toth and Schick, 1993). As such, these observations strongly suggest that lateralization in the hominin brain has a very ancient history. In addition, in all cases in which right and left upper arm bones are preserved, humeral asymmetry of right and left humeri indicates that these Neandertal individuals were right handed (Trinkaus et al., 1994).

[12]However, a recently discovered *H. erectus* calvaria from Java (Sm 4) suggests that any causal relationship between a more globular braincase and basicranial flexion is quite complex. The cranial base flexion of Sm 4 is as strong as in modern humans, yet the cranial vault is platycephalic (long and low), not globular as one might expect with such a high degree of cranial base flexion (Baba et al., 2003).

Biomechanical models indicate that the entire Neandertal masticatory apparatus was designed for generating and withstanding high or repeated forces on the anterior dentition, particularly on the incisors. Several lines of morphological evidence support this view, including relatively large anterior tooth dimensions, excessive amounts of anterior dental attrition, and the presence of dental chipping and pitting on the incisors (Brace, 1964; Demes, 1987; Smith and Paquette, 1989; Spencer and Demes, 1993; Trinkaus, 1987).

Two of the more influential biomechanical models of Neandertal facial morphology have been dubbed the "Infraorbital Plate Model" (Rak, 1986) and the "Zygomatic Retreat Model" (Trinkaus, 1987). Both models agree that the total morphological pattern of the Neandertal face is unique and that (1) the pronounced facial prognathism characteristic of Neandertals is a primitive, or plesiomorphic, feature; (2) both the large size and the extensive wear features of Neandertal anterior teeth indicate that they placed heavy loads on their anterior dentition for purposes other than just chewing food, resulting in elevated and/or repetitive levels of stress through the facial skeleton; and (3) features of the Neandertal face such as the absence of canine fossae, the anterolateral flattening of the body of the zygomatic bone, and the absence of a notch in the zygomatic root would have maximized the strength of the infraorbital region against bending and/or torsion produced through anterior dental loading.

According to the Infraorbital Plate Model, the pronounced facial prognathism characteristic of Neandertals is considered to be an adaptation to better withstand sagittally oriented rotary moments induced by heavy anterior dental loading. In the Zygomatic Retreat Model, the Neandertal face is seen as a compromise between maintaining the ancestral condition of facial prognathism and the derived condition of posterior migration of the masticatory muscle region (zygomatic retreat). In this model, Neandertal facial features that reflect this spatial reorganization, or retreat, include the positioning of the zygomatic root above M^2–M^3 instead of above M^1–M^2, as in most early and recent hominins, and the frequent presence of a retromolar space between the distal M_3 and the anterior margin of the mandibular ramus.

The Neandertal postcranial skeleton is just as distinctive as the cranium and is characterized by a number of features (Fig. 13.9):
- Heavily built vertebral column
- Cervical vertebrae with long, horizontally projecting spinous processes
- Broad scapula, with a sulcus on the dorsal aspect of the axillary border
- Robust humerus, with massive head
- Pronounced lateral bowing of the radius
- Distal phalanx of the thumb approximately as long as the proximal one (unlike modern humans, in whom the distal phalanx is much shorter than the proximal one); large and rounded tips, or apical tufts, on the fingers
- Pelvis with more dorsally rotated ilia
- Thin, elongated superior pubic ramus

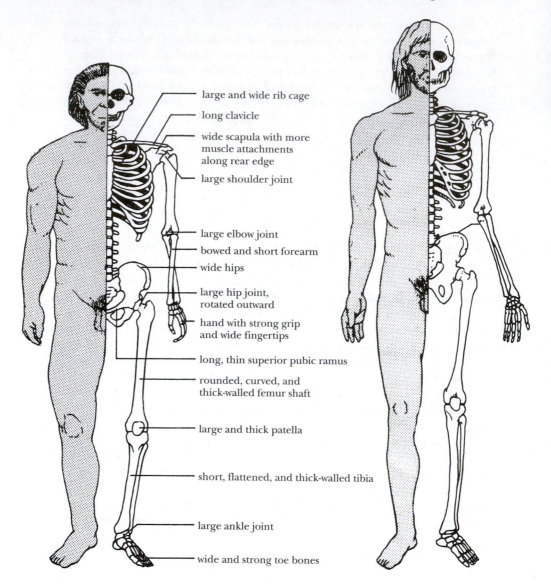

large and wide rib cage

long clavicle

wide scapula with more
muscle attachments
along rear edge

large shoulder joint

large elbow joint

bowed and short forearm

wide hips

large hip joint,
rotated outward

hand with strong grip
and wide fingertips

long, thin superior pubic ramus

rounded, curved, and
thick-walled femur shaft

large and thick patella

short, flattened, and thick-walled tibia

large ankle joint

wide and strong toe bones

Fig. 13.9. Some distinguishing features of the Neandertal postcranial skeleton. (Stringer and Gamble, 1993.)

- Femora with massive, cortically thick cylindrical shafts that lack a distinct pilaster; low femoral neck-shaft angle
- Short and strong tibias with retroverted proximal heads; supplementary facets on the distal tibia for articulation with the talus, or ankle bone (squatting facets)
- Large and thick kneecaps
- Low brachial and crural indices

The most obvious difference between the Neandertal skeleton and that of later more modern-looking hominins is the general level of skeletal robusticity in the former. To put this into some perspective, overall body mass in Neandertals is estimated to be about 30% larger than the average body mass of humans living today (Ruff et al., 1997). In short, Neandertals were powerfully built. The cervical, or neck, vertebrae had horizontally long, robust spines. Even the ribs are particularly thick in cross section. The scapula was very broad with a peculiar sulcus on the dorsal side of the axillary border, suggesting that the rotator cuff muscles, involved in rotating the upper limb, were particularly well developed (Stewart, 1962). One of the bones of the forearm, the radius, is highly bowed, giving greater leverage to muscles that help pronate and supinate the forearm. All of the wrist and hand bones are robust with strong muscular markings—not a hand adapted for limp-wristed handshakes (Musgrave, 1971).

Features of the lower limb also display this same level of robustness, particularly in the size and cross-sectional shape of the femoral and tibial shafts. The thickened cortical bones in the femur and tibia reflect overall muscularity of the lower limbs and are obvious adaptations to maximizing torsional and bending strengths within these bones. By contrast, early modern humans do not show such extremes of skeletal and muscular robusticity. In fact, the oldest reasonably complete early modern postcrania from the Near East (Qafzeh and Skhul) are quite gracile by comparison (Trinkaus et al., 1991).

One suggestion put forward to help explain the general overall robustness of Neandertals is that the timing and intensity of endocrine production (e.g., osteogenic hormones) may have differed between Neandertals and anatomically modern humans. For example, the clinical condition known as precocious puberty, in which there is an early onset and elevated levels of sex steroid production, sometimes produces Neandertal-like symptoms in modern children (e.g., robust and heavily muscled limb bones with large joint surfaces, thick cranial vault bones, large browridges, projecting midfaces, and limb bones with narrow medullary cavities) (Churchill, 1998).

Neandertal pelvic morphology is quite distinctive from that of anatomically modern humans. Specifically, their superior pubic bones are long and thin (a feature we also noticed in the non-Neandertal Jinniu Shan pelvis from China), contributing to birth canals that are large compared to those of modern humans. This elongated pubis is even evident in Neandertal children as young as 3–5 years of age (e.g., La Ferrassie 6) (Tompkins and Trinkaus, 1987). This unusual pelvic morphology has led to several hypotheses concerning Neandetal reproductive biology.

The first, known as the Gestation-Length Model, suggests that an elongated superior pubic ramus gave Neandertals a larger pelvic aperture that could have accommodated a neonatal cranium 15–25% larger than in modern humans. This in turn suggested that Neandertal newborns were large compared to modern neonates because they were born at a comparatively later stage in their development and, therefore, most likely had elongated gestation periods as well, perhaps 12 months rather than 9 (Trinkaus, 1984a). The second, known as the Accelerated Fetal Growth Model, suggests that dental eruption schedules were accelerated in Neandertals relative to modern humans, indicating that Neandertals had accelerated growth, including brain growth, compared to modern humans, but within normal human gestation times (Dean et al., 1986; Thompson and Nelson, 2000). The third, known as the Maternal Body Weight Model, focuses more on maternal body weight as a critical determinant of infant size and, therefore, of birth canal size. While the first two models propose that Neandertal infants were large at birth as a consequence of developmental timing or rates that differed from those of modern humans, the latter model proposes that Neandertal newborns were large because of the great body size and weight of their mothers and not because they were born at a later stage of development or because they developed at a different rate in utero (Rosenberg, 1988).

It is interesting to note that many of these distinctive Neandertal features seem to result from differences in the relative timing and rates of activity at specific growth fields during early ontogeny (Ponce de León and Zollikofer, 2001).[13] For example, the midfacial projection so characteristic of Neandertals probably results from less basicranial flexion at the spheno-occipital synchondrosis during early postnatal or possibly even prenatal ontogeny. Other characteristic Neandertal features such as the suprainiac fossa, shovel-shaped upper incisors, elongated pubis, and bowing of the femoral and tibial shafts, also appear very early in development, as the 2-year-old Neandertal skeleton from Dederiyeh Cave, Syria, clearly demonstrates (Akazawa et al., 1995). In fact, the recent rediscovery of an approximately 4-month-old Neandertal (Le Moustier 2), which had been misplaced for almost a century, shows that many Neandertal features were present even at this young age (Maureille, 2002).

Neandertal limb proportions also differ substantially from most modern populations in that these individuals tend to have relatively short distal limb segments. For this reason, Neandertal crural (tibia length/femur length) and brachial (radius length/humerus length) indices are low.

What can be the functional explanation for such limb proportions? It turns out that brachial and crural indices are correlated with mean annual temperature in modern populations—those populations living in the coldest climates, for example, Lapps and Eskimos, have the lowest indices as an adaptation to reduce heat loss, whereas those living in hotter regions, for example, Egyptians and equatorial Africans, have higher indices as an adaptation to facilitate heat loss. This is an example of what is known in

---

[13]The immature Neandertal sample that forms the bases for these studies includes Amud 7, Pech de l'Aze, Barakai, Subalyuk, Roc de Marsal, Devil's Tower (Gibraltar 2), Engis 2, La Quina 18, Teshik Tash, La Naulette, and Le Moustier 1.

biology as Allen's rule. Two nineteenth-century biological rules relating body form to cold stress are known as Allen's rule and Bergmann's rule. Allen's rule states that in a given species animals living in cold areas tend to have shorter extremities than those in warmer climates. Bergmann's rule states that in a given species the warm-blooded animals living in colder places tend to have greater body bulk than those living in warmer regions. The shift in limb proportions seen in post-Neandertal populations suggests that these Upper Pleistocene hominins may have been under less thermal stress than Neandertals, possibly because of their ability to better control fire and to make more effective clothing and shelters (Trinkaus, 1981, 1984b, 1989c). But Neandertals were certainly not devoid of such cultural amenities, as we shall see below.

Cultural Capacities of Neandertals

No hominin group has been more maligned in the history of paleoanthropology than the Neandertals. The trend to dehumanize them continues (Hayden, 1993):

> Neandertals have been portrayed as incompetent users of language and symbolic thought, . . . as incompetent hunters, . . . as incapable of anticipating patterned animal movements, . . . as incapable of anticipating future needs for tools and therefore only employing expedient technologies, . . . as incapable of using future tenses or clauses and therefore lacking alliances and even extended families, . . . as incapable of forming ethnic identities, ... as possibly lacking aggregation sites or even home bases, . . . as incapable of abstract or realistic artistic expression, . . . as lacking values or symboling ability related to the intentional interment of the dead and by inference lacking any developed religious thought, . . . as lacking the motor and mental conceptual wherewithal to manufacture stone blades and bone tools, . . . and as generally lacking culture as we recognize it.

Whew! What a litany of alleged sins.

As Brian Hayden of Simon Fraser University points out in the above quotation, there are two major implications that follow from these views: that Neandertals were genetically incapable of language, symbolic behavior, religion, foresight, tool curation, ethnicity, art, hunting, and blade and bone tool production—all of which had to wait until the emergence of anatomically modern *H. sapiens* of the Upper Paleolithic—and that even if Neandertals did have the capacity for these behaviors, they were not a significant part of their worldview, and thereby failed to avail themselves of this potential. However, Hayden notes that, in contrast to these dehumanizing views, there is a reasonable body of archeological evidence showing that Neandertals were not significantly different from early *H. sapiens* in their capacity for cultural behavior and that symbolic behavior was indeed a part of their adaptation in the Middle Paleolithic.

For example, there is now abundant archeological evidence for hafting on Levallois and Mousterian points and scrapers in the Middle Paleolithic (remember, virtually all archeologists agree that Mousterian assemblages were produced by Neandertals) (Fig. 13.10). Some of this hafted lithic material came from up to 30–80 km away from the sites where they were found, a strong indicator that hafting involved curation, foresight, and mental templates of tool designs that had to be shaped to certain predetermined specifications. In addition, it appears that at least some Middle Paleolithic Neandertal populations were already experimenting with the use of bitumen as a glue for hafting handles onto their tools (Boeda et al., 1996). Most important, tool types and patterns of raw material procurement do not necessarily change at the first appearance of anatomically modern *H. sapiens*. It is clear that both wood and bone tools were manufactured by hominins before the appearance of anatomically modern *H. sapiens*. These tools include several spruce throwing spears from Schöningen, Germany, found in association with the butchered remains of more than 10 horses, dated to about 400 kya (Thieme, 1997); a yew spear from Clacton, England, dated to about 300 kya; a spear end found in the rib cage of an elephant at Lehringen, Germany, dating to about 120 kya; and wood tools from the Acheulean at Kalambo Falls. That Neandertals were familiar with working both bone and ivory for making tools and personal ornaments is evidenced by occasional finds of bone points, awls, perforated bones and teeth, ivory rings, cut antlers, and antler digging picks. As far as blade production is concerned, this lithic technology occurs in the Acheulean as well as the later Mousterian. The relatively high percentage of Levallois (spear) points found at Neandertal sites, particularly in the Levant, strongly suggests an increased emphasis on intercept hunting. This, combined with many of the hyperrobust skeletal features and evidence of skeletal trauma, could be interpreted as evidence of close-quarters confrontational hunting of large terrestrial mammals (Shea, 1998).

In accepting the notion that Neandertals were incapable of art and ritual, some have doubted that Neandertals buried their dead (Gargett, 1989). However, the evidence, particularly from Shanidar, is suggestive that not only were some Neandertals buried but also that flowers were used in some of these burials—if so, a clear example of symbolic and religious behavior (Leroi-Gourhan, 1975). Another indication that an appreciation of art was present even before Neandertals emerged is demonstrated by (1) a sophistication and beauty in some Acheulean bifaces that far exceeded any possible functional requirements; (2) the selection, in some cases, of particularly attractive fossiliferous chert (a type of

Fig. 13.10.   (a) Typical Mousterian tools made by Neandertals: (i) Mousterian point, (ii) elongated Mousterian point, and (iii) sidescraper. (b) Stages in the manufacture of (i) a Levallois flake and (ii) a Levallois point. (Gowlett, 1992.)

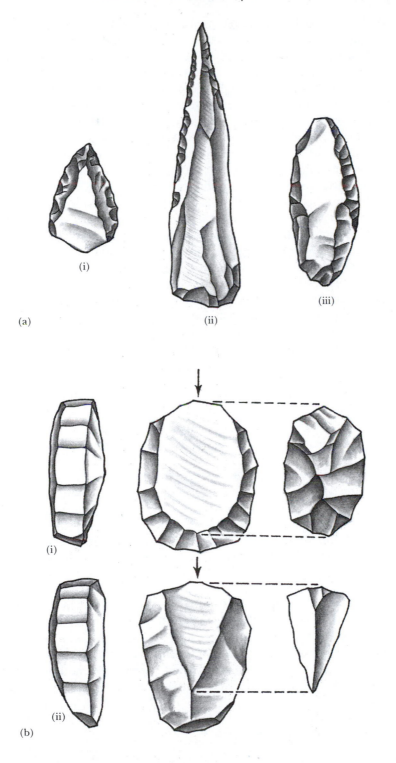

(a)

    (i)

    (ii)

    (iii)

(b)

    (i)

    (ii)

flint) or rock crystals for tools; (3) the flaking of handaxes in such a way that prominent single fossils were centrally located in the finished tool; and (4) the transport over long distance of nonfunctional items such as fossiliferous cherts and the teeth of whales and seals.

It is also important to note that Neandertals had achieved a level of social caring and responsibility in which disabled members of the community were cared for by other members of the group long after they could have contributed in any substantial way to the group's material welfare. Despite the fact that virtually every reasonably complete skeleton of an elderly Neandertal shows evidence of some trauma, all of these individuals clearly survived for extended post-traumatic periods, as they all show extensive wound healing usually with little or no evidence of infection. It is fascinating to speculate on just what type of indirect value these elderly individuals must have had to the social group that cared for them over such extended periods of time. Perhaps it is not surprising, then, that many of these same individuals were found in intentional burials (Trinkaus and Shipman, 1992; Trinkaus and Zimmerman, 1982).

But certainly the Neandertal world was a violent one.[14] Some Neandertal specimens reveal wounds that were presumably caused by interpersonal violence. For example, the St. Césaire 1 skeleton of a young adult has a healed fracture in the cranial vault that bears all the hallmarks of trauma induced by the impact of a sharp implement; the Shanidar 3 individual has a slash wound in the superior margin of the ninth rib from a penetrating implement that must have remained stuck between the ribs of this individual until his death (Zollikofer et al., 2002).

One site well known for alleged indications of ritual Neandertal behavior is Monte Circeo (Grotta Guattari), Italy, that is best known for its three Neandertal remains. The Circeo 1 cranium, found in a small chamber amid what has been described as a "ring" of stones, had what appeared to be an artificially enlarged foramen magnum, possibly indicative of cannibalism. A Neandertal mandible (Circeo 2) was found within the bone scatter in 1939, and another mandible (Circeo 3) was discovered in 1950 in the breccia lining one of the cave entrances. Radiometric analyses (U/Th and ESR) suggest that bone accumulation ceased about 50 kya (Schwarcz et al., 1991). Based on more recent taphonomic studies, the surface fauna at the site, once interpreted as the contents of a Neandertal ritual chamber, now appears to represent the remains of a spotted hyena maternity den. There is, however, clear evidence of hominin occupation of the cave at certain levels. These occupations levels are relatively poor in bone compared to the number of Mousterian artifacts and are dominated by head parts of common ungulate species, biased toward older adults, suggesting scavenging as the main means for procurement. Detailed study of the

---

[14]Why shouldn't it be—ours still is!

damage to the Monte Circeo 1 cranium indicates no unequivocal evidence of cannibalism but rather is more consistent with damage produced by carnivores (Stiner, 1991; White and Toth, 1991).

A much clearer case of Neandertal cannibalism is found in the cave site of Moula-Guercy, France (Defleur et al., 1999). The cave was occupied by Neandertals about 100 kya. There, 78 hominin bones, including cranial, dental, and postcranial remains, are attributed to at least six individuals. Associated with the hominin remains are a number of Mousterian tools (a high frequency of scrapers and Levallois prepared cores) as well as evidence of three hearths and a stone wall. The most common non-hominin in the fauna is *Cervus elephus* (red deer). Both hominin and deer bones show clear modification by other hominins and indicate that both taxa were defleshed and disarticulated before their marrow cavities were smashed open.

Hand in hand with controversies regarding Neandertal's cultural capacities are recurring debates about Neandertal abilities regarding faunal exploitation—that is, were they efficient hunters? scavengers? or something in-between? Given that Neandertal's overall skeletal robusticity indicates high activity levels, it is virtually unthinkable (at least in energetics terms) that they could have maintained such energy levels without being extremely efficient foragers and hunters (Sorensen and Leonard, 2001).

Indeed, there is ample archeological evidence, particularly at a number of circum-Mediterranean sites (e.g., Israel, Italy) that Middle and Upper Paleolithic hunters successfully exploited both small animals and ungulates for meat (Stiner et al., 1999). The most commonly eaten small animals were tortoises, shellfish, partridges, hares, and rabbits, followed in frequency by doves, waterfowl, hedgehogs, marmots, squirrels, legless lizards, large snakes, and ostrich eggs. Even though the proportion of small to large game animals taken by Paleolithic hunters didn't seem to change much from about 200–10 kya, the types of small animals most often consumed by these hunters did. Animals with low metabolism and long life spans like tortoises and marine shellfish tend to dominate Middle Paleolithic small game menus, whereas more agile, warm-blooded animals that mature rapidly (mainly hares and partridges) dominate Upper Paleolithic ones. The mean size of these slow-growing prey species were also decreasing over this time period—a clear indication that human hunting pressures were increasing, most probably due to pulses in Paleolithic population growth.

Over the past few decades four basic models of Neandertal faunal exploitation have been offered: the Obligate Scavenger Model, the Flexible Hunter-Scavenger Model, the Less-Adept Hunter Model, and the Fully Adept Hunter Model (Marean and Assefa, 1999). We shall briefly consider each of these in turn.

The Obligate Scavenger Model argues that scavenging was the major method of meat procurement during the Middle Paleolithic, with a bias toward meat scavenging versus bone marrow exploitation (Binford, 1981).

According to this model, hunting of moderate-size animals did not become frequent until after about 35 kya. It follows, then, that this model views Neandertals as being nearly as behaviorally primitive as Plio-Pleistocene early *Homo*. Given that Neandertals successfully endured and prospered in some of the harshest climates ever inhabited by hominins for a span of tens, or hundreds of thousands of years, this model seems, quite frankly, logically absurd. Neandertals were not surviving by tending vegetable gardens or stuffing themselves with juniper berries.

The Flexible Hunter-Scavenger Models propose that Neandertals practiced both regular hunting and scavenging (Stiner, 1991). Although Neandertals are not regarded as obligate scavengers in this model, they tended more toward scavenging, as opposed to hunting, when plant foods were abundant. During times when plant foods were not abundant, Neandertals shifted to more hunting oriented faunal exploitation.

The Less-Adept Hunter Model argues that while Middle Stone Age hominins were undoubtedly hunters, they were much less effective at it than modern humans (Klein, 2003; Klein and Cruz-Uribe, 2000). As this argument is generally presented, around 50 kya some genetic change related to language development suddenly arose, thereby initiating the behaviorally modern features characteristic of Upper Paleolithic modern humans. Somehow this neurological change allowed more sophisticated and effective hunting practices to emerge. Much of the evidence for this model is based on faunal analyses of African Middle and Later Stone Age sites. Middle Stone Age sites show that less dangerous animals, like the eland, was the predominant prey species, and the more dangerous buffalo and bushpig were less abundant. Middle Stone Age sites also show lower frequencies of fish and flying seabirds compared to Later Stone Age ones, again suggesting that Middle Stone Age hunters were less capable of catching these more elusive animals. These trends tend to be reversed in Later Stone Age sites. This is taken to mean that Middle Stone Age hunters focused on less dangerous game (eland) because they were less capable of killing the more dangerous game (buffalo and bushpig). Later Stone Age hunters could successfully hunt both kinds of game, as well as fish and flying seabirds, with equal facility.

Some tantalizing support for the genetic change noted above is the recent identification of FOXP2, a gene involved with normal speech and language abilities in humans (Enard et al., 2002). Individuals with disruption of this gene also have impairment of fine orofacial movements necessary for articulate speech. A point mutation in the gene is associated with a disorder in which those afflicted have severe articulation difficulties as well as linguistic and grammatical impairment. Chimpanzees, gorillas, and rhesus macaques all have identical FOXP2 genes and have only one amino acid difference from the mouse and two from the human protein. Two of the three amino acid differences between humans and mice occurred in the human lineage after the separation from the common ancestor with the chimpanzee. In other words, since the human/chimpanzee split about 5–7 mya, two fixed amino acid changes occurred in the human lineage, whereas none occurred in the chimpanzee and other primate lineages (except for one change on the orangutan lineage). Under certain population genetic models, fixation of this beneficial allele in humans occurred within the past 120,000 years or so.

The last model, the Fully Adept Hunter Model, simply argues that Middle Stone Age hunters had effective and full hunting capabilities (Chase, 1990).

A recent assessment of these competing models suggests that zooarcheological data do not support any model that views scavenging as a regular method of faunal exploitation by Neandertals or asserts that regular meat acquisition by Neandertals inhabiting temperate and cold zones was not essential. The fact that Middle Stone Age hunters concentrated on eland (in Southern Africa) does not necessarily mean that they were less adept hunters than Later Stone Age peoples. An emphasis on single-species hunting is characteristic of many modern hunter-gatherer people (e.g., Eskimo) who practice sophisticated tactical landscape strategies that are focused on one prey species. The rarity of fish, flying seabirds, buffalo and bush pig in Middle Stone Age sites and their relative abundance in Later Stone Age ones may simply imply that the more accessible and less dangerous game, like eland, had become overexploited by Later Stone Age times and that these later hunters had to rely on more dangerous, and/or, elusive game in order to satisfy their dietary needs (Marean and Assefa, 1999).

Some of this controversy about Neandertal food preferences can finally be put to rest by recent stable carbon isotope analyses of Neandertal remains from Vindija Cave (Croatia), Marillac (France), and Scladina Cave (Belgium) (Bocherens et al., 2001; Richards et al., 2000). These emerging studies clearly show that Neandertals were behaving as top-level carnivores in their environment, receiving most of their dietary protein from open-country herbivores. This could be accomplished only if they were extremely efficient hunters.

Finally, we return to the long-running debate about whether or not Neandertals were capable of fully sapient speech. A most articulate and persistent spokesperson for the view that Neandertals lacked "the speech producing anatomy that is necessary for sounds like the vowels (i), (u), and (a), for nasal versus nonnasal distinctions, and certain velar consonants" is Philip Lieberman (1976, 1989) of Brown University. Much of Lieberman's argument rests on perceived similarities between the anatomy of the Neandertal supralaryngeal tract (based mainly on a reconstruction of the La Chapelle-aux-Saints Neandertal) to that of chimpanzees and human newborns. These reconstructions purportedly show that the size of the Neandertal neck could not possibly accommodate the vocal apparatus of modern humans, thereby limiting the sapient quality of speech. However, Lieberman's reconstruction of the Neandertal supralaryngeal tract and the linguistic conclusions drawn from it have been challenged (Houghton, 1993). This interpretation suggests that, while Neandertal craniofacial anatomy is indeed distinctive, there is no osteological evidence to suggest that they could not have had the same linguistic abilities as modern humans. Lending some credence to this is the discovery of an intact Neandertal hyoid bone from Kebara (see below), the small bone that anchors some of the tongue muscles. It is virtually indistinguishable from the same bone in modern humans (Arensburg et al., 1989, 1990; Bar-Yosef and Vandermeersch, 1993). This hyoid bone has not settled the debate, however, since the human hyoid looks very similar to the same bone in pigs! Thus the issue of Neandertal linguistic capabilities still generates heated, and mutually contradictory, claims (Arensburg, 1994; Lieberman, 1993, 1994).

One further line of evidence regarding language capabilities in Neandertals comes from the size of the hypoglossal canal, the small foramen in the base of the cranium through which the nerve of the same name passes to supply motor innervation to the tongue muscles. It was initially reported that this canal was both absolutely and relatively larger in modern humans than in African apes, reflecting the rich innervation of the human tongue necessary for speech. Hypoglossal canal size in gracile *Australopithecus* and early *Homo* was said to fall within the ape size range, whereas that of Neandertals (La Chapelle and La Ferrassie 1) and early anatomical modern humans (Skhul V) was said to fall within the extant *Homo* size range. Thus it was concluded that the vocal capabilities of Neandertals were the same as those of modern humans (Kay et al., 1998).

Unfortunately, a more recent study has shown that this is not the case at all. It turns out that many nonhuman primates have hypoglossal canals within the modern human size range, both absolutely and relative to oral cavity volume. Furthermore, *A. afarensis, A. africanus,* and *A. boisei* all have hypoglossal canals that are equal in size to those of modern humans, both absolutely and relative to oral cavity volume. It was further observed that hypoglossal *canal* size is not even correlated with hypoglossal *nerve* size—the main argument of the original hypothesis. Thus the timing of human language origins in general (at least based on hypoglossal canal size), and of Neandertals in particular, is still an open and contentious question (DeGusta et al., 1999; Lieberman, 1999).

Neandertal mtDNA

The question of how much, if any, of the Neandertal gene pool found its way into anatomical populations of Europe has vexed paleoanthropologists for a very long time. Recent discoveries from Lagar Velho (Portugal) have shed some interesting, if controversial, insights into this question (Duarte et al., 1999; Tattersall and Schwartz, 1999). There, the remains of an approximately

4-year-old child were found buried in association with red ochre and pierced shell. The fossil is dated to about 24 kya. What is particularly intriguing about the specimen is that the cranium, mandible, dentition, and postcrania are said to present a mosaic of European early modern human and Neandertal features. Features that align the skeleton with modern humans include the configuration of the mental foramen, the size and proportions of the teeth, various features of the mandibular rami, the orientation of the radial tuberosity and the radial diaphyseal curvature, and the proportions of the pubic bone. Features more reminiscent of Neandertal morphology include body proportions (reflected in the femorotibial length), overall femoral and tibial diaphyseal robusticity, tibial condylar displacement, mandibular symphyseal retreat, and the overall robusticity of thorocohumeral muscle insertions.

Some researchers suggest that this combination of morphological features indicate admixture between regional Neandertal and early modern human populations who were dispersing into southern Iberia in the early Upper Paleolithic (Duarte et al., 1999). However, could this child possibly be the result of a rare Neandertal/early modern human interbreeding event rather than the descendant of an extensively admixed population? This is doubtful since the dating of the child's skeleton to several thousand years *after* the (probable) transition from Neandertal to early modern humans in southern Iberia (about 28–30 kya) indicated that this morphological mosaic persisted for a substantial period of time in this region. It is clear that this interpretation of events runs counter to the view that the transition from Neandertals to modern humans in western Europe involved the extinction without descent of European Neandertals and their complete replacement by early modern humans. This, of course, also implies a rejection of a strict Out of Africa Model.

If anatomically modern humans and Neandertals coexisted for tens of thousands of years, what was their phylogenetic relationship to one another? Did one evolve from the other? Were they separate species? Did Neandertals go extinct without contributing anything to the modern human gene pool? Several startling breakthroughs help put the answer into the framework of modern molecular genetics.

The DNA sequences of the first and second hypervariable regions of Neandertal mtDNA have now been determined from material extracted from a small sample of the humerus of the original 1856 Neandertal skeleton from the Neandertal Valley (Feldhofer) and compared to modern human mtDNA sample (Krings et al., 1997, 1999.)[15] In the original study,

---

[15]Genetic analyses have recently shown that plant and animal DNA may be preserved for long periods of time in certain permafrost and temperate sediments. For example, in Siberia five permafrost cores ranging in age from 400 to 10 kya were found to contain DNA signatures of at least 19 different plant taxa, including the oldest authenticated ancient DNA sequences known, as well as DNA signatures of mammoth, bison, and horse. Thus many sedimentary deposits may soon actually start to yield unique genetic records of past faunal and floral environments (Willerslev et al., 2003).

the Neandertal sequence was compared to 994 contemporary human mtDNA lineages—that is, distinct sequences found in one or more individuals from a sample consisting of 478 Africans, 510 Europeans, 167 Native Americans, and 20 individuals from Australia and Oceania. These modern human sequences differed among themselves by an average of 8 substitutions (ranging from 1 to 24 substitutions), whereas the difference between humans and the Neandertal sequence was 27.2 (ranging from 22 to 36 substitutions). Thus the largest difference between any two modern human sequences was two subsitutions larger than the smallest difference between a modern human and the Neandertal specimen. In addition, the Neandertal sequence differed by approximately the same amount from the modern populations in each of the geographical regions. Thus, even though Neandertals inhabited the same geographic region as contemporary Europeans, their mtDNA does not appear to be any more closely related to them than to any other modern population (as we saw earlier, this is not an assumption of the Multiregional Continuity Model and thus this observation, in and of itself, does *not* refute that model). The age of the common ancestor of the Neandertal and modern human mtDNA was estimated to be four times greater than that of the common ancestor of modern human mtDNA. Using an estimated divergence date between humans and chimpanzees of 4–5 mya yielded a date of 550–690 kya for the divergence of Neandertal and contemporary human mtDNA.

The DNA sequence of hypervariable region II augmented the conclusions reached from the original hypervariable I region, but this time the date of divergence between Neandertal and contemporary human mtDNA was estimated to be about 465 kya (with confidence limits of 317–741 kya). The extent of mtDNA sequence divergence between Neandertals and modern humans was found to exceed that found within current chimpanzee subspecies, thus suggesting that Neandertal and ancestral human mtDNA gene pools evolved separately over a long period of time.

More recently, molecular analysis of DNA extracted from the ribs of a 29,000-year-old Neandertal specimen from the northern Caucasus site of Mizmaiskaya Cave has also been reported (Ovchinnikov et al., 2000). A comparison of the Mizmaiskaya Cave sample (345-base-pair fragment) to both a modern reference sample and the Feldhofer Neandertal showed that the two Neandertals differ by only about 3.48%, about half the amount they differ from the modern human reference sample. These studies also indicate that Neandertal mtDNA is equally distant from all modern sequences, regardless of geographic region of origin; and this observation is again (mis)interpreted by some Out of Africa Model supporters to bolster their view that Neandertal mtDNA types did not contribute to the modern human mtDNA gene pool. In this study the age of the most recent common ancestor of the Feldhofer and Caucasus Neandertal mtDNA is estimated at 151–352 kya, that of the common mtDNA ancestor of modern humans and Neandertals at 365–853 kya, and that of the earliest modern human mtDNA divergences at 106–246 kya. The mtDNA analysis of a third Neandertal from Vindija Cave, Croatia, basically reaches these same general conclusions (Krings et al., 2000).

As technically brilliant as the above studies are, do they really resolve the question of whether or not Neandertals are a separate species from *H. sapiens,* one that did not contribute any genetic legacy to modern human populations? In spite of what one often reads in the press, the answer is, unfortunately, not yet.

First of all, species are not defined on the basis of similarities and/or differences in small fragments of mtDNA so we don't really know what the differences between Neandertal and modern human mtDNA really mean in a taxonomic sense. For example, although the average number of sequence differences found between Neandertals and living humans exceeds the amount found *within* chimpanzee subspecies, it is less than the number of differences found *between* two out of three chimpanzee subspecies. Thus it is not at all intuitively obvious whether the mtDNA differences between Neandertals and modern humans are best interpreted as evidence of separate species or subspecies status within a single evolving lineage (Relethford, 2001a).

Second, until recently we didn't have any idea of how variable mtDNA sequences were among anatomically modern humans—both ancient and recent. In order to show that mtDNA sequence differences are really distinctive between Neandertals and anatomically modern *H. sapiens,* one needs to demonstrate such differences between Neanderals and *contemporary* anatomically modern *H. sapiens* (e.g., Cro-Magnon, Lake Mungo)—not between fossils that differ in age by tens of thousands of years during which time modern human mtDNA continued to mutate while Neandertal mtDNA obviously did not. For example, recent mtDNA analyses on 10 ancient Australians, all of whom are anatomically modern and who date to between 0.2 and 62 kya, provide some surprising evidence on this score (Adcock et al., 2001). The oldest specimen, Lake Mungo 3, is possibly older than two (and quite possibly all three) of the Neandertal specimens from which mtDNA has been extracted.[16] Its mtDNA sequence is the most divergent of all the Australian fossils examined and is an example of a mtDNA lineage that is now absent (i.e., extinct) in modern populations. Ironically, instead of the deepest mtDNA branch in living humans being from Africa (Eve), this evidence indicates that it is from Australia! This mtDNA evidence does not mean, however, that modern humans originated in Australia any more than a deep African mtDNA root necessarily demonstrates that modern humans originated in Africa: The "deepest" geographic root could exist in different times and places, depending on ancient population dynamics. What this study *does* demonstrate is that ancient mtDNA lineages belonging to anatomically modern humans can,

---

[16]See C. Smith et al. (2003) for a cautionary view about this mtDNA sequence.

and do, become extinct—but that such extinctions need not necessarily imply any population replacement such as predicted by the Out of Africa model. The fossil evidence from Australia shows a continuity of modern humans over the past 60,000 years; however, ancient mtDNA lineages do not necessarily show such continuity. Instead what they show is that some mtDNA lineages went extinct through such processes as genetic drift and/or selective sweeps. This, then, is an excellent demonstration of why the history of any particular genetic locus or DNA sequence does not necessarily represent the history of a population. Thus comparing Neandertal DNA only to that of *living* humans does not adequately test whether or not Neandertals were distinct at the species level.

Third, if some amount of mtDNA recombination does take place—as some evidence is just beginning to suggest (Awadalla et al., 1999)—then all bets are off. Since mtDNA recombination tends to create more homogeneous populations of DNA sequences over time, one might expect greater amounts of mtDNA sequence diversity in the past, and therefore greater disparity between ancient hominin sequences and the more homogeneous sequences seen in modern humans. If true, this would suggest that the Neandertals might be more closely related to present-day humans than current interpretations of the mtDNA data suggest.

Fourth, the lack of regional affinity of Neandertal DNA to that of living Europeans does not necessarily invalidate the Multiregional Continuity Model since, as we saw earlier, one would actually expect to see similar levels of Neandertal ancestry in all contemporary regions under certain models of interregional gene flow. In other words, continued interregional gene flow will ultimately lead to a state of equilibrium in which it would be expected that all living humans would have the same degree of Neandertal ancestry (Relethford, 1998, 2001a).

Fifth, even if Neandertals went extinct, this would not, in and of itself, invalidate the Multiregional Continuity Model. The Out of Africa Model is only true if *all* archaic *Homo* populations were replaced, not just Neandertals, and there is absolutely no evidence of that in any other part of the Old World.

Sixth, data from single loci do not have enough power of resolution to answer the question of whether Neandertal genes contributed to the modern human gene pool. In fact, the mtDNA data can actually be seen as consistent with a high level of interbreeding between humans and Neandertals. It has been calculated that even if Neandertal mtDNA made up only 25% of the ancestry of extant human mtDNA some 68 kya, there would still be a more than 50% chance that all Neandertal mtDNA would have been lost because of genetic drift by the present day. To have any power, anthropologists need data from multiple unlinked genetic loci (Nordberg, 1998; Wall, 2000).

And last, but not least, is the little problem of whether or not sequencing ancient hominin DNA may even be technically possible due to the very real danger of contamination of fossil samples through excessive handling of specimens by modern researchers.[17]

Thus, after all the dust has settled, what is our final mental image of Neandertals? It is best summed up in the words of two prominent anatomists who were moved to write that "a healthy, normal Neanderthalian, . . . reincarnated and placed in a New York subway—provided that he were bathed, shaved, and dressed in modern clothing—would [be unlikely to] attract any more attention than some of its other denizens" (Straus and Cave, 1957).[18]

Given all that, it is still probably fair to say that a majority of Old World archeologists hold that the Out of Africa Model, rather than the Multiregional Continuity Model, best explains the archeological and paleontological data from Europe. Pivotal to this view is the conclusion that all of the earliest modern humans in Europe are associated with Aurignacian assemblages. There seems little doubt that this is the case for such geographically widespread regions as Germany (Vogelherd), Czechoslovakia (Mladec), and France (Les Rois). Certainly no evidence in Europe directly associates Aurignacian industries with Neandertals. Of course, the relevant question here is whether the Aurignacian industries reflect the dispersal of an anatomically modern population over the entire continent or local cultural developments that emerged independently within each region from preceding Middle Paleolithic Neandertal populations. As mentioned above, most archeologists favor the former hypothesis (population replacement) based on the following observations (Mellars, 1992):

- The Aurignacian seems to be a remarkably uniform technology that extends all the way from western Europe through central, eastern, and southern Europe and even into northern portions of the Near East. This implies that Aurignacian populations maintained social/cultural links over large geographic areas. This pattern of cultural uniformity in the Aurignacian is very different from the highly varied technologies (like the Mousterian of Acheulean tradition in western Europe or the Micoquian, eastern Charentian, and various leaf point industries in central and eastern Europe) found within the same areas of Europe during the preceding Middle Paleolithic.

- A local European origin for the Aurignacian cannot be convincingly demonstrated because the Aurignacian appears relatively suddenly without any clear local Middle Paleolithic antecedents. In any event, it would be difficult to explain how a rather uniform Aurignacian could emerge suddenly from the varied Middle Paleolithic industries. At present, the

[17]Thus if "Neandertal" DNA turned out to be very similar to that of Erik Trinkaus, Chris Stringer, or Milford Wolpoff, what would we conclude from that!

[18]Is this a commentary on Neandertals or New Yorkers? "New York—A city . . . so decadent that when I leave it I never dare look back lest I turn into salt and the conductor throw me over his left shoulder for good luck" (Frank Sullivan).

most likely source of the Aurignacian is in the Middle East (e.g., at Ksar Akil, Lebanon).

- It is fairly well established that early forms of the Aurignacian were present in most of Europe by 40–35 kya, and the available radiocarbon dates suggest an overall "cline" of older to younger dates running east to west across Europe (Fig. 12.3).

- Finally, it is now generally accepted that Aurignacian assemblages include the earliest well-documented occurrences of most, if not all, of the distinctive technological, "symbolic," and other cultural innovations diagnostic of the Upper Paleolithic. The dissemination of such technological breakthroughs throughout Eurasia is hard to imagine without the development of a relatively complex, structured language among these Aurignacian peoples.

If indeed there was replacement of early populations by more modern humans, then we should expect to see some chronological overlap between the two. In fact, this appears to be the case from sites in the Perigord and adjacent provinces of southwest France, where two quite distinct technological patterns, the Aurignacian and Châtelperronian (which has clear links to Middle Paleolithic Mousterian technologies), clearly overlap in time and are associated with anatomically modern and Neandertal morphologies (e.g., Saint-Césaire, Arcy-sur-Cure), respectively.

Central Europe

A number of sites in central Europe have yielded remains of early modern human types, the most notable being Mladec, Zlaty Kun, Vindija, Brno, Predmosti, and Dolni Vestonice. As noted earlier, these sites are of particular importance to those who argue the case of evolutionary continuity between Neandertals and modern humans.

Upper Paleolithic human fossils and Aurignacian tools were discovered at Mladec (Moravia) as early as 1881 (Fig. 13.11). Of particular interest is a necklace of drilled animal teeth and numerous distinctive flat bone (Mladec) points characteristic of the early Aurignacian in the region. The cranial and postcranial material indicates varying degrees of robusticity and size for this population, presumably indicative of sexual dimorphism. The important point about the skeletal biology of this population is that, although they are clearly *H. sapiens,* some individuals still have a number of features that are reminiscent of Neandertal morphology, including lambdoidal flattening, occipital bunning, thick cranial bones, and massive supraorbitals. These Neandertal-like features are found in a number of early Aurignacian modern humans from central Europe (Smith, 1982).

A number of other dental and cranial fragments from the region, including those from Zlaty Kun (Moravia), Vindija (upper cave), and Brno (Moravia), reinforce the comments made above about the "mosaic" nature

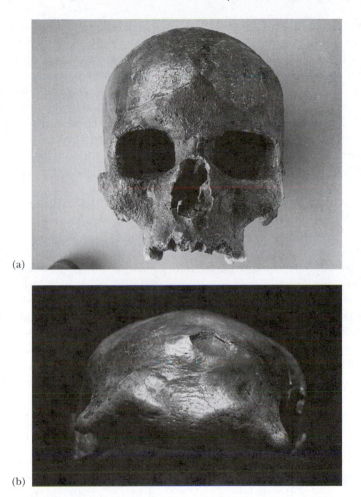

(a)

(b)

Fig. 13.11. Frontal views of (a) Mladec 1 and (b) Mladec 5. Upper Paleolithic human fossils and Aurignacian tools were first discovered at Mladec (Moravia) in 1881. The crania still have a number of features reminiscent of Neandertal morphology, such as thick cranial bones and massive supraorbitals. These Neandertal-like features are found in a number of early Aurignacian modern humans from central Europe. (Photos courtesy of B. Schumann.)

of the Mladec hominins. For example, the Zlaty Kun and Brno crania are also quite robust, with well-developed occipital bunning and thick, projecting supraorbital tori. However, the zygomatics lack the columnar, pillar-like frontal processes so characteristic of Neandertals. In addition, a distinct chin is usually present and the typical Neandertal-like retromolar space is less frequent.

From another late Mousterian (Micoquian) complex at Kulna, not far from Brno, has come a right maxillary fragment found in 1965 that preserves the canine through M^1. Subsequent excavations have yielded a right parietal fragment and a few isolated deciduous teeth. All these specimens have usually been considered Neandertal-like and date to about 50 kya based on ESR dating techniques (Rink et al., 1996).

The largest sample of Upper Paleolithic hominins yet discovered from central Europe comes from the open-air site of Predmosti (Moravia) (Fig. 13.12). In 1894 a communal grave was discovered containing the remains of 18 individuals, most with their heads oriented to the north. The grave was covered with limestone slabs and mammoth bones. There may be as many as 29 individuals represented at the site: 15 subadults ranging from a few months to midteens, 6 adult males, 2 to 4 adult females, and 4 unsexed individuals.[19] The hominins were associated with thousands of stone tools and a diverse bone and antler industry. The predominance of mammoth remains strongly suggests that these animals were the primary prey of the Predmosti hunters. The hominin specimens are quite variable, showing the same mosaic of modern human and Neandertal features noted earlier for this region. One interesting postcranial difference between this population and Neandertals is that the Predmosti population has higher brachial and crural indices, indicating that their distal limb segments were relatively longer than the corresponding bones in classic western European Neandertals.

Dolni Vestonice (Moravia) is a particularly interesting Upper Paleolithic site dated to about 30–25 kya (Tomaskova, 1995). The site consists of the traces of several tent-like huts, a large collection of mammoth bones, and large central hearths. Since excavations commenced in 1924, at least 35 individuals, 6 of whom have been found in proper graves associated with extensive ritual, have been recovered. In 1986 a triple burial was discovered at the site. Two men and one woman lay side by side, their bodies strewn with red ocher. A fragment of a charred horse rib in the mouth of one of the skeletons (DV 15) who clearly suffered from some severe illness may have served as a biting device used to overcome pain (Fig. 13.13). From pathological changes in this skeleton, including asymmetric shortening of the femur, bowing of femur and humerus, and dysplasias of sacrum, pubis and vertebral column, this individual may have suffered from chondrodysplasia calcificans punctata (CCP), a rare inherited disorder of bony epiphyses (Formicola et al., 1998, 2001). The three skeletons were submitted to a systematic kinship analysis using dental and other non-metric traits. These studies indicate a high probability that the three individuals were genetically related and actually belonged to one family (Alt et al., 1997).

Stone and bone tools, decorative items like beads and pendants, evidence of nets used for hunting, and clay figurines are numerous. One of

---

[19]Unfortunately, these were all destroyed in the 1945 fire at Mikulov Castle.

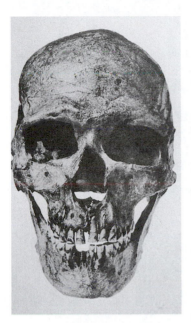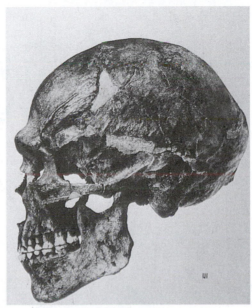

Fig. 13.12. Frontal and lateral views of Predmost 3, which displays a mosaic of Neandertal and modern human features, such as enlarged browridges combined with a gracile dental size. The largest sample of Upper Paleolithic hominins discovered from central Europe comes from this open-air site at Predmosti (Moravia). (Photos courtesy of F. Smith.)

the clay figurines is of a human head with very asymmetrical left facial features. One of the specimens found at the site (Dolni Vestonice 3) is a virtually complete female skeleton showing severe facial deformation on the left side. Could it be that the clay figurine was an artistic rendering of this individual? If so, it would be the first "portrait" of a human being from the archeological record. Some burials seem to provide evidence of some type of ritual behavior. For example, bodies are often laid on their right sides with knees strongly flexed and are oriented in an east-west direction with the head toward the east, some are placed within a central settlement area facing the hearth, some are associated with perforated carnivore canines and pendants of mammoth ivory, and some have their head and pelvic areas covered by ochre (a dark yellow or reddish pigment) (Klima, 1987; Svoboda, 1987b). Pollen analysis indicates a forest-steppe environment for the site (Mason et al., 1994).

As noted earlier, those who favor the idea of evolutionary continuity between Neandertal and modern human populations in Europe often turn to the paleontological and archeological records of central Europe for support (Brose and Wolpoff, 1971; Frayer, 1992; Jelinek, 1969; Lindly and Clark, 1990; Smith, 1982; Wolpoff, 1989b). They argue that the usual

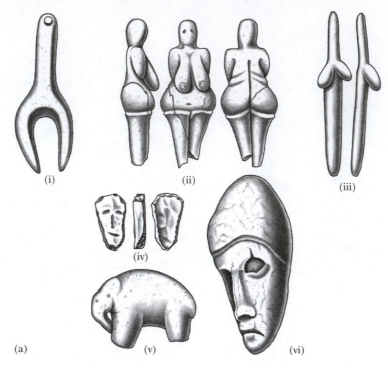

Fig. 13.13. (a) Examples of clay figurines found at a triple burial at Dolni Veston-ice, Moravia. Scale: (i), (iii), and (vi) 34% actual size; (ii), (iv), (v) 25% actual size. (b) In the burial, the individual in the middle (of undetermined sex) is flanked by two males, both of whom had ivory pendants around their teeth. (Coles and Higgs, 1969; Stringer and Gamble, 1993.)

comparisons made between Neandertals and the first anatomically mod-ern western European populations, known as **Cro-Magnons** (Fig. 13.14) after the site where their remains were first identified ("big cliffs" in French), are potentially misleading because the latter are not necessarily the earliest representatives of post-Neandertal Europeans. According to this line of reasoning, the earliest putative descendants of European Nean-dertals from eastern and central Europe at Mladec, Vindija, Brno, Pred-mosti, Dolni Vestonice, and Zlaty Kun predate Cro-Magnons from western Europe and are more archaic looking as well. These researchers also argue that there is archeological continuity between Middle and Upper Pale-olithic assemblages as well, thus further attesting to the continuity of the Neandertal–modern human transition in Europe.

There is little doubt that, historically at least, studies of the Neandertal Question have overemphasized the western European fossil record at the expense of the central European one, particularly at sites in Hungary, east-ern Austria, western Rumania, northern Croatia, and southern portions of

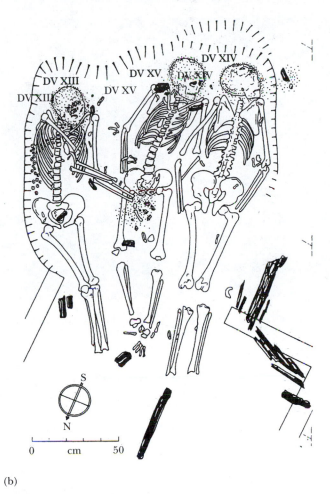

(b)

Moravia and Slovakia.[20] In fact, some of the first Neandertal fossils ever discovered were from central Europe (at Ochoz and Sipka) and the Krapina
fossils still remain the largest sample of Neandertals known from a single
locality. Similarly, the largest sample of early Upper Paleolithic skeletons
comes from Predmosti, yet it has often been overshadowed in the literature by such western European sites as Cro-Magnon and Grimaldi.

Upper Pleistocene hominins from central Europe are associated with
both Middle and Upper Paleolithic assemblages. The Szeletian and Aurignacian are the earliest Upper Paleolithic assemblages in the region, with
the former being slightly older than the latter. The Szeletian, found mainly

[20]Important sites in central Europe include Moravia (Predmosti, Dolni Vestonice, Sipka,
Kulna, Mladec, and Brno), Croatia (Krapina, Vindija, Veternica), Slovakia (Sala, Ganovce),
Hungary (Subalyuk), and Austria (Willendorf, Miesslingstal) (Smith, 1982).

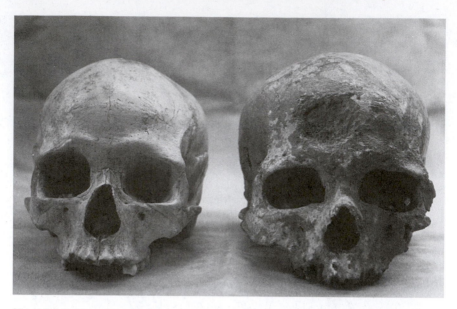

Fig. 13.14.   Frontal view of Upper Pleistocene hominins from (left) Abri Pataud and (right) Cro Magnon. (Photo courtesy of B. Schumann.)

in the eastern part of central Europe, is described as having a strong Middle Paleolithic "flavor" and some archeologists believe that it evolved directly out of the local Middle Paleolithic. The Gravettian follows the Aurignacian in central Europe and consists of the usual array of Upper Paleolithic blade tools, including burins, Gravettian points (distinctive small, pointed points with straight blunted backs), extensive and intricate bone and ivory items, and evidence of ritual burials.

As mentioned, one of the earliest Neandertal discoveries was the symphyseal, or chin, fragment found in 1880 at Sipka (unfortunately, this and many other human fossils were destroyed by fire in 1945). Of more anthropological importance, however, are the larger Neandertal samples from a number of central European sites, all apparently dating to the end Riss-Würm or early Würm and all associated with Mousterian assemblages.

The richest of these sites, Krapina, was excavated between 1899 and 1905 and has yielded an extensive faunal and archeological assemblage. The hominin sample consists of over 800 fragments, including nearly 200 isolated teeth representing about 80 individuals, the greatest number of Neandertal remains ever recovered from a single locality (Fig. 13.15). The site is divided into 13 stratigraphic units, of which the upper 9 contain Middle Paleolithic artifacts. Most of the human fossils are from levels 3 and 4 and appear to date to the end of the Riss-Würm interglacial. ESR and U-S dates on hominin tooth enamel from the site indicate that the hominins date to about 130 kya. Both cranial and postcranial remains

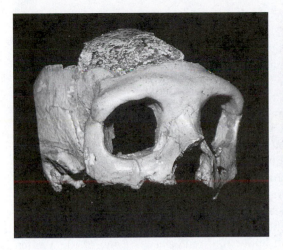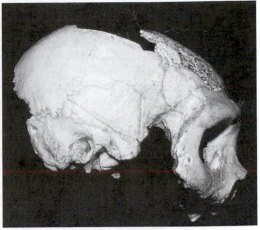

Fig. 13.15. Two views of the Krapina C (or 3) cranium. (Photos courtesy of F. Smith.)

show most of the distinctive Neandertal features listed earlier and clearly align the Krapina hominins with Neandertals from western Europe (Minugh-Purvis et al., 2000). One unusual feature of the Krapina Neandertals is the size of their anterior dentition, perhaps the largest of any Pleistocene hominin sample. Estimated stature for the Krapina Neandertals averages 5 feet 3 inches. It is interesting that several specimens from level 8, in particular cranial elements of a 6- to 8-year-old juvenile (Krapina 1) and a partial occipital bone (Krapina 11), lack features usually found in Neandertals (such as the suprainiac fossa) and suggest to some that these fossils from the upper layers at Krapina may be transitional to anatomically modern hominins (Rink et al., 1995; Smith, 1978, 1982; Wolpoff, 1979).

Because all of the Neandertal remains from Krapina are extremely fragmented, some have suggested that the Krapina Neandertals may have practiced cannibalism, breaking the bones to obtain brains, marrow, and other soft tissues for ritual or dietary purposes. However, careful analysis of the hominin sample reveals that none of the damage patterns can be explained solely as a product of cannibalism, and it may be just as likely that the damage was caused by normal geological and biological processes (Trinkaus, 1985; Villa, 1992). However, remains of 13 Neandertals found near Valence, France, clearly had cut marks produced by flint tools on both cranial fragments and a proximal radius (Defleur et al., 1993). Again, it is tantalizing, if unproven, evidence of cannibalism among at least some Neandertals.

Another nearby site, Vindija, is only about 50 km from Krapina and has yielded over 80 Neandertal fragments since 1974 (Ahern, 2004). The earliest hominins at the site (from level G_3) date to the lower Würm and are associated with a Mousterian industry. It is interesting that a case can be made for the presence of both late Mousterian and Upper Paleolithic tool types in this layer. A few isolated human teeth, a radial fragment, and cranial fragments are associated in higher stratigraphic levels (G_1) with Aurignacian and Gravettian assemblages, including some bone tools (Crummett and Miracle, 1995; Karavanic and Smith, 1998). The G_3 hominin sample is clearly Neandertal-like in all relevant features. Furthermore, the Vindija hominins show some features foreshadowing early modern *H. sapiens,* such as the reduction in size of the supraorbital tori, reduced midfacial prognathism, incipient chin development, and the lack of both occipital bunning and lambdoidal flattening. For this reason, some anthropologists suggest that the Vindija sample may be an intermediate form between Neandertals and more modern-looking Europeans. Of particular interest is the description of two hominin cranial fragments from the G_1 level: a zygomatic bone that provides the first information about the midfacial anatomy of the Vindija hominins, and a frontal/supraorbital torus fragment (Smith and Ahern, 1994). Both specimens exhibit Neandertal-like morphology and both are presumably associated with the Aurignacian industry, based on the presence of a single split-based bone point. This is significant because it has often been assumed that only early modern Europeans produced the Aurignacian. These later Vindija Neandertal-like hominins may date to as young as 29 kya. If so, these would be the latest surviving Neandertals in the fossil record. However, the apparent association of Neandertal remains with Aurignacian tools remains problematic at this site, given that postdepositional processes, such as cryoturbation and cave bear denning, are evident (d'Errico et al., 1998; Smith et al., 1999).

Another interesting Neandertal fossil comes from the site of Ganovce in northern Slovakia. There, in 1926, a Neandertal endocast with a few adhering segments of the cranial vault was discovered. The endocast reveals that the overall shape of the cranium was distinctly Neandertal-like. Estimated cranial capacity is about 1320 cc, near the average for Riss-Würm Neandertals.

Further information about cranial anatomy of central European Neandertals comes from a frontal bone recovered at Sal'a in western Slovakia. It is interesting that this individual survived trauma over the right orbit, where there is a healed lesion. In terms of the morphology of its supraorbital region and overall proportions, the specimen is clearly Neandertal-like. However, this specimen, like some of those from Vindija, also shows more "transitional" features, such as a greater frontal curvature than is commonly seen in most western Neandertals and Krapina Neandertals (Sládek et al., 2002).

Another early Neandertal discovery (1905), the mandible from Ochoz, southern Moravia, preserves the alveolar region and complete dentition (except for the right M_3). Further excavations in the 1960s produced two small human cranial fragments (portions of a parietal and temporal squama) and an isolated right M_3 found associated with an end Riss-Würm age fauna. The mandible and teeth have all the features normally associated with western European Neandertals: a retromolar space, large anterior teeth, and taurodont molars.

Similar features are found in a Neandertal mandible from Subalyuk, Hungary. Here, fragmentary remains of a Neandertal adult and child were found in association with a Mousterian assemblage. The adult specimen consists of a mandible preserving the left canine through M_3, molars on the right side, and a few postcranial elements, including a sacrum and the upper part of the sternum, or manubrium. Many western European Neandertals are characterized by a "barrel-shaped" upper thorax, and the ventrally concave Subalyuk manubrium indicates a similar morphology for this central European Neandertal.[21] The Subalyuk child is represented by a calvaria, most of both maxillas, and most of the deciduous dentition. The individual was probably about 3 years old when it died. The calvaria is long, low, and broad and already there is evidence of lambdoidal flattening and incipient occipital bunning. The suture between the frontal bones (metopic suture) is still present, as it is in most other Neandertal children.

Thus, given the paleontological and archeological richness and complexity of these central European sites, it is easy to see how proponents of both the Out of Africa Model and the Multiregional Continuity Model can manipulate data to support their respective views, the former to argue that the transition from Middle to Upper Paleolithic industries was the result of anatomically modern populations sweeping across Europe from east to west and the latter to argue that there was both technological and anatomical continuity between Middle Paleolithic Neandertals and Upper Paleolithic modern populations.

To help sort out these issues, we next turn to the important fossils of the Near East.

FOSSIL EVIDENCE FROM THE NEAR EAST

Hominin fossils from the Near East are extremely relevant to the issue of modern human origins. As previously mentioned, Upper Paleolithic cultures first appear in western Asia (the Near East) about 40 kya; and the associated hominins, like a child's cranium from Ksar Akil, Lebanon, dated to about 37 kya, are anatomically modern. As in western Europe, Middle Paleolithic (Mousterian) assemblages in the Near East (and even into southern Siberia) are also associated with Neandertals (e.g., Tabun, Amud, and Kebara Caves in Israel; Shanidar Cave in Iraq; Teshik-Tash Cave in Uzbekistan; and Okladnikov and Denisova caves in Siberia) (Fig. 13.16) (Goebel, 1999).

---

[21]Although see Franciscus and Churchill (2002) regarding the shape of the thorax in one of the Shanidar specimens.

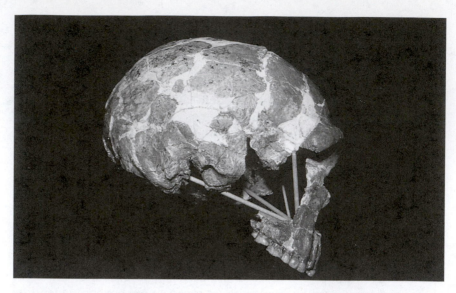

Fig. 13.16.   Lateral view of the Tabun 1 cranium.   (Photo courtesy of F. Smith.)

However, unlike the situation prevailing in western Europe, anatomically modern humans in the Near East are also associated with Middle Paleolithic (Mousterian) assemblages at several sites, the best known being Mugharet es Skhul and Jebel Qafzeh Caves in northern Israel (Valladas et al., 1987, 1988) (see below).

Within the past decade or so, new advances in dating techniques, particularly TL, ESR, and U-S, have virtually revolutionized views of modern human origins, particularly as they relate to many of these Levantine sites. Specifically, these new dates indicate that hominins associated with the Acheulo-Yabrudian and Mousterian industries, such as those at Zuttiyeh, Tabun, Skhul, Qafzeh, Kebara, Shanidar, and Amud, span both the late Middle and Upper Paleolithic and, most important, that the archeological "revolution" characterizing the Middle/Upper Paleolithic transition post-dated by tens of thousands of years the first appearance of anatomically modern humans in the region (Bar-Yosef, 1992; Bar-Yosef and Vandermeersch, 1993).[22] It now seems apparent that Neandertals and early modern humans coexisted (or alternated) in Eurasia for tens of thousands of years, perhaps from before 100 kya to just under 35 kya. For example, TL dating of burnt flints and ESR and U-S dating of dental samples at Qafzeh reveal that the early modern *H. sapiens* from this site (the remains of at least 20 hominins are represented), which had previously been assumed to be only about 40–50 kya, are actually on the order of about 90 kya (Aitken

---

[22]The middle to earlier Late Pleistocene archeological sequence in the Near East (Levant) is divided into the Upper or Late Acheulean, the Mugharan (Acheulo-Yabrudian), and the Mousterian traditions.

and Valladas, 1992; McDermott et al., 1993; Schwarcz and Grün, 1992; Schwarcz et al., 1988b; Stringer et al., 1989; Valladas et al., 1987, 1988). At the other extreme, Neandertal remains from Saint-Césaire, France, have been dated to about 35 kya (Mercier et al., 1991). Proponents of the Out of Africa Model use this type of evidence to bolster the view that Neandertals could not have evolved into anatomically modern humans as the Multiregional Continuity Model proposes, but must have been replaced by them instead.

Mount Carmel Caves (Skhul and Tabun)

Although archeological evidence indicates that early hominins were using the Levant as an Out of Africa corridor through much of the Lower Pleistocene (e.g., Ubeidiya at about 1.4 mya, Evron Quarry at about 1.0 mya, Gesher Benot Ya'aqov at about 0.8 mya), hominin skeletal remains at these sites are scarce (Goren-Inbar et al., 2000). Actually, the earliest evidence for hominin control of fire is the presence of burnt seeds, wood, and flint at the Acheulean site of Gesher Benot Ya'aqov dated to approximately 800,000 years ago (Goren-Inbar et al., 2004). The hominin fossil record substantially improves with the discoveries from Israel's Mount Carmel caves. When fossil hominins from the Mount Carmel caves of Tabun and Skhul were first described in the 1930s by Theodore McCown and Arthur Keith, it was thought that the Skhul hominins represented a population characterized by a mosaic of modern and primitive anatomical features and that the Tabun hominins represented a more primitive, "Neanderthaloid" population (Fig. 13.17). Later, they reversed their opinion and concluded that the Skhul and Tabun populations represented the morphological extremes of a single people in the "throes of evolutionary change" (McCown and Keith, 1939).

Skhul is one of the most important of the Near Eastern sites from which more modern-like humans have been recovered. However, it should be noted that the Skhul V cranium is usually the one specimen specifically mentioned as being more modern looking—there is a great deal of morphological variation among the Skhul hominin sample, with some specimens, like Skhul IV and IX, being much more Neandertal-like (Corruccini, 1992, 1994).

The site consists of three successively older units: layer A, which contains a mixed assemblage of Middle and Upper Paleolithic artifacts and some potsherds; layer B, which contains cranial and postcranial remains of at least 10 individuals (3 of whom were children) associated with a Levallois-Mousterian (Middle Paleolithic) industry; and layer C, which also has a stone tool industry similar to layer B. The hominins from layer B, most of which appear to have been intentionally buried, represent an early form of what most paleoanthropologists regard as anatomically modern humans. Morphologically, the Skhul hominins are most similar to those from the nearby site of Qafzeh near Nazareth. Recent ESR and U-S dating methods suggest that the Skhul hominins may fall into two faunal ages within layer B, an older assemblage of

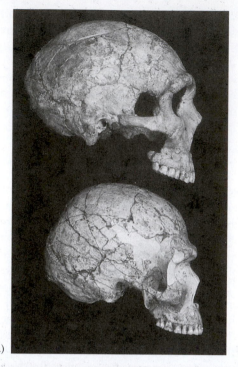

(a)

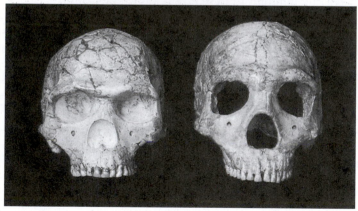

(b)

Fig. 13.17.   (a) Right lateral views of *Homo sapiens neanderthalensis*, Amud 1 (*above*), and early *Homo sapiens sapiens*, Skhul 5 (*below*). (b) Frontal views of Skhul 5 (*left*) and Amud 1 (*right*). (Photos by C. Tarka, courtesy E. Delson and Israel Antiquities Authority and Peabody Museum, Harvard University.)

about 80–119 kya and a younger assemblage about 40 kya (McDermott et al., 1993; Mercier et al., 1993; Stringer et al., 1989).

It is interesting to note that the stone-tool traditions of these more anatomically modern hominins found in Skhul and Qafzeh are practically indistinguishable from those used at a later date by the morphologically distinct Neandertal-like hominins from the same region (e.g., at Kebara), and both hominin groups apparently practiced intentional burials as well.[23] The only major "cultural" distinctions between the two groups seem to be that the Neandertal assemblages (e.g., Kebara) have a higher percentage of points (presumably hafted to wooden shafts as spear heads) than the Qafzeh assemblages[24] and that the more anatomically modern human assemblages (e.g., Qafzeh and Skhul) include more evidence of deliberate burials (Skhul 1, 4, 5 and Qafzeh 8–11, 15 are in anatomical articulation) and body decorations—such as the use of red ochre (at Qafzeh) and *Glycymeris* shells (at Qafzeh and Skhul) for necklaces, a nonedible molluscan species that must have been brought in from at least 50 km away (Bar-Yosef, 1992; Shea, 2003).

Although the cultural distinctions between the more modern Qafzeh/Skhul group and the more Neandertal-like Amud/Shanidar/Tabun group may not be so great, some of their morphological differences may reflect subtle, yet significant, biosocial distinctions (Churchill, 1996). For example, the femoral neck-shaft angles in the Near Eastern Neandertal-like sample are much lower than in the Qafzeh/Skhul sample. This difference in femoral neck angulation parallels that seen between modern foragers and more sedentary human populations, with the Qafzeh/Skhul group reflecting the sedentary pattern and the Neandertal group the foragers pattern. Of course, both of these Middle Paleolithic groups were undoubtedly foragers, but because the femoral neck-shaft angle decreases with age and level of activity, the suggestion has been made that *immature* Qafzeh/Skhul individuals may have participated less in foraging-related locomotor activity than the *immature* individuals of the Neandertal-like group. If true, this implies that the immature Qafzeh/Skuhl individuals were being cared for by some of the adult population in or near a primary site location, suggesting in turn a more elaborate social organizational system in this group than in the more Neandertal-like groups. Some support for this idea comes from the fact that commensal rodents are much more common at Qafzeh than at Neandertal sites like Tabun, Amud, and Kebara, a zooarcheological pattern expected at sites with relatively longer periods of residence at any one time (Trinkaus, 1993).

It is also seems that even though the stone-tool traditions of the more anatomically modern hominins from Skhul and Qafzeh are similar to those of the Neandertal-like hominins from the same region, there are subtle differences in hand morphology between the two groups. The Skhul/Qafzeh group shows detailed similarities to the hands of Upper Paleolithic modern humans (Niewoehner, 2001).

Other subtle behavioral differences between anatomically modern and Neandertal-like populations from the Near East can also be teased out of

---

[23]For an opposing view of intentional burial at such Middle Paleolithic burial sites as Qafzeh, Saint-Césaire, Kebara, Amud, Dederiyeh, and others, see Gargett (1999).

[24]Wooden spears are known from the Lower Paleolithic of Europe—for example at Clacton-on-Sea, England, and at Lehringen and Schöningen, Germany.

the fossil record. For example, dental evidence from remains of mountain gazelles at some sites have been used as an indicator of seasonality because of the strong correlation between the nature of acellular cementum bands in their teeth and their seasonal diet, which consists primarily of grazing during the winter rain season and browsing during the summer dry season. The pattern of seasonal gazelle use from Kebara, Qafzeh, and Tabun reveals two different patterns. In the Kebara Mousterian levels, gazelle were apparently hunted in both the dry and the wet seasons, whereas at Qafzeh the evidence suggests only single seasonal hunting of gazelle during the dry season. Tabun B shows a multiseasonal pattern (like Kebara) and Tabun C shows a more seasonal one (like Qafzeh), except hunting here was in the wet season.

Thus gazelles associated with the more modern hominin sample at Qafzeh suggests that these hominins probably had what is known as a circulating residential mobility strategy in contrast to the more locally intensive radiating mobility pattern inferred for the more Neandertal-like humans at Kebara. Circulating mobility strategies involve seasonal movements by hunter-gatherer bands from one temporary residential camp to another in a recurrent annual cycle. This contrasts with radiating strategies that involve movements between more permanent (multiseasonal) residential base-camps and less permanent (highly seasonal) logistic camps positioned near important resources. It is hypothesized that these two strategies may help explain some of the lithic patterns seen in the Levantine Mousterian. For example, if Qafzeh was a highly seasonal occupation site, then the relatively low frequencies of pointed artifacts there may reflect the abandonment of these sites before resource depletion required increased investment in the production of hunting tools. By contrast, the Neandertal-like humans at Kebara were presumably less seasonally mobile and, therefore, hunted more frequently than did the early modern humans at Qafzeh. The multiseasonal occupation sites such as Kebara probably required the Neandertal-like humans to forage for considerably longer periods than their more modern human counterparts and was thus a less energetically efficient method of resource exploitation (Lieberman and Shea, 1994).

The nearby cave at Tabun provides one of the best, or at least one of the longest, yardsticks of stone-tool changes through the Middle/Upper Pleistocene sequence. The dating of the cave deposits has been controversial (Fig. 13.18) (Grün and Stringer, 2000; Grün et al., 1991; Jelinek, 1982; McDermott et al., 1993). Pre-Mousterian layers at Tabun contain both upper Acheulean levels and Mugharan assemblages (locally referred to as the "Acheulo-Yabrudian tradition"), an industry characterized by the predominance of sidescrapers made from thick flakes with little evidence of Levallois technique. This Acheulo-Yabrudian industry is now thought to be older than 200 kya in the region and may date back to well over 400 kya (Bar-Yosef, 1995).

A revised chronology of Tabun's layers has recently been determined based on ESR and TL methods (Grün and Stringer, 2000). Levallois techniques become more frequent in level Tabun D, dating back to some 133 ± 13 kya; unfortunately, no human fossils have yet been discovered in association with this industry. The overlying layer, Tabun C, is distinguished by more ovate Levallois flakes and a lower frequency of points. Neandertal remains associated with this industry, which date to 120 ± 16 kya, include a

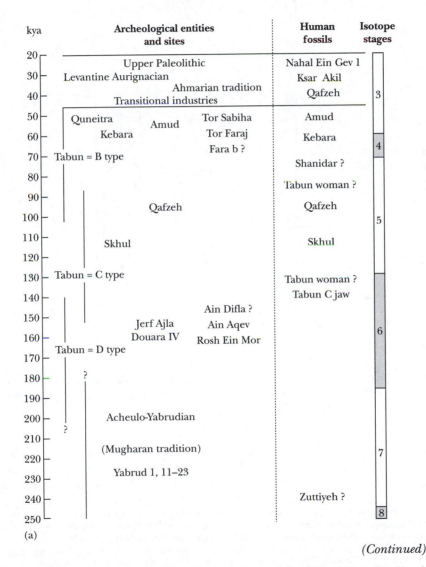

(a)

(Continued)

Fig. 13.18.   (a) Chronology for Near Eastern sites and fossil hominins. (Bar-Yosef, 1992.)

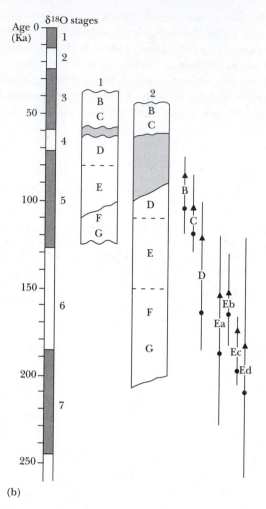

(b)

Fig. 13.18. *(Continued)* (b) Three suggested chronologies for Tabun. Scheme 1 (Jelinek, 1982) and scheme 2 (Bar-Yosef, 1989) are compared with recent ESR results (Grün and Stringer, 2000.)

nearly complete adult female skeleton (Tabun C I),[25] a virtually complete adult mandible (Tabun C II), and some isolated postcranial pieces (the hominins from Qafzeh and Skhul are also associated with this tool industry). An

[25]Unfortunately, it is not altogether certain whether this skeleton actually came from layer C or B (Bar-Yosef and Callander, 1999; Garrod and Bate, 1937). Recent U-S dating suggests that the skeleton may be only about 32,000–75,000 years old, depending on which uranium-uptake model is used for the analysis. If these younger dates hold up, it would indicate that the Tabun C 1 skeleton was either buried into layer C or was actually from a younger stratigraphic level (Schwarcz et al., 1998). However, others suggest the skeleton is actually from layer B and is closer to 122,000 years old (Grün and Stringer, 2000).

adult femoral shaft and lower molar were also recovered from layer E. Thus the estimated age of the Tabun Neandertals lies mainly within ^{18}O stage 5, close to the dates obtained for the more modern-looking hominins from Skhul and Qafzeh. Layer B at Tabun is recognized by the predominance of long, narrow flakes and short, broad-based Levallois points and dates to 102 ± 17 kya. This tool tradition is known from several other sites that also yield Neandertal-like hominins, including Kebara and Amud.

Since the stone-tool industries at Tabun seem to show certain progressive changes through time (particularly in the ratio of width to thickness of unretouched flakes), these tool types have been used as a sort of master chronology for correlation of other Near Eastern sites. For example, Tabun B–type Mousterian industries are found in the hominin-bearing layers of Kebara and possibly Skhul, while Tabun C is found at Qafzeh.

Qafzeh and Kebara

The site at Qafzeh preserves at least three burials of anatomically modern humans: (1) an adult lying on its right side with knees partially drawn up; (2) a double burial consisting of a young woman lying on her right side with a small child at her feet; and (3) a young boy with deer antlers placed over his hands (Fig. 13.19). Also present are the perforated shells of *Glycymeris*,

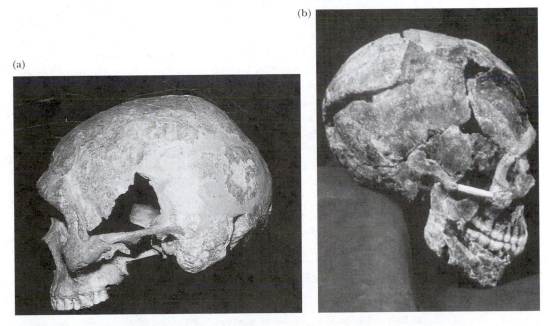

Fig. 13.19.   (a) Cranium of Jebel Qafzeh 6. (Photo courtesy of F. Smith.) (b) Cranium of Jebel Qafzeh 9. (Photo courtesy of E. Delson and and Israel Antiquities Authority.)

which were apparently designed for use as amulets or necklaces. As noted earlier, both TL and ESR dates suggest an age for the Qafzeh hominins of about 90–100 kya. Several of the Qafzeh hominins (Qafzeh 8, 9, 11) have human-like chins, although it is interesting that none of the roughly contemporaneous Skhul specimens do (Schwartz and Tattersall, 2000).

The Kebara Cave is located on the western side of Mount Carmel. Artifacts from the site resemble those from Tabun B. Both TL and ERS dating techniques give an age of approximately 60 kya for the site (Bar-Yosef et al., 1992; Schwarz et al., 1989; Valladas et al., 1987). In 1983 an adult male skeleton, probably between 25 and 35 years old, was recovered from a dugout grave pit. The cranium appears to have been removed from the body after the flesh had decayed, perhaps many months after the individual had died. This is thought to represent the first clear case of later human intervention in a primary burial. It is hard to imagine what (religious?) motive might have inspired such an act.[26] Below the well-preserved lower jaw was an intact hyoid bone, the small bone that anchors some of the tongue muscles. The bone is identical in size and shape to the same bone in modern humans and suggests to some that the morphological basis for human speech was fully developed in the Near East by the Middle Paleolithic (Arensburg et al., 1989, 1990; Bar-Yosef and Vandermeersch, 1993; Houghton, 1993).[27]

All 24 of the presacral vertebrae—7 cervical, 12 thoracic, and 5 lumbar—are preserved in the Kebara skeleton. These vertebrae are morphologically similar to, and within the size range of, modern human populations. As seen in other Neandertal individuals, the spinous processes of the 6th and 7th cervical (neck) vertebrae are more horizontal than in modern populations. In addition, the cervical segment of the Kebara individual is short relative to thoracic and lumbar vertebral lengths, although the functional significance of this feature is unclear.

The pelvis is the most complete of any Neandertal discovered to date and is characterized by an elongated iliopubic ramus, a morphology not usually seen in modern humans (Fig. 13.9). The pelvic inlet is modern in size, but the pelvic outlet is confined relative to modern females, although it should be remembered that this is a male pelvis, not a female one (Tague, 1992). This supports the view that Neandertals did not have elongated gestation periods or bigger neonates necessitating enlarged pelvic diameters, as had been earlier hypothesized (Rosenberg, 1992; Trinkaus, 1984a). This peculiar pelvic morphology is restricted to other Neandertal specimens, such as those from Europe and at Shanidar and does not characterize the more modern specimens from Skhul and Qafzeh (Stewart, 1960).

[26]Frank Hole notes that later Natufians sometimes detached the crania from skeletons and asks the interesting question of whether an early Natufian grave digger discovered this burial and removed the cranium (Bar-Yosef et al., 1992).
[27]For a different viewpoint see Lieberman (1989).

As we noted above, McCown and Keith (1939) reversed their earlier opinion of the Skhul and Tabun populations by finally concluding that they represented the morphological extremes of a single, highly variable, species. This conclusion is of some importance to the logic of the Out of Africa debate, for if anatomically modern humans first evolved in Africa, one of the first early populations they would have met as they moved out of Africa would have been the more Neandertal-like populations of the Levant (as represented by the Tabun and Amud populations). Therefore, Out of Africa supporters necessarily regard these two Levant populations as being distinct at the specific level. In order to test the distinctiveness of these two populations, non-metric cranial features of eight of the most complete specimens from the Levant were analyzed to see if two distinct populations, one modern and one Neandertal-like, could actually be identified in this sample using phylogenetic analyses (Kramer et al., 2001). As it turns out, not a single one of the 17 most parsimonious trees revealed a Neandertal clade at Tabun and Amud distinct from the early modern sample from Skhul and Qafzeh, this in spite of the fact that the 12 cranial features used could clearly cladistically distinguish European Neandertal cranial morphology from that of anatomically modern humans from the early Upper Paleolithic of Europe. The conclusion of this study is that neither Levantine Neandertals nor early moderns were characterized by a set of uniquely derived characters. Instead, many of the so-called Neandertal autapomorphies were not unique to Levant Neandertals and were variably present in the early moderns from Skhul and Qafzeh. Instead of complete replacement (as a strict Out of Africa theory demands), the extreme variation seen in the Skhul and Qafzeh samples suggest that while anatomically moderns may have first originated in Africa, they mixed with other populations (i.e., Neandertals) as they spread and expanded their range into the Levant.

Shanidar

Probably the most informative sample of Near Eastern Neandertal remains comes from the Shanidar Cave in the Zagros Mountains of Iraq, excavated by Ralph Solecki between 1951 and 1960 (Fig. 13.20). This is the largest sample of Neandertal partial skeletons and consists of the remains of seven adults (Shanidar 1–6, 8) and two infants (Shanidar 7, 9) associated with a Mousterian industry. Two radiocarbon dates on charcoal associated with Shanidar crania 1 and 5 range from 50 to 45 kya. The Shanidar 2 cranium may be closer to 60 kya. An important lesson to be learned from this sample is how variable Neandertal morphology can be. For example, the Shanidar 1 cranium has the highest cranial vault of any Neandertal, whereas the Shanidar 5 cranium has one of the lowest. Similarly, Shanidar 5 displays the typical Neandertal condition of inflated maxilla containing large air sinuses, whereas Shanidar 1, 2, and 4 have relatively flat maxillas. The Shanidar mandibles are typically Neandertal in morphology in that

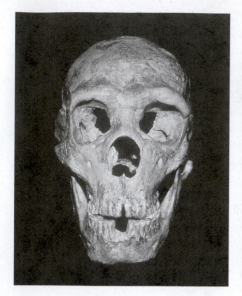
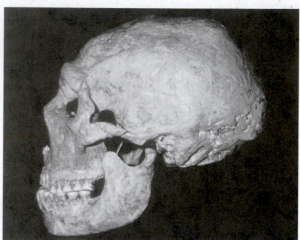

Fig. 13.20.   The cranium of Shanidar 1.   (Photo courtesy of E. Trinkaus.)

they possess an anteriorly placed dental arcade to match the corresponding facial projection, mental foramina located posteriorly below the first molar, and large retromolar spaces behind the third molars (Stewart, 1961; Stringer and Trinkaus, 1981; Trinkaus, 1983, 1984b; Trinkaus and Shipman, 1992).

Analysis of the costal skeleton (rib cage) of Shanidar 3 shows that the Neandertal rib cage was larger and more rounded and rugose; it enclosed a larger thoracic volume than other early modern humans and recent Europeans. This may reflect relatively elevated ventilatory levels in this group (compared to modern humans), which may be associated with increased activity levels in this population. However, since lung volume scales isometrically to body mass in mammals, this may also simply reflect greater body mass in Neandertals compared to the modern sample (Franciscus and Churchill, 2002).

There is an extremely high incidence of antemortem trauma in the Shanidar sample (Trinkaus and Zimmerman, 1982; Trinkaus et al., 1994). Of the six reasonably complete adults, four show evidence of past injury, and two of them (Shanidar 1 and 3) must have been at least partially incapacitated. Shanidar 1 had injuries to the right side of the head, the right humerus, and the right fifth metatarsal as well as atrophy of the right clavicle, scapula, and humerus; osteomyelitis of the right clavicle; degenerative joint disease of the right knee, ankle, and first tarsometatarsal joint; and injuries to the left tibia. Shanidar 3 had trauma-induced injuries to the right ankle joint and a penetrating wound in the right side of the rib cage.

Shanidar 4 suffered a fracture of the right rib cage, and Shanidar 5 had a scalp wound over the left frontal. The importance of these facts, besides verifying that Neandertal habitats were just as violent as modern urban America seems to be, is that Neandertals had already evolved social mechanisms to care for such disabled members of their group, since many of these injured individuals show evidence of wound healing and apparently lived to old age.[28]

Zuttiyeh

The oldest reasonably complete hominin specimen from the Near East is the frontal/facial fragment from Zuttiyeh, Israel. The specimen is associated with the Acheulo-Yabrudian tradition and is estimated to be between 250 and 350 kya. As the oldest specimen from the region, it assumes great importance in the debate surrounding the Multiregional Continuity and Out of Africa Models of modern human origins. Phylogenetic inferences drawn from the Zuttiyeh specimen have been diverse: some have regarded it as an ancestral Neandertal, others as being uniquely ancestral to modern hominins in the Levant and not ancestral to Levant Neandertals, and still others as a more generalized ancestor of all more recent West Asian hominins (Simmons et al., 1991). More recently, some proponents of the Multiregional Continuity Model have suggested that Zuttiyeh shares significant morphological features with east Asian Middle Pleistocene hominins found in Zhoukoudian, Gongwangling, or Hexian, most of which do not characterize Middle Pleistocene hominins from either Europe or Africa; if true, this would seriously undermine the Out of Africa Model (Sohn and Wolpoff, 1993).

As we have seen, the Out of Africa Model contends that Middle and/or early Upper Pleistocene Africans are uniquely ancestral to all modern humans. Therefore, it should follow that the earliest Levantine hominins ancestral to the Skhul/Qafzeh moderns at Zuttiyeh, for example, should be more morphologically similar to Middle and/or early Upper Pleistocene Africans than to similarly aged hominins from any other geographical region. However, if the above-mentioned analysis of Zuttiyeh is correct, then the East Asian features found not only in Zuttiyeh but also from Tabun and Qafzeh falsify one of the expectations of the Out of Africa Model and support a model of local morphological continuity in the Levant. The Multiregional Continuity Model proponents conclude that (1) The Neandertal and non-Neandertal populations of the Levant are only racially distinct and cannot be differentiated at the species level and (2) the significant levels of

---

[28]Neandertals clearly had a tough time of it. Trauma has been reported in the original Neandertal specimen (fractured ulna), La Chapelle-aux-Saints 1 (broken rib), La Ferrassie 1 (injury to the right proximal femur), Krapina 180 (nonunion fracture of the ulna), La Quina 5 (injury producing some atrophy of the left humerus), and Sala 1 (injury to the right supraorbital torus) (Trinkaus and Zimmerman, 1982; Trinkaus et al., 1994).

East Asian ancestry in the Levant populations (Neandertal, non-Neandertal, or both) demonstrate that "no known African population can be the unique ancestor of all modern populations" (Sohn and Wolpoff, 1993). However, given the strong "Ethiopian" component of the Qafzeh fauna, one other interpretation might be that the more modern-like Skhul and Qafzeh hominins actually represent African populations on the northwestern frontier of their range, rather than examples of a major Out of Africa event (Klein, 1996).

Summing up the Near East Record

As we have noted above, archeological evidence indicates that the transition from Middle to Upper Paleolithic industries in the Levant occurred about 40 kya and is marked by less reliance on flat unipolar and bipolar Levallois core reduction techniques and increasing use of prismatic cores, ultimately leading to such blade and bladelet–dominated industries as the **Ahmarian.** The Upper Paleolithic cultures mainly differ from underlying Middle Paleolithic cultures in their greater production of bone and antler objects, greater use of worked marine shells (possibly for body decorations), production of art objects, more frequent use of red ochre, use of grinding tools, and the practice of encircling hearths with stones and using rocks for reflecting warmth.

Before the revised radiometric dates became available for the Near East, anthropologists had thought that the apparent morphological resemblances between early modern humans in Europe (e.g., Cro-Magnons) and those from the Near East (Qafzeh and Skhul) reflected a close temporal relationship as well. It was also thought that the Near Eastern Neandertals from Tabun, Amud, Zuttiyeh, and Kebara dated to only about 50 kya, whereas the earliest anatomically modern humans from Qafzeh and Skhul were younger, perhaps dating to less than 40 kya (Garrod, 1958; Howell, 1958; Valladas et al., 1987, 1988). This was used as evidence that the earlier Neandertal-like hominins of the area gradually evolved into the more modern-like populations. This view is now no longer tenable, at least as far as the Near East is concerned, because, as we have seen, TL, ESR, and U-S age determinations show that the Qafzeh hominins date to the earlier part of the late Pleistocene, probably more than 90 kya, and that at least some of the Skhul hominins may date to about 80 kya (McDermott et al., 1993; Schwarcz et al., 1988b; Stringer et al., 1989; Valladas et al., 1988). Conversely, some Neandertal-like hominins (Kebara, Amud, Tabun) are associated with the Tabun B industry dated to between 100 and 46 kya. Thus some of the more anatomically modern humans, like those from Qafzeh, actually *predate* some of the Neandertals such as those from Kebara by tens of thousands of years! In fact, dates from other sites, such as Tabun, now seem to indicate that anatomically modern humans coexisted with Neandertals in the Near East for over 50,000 years. These findings refute not only the view that Neandertals gradually evolved in situ into modern *H. sapiens* in the Near East but also the notion that the appearance of modern *H. sapiens* coincided with the technological revolution of the Upper Paleolithic, since the cultural traditions of both hominin groups were indistinguishable variants of the Mousterian (Bar-Yosef and Vandermeersch, 1993).

Perhaps this alternating pattern of Neandertal-like–modern lineages in the Levant reflects contrasting associations with faunal and ecozones within the Levant. Recent research indicates that in this region the late Neandertal-like lineages such as those from Amud, Kebara, Shanidar, and Tabun appear to be associated more with Paleartic faunas whereas the early modern humans lineages like those from Skhul and Qafzeh are associated more with Afro-Arabian ones. The idea that these different lineages were adapted to different ecogeographical zones is supported by the observation that body proportions in the two groups differ, the late Neandertal-like groups being more cold adapted compared to the more tropically adapted modern groups (Ruff, 1994; Stefan and Trinkaus, 1998; Trinkaus, 1981).

Did these Middle Paleolithic Neandertals and early anatomically modern humans from western Asia engage in symbolic behavior? The clear signs of deliberate burials at Qafzeh, Skhul, Amud, Kebara, Dederiyeh, and Shanidar as well as the use of marine shells and red ochre for body decorations at Skhul and Qafzeh strongly suggest that they did (Akazawa et al., 1995; Belfer-Cohen and Hovers, 1992; Rak et al., 1994).

Fossil evidence of human populations morphologically and archeologically similar to the Levant sites occurs sporadically throughout adjacent regions, attesting to the fact that these populations were widespread (Hoffecker, 1999). For example, sites in the Crimea, Kiik-Koba and Tartar provide evidence of human populations associated with Mousterian industries. The Kiik-Koba evidence consists of hand, leg, and foot bones associated with a Mousterian industry of sidescrapers and small handaxes. The skeletal elements are said to resemble similar bones from Krapina and Tabun. Likewise, the ritually buried child's skeleton from Teshik-Tash in Uzbekistan also differs from that of classic Neandertal children such as that of La Quina (Fig. 13.21).

We can sum up the Near Eastern evidence of Neandertals and modern humans as follows (Klein, 1996):

- Near-modern (e.g., Skhul, Qafzeh) and Neandertal (e.g, Tabun, Kebara) populations occupied West Asia between approximately 130 and 40 kya.
- Early near-modern populations were predominant before 80 kya and Neandertals after 80 kya.
- It is unlikely that either population gave rise to the other: The early near-modern populations probably migrated from Africa during the last interglacial (^{18}O stage 5); the Neandertals probably originated in western Europe and migrated to West Asia during the opening stages of the last glaciation (^{18}O stage 4).
- The two populations were archeologically indistinct from each other.

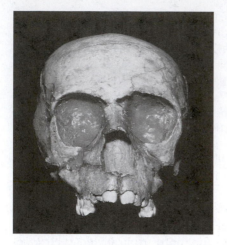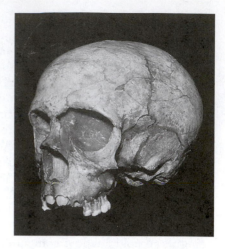

Fig. 13.21. Frontal and oblique views of the Neandertal child's cranium, La Quina 18. (Photos courtesy of F. Smith.)

FOSSIL EVIDENCE FROM AUSTRALASIA

Franz Weidenreich (1939, 1943) first explored the possibility of regional continuity between Far Eastern *H. erectus* populations and modern Australasian populations over a half century ago, and paleoanthropologists have been arguing the case for and against this concept ever since. Weidenreich envisioned an "Australoid" lineage passing from Indonesian *H. erectus* to Australian Aborigines via intermediaries like Ngandong (Solo) and Wajak. He didn't mince words when he noted (Weidenreich, 1943):

> The ancient Javanese forms, *Pithecanthropus* and *Homo soloensis,* agree in typical but minor details with certain fossil and recent Australian types of today so perfectly that they give evidence of a continuous line of evolution leading from the mysterious Java forms to the modern Australian bushman.

Likewise, he envisioned a "Mongoloid" lineage passing from Chinese *H. erectus* via such "intermediaries" as Dali, Maba, Zhoukoudian Upper Cave, and Liujiang to modern Mongoloid populations of East Asia.

If such regional continuity can be proven beyond a reasonable doubt (or what passes for "reasonable doubt" in paleoanthropological circles), then the implications are obvious—anatomically modern Australasians evolved in situ and did not migrate into the region from other geographical areas as the Out of Africa Model contends. We will shortly examine the arguments, both pro and con, for regional continuity in Australasia, but first we must briefly survey the available fossil evidence bearing on the question.

East Asia

The first appearance of anatomically modern *H. sapiens* in east Asia continues to be problematic. The earliest well-preserved hominins from China that unequivocally exhibit anatomically modern morphology is the Liujiang material. The Liujiang specimens, consisting of a cranium and some postcranial material, were found in association with a characteristic giant panda–primitive elephant (*Ailuropoda–Stegodon*) fauna usually interpreted as being from the Middle Pleistocene. However (as is usual with the Chinese material), the contemporaneity of the hominins and the fauna has not been definitely established. More recently, U-S dates of about 139–111 kya have been reported for this site (with some estimates more than 153 kya), but again, the stratigraphic relationship between the dated stalactite layers and the hominins are problematic (Shen et al., 2002; Wu, 1990). If the radiometric dating can be believed, it implies that anatomically modern humans in China were as old, or older than, anatomically modern humans from anywhere else in the Old World (Pope, 1992).

It has been claimed that the Liujiang cranium has many traits that can be traced back to both Chinese *H. erectus* and early *H. sapiens,* such as rectangular orbits, frontal bossing, a flat midface with a distinct incisura malaris, a relatively short maxilla, and no lateral alveolar prognathism. As might be expected, the presence of these early traits in an otherwise anatomically modern sample has been seized upon by supporters of the Multiregional Continuity Model.

Another important early modern hominin sample from China comes from Zhoukoudian Upper Cave. A series of radiocarbon dates from Zhoukoudian gives ages of about 10–18 kya for the Upper Cave levels. More recent dates, again on nonhuman bone, range from 33 to 13 kya, with a suggested age of 24–29 kya for the archeological occurrences. Again however, the stratigraphic relationship between the human burials and the dated faunal material is insecure.

Hominin material from East Asia that may be of early modern *H. sapiens* include fossils from Niah Cave, Borneo; Wajak 1 and II, Java; Yamashita-cho, Okinawa; and Tabon, Philippines. The fragmentary cranium from Niah has been radiocarbon dated on the basis of charcoal possibly associated with the cranium to about 40 kya. The reconstructed cranium is characterized by thin cranial vault walls, a relatively steep supraglabellar region behind which the frontal gently recedes, slightly developed supraorbitals, squarish orbits, prominent parietal bosses, a rounded occipital, and well-marked temporal lines. The face is short, broad, and prognathic, with a moderately developed canine fossa. Many of these features are commonly found on Australian aboriginal crania.

The Wajak crania are undated but are considered Late Pleistocene solely on the basis of perceived morphological similarity with prehistoric Australian aboriginal crania (which is incompatible with faunal analyses that suggest Wajak is essentially recent in age). The Wajak 1 cranium is similar to the Australian cranium from Keilor (see below) in terms of size, proportions, and facial flatness and has been used as evidence documenting regional continuity of fossils from East Asia and Australia (Fig. 13.22).

The fossils from Yamashita-cho, Okinawa, consist of a femur and tibia of a 6-year-old child dated by radiocarbon to greater than 32 kya (Trinkaus and Ruff, 1996). Their morphology shows a mosaic pattern, with some features (diaphyseal robusticity) more similar to early human values, and other features (femoral neck-shaft angles) more similar to modern human values.

The Tabon sample consists of the remains of at least five individuals and includes cranial, mandibular, and postcranial elements radiocarbon dated to about 23 kya. The frontal bone is quite gracile and thin with little postorbital constriction, a relatively steep supraglabellar region, and a gently receding frontal profile. The supraorbitals are only moderately developed and the glabella region is prominent. One mandible shows slight chin development and congenital absence of the third molar. Some features of the mandible, like the three-rooted molars and agenesis of the third molar, suggest "Mongoloid" affinities.

Far East paleolithic sites older than about 20 kya are summarized in Figure 10.12. One interesting sidelight to these dates is that if they are anywhere near correct, then *H. erectus* and *H. sapiens* coexisted in China over a substantial period of time (e.g., the presence of *H. erectus* at Hexian and *H. sapiens* at Chaohu) (Chen and Zhang, 1991).

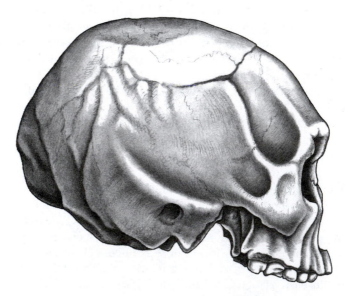

Fig. 13.22. The cranium of Wajak 1.   (Larsen et al., 1991.)

Australia

Until recently, the earliest widely accepted evidence for human occupation of Greater Australia (Australia, New Guinea, Tasmania) was a radiocarbon date of about 39 kya for charcoal associated with stone tools from western Australia (Carpenter's Gap rock shelter). However, on the basis of TL dates from Malakunanka II rock shelter, some paleoanthropologists argue that human occupation of Australia may actually predate 50 kya (Roberts et al., 1990), and U-S dates suggest human occupation of Papua New Guinea some 40 kya (Groube et al., 1986). Indeed, the oldest rock art thus far known in the Old World comes from several sites in Australia; these include a date of 32 kya for a *Conus* shell necklace from Mandu Mandu Creek, Western Australia, and dates of approximately 42 kya for rock varnish covering petroglyphs at Wharton Hill and Panaramitee North, South Australia (Bahn, 1996b).

These dates may soon be exceeded dramatically by the discovery in northwestern Australia at Jinmium rock shelter of a rock face, and many surrounding boulders, engraved with thousands of circles dated by TL techniques to earlier than 58 kya (Bahn, 1996a; Fullagar et al., 1996). If verified by further research, this (and the abstract representations engraved on pieces of red ochre from Middle Stone Age layers at Blombos Cave, South Africa), would be by far the earliest known record of artistic behavior in the archeological record, more than twice the age of any European cave painting and at least 15,000 years older than any previous Australian rock art.[29] Even more astounding, archeologists report the discovery of red ochre and stone artifacts in deeper sediments at Jinmium rock shelter dated by TL to 116 ± 12 kya and perhaps to as much as 176 kya (Fullagar et al., 1996). If this older date is accurate, then who made these tools? Could it be that in some rare cases, artistic expression began before the emergence of modern *Homo sapiens*? We can't be certain, since no skeletal material has yet been found associated with these archeological discoveries.[30]

Although intriguing, there are some good reasons to be sceptical about these claims. As archeologists James O'Connell and Jim Allen (1998) point out, such ancient dates "require significant changes in current ideas, not just about the initial colonization of Australia, but about the entire chronology of human evolution in the late Middle and early Upper Pleistocene. Either fully modern humans were present well outside

---

[29]There is some suggestion in the archeological record that even older art may be attributed to *H. erectus*. For example, a small piece of volcanic tuff resembling a female figurine from the site at Berekhat Ram on the Golan Heights has been dated to between 233,000 and 800,000 years ago; several bones from the Middle Pleistocene site of Bilzingsleben, Germany, seem to bear a series of decorative parallel incisions; and two petroglyphs have been found in a cave at Bhimbetka, India, covered by an Acheulean occupation layer thought to be several hundred thousand years old (Bahn, 1996b).

[30]For a cautionary note on the reliability of these TL derived dates, see Gibbons (1997).

Africa at a surprisingly early date or the behavioral capabilities long thought to be uniquely theirs were also associated, at least to some degree, with other hominins."

The dating of these early Australian sites are suspect on several grounds. First, these older dates, based exclusively on luminescence techniques (e.g., TL), are, in many cases, incompatible with ^{14}C-derived dates from other archeological sites in Australia. One possibility might be that in situ decay of older sediments may have influenced the TL dates to make them appear artificially old. Second, stone tools at these "older" sites are found not far below much younger dated sediments, in some cases within the range of vertical displacement caused by various bioturbation factors, such as termites. Third, of the more than 40 archeological sites in Australia known to be older than 30 kya based on radiocarbon, none dates to greater than 40 kya. Recently, these concerns about the dating have been shown to be well founded, since more recent optical luminescence and ^{14}C dates indicate that the Jinmium site may be only Holocene in age (less than 10,000 years old) (Roberts et al., 1998).

The oldest reasonably well dated skeletal remains are the Lake Mungo 1 cremation dated to about 25 kya. It has been argued on geological grounds that the extended burial Lake Mungo 3 may be on the order of about 40 kya, although recent ESR and U-Series dates have suggested ages as old as 61 ± 2 years kya (Thorne et al., 1999). This age determination is still a matter of some dispute (Bowler and Magee, 2000; Gillespie and Roberts, 2000; Grün et al., 2000). Others have suggested, solely on morphological grounds, that the Willandra Lakes specimen (WLH 50) is considerably older than Lake Mungo 1. WLH 50 has now been dated to about 15 kya by U-Series analysis and to about 30 kya by ESR. Kow Swamp is bracketed by radiocarbon dates on shell to about 13–9.5 kya and by optically stimulated luminescence to about 26–19 kya, and the hominins from Coobool Creek, Nacurrie 1, and Keilor all appear to be of a similar age (Brown, 1992; Stone and Cupper, 2003).

Cranial material from the terminal Pleistocene of Australia, found in Coobool Creek, Nacurrie, Keilor, Cohuna, Lake Mungo, Kow Swamp, and Tandou, are highly variable but are much larger overall than recent crania from the same region (Fig. 13.23). These crania are dominated by the functional requirements of a large dentition. By the Holocene, a reduction in tooth size and associated alveolar region has resulted in significantly shorter and less prognathic faces.

Because of the great deal of variability in the early hominin sample from Australia, some Australian paleoanthropologists have argued that the continent was populated by two hominin groups, each with a distinct evolutionary origin, that coexisted for long periods of time in the late Pleistocene (Thorne, 1980). According to this theory, one group is represented by the robust Talgai, Cohuna, and Kow Swamp specimens, which are seen as being derived from Indonesian *H. erectus* through such intermediaries

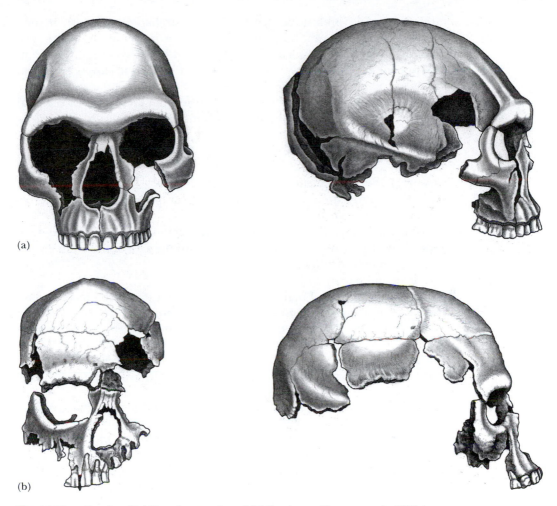

Fig. 13.23. Crania of (a) Kow Swamp 1 and (b) Tandou.   (Larsen et al., 1991.)

as Ngandong. The second group is represented by the more gracile Mungo and Keilor fossils, which are seen as being derived from the Chinese *H. erectus* populations. However, it should be noted that multivariate tests have demonstrated that these so-called robust and gracile groups are more similar to one another than they are to hominins from any other geographical area (Habgood, 1989).

Let us now go back and analyze the fossil data as they pertain to the Multiregional Continuity Model. The crux of the matter is this: If the Multiregional Continuity Model is true, then there must be a number of identifiable and unique "regional features" characterizing both archaic hominins from Australasia (*H. erectus* or early *H. sapiens*) and the later modern sample (prehistoric and modern Australian aborigines). If such regional features cannot be demonstrated to be truly unique to the Australasian sample—that is, if they can be found in archaic hominins from other geographical regions—then they cannot be used to support regional continuity.

Weidenreich (1943) was one of the first to offer such a list of regional features, linking Indonesian archaic hominins, specifically Ngandong (Solo) crania, to Australian aborigines:

- Well-developed superciliary ridges
- A flat, receding forehead
- A prelambdoid depression
- A sharply angled occipital bone with a torus-like demarcation line between the occiput and the nuchal plane
- A short sphenoparietal articulation in the region where the frontal, temporal, parietal, and sphenoid bones meet on the side of the cranial vault (a region known as pterion)
- A deep and narrow infraglabellar notch

Weidenreich's list of regional features was later expanded to 12 and includes a number of other features linking Indonesian *H. erectus* (based mainly on a reconstruction of Sangiran 17) to Australian hominins (Wolpoff et al., 1984):

- Flatness of the frontal bone in the sagittal plane
- Posterior position of the minimum frontal breadth well behind the orbits
- A relatively horizontal orientation of the inferior supraorbital border
- Presence of a distinct prebregmatic eminence (bregma being the ectocranial point where the coronal and sagittal sutures intersect)
- A low position of maximum parietal breadth
- Marked facial prognathism
- Presence of a malar tuberosity
- Eversion of the lower border of the malar
- Rounding of the inferolateral border of the orbit
- The lower border of the nasal aperture lacking a distinct line dividing the nasal floor from the subnasal face of the maxillas
- Marked expression of curvature of the posterior alveolar plane of the maxillas
- The degree of facial and dental (especially posterior) reduction

However, several paleoanthropologists have argued that many of these same so-called Australasian regional features are actually primitive retentions found in many *H. erectus* and archaic *H. sapiens* crania from other parts of the Old World and thus are not indicative of any special cladistic relationship between Indonesian *H. erectus* and modern Australians (Groves, 1989a; Habgood, 1989; Lahr, 1994) As Table 13.3 indicates, if these 12 features are considered *individually*, then they clearly do not define an Indonesian-Australian clade. However, what if they are considered in *combination?* That is to say, can the combination of these Australasian features be matched in single specimens outside of Australasia? The answer is, apparently, no. Thus, while it is possible that the presence of a certain combination of the above-listed traits may support a regional continuity model, the individual traits cannot.

This conclusion is reinforced by a recent comparison of the Willandra Lakes Hominid (WLH 50) and the Ngandong sample (Hawks et al., 2000b; Wolpoff et al., 2001). Although WLH 50 shares many cranial features with the Ngandong sample, it is regarded as a modern human specimen by virtually all workers. By contrast, the Ngandong sample is regarded either as members of a late surviving *H. erectus* population or as an archaic *H. sapiens* population.

If the multiregional model pertains to the Australasian hominins, then WLH 50 would be expected to share more morphological features with the earlier Javanese Ngandong sample than with earlier modern human samples from Africa or the Levant. However, if the Out of Africa Model pertains, then just the opposite should be true. In other words, the complete replacement model (Out of Africa Model) requires that a unique relationship should exist between the early modern humans of Australia (WLH 50) and their putative archaic *H. sapiens* ancestors from Africa and/or the Levant.[31] If, on the other hand, the evidence shows significant local geographic (regional) ancestry for WLH 50, then the complete replacement model must be wrong. Using pair-wise differences in 16 nonmetric cranial features between WLH 50 and each of its putative ancestors (Ngandong vs. Africa/Levant), it was found that WLH 50 was much closer to the Ngandong sample than to the African/Levant sample. Hawks et al. (2000b) and Wolpoff et al. (2001) found that six of seven Ngandong crania are closer to WLH 50 than are any other specimens. On average, WLH 50 possesses fewer differences from the Ngandong group (3.7 pairwise differences) than from either the African (9.3) or Levantine (7.3) groups.

However, three nagging questions further confuse the issue: (1) If regional continuity is true, then why do some of the earliest anatomically modern hominins from the region, like WLH 50, share these regional features with earlier Indonesian hominins, whereas others (Lake Mungo 1 and 3, Niah Cave) do not, either individually or in combination? (2) If the rapid replacement model is true, why is there no evidence of an influx of new archeological assemblages into Australia during the late Upper Pleistocene? and (3) Why do three biallelic markers on the Y chromosome in East Asian men (YAP, M89, M130) coalesce to another mutation (M168T) that originated in Africa about 35–89 kya (Ke et al., 2001)?

---

[31] The African sample includes Jebel Irhoud 1 and 2, Omo 1 and 2, Laetoli 18, and Singa. The Levantine sample includes Qafzeh (6 and 9) and Skhul (5 and 9).

Table 13.3   The Occurrence of Proposed Regional Features in Fossil Hominins

	Features[a]											
	1	2	3	4	5	6	7	8	9	10	11	12
H. erectus												
KNM-ER 3733	—	—	—	—?	X	X	—	—	—	X	?	?
KNM-ER 3883	X	—	—	—	X	?	—	—?	—	?	?	
Olduvai H9	X	—	X	?	X	?	?	?	?	?	?	?
Sangiran 17	X	X	X	X/—	X	X	X/—	X	X/—	X	?	X
Solo 12	X	X	X	X	X	?	?	?	?	?	?	?
Zhoukoudian reconstruction	X/—	—	—	—	X	X	—	—	X	X	—	X
Australian												
WLH 50	X	X	X	—	X	?	X	X	X	?	?	?
Kow Swamp 1	X	X	X	—	X	X	X	X	X	X	X	X
Kow Swamp 5	X	X	X	?	X	X	X	X	X	X	?	X
Kow Swamp 15	—	X?	X	?	?	X	X	X	X	X	X?	X
Cohuna	X	X	X	X	X	X	X	X	X	X	X	X
Talgai	X	X?	X?	?	X	X	?	X?	X?	X	X?	X
Cossack	X	X	?	?	X	X	X	?	?	?	X	X
Mossgiel	X	X	X	—	X	X?	X	X	X	?	X?	X
Lake Nitchie	—	—	X	—	X	X	X	X	X	X	X	X
Keilor	—	—	X	—	X	X	X?	X	X	X	?	X
Lake Mungo 1	—	—	X	—	—?	?	—	?	?	?	?	?
Lake Mungo 3	—	—	X	—	X	?	?	?	?	?	?	?
Lake Tandou	—	—	X	—	X?	X	X?	X	X	?	X	X
Southeast Asia												
Niah	—	?	?	—	?	X	—	—	X	X	?	?
Wajak 1	—	—	X?	—	X	X	—	—	X	X	?	?
Wajak 2	?	?	X?	?	?	?	?	?	?	X	—	X
East Asia												
Maba	—	—	—	?	?	?	?	?	?	?	?	?
Liujiang	—	—	X?	—	—	X	—?	—	X	X	—	X
Upper Cave 101	—	—	X	—	X	X	—?	—	X	X	—	—
Upper Cave 102	X	—	X?	X	X	X	—?	—	X	X	?	?
Upper Cave 103	—	—	X	—	X	X	—?	X	X	X	?	?

(Continued)

Other rigorous tests of the Multiregional Continuity and the Out of Africa Models have been presented based on the fossil evidence, but unfortunately they come to different conclusions. The first compares several nonmetric features of six *H. erectus* mandibles from Sangiran and Java to modern mandibles from East African and Australian hunter-gatherer populations (Kramer, 1991). The Out of Africa Model would predict that the Sangiran mandibles would not display any particular morphological continuity with the modern Australian sample

	Features[a]											
	1	2	3	4	5	6	7	8	9	10	11	12
Sub-Saharan Africa												
Bodo 1	—?	—	X	?	?	X	—	X	X	X?	?	?
Ndutu	?	—	—	?	X	X	?	—	?	?	?	?
Kabwe 1	X	—	X	—	X	X	X	—	X	X	X	X
Laetoli H18	X	—	X	—	X	X	?	?	?	X	?	?
Omo 1	—	—	?	—	?	?	—?	?	X	?	?	?
Border Cave 1	—	—	—	—	?	?	X?	?	X	?	?	?
Florisbad	—	—	—	—	?	?	—?	?	X	—	?	?
North Africa and Western Asia												
Jebel Irhoud 1	—	—	—?	—	X	X	—	—	X	X	?	?
Wadi Halfa Sample	X/—	—	—	—	X/—	X	X	X	X?	?	—	X
Zuttiyeh	—	—	—	—	?	?	—?	—	—	?	?	?
Skhul 4	—	—	?	?	X	X	—	—	X	X	—	X
Skhul 5	—	—	X	—	—	X	—	—	X?	?	—	X
Jebel Qafzeh 9	—	—	X	?	—	X	—?	—	X	X	—	X
Amud I	X	—	—	—	—	X	—?	—	—	—?	—	X
Europe												
Petralona	X	—	X	—	X	X	—?	—	X	—	—	X
Arago 21	X	X	—	—	X	X	—	—	X	—	—	X
Steinheim	X	—	—	—	X	X	—	—	X	?	—?	X
La Ferrassie 1	X	—	—	—	—	X	—	—	X	—	—	X
Cro-Magnon 1	—	—	X	—	—	—	?	—	X	?	?	?
Oberkassel 1	—	—	X	—	—	—	X	X	X	?	—	?
Oberkassel 2	—	—	X	—	—	—	—	—	—	?	—	X
Dolni Vestoniče 3	—	—	X	—	—	—	—	—	—	?	X?	X
Předmosti 3	—	—	—	—	—	—	—	—	—	—	—	X
Předmosti 4	—	—	—	—	—	—	—	—	—	—	—	X
Mladeč 1	—	—	—	—	—	—	—	—	—	—	?	?

From Habgood (1989).

[a]The numbering of the features follows the list in the text.

x, present; —, absent; ?, questionable identification or area not preserved.

and that the two modern human samples should share more features than either would with the million-year-old *H. erectus* specimens from Indonesia. The Multiregional Continuity Model would predict that the Indonesian *H. erectus* sample should share more features with the modern Australian sample than with the modern African sample. The results of the study favor the Multiregional Continuity Model of regional evolution of *H. erectus* into modern humans in southeast Asia and Australia. Of the 17 features analyzed, 8 supported a grouping of Sangiran and the Australian aborigines to the exclusion of the modern Africans (Kenyans in this case).

The second rigorous morphological test of the multiregional model has come to just the opposite conclusion (Lahr, 1994). More specifically, this study addressed two particular hypotheses that should follow from the multiregional model: (1) that certain cranial traits should occur exclusively or with a higher incidence in Australia and East Asia, reflecting morphological continuity from *H. erectus* populations in these regions, and (2) that modern *H. sapiens* fossils in each area of the world should strongly resemble modern inhabitants of those same regions. This study rejected those two hypotheses by concluding that (1) many of the regional features claimed by the Multiregional Continuity Model to characterize the East Asian and Australasian evolutionary lines are not exclusive to these regions, with some even occurring at higher frequencies in other populations; (2) some cranial features are clearly related to overall robusticity and related functional demands and may, therefore, be of less phylogenetic value; and (3) the differences between some fossil and recent African specimens argue against the maintenance of morphological regional patterns through time and suggest instead high levels of population differentiation. However, remember the caveat we mentioned in an earlier chapter—the finding that some fossil hominins may show certain similarities to earlier African fossils rather than to earlier hominins from the same geographical region does not necessarily support the Out of Africa Model to the exclusion of the Multiregional Continuity Model given that African populations were much larger than other Eurasian populations through most of human history (Relethford, 1999, 2001a, 2001b, 2001c).

The third fossil study employed a sophisticated quantitative test, called matrix correlation, to the question of modern human origins (Waddle, 1994). A sample of 83 Middle to Late Pleistocene hominin crania were divided into 12 operational taxonomic units based on geographical location and chronological age. Morphological distances were calculated between each pair of samples based on 74 metric traits (including cranial lengths and breadths), 52 discrete traits (defined as present or absent), and 39 angles and indices. These values were then arranged in a morphological distance correlation matrix. When this morphological distance matrix was correlated to design matrices representing both the Out of Africa and the Multiregional Continuity Models of modern human origins, it was found that the Out of Africa Model provided a better explanation for cranial variation and refuted the notion of evolutionary continuity in Europe and for the Neandertals of southwest Asia.

Finally, a fourth study carefully evaluated 33 craniodental characters usually used to support either the Out of Africa or the Multiregional Continuity Model. It concluded that most of these features were actually of little phylogenetic value in that most were either non-homologous and/or shared-primitive characters present in both early African *H. erectus* and archaic *H. sapiens* populations. As we have stressed many times, such symplesiomorphic features do not resolve evolutionary relationships. In fact, of the 33 characters only 4 provided qualified support for the multiregional hypothesis and only 6 provided support for the Out of Africa hypothesis (Lieberman, 1995).

As mentioned earlier, Weidenreich (1939) also argued for regional continuity in the Chinese hominin fossil record. Again, his (and others') arguments rest mainly on the identification of what are considered to be Mongoloid skeletal features in the Zhoukoudian *H. erectus* sample and in modern northern Chinese:

- Midsagittal crest and parasagittal depression
- High frequency of metopic sutures
- High frequency of accessory bones that form within the cranial sutures (known as Inca bones)
- Mongoloid features of the cheek region (i.e., facial flatness)
- Mandibular, ear, and maxillary exostoses
- Femoral platymeria
- Strong deltoid tuberosity of the humerus
- Shovel-shaped incisors
- A horizontal course of the nasofrontal and frontomaxillary sutures
- Rounded profile of nasal saddle and nasal roof
- Rounded infraorbital margin
- Reduced posterior teeth
- High frequency of third molar agenesis
- Small frontal sinuses

However, in an exhaustive survey of the morphological evidence relating to these features, Colin Groves (1989a) of the Australian National University has questioned the evidence for special likeness of modern Mongoloids to Chinese *H. erectus*. Any correlation can be explained by a similarity of Zhoukoudian *H. erectus* to some modern Mongoloid populations, but not to others, and, perhaps, even in these cases, by retention in some Mongoloid groups of primitive character states.

In the final analysis, we must not lose sight of the fact that the great number of craniofacial features clearly distinguishing most fossil Asian hominins from their European and African counterparts cannot simply be wished away. All these features are still found today in higher frequencies among extant Mongoloid populations than among extant African and/or Eurasian populations. Both European and Australasian samples diverge from the conditions seen in specimens of archaic hominins from Africa, and many of the morphological traits previously restricted only to fossil Asians now occur in all populations of modern humans (however, their frequency remains higher in populations deriving from or occupying the Far East). This worldwide dissemination of morphological traits that first appeared in the Asian fossil record strongly implies that at least some of the craniofacial traits associated with the emergence of modern humans could not have resulted from a single African origin, as extreme versions of the Out of Africa Model propose, but rather from admixture and gene flow between different regions of the Old World (Pope, 1991).

The bottom line is this: If anyone tries to tell you that the issue of modern human origins has been "solved," don't buy it!

In the last two chapters we reviewed an array of data pertinent to the question of modern human origins and have seen that the evidence is both complex and sometimes contradictory. Perhaps it is appropriate to conclude our story of human evolution by acknowledging another difficulty that has stalled progress on this important issue, a problem that Arizona State University anthropologists Catherine Willermet and Geoffrey Clark refer to as the "paradigm crisis" in modern human origins research (Clark, 1999; Willermet and Clark, 1995). As they point out, an anthropological paradigm is not a specific scientific theory but an intellectual or philosophical worldview that determines how anthropologists perceive what may be learned, and is worth learning, from the prehistoric record and what kinds of evidence and analytical tools are necessary in order to learn it. Clearly, if supporters of either the Multiregional Continuity or Out of Africa model endorse different underlying paradigms about what causes patterns in the human fossil record and about what data sets should be measured and evaluated to support their particular paradigm, then it should not be surprising that consensus about modern human origins still eludes us. For example, Willermet and Clark determined that proponents of the Multiregional Continuity and Out of Africa models have used at least 680 craniometric datum points, representing 61 variables on 55 fossils, in order to "prove" their respective paradigms about modern human origins; however, of this total only 72 variables on 11 fossils, or 11% of the entire reported database, are common to both paradigms! In other words, 89% of the data were used by supporters of only one paradigm. Thus in evaluating the debate about modern human origins, we should be cognizant of the fact "that there is relatively little overlap between the metaphysical paradigms of 'continuity' and 'replacement' researchers, and they, as a consequence, are using different data sets in their analyses . . . and that consciously or unconsciously, researchers tend to select those fossils and variables that lend support to their respective positions" (Willermet and Clark, 1995).

Willermet and Clark (1995) conclude their provocative article by asking: "In light of the plethora of articles and books that have appeared in the last 10 years, it is worth asking ourselves whether we are any closer to solving the question of our origins than we were a century ago."

I hope, now that you have reached the end of this book, your answer will be a resounding yes and that you will also agree that there is still much exciting work to be done.

Epilogue

In his novella *A River Runs Through It*, Norman Maclean (1976) wrote, "Eventually all things merge into one, and a river runs through it. The river was cut by the world's great flood and runs over rocks from the basement of time. On some of the rocks are timeless raindrops. Under the rocks are the words, and some of the words are theirs. I am haunted by waters." Norman Maclean was haunted by waters; I am haunted by time—time that ranges from the very short durations of unstable elementary particles to the Universe's life span of several billion years. This vast range of time is incomprehensible in terms of our everyday experience. Even the limited time span of human evolution reviewed in the previous chapters needs to be expressed on some reduced scale that we can relate to.

In order to visualize such a reduced time axis, the Japanese physicist Akiyoshi Wada (1995) devised a simple slide rule in time dimensions (Fig. E.1). The slide rule consists of a main time rule (on the left), which carries a logarithmic time scale on which various historical events are noted, and a reference time rule (on the right). Like any slide rule, the left and right sides of the ruler can slide with respect to one another. This so-called Wada ruler is easy to use. Simply photocopy the figure, separate the main rule (left) from the reference rule (right) and mount each part on a stiff card in such a way as to be able to slide the latter against the former. For example, Figure E.1 shows a time reduction in which the age of the universe ("Big Bang") on the main time rule is set equal to the appearance of Egyptian civilization about 4000 years ago on the reference time rule. On this scale, australopiths and early *Homo* first appear about a year ago and Isaac Newton's *Principia* and the Declaration of Independence were written less than an hour ago. Similarly, if we slide the rule so that the age of the universe is set to 1 year, we would find that Egyptian civilization began less than a minute ago and that Newton's *Principia* and the Declaration of Independence were written less than a second ago.

As we contemplate time—5 million years of human history to be exact—is there any single conclusion to be drawn? Yes, that in both a geological

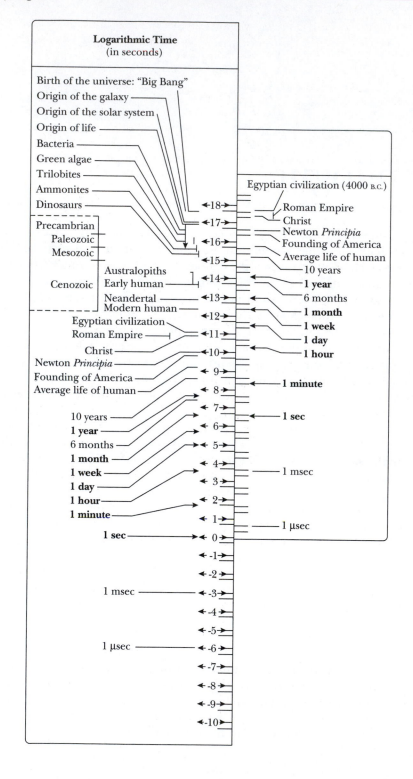

instant and in a restricted Darwinian sense, humankind has been successful, perhaps too much so. As the writer John McPhee (1980) expressed it:

> For establishing our bearings through time, we obviously owe an incalculable
> debt to vanished and endangered species. . . . The opossum may be Cretaceous,
> certain clams Devonian, and oysters Triassic, but for each and every oyster in the
> sea, it seems, there is a species gone forever. Be a possum is the message, and
> you may outlive God.

I sometimes imagine the sound of a shot ringing out and turn in time
to see the last elephant, black rhino, or mountain gorilla slowly sink to its
knees in the red African dust. In time, that will come to pass; and on that
day an unbearable loneliness will descend over humankind. To all creatures still wild and free, I dedicate this book. The success of human evolution has not been kind to you.

BRAINTEASERS

A few years ago, John Fleagle, editor of *Evolutionary Anthropology* and author
of the second-finest book on primate evolution,[1] asked me to write a short
essay on what I thought were the hot issues or nonissues in human evolution these days (Conroy, 1998). It is reprinted here for your entertainment.

My initial response to John's request was: "What hot issues?"—haven't
we simply been filling in the gaps since Darwin's *Origin of Species*? Didn't
the discovery of *Otavipithecus* pretty much solve whatever was left to solve?
To some, apparently not! Thus I offer the following musings and brain-
teasers for your intellects to munch on. I have had fun thinking about
them; I hope you do too. There is more here than meets the eye, so tread
carefully. I'd love to hear your answers.

• There is, apparently, no type specimen for *Homo sapiens* (you are
nothing but a nomen nudum). Therefore, what exactly is "an anatomically
modern human"?

• Now let me see if I have this Out of Africa story straight. Anatomically modern humans first evolved along the garden route of South Africa
a little over 100,000 years ago, leaving no archeological trace as to what
might have triggered this astounding evolutionary achievement. They
then must have quickly left the glorious Cape of Good Hope and quickly
marched through the rest of Africa, quickly subduing all the early *Homo*
in sub-Saharan Africa along the way with their newly evolved mental
trigones, since, once again, there is no archeological trace of this event.
At this point, they must have stayed put for a while in order to build up

---

[1]Fleagle (1999), not to be confused with *Primate Evolution* (Conroy, 1990).

the mtDNA diversity that seems to characterize sub-Saharan African populations relative to Eurasian ones. Then a small mtDNA subset of this group invaded Eurasia and commingled with Neandertals in the Near East for tens of thousands of years before totally wiping them out, as well as everyone else, during the last glacial period. Now my question is this: If the mtDNA homogeneity in Eurasian populations and heterogeneity in African populations is used as an argument in favor of an African Eve hypothesis, then why didn't this little band of mtDNA Africans also turn south from the Near East, from whence they originally came, and wipe out the genetically diverse African populations they left behind? Am I missing something here?

• If large-bodied early/middle Miocene apes share many postcranial features with semiterrestrial quadrupeds, and if modern hominoids (apes and humans) share many hanging adaptations of the limbs and vertebral column, then just where, when, and how could such hanging adaptations have developed just as some of these late Miocene hominoids supposedly were leaving the forests to become bipeds in the expanding Pliocene savannas of Africa?

• Assuming that the trichotomy among chimps, gorillas, and humans is resolved in favor of chimps-humans, then shouldn't gorillas be used as an outgroup in comparing hominin (chimp-human clade) morphological and genetic synapomorphies and symplesiomorphies?

• Still on the subject of trichotomies: If our molecular friends are right and humans are more closely related to chimps than chimps are to gorillas, then I challenge any reader to come up with a cladogram of craniodental or postcranial features (or both) in humans, chimps, and gorillas that would demonstrate this relationship.

• A small segment of Neandertal mtDNA apparently doesn't look much like a small segment of modern human mtDNA. Given the fast mutation rate of mtDNA, would any human mtDNA from 100,000–200,000 years ago resemble that of modern humans?

• Ted Williams batted 406 in 1941. Thus, using the logic of molecular clock advocates predicting relatively recent divergence dates, we should be able to predict with confidence that when Williams had two base hits in the 1941 season he had been at bat only five times, not counting walks. This would be unlikely. For all we know, he went 0 for 5 his first game and 4 for 5 his second game, or anything in between. His overall season batting average has no predictive value for early season games. The predictive value increases only as one approaches the end of the season. It is only when we are told that he has 200 base hits near the end of the season that we would be fairly confident in predicting that he had been to bat about 500 times.

• Why is it surprising that human mtDNA haplotypes seem so homogeneous? What else could they be? What are the odds that females will beget females who beget females for more than four or five generations? Wouldn't you think the human mtDNA genome must be getting pruned constantly and dramatically every century or so and that mtDNA heterogeneity could increase in a population only if the rate of mtDNA mutation within lineages exceeded that of female lineages dying out? Go figure.

• How many different mtDNA haplotypes are there anyway in the human genome? Do mtDNA haplotypes really coalesce to one individual (Eve) or to one haplotype that may be found in one, tens, hundreds, or thousands of individuals?

• And speaking of coalescence time, why do some writers keep equating modern human mtDNA coalescence time with the origins of anatomically modern humans? Why couldn't human mtDNA coalesce back to early *H. sapiens, H. erectus, Otavipithecus* (my personal choice), or sea cucumbers? Why should the two necessarily have anything to do with one another? Answer: They don't!

• If mtDNA Eve was the mother of us all in a mtDNA sense, then who was Eve's mother?

• Let's check a cladogram against a known phylogeny: me, my mother, my grandmother. How do I draw a cladogram of this with the three of us as end points? Is my mother more closely related to me than she is to her own mother? Perhaps my grandmother was just a hypothetical ancestor? No wonder I wasn't in Granny's will.

• Let's assume that Neandertals diverged from the modern human lineage 250,000 years ago. Are a Neandertal and a modern human, each dated to 249,000 years ago, more closely related to one another than the 249,000-year-old modern human is to a modern human living today?

• Your first molar hasn't changed in size since it first popped into your oral cavity when you were about 6 years old. I bet your body weight has changed dramatically since then. So has the size of your femoral head, although, of course, the age of attainment of adult femoral head size would have occurred later. So how come regression equations relating first molar size or femoral head size to body weight in fossil hominins (or any primate, for that matter) are used to predict adult body size? Some biologists seem puzzled that intraspecific regression slopes are much lower than interspecific ones. How could it be otherwise?

• The human body, or any body, can be divided into an infinite number of characters, limited only by the imagination of the investigator. Thus no matter how large a cladistic character matrix may be, isn't it, by definition, an infinitesimally small part of the organism? How sound are phylogenetic assessments based on infinitesimally small samples? Let's look at it another way. There is no such thing as an independent character: The body is a morphologically integrated whole. Thus the infinite characters of the human body can be reduced to one. (As the gurus say, we are all one. But I would add, one *what?*) How sound are phylogenetic assessments based on a sample of one?

• Sciences that, like molecular biology, progress by leaps and bounds, actually force their practitioners to share data by requiring them to publish their raw data in an internationally retrievable way—for example, the base pair sequences of the genomic material used in a study. Wouldn't it be nice if paleoanthropology worked the same way? One argument used by the paleontology community to lambast Sotheby's for its auctioning "Sue" the *Tyrannosaurus rex* for $8 million was that someone could buy it and then hide it away in a locked room so that the scientific community would no longer have access to it. Excuuuuse me, but isn't that what some (many?) of our paleoanthropological colleagues do to the rest of us? Let's see a show of hands. How many of you would like, someday, to study the original fossils of _____ [fill in the blank]? How many of you believe that you will ever get permission to do so in your lifetime?

• A major problem in paleoanthropology is that access to, and interpretation of, its raw material, the fossils, is restricted to a precious few. Thus I offer for the reader's consideration a call to arms to deal with the situation.

CONROY'S MANIFESTO

1. There should be a statute of limitations on describing fossil hominins and other important primate fossil material. If their discoverers do not publish them within _____ [fill in the blank], they become fair game for the rest of us.

2. If, after publishing their results, investigators do not share their raw data (e.g., casts, photos, and measurements) with colleagues, they should be barred from further taxpayer support (read "National Science Foundation"), publishing in society journals, and presenting their toys at society meetings. Offenders should also be forced to serve a 3-year term as postmodernist film review editors for the American Anthropological Association.

3. The anthropology section of the National Science Foundation, or any interested philanthropic organization, should establish and financially support the paleoanthropological equivalent of a genetic bank. After publication of the descriptions of major fossils, high-quality casts of the fossils should be made. The casts should be deposited and curated in a central repository, such as the Smithsonian or the American Museum of Natural History (or better yet, Washington University), and be available to all colleagues for study.

4. New hominin taxa should be described and named only in internationally acceptable, refereed journals (no more *H. ergaster* in things like *Ca-*

sopsis SPro Mineralogii a Geologii). The same goes for wholesale taxonomic revisions of well-established, or at least time-honored, hominin taxa.

5. Species names should be banned as end points in cladograms. Cladograms do not document evolutionary changes in whole animals or species. Instead, they document only changes in the character (usually few) under consideration. If there are many characters in the analysis, the numbers of reversals, parallelisms, and so forth become mind-numbing. In other words, stop messing with our heads!

Glossary

absolute dating   methods for determining the age, in years before present, of artifacts, fossils, or rocks, usually based on the amount of radioactive change in the specimen

Acheulean industry   early Paleolithic industry characterized by handaxes and cleavers

aeolian   pertaining to or caused by wind

Ahmarian   a Middle to Upper Paleolithic blade and bladelet–dominated industry of the Levant, dating to about 40 kya

allopatric   pertaining to taxa occupying different and disjunct geographical areas (see **punctuated equilibrium**)

allopatric speciation   evolutionary model based on the idea that most evolutionary change is concentrated in comparatively rapid speciation events in small isolated subpopulations of the ancestral species

alpha decay   radioactive decay in which the nucleus of the parent atom loses two protons and two neutrons; thus its mass number decreases by four and its atomic number decreases by two (e.g., the decay of ^{238}U to ^{234}Th)

alveolus   tooth socket

anagenesis   an evolutionary process involving the gradual accumulation of changes in ancestor to descendant lineages through time (also called phyletic evolution)

analogy   a similarity of form or structure between two taxa that is not shared with their nearest common ancestor—that is, the similar structure has evolved independently in the two taxa and is due to convergent evolution

anterior pillars   two massive bony columns that support the anterior portion of the palate on both sides of the nasal aperture

Anthropoidea   suborder of Primates that includes monkeys, apes, and humans

anvil percussion   a stone-tool-making technique in which a large flat stone is placed on the ground and used as an anvil for breaking off stone flakes

apatite   important mineral component of bones and teeth consisting mainly of calcium phosphate

apomorphies   the evolutionary later state of a character, relative to its ancestral state

appendicular skeleton   the bones of the limbs, including the shoulder girdle

582

arboreal   relating to life in the trees

association areas   regions of the cerebral cortex involved with complex functions of comprehension, communication, and consciousness

asthenopshere   the layer of the Earth directly below the lithosphere, about 100–300 km below the Earth's surface

Aterian   a Middle Paleolithic tool industry in North Africa characterized by tools with tanged points and bifacially worked leaf-shaped points

atomic mass number   total number of protons and neutrons in an atom

atomic number   the number of protons in an atom

autapomorphy   a derived character that arose for the first time in a particular group; autapomorphic characters of a taxon are those not shared by its sister groups or by their most recent common ancestor

axial precession   see **precession**

axial skeleton   the bones of the trunk, including the vertebrae, pelvis, ribs, and sternum

badlands   refers to a complex, stream-dissected topography

basicranium   the base of the cranium

basion   the midline point on the anterior margin of the foramen magnum

beta decay   radioactive decay in which one of the neutrons in the nucleus turns into a proton; the atomic number increases by one, but the mass number remains unchanged (e.g., ^{87}Rb to ^{87}Sr)

bicuspids   premolars

binocular vision   vision in which both visual axes focus on a distant object to produce a stereoscopic (three-dimensional) image

biogenic carbonate   a sediment or rock composed of calcium, magnesium, and/ or iron that is produced directly by the life activities or processes of organisms

bipolar percussion   a stone-tool-making technique in which an anvil is set on the ground, a piece of quartz held upright on it, and flakes chipped off both ends (bipolar flakes) by striking it with a hammerstone

blades   a long parallel-sided flake struck from a specially prepared core

brachycephalic   having a disproportionately short head, usually with a cephalic index (breadth/length) over 80

bregma   the point on the midline of the cranium corresponding to the intersection of the coronal and sagittal sutures

Broca's area   the posterior part of the inferior frontal gyrus of the left or dominant hemisphere in the brain; a critical brain area for motor mechanisms governing articulate speech

Brunhes   long interval of geologic time from about 780 kya to the present in which the polarity of Earth's magnetic field was (for the most part) normal

buccal   toward the lateral (cheek) side of a tooth

burin   a pointed tool made of chipped flint or stone used to engrave bone, antler, ivory and wood

calcrete   a limestone precipitated as surface or near-surface crusts and nodules by the evaporation of soil moisture in semiarid climates

calotte   the calvaria without the base of the cranium

calvaria   top of the cranium; calotte

canine   the pointed tooth between the incisors and the premolars

carbon isotope analyses   studies comparing the relative abundance of two carbon isotopes, ^{12}C and ^{13}C, in tissues of animals; distinct carbon isotope "signatures" are passed along the food chain from the plants to the tissues, including tooth enamel, of herbivores.

carpometacarpal joint   articulation between the wrist bones, or carpus, and the metacarpal bones

cave breccia   a term used to describe sediments in caves that are calcified by lime-bearing solutions dripping from the cave roof

cementum   bone-like tissue that covers the external surface of tooth roots

Cenozoic Era   that portion of Earth's history covering the last 65 million years or so ("recent life")

cephalic index   the ratio of the maximal breadth to the maximal length of the head multiplied by 100

character   morphological feature or trait chosen for study

character weighting   assigning more importance to certain characters than to others to elucidate evolutionary relationships

chronospecies   a species represented in more than one geological time horizon; a time-successive species

cingulum   thickened ring of enamel around the base of a tooth

clade   group comprising all the species descended from a single common ancestor

cladistics   a method of classification employing phylogenetic hypotheses as the basis for classification and using recency of common ancestry as the sole criterion for grouping taxa, rather than data on phenetic similarity (sometimes referred to as phylogenetic systematics)

cladogenesis   a branching type of evolutionary progress involving the splitting and subsequent divergence of populations (also called dendritic evolution)

cladogram   a branching tree diagram used to represent phyletic relationships (also called a cladistic tree)

classification   the process of establishing, defining, and ranking taxa within some hierarchical series of groups

clavicles   the collarbones

cleaver   large, usually bifacially flaked artifact with a straight, sharp-edged bit on one end

climatic forcing model   any of several hypotheses that attempt to relate widespread climatic and associated environmental change, in particular the widespread cooling that occurred around 2.5 mya and affected faunas and floras worldwide, to important events in Plio-Pleistocene hominin evolution

conceptual models   models that reconstruct early hominin behavior using principles from behavioral ecology and evolutionary theory and information on the behavior of particular primate species, including humans

continental drift   slow movements of continents (and the crustal plates to which they are attached) over the surface of the Earth

convergent evolution   the independent evolution of structural or functional similarity in two or more unrelated or distantly related lineages or forms that is not based on genotypic similarity

cores   lumps of stone from which flakes have been removed; sometimes a core is the by-product of tool making, but it may also be shaped and modified to serve as a tool in its own right

coronal   the suture between the frontal and parietal bones

cranium   the skull without the lower jaw or mandible

Cro-Magnons   first anatomically modern western European populations

cross striations   daily microscopic increments of enamel laid down as teeth are formed

crown clade   the clade stemming from the most recent common ancestor of sister taxa with extant representatives (i.e., the clade containing only living taxa and their last common ancestor)

culture   a system of shared meanings, symbols, customs, beliefs, and practices that are learned, either by teaching or by imitation, and used to cope with the environment, to communicate with others, and to transmit information through the generations

decay constant   constant rate by which radioactive elements change spontaneously to lower energy states

deciduous   refers to teeth that are shed and replaced by other teeth during the normal course of an animal's lifetime

dendrochronology   dating by tree rings

dental arch   the teeth and their supporting structures

dental comb   the special alignment of canines and incisors for fur grooming in some prosimian primates

dental formula   shorthand notation denoting the numbers and pattern of teeth in each quadrant of the upper and lower jaws

dentine   the avascular tissue forming the core of teeth; 80% inorganic (mostly hydroxyapatite) and 20% organic (mostly collagen)

Developed Oldowan tradition   a continuation of the Oldowan tool tradition that includes simple pointed choppers, or proto-handaxes, rough bifacial forms, and rare handaxes together with some more evolved scraper forms

diagenesis   the sum of all physical, chemical, and biological changes to which a sediment is subjected after deposition

diaphysis   shaft of a long bone

diastema   space or gap between adjacent teeth in the tooth row

diploic veins   small veins that run between the outer and inner tables of cranial bones

direct percussion   a stone-tool-making technique in which a core flint is held and flakes are detached by striking it with a hammerstone

distal   refers to the side of the tooth or portion of the jaw toward the back of the mouth; also used as a directional term when contrasting positions nearer the attachment (proximal) or origin of a limb or structure and away from its attachment (distal) or origin.

dolichocephalic   having a long, narrow cranium; usually with a cephalic index below 75

dolomitic   a type of limestone in which magnesium replaces calcite

Early Paleolithic   see **Lower Paleolithic**

East African rift system   an elongated trough in the Earth's crust bounded on either side by faults, stretching all the way from the Red Sea in the north to the southern end of Lake Malawi (bordering Mozambique, Tanzania, and Malawi) in the south

eccentricity of the orbit   the deviation of the Earth's orbit around the sun from near circularity to more pronounced ellipticity at periods of about 100,000 years and 400,000 years

electron capture   a radioactive decay process in which a proton in the nucleus turns into a neutron, thus decreasing the atomic number by one; the mass number remains unchanged (e.g., ^{40}K to ^{40}Ar)

electron spin resonance   a method of dating in which the number of trapped electrons is determined by measuring their absorption of microwave radiation; the theoretical age range of ESR dating is from a few thousand years to more than 1 million years ago, but in practical terms most age estimates beyond about 300 kya are very uncertain

elliptical precession   see **precession**

emissary veins   veins that course directly through the bones of the cranium

enamel   the specialized avascular and acellular hard tissue that covers the crowns of teeth

endocranial cast   a naturally occurring (fossilized) or artificially made mold of the external surface of the brain

entoconid   cusp on the lingual rim of the talonid of lower molars

epochs   subdivisions of the Cenozoic Era into the Paleocene, Eocene, Oligocene, Miocene, Pliocene, and Pleistocene

estrus   that phase of the sexual cycle of female animals characterized by willingness to permit coitus

evolutionary systematics   a method of classification employing hypothetical reconstructions of evolutionary history incorporating both cladistic data (on the sequence of branching events) and morphological divergence data

exostosis   a benign bony growth projecting outward from the surface of a bone

external auditory meatus   the ear canal and its opening on the lateral side of the cranium

facial prognathism   forward projection of the face and/or jaws

flourine test   a relative dating technique based on the fact that bones absorb flourine from surrounding groundwater that then combines with bone calcium to form the compound fluoroapatite; the longer the bone has been in the ground, the more fluoroapatite is present

foramen magnum   large hole in the base of the cranium through which the spinal cord passes, joining the base of the brain

Frankfurt Horizontal   plane of orientation of the cranium in side view from the superior margin of the external acoustic meatus to the lower portion of the orbit (orbitale)

frontal keel   a midline thickening in the frontal bone

Gauss   long interval of geologic time from about 3.5 to 2.5 mya in which the polarity of the Earth's magnetic field was (for the most part) normal

geomagnetic polarity reversal time scale   the magnetic histories of rocks and sediments

geophytes   plants having underground bulbs

Gilbert   long interval of geologic time from about 5.8 to 3.5 mya in which the polarity of the Earth's magnetic field was (for the most part) reversed

glabella   area on the frontal bone between the browridges

glacial drift   deposits of rock material transported by glacial ice and then "dumped" by the melting ice on the land surface

glacial periods   portions of geologic time in which the total area covered by glaciers greatly exceeded that of the present

glacial theory   the idea that extensive glaciers formerly covered much of the Northern Hemisphere

glenoid cavity   the socket on the scapula that articulates with the head of the humerus

glenoid fossa   area on the temporal bone for articulation with the condyle of the mandible

Gondwanaland   see **Tethys Sea**

gracile   describes any slender, lightly built body or body part; often used to categorize the less robust australopith species

grade   groups of organisms characterized by a certain level of organization and/or adaptation

graminivorous   grass-eating diet

greenhouse effect   the trapping of heat in the Earth's atmosphere by carbon dioxide

half-life   the time required for half of the atoms of any particular radioactive element to decay

hallux   first toe

handaxe   a large bifacially worked core tool, normally oval or pear shaped

heterodonty   regional differention of teeth into incisors, canines, premolars, and molars

home base   an area to which hominins return to meet other group members, share food, and make tools

hominoid primates   the lesser apes (gibbons and siamangs of eastern Asia), the great apes (chimpanzees and gorillas of Africa and the orangutan of Southeast Asia), and humans

homologous   pertaining to structures shared between two species and their common ancestor

homoplasy   any resemblance not due to inheritance from a common ancestry, for example, similarities due to parallel evolution, convergence, or mimicry

Howiesons Poort   a distinctive South African artifact assemblage that contains many tools specifically designed for hafting as replaceable bits or inserts in composite tools

humerofemoral index   the measure of the ratio of the length of the humerus divided by the length of the femur multiplied by 100

hypocone   the main cusp on the distolingual side of the upper molars

hypoconid   cusp on the lateral rim of the talonid of lower molars

hypoconulid   cusp on the middle of the distal margin of the rim of the talonid on lower molars

hypodigm   the entire known material of a species available to a taxonomist for study

hypsodonty   high-crowned teeth

igneous rock   one of the main groups of rocks that make up the Earth's crust, formed of molten material that flows up from the deeper part of the crust

iliofemoral ligament   ligament that runs from the anterior inferior spine of the ilium to the proximal femur

incisors   the cutting teeth at the front of the upper and lower jaws

inferior transverse torus   shelf-like buttress of bone on the inside of the mandibular symphysis

insolation   the geological effect of solar rays on the surface materials of the earth

interglacial periods   periods of glacial ice retreat

intermembral index   ratio of the length of the forelimb (humerus plus radius) divided by the length of the hindlimb (femur plus tibia) multiplied by 100

interstadials   irregular but well-defined episodes of somewhat milder climatic conditions occurring during glacial periods

intron   a part of a gene that is not translated into a protein

ischial callosities   well-developed sitting pads on the ischium of all Old World monkeys and gibbons

ischial tuberosity   a bony expansion of the ischium that support ischial callosities

isotopes   two atoms that have the same number of protons but a different number of neutrons

Late Paleolithic   see **Upper Paleolithic**

Late Pleistocene   subdivision of the Pleistocene from about 127 to 10 kya (also called Upper Pleistocene)

Late Stone Age   the Upper Paleolithic of southern Africa that generally postdates 40 kya; characterized by a predominance of blade tools and microliths and tiny geometrically shaped blades often set in handles made of bone or wood

Laurasia   see **Tethys Sea**

Law of Superposition   a geological rule that, assuming strata are relatively undisturbed, fossils contained in lower strata will be older than those higher up in the stratigraphic sequence; it is assumed that fossils found in the same stratigraphic level are roughly contemporaneous, the degree of contemporaneity depending on how quickly that particular strata was laid down

Levallois cores   a stone-tool core that is extensively preshaped in order to produce one or more flakes having a predetermined shape

lingual   toward the tongue

lithosphere   the top 70 km layer of the Earth, including oceanic and continental crust

living floor   in archeology, an occupation site

loess   extensive deposits of windblown glacial dust produced by the grinding down of boulders within glacial ice against bedrock

Lower Paleolithic   an archeological subdivision of the Plio-Pleistocene between the first evidence of stone-tool manufacture about 2.6 mya in East Africa and the first appearance, or predominance, of prepared-core flake technologies and flake tools about 300–40 kya (also referred to as the Early Paleolithic)

Lower Pleistocene   subdivision of the Pleistocene from about 1.6 to 0.9 mya

mammae   mammary, or milk-producing, glands

manuports   unaltered objects carried some distance before use

manus   hand

Matuyama   long interval of geologic time from about 2.5 to 0.7 mya in which the polarity of the Earth's magnetic field was (for the most part) reversed

member   in geology, a rock unit that is a subdivision of a formation

mesial   toward the anterior side of a molar or premolar tooth or to the side of an incisor tooth nearest the midline of the jaw

mesocephalic   having a head shape between dolichocephalic and brachycephalic, usually with a cephalic index between 75 and 80

Messinian salinity crisis   dropping of sea levels worldwide that caused the temporary desiccation of the Mediterranean Sea about 5.3 mya

metacone   the main cusp on the distobuccal side of the upper molars

metaconid   cusp on the distolingual corner of the trigonid

Middle Paleolithic   an archeological subdivision of the Plio-Pleistocene about 300–35 kya often referred to (in Europe at least) as the Mousterian, after the site of Le Moustier in France where it was first recognized; characterized by increasing sophistication of stone-tool technology, particularly in the use of flake tools made from prepared cores (e.g., Levallois cores)

Middle Pleistocene   subdivision of the Pleistocene from about 900 to 127 kya

Middle Stone Age   stone-tool tradition in Africa generally dated from over 100 to about 40 kya and characterized by the use of carefully prepared stone cores for the production of flake tools; also the time in Africa when regional variation in stone-tool technologies became most evident

mitochondria   organelles in the cell's cytoplasm made up of single, circular strands of DNA, each having their own genetic coding system; mtDNA has a clonal mode of inheritance that is passed down only through the maternal line

mode   the process of evolution

molars   large grinding teeth at the back of the jaw

molecular clocks   a system of dating based on the premise that many molecular differences among taxa are neutral mutations that accumulate at a relatively constant rate when averaged over geologic time

monogamous pair bonding   a social system based on mated pairs and their offspring

monophyletic group   refers to a group containing all the known descendants of an ancestral species; also a group of species that share a common ancestor that would be classified as a member of the group (clade)

moraines   ridges of glacial drift built up from the material riding on the ice that delineates the melting zones along the margins and bottom of glaciers

morphocline   arrangement of the morphological variations of a homologous character into a continuum of primitive to derived states

mosaic evolution   the appearance at different times in regionally disparate populations of various characters

Mousterian   the tool industry associated most closely with Neandertals, synonymous with the Middle Paleolithic at least in Europe; named for the site of Le Moustier in France where it was first recognized

Multiregional Continuity Model   the evolutionary model that posits humans evolved as an interconnected polytypic species from a single origin in Africa, the small population effects during initial colonizations outside Africa, and adaptations to local conditions, helping establish regional differences that were subsequently maintained through isolation by distance and adaptive variation; advantageous changes spread widely because of genic exchanges and the common background of the evolving cultural system whose elements also could spread; most modernizing features arose at different times and places and diffused independently

Neogene   in geology, the time-stratigraphic unit composed of the Miocene, Pliocene, and Pleistocene

neurocranium   portion of the cranium enclosing the brain

nitrogen test   a means to measure how long a bone has been in the fossilization process based on the amount of nitrogen remaining in it

nuchal crest   bony shelf on the back of the cranium for the attachment of powerful neck muscles

obliquity   in this text, refers to the tilt of the Earth's axis

occipital lobes   posterior portion of the cerebral cortex, mostly involved with vision

occipital/marginal venous sinus   one pathway for venous blood leaving the brain; typically seen in robust australopiths and *A. afarensis*

occlusal   refers to the surfaces of the teeth that meet during occlusion, or chewing

Oldowan tradition   oldest formally recognized stone artifact assemblage of the early Paleolithic; originally defined from Beds I and II of Olduvai Gorge, Tanzania

ontogenetic   relating to the growth and development of an individual organism

opportunistic tools   simple unaltered objects

optical isomers   two amino acids that have different structures but identical formulas

orthognathous   more vertical, nonprotruding face; opposite of prognathous

Osteodontokeratic Culture   the idea proposed by Raymond Dart that many of the bones and jaws at Makapansgat had been utilized as tools by the early hominins at the cave; teeth as saws and scrapers, long bones as clubs, etc.

Out of Africa Model   model of modern human origins that holds that the biocultural transition from late early humans to early modern humans was restricted to Africa, after which radiation outward to the rest of the Old World occurred

oxygen-isotope study   a measure of the oxygen isotope ratios in the calcareous shells of deep-sea marine organisms used to determine both ice volume and ocean temperature; it is based on the fact that there are two isotopes of oxygen in ocean water, the heavier ^{18}O and the lighter ^{16}O; since the overall quantity of the two isotopes is unchanging on Earth, more of ^{16}O tends to be locked up in continental ice during glacial periods, making less available in the oceans. Over time this process leads to an increase in the $^{18}O:^{16}O$ ratio of seawater during glacial periods.

paleomagnetic column   magnetostratigraphic profile of a region

paracone   the main cusp on the mesiobuccal side of the upper molars

paraconid   cusp on the mesial lingual surface of the lower molars

parallel evolution   the independent acquisition in two or more related descendant species of similar derived character states evolved from a common ancestral condition

paraphyletic   refers to a group containing some but not all the known descendants of the common ancestor of the group

parasagittal depressions   slight depressions on either side of the midsagittal keel along the parietal bones

perihelion   the point of closest approach of the earth to the sun

perikymata   enamel ridges visible on teeth that represent weekly microscopic increments of enamel laid down as teeth are formed (see **striae of Retzius**)

pes   foot

phyletic gradualism   a view of evolution that holds that daughter species usually originate through a progressive series of small, gradual transformations of parental species through anagenesis

phylogenetic systematics   see **cladistics**

phylogeny   evolutionary or genealogical history of a group of organisms

phylogram   branching diagram for a set of species that shows their ancestral relationships; one direction, usually the vertical axis, represents time (also called a phylogenetic tree)

plate tectonics   in geology, the movement of segments of the lithosphere that float on the underlying, more gelatinous asthenosphere

platymeric   having an anteroposteriorly flattened femoral shaft

platypelloid   pelvic shape that is wide from side to side and narrow from front to back

pneumatized   filled with air spaces, as in pneumatized portions of the cranium

polarity   the direction of a morphocline from primitive to derived

polarity epochs   extended intervals during which the geomagnetic field has predominantly one polarity

polarity events   short-lived geomagnetic polarity reversal occurring within a polarity epoch

polygynous   the mating of one male with more than one female

polymorphic   showing a variety of forms

polyphyletic group   a taxonomic group whose resemblances are based on convergences

polytypic   comprising several geographical and/or morphological variants

postorbital bar   bony ring surrounding the lateral side of the orbit in lower primates and many other mammals

postorbital closure   "walling off" of the orbit posteriorly by means of a bony partition so that the orbit forms a cup-shaped structure

postorbital constriction narrowing of the cranium behind the orbits

precession perturbations of the Earth's orbit are strongly influenced by gravitational effects of planetary bodies, and these perturbations periodically alter the geographic distribution of incoming solar radiation; one of these effects is known as precession, which changes the distance between the Earth and the Sun at any given season (two components of precession are axial precession, in which the Earth's axis of rotation "wobbles" like that of a spinning top and elliptical precession in which the elliptical orbit itself rotates slightly)

precession of the equinox the equinox is the time when the Sun crosses the plane of the Earth's equator, making night and day all over the Earth of equal length (see **precession**)

prehensile capable of grasping, as hands, feet, or, in some cases, tails

premolars bicuspids

Primates order of mammals that includes prosimians (lemurs, lorises, tarsiers), monkeys, apes, and humans

pronograde quadrupedal locomotion with palms toward the ground

Prosimii suborder of Primates that includes lemurs, lorises, and tarsiers

protocone the main cusp on the mesiolingual side of the upper molars

protoconid one of three main cusps on the trigonid, found on the buccal side of the tooth

pulp cavity the neurovascular space within the dentine that extends for a variable distance into the roots

punctuated equilibrium a view of evolution holding that the creation of new species is more often than not a comparatively rapid event and that most evolutionary change is concentrated in comparatively rapid speciation events in small isolated subpopulations of the ancestral species, a process known as allopatric speciation

racemization the process by which L-amino acids slowly undergo a conversion from the active L-amino acid form into the inactive D-amino acid form over long periods of time

radiometric dating techniques that make use of the fact that many kinds of atoms are unstable and change spontaneously into a lower energy state by radioactive emission; each radioactive element has one particular mode of decay and its own unique constant rate of decay; measuring ratios of undecayed atoms to the products of decay allows one to extrapolate back to the ages of many fossil-bearing rocks

Red Queen Model hypothesis that views evolutionary change leading to new species as being driven by competition among populations that share the same habitat and that sexual recombination is an adaptation to augment a population's capacity to evolve quickly

referential models models that use the social system of a particular nonhuman primate species to model early hominin behavioral evolution

relative dating dating methods that seek to put human fossils and artifacts into a temporal context with other locally associated archeological, faunal and floral materials

rift valleys valleys formed by depression of continental crust

robust describes any large, or heavily built body or body part; often used to categorize the robust australopith species

sagittal crest   bony crest running along the midline of the cranium for attachment of enlarged temporalis muscles

scenario   an historical narrative that attempts to describe not only phylogenetic relationships among taxa but also the ecological and/or evolutionary forces that most directly influenced the character state(s) under discussion

sclerophyllous vegetation   vegetation adapted to dry conditions

sectorial   tooth in the lower jaw (usually the anterior premolar) with a honing facet for sharpening the upper canine during occlusion

secular radioactive equilibrium   in any uranium-bearing material that has lain undisturbed for millions of years, the radioactive decay rate of each of the daughter isotopes will equal the decay rate of any other uranium isotope in the same sample

seed-eating hypothesis   a hypothesis that makes an analogy between anatomical and behavioral characters shared by living gelada baboons (*Theropithecus gelada*) and some early hominins by suggesting that early hominin populations relied on small-object feeding, that this dietary specialization resulted in a suite of adaptations to feeding in grassland savanna, and that bipedalism developed in response to such feeding posture

sexual-and-reproductive-strategy model   a model of human origins based on the trend toward prolonged life span in the primate evolutionary record and its implications for primate physiology, population dynamics, and behavior

simian shelf   distinct mandibular torus that projects posteriorly from the inferior surface of the mandibular symphysis (see also **inferior transverse torus**)

single-crystal fusion   a method of potassium-argon dating in which a laser is used to melt crystals to release the argon gas; this technique has two important advantages over other methods: (1) the laser beam allows such a localized heating of the crystals that there is much less chance of background atmospheric argon confounding the final age calculations and (2) it greatly reduces the amount of sample needed for the age determination

sister groups   two groups that result from a single split in a cladogram—that is, they (and only they) share the same parent taxon

Siwalik Group   the thick sequence of fossiliferous sediments deposited at the base of the rising Himalayas

speleothem   any one of a number of variously shaped mineral deposits formed in caves by the action of water (e.g., stalagmites, stalactites, and flowstones)

spontaneous fission   during spontaneous fission the nucleus within the atomic nucleus of ^{238}U splits into two or more high-energy fragments, and these fragments leave damage tracks within the rock crystals that can be enlarged and studied

stasis   a time of little evolutionary change

stem-based clade   the clade that includes all species, living or extinct, that are more closely related to the living members of that group than to any other living taxon

stomata   the minute respiratory orifices in the epidermis of leaves

striae of Retzius   weekly microscopic increments of enamel laid down as teeth are formed

sulcal patterns   the configuration of the grooves on the external surface of the brain

suprainiac fossa   a midline depression on the occipital bone

supralaryngeal vocal tract   the airspace above the vocal cords

supraorbital tori   projecting browridges that are united medially by a distinct glabellar prominence

supratoral sulcus   trough-like depression between the supraorbital torus and the frontal squama

suture   form of fibrous joint in which two bones formed in membrane are united by a fibrous membrane

sympatric   occurring together in the same geographical area

symplesiomorphy   describes a shared primitive character (symplesiomorph)

synapomorphy   describes a shared derived character (synapomorph)

synchronic   existing or occurring at the same time

talonid   posterior heel-like portion of lower molars

talus cone   sediment, often containing the bones of animals, washed in from the surface in caves where there is a direct passageway between the cave floor and the surface

taphonomy   study of the processes by which animal bones become fossilized

taurodont   having large pulp cavities in the teeth

tempo   the rate of evolution

temporal fossa   the space between the zygomatic arch and the side of the cranium through which the temporalis muscle passes to its insertion point on the coronoid process of the mandible

Tethys Sea   initially a broad waterway that originally divided the northern supercontinent Laurasia (consisting of what is now North America, Europe, and Asia) from the southern supercontinent Gondwanaland, consisting of South America, Africa, Antarctica, India, Madagascar, and Australia

thermoluminescence   the light emitted by trapped electrons as they return to their stable energy states

till   stratified layers of glacial drift

transgression   incursion of the sea over land that converts initially shallow-water conditions to deeper-water conditions

transverse occipital torus   a transverse bony ridge along the occipital bone where the upper (occipital) and lower (nuchal) portions of the bone meet at an angle

travertine   a crystalline calcium carbonate deposit precipitated in solution by inorganic chemical processes

trigonid   anterior triangular portion of the lower molars

tufas   chemical sedimentary deposits rich in calcium carbonate typically occurring as incrustations around the mouths of springs

tuff   general term for rock composed of volcanic ash cemented or consolidated by the pressure of overlying material

type   in systematics, the specimen that serves as the basis for the name of a taxon

Upper Paleolithic   an archeological subdivision of the Plio-Pleistocene about 45–10 kya characterized by the predominance of well-made blades, microliths, distinctive bone points, and the use of burins and other tools to work bone, antler, ivory, teeth, and shells

Upper Pleistocene   see **Late Pleistocene**

varves layers of glacial till that reflect annual cycles of summer melt-off

Villafranchian a distinctive mammalian fauna of Europe that includes animals particularly well adapted to highly seasonal, drought-resistant grasslands; recognized by the presence of mammoths (*Mammuthus*), true bovines (cattle, bison, buffalo), and one-toed horses (*Equus*)

Weak Garden of Eden hypothesis posits that modern humans appeared in a subpopulation and spread slowly over several tens of thousands of years, then later expanded from separated daughter populations bearing modern technologies, such as those of the African Late Stone Age or the European Upper Paleolithic

xeric adapted to dry conditions

References

Abbate E, Albianelli A, et al. 1998. A one-million-year-old *Homo* cranium from the Danakil (Afar) Depression of Eritrea. Nature 393:458–460.

Abbey E. 1989. A voice crying in the wilderness. New York, St. Martin's Press.

Adam KD. 1985. The chronological and systematic position of the Steinheim skull. In: Delson E, editor. Ancestors: The hard evidence. New York: Liss. p 272–276.

Adcock G, Dennis E, et al. 2001. Mitochondrial DNA sequences in ancient Australians: Implications for modern human origins. Proc Natl Acad Sci USA 98: 537–542.

Ahern J, Karavanic I, et al. 2004. New discoveries and interpretations of hominid fossils and artifacts from Vindija Cave, Croatia. J Hum Evol 46:27–67.

Aiello L and Dunbar R. 1993. Neocortex size, group size, and the evolution of language. Curr Anthropol 34:184–193.

Aiello L and Wheeler P. 1995. The expensive-tissue hypothesis. Curr Anthropol 36:199–221.

Aiello L and Collard M. 2001. Our newest oldest ancestor? Nature 410:526–527.

Aiello L and Key C. 2002. Energetic consequences of being a *Homo erectus* female. Am J Hum Biol 14:551–565.

Aitken M, and Valladas H. 1992. Luminescence dating relevant to human origins. Phil Trans R Soc Biol Sci 337:139–144.

Akazawa T, Muhesen S, et al. 1995. Neanderthal infant burial. Nature 377:586–587.

Alba D, Moya–Sola S, et al. 2003. Morphological affinities of the *Australopithecus afarensis* hand on the basis of manual proportions and relative thumb length. J Hum Evol 44:225–254.

Alemseged Z. 2003. An integrated approach to taphonomy and faunal change in the Shungura Formation (Ethiopia) and its implication for hominid evolution. J Hum Evol 44:451–478.

Alemseged Z, Coppens Y, et al. 2002. Hominid cranium from Omo: Description and taxonomy of Omo-323-1976-896. Am J Phys Anthropol 117:103–112.

Allen J, Brandt U, et al. 1999. Rapid environmental changes in southern Europe during the last glacial period. Nature 400:740–743.

Alpagut B, Andrews P, et al. 1990. New hominoid specimens from the middle Miocene site at Pasalar, Turkey. J Hum Evol 19:397–422.

Alpagut B, Andrews P, et al. 1996. A new specimen of *Ankarapithecus meteai* from the Sinap Formation of central Anatolia. Nature 382:349–351.

Alsonso S and Armour J. 2001. A highly variable segment of human subterminal 16p reveals a history of population growth for modern humans outside Africa. Proc Natl Acad Sci USA 98:864–869.

Alt K, Pichler S, et al. 1997. Twenty-five thousand-year-old triple burial from Dolni Vestonice: An ice-age family? Am J Phys Anthropol 102:123–131.

Ambrose S. 1998. Late Pleistocene human population bottlenecks, volcanic winter, and differentiation of modern humans. J Hum Evol 34:623–651.

Ambrose S. 2003. Did the super-eruption of Toba cause a human population bottleneck? Reply to Gathorne-Hardy and Harcourt-Smith. J Hum Evol 45:231–237.

An Z. 1990. The proto-handaxe and its tradition in China. Acta Anthropol Sinica 9:311.

An Z, Gao W, et al. 1990. Magnetostratigraphic dates of Lantian *Homo erectus*. Acta Anthropol Sinica 9:7.

Andersson J. 1996. Finding Beijing man. In: Fagan, B, editor. Eyewitness to discovery. Oxford, UK: Oxford University Press. p 29–36.

Andrews P. 1978. A Revision of the Miocene Hominoidea of East Africa. Bull Br Mus Nat Hist Geol 30:85–224.

Andrews P. 1981. Species diversity and diet in monkeys and apes during the Miocene. In: Stringer C, editor. Aspects of human evolution. London: Taylor & Francis. p 25–61.

Andrews P. 1984. An alternative interpretation of the characters used to define *Homo erectus*. Cour Forsch Inst Senckenberg 69:167–175.

Andrews P. 1990. Lining up the ancestors. Nature 345:664–665.

Andrews P. 1992. Reconstructing past environments. In: Jones S, Martin R, et al., editors. The Cambridge encyclopedia of human evolution. Cambridge, UK: Cambridge University Press. p 191–195.

Andrews P and Van Couvering J. 1975. Paleoenvironments in the East African Miocene. In: Szalay F, editor. Approaches to primate paleobiology. Basel: Karger. p 62–103.

Andrews P and Walker A. 1976. The primate and other fauna from Fort Ternan, Kenya. In: Isaac G, McCown E, editors. Human origins: Louis Leakey and the East African evidence. Menlo Park, CA: Benjamin-Cummings. p 279–304.

Andrews P and Tekkaya I. 1980. A revision of the Turkish Miocene hominoid *Sivapithecus meteai*. Palaeontology 23:85–95.

Andrews P, Meyer G, et al. 1981. The Miocene fossil beds of Maboko Island, Kenya: Geology, age, taphonomy and paleontology. J Hum Evol 10:35–48.

Andrews P and Cronin J. 1982. The relationships of *Sivapithecus* and *Ramapithecus* and the evolution of the orang-utan. Nature 297:541–546.

Andrews P and Martin L. 1987. Cladistic relationships of extant and fossil hominoids. J Hum Evol 16:101–118.

Andrews P and Martin L. 1991. Hominoid dietary evolution. Phil Trans R Soc Lond B 334:199–209.

Andrews P and Jalvo Y. 1997. Surface modifications of the Sima de los Huesos fossil humans. J Hum Evol 33:191–217.

Anklin M, Barnola J, et al. 1993. Climate instability during the last interglacial period recorded in the GRIP ice core. Nature 364:203–207.

Antón S. 1994. Mechanical and other perspectives on Neandertal craniofacial morphology. In: Corruccini RS, Ciochon RL, editors. Integrative paths to the past. Englewood Cliffs, NJ: Prentice Hall. p 677–695.

Antón S. 1997a. Developmental age and taxonomic affinity of the Mojokerto child, Java, Indonesia. Am J Phys Anthropol 102:497–514.

Antón S. 1997b. Endocranial hyperostosis in Sangiran 2, Gibralter 1, and Shanidar 5. Am J Phys Anthropol 102:111–122.

Antón S. 1999. Cranial growth in *Homo erectus:* How credible are the Ngandong juveniles? Am J Phys Anthropol 108:223–236.

Antón S, Márquez S, et al. 2002. Sambungmacan 3 and cranial variation in Asian *Homo erectus*. J Hum Evol 43:555–562.

Antón S. 2003. Natural history of *Homo erectus*. Year Phys Anthropol 46:126–170.

Ardrey R. 1961. African genesis. New York: Dell.

Arensburg B. 1994. Middle Paleolithic speech capabilities: A response to Dr. Lieberman. Am J Phys Anthropol 94:279–280.

Arensburg B, Tillier AM, et al. 1989. A Middle Palaeolithic human hyoid bone. Nature 338:758–760.

Arensburg B, Schepartz LA, et al. 1990. A reappraisal of the anatomical basis for speech in Middle Palaeolithic hominids. Am J Phys Anthropol 83:137–146.

Aronson J and Taieb M. 1981. Geology and paleogeography of the Hadar hominid site, Ethiopia. In: Rapp G, Vondra C, editors. Hominid sites: Their geologic settings. Boulder, CO: Westview Press. p 165–196.

Arsuaga J, Carretero JM, et al. 1991. Cranial remains and long bones from Atapuerca/Ibeas Spain. J Hum Evol 20:191–230.

Arsuaga J, Martínez I, et al. 1993. Three new human skulls from the Sima de los Huesos Middle Pleistocene site in Sierra de Atapuerca, Spain. Nature 362: 534–537.

Arsuaga J, Carretero J, et al. 1997a. Size variation in Middle Pleistocene humans. Science 277:1086–1088.

Arsuaga J, Martínez I, et al. 1997b. Sima de los Huesos (Sierra de Atapuerca, Spain). The site. J Hum Evol 33:109–127.

Arsuaga J, Martínez I, et al. 1997c. The Sima de los Huesos crania (Sierra de Atapuerca, Spain). A comparative study. J Hum Evol 33:219–281.

Arsuaga J, Lorenzo C, et al. 1999a. A complete human pelvis from the Middle Pleistocene of Spain. Nature 399:255–258.

Arsuaga J, Martínez I, et al. 1999b. The human cranial remains from Gran Dolina Lower Pleistocene site (Sierra de Atapuerca, Spain). J Hum Evol 37:431–457.

Ascenzi A, Biddittu I, et al. 1996. A calvarium of late *Homo erectus* from Ceprano, Italy. J Hum Evol 31:409–423.

Asfaw B. 1983. A new hominid parietal from Bodo, Middle Awash Valley, Ethiopia. Am J Phys Anthropol 61:367–371.

Asfaw B. 1987. The Belohdelie frontal: New evidence of early hominid cranial morphology from the Afar of Ethiopia. J Hum Evol 16:611–624.

Asfaw B. 1995. Progress in paleoanthropology at Konso Gardula. Am J Phys Anthropol Suppl 20:60.

Asfaw B, Beyene Y, et al. 1992. The earliest Acheulean from Konso-Gardula. Nature 360:732–735.

Asfaw B, Beyene Y, et al. 1995. Three seasons of hominid paleontology at Aramis, Ethiopia. Paper presented at the Paleoanthropology Society Conference, Oakland, CA.

Asfaw B, White T, et al. 1999. *Australopithecus garhi:* A new species of early hominid from Ethiopia. Nature 284:629–635.

Asfaw B, Gilbert W, et al. 2002. Remains of *Homo erectus* from Bouri, Middle Awash, Ethiopia. Nature 416:317–320.

Ashlock P. 1974. The uses of cladistics. Ann Rev Ecol Syst 5:81–99.

Avery D. 2001. The Plio-Pleistocene vegetation and climate of Sterkfonetin and Swartkrans, South Africa, based on micromammals. J Hum Evol 41:113–132.

Avise J. 1994. Molecular markers, natural history and evolution. London: Chapman & Hall.

Awadalla P, Eyre-Walker A, et al. 1999. Linkage disequilibrium and recombination in hominid mitochondrial DNA. Science 286:2524–2525.

Ayala F. 1995. The myth of Eve: Molecular biology and human origins. Science 270:1930–1936.

Baba H, Aziz F, et al. 2003. *Homo erectus* calvarium from the Pleistocene of Java. Science 299:1384–1388.

Backwell L and d'Errico F. 2001. Evidence of termite foraging by Swartkrans early hominids. Proc Natl Acad Sci USA 98:1358–1363.

Bada J 1985. Amino acid racemization dating of fossil bones. Ann Rev Earth Planetary Sci 13:241–268.

Bada J, Schroeder R, et al. 1974. New evidence for the antiquity of man in North America deduced from aspartic acid racemization. Science 184:791–793.

Bahn P. 1996a. Further back down under. Nature 383:577–578.

Bahn P. 1996b. New developments in Pleistocene art. Evol Anthropol 4:204–215.

Bailey WJ. 1993. Hominoid trichotomy: A molecular overview. Evol Anthropol 2:100–108.

Baker B and Wohlenberg J 1971. Structure and evolution of the Kenya rift valley. Nature 229:538–542.

Baksi AK, Hsu V, et al. 1992. ^{40}Ar/^{39}Ar dating of the Brunhes-Matuyama geomagnetic field reversal. Science 256:356–357.

Bard E, Hamelin B, et al. 1990a. U-Th ages obtained by mass spectrometry in corals from Barbados: Sea level during the past 130,000 years. Nature 346:456–458.

Bard E, Hamelin B, et al. 1990b. Calibration of the ^{14}C timescale over the past 30,000 years using mass spectrometric U-Th ages from Barbados corals. Nature 345:405–410.

Barham L. 2002. Backed tools in Middle Pleistocene central Africa and their evolutionary significance. J Hum Evol 43:585–603.

Barham L and Smart P. 1996. An early date for the Middle Stone Age of central Zambia. J Hum Evol 30:287–290.

Barrett P, Adams C, et al. 1992. Geochronological evidence supporting Antarctic deglaciation three million years ago. Nature 359:816–818.

Barry J. 1986. A review of the chronology of Siwalik hominoids. In: Else JG, Lee PC, editors. Primate evolution. Cambridge, UK: Cambridge University Press. p 93–106.

Bartholomew G and Birdsell J. 1953. Ecology and the protohominids. Am Anthropol 55:481–498.

Bartsiokas A and Day MH. 1993. Lead poisoning and dental caries in the Broken Hill hominid. J Hum Evol 24:243–249.

Bartstra G-J, Soegondho S, et al. 1988. Ngandong man: Age and artifacts. J Hum Evol 17:325–337.

Bar-Yosef O. 1989. Geochronology of the Levantine Middle Palaeolithic. In: Mellars P, Stringer C, editors. The human revolution: Behavioural and biological perspectives on the origin of modern humans. Edinburgh, UK: Edinburgh University Press. p 589–610.

Bar-Yosef O. 1992. The role of western Asia in modern human origins. Phil Trans R Soc Biol Soc 337:193–200.

Bar-Yosef O. 1995. The Lower and Middle Palaeolithic in the Mediterranean Levant: Chronology, and cultural entities. In: Ullrich H, editor. Man and environment in the Palaeolithic. Liege: E.R.A.U.L. p 247–263.

Bar-Yosef O, Vandermeersch B, et al. 1992. The excavations in Kebara Cave, Mt. Carmel. Curr Anthropol 33:497–550.

Bar-Yosef O and Vandermeersch B. 1993. Modern humans in the Levant. Sci Amer 268:94–100.

Bar-Yosef O. and Callander J. 1999. The women from Tabun: Garrod's doubts in historical perspective. J Hum Evol 37:879–885.

Beard KC. 1990. Gliding behavior and palaeoecology of the alleged primate family Paromomyidae (Mammalia, Dermoptera). 345:340–341.

Beard KC, Teaford M, et al. 1986. New wrist bones of *Proconsul africanus* and *P. nyanzae* from Rusinga Island, Kenya. Folia Primatol 47:97–118.

Bednarik R. 1995. Concept-mediated marking in the Lower Palaeolithic. Curr Anthropol 36:605–634.

Begun D. 1992. Miocene fossil hominids and the chimp-human clade. Science 257:1929–1933.

Begun D. 1994a. Relations among the great apes and humans: new interpretations based on the fossil great ape *Dryopithecus*. Yearbk Phys Anthropol 37:11–63.

Begun D. 1994b. The significance of *Otavipithecus namibiensis* to interpretations of hominoid evolution. J Hum Evol 27:385–394.

Begun D. 1995. Late Miocene European orang-utans, gorillas, humans, or none of the above? J Hum Evol 29:169–180.

Begun D. 2002. European hominoids. In: Hartwig W, editor. The primate fossil record. Cambridge, UK: Cambridge University Press. p 339–368.

Begun, D. 2004. The earliest hominins—Is less more? Science 303:1478–1480.

Begun D and Walker A. 1993. The endocast of the Nariokotome hominid. In: Walker A, Leakey RE, editors. The Nariokotome *Homo erectus* skeleton. Cambridge, MA: Harvard University Press. p 326–358.

Begun D, Teaford MF, et al. 1994. Comparative and functional anatomy of *Proconsul* phalanges from the Kaswanga primate site, Rusinga Island, Kenya. J Hum Evol 26:89–165.

Begun D and Kordos L. 1997. Phyletic affinities and functional convergence in *Dryopithecus* and other Miocene and living hominids. In: Begun D, Ward C, et al., editors. Function, phylogeny, and fossils: Miocene hominoid evolution and adaptations. New York: Plenum. p 291–316.

Begun D and Gülec E. 1998. Restoration of the type and palate of *Ankarapithecus meteai:* Taxonomic and phylogenetic implications. Am J Phys Anthropol 105:279–314.

Behrensmeyer A. 1976. Lothagam Hill, Kanapoi, and Ekora: A general summary of stratigraphy and faunas. In: Coppens Y, Howell FC, et al., editors. Earliest man and environments in the Lake Rudolf Basin. Chicago: University of Chicago Press. p 163–170.

Behrensmeyer A. 1978. Correlation of Plio–Pleistocene sequences in the northern Lake Turkana Basin: A summary of evidence and issues. In: Bishop W, editor. Geological background to fossil man: Recent research in the Gregory Rift Valley, East Africa. Edinburgh, UK: Scottish Academic Press. p 421–440.

Behrensmeyer A. 1992. Fossil deposits and their investigation. In: Jones S, Martin R, et al., editors. The Cambridge encyclopedia of human evolution. Cambridge, UK: Cambridge University Press. p 187–190.

Behrensmeyer A, Todd N, et al. 1997a. Paleoecological implications of faunas associated with hominids in the Turkana Basin, Kenya. J Hum Evol 32:A2–A3.

Behrensmeyer A, Todd N, et al. 1997b. Late Pliocene faunal turnover in the Turkana Basin, Kenya and Ethiopia. Science 278:1589–1594.

Belfer-Cohen A and Hovers E. 1992. In the eye of the beholder: Mousterian and Natufian burials in the Levant. Curr Anthropol 33:463–471.

Benefit B. 1995. Earliest Old World monkey skull. Am J Phys Anthropol Suppl. 20:64.

Benefit B and McCrossin M. 1989. New primate fossils from the middle Miocene of Maboko Island, Kenya. J Hum Evol 18:493–497.

Benefit B and McCrossin M. 1997. Earliest known Old World monkey skull. Nature 388:368–371.

Berge C. 1994. How did the australopithecines walk: A biomechanical study of the hip and thigh of *Australopithecus afarensis.* J Hum Evol 26:259–273.

Berger L, Keyser A, et al. 1993. Gladysvale: First early hominid site discovered in South Africa since 1948. Am J Phys Anthropol 92:107–111.

Berger L and Clarke R. 1994. Eagle involvement in accumulation of the Taung child fauna. J Hum Evol 29:275–299.

Berger L, Menter C, et al. 1994. The renewal of excavation activities at Kromdraai, South Africa. South Afr J Sci 90:209–210.

Berger L and Tobias P. 1994. New discoveries at the early hominid site of Gladysvale, South Africa. South Afr J Sci 90:223–226.

Berger L and Parkington J. 1995. A new Pleistocene hominid-bearing locality at Hoedjiespunt, South Africa. Am J Phys Anthropol 98:601–609.

Berger L and Clarke R. 1996. The load of the Taung child. Nature 379:778–779.

Berger L and Tobias P. 1996. A chimpanzee-like tibia from Sterkfontein, South Africa and its implications for the interpretation of bipedalism in *Australopithecus africanus.* J Hum Evol 30:343–348.

Berger L, Lacruz R, et al. 2002. Revised age estimates of *Australopithecus*-bearing deposits at Sterkfontein, South Africa. Am J Phys Anthropol 119:192–197.

Bernor R. 1983. Geochronology and zoogeographic relationships of Miocene Hominoidea. In: Ciochon R, Corruccini R, editors. New interpretations of ape and human ancestry. New York: Plenum. p 21–64.

Bernor R, Flynn L, et al. 1988. *Dionysopithecus* from southern Pakistan and the biochronology and biogeography of early Eurasian catarrhines. J Hum Evol 17:339–358.

Bernor R and Tobien H. 1990. The mammalian geochronology and biogeography of Pasalar (Middle Miocene, Turkey). J Hum Evol 19:551–568.

Beynon A and Dean M. 1988. Distinct dental development patterns in early fossil hominids. Nature 335:509–514.

Bicchieri MG, ed. 1972. Hunters and gatherers today. New York: Holt, Rinehart & Winston.

Biewener AA. 1990. Biomechanics of mammalian terrestrial locomotion. Science 250:1097–1103.

Binford L. 1981. Bones: Ancient men and modern myths. New York: Academic Press.

Binford L. 1985. Human ancestors: Changing views of their behavior. J Anthropol Archaeol 4:292–327.

Binford L. 1989. Isolating the transition to cultural adaptations: An organizational approach. In: Trinkaus E, editor. The emergence of modern humans. Cambridge, UK: Cambridge University Press. p 18–41.

Binford L and Stone N. 1986. Zhoukoudian: A closer look. Curr Anthropol 27:453–460.

Binford L and Ho C. 1985. Taphonomy at a distance: Zhoukoudian, "The cave home of Beijing man"? Curr Anthropol 26:413–443.

Bischoff J, Fitzpatrick J, et al. 1997. Geology and preliminary dating of the hominid-bearing sedimentary fill of the Sima de los Huesos Chamber, Cueva Mayor of the Sierra de Atapuerca, Burgos, Spain. J Hum Evol 33:129–154.

Bischoff J and Shamp D. 2003. The Sima de los Huesos hominids date to beyond U/Th equilibrium (>350 kyr) and perhaps to 400–500 kyr: New radiometric dates. J Archeol Sci 30:275–280.

Bishop LC and Plummer TW. 1995. Modern analogues for Olduvai Bed I environments based on artiodactyl habitat preferences. Paper presented at the Paleoanthropology Society Conference, Oakland, CA.

Bishop W. 1964. More fossil primates and other Miocene mammals from northeast Uganda. Nature 203:1327–1331.

Bishop W. 1967. The later Tertiary in East Africa: Volcanics, sediments, and faunal inventory. In: Bishop W, Clark J, editors. Background to evolution in Africa. Chicago: University of Chicago. p 31–56.

Bishop W, ed. 1978. Geological background to fossil man: Recent research in the Gregory rift valley, East Africa. Edinburgh, UK: Scottish Academic Press.

Bishop W. 1980. Paleogeomorphology and continental taphonomy. In: Behrensmeyer AK, and Hill AP, editors. Fossils in the making. Chicago: University of Chicago Press. p 20–37.

Bishop W, Miller J, et al. 1969. New potassium-argon age determinations relevant to the Miocene fossil mammal sequence in East Africa. Am J Sci 267:669–699.

Black D. 1927. On a lower molar hominid tooth from the Chou Kou Tien deposit. Palaeontol Sinica Ser D 7:1.

Blackwell B and Rutter N. 1990. Amino acid racemization in mammalian bones and teeth from La Chaise-de-Vouthon (Charente), France. Geoarchaeol 5:121–147.

Blumenschine R. 1987. Characteristics of an early hominid scavenging niche. Curr Anthropol 28:383–407.

Blumenschine R. 1995. Percussion marks, tooth marks, and experimental determinations of the timing of hominid and carnivore access to long bones at FLK *Zinjanthropus*, Olduvai Gorge, Tanzania. J Hum Evol 29:21–51.

Blumenschine R, Masao F, et al. 1997. New paleoanthropological discoveries and tests of hominid land use models in the Western Lacustrine Plain of the lowermost Bed II (Olduvai Basin). J Hum Evol 32:A5.

Blumenschine R and Cavallo J. 1992. Scavenging and human evolution. Sci Am 266:90–96.

Blumenschine R, Peters C, et al. 2003. Late Pliocene *Homo* and hominid land use from western Olduvai Gorge, Tanzania. Science 299:1217–1221.

Blunier T, Chappellaz J, et al. 1998. Asynchrony of Antarctic and Greenland climate change during the last glacial period. Nature 394:739–743.

Boaz N and Howell F. 1977. A gracile hominid cranium from upper member G of the Shungura Formation, Ethiopia. Am J Phys Anthropol 46:93–108.

Bobe R. 1997. Hominid environments and paleoecology in the East African Pliocene. Am J Phys Anthropol Suppl 24:78.

Bobe R, Behrensmeyer A, et al. 2002. Faunal change, environmental variability and late Pliocene hominin evolution. J Hum Evol 42:475–498.

Bocherens H, Billiou D, et al. 2001. New isotopic evidence for dietary habits of Neandertals from Belgium. J Hum Evol 40:497–505.

Boeda E, Connan J, et al. 1996. Bitumen as a hafting material on Middle Palaeolithic artifacts. Nature 380:336–338.

Boesch C and Boesch H. 1984. Possible causes of sex differences in the use of natural hammers by wild chimpanzees. J Hum Evol 13:415–440.

Boesch C and Boesch H. 1989. Hunting behavior of wild chimpanzees in the Tai National Park. Am J Phys Anthropol 78:547–573.

Boesch C, Marchesi P, et al. 1994. Is nut cracking in wild chimpanzees a cultural behavior? J Hum Evol 26:325–338.

Boesch-Achermann H and Boesch C. 1994. Hominization in the rainforest: The chimpanzee's piece of the puzzle. Evol Anthropol 3:9–16.

Bonnefille R. 1976. Palynological evidence for an important change in the vegetation of the Omo Basin between 2.5 and 2 million years. In: Copens Y, Howell F, et al., editors. Earliest man and environments in the Lake Rudolf basin. Chicago: University of Chicago Press. p 421–431.

Bonnefille R. 1994. Palynology and paleoenvironment of East African hominid sites. In: Corruccini RS, and Ciochon RL, editors. Integrative paths to the past. Englewood Cliffs, NJ: Prentice Hall. p 415–427.

Boschetto HG, Brown FH, et al. 1992. Stratigraphy of the Lothidok Range, northern Kenya, and K/Ar ages of its Miocene primates. J Hum Evol 22:47–71.

Boule M. 1923. Fossil men: Elements of human paleontology. London: Gurney & Jackson.

Bowen DQ and Sykes GA. 1994. How old is "Boxgrove man"? Nature 371:751.

Bowler J and Magee J. 2000. Redating Australia's oldest human remains: A sceptic's view. J Hum Evol 38:719–726.

Brace CL. 1964. The fate of the classic Neandertals: A consideration of hominid catastrophism. Curr Anthropol 5:3–43.

Brace CL. 1967. The stages of human evolution. Englewood Cliffs, NJ: Prentice Hall.

Brace CL. 1979. Krapina, "classic" Neanderthals, and the evolution of the European face. J Hum Evol 8:527–550.

Brace CL. 1995. Biocultural interaction and the mechanism of mosaic evolution in the emergence of "modern" morphology. Am Anthropol 97:711–721.

Brain C. 1970. New finds at the Swartkrans Australopithecine site. Nature 225:1–7.

Brain C. 1981a. Hominid evolution and climatic change. South Afr J Sci 77:104–105.

Brain C. 1981b. The hunters or the hunted? Chicago: University of Chicago Press.

Brain C. 1983. The terminal Miocene event: A critical environmental and evolutionary episode. In: Vogel J, editor. SASQUA international symposium. Rotterdam: Balkema. p 491–498.

Brain C. 1988. New information from the Swartkrans cave or relevance to "robust" australopithecines. In: Grine F, editor. Evolutionary history of the "robust" australopithecines. New York: de Gruyter. p 311–316.

Brain C. 1993a. The occurrence of burnt bones at Swartkrans and their implications for the control of fire by early hominids. In: Brain CK, editor. Swartkrans: A cave's chronicle of early man. Pretoria: Transvaal Museum. p 229–242.

Brain C. 1993b. Structure and stratigraphy of the Swartkrans cave in the light of the new excavations. In: Brain CK, editor. Swartkrans: A cave's chronicle of early man. Pretoria: Transvaal Museum. p 23–33.

Brain C, ed. 1993c. Swartkrans: A cave's chronicle of early man. Pretoria: Transvaal Museum Monographs.

Brain C. 1994. The Swartkrans palaeontological research project in perspective: Results and conclusions. South Afr J Sci 90:220–223.

Brain C, van Riet Lowe C, et al. 1955. Kafuan stone artefacts in the post australopithecine breccia at Makapansgat. Nature 175:16.

Brain C and Sillen A. 1988. Evidence from the Swartkrans cave for the earliest use of fire. Nature 336:464–466.

Brain C and Watson V. 1992. A guide to the Swartkrans early hominid cave site. Ann Transvaal Mus 35:343–365.

Brain C and Shipman P. 1993. The Swartkrans bone tools. In: Brain CK, editor. Swartkrans: A cave's chronicle of early man. Pretoria: Transvaal Museum. p 195–215.

Bräuer B and Mbua E. 1992. *Homo erectus* features used in cladistics and their variability in Asian and African hominids. J Hum Evol 22:79–108.

Bräuer G. 1989. The evolution of modern humans: A comparison of the African and non-African evidence. In: Mellars P, Stringer C, editors. The human revolution: Behavioral and biological perspectives on the origins of modern humans. Edinburgh, UK: Edinburgh University Press, p 123–154.

Bräuer G. 1990. The occurrence of some controversial *Homo erectus* cranial features in the Zhoukoudian and East African hominids. Acta Anthropol Sinica 9:352–358.

Bräuer G. 1994. How different are Asian and African *Homo erectus*? Cour Forsch Inst Senckenberg 171:301–318.

Bräuer G and Leakey RE. 1980. The ES–1693 cranium from Eliye Springs, West Turkana, Kenya. J Hum Evol 15:289–312.

Bräuer G and Rimbach KW. 1990. Late archaic and modern *Homo sapiens* from Europe, Africa, and Southwest Asia: Craniometric comparisons and phylogenetic implications. J Hum Evol 19:789–807.

Bräuer G, Deacon HJ, et al. 1992. Comment on the new maxillary finds from Klasies River, South Africa. J Hum Evol 23:419–422.

Bräuer G and Schultz M. 1996. The morphological affinities of the Plio-Pleistocene mandible from Dmanisi, Georgia. J Hum Evol 30:445–481.

Bräuer G, Yokoyama Y, et al. 1997. Modern human origins backdated. Nature 386:337–338.

Bräuer G, Groden C, et al. 2004. Virtual study of the endocranial morphology of the matrix-filled cranium from Eliye Springs, Kenya. Anat Rec 276A:113–133.

Britten R. 1986. Rates of DNA sequence evolution differ between taxonomic groups. Science 231:1393–1398.

Britten R. 2002. Divergence between samples of chimpanzee and human DNA sequences is 5%, counting indels. Proc Nat Acad Sci 99:13633–13635.

Bromage T. 1987. The biological and chronological maturation of early hominids. J Hum Evol 16:257–272.

Bromage T and Dean M. 1985. Re-evaluation of the age at death of immature fossil hominids. Nature 317:525–527.

Bromage T, Schrenk F, et al. 1995. Paleoanthropology of the Malawi Rift: An early hominid mandible from the Chiwondo Beds, northern Malawi. J Hum Evol 28:71–108.

Brookfield J. 1997. Importance of ancestral DNA ages. Nature 388:134.

Brooks A. 1988a. Middle Paleolithic. In: Tattersall I, Delson E, et al., editors. Encyclopedia of human evolution and prehistory. New York: Garland. p 341–346.

Brooks A. 1988b. Paleolithic. In: Tattersall I, Delson E, et al., editors. Encyclopedia of human evolution and prehistory. New York: Garland. p 415–419.

Brooks A, Hare P, et al. 1990. Dating Pleistocene archeological sites by protein diagenesis in ostrich eggshell. Science 248:60–64.

Brooks A, Helgren D, et al.1995. Dating and context of three Middle Stone Age sites with bone points in the Upper Semliki Valley, Zaire. Science 268:548–553.

Broom R. 1936. A new fossil anthropoid skull from South Africa. Nature 138:486–488.

Broom R. 1937. Discovery of a lower molar of *Australopithecus*. Nature 140:681–682.

Broom R. 1938. The Pleistocene anthropoid apes of South Africa. Nature 142:377–379.

Broom R. 1949. Another new type of fossil ape-man. Nature 163:57.

Broom R and Robinson J. 1947. Further remains of the Sterkfontein ape-man, *Plesianthropus*. Nature 160:430–431.

Broom R and Robinson J. 1949. A new type of fossil man. Nature 164:322–323.

Broom R and Robinson JT. 1950. Man contemporaneous with the Swartkrans ape-man. Am J Phys Anthropol 8:151–156.

Broom R and Robinson J. 1951. Eruption of the permanent teeth in the South African fossil ape-men. Nature 167:443.

Brose D and Wolpoff M. 1971. Early Upper Paleolithic man and late Middle Paleolithic tools. Am Anthropol 73:1156–1194.

Brown B, Walker A, et al. 1993. New *Australopithecus boisei* calvaria from East Lake Turkana, Kenya. Am J Phys Anthropol 91:137–159.

Brown F. 1992. Methods of dating. In: Jones S, Martin R, et al., editors. The Cambridge encyclopedia of human evolution. Cambridge, UK: Cambridge University Press. p 179–186.

Brown F. 1994. Development of Pliocene and Pleistocene chronology of the Turkana Basin, East Africa, and its relation to other sites. In: Corruccini RS, Ciochon RL, editors. Integrative paths to the past. Englewood Cliffs, NJ: Prentice Hall. p 285–312.

Brown F, Howell F, et al. 1978. Observations on problems of correlation of late Cenozoic hominid-bearing formations in the North Lake Turkana Basin. In: Bishop W, editor. Geological background to fossil man: Recent advances in the Gregory rift valley, East Africa. Edinburgh, UK: Scottish Academic Press. p 473–498.

Brown F, Harris J, et al. 1985a. Early *Homo erectus* skeleton from west Lake Turkana, Kenya. Nature 316:788–792.

Brown F, McDougall I, et al. 1985b. An integrated Plio-Pleistocene chronology for the Turkana Basin. In: Delson E, editor. Ancestors: The hard evidence. New York: Liss, p 82–90.

Brown F and Feibel C. 1986. Revision of lithostratigraphic nomenclature in the Koobi Fora region, Kenya. J Geol Soc 143:297–310.

Brown F and Feibel C. 1988. "Robust" hominid and Plio-Pleistocene paleogeography of the Turkana Basin, Kenya and Ethiopia. In: Grine FE, editor. Evolutionary history of the "robust" australopithecines. New York: de Gruyter. p 325–341.

Brown P. 1992. Recent human evolution in East Asia and Australasia. Phil Trans R Soc Biol Sci 337:235–242.

Brown P, Sutikna T, et al. (2004) A new small-bodied hominin from the Late Pleistocene of Flores, Indonesia. Nature 431:1055–1061.

Brunet M, Beauvilain A, et al. 1995. The first australopithecine 2,500 kilometres west of the rift valley (Chad). Nature 378:273–275.

Brunet M, Beauvilain A, et al. 1996. *Australopithecus bahrelghazali,* une nouvelle espece d'hominide ancien de la region de Koro Toro (Tchad). CR Acad Sci Paris 322:907–913.

Brunet M, Guy F, et al. 2002. A new hominid from the Upper Miocene of Chad, central Africa. Nature 418:145–151.

Buchardt B. 1978. Oxygen isotope palaeotemperatures from the Tertiary period in the North Sea area. Nature 275:121–123.

Burbank DW, Derry LA, et al. 1993. Reduced Himalayan sediment production 8 myr ago despite an intensified monsoon. Nature 364:48–50.

Burrows W and Ryder O. 1997. Y-chromosome variation in great apes. Nature 385:125–126.

Burton JH and Wright LE. 1995. Nonlinearity in the relationship between bone Sr/Ca and diet: paleodietary implications. Am J Phys Anthropol 96:273–282.

Butzer KW and Isaac GL, eds. 1975. After the australopithecines. The Hague: Mouton.

Cachel S and Harris J. 1995. Ranging patterns, land-use and subsistence in *Homo erectus,* form the perspective of evolutionary ecology. In: Bower J, Sartono S, editors. Human evolution in its ecological context. Leiden: Leiden University. p 51–47.

Cadman A and Rayner RJ. 1989. Climatic change and the appearance of *Australopithecus africanus* in the Makapansgat sediments. J Hum Evol 18:107–113.

Calcagno J. 1995. Dental crowding in the South African early hominids. Am J Phys Anthropol Suppl 20:71–72.

Calcagno J, Cope D, et al. 1997. Is *A. africanus* the only hominid species in Sterkfontein member 4? Am J Phys Anthropol Suppl 24:86.

Cande S and Kent D. 1995. Revised calibration of the geomagnetic polarity time scale for the late Cretaceous and Cenozoic. J Geophys Res 100:6093–6095.

Cane M and Molnar P. 2001. Closing of the Indonesian seaway as a precursor to east African aridification around 3–4 million years ago. Nature 411:157–162.

Cann R, Stoneking M, et al. 1987. Mitochondrial DNA and human evolution. Nature 325:31–36.

Cant JGH. 1987. Effects of sexual dimorphism in body size on feeding postural behavior of Sumatran orangutans (*Pongo pygmaeus*). Am J Phys Anthropol 74:143–148.

Capaldo S. 1997. Experimental determinations of carcass processing by Plio-Pleistocene hominids and carnivores at FLK 22 (*Zinjanthropus*), Oduvai Gorge, Tanzania. J Hum Evol 33:555–597.

Carbonell E, de Castro JMB, et al. 1995. Lower Pleistocene hominids and artifacts from Atapuerca-TD 6 (Spain). Science 269:826–830.

Carbonell E, Esteban M, et al. 1999a. The Pleistocene site of Gran Dolina, Sierra de Atapuerca, Spain: A history of the archaeological investigations. J Hum Evol 37:313–324.

Carbonell E, Garcia-Antón M, et al. 1999b. The TD6 level lithic industry from Gran Dolina, Atapuerca, (Burgos, Spain): Production and use. J Hum Evol 37:653–693.

Carretero J, Arsuaga J, et al. 1997. Clavicles, scapulae and humeri from the Sima de los Huesos site (Sierra de Atapuerca, Spain). J Hum Evol 33:357–408.

Carretero J, Lorenzo C, et al. 1999. Axial and appendicular skeleton of *Homo antecessor.* J Hum Evol 37:459–499.

Carter B, Dunnell R, et al. 1997. The effect of reproductive status on Sr/Ca ratios: Experimental data from *Macaca nemistrina.* Am J Phys Anthropol Suppl 24:89.

Cartmill M. 1990. Human uniqueness and theoretical content in paleoanthropology. Int J Primatol 11:173–192.

Cartmill M. 1993. A view to a death in the morning. Cambridge, MA: Harvard University Press.

Cartmill M and Schmitt D. 1997. The effect of pelvic width on pelvic rotation during bipedalism in modern and fossil hominids. Am J Phys Anthropol Suppl 24:89.

Caspari R and Wolpoff MH. 1990. The morphological affinities of the Klasies River mouth skeletal remains. Am J Phys Anthropol 81:203.

Cavalieri D, Gloersen P, et al. 1997. Observed hemispheric asymmetry in global sea ice changes. Science 278:1104–1106.

Cavalli-Sforza L, Menozzi P, et al. 1993. Demic expansions and human evolution. Science 259:639–646.

Cavallo J and Blumenschine R. 1989. Tree-stored leopard kills: Expanding the hominid scavenging niche. J Hum Evol 18:393–399.

Cela-Conde C and Ayala F. 2003. Genera of the human lineage. Proc Nat Acad Sci 100:7684–7689.

Cerling T. 1992. Development of grasslands and savannas in East Africa during the Neogene. Paleogeog Paleoclimatol Paleoecol 97:241–247.

Cerling T, Quade J, et al. 1991. Fossil soils, grasses, and carbon isotopes from Fort Ternan, Kenya: Grassland or woodland? J Hum Evol 21:295–306.

Cerling T, Harris J, et al. 1997. Global vegetation change through the Miocene/Pliocene boundary. Nature 389:153–158.

Chamberlain A and Wood B. 1987. Early hominid phylogeny. J Hum Evol 16:119–133.

Chaplin G, Jablonski NG, et al. 1994. Physiology, thermoregulation and bipedalism. Am J Phys Anthropol 27:497–510.

Chase P. 1990. Tool-making tools and Middle Paleolithic behavior. Curr Anthropol 31:443–447.

Chazan M. 1995a. Conceptions of time and the development of Paleolithic chronology. Am Anthropol 97:457–467.

Chazan M. 1995b. The language hypothesis for the Middle-to-Upper Paleolithic transition. Curr Anthropol 36:749–768.

Chen T, Hedges R, et al. 1989. Accelerator radiocarbon dating from upper cave of Zhoukoudian. Acta Anthropol Sinica 8:221.

Chen T and Zhang Y. 1991. Palaeolithic chronology and the possible coexistence of *Homo erectus* and *Homo sapiens* in China. World Archeol 23:147–154.

Chen T, Yang Q, et al. 1993. Electron spin resonance dating of teeth enamel samples from Jingniushan palaeoanthropological site. Acta Anthropol Sinica 12:346.

Chen T, Yang Q, et al.1996. ESR dating on the stratigraphy of Yunxian *Homo erectus,* Hubei, China. Acta Anthropol Sinica 15:114–118.

Chen Y-S, Torroni A, et al. 1995. Analysis of mtDNA variation in African populations reveals the most ancient of all human continent-specific haplogroups. Am J Hum Genet 57: 133–149.

Chung S-L, Lo C-H, et al. 1998. Diachronous uplift of the Tibetan plateau starting 40 myr ago. Nature 394:769–773.

Churchill S. 1996. Particulate versus integrated evolution of the upper body in Late Pleistocene humans: A test of two models. Am J Phys Anthropol 100:559–83.

Churchill S. 1998. Cold adaptation, heterochrony, and Neandertals. Evol Anthropol 7:46–61.

Churchill S, Pearson O, et al. 1996. Morphological affinities of the proximal ulna from Klasies River main site: Archaic or modern? J Hum Evol 31:213–237.

Churchill S. and Smith F. 2000. Makers of the Early Aurignacian. Am J Phys Anthropol 43:61–115.

Ciochon R, Olsen J, et al. 1990. Other origins: The search for the giant ape in human prehistory. New York: Bantam.

Clark A, Glanowksi S, et al. 2004. Inferring nonneural evolution from human-chimp-mouse orthologous gene trios. Science 302:1960–1963.

Clark G. 1999. Highly visible, curiously intangible. Science 283:2029–2032.

Clark JD. 1970. The prehistory of Africa. New York: Praeger.

Clark JD. 1985. Leaving no stone unturned: archaeological advances and behavioral adaptation. In: Tobias P, editor. Hominid evolution: Past, present, and future. New York: Liss, p 6–88.

Clark JD. 1992. African and Asian perspectives on the origins of modern humans. Phil Trans R Soc Biol Sci 337:201–215.

Clark JD. 1993. Stone artefacts assemblages from members 1–3, Swartkrans cave. In: Brain CK, editor. Swartkrans: A cave's chronicle of early man. Pretoria: Transvaal Museum. p 167–194.

Clark JD. 1994. The Acheulian industrial complex in Africa and elsewhere. In: Corruccini RS, Ciochon RL, editors. Integrative paths to the past. Englewood Cliffs, NJ: Prentice Hall. p 451–469.

Clark JD, Brothwell DR, et al. 1968. Rhodesian man: Notes on a new femur fragment. Man 3:105–111.

Clark JD, Asfaw B, et al. 1984. Palaeoanthropological discoveries in the Middle Awash valley, Ethiopia. Nature 307:423–428.

Clark JD, de Heinzelin J, et al. 1994. African *Homo erectus:* Old radiometric ages and young Oldowan assemblages in the Middle Awash valley, Ethiopia. Science 264:1907–1910.

Clark JD, Beyene Y, et al. 2003. Stratigraphic, chronologial and behavioural contexts of Pleistocene *Homo sapiens* from Middle Awash, Ethiopia. Nature 423:747–752.

Clark P, Alley R, et al. 1999. Northern Hemisphere ice-sheet influences on global climate change. Science 286:1104–1111.

Clarke R. 1976. New cranium of *Homo erectus* from Lake Ndutu, Tanzania. Nature 262:485–487.

Clarke R. 1985a. *Australopithecus* and early *Homo* in southern Africa. In: Delson E, editor. Ancestors: The hard evidence. New York: Liss., p 171–177.

Clarke R. 1985b. A new reconstruction of the Florisbad cranium, with notes on the site. In: Delson E, editor. Ancestors: The hard evidence. New York: Liss. p 301–305.

Clarke R. 1988. A new *Australopithecus* cranium from Sterkfontein and its bearing on the ancestry of *Paranthropus.* In: Grine FE, editor. Evolutionary history of the "robust" australopithecines. New York: de Gruyter. p 285–292.

Clarke R. 1990. The Ndutu cranium and the origin of *Homo sapiens.* J Hum Evol 19:699–736.

Clarke R. 1994a. Advances in understanding the craniofacial anatomy of South African early hominids. In: Corruccini RS, Ciochon RL, editors. Integrative paths to the past. Englewood Cliffs, NJ: Prentice Hall. p 205–222.

Clarke R. 1994b. On some new interpretations of Sterkfontein stratigraphy. South Afr J Sci 90:211–214.

Clarke R. 1994c. The significance of the Swartkrans *Homo* to the *Homo erectus* problem. Cour Forsch Inst Senckenberg 171:185–193.

Clarke R. 1998. First ever discovery of a well-preserved skull and associated skeleton of *Australopithecus*. South Afr J Sci 94:460–463.

Clarke R. 1999. Discovery of complete arm and hand of the 3.3 million-year-old *Australopithecus* skeleton from Sterkfontein. South Afr J Sci 95:477–480.

Clarke R. 2002a. Newly revealed information on the Sterkfontein member 2 *Australopithecus* skeleton. South Afr J Sci 98:523–526.

Clarke R and Howell F. 1972. Affinities of the Swartkrans 847 hominid cranium. Am J Phys Anthropol 37:319–336.

Clarke R. 2002b. On the unrealistic "revised age estimates" for Sterkfontein. South Afr J Sci 98:415–418.

Clarke R, Howell F, et al. 1970. More evidence of an advanced hominid at Swartkrans. Nature 225:1219–1222.

Clarke R and Tobias P. 1995. Sterkfontein member 2 foot bones of the oldest South African hominid. Science 269:521–524.

Clegg M and Aiello L. 1999. A comparison of the Nariokotome *Homo erectus* with juveniles from a modern human population. Am J Phys Anthropol 110:81–93.

Clemens S and Tiedemann R. 1997. Eccentricity forcing of Pliocene-Early Pleistocene climate revealed in a marine oxygen-isotope record. Nature 385:801–804.

Clutton-Brock T and Harvey P. 1977. Primate ecology and social organisation. J Zool Lond 183:1–39.

Coe RS, Prevot M, et al. 1995. New evidence for extraordinarily rapid change of the geomagnetic field during a reversal. Nature 374:687–692.

Coffing K, Feibel C, et al. 1994. Four-million-year-old hominids from East Lake Turkana, Kenya. Am J Phys Anthropol 93:55–65.

Cohen P. 1996. Fitting a face to Ngaloba. J Hum Evol 30:373–379.

Coleman M and Hodges K. 1995. Evidence for Tibetan plateau uplift before 14 myr ago from a new minimum age for east-west extension. Nature 374:49–52.

Coles J and Higgs E. 1969. The archaeology of early man. New York: Praeger.

Collard M and Wood B. 2000. How reliable are human phylogenetic hypotheses? Proc Nat. Acad Sci USA 97:5003–5006.

Collard M and Wood B. 2001. Homoplasy and the early hominid masticatory system: Inferences from analyses of extant hominoids and papionins. J Hum Evol 41:167–194.

Combourieu-Neubout N, Semah F, et al. 1990. The Plio-Pleistocene boundary: Magnetostratigraphic and climatic information from a detailed analysis of the Vrica stratotype (Crotona, Italy). CR Acad Sci (Paris) 311:851–857.

Conard N and Bolus M. 2003. Radiocarbon dating the appearance of modern humans and timing of cultural innovations in Europe: New results and new challenges. J Hum Evol 44: 331–371.

Conroy G. 1980. New evidence of Middle Pleistocene hominids from the Afar Desert, Ethiopia. Anthropos 7:96–107.

Conroy G. 1987. Problems of body-weight estimation in fossil primates. Int J Primatol 8:115–137.

Conroy G. 1988. Alleged synapomorphy of the M1/I1 eruption pattern in robust australopithecines and *Homo:* Evidence from high-resolution computed tomography. Am J Phys Anthrop 75:487–492.

Conroy G. 1990. Primate Evolution. New York: Norton.

Conroy G. 1991. Enamel thickness in South African australopithecines: Non-invasive evaluation by computed tomography. Palaeont Afr 28:53–58.

Conroy G. 1994. *Otavipithecus:* Or how to build a better hominid—Not. J Hum Evol 27:373–383.

Conroy G. 1998. Paleoanthropology today. Evol Anthropol 6:155–156.

Conroy G. 2002. Speciosity in the early *Homo* lineage: Too many, too few, or just about right? J Hum Evol 43:759–766.

Conroy G. 2003. The inverse relationship between species diversity and body mass: Do primates play by the "rule"? J Hum Evol 45:43–55.

Conroy G and Pilbeam D. 1975. *Ramapithecus,* a review of its hominid status. In: Tuttle R, editor. Paleoanthropology: Morphology and paleoecology. The Hague: Mouton. p 59–86.

Conroy G, Jolly C, et al. 1978. Newly discovered fossil hominid skull from the Afar depression, Ethiopia. Nature 275:67–70.

Conroy G and Vannier M. 1987. Dental development of the Taung skull from computerized tomography. Nature 329:625–627.

Conroy G and Vannier M. 1988. The nature of Taung dental maturation continued. Nature 333:808.

Conroy G, Vannier M, et al. 1990. Endocranial features of *Australopithecus africanus* revealed by 2 and 3-D computed tomography. Science 247:838–841.

Conroy G and Mahoney C. 1991. A mixed longitudinal study of dental emergence in the chimpanzee, *Pan troglodytes* (Primates, Pongidae). Am J Phys Anthropol 86:243–254.

Conroy G and Vannier M. 1991a. Dental development in South African australopithecines: Part I: Problems of pattern and chronology. Am J Phys Anthropol 86:121–136.

Conroy G and Vannier M. 1991b. Dental development in South African australopithecines Part II: Dental stage assessment. Am J Phys Anthrop 86:137–156.

Conroy G, Pickford M, et al. 1992. *Otavipithecus namibiensis,* first Miocene hominoid from southern Africa. Nature 356:144–148.

Conroy G, Pickford M, et al. 1993. Diamonds in the desert: The discovery of *Otavipthecus namibiensis.* Evol Anthropol 2:46–52.

Conroy G and Kuykendall K. 1995. Paleopediatrics: Or when did human infants really become human? Am J Phys Anthropol 98:121–131.

Conroy G, Weber G, et al. 1998. Endocranial capacity in an early hominid cranium from Sterkfontein, South Africa. Science 280:1730–1731.

Conroy G, Weber G, et al. 2000. Endocranial capacity of the Bodo cranium determined from three-dimensional computed tomography. Am J Phys Anthropol 113:111–118.

Constable C. 1992. Link between geomagnetic reversal paths and secular variation of the field over the past 5 myr. Nature 358:230–233.

Cook J, Stringer C, et al. 1982. A review of the chronology of the European Middle Pleistocene hominid record. Yearbk Phys Anthropol 25:19–65.

Cooke H. 1976. Suidae from Pliocene-Pleistocene strata in the Rudolf Basin. In: Coppens Y, Howell FC, et al., editors. Earliest man and environments in the Lake Rudolf Basin. Chicago: University of Chicago Press, p 251–263.

Cooke H. 1997. Plio-Pleistocene deposits and the Quaternary boundary in sub-Saharan Africa. In: Van Couvering J, editor. The Pleistocene boundary and the beginning of the Quaternary. Cambridge, UK: Cambridge University Press. p 254–263.

Coon CS. 1962. The origin of races. New York: Knopf.

Corkern M. 1997. Phalangeal curvature as a prediction of locomotor behavior in extinct primates. Am J Phys Anthropol Suppl 24:95.

Corruccini R. 1978. Comparative osteometrics of the hominoid wrist joint, with special reference to knuckle-walking. J Hum Evol 7:307–321.

Corruccini R. 1992. Metrical reconsideration of the Skhul IV and IX and Border Cave 1 crania in the context of modern human origins. Am J Phys Anthrop 87:433–445.

Corruccini R. 1994. Reaganomics and the fate of the progressive Neandertals. In: Corruccini RS, Ciochon RL, editors. Integrative paths to the past. Englewood Cliffs, NJ: Prentice Hall, p 697–708.

Corruccini R and McHenry H. 1980. Cladometric analysis of Pliocene hominids. J Hum Evol 9:209–221.

Cracraft J. 1983. Species concepts and speciation analysis. In: Johnston R, editor. Current ornithology. New York: Plenum. p 159–187.

Crompton R, Yu L, et al. 1998. The mechanical effectiveness of erect and "bent-hip, bent-knee" bipedal walking in *Australopithecus afarensis*. J Hum Evol 35:55–74.

Cronin J, Boaz N, et al. 1981. Tempo and mode in human evolution. Nature 292:113–122.

Crowley TJ and North GR. 1991. Paleoclimatology. New York: Oxford University Press.

Crummett TL and Miracle PT. 1995. Aurignacian Neandertals? The case of Vindija, Croatia. Paper presented at the Paleoanthropology Society Conference, Oakland, CA.

Curnoe D, Grun R, et al. 2001. Direct ESR dating of a Pliocene hominin from Swartkrans. J Hum Evol 40:379–391.

Curnoe D and Thorne A. 2003. Number of ancestral human species: A molecular perspective. Homo 53:201–224.

Curtis G, Drake R, et al. 1975. Age of KBS tuff in Koobi Fora Formation, East Rudolf, Kenya. Nature 258:395–398.

Czarnetzki A, Jakob T, et al. 2003. Palaeopathological and variant conditions of the *Homo heidelbergensis* type specimen (Mauer, Germany). J Hum Evol 44:479–495.

Dainton M and Macho G. 1999. Did knuckle walking evolve twice? J Hum Evol 36:171–194.

Dansgaard W, Johnsen SJ, et al. 1993. Evidence for general instability of past climate from a 250-kyr ice-core record. Nature 364:218–220.

Dart R. 1925a. *Australopithecus africanus:* The man-ape of South Africa. Nature 115:195–199.

Dart R. 1925b. Note on Makapansgat: A site of early human occupation. South Afr J Sci 22:454.

Dart R. 1948a. The adolescent mandible of *Australopithecus prometheus*. Am J Phys Anthropol 6:391–412.

Dart R. 1948b. An adolescent promethean australopithecine mandible from Makapansgat. South Afr J Sci 45:73–75.

Dart R. 1949. Adventures with *Australopithecus*. Rationalist Ann 1949:15–25.

Dart R. 1957. The Osteodontokeratic culture of *Australopithecus prometheus*. Pretoria: Transvaal Museum Memoir.

Dart R and Craig D. 1959. Adventures with the missing link. New York: Harper & Brothers.

Darwin C. 1859. The origin of species by means of natural selection or the preservation of favored races in the struggle for life. London: Murray.

Darwin C. 1871. The descent of man, and selection in relation to sex. London: Murray.

Dawson A. 1992. Ice age earth. London: Routledge.

Day M. 1971. Postcranial remains of *Homo erectus* from Bed IV Olduvai Gorge, Tanzania. Nature 232:384–387.

Day M. 1984. The postcranial remains of *Homo erectus* from Africa, Asia, and possibly Europe. Cour Forsch Inst Senckenberg 69:113–122.

Day M. 1985. Hominid locomotion-from Taung to the Laetoli footprints. In: Tobias P, editor. Hominid evolution: Past, present and future. New York: Liss. p 115–127.

Day M. 1988. Guide to fossil man. Chicago: University of Chicago Press.

Day M and Molleson T. 1973. The Trinil femora. In: Day MH, editor. Human evolution. London: Taylor & Francis, p 127–154.

Day M, Leakey MD, et al. 1980. A new hominid fossil skull (LH18) from the Ngaloba Beds, Laetoli, northern Tanzania. Nature 284:55–56.

Deacon HJ. 1983. The comparative evolution of Mediterranean-type ecosystems: A southern perspective. In: Kruger FJ, Mitchell DT, et al., editors. Ecological studies: Mediterranean-type ecosystems. Berlin: Springer-Verlag. p 3–40.

Deacon HJ, Talma AS, et al. 1988. Biological and cultural development of Pleistocene people in an Old World southern continent. In: Prescott JR, editor. Early man in the southern hemisphere. Supplement to archaeometry: Australasian studies. Adelaide: University of Adelaide. p S23–S31.

Deacon HJ. 1992. Southern Africa and modern human origins. Phil Trans R Soc Biol Sci 337:177–183.

Deacon HJ and Geleijnse VB. 1988. The stratigraphy and sedimentology of the main site sequence, Klasies River, South Africa. South Afr Arcaeol Bull 43:5–14.

Deacon HJ and Shuurman R. 1992. The origins of modern people: The evidence from Klasies River. In: Bräuer G, Smith FH, editors. Continuity or replacement: Controversies in *Homo sapiens* evolution. Rotterdam: Balkema. p 121–129.

Dean D, Hublin J-J, et al. 1998. On the phylogenetic position of the pre-Neandertal specimen from Reilingen, Germany. J Hum Evol 34:485–508.

Dean MC. 1985. The eruption pattern of the permanent incisors and first permanent molars in *Australopithecus (Paranthropus) robustus*. Am J Phys Anthrop 67:251–258.

Dean MC. 1987. The dental developmental status of six East African juvenile fossil hominids. J Hum Evol 16:197–214.

Dean MC, Beynon AD, et al. 1993. Histological reconstruction of dental development and age at death of a juvenile *Paranthropus robustus* specimen, SK 63, from Swartkrans, South Africa. Am J Phys Anthropol 91:401–419.

Dean MC, Leakey M, et al. 2001. Growth processes in teeth distinguish modern humans from *Homo erectus* and earlier hominins. Nature 414:628–631.

Dean M, Stringer C, et al. 1986. Age at death of the Neanderthal child from Devils Tower, Gibraltar and the implications for studies of general growth and development in Neanderthals. Am J Phys Anthropol 70:301–309.

de Bonis L and Melentis J. 1982. L'homme de Petralona: Comparaisons avec l'homme de Tautavel. Prem Congr Int Paleo Hum Nice 2:847–874.

de Bonis L, Bouvrain G, et al. 1990. New hominid skull material from the late Miocene of Macedonia in northern Greece. Nature 345:712–714.

de Bonis L and Koufos GD. 1993. The face and the mandible of *Ouranopithecus macedoniensis*: Description of new specimens and comparisons. J Hum. Evol 24:469–491.

de Bonis L and Koufos GD. 1995. Our ancestors ancestor: *Ouranopithecus* is a Greek link to human ancestry. Evol Anthropol 3:75–83.

de Castro J. 1988. Dental remains from Atapuerca/Ibeas (Spain) II. Morphology. J Hum Evol 17:279–304.

de Castro J, Bromage T, et al. 1988. Buccal striations on fossil human anterior teeth: Evidence of handedness in the Middle and early Upper Pleistocene. J Hum Evol 17:403–412.

de Castro J and Rosas A. 1992. A human mandibular fragment from the Atapuerca Trench (Burgos, Spain). J Hum Evol 22:41–46.

de Castro J, Durand AI, et al. 1993. Sexual dimorphism in the human dental sample from the SH site (Sierra de Atapuerca, Spain): A statistical approach. J Hum Evol 24:43–56.

de Castro J, Arsuaga J, et al. 1997a. A hominid from the Lower Pleistocene of Atapuerca, Spain: Possible ancestor to Neandertals and modern humans. Science 276:1392–1395.

de Castro J, Arsuaga J, et al. 1997b Interproximal grooving in the Atapuerca-SH hominid dentitions. Am J Phys Anthropol 102:369–376.

de Castro J, Carbonell E, et al. 1999a. The TD6 (Aurora stratum) hominid site. Final remarks and new questions. J Hum Evol 37:695–700.

de Castro J, Rosas A, et al. 1999b. A modern human pattern of dental development in Lower Pleistocene hominids from Atapuerca-TD6 (Spain). Proc Natl Acad Sci 96:4210–4213.

de Castro J and Rosas A. 2001. Pattern of dental development in hominid XVIII from the Middle Pleistocene Atapuerca-Sima de los Huesos site (Spain). Am J Phys Anthropol 114:325–330.

de Castro J, Sarmiento S, et al. 2001. Dental size variation in the Atapuerca-SH Middle Pleistocene hominids. J Hum. Evol 41:195–209.

de Castro J, Martinón-Torres M, et al. 2004. The Atapuerca sites and their contribution to the knowledge of human evolution in Europe. Evol Anthropol 13:25–41.

Defleur A, Dutour O, et al. 1993. Cannibals among the Neanderthals? Nature 362:214.

Defleur A, White T, et al. 1999. Neanderthal cannibalism at Moula-Guercy, Ardèche, France. Science 286:128–131.

DeGusta D, Gilbert W, et al. 1999. Hpoglossal canal size and hominid speech. Proc Nat Acad Sci USA 96:1800–1804.

de Heinzelin J. 1994. Rifting, a long-term African story, with considerations on early hominid habitats. In: Corruccini RS, Ciochon RL, editors. Integrative paths to the past. Englewood Cliffs, NJ: Prentice Hall, p 313–320.

de Heinzelin J, Clark J, et al. 1999. Environment and behavior of 2.5-million-year-old Bouri hominids. Science 284:625–629.

Deinard A and Kidd K. 1999. Evolution of a HOXB6 intergenic region within the great apes and humans. J Hum Evol 36:687–703.

Deino A, Renne P, et al. 1998. ^{40}Ar/^{39}Ar dating in paleoanthropology and archeology. Evol Anthropol 6:63–75.

Deloison Y. 1997. The foot bones from Hadar, Ethiopia and the Laetoli, Tanzania footprints. Am J Phys Anthropol Suppl 24:101.

Delson E. 1984. Cercopithecoid biochronology of the African Plio-Pleistocene: Correlation among eastern and southern hominid-bearing localities. Cour Forschunginst Senckenb 69:199–218.

Delson E. 1988. Chronology of South African australopith site units. In: Grine F, editor. Evolutionary history of the "robust" australopithecines. New York: de Gruyter. p 317–324.

de Lumley M-A. 1975 Ante-Neanderthals of western Europe. In: Tuttle RH, editor. Paleoanthropology: Morphology and paleoecology. The Hague: Mouton. p 381–387.

deMenocal P. 1995. Plio-Pleistocene African climate. Science 270:53–59.

Demes B. 1987. Another look at an old face: Biomechanics of the Neandertal facial skeleton reconsidered. J Hum Evol 16:297–303.

Demes B and Creel N. 1988. Bite force, diet, and cranial morphology of fossil hominids. J Hum Evol 17:657–670.

Dennell R. 1994. Son of Piltdown man found at Boxgrove. Antiquity 68:482–483.

Dennell R and Roebroeks W. 1996. The earliest colonization of Europe: The short chronology revisited. Antiquity 70:535–542.

d'Errico F. 2003. The invisible frontier. A multiple species model for the origin of behavioral modernity. Curr Anthropol 12:188–202.

d'Errico F, Zilhão J, et al. 1998. Neanderthal acculturation in western Europe? Curr Anthropol 39:S1–S44.

DeVore I and Washburn SL. 1963. Baboon ecology and human evolution. In: Howell FC, Bourliere F, editors. African ecology and human evolution. Chicago: Aldine. p 335–367.

de Vos J. 1985. Faunal stratigraphy and correlation of the Indonesian hominid sites. In: Delson E, editor. Ancestors: The hard evidence. New York: Liss, p 215–220.

de Vos J. 1994. Dating hominid sites in Indonesia. Science 266:1726.

Disotell T. 1999. Origins of modern humans still look recent. Curr Biol 9:R647–R650.

Dobzhansky T. 1962. Mankind evolving. New Haven, CT: Yale University Press.

Dominguez-Rodrigo M, Serrallonga J, et al. 2001. Woodworking activities by early humans: A plant residue analysis on Acheulian stone tools from Peninj (Tanzania). J Hum Evol 40:289–299.

Donnelly P, Tavaré S, et al. 1996. Estimating the age of the common ancestor of men from the ZFY intron. Science 272:1357–1358.

Dorit R, Akashi H, et al. 1995. Absence of polymorphism at the ZFY locus on the human Y chromosome. Science 268:1183–1185.

Dorit R, Akashi H, et al. 1996. Estimating the age of the common ancestor of men from the ZFY intron. Science 272:1361–1362.

Dowsett H, Cronin T, et al. 1992. Micropaleontological evidence for increased meridional heat transport in the North Atlantic Ocean during the Pliocene. Science 258:1133–1135.

Duarte C, Maurício J, et al. 1999. The early Upper Paleolithic human skeleton from the Abrigo do Lagar Velho (Portugal) and modern human emergence in Iberia. Proc Natl Acad Sci USA 96:7604–7609.

Dubois E. 1894. *Pithecanthropus erectus*: Eine Menschenaehnliche Vebergangsform aus Java. Batavia: Landesdruckerei.

Dubois E. 1922. The proto-Australian fossil man of Wadjak, Java. Proc Sect Sci K Akad Weten-sch Amsterdam 23:1013–1051.

Dubois E. 1924. Figures of the calvarium and endocranial cast, a fragment of the mandible and three teeth of *Pithecanthropus erectus*. Proc Koninklijke Nederlandse Akad Wetansch Amsterdam 27:459–464.

Duncan AS, Kappelman J, et al. 1994. Metatarsophalangeal joint function and positional behavior in *Australopithecus afarensis*. Am J Phys Anthrop 93:67–81.

Durband A. 1998. The cranial base of the Ngandong hominids: Implications for modern human origins. Am J Phys Anthropol Suppl 26:79.

Ebinger C and Sleep N. 1998. Cenozoic magmatism throughout east Africa resulting from impact of a single plume. Nature 395:788–791.

Eckhardt R. 1977. Hominid origins: The Lothagam mandible. Curr Anthropol 18:356.

Eckhardt R. 1987. Hominoid nasal region polymorphism and its phylogenetic significance. Nature 328:333–335.

Effremov IA. 1940. Taphonomy: A new branch of paleontology. Pan-Am Geol 74:81–93.

Eicher D. 1976. Geologic time. Englewood Cliffs, NJ: Prentice Hall.

Eldredge N and Gould S. 1972. Punctuated equilibria: An alternative to phyletic gradualism. In: Schopf T, editor. Models in paleobiology. San Francisco: Freeman, Cooper. p 82–115.

Eldredge N and Tattersall I. 1975. Evolutionary models, phylogenetic reconstruction and another look at hominid phylogeny. In: Szalay FS, editor. Approaches to primate paleobiology. Basel: Karger. p 218–242.

Enard W, Przeworski M, et al. 2002. Molecular evolution of FOXP2, a gene involved in speech and language. Nature 418:869–872.

Etler D. 1984. The fossil hominoids of Lufeng, Yunnan Province, The People's Republic of China: A series of translations. Yearbk Phys Anthropol 27:1–55.

Etler D and Li T. 1994. New archaic human fossil discoveries in China and their bearing on hominid species definition during the middle Pleistocene. In: Corruccini RS, Ciochon RL, editors. Integrative paths to the past. Englewood Cliffs, NJ: Prentice Hall, p 639–675.

Etler D and Guoxing Z. 1998. Asian fossils and African origins. J Hum Evol 34:A6.

Evans E, Van Couvering J, et al. 1981. Paleoecology of Miocene sites in western Kenya. J Hum Evol 10:99–116.

Falguères C, Bahain J, et al. 1999. Earliest humans in Europe: The age of TD6 Gran Dolina, Atapuerca, Spain. J Hum Evol 37:343–352.

Falk D. 1980. Hominid brain evolution: The approach from paleoneurology. Yearbk Phys Anthropol 23:93–107.

Falk D. 1983a. Cerebral cortices of east African early hominids. Science 221:1072–1074.

Falk D. 1983b. The Taung endocast: A reply to Holloway. Am J Phys Anthropol 60:479–489.

Falk D. 1985 Apples, oranges and the lunate sulcus. Am J Phys Anthropol 67:313–315.

Falk D. 1986. Evolution of cranial blood drainage in hominids: enlarged occipital/marginal sinuses and emissary foramina. Am J Phys Anthropol 70:311–324.

Falk D. 1987a. Brain lateralization in primates and its evolution in hominids. Yearbk Phys Anthropol 30:107–125.

Falk D. 1987b. Hominid paleoneurology. Ann Rev Anthropol 16:13–30.

Falk D. 1989. Ape-like endocast of "ape-man" Taung. Am J Phys Anthropol 80:335–339.

Falk D. 1990. Brain evolution in *Homo:* The "radiator" theory. Behavioral Brain Sci 13:333–381.

Falk D. 1991a. Breech birth of the genus *Homo:* Why bipedalism preceded the increase in brain size. In: Coppens Y, Senut B, editors. Origine(s) de la bipedie chez les hominides. Paris: CNRS. p 259–266.

Falk D. 1991b. Reply to Dr. Holloway: shifting positions on the lunate sulcus. Am J Phys Anthropol 84:89–91.

Falk D and Conroy GC. 1983. The cranial venous sinus system in *Australopithecus afarensis*. Nature 306:779–781.

Falk D, Hildebolt C, et al. 1989. Reassessment of the Taung early hominid from a neurological perspective. J Hum Evol 18:485–492.

Falk D and Baker E. 1992. Earliest *Homo* debate. Nature 358:290.

Falk D, Gage T, et al. 1995. Did more than one species of hominid coexist before 3.0 ma?: Evidence from blood and teeth. J Hum Evol 29:591–600.

Falk D, Redmond J, et al. 2000. Early hominid brain evolution: A new look at old endocasts. J Hum Evol 38:695–717.

Faupl P, Richter W, et al. 2004. Geochronology: Dating of the Herto hominin fossils. Nature 426:621–622.

Faure G. 1986. Principles of isotope geology. New York: Wiley.

Feathers J. 1996. Luminescence dating and modern human origins. Evol Anthropol 5:25–36.

Feathers J and Bush D. 2000. Luminescence dating of Middle Stone Age deposits at Die Kelders. J Hum Evol 8:91–119.

Fedigan L. 1982. Primate paradigms: Sex roles and social bonds. Montreal: Eden Press.

Fedigan L. 1986. The changing role of women in models of human evolution. Ann Rev Anthropol 15:25–66.

Feibel C. 1992. Earliest *Homo* debate. Nature 358:289.

Feibel C. 1999. Tephrostratigraphy and geological context in paleoanthropology. Evol Anthropol 8:87–100.

Feibel C, Brown F, et al. 1989. Stratigraphic context of fossil hominids from the Omo Group deposits: Northern Turkana basin, Kenya and Ethiopia. Am J Phys Anthrop 78:595–622.

Feibel C and Brown FH. 1991. Age of the primate-bearing deposits on Maboko Island, Kenya J Hum Evol 21:221–225.

Feibel C, Agnew N, et al. 1996. The Laetoli hominid footprints—A preliminary report on the conservation and scientific restudy. Evol Anthropolol 4:149–154.

Feldesman M. 1979. Further morphometric studies of the ulna from the Omo Basin, Ethiopia. Am J Phys Anthropol 51:409–416.

Feldesman M and Lundy J. 1988. Stature estimates for some African Plio-Pleistocene fossil hominids. J Hum Evol 17:583–596.

Fernández-Jalvo Y, Denys C, et al. 1998. Taphonomy and palaeoecology of Olduvai Bed-I (Pleistocene, Tanzania). J Hum Evol 34:137–172.

Fernández-Jalvo Y, Díaz J, et al. 1999. Human cannabilism in the Early Pleistocene of Europe (Gran Dolina, Sierra de Atapuerca, Burgos, Spain). J Hum Evol 37:591–622.

Field MH, Huntley B, et al. 1994. Eemian climate fluctuations observed in a European pollen record. Nature 371:779–783.

Fields W. 1990. What the river knows: An angler in midstream. New York: Poseidon Press.

Fitch F. 1972. Selection of suitable material for dating and the assessment of geological error in potassium-argon age determination. In: Bishop W, Miller J, editors. Calibration of hominoid evolution: Recent advances in isotopic and other dating methods applicable to the origin of man. Edinburgh, UK: Scottish Academic Press. p 77–92.

Fitch F, Findlater I, et al. 1974. Dating of the rock succession containing fossil hominids at East Rudolf, Kenya. Nature 251:213–215.

Fitch F, Miller J, et al. 1996. Dating of the KBS Tuff and *Homo rudolfensis*. J Hum Evol 30:277–286.

Fleagle J. 1999. Primate adaptation and evolution. New York: Academic Press.

Fleagle J, Kay R, et al. 1980. Sexual dimorphism in early anthropoids. Nature 287:328–330.

Fleagle J, Rasmussen D, et al. 1991. New hominid fossils from Fejej, southern Ethiopia. J Hum Evol 21:145–152.

Flint R. 1971. Glacial and quaternary geology. New York: Wiley.

Foley R. 1987. Another unique species: Patterns in human evolutionary ecology. New York: Wiley.

Foley R. 1991. How many species of hominid should there be? J Hum Evol 20:413–427.

Foley R. 1994. Speciation, extinction and climatic change in hominid evolution. J Hum Evol 26:275–289.

Foley R and Lee PC. 1989. Finite social space, evolutionary pathways, and reconstructing hominid behavior. Science 243:901–905.

Formicola V, Pontrandolfi A, et al. 1998. The Upper Paleolithic triplex burial of Dolni Vestonice: Pathology and funerary behavior. Am J Phys Anthropol Suppl 26:83.

Formicola V, Pontrandilfi A, et al. 2001. The Upper Paleolithic triple burial of Dolní Vestonice: Pathology and funerary behavior. Am J Phys Anthropol 115:372–379.

Franciscus R and Churchill S. 2002. The costal skeleton of Shanidar 3 and a reappraisal of Neandertal thoracic morphology. J Hum Evol 42:303–356.

Frayer D. 1978. Evolution of the dentition in Upper Paleolithic and Mesolithic Europe. Univ Kansas Publ Anthropol 10:1–201.

Frayer D. 1992. The persistence of Neanderthal features in post-Neanderthal Europeans. In: Bräuer G, Smith FH, editors. Continuity or replacement. Rotterdam: Balkema. p 179–188.

Frayer D, Wolpoff M, et al. 1993. Theories of modern human origins: The paleontological test. Am Anthropol 95:14–50.

Frayer D and Fox C. 1998. Anterior tooth scratches, handedness and manual dexterity in fossil Europeans. J Hum Evol 34:A7–8.

Friday A. 1992. Measuring relatedness. In: Jones S, Martin R, et al., editors. The Cambridge encyclopedia of human evolution. Cambridge, UK: Cambridge University Press. p 295–297.

Fu Y-X and Li W-H. 1996. Estimating the age of the common ancestor of men from the ZFY intron. Science 272:1356–1357.

Fu Y-X and Li W-H. 1997. Estimating the ages of the common ancestor of a sample of DNA sequences. Mol Biol Evol 14:195–199.

Fullagar R, Price D, et al. 1996. Early human occupation of northern Australia: Archaeology and thermoluminescence dating of Jinmium rock-shelter, Northern Territory. Antiquity 70:751–773.

Fullerton SM, Schneider JA, et al. 1995. DNA sequence variation at the β-globin locus and human evolutionary origins. Am J Phys Anthropol Suppl 20:94.

Gabunia L and Vekua A. 1995. A Plio-Pleistocene hominid from Dmanisi, East Georgia, Caucasus. Nature 373:509–512.

Gabunia L, Vekua A, et al. 2000. Earliest Pleistocene hominid cranial remains from Dmanisi, Republic of Georgia: Taxonomy, geological setting, and age. Science 288:1019–1025.

Gabunia L, Anton S, et al. 2001. Dmanisi and dispersal. Evol Anthropol 10:158–170.

Gagneux P, Wills C, et al. 1999. Mitochondrial sequences show diverse evolutionary histories of African hominoids. Proc Nat Acad Sci USA 96:5077–5082.

Gallup CD, Edwards RL, et al. 1994. The timing of high sea levels over the past 200,000 years. Science 263:796–800.

Gamble C. 1986. The Palaeolithic settlement of Europe. Cambridge, UK: Cambridge University Press.

Gannon P, Holloway R, et al. 1998. Asymmetry of chimpanzee planum temporale: Humanlike pattern of Wernike's brain language area homolog. Science 279:220–222.

Gargett R. 1989. Grave shortcomings: The evidence for Neanderal burial. Curr Anthropol 30:157–190.

Gargett R. 1999. Middle Palaeolithic burial is not a dead issue: The view from Zafzeh, Saint-Césaire, Kebara, Amud, and Dederiheh. J Hum Evol 37:27–90.

Garrod D. 1958. The ancient shore-lines of the Lebanon, and the dating of Mt. Carmel man. In: von Koenigswald GHR, editor. Hundert Jahre Neanderthaler. Utrecht: Kemink & Zoon. p 182–184.

Garrod D and Bate D. 1937. The stone age of Mount Carmel: Excavations of the Wadi el Mughara. Oxford, UK: Clarendon Press.

Gartner S and McGuirk J. 1979. Terminal cretaceous extinction scenario for a catastrophe. Science 206:1272–1276.

Gathorne-Hardy F and Harcourt-Smith W. 2003. The super-eruption of Toba, did it cause a human bottleneck? J Hum Evol 45:227–230.

Gauld S. 1996. Allometric patterns of cranial bone thickness in fossil hominids. Am J Phys Anthropol 100:411–426.

Gebo D, MacLatchy L, et al. 1997. A hominoid genus from the Early Miocene of Uganda. Science 276:401–404.

Gee H. 1996. Box of bones "clinches" identity of Piltdown palaeontology hoaxer. Nature 381:261–262.

Gentry A. 1970. The Bovidae (mammalia) of the Fort Ternan fossil fauna. In: Leakey L, Savage R, editors. Fossil vertebrates of Africa. London: Academic Press. p 243–323.

Gentry A. 1976. Bovidae of the Omo Group deposits. In: Coppens Y, Howell F, et al., editors. Earliest man and environments in the Lake Rudolf Basin. Chicago: University of Chicago Press. p 293–301.

Geraads D, Hublin J, et al. 1986. The Pleistocene hominid site of Ternifine, Algeria: New results on the environment, age, and human industries. Quaternary Res. 25:380–386.

Gibbons A. 1997. Doubts over spectacular dates. Science 278:220–222.

Gibson KR and Jessee SA. 1994. Cranial base shape and laryngeal position: Implications for Neanderthal language debates. Am J Phys Anthropol Suppl 18:93.

Gilbert W, White T, et al. 2003. *Homo erectus, Homo ergaster, Homo "cepranensis,"* and the Daka cranium. J Hum Evol 45:255–259.

Gillespie R. 1984. Radiocarbon user's handbook. Oxford, UK: Oxbow Books.

Gillespie R and Roberts R. 2000. On the reliability of age estimates for human remains at Lake Mungo. J Hum Evol 38:727–732.

Gingerich PD. 1991. Fossils and evolution. In: Osawa S, Honjo T, editors. Evolution of life: Fossils, molecules and culture. Tokyo: Springer-Verlag. p 3–20.

Gingerich PD. 1993. Quantification and comparison of evolutionary rates. Am J Sci 293-A:453–478.

Gitau SN and Benefit BR. 1995. New evidence concerning the facial morphology of *Simiolus leakeyorum* from Maboko Island. Am J Phys Anthropol Suppl 20:99.

Gleadow A. 1980. Fission track age of the KBS tuff and associated hominid remains in northern Kenya. Nature 284:225–230.

Godfrey L and Jacobs K. 1981. Gradual, autocatalytic and punctuational models of hominid brain evolution: A cautionary tale. J Hum Evol 10:255–272.

Goebel T. 1999. Pleistocene human colonization of Siberia and peopling of the Americas: An ecological approach. Evol Anthropol 8:208–227.

Goebel T, Derevianko A, et al. 1993. Dating the Middle-to-Upper Paleolithic transition at Kara-Bom. Curr Anthropol 34:452–458.

Goebel T and Aksenov M. 1995. Accelerator radiocarbon dating of the initial Upper Palaeolithic in southeast Siberia. Antiquity 69:349–357.

Goldberg P, Weiner S, et al. 2001. Site formation processes at Zhoukoudian, China. J Hum Evol 41:483–530.

Goldman N and Barton NH. 1992. Genetics and geography. Nature 357:440–441.

Goodall J. 1976. Continuities between chimpanzee and human behavior. In: Isaac G, McCown T, editors. Human origins: Louis Leakey and the East African evidence. Menlo Park, CA: Benjamin. p 81–95.

Goodall J. 1986. Chimpanzees of Gombe: Patterns of behavior. Cambridge, MA: Harvard University Press.

Goodfriend G. 1992. Rapid racemization of aspartic acid in mollusc shells and potential for dating over recent centuries. Nature 357:399–401.

Goodman M. 1992. Reconstructing human evolution from proteins. In: Jones S, Martin R, et al., editors. The Cambridge encyclopedia of human evolution. Cambridge, UK: Cambridge University Press, p 307–312.

Goodman M, Baba M, et al. 1983. The bearing of molecular data on the cladogenesis and times of divergence of hominoid lineages. In: Ciochon R, Corruccini R, editors. New Interpretations of ape and human ancestry. New York: Plenum. p 67–86.

Goodman M, Bailey WJ, et al. 1994. Molecular evidence on primate phylogeny from DNA sequences. Am J Phys Anthrop 94:3–24.

Goodman M, Czelusniak J, et al. 2001. Where DNA sequences place *Homo sapiens* in a phylogenetic classification of primates. In: Tobias P, Rath M, et al., editors. Humanity from African naissance to coming millennia. Firenze, Italy: Firenze University Press, p 279–289.

Goren-Inbar N, Feibel C, et al. 2000. Pleistocene milestones on the out-of-Africa corridor at Gesher Benot Ya'aqov, Israel. Science 289:944–947.

Goren-Inbar N, Alperson N, et al. 2004. Evidence of hominin control of fire at Gesher Benot Ya'aqov, Israel. Science 304:725–727.

Gould SJ and Eldredge N. 1993. Punctuated equilibrium comes of age. Nature 366:223–227.

Gowlett J. 1992. Tools—The Palaeolithic record. In: Jones S, Martin R, et al, editors. The Cambridge encyclopedia of human evolution. Cambridge, UK: Cambridge University Press. p 350–360.

Gowlett J, Harris J, et al. 1981. Early archaeological sites, hominid remains and traces of fire from Chesowanja, Kenya. Nature 294:125–129.

Grausz HM, Leakey REF, et al. 1988. Associated cranial and postcranial bones of *Australopithecus boisei*. In: Grine FE, editor. Evolutionary history of the "robust" australopithecines. New York: de Gruyter. p 127–132.

Green H and Djian P. 1995. The involucrin gene and hominoid relationships. Am J Phys Anthropol 98:213–216.

Green M and Smith F. 1991. Heterochrony, life history and Neandertal morphology. Am J Phys Anthropol Suppl 12:164.

Greenfield L. 1992. Origin of the human canine: A new solution to an old enigma. Yearbk Phys Anthropol 35:153–185.

Gregory J. 1896. The great rift valley. London: Seeley.

Grine F. 1987. On the eruption pattern of the permanent incisors and first permanent molars in *Paranthropus*. Am J Phys Anthrop 72:353–360.

Grine F. 1988. Evolutionary history of the "robust" australopithecines: A summary and historical perspective. In: Grine FE, editor. Evolutionary history of the "robust" australopithecines. New York: de Gruyter. p 509–519.

Grine F. 1989. New hominid fossils from the Swartkrans Formation (1979–1986 excavations): Craniodental specimens. Am J Phys Anthropol 79:409–449.

Grine F. 1993a. Australopithecine taxonomy and phylogeny: Historical background and recent interpretation. In: Ciochon RL, Fleagle JG, editors. The human evolution source book. Inglewood Cliffs, NJ: Prentice Hall. p 198–210.

Grine F. 1993b. Description and preliminary analysis of new hominid craniodental fossils from the Swartkrans Formation. In: Brain CK, editor. Swartkrans: A cave's chronicle of early man. Pretoria: Transvaal Museum. p 75–116.

Grine F. 2000. Middle Stone Age human fossils from Die Kelders Cave 1, Western Cape Province, South Africa. J Hum Evol 38:129–145.

Grine F and Klein R. 1985. Pleistocene and Holocene human remains from Equus Cave, South Africa. Anthropology 8:55–98.

Grine F and Kay R. 1988. Early hominid diets from quantitative image analysis of dental microwear. Nature 333:765–768.

Grine F and Martin L. 1988. Enamel thickness and development in *Australopithecus* and *Paranthropus*. In: Grine FE, editor. Evolutionary history of the "robust" australopithecines. New York: de Gruyter. p 3–42.

Grine F, Klein R, et al. 1991. Dating, archaeology and human fossils from the Middle Stone Age levels of Die Kelders, South Africa. J Hum Evol 21:363–395.

Grine F and Susman R. 1991. Radius of *Paranthropus robustus* from member 1, Swartkrans Formation, South Africa. Am J Phys Anthropol 84:229–248.

Grine F and Daegling D. 1993. New mandible of *Paranthropus robustus* from member 1, Swartkrans Formation, South Africa. J Hum Evol 24:319–333.

Grine F, Demes B, et al. 1993. Taxonomic affinity of the early *Homo* cranium from Swartkrans, South Africa. Am J Phys Anthropol 92:411–426.

Grine F and Strait D. 1994. New hominid fossils from member 1 "Hanging Remnant," Swartkrans Formation, South Africa. J Hum Evol 26:57–75.

Grine F, Jungers W, et al. 1996. Phenetic affinities among early *Homo* crania from East and South Africa. J Hum Evol 30:189–225.

Grine F, Pearson O, et al. 1998. Additional human fossils from Klasies River mouth, South Africa. J Hum Evol 35:95–107.

Grine F and Henshilwood C. 2002. Additional human remains from Blombos Cave, South Africa (1999–2000 excavations). J Hum Evol 42:293–302.

Grootes PM, Stuiver M, et al. 1993. Comparison of oxygen isotope records from the GISP2 and GRIP Greenland ice cores. Nature 366:552–554.

Groube L, Chappell J, et al. 1986. A 40,000 year-old human occupation site at Huon Peninsula, Papua New Guinea. Nature 324:453–455.

Groves C. 1989a. A regional approach to the problem of the origin of modern humans in Australasia. In: Mellars P, Stringer C, editors. The human revolution. Princeton, NJ: Princeton University Press. p 274–285.

Groves C. 1989b. A theory of human and primate evolution. Oxford, UK: Clarendon Press.

Groves C and Mazak V. 1975. An approach to the taxon of Hominidae: Gracile Villafranchian hominids of Africa. Casopsis SPro Mineral Geol 20:225–246.

Grün R. 1993. Electron spin resonance dating in paleoanthropology. Evol Anthropol 2:172–181.

Grün R. 1996. A re-analysis of electron spin resonance dating results associated with the Petralona hominid. J Hum Evol 30:227–241.

Grün R, Beaumont P, et al. 1990a. ESR dating evidence for early modern humans at Border Cave in South Africa. Nature 344:537–539.

Grün R, Shackleton N, et al. 1990b. Electron-spin-resonance dating of tooth enamel from Klasies River mouth cave. Curr Anthropol 31:427–432.

Grün R and Stringer C. 1991. Electron spin resonance dating and the evolution of modern humans. Archaeometry 33:153–199.

Grün R, Stringer CB, et al. 1991. ESR dating of teeth from Garrod's Tabun cave collection. J Hum Evol 20:231–248.

Grün R, Brink J, et al. 1996. Direct dating of the Florisbad hominid. Nature 382:500–501.

Grün R, Huang P, et al. 1997. ESR analysis of teeth from the palaeoanthropological site of Zhoukoudian, China. J Hum Evol 32:83–91.

Grün R and Thorne A. 1997. Dating the Ngandong humans. Science 276:1575.

Grün R, Huang P-H, et al. 1998. ESR and U-series analyses of teeth from the palaeoanthropological site of Hexian, Anhui Province, China. J Hum Evol 34:555–564.

Grün R, Spooner N, et al. 2000. Age of the Lake Mungo 3 skeleton, reply to Bowler & Magee and to Gillespie & Roberts. J Hum Evol 38:733–741.

Grün R and Stringer C. 2000. Tabun revisited: Revised ESR chronology and new ESR and U-series analyses of dental material from Tabun C1. J Hum Evol 39:601–612.

Grün R and Beaumont P. 2001. Border Cave revisited: A revised ESR chronology. J Hum Evol 40:467–482.

Grün R, Beaumont P, et al. 2003. On the age of Border Cave 5 human mandible. J Hum Evol 45:155–167.

Guoqin Q. 1993. The environment and ecology of the Lufeng hominoids. J Hum Evol 24:3–11.

Habgood PJ. 1989. The origin of anatomically modern humans in Australasia. In: Mellars P, Stringer C, editors. The human revolution. Princeton, NJ: Princeton University Press. p 245–273.

Haeckel E. 1866. Generelle morphologie der organismen. Berlin: Reimer.

Haeckel E. 1896. The evolution of man. New York: Appleton.

Haeusler M, Martelli S, et al. 2002. Vertebrae numbers of the early hominid lumbar spine. J Hum Evol 43:621–643.

Haileab B and Brown F. 1992. Turkana basin-Middle Awash Valley correlations and the age of the Sagantole and Hadar Formations. J Hum Evol 22:453–468.

Haile-Selassie Y. 2001. Late Miocene hominids from the Middle Awash, Ethiopia. Nature 412:178–181.

Haile-Selassie Y, Asfaw B, et al. 2004a. Hominid cranial remains from upper Pleistocene deposits at Aduma, Middle Awash, Ethiopia. Am J Phys Anthropol 123:1–10.

Haile-Selassie Y, Suwa G, et al. 2004b. Late Miocene teeth from Middle Awash, Ethiopia, and early hominid dental evolution. Science 303:1503–1505.

Hamai M, Nishida T, et al. 1992. New records of within-group infanticide and cannibalism in wild chimpanzees. Primates 33:151–162.

Hammer M. 1995. A recent common ancestry for human Y chromosomes. Nature 378: 376–378.

Hammer M and Zegura S. 1996. The role of the Y chromosome in human evolutionary studies. Evol Anthropol 5:116–134.

Hamrick M, Churchill S, et al. 1997. EMG of the human flexor pollicis longus: Implications for the evolution of hominid tool use. Am J Phys Anthropol Suppl 24:123.

Hamrick M, Churchill S, et al. 1998. EMG of the human flexor pollicis longus muscle: Implications for the evolution of hominid tool use. J Hum Evol 34:123–136.

Harland W, Armstrong R, et al. 1990. A geologic time scale (1989). Cambridge, UK: Cambridge University Press.

Harmon RS, Glazek J, et al. 1980. 230Th/234U dating of travertine from the Bilzingsleben archaeological site. Nature 284:132–135.

Harpending H, Sherry S, et al. 1993. The genetic structure of ancient human populations. Curr Anthropol 34:483–496.

Harris E and Hey J. 1999a. Human demography in the Pleistocene: Do mitochondrial and nuclear genes tell the same story? Evol Anthropol 8:81–86.

Harris E and Hey J. 1999b. X chromosome evidence for ancient human histories. Proc Natl Acad Sci USA 96:3320–3324.

Harris J, Brown F, et al. 1988. Pliocene and Pleistocene hominid-bearing sites from west of Lake Turkana, Kenya. Science 239:27–33.

Harrison T. 1989. A new species of *Micropithecus* from the middle Miocene of Kenya. J Hum Evol 18:537–557.

Harrison T. 1998. Evidence for a tail in *Proconsul heseloni*. Am J Phys Anthropol Suppl 26:93–94.

Harrison T. 2002. Late Oligocene to middle Miocene catarrhines from Afro-Arabia. In: Hartwig W, editor. The primate fossil record. Cambridge, UK: Cambridge University Press. p 311–338.

Harrison T and Rook L. 1997. Enigmatic anthropoid or misunderstood ape? The phylogenetic status of *Oreopithecus bambolii* reconsidered. In: Begun D, Ward C, et al., editors. Function, phylogeny and fossils: Miocene hominoid evolution and adaptations. New York: Plenum. p 327–362.

Hartwig W, ed. 2002. The primate fossil record. Cambridge, UK: Cambridge University Press.

Hartwig-Scherer S and Martin R. 1991. Was "Lucy" more human than her "child"? Observations on early hominid postcranial skeletons. J Hum Evol 21:439–449.

Hartwig-Scherer S. 1993. Body weight prediction in early fossil hominids: Towards a taxon-"independent" approach. Am J Phys Anthropol 92:17–36.

Hasegawa M and Horai S. 1991. Time of the deepest root for polymorphism in human mitochondrial DNA. J Mol Evol 32:37–42.

Häusler M and Schmid P. 1995. Comparison of the pelves of Sts 14 and AL 288-1: Implications for birth and sexual dimorphism in australopithecines. J Hum Evol 29:363–383.

Häusler M and Schmid P. 1997. Assessing the pelvis of AL 288-1: A reply to Wood and Quinney. J Hum Evol 32:99–102.

Häusler M and Berger L. 2001. Stw 441/465: A new fragmentary ilium of a small-bodied *Australopithecus africanus* from Sterkfontein, South Africa. J Hum Evol 40:411–417.

Hawkes K. 1993. Why hunter-gatherers work: An ancient version of the problem of common goods. Curr Anthrop 34:341–361.

Hawkes K, O'Connell JF, et al. 1991. Hunting income patterns among the Hadza: Big game, common goods, foraging goals and the evolution of the human diet. Phil Trans R Soc Lond B 334:243–251.

Hawkes K, O'Connell J, et al. 1998. Grandmothering, menopause, and the evolution of human life histories. Proc Nat Acad Sci USA 95:1336–1339.

Hawks J, Hunley K, et al. 2000a. Population bottlenecks and Pleistocene human evolution. Mol Biol Evol 17:2–22.

Hawks J, Oh S, et al. 2000b. An Australasian test of the recent African origin theory using the WLH-50 calvarium. J Hum Evol 39:1–22.

Hay R. 1971. Geologic background of Beds I and II. In: Leakey M, editor. Olduvai Gorge. Cambridge, UK: Cambridge University Press, p 9–20.

Hay R. 1973. Lithofacies and environments of Bed I, Olduvai Gorge, Tanzania. Quaternary Res 3:541–560.

Hay R. 1981. Paleoenvironments of the Laetolil Beds, Northern Tanzania. In: Rapp G, Vondra C, editors. Hominid sites: Their geologic settings. Boulder, CO: Westview Press. p 7–23.

Hayden B. 1993. The cultural capacities of Neandertals: A review and re-evaluation. J Hum Evol 24:113–146.

Hays J, Imbrie J, et al. 1976. Variations in the earth's orbit: pacemaker of the ice ages. Science 194:1121–1132.

Hedenstrom A. 1995. Lifting the Taung child. Nature 378:670.

Hedges SB, Kumar S, et al. 1991. Human origins and analysis of mitochondrial DNA sequences. Science 255:737–739.

Heinrich RE, Rose MD, et al. 1993. Hominid radius from the Middle Pliocene of Lake Turkana, Kenya. Am J Phys Anthropol 92:139–148.

Heizmann E and Begun D. 2001. The oldest Eurasian hominoid. J Hum Evol 41:463–481.

Hennig GJ, Herr W, et al. 1981. ESR-dating of the fossil hominid cranium from Petralona Cave, Greece. Nature 292:533–536.

Hennig W. 1965. Phylogenetic systematics. Ann Rev Entomol 10:97–116.

Henshilwood C, d'Errico F, et al. 2001. An early bone tool industry from the Middle Stone Age at Blombos Cave, South Africa: Implications for the origins of modern human behaviour, symbolism and language. J Hum Evol 41:631–678.

Henshilwood C, d'Errico F, et al. 2002. Emergence of modern human behavior: Middle Stone Age engraving from South Africa. Science 295:1278–1280.

Henshilwood C, d'Errico F, et al. 2004. Middle Stone Age shell beads from South Africa. Science 304:404.

Herman Y and Hopkins D. 1980. Arctic oceanic climate in late Cenozoic time. Science 209:557–562.

Hill A. 1987. Causes of perceived faunal change in the later Neogene of East Africa. J Hum Evol 16:583–596.

Hill A. 1994. Late Miocene and Early Pliocene hominoids from Africa. In: Corruccini RS, Ciochon RL, editors. Integrative paths to the past. Englewood Cliffs, NJ: Prentice Hall. p 123–145.

Hill A. 2002. Paleoanthropological research in the Tugen Hills, Kenya. J Hum Evol 42:1–10.

Hill A and Ward S. 1988. Origin of the Hominidae: The record of African large hominoid evolution between 14 my and 4 my. Yearbk Phys Anthropol 31:49–83.

Hill A, Behrensmeyer K, et al. 1991. Kipsaramon: A lower Miocene hominoid site in the Tugen Hills, Baringo District, Kenya. J Hum Evol 20:67–75.

Hill A, Ward S, et al. 1992a. Anatomy and age of the Lothagam mandible. J Hum Evol 22:439–451.

Hill A, Ward S, et al. 1992b. Earliest *Homo*. Nature 355:719–722.

Hillhouse J, Ndombi J, et al. 1977. Additional results on palaeomagnetic stratigraphy of the Koobi Fora Formation, east of Lake Turkana (Lake Rudolf), Kenya. Nature 265:411–415.

Hoberg E, Alkire N, et al. 2001. Out of Africa: Origins of the Taenia tapeworms in humans. Proc R Soc Lond B 268:781–787.

Hodell D, Elmstrom K, et al. 1986. Latest Miocene benthic O-18 changes, global ice volume, sea level and the "Messinian salinity crisis." Nature 320:411–414.

Hoffecker J, Powers WR, et al. 1993. The colonization of Beringia and the peopling of the New World. Science 259:46–53.

Hoffecker J. 1999. Neanderthals and modern humans in eastern Europe. Evol Anthropol 7:129–141.

Holloway R. 1965, Cranial capacity of the hominine from Olduvai Bed I. Nature 208:205–206.

Holloway R. 1975. Early hominid endocasts: volumes, morphology and significance for hominid evolution. In: Tuttle RH, editor. Primate functional morphology and evolution. The Hague: Mouton. p 393–415.

Holloway R. 1981a. The Indonesian *Homo erectus* brain endocasts revisited. Am J Phys Anthropol 55:503–522.

Holloway R. 1981b. Revisiting the South African Taung australopithecine endocast: The position of the lunate sulcus as determined by the stereoplotting technique. Am J Phys Anthrop 56:43– 58.

Holloway R. 1981c. Volumetric and asymmetry determinations on recent hominid endocasts: Spy 1 and 2, Djebel Irhoud 1, and the Sale *Homo erectus* specimens, with some notes on Neanderthal brain size. Am J Phys Anthropol 55:385–393.

Holloway R. 1983. Human brain evolution: A search for units, models and synthesis. Can J Anthropol 3:215–230.

Holloway R. 1984. The Taung endocast and the lunate sulcus: A rejection of the hypothesis of its anterior position. Am J Phys Anthropol 64:285–287.

Holloway R. 1991. On Falk's 1989 accusations regarding Holloway's study of the Taung endocast: A reply. Am J Phys Anthropol 84:81–88.

Holmes A. 1965. Principles of physical geology. London: Nelson.

Hooghiemstra H. 1986. A high-resolution palynological record of 3.5 million years of northern Andean climatic history: The correlation of 26 "glacial cycle" with terrestrial, marine and astronomical data. Zbl Geol Palaont 1:1363–1366.

Hooten E. 1946. Up from the ape. New York: Macmillan.

Hopwood A. 1933. Miocene primates from Kenya. J Linn Soc London Zool 38:437–464.

Houghton P. 1993. Neandertal supralaryngeal vocal tract. Am J Phys Anthropol 90:139–146.

Howell F. 1951. The place of Neanderthal man in human evolution. Am J Phys Anthropol 9:379–416.

Howell F. 1952. Pleistocene glacial ecology and the evolution of "classic Neandertal" man. Southwest J Anthropol 8:377–410.

Howell F. 1958. Upper Pleistocene men of the Southwest Asian Mousterian. In: von Koenigswald GHR, editor. Hundert Jahre Neanderthaler. Utrecht: Kemink & Zoon. p 185–198.

Howell F. 1965. New discoveries in Tanganyika: Their bearing on hominid evolution (reply to Tobias). Curr Anthropol 6:399–401.

Howell F. 1978. Hominidae. In: Maglio VJ, Cooke HBS, editors. Evolution of African mammals. Cambridge, MA: Harvard University Press. p 154–248.

Howell F. 1981. Some views of *Homo erectus* with special reference to its occurrence in Europe. In: Sigmon BA, Cybulski JS, editors. *Homo erectus*: Papers in honor of Davidson Black. Toronto: University of Toronto Press. p 153–157.

Howell F. and Coppens Y. 1976. An overview of Hominidae from the Omo succession, Ethiopia. In: Coppens Y, Howell F, et al., editors. Earliest man and environments in the Lake Rudolf Basin. Chicago: University of Chicago Press. p 522–532.

Howell F, Haesaerts P, et al. 1987. Depositional environments, archeological occurrences, and hominids from members E and F of the Shungura Formation (Omo basin, Ethiopia). J Hum Evol 16:665–700.

Howells W. 1973. Evolution of the genus *Homo*. Reading, MA: Addison-Wesley.

Howells W. 1980. *Homo erectus*—Who, when and where: A survey. Yearbk Phys Anthropol 23:1–23.

Howells W. 1981. *Homo erectus* in human descent: Ideas and problems. In: Sigmon BA, Cybulski JS, editors. *Homo erectus:* Papers in honor of Davidson Black. Toronto: University of Toronto Press. p 64–85.

Howells W. 1992. The dispersion of modern humans. In: Jones S, Martin R, et al., editors. The Cambridge encyclopedia of human evolution. Cambridge, UK: Cambridge University Press. p 389–401.

Hrdlicka A. 1927. The Neanderthal phase of man. J Roy Soc Anthropol Inst 57:249–273.

Hrdy S. 1981. The woman that never evolved. Cambridge, MA: Harvard University Press.

Hsu K, Montadert L, et al. 1977. History of the Mediterranean salinity crises. Nature 267:399–403.

Huang P, Jin S, et al. 1991. Study of ESR dating for burying age of the first skull of Peking man and chronological scale of the cave deposit in Zhoukoudian site Loc. 1. Acta Anthropol Sinica 10:115.

Hublin J. 1985. Human fossils from the North African Middle Pleistocene and the origin of *Homo sapiens*. In: Delson E, editor. Ancestors: The hard evidence. New York: Liss. p 283–288.

Hublin J. 1992. Recent human evolution in northwestern Africa. Phil Trans R Soc London B 337:185–191.

Hublin J and Tillier A. 1981. The Mousterian juvenile mandible from Irhoud (Morocco): A phylogenetic interpretation. In: Stringer C, editor. Aspects of human evolution. London: Taylor & Francis. p 167–185.

Hublin J, Spoor F, et al. 1996. A late Neanderthal associated with Upper Palaeolithic artefacts. Nature 381:224–226.

Huffman O. 2001. Geologic context and age of the Perning/Mojokerto *Homo erectus*, East Java. J Hum Evol 40:353–362.

Hughen K, Lehman S, et al. 2004. [14]C activity and global carbon cycle changes over the past 50,000 years. Science 303:202–210.

Hughes A and Tobias P. 1977. A fossil skull probably of the genus *Homo* from Sterkfontein, Transvaal. Nature 265:310–312.

Hull D. 1979. The limits of cladism. Syst Zool 28:416–440.

Hunley K. 1998. Vertebral canal size and function: A comparison of extant and fossil hominoids. J Hum Evol 34:A10.

Hunt K. 1994. The evolution of human bipedality: Ecology and functional morphology. J Hum Evol 26:183–202.

Hunt K. 2003. The single species hypothesis: Truly dead and pushing up bushes, or still twitching and ripe for resuscitation? Hum Biol 75:485–502.

Hunt K and Vitzthum V. 1986. Dental metric assessment of the Omo Fossils: Implications for the phylogenetic position of *Australopithecus africanus*. Am J Phys Anthrop 71:141–156.

Huxley J. 1958. Evolutionary processes and taxonomy with special reference to grades. Uppsala Univ Arssks 1958:21–38.

Hylander WL. 1975. Incisor size and diet in anthropoids with special reference to Cercopithecidae. Science 189:1095–1098.

Hyodo M, Watanabe N, et al. 1993. Magnetostratigraphy of hominid fossil bearing formations in Sangiran and Mojokerto, Java. Anthropol Sci 101:157–186.

Ikeya M and Miki T. 1980. Electron spin resonance dating of animal and human bones. Science 207:977–979.

Ingman M, Kaessmann H, et al. 2000. Mitochondrial genome variation and the origin of modern humans. Nature 408:708–713.

Inouye S and Shea B. 1997. What's your angle? Size correction and bar-glenoid orientation in "Lucy" (A.L. 288-1). Int J Primtol 18:629–650.

Isaac G. 1971. The diet of early man: Aspects of archaeological evidence from lower and Middle Pleistocene sites in Africa. World Archaeol 2:278–299.

Isaac G. 1978. The Olorgesailie Formation: Stratigraphy, tectonics, and the palaeogeographic context of the Middle Pleistocene archeolgoical sites. In: Bishop W, editor. Geological background to fossil man: Recent research in the Gregory Rift Valley, East Africa. Edinburgh, UK: Scottish Academic Press. p 173–206.

Isaac G. 1983. Aspects of human evolution. In: Bendall D, editor. Evolution from molecules to men. New York: Cambridge University Press. p 509–543.

Ishida H. 1991. A strategy for long distance walking in the earliest hominids: Effect of posture on energy expenditure during bipedal walking. In: Coppens Y, Senut B, editors. Origine(s) de le bipedie chez les hominides. Paris: CNRS. p 9–15.

Ishida H, Kunimatsu Y, et al. 2004. *Nacholapithecus* skeleton from the Middle Miocene of Kenya. J Hum Evol 46:69–103.

Jablonski NG and Chaplin G. 1993. Origin of habitual terrestrial bipedalism in the ancestor of the Hominidae. J Hum Evol 24:259–280.

Jackson A. 1992. Still poles apart on reversals? Nature 358:194–195.

Jacob T. 1981. Solo man and Peking man. In: Sigmon BA, Cybulski JS, editors. *Homo erectus:* Papers in honor of Davidson Black. Toronto: University of Toronto Press. p 87–104.

Jacob T, Soejono R, et al. 1978. Stone tools from Mid-Pleistocene sediments in Java. Science 202:885–887.

Jacobs BF and Kabuye C. 1987. A middle Miocene (12.2 my old) forest in the East African Rift Valley, Kenya. J Hum Evol 16:147–155.

Jacobs Z, Wintle A, et al. 2003. Optical dating of dune sand from Blombos Cave, South Africa: 1—Multiple grain data. J Hum Evol 44:599–612.

Jaeger JJ. 1981. Les hommes fossiles du Pleistocene moyen du Maghreb dans leur cadre geologique, chronologique, et paleoecologique. In: Sigmon BA, Cybulski JS, editors. *Homo erectus:* Papers in honor of Davidson Black. Toronto: University of Toronto Press. p 159–187.

James S. 1989. Hominid use of fire in the Lower and Middle Pleistocene: A review of the evidence. Curr Anthropol 30:1–26.

Jansen J, Kuijpers A, et al. 1986. A mid-Brunhes climatic event: Long-term changes in global atmosphere and ocean circulation. Science 232:619–622.

Janus C. 1975. The Peking man fossils: Progress of the search. In: Tuttle RH, editor. Paleoanthropology, morphology and paleoecology. The Hague: Mouton. p 291–300.

Jasper J and Hayes J. 1990. A carbon isotope record of CO_2 levels during the late Quaternary. Nature 347:462–464.

Jelinek J. 1969. Neanderthal man and *Homo sapiens* in central and eastern Europe. Curr Anthropol 10:475–503.

Jelinek J. 1982. The Tabun cave and Paleolithic man in the Levant. Science 216:1369–1375.

Jenkins FA and Fleagle JG. 1975. Knuckle-walking and the functional anatomy of the wrists in living apes. In: Tuttle RH, editor. Primate functional morphology and evolution. The Hague: Mouton. p 213–227.

Johanson D. 1989. A partial *Homo habilis* skeleton from Olduvai Gorge, Tanzania: A summary of preliminary results: Hominidae. In: Giacobini G, editor. Proceedings of the Second International Congress of Human Paleontology Milan: Editoriale Jaca Book. p 155–166.

Johanson D and Coppens Y. 1976. A preliminary anatomical diagnosis of the first Plio/Pleistocene hominid discoveries in the central Afar, Ethiopia. Am J Phys Anthropol 45:217–234.

Johanson D, White T, et al. 1978. A new species of the genus *Australopithecus* (Primates: Hominidae) from the Pliocene of eastern Africa. Kirtlandia 28:1–15.

Johanson D and White T. 1979. A systematic assessment of early African hominids. Science 202:321–330.

Johanson D, Taieb M, et al. 1982. Pliocene hominids from the Hadar Formation, Ethiopia (1973–1977): Stratigraphic, chronologic, and paleoenvironmental contexts, with notes on hominid morphology and systematics. Am J Phys Anthropol 57:373–402.

Johanson D, Masao F, et al. 1987. New partial skeleton of *Homo habilis* from Olduvai Gorge, Tanzania. Nature 327:205–209.

Johnsen S, Clausen H, et al. 1992. Irregular glacial interstadials recorded in a new Greenland ice core. Nature 359:311–313.

Jolly C. 1970. The seed-eaters: A new model of hominid differentiation based on a baboon analogy. Man 5:5–26.

Jolly C. 2001. A proper study for mankind: Analogies from the Papionin monkeys and their implications for human evolution. Am J Phys Anthropol 44:177–204.

Jolly C and Plog F. 1986. Physical anthropology and archeology. New York: McGraw-Hill.

Jorde L, Bamshad M, et al. 1995. Origins and affinities of modern humans: A comparison of mitochondrial and nuclear genetic data. Am J Hum Genet 57:523–538.

Jorde L, Rogers A, et al. 1997. Microsatellite diversity and the demographic history of modern humans. Proc Nat Acad Sci USA 94:3100–3103.

Jorde L, Bamshad M, et al. 1998. Using mitochondrial and nuclear DNA markers to reconstruct human evolution. BioEssays 20:126–136.

Jungers W. 1982. Lucy's limbs: Skeletal allometry and locomotion in *Australopithecus afarensis*. Nature 297:676–678.

Jungers W. 1988a. Lucy's length: Stature reconstruction in *Australopithecus afarensis* (AL288-1) with implications for other small-bodied hominids. Am J Phys Anthropol 76:227–231.

Jungers W. 1988b. New estimates of body size in australopithecines. In: Grine F, editor. Evolutionary history of the "robust" australopithecines. New York: de Gruyter. p 115–125.

Jungers W. 1991. A pygmy perspective on body size and shape in *Australopithecus afarenis* (AL 288-1, "Lucy"). In: Coppens Y, Senut B, editors. Origine(s) de la bipedie chez les hominides. Paris: CNRS. p 215–224.

Jungers W. and Stern J. 1983. Body proportions, skeletal allometry and locomotion in the Hadar hominids: A reply to Wolpoff. J Hum Evol 12:673–684.

Kaessmann H, Wiebe V, et al. 1999. Extensive nuclear DNA sequence diversity among chimpanzees. Science 286:1159–1162.

Kalb J. 1993. Refined stratigraphy of the hominid-bearing Awash group, Middle Awash Valley, Afar Depression, Ethiopia. Newslett Stratigr 29:21–62.

Kalb J. 1995. Fossil elephantoids, Awash paleolake basins, and the Afar triple junction, Ethiopia. Palaeogeog Palaeoclim Palaeoecol 114:357–368.

Kalb J. 2001. Adventures in the bone trade. New York: Copernicus Books.

Kalb J, Jolly C, et al. 1982a. Fossil mammals and artifacts from the Middle Awash valley, Ethiopia. Nature 298:25–29.

Kalb J, Oswald E, et al. 1982b. Geology and stratigraphy of Neogene deposits, Middle Awash valley, Ethiopia. Nature 298:17–25.

Kalb J, Jolly C, et al. 1984. Early hominid habitation in Ethiopia. Am Sci 72:168–178.

Kalb J and Mebrate A. 1993. Fossil Elephantoids from the hominid-bearing Awash group, Middle Awash valley, Afar Depression, Ethiopia. Trans. Am Philos Soc 83:1–113.

Kamminga J and Wright R. 1988. The upper cave at Zhoukoudian and the origins of the Mongoloids. J Hum Evol 17:739–767.

Kaplan N, Hudson R, et al. 1989. The "hitch-hiking effect" revisited. Genetics 13:887–899.

Kappelman J. 1993. The attraction of paleomagnetism. Evol Anthropol 2:89–99.

Kappelman J, Kelley J, et al. 1991. The earliest occurrence of *Sivapithecus* from the middle Miocene Chinji Formation of Pakistan. J Hum Evol 21:61–73.

Kappelman J, Swisher C, et al. 1996. Age of *Australopithecus afarensis* from Fejej, Ethiopia. J Hum Evol 30:139–146.

Kappelman J, Plummer T, et al. 1997. Bovids as indicators of Plio–Pleistocene paleoenvironments in East Africa. J Hum Evol 32:229–256.

Karavanic I and Smith F. 1998. The Middle/Upper Paleolithic interface and the relationship of Neanderthals and early modern humans in the Hrvatsko Zagorje, Croatia. J Hum Evol 34:223–248.

Kay R. 1985. Dental evidence for the diet of *Australopithecus*. Ann Rev Anthropol 14:315–341.

Kay R and Grine F. 1988. Tooth morphology, wear and diet in *Australopithecus* and *Paranthropus* from southern Africa. In: Grine FE, editor: The evolutionary history of the robust australopithecines. New York: de Gruyter. p 427–447.

Kay R, Cartmill M, et al. 1998. The hypoglossal canal and the origin of human vocal behavior. Proc Natl Acad Sci USA 95:5417–5419.

Ke Y, Su B, et al. 2001. African origin of modern humans in East Asia: A tale of 12,000 Y chromosomes. Science 292:1151–1153.

Keates S. 1996. On earliest human occupation in central Asia. Curr Anthropol 37:129–130.

Keith A. 1931. New discoveries relating to the antiquity of man. London: Williams & Norgate.

Keith A. 1948. A new theory of human evolution. London: Watts.

Kelley J. 1992. Evolution of apes. In: Jones S, Martin R, et al., editors. The Cambridge encyclopedia of human evolution. Cambridge, UK: Cambridge University Press. p 223–230.

Kelley J. 1993. Taxonomic implications of sexual dimorphism in *Lufengpithecus*. In: Kimbel WH, Martin LB, editors. Species, species concepts, and primate evolution. New York: Plenum. p 429–458.

Kelley J. 2002. The hominoid radiation in Asia. In: Hartwig W, editor. The primate fossil record. Cambridge, UK: Cambridge University Press, p 369–384.

Kennedy G. 1983. A morphometric and taxonomic assessment of a hominine femur from the lower member, Koobi Fora, Lake Turkana. Am J Phys Anthrop 61:429–436.

Kennedy G. 1991. On the autapomorphic traits of *Homo erectus*. J Hum Evol 20:375–412.

Kennedy K. 1999. Paleoanthropology of South Asia. Evol Anthropol 8:165–185.

Kennedy K, Sonakia A, et al. 1991. Is the Narmada hominid an Indian *Homo erectus*? Am J Phys Anthropol 86:475–496.

Kennett J. 1977. Cenozoic evolution of Antarctic glaciation, the circum-Antarctic Ocean, and their impact on global paleoceanography. J Geophys Res 82:3843–3860.

Keyser A. 2000. The Drimolen skull: The most complete australopithecine cranium and mandible to date. South Afr J Sci 96:189–193.

Keyser A, Menter C, et al. 2000. Drimolen: A new hominid-bearing site in Gauteng, South Africa. South Afr J Sci 96:193–197.

Kidd R, O'Higgins P, et al. 1996. The OH8 foot: A reappraisal of the functional morphology of the hindfoot utilizing a multivariate analysis. J Hum Evol 31:269–291.

Kimbel W. 1984. Variation in the pattern of cranial venous sinuses and hominid phylogeny. Am J Phys Anthro 63:243–263.

Kimbel W, White T, et al. 1988. Implications of KNM-WT 17000 for the evolution of "robust" australopithecines. In: Grine F, editor. Evolutionary history of the "robust" australopithecines. New York: de Gruyter. p 259–268.

Kimbel W, Johanson D, et al. 1994. The first skull and other new discoveries of *Australopithecus afarensis* at Hadar, Ethiopia. Nature 368:449–451.

Kimbel W, Walter R, et al. 1996. Late Pliocene *Homo* and Oldowan tools from the Hadar Formation (Kada Hadar member), Ethiopia. J Hum Evol 31:549–561.

Kimbel W, Johanson D, et al. 1997. Systematic assessment of a maxilla of *Homo* from Hadar, Ethiopia. Am J Phys Anthropol 103:235–262.

King M and Motulsky A. 2002. Mapping human history. Science 298:2342–2343.

King W. 1864. The reputed fossil man of the Neanderthal. Rev Sci 1:88–97.

Kingston JD, Marino BD, et al. 1994. Isotopic evidence for Neogene hominid paleoenvironments in the Kenya rift valley. Science 264:955–959.

Kittler R, Kayser M, et al. 2003. Molecular evolution of *Pediculus humanus* and the origin of clothing. Curr Biol 13:1414–1417.

Klein R. 1973. Geological antiquity of Rhodesian man. Nature 244:311–312.

Klein R. 1975. Middle stone age man-animal relationships in southern Africa: Evidence from Die Kelders and Klasies River mouth. Science 190:265–267.

Klein R. 1979. Stone age exploitation of animals in southern Africa. Am Sci 67:151–160.

Klein R. 1987. Reconstructing how early people exploited animals: Problems and prospects. In: Nitecki MH, Nitecki DV, editors. The evolution of human hunting. New York: Plenum. p 11–45.

Klein R. 1989a. Biological and behavioural perspectives on modern human origins in southern Africa. In: Mellars P, Stringer C, editors. The human revolution: Behavioural and biological perspectives on the origins of modern humans. Edinburgh, UK: Edinburgh University Press. p 529–546.

Klein R. 1989b. The human career. Chicago: University of Chicago Press.

Klein R. 1992. The archeology of modern human origins. Evol Anthropol 1:5–14.

Klein R. 1996. Neanderthals and modern humans in West Asia: A conference summary. Evol Anthropol 4:187–193.

Klein R. 2000. Archeology and the evolution of human behavior. Evol Anthropol 9:17–36.

Klein R. 2003. Whither the Neanderthals? Science 299:1525–1527.

Klein R, Cruz-Uribe K, et al. 1991. Environmental, ecological, and paleoanthropological implications of the late Pleistocene mammalian fauna from Equus Cave, Northern Cape Province, South Africa. Quaternary Res 36:94–119.

Klein R and Cruz-Uribe K. 1996. Exploitation of large bovids and seals at Middle and Later Stone Age sites in South Africa. J Hum Evol 31:315–334.

Klein R and Cruz-Uribe K. 2000. Middle and Later Stone Age large mammal and tortoise remains from Die Kelders Cave 1, Western Cape Province, South Africa. J Hum Evol 38:169–195.

Klima B. 1987. A triple burial from the Upper Paleolithic of Dolni Vestonice, Czechoslovakia. J Hum. Evol 16:831–835.

Knight A, Batzer M, et al. 1996. DNA sequences of *Alu* elements indicate a recent replacement of the human autosomal genetic complement. Proc Natl Acad Sci 93:4360–4364.

Koch P, Zachos J, et al. 1992. Correlation between isotope records in marine and continental carbon reservoirs near the Palaeocene/Eocene boundary. Nature 358:319–322.

Kordos L and Begun D. 1998. Encephalization and endocranial morphology in *Dryopithecus brancoi:* Implications for brain evolution in early hominids. Am J Phys Anthropol Suppl 26:141–142.

Kortlandt A. 1983. Facts and fallacies concerning Miocene ape habitats. In: Ciochon R, Corruccini R, editors. New interpretations of ape and human ancestry. New York: Plenum. p 465–515.

Kotilainen AT and Shackleton NJ. 1995. Rapid climate variability in the north Pacific ocean during the past 95,000 years. Nature 377:323–326.

Kraatz R. 1985. A review of recent research on Heidelberg man, *Homo erectus heidelbergensis.* In: Delson E, editor. Ancestors: The hard evidence. New York: Liss. p 268–271.

Kramer A. 1986. Distinctiveness in the Miocene-Pliocene fossil record: The Lothagam mandible. Am J Phys Anthro 70:457–474.

Kramer A. 1991. Modern human origins in Australasia: Replacement or evolution? Am J Phys Anthropol 86:455–473.

Kramer A. 1993. Human taxonomic diversity in the Pleistocene: Does *Homo erectus* represent multiple hominid species? Am J Phys Anthropol 91:161–171.

Kramer A. 1994. A critical analysis of claims for the existence of Southeast Asian australopithecines. J Hum Evol 26:3–21.

Kramer A, Donnelly S, et al. 1995. Craniometric variation in large-bodied hominoids: Testing the single-species hypothesis for *Homo habilis.* J Hum Evol 29:443–462.

Kramer P and Eck G. 2000. Locomotor energetics and leg length in hominid bipedality. J Hum Evol 38:651–666.

Kramer A, Crummett T, et al. 2001. Out of Africa and into the Levant: Replacement of admixture in western Asia? Q Int 75:51–63.

Kretzoi M and Vertes L. 1965. Upper Biharian (Intermindel) pebble-industry occupation site in western Hungary. Curr Anthropol 6:74–87.

Krings M, Stone A, et al. 1997. Neandertal DNA sequences and the origin of modern humans. Cell 90:19–30.

Krings M, Geisert H, et al. 1999. DNA sequence of the mitochondrial hypervariable region II from the Neandertal type specimen. Proc Nat Acad Sci 96:5581–5585.

Krings M, Capelli C, et al. 2000. A view of Neandertal genetic diversity. Nature Gen 26:144–146.

Kukla G. 1987. Loess stratigraphy in central China. Q Sci Rev 6:191–219.

Kullmer O, Sandrock O, et al. 1999. The first *Paranthropus* from the Malawi Rift. J Hum Evol 37:121–127.

Kuman K. 1994a. The archaeology of Sterkfontein—past and present. J Hum Evol 27:471–495.

Kuman K. 1994b. The archaeology of Sterkfontein: Preliminary findings on site formation and cultural change. South Afr J Sci 90:215–219.

Kuman K. 1996. Recent findings on the archaeology of Sterkfontein. Darmstädter Beit Naturgeschichte 6:31–36.

Kuman K, Field A, et al. 1997. Discovery of new artefacts at Kromdraai. South Afr J Sci 93:187–193.

Kuman K and Clarke R. 2000. Stratigraphy, artifact industries and hominid associations for Sterkfontein, member 5. J Hum Evol 38:827–847.

Kumar S and Hedges S. 1998. A molecular timescale for vertebrate evolution. Nature 392:917–920.

Kummer B. 1991. Biomechanical foundations of the development of human bipedalism. In: Coppens Y, Senut B, editors. Origine(s) de la bipedie chez les hominides. Paris: CNRS. p 1–8.

Kuniholm P, Kromer B, et al. 1996. Anatolian tree rings and the absolute chronology of the eastern Mediterranean, 2220–718 BC. Nature 381:780–783.

Kunz M and Reaniert R. 1994. Paleoindians in Beringia: Evidence from Arctic Alaska. Science 263:660–662.

Kurten B and Poulianos A. 1977. New stratigraphic and faunal material from Petralona cave with special reference to the Carnivora. Anthropos 4:47–130.

Kuykendall K. 1992. Dental development in chimpanzees (*Pan troglodytes*) and implications for dental development patterns in fossil hominids. Ph.D. thesis. St. Louis: Washington University.

Kuykendall K, Mahoney C, et al. 1992. Probit and survival analysis of tooth emergence ages in a mixed-longitudinal sample of chimpanzees (*Pan troglodytes*). Am J Phys Anthropol 89:379–399.

Labuda D, Zietkiewicz E, et al. 2000. Archaic lineages in the history of modern humans. Genetics 156:799–808.

Lague M and Jungers W. 1996. Morphometric variation in Plio–Pleistocene hominid distal humeri. Am J Phys Anthropol 101:401–427.

Lahr M. 1994. The multiregional model of modern human origins: A reassessment of its morphological basis. J Hum Evol 26:23–56.

Lahr M and Foley R. 1994. Multiple dispersals and modern human origins. Evol Anthropol 3:48–60.

Laitman J. 1984. The anatomy of human speech. Nat Hist 92:20–27.

Laitman J. 1985. Evolution of the hominid upper respiratory tract: The fossil evidence. In: Tobias P, editor. Human evolution: Past, present, and future. New York: Liss. p 281–286.

Laitman J and Heimbuch R. 1982. The basicranium of Plio-Pleistocene hominids as an indicator of their upper respiratory systems. Am J Phys Anthropol 59:323–343.

Laitman J, Heimbuch R, et al. 1979. The basicranium of fossil hominids as an indicator of their upper respiratory systems. Am J Phys Anthropol 51:15–34.

Lam Y, Pearson O, et al. 1996. Chin morphology and sexual dimorphism in the fossil hominid mandible sample from Klasies River Mouth. Am J Phys Anthropol 100:545–557.

Landau M. 1984. Human evolution as narrative. Am Sci 72:262–267.

Landau M. 1991. Narratives of Human evolution. New Haven, CT: Yale University Press.

Langbroek M and Roebroeks W. 2000. Extraterrestrial evidence on the age of the hominids from Java. J Hum Evol 38:595–600.

Langdon J, Bruckner J, et al. 1991. Pedal mechanics and bipedalism in early hominids. In: Coppens Y, Senut B, editors. Origine(s) de la bipedie chez les hominides. Paris: CNRS. p 159–167.

Langereis C, van Hoof A, et al. 1992. Longitudinal confinement of geomagnetic reversal paths as a possible sedimentary artifact. Nature 358:226–230.

Larsen CS, Matter RM, et al. 1991. Human origins: The fossil record. Prospect Heights, IL: Waveland Press.

Larsen HC, Saunders AD, et al. 1994. Seven million years of glaciation in Greenland. Science 264:952–955.

Latimer B. 1991. Locomotor adaptations in *Australopithecus afarensis:* The issue of arboreality. In: Coppens Y, Senut B, editors. Origine(s) de la bipedie chez les hominides. Paris: CNRS. p 169–176.

Latimer B and Lovejoy O. 1989. The calcaneus of *Australopithecus afarensis* and its implications for the evolution of bipedality. Am J Phys Anthropol 78:369–386.

Latimer B and Lovejoy O. 1990a. Hallucal tarsometatarsal joint in *Australopithecus afarensis.* Am J Phys Anthropol 82:125–133.

Latimer B and Lovejoy O. 1990b. Metatarsophalangeal joints of *Australopithecus afarensis.* Am J Phys Anthropol 83:13–23.

Latimer B and Ward C. 1993. The thoracic and lumbar vertebrae. In: Walker A, Leakey RE, editors. The Nariokotome *Homo erectus* skeleton. Cambridge, MA: Harvard University Press. p 266–293.

Le Gros Clark WE. 1959. The antecedents of man. Edinburgh, UK: University Press.

Leakey L. 1935. Adam's ancestors. New York: Longmans, Green.

Leakey L. 1936. A new fossil skull from Eyassi, East Africa: Discovery by a German expedition. Nature 138:1082–1084.

Leakey L. 1959. A new fossil skull from Olduvai. Nature 184:491–493.

Leakey L. 1960. The affinities of the new Olduvai australopithecine (reply to J.T. Robinson). Nature 186:458.

Leakey L. 1962. A new lower Pliocene fossil primate from Kenya. Ann Mag Nat Hist 4:689–696.

Leakey L. 1966. *Homo habilis, Homo erectus* and the australopithecines. Nature 209:1279–1281.

Leakey L. 1967a. An early Miocene member of Hominidae. Nature 213:155–163.

Leakey L. 1967b. Olduvai Gorge 1951–1961: Fauna and background. Cambridge, UK: Cambridge University Press.

Leakey L, Tobias P, et al. 1964. A new species of the genus *Homo* from Olduvai Gorge. Nature 202:7–9.

Leakey M. 1971. Discovery of postcranial remains of *Homo erectus* and associated artifacts in Bed IV at Olduvai Gorge, Tanzania. Nature 232:380–383.

Leakey M. 1981. Olduvai Gorge. Cambridge, UK: Cambridge University Press.

Leakey M, Tobias P, et al. 1969. An Acheulian Industry with prepared core technique and the discovery of a contemporary hominid mandible at Lake Baringo, Kenya. Proc Prehist Soc 35:48–76.

Leakey M, Clarke R, et al. 1971. New hominid skull from Bed 1, Olduvai Gorge, Tanzania. Nature 232:308–312.

Leakey M and Hay R. 1979. Pliocene footprints in the Laetoli beds at Laetoli, northern Tanzania. Nature 278:317–328.

Leakey M and Harris J. 1987. Laetoli: A Pliocene site in northern Tanzania. Oxford, UK: Oxford University Press.

Leakey M, Leakey RE, et al. 1991. Similarities in *Aegyptopithecus* and *Afropithecus* facial morphology. Folia Primatol 56:65–85.

Leakey M, Feibel C, et al. 1995. New four-million-year-old hominid species from Kanapoi and Allia Bay, Kenya. Nature 376:565–571.

Leakey M, Feibel C, et al. 1996. Lothagam: A record of faunal change in the late Miocene of East Africa. J Vert Paleontol 16:556–570.

Leakey M, Feibel C, et al. 1998. New specimens and confirmation of an early age for *Australopithecus anamensis.* Nature 393:62–66.

Leakey M, Spoor F, et al. 2001. New hominin genus from eastern Africa shows diverse Middle Pliocene lineages. Nature 410:433–440.

Leakey R. 1969. Early *Homo sapiens* remains from the Omo River region of south-west Ethiopia: Faunal remains from the Omo Valley. Nature 222:1132–1133.

Leakey R. 1971. Further evidence of lower Pleistocene hominids from East Rudolf, North Kenya. Nature 231:241–245.

Leakey R. 1972. Further evidence of lower Pleistocene hominids from East Rudolf, North Kenya, 1971. Nature 237:264–269.

Leakey R. 1973. Evidence for an advanced Plio-Pleistocene hominid from East Rudolf, Kenya. Nature 242:447–450.

Leakey R. 1974. Further evidence of lower Pleistocene hominids from East Rudolf, North Kenya, 1973. Nature 248:653–656.

Leakey R and Wood B. 1973. New evidence of the genus *Homo* from East Rudolf Kenya. II. Am J Phys Anthropol 39:355–368.

Leakey R and Wood B. 1974. New evidence of the genus *Homo* from East Rudolf, Kenya. IV. Am J Phys Anthropol 41:237–244.

Leakey R and Walker A. 1976. *Australopithecus, Homo erectus* and the single species hypothesis. Nature 261:572–574.

Leakey R and Walker A. 1985. New higher primates from the early Miocene of Buluk, Kenya. Nature 318:173–175.

Leakey R and Leakey MG. 1986a. A new Miocene hominoid from Kenya. Nature 324:143–146.

Leakey R and Leakey MG. 1986b. A second new Miocene hominoid from Kenya. Nature 324:146–148.

Leakey R and Leakey MG. 1987. A new Miocene small-bodied ape from Kenya. J Hum Evol 16:369–387.

Leakey R, Leakey MG, et al. 1988a. Morphology of *Afropithecus turkanensis* from Kenya. Am J Phys Anthrop 76:289–307.

Leakey R, Leakey MG, et al. 1988b. Morphology of *Turkanapithecus kalakolensis* from Kenya. Am J Phys Anthrop 76:277–288.

Leakey R and Lewin R. 1992. Origins reconsidered: In search of what makes us human. Boston: Little, Brown.

Lee RB and DeVore I, eds. 1968. Man the hunter. Chicago: Aldine.

Lee-Thorp J, van der Merwe N, et al. 1989. Isotopic evidence for dietary differences between two extinct baboon species from Swartkrans. J Hum Evol 18:183–189.

Lee-Thorp J and van der Merwe N. 1993. Stable carbon isotope studies of Swartkrans fossils. In: Brain CK, editor. Swartkrans: A cave's chronicle of early man. Pretoria: Transvaal Museum. p 251–264.

Lee-Thorp J, van der Merwe N, et al. 1994. Diet of *Australopithecus robustus* at Swartkrans from stable carbon isotopic analysis. J Hum Evol 27:361–372.

Lee-Thorp J and Beaumont P. 1995. Vegetation and seasonality shifts during the Late Quaternary deduced from $^{13}C/^{12}C$ ratios of grazers at Equus Cave, South Africa. Quaternary Res 43:426–432.

Lee-Thorp J, Thackeray J, et al. 2000. The hunters and the hunted revisited. J Hum Evol 39:565–576.

LeGros Clark W. 1955. The fossil evidence for human evolution. Chicago: University of Chicago Press.

Leonard W and Robertson M. 1997a. Comparative primate energetics and hominid evolution. Am J Phys Anthropol 102:265–281.

Leonard W and Robertson M. 1997b. Rethinking the energetics of bipedality. Curr Anthropol 38:304–309.

Leroi-Gourhan A. 1975. The flowers found with Shanidar IV, a Neanderthal burial in Iraq. Science 190:562–565.

Leute U. 1987. Archaeometry: An introduction to physical methods in archaeology and the history of art. Weinheim: VCH.

Leutenegger W. 1982. Scaling of sexual dimorphism in body weight and canine size in primates. Folia Primatol 37:163–176.

Leutenegger W. 1987. Neonatal brain size and neurocranial dimensions in Pliocene hominids: Implications for obstetrics. J Hum Evol 16:291–296.

Leutenegger W and Cheverud J. 1985. Sexual dimorphism in primates: The effects of size. In: Jungers WL, editor. Size and scaling in primate biology. New York: Plenum. p 33–50.

Leutenegger W and Shell B. 1987. Variability and sexual dimorphism in canine size of *Australopithecus* and extant hominoids. J Hum Evol 16:359–367.

Levinton J and Simon C. 1980. A critique of the punctuated equilibria model and implications for the detection of speciation in the fossil record. Syst Zool 29:130–142.

Lewis M. 1995. Plio-Pleistocene carnivorans and carcass processing in East Africa. Paper presented at the Paleoanthropology Society Conference, Oakland, CA.

Lewis M. 1997. Carnivoran paleoguilds of Africa: Implications for hominid food procurement strategies. J Hum Evol 32:257–288.

Lewontin R. 1972. The apportionment of human diversity. Evol Biol. 6:381–398.

Li T and Etler D. 1992. New Middle Pleistocene hominid crania from Yunxian in China. Nature 357:404–407.

Lieberman D. 1995. Testing hypotheses about recent human evolution from skulls. Curr Anthropol 36:159–197.

Lieberman D. 1996. How and why humans grow thin skulls: Experimental evidence for systemic cortical robusticity. Am J Phys Anthropol 101:217–236.

Lieberman D. 1998. Sphenoid shortening and the evolution of modern human cranial shape. Nature 393:158–162.

Lieberman D. 2001. Another face in our family tree. Nature 410:419–420.

Lieberman D and Shea J. 1994. Behavioral differences between archaic and modern humans in the Levantine Mousterian. Am Anthropol 96:300–332.

Lieberman D, Wood B, et al. 1996. Homoplasy and early *Homo:* An analysis of the evolutionary relationships of *H. habilis sensu stricto* and *H. rudolfensis.* J Hum Evol 30:97–120.

Lieberman D, McCarthy R, et al. 1998. New estimates of fossil hominid vocal tract dimensions. J Hum Evol 34:A12–13.

Lieberman D, McBratney B, et al. 2002. The evolution and development of cranial form in *Homo sapiens.* Proc Nat Acad Sci USA 99:1134–1139.

Lieberman P. 1976. Interactive models for evolution: Neural mechanisms, anatomy, and behaviour. Ann NY Acad Sci 280:660–672.

Lieberman P. 1989. The origins of some aspects of human language and cognition. In: Mellars P, Stringer C, editors. The human revolution. Princeton, NJ: Princeton University Press. p 391–414.

Lieberman P. 1992. Human speech and language. In: Jones S, Martin R, et al., editors. The Cambridge encyclopedia of human evolution. Cambridge, UK: Cambridge University Press, p 134–137.

Lieberman P. 1993. On the Kebara KMH 2 hyoid and Neanderthal speech. Curr Anthropol 34:172–175.

Lieberman P. 1994. Hyoid bone position and speech: Reply to Dr. Arensburg et al. (1990). Am J Phys Anthropol 94:275–278.

Lieberman P. 1999. Silver-tongued Neandertals? Science 283:175.

Lieberman P. 2002. On the nature and evolution of the neural bases of human language. Am J Phys Anthropol 45:36–62.

Lieberman P, Laitman J, et al. 1992. The anatomy, physiology, acoustics and perception of speech: Essential elements in analysis of the evolution of human speech. J Hum Evol 23:447–467.

Lieberman S, Gelvin B, et al. 1985. Dental sexual dimorphism in some extant hominoids and ramapithecines from China: A quantitative approach. Am J Primatol 9:305–326.

Lincoln R, Boxshall G, et al. 1990. A Dictionary of ecology, evolution and systematics. Cambridge, UK: Cambridge University Press.

Lindly J and Clark G. 1990. Symbolism and modern human origins. Curr Anthropol 31:233–262.

Linnaeus C. 1758. Systema naturae per regna tria naturae, secundum classes, ordines genera, species cum characteribus, differentris, synonymis, locis. Stockholm: Laurentii Salvii.

Liu Z. 1983. The palaeoclimatic changes inferred from Peking man cave deposits in comparison with the climatic sequence of other formations. Acta Anthropol Sinica 2:183.

Lockwood C. 1999. Sexual dimorphism in the face of *Australopithecus africanus.* Am J Phys Anthropol 108:97–127.

Lockwood C, Richmond B, et al. 1996. Randomization procedures and sexual dimorphism in *Australopithecus afarensis.* J Hum Evol 31:537–548.

Lockwood C and Tobias P. 1999. A large male hominin cranium from Sterkfontein, South Africa, and the status of *Australopithecus africanus*. J Hum Evol 36:637–685.

Lockwood C, Kimbel W, et al. 2000. Temporal trends and metric variation in the mandibles and dentition of *Australopithecus afarensis*. J Hum Evol 39:23–55.

Lockwood C and Tobias P. 2002. Morphology and affinities of new hominin cranial remains from member 4 of the Sterkfontein Formation, Gauteng Province, South Africa. J Hum Evol 42:389–450.

Lorenzo C, Arsuaga J, et al. 1999. Hand and foot remains from the Gran Dolina Early Pleistocene site (Sierra de Atapuerca, Spain). J Hum Evol 37:501–522.

Loth S and Henneberg M. 1996. The Taung child—it's a boy! Sexually dimorphic morphology in the immature human mandible and its application to fossil hominids. Am J Phys Anthropol Suppl 22:152.

Lovejoy O. 1975. Biomechanical perspectives on the lower limbs of early hominids. In: Tuttle R, editor. Primate functional morphology and evolution. The Hague: Mouton. p 291–326.

Lovejoy O. 1981. The origin of man. Science 211:341–350.

Lovejoy O. 1988. Evolution of human walking. Sci Am 259:118–125.

Lovejoy O. 1993. Modeling human origins: Are we sexy because we're smart, or smart because we're sexy? In: Rasmussen DT, editor. The origin and evolution of humans and humanness. Boston: Jones & Bartlett. p 1–28.

Lovejoy O, Heiple K, et al. 2001. Did our ancestors knuckle-walk? Nature 410:325–326.

Ludwig K and Renne P. 2000. Geochronology on the paleoanthropological time scale. Evol Anthropol 9:101–110.

Macchiarelli R, Bondioli L, et al. 1999. Hip bone travecular architecture shows uniquely distinctive locomotor behavior in South African australopithecines. J Hum Evol 36:211–232.

MacDougall J. 1976. Fission-track dating. Sci Am 235:114–122.

Maclean, N. 1976. A river runs through it and other stories. Chicago: University of Chicago Press.

MacLarnon A. 1993. The vertebral canal. In: Walker A, Leakey R, editors. The Nariokotome *Homo erectus* skeleton. Cambridge, MA: Harvard University Press. p 359–390.

MacLatchy L. 1996. Another look at the australopithecine hip. J Hum Evol 31:455–4776.

MacLatchy L, Gebo DL, et al. 1995. New primate fossils from the lower Miocene of northeast Uganda. Am J Phys Anthropol Suppl 20:139.

Madar S, Rose M, et al. 2002. New *Sivapithecus* postcranial specimens from the Siwaliks of Pakistan. J Hum Evol 42:705–752.

Maddison DR. 1991. African origin of human mitochondrial DNA reexamined. Syst Zool 40:355–363.

Maddison DR, Ruvolo M, et al. 1992. Geographic origins of human mitochondrial DNA: Phylogenetic evidence from control region sequences. Syst Biol 41:111–124.

Mahoney S. 1980. Cost of locomotion and heat balance during rest and running from 0 to 55°C in a patas monkey. J Appl Physiol 49:789–800.

Maier W and Nkini A. 1984. Olduvai hominid 9: New results of investigation. Cour Forsch Inst Senckenberg 69:123–130.

Mallegni F, Carnieri E, et al. 2003. *Homo cepranensis* and the evolution of African–European Middle Pleistocene hominids. CR Palevol 2:153–159.

Mania D and Vlcek E. 1981. *Homo erectus* in middle Europe: The discovery from Bilzingsleben. In: Sigmon BA, Cybulski JS, editors. *Homo erectus:* Papers in honor of Davidson Black. Toronto: University of Toronto Press. p 133–151.

Mann A. 1975. Some paleodemographic aspects of the South African australopithecines. Philadelphia: University of Pennsylvania Publications in Anthropology.

Mann A. 1981. The significance of the *Sinanthropus* casts, and some paleodemographic notes. In: Sigmon BA, Cybulski JS, editors. *Homo erectus:* Papers in honor of Davidson Black. Toronto: University of Toronto Press, p 41–62.

Manzi G. 2004. Human evolution at the Matuyama-Brunhes boundary. Evol Anthropol 13:11–24.

Manzi G, Mallegni F, et al. 2001. A cranium for the earliest Europeans: Phylogenetic position of the hominid from Ceprano, Italy. Proc Natl Acad Sci USA 98:10011–10016.

Marchant DR, Swisher CC, et al. 1993. Pliocene paleoclimate and east Antarctic ice-sheet history from surficial ash deposits. Science 260:667–670.

Marean C. 1989. Sabertooth cats and their relevance for early hominid diet and evolution. J Hum Evol 18:559–582.

Marean C and Ehrhardt C. 1995. Paleoanthropological and paleoecological implications of the taphonomy of a sabertooth's den. J Hum Evol 29:515–547.

Marean C and Assefa Z. 1999. Zooarcheological evidence for the faunal exploitation behavior of Neandertals and early modern humans. Evol Anthropol 8:22–37.

Marks J. 1994. Blood will tell (won't it?): A century of molecular discourse in anthropological systematics. Am J Phys Anthropol 94:59–79.

Marks J. 1995. Learning to live with a trichotomy. Am J Phys Anthropol 98:211–213.

Marks J, Schmid CW, et al. 1988. DNA hybridization as a guide to phylogeny: Relations of the Hominoidea. J Hum Evol 17:769–786.

Marquez S, Mowbray K, et al. 2001. New fossil hominid calvaria from Indonesia—Sambungmacan 3. Anat Rec 262:34–368.

Marth G, Schuler G, et al. 2003. Sequence variation in the public human genome data reflect a bottlenecked population history. Proc Nat Acad Sci USA 100:376–381.

Martin, LB. 1995. Oldest known thick-enamelled ape. Am J Phys Anthropol Suppl 20:144.

Martin LB and Andrews PJ. 1991. Species recognition in middle Miocene hominoids. Am J Phys Anthropol Suppl 12:126.

Martin LB and Andrews P. 1993. Species recognition in middle Miocene hominoids. In: Kimbel WH, Martin LB, editors. Species, species concepts, and primate evolution. New York: Plenum. p 393–427.

Martin R. 1981. Relative brain size and basal metabolic rate in terrestrial vertebrates. Nature 293:57–60.

Martin R. 1983. Human brain evolution in an ecological context. New York: American Museum of Natural History.

Martin R. 1986. Primates: A definition. In: Wood B, Martin L, et al., editors. Major topics in primate and human evolution. Cambridge, UK: Cambridge University Press. p 1–31.

Martin R. 1992a. Classification and evolutionary relationships. In: Jones S, Martin R, et al., editors. The Cambridge encyclopedia of human evolution. Cambridge, UK: Cambridge University Press. p 17–23.

Martin R. 1992b. Walking on two legs. In: Jones S, Martin R, et al., editors. The Cambridge encyclopedia of human evolution. Cambridge, UK: Cambridge University Press. p 78.

Marzke M. 1983. Joint functions and grips of the *Austalopithecus afarensis* hand, with special reference to the region of the capitate. J Hum Evol 12:197–211.

Marzke M. 1997. Precision grips, hand morphology, and tools. Am J Phys Anthropol 102:91–110.

Marzke M and Shackley M. 1986. Hominid hand use in the Pliocene and Pleistocene: Evidence from experimental archaeology and comparative morphology. J Hum Evol 15:439–460.

Mason S, Hather J, et al. 1994. Preliminary investigation of the plant macro-remains from Dolni Vestonice II, and its implications for the role of plant food in Palaeolithic and Mesolithic Europe. Antiquity 68:48–57.

Maureille B. 2002. A lost Neanderthal neonate found. Nature 419:33–34.

Maureille B and Bar D. 1999. The premaxilla in Neandertal and early modern children: Ontogeny and morphology. J Hum Evol 37:137–152.

Mayr E. 1963. Animal species and evolution. Oxford, UK: Oxford University Press.

Mayr E. 1981. Biological classification: Toward a synthesis of opposing methodologies. Science 214:510–516.

McBrearty S and Brooks A. 2000. The revolution that wasn't: A new interpretation of the origin of modern human behavior. J Hum Evol 39:453–563.

McBurney C. 1958. Evidence for the distribution in space and time of Neanderthaloids and allied strains in northern Africa. In: Von Koenigswald GHR, editor. Hundert Jahre Neanderthaler. Utrecht: Kemink & Zoon. p 253–264.

McCarthy, C. 1985. Blood Meridian: or the Evening Redness in the West. New York: Vintage Books.

McCarthy, C. 1993. The Orchard Keeper. New York: Vintage.

McCollum M. 1994. Mechanical and spatial determinants of *Paranthropus:* facial form. Am J Phys Anthropol 93:259–273.

McCollum M. 1997. Palatal thickening and facial form in *Paranthropus:* Examination of alternative developmental models. Am J Phys Anthropol 103:375–392.

McCollum M. 1999. The robust australopithecine face: A morphogenetic perspective. Science 284:301–305.

McCollum M. 2000. Subnasal morphological variation in fossil hominids: A reassessment based on new observations and recent developmental findings. Am J Phys Anthropol 112:275–283.

McCollum M, Grine F, et al. 1993. Subnasal morphological variation in extant hominoids and fossil hominids. J Hum Evol 24:87–111.

McCollum M and Ward S. 1997. Subnasoalveolar anatomy and hominid phylogeny: Evidence from comparative ontogeny. Am J Phys Anthropol 102:377–405.

McCown T and Keith A. 1939. The Stone Age of Mount Carmel. Oxford, UK: Clarendon Press.

McCown T and Kennedy K, eds. 1972. Climbing man's family tree: A collection of major writings on human phylogeny, 1699–1971. Englewood Cliffs, NJ: Prentice-Hall.

McCrossin M. 1992. An oreopithecid humerus from the middle Miocene of Maboko Island, Kenya. Int J Primatol 13:659–677.

McCrossin M and Benefit B. 1993. Recently recovered *Kenyapithecus* mandible and its implications for great ape and human origins. Proc Natl Acad Sci USA 90:1962–1966.

McCrossin M and Benefit B. 1994. Maboko Island and the evolutionary history of Old World monkeys and apes. In: Corruccini RS, Ciochon RL, editors. Integrative paths to the past. Englewood Cliffs, NJ: Prentice-Hall. p 95–122.

McCrossin M and Benefit B. 1997. On the relationships and adaptations of *Kenyapithecus,* a large-bodied hominoid from the middle Miocene of eastern Africa. In: Begun D, Ward C, et al., editors. Function, phylogeny, and fossils: Miocene hominoid evolution and adaptation. New York: Plenum. p 241–267.

McDermott F, Grün R, et al. 1993. Mass-spectrometric U-series dates for Israeli Neanderthal/early modern hominid sites. Nature 363:252–255.

McDermott F, Stringer C, et al. 1996. New late-Pleisotocene uranium-thorium and ESR dates for the Singa homind (Sudan). J Hum Evol 31:507–516.

McDougall I. 1981. ^{40}Ar/^{39}Ar age spectra from the KBS tuff, Koobi Fora Formation. Nature 294:120–124.

McDougall I, Maier R, et al. 1980. K-Ar age estimate for the KBS tuff, east Turkana, Kenya. Nature 284:230–234.

McFadden P and Brock A. 1984. Magnetostratigraphy at Makapansgat. South Afr J Sci 80:482–483.

McHenry H. 1975. Fossil hominid body weight and brain size. Nature 254:686–688.

McHenry H. 1976. Early hominid body weight and encephalization. Am J Phys Anthropol 45:77–84.

McHenry H. 1984. Relative cheek-tooth size in *Australopithecus.* Am J Phys Anthropol 64:297–306.

McHenry H. 1985. Implications of postcanine megadontia for the origin of *Homo.* In: Delson E, editor. Ancestors: The hard evidence. New York: Liss. p 178–183.

McHenry H. 1988. New estimates of body weight in early hominids and their significance to encephalization and megadontia in robust australopithecines. In: Grine F, editor. Evolutionary history of the "robust" australopithecines. New York: de Gruyter. p 133–148.

McHenry H. 1991a. Femoral lengths and stature in Plio-Pleistocene hominids. Am J Phys Anthropol 85:149–158.

McHenry H. 1991b. First steps? Analyses of the postcranium of early hominids. In: Coppens Y, Senut B, editors. Origine(s) de la bipedie chez les hominides. Paris: CNRS. p 133–141.

McHenry H. 1992a. Body size and proportions in early hominids. Am J Phys Anthropol 87:407–431.

McHenry H. 1992b. How big were early hominids? Evol Anthropol 1:15–20.

McHenry H and Berger L. 1996. Ape-like body proportions in *A. africanus* and their implications for the origin of the genus *Homo*. Am J Phys Anthropol Suppl 22:163–164.

McHenry H and Berger L. 1998a. Body proportions in *Australopithecus afarensis* and *A. africanus* and the origin of the genus *Homo*. J Hum Evol 35:1–22.

McHenry H and Berger L. 1998b. Limb lengths in *Australopithecus* and the origin of the genus *Homo*. South Afr J Sci 94:447–450.

McKee J. 1989. Australopithecine anterior pillars: Reassessment of the functional morphology and phylogenetic relevance. Am J Phys Anthropol 80:1–9.

McKee J. 1997. East African confirmation of constant turnover among Plio-Pleistocene large mammals. Am J Phys Anthropol Suppl 24:167.

McKee J. 1993a. Faunal dating of the Taung hominid fossil deposit. J Hum Evol 25:363–376.

McKee J. 1993b. Formation of geomorphology of caves in calcareous tufas and implications for the study of the Taung fossil deposits. Trans R Soc South Afr 48:307–322.

McKee J. 1994. Hominid evolution in the context of gradual change among the mammals of southern Africa. Am J Phys Anthropol Suppl 18:145.

McKee J, Thackeray J, et al. 1995. Faunal assemblage seriation of southern African Pliocene and Pleistocene fossil deposits. Am J Phys Anthropol 96:235–250.

McKee J and Tobias P. 1994. Taung stratigraphy and taphonomy: Preliminary results based on the 1988–93 excavations. South Afr J Sci 90:233–235.

McPhee J. 1980. Basin and range. New York: Farrar Straus Giroux.

McPhee J. 1998. Annals of the former world. New York: Farrar, Straus and Giroux.

Meehl GA and Washington WM. 1993. South Asian summer monsoon variability in a model with doubled atmospheric carbon dioxide concentration. Science 260:1101–1104.

Mellars P. 1992. Archaeology and the population-dispersal hypothesis of modern human origins in Europe. Phil Trans R Soc Biol Sci 337:225–234.

Mellars P, Aitken M, et al. 1992. Outlining the problem. Phil Trans R Soc Biol Sci 337:127–130.

Melnick DJ and Hoelzer GA. 1993. What is mtDNA good for in the study of primate evolution? Evol Anthropol 2:2–10.

Melosh H, Schneider N, et al. 1990. Ignition of global wildfires at the Cretaceous/Tertiary boundary. Nature 343:251–254.

Menter C, Keyser A, et al. 1999. First record of hominid teeth from the Plio-Pleistocene site of Gondolin, South Africa. J Hum Evol 37:299–307.

Mercier N, Valladas H, et al. 1991. Thermoluminescence dating of the late Neanderthal remains from Saint-Césaire. Nature 351:737–739.

Mercier N, Valladas H, et al. 1993. Thermoluminescence date for the Mousterian burial site of Es-Skhul, Mt. Carmel. J Archaeol Sci 20:169–174.

Miller G, Beaumont P, et al. 1992. Pleistocene geochronology and palaeothermometry from protein diagenesis in ostrich eggshells: Implications for the evolution of modern humans. Phil Trans R Soc Biol Sci 337:149–157.

Miller G, Magee J, et al. 1997. Low-latitude glacial cooling in the Southern Hemisphere from amino-acid racemization in emu eggshells. Nature 385:241–244.

Miller J. 1991. Does brain size variability provide evidence of multiple species in *Homo habilis?* Am J Phys Anthropol 84:385–398.

Miller J. 1994. *Homo habilis:* Is the degree of craniofacial variation excessive? Am J Phys Anthropol Suppl 18:147.

Miller J. 2000. Craniofacial variation in *Homo habilis:* An analysis of the evidence for multiple species. Am J Phys Anthropol 112:103–128.

Miller J, Albrecht G, et al. 1997. An hierarchical analysis of craniofacial variation in *Homo habilis* using a *Gorilla* analog. Am J Phys Anthropol Suppl 24:170.

Milton K. 1999. A hypothesis to explain the role of meat-eating in human evolution. Evol Anthropol 8:11–21.

Minugh-Purvis N. 1993. Reexamination of the immature hominid maxilla from Tangier, Morocco. Am J Phys Anthropol 92:449–461.

Minugh-Purvis N, Radovcic J, et al. 2000. Krapina 1: A juvenile Neandertal from the early Late Pleistocene of Croatia. Am J Phys Anthropol 111:393–424.

Mishra S, Venkatesan T, et al. 1995. Earliest Acheulian industry from Peninsular India. Curr Anthropol 36:847–851.

Mitani J, Watts D, et al. 2002. Recent developments in the study of wild chimpanzee behavior. Evol Anthropol 11:9–25.

Mivart SG. 1873. On *Lepilemur* and *Cheirogaleus* and on the zoological rank of the Lemuroidea. Proc Zool Soc Lond 1873:484–510.

Moggi-Checchi J and Collard M. 2002. A fossil stapes from Sterkfontein, South Africa, and the hearing capabilities of early hominids. J Hum Evol 42:259–265.

Molnar P and England P. 1990. Late Cenozoic uplift of mountain ranges and global climate change: Chicken or egg? Nature 346:29–34.

Montgomery P, Williams H, et al. 1994. An assessment of the temporal bone lesions of the Broken Hill cranium. J Archaeol Sci 21:331–337.

Moore J. 1996. Savanna chimpanzees, referential models and the last common ancestor. In: McGrew W, Marchant L, et al., editors. Great ape societies. Cambridge, UK: Cambridge University Press. p 275–292.

Morell V. 1994. Did early humans reach Siberia 500,000 years ago? Science 263:611–612.

Morell V. 1995. Siberia: Surprising home for early modern humans. Science 268:1279.

Morgan ME, Kingston JD, et al. 1994. Carbon isotopic evidence for the emergence of C_4 plants in the Neogene from Pakistan and Kenya. Nature 367:162–165.

Morris A. 1991. Biological relationships between Upper Pleistocene and Holocene populations in southern Africa. In: Bräuer G, Smith FH, editors. Continuity or replacement: Controversies in *Homo sapiens* evolution. Rotterdam: Balkema. p 131–143.

Morwood M, O'Sullivan P, et al. 1998. Fission-track ages of stone tools and fossils on the east Indonesian island of Flores. Nature 392:173–176.

Morwood M, Soejono R, et al. (2004) Archaeology and age of a new hominin from Flores in eastern Indonesia. Nature 431:1087–1091.

Mountain JL, Lin AA, et al. 1992. Evolution of modern humans: Evidence from nuclear DNA polymorphisms. Phi Trans R Soc Biol Sci 337:159–165.

Movius H. 1944. Early man and Pleistocene stratigraphy in southern and eastern Asia. Trans Am Philos Soc 38:329–420.

Moya-Sola S and Kohler M. 1996. A *Dryopithecus* skeleton and the origins of great-ape locomotion. Nature 379:156–159.

Mturi AA. 1976. New hominid from Lake Ndutu, Tanzania. Nature 262:484–485.

Muller R and MacDonald G. 1997. Glacial cycles and astronomical forcing. Science 277:215–218.

Musgrave JH. 1971. How dextrous was Neanderthal man? Nature 233:538–541.

Nakatusukasa M, Tsujikawa H, et al. 2003. Definitive evidence for tail loss in *Nacholapithecus*, an East African Miocene hominoid. J Hum Evol 45:179–186.

Napier J and Davis P. 1959. The fore-limb skeleton and associated remains of *Proconsul africanus*. Br Mus Nat Hist Fossil Mamm Afr 16:1–69.

Napier JR and Tobias PV. 1964. The case for *Homo habilis:* London: The Times.

Navarro A and Barton N. 2003. Chromosomal speciation and molecular divergence—Accelerated evolution in rearranged chromosomes. Science 300:321–324.

Nei M. 1987. Molecular evolutionary genetics. New York: Columbia University Press.

Nengo I and Rae R. 1992. New hominoid fossils from the early Miocene site of Songhor, Kenya. J Hum Evol 23:423–429.

Niewoehner W. 2001. Behavioral inferences from the Skhul/Qafzeh early modern human hand remains. Proc Natl Acad Sci USA 98:2979–2984.

Nishimura T, Mikami A, et al. 2003. Descent of the larynx in chimpanzee infants. Proc Natl Acad Sci USA 100:6930–6933.

Nordberg M. 1998. On the probability of Neanderthal ancestry. Am J Hum Gen 63:1237–1240.

Oakley KP. 1958a. The dating of Broken Hill (Rhodesian man). In: von Koenigswald GHR, editor. Hundert Jahre Neanderthaler. Utrecht: Kemink & Zoon. p 265–266.

Oakley KP. 1958b. Use of fire by Neandertal man and his precursors. In: Von Koenigswald GHR, editor. Hundert Jahre Neanderthaler. Utrecht: Kemink & Zoon. p 267–269.

Oakley KP. 1966. Exhibit: Discovery of part of skull of *Homo erectus* with Buda industry at Vértesszöllös, north-west Hungary. Proc Geol Soc London 1630:31–34.

O'Connell J and Allen J. 1998. When did humans first arrive in greater Australia and why is it important to know? Evol Anthropol 6:132–146.

O'Connell J, Hawkes K, et al. 2002. Male strategies and Plio-Pleistocene archaeology. J Hum Evol 43:831–872.

Oerlemans J and Fortuin J. 1992. Sensitivity of glaciers and small ice caps to greenhouse warming. Science 258:115–117.

Ohman J, Krochta T, et al. 1997. Cortical bone distribution in the femoral neck of hominoids: Implications for the locomotion of *Australopithecus afarensis*. Am J Phys Anthropol 104:117–131.

Oliva M. 1988. Discovery of a Gravettian mammoth bone hut at Milovice (Moravia, Czechoslovakia). J Hum Evol 17:787–790.

Olsen J and Ciochon R. 1990. A review of evidence for postulated Middle Pleistocene occupations in Viet Nam. J Hum Evol 19:761–788.

Olson EC. 1980. Taphonomy: Its history and role in community evolution. In: Behrensmeyer AK, Hill AP, editors. Fossils in the making. Chicago: University of Chicago Press. p 5–19.

Olson T. 1978. Hominid phylogenetics and the existence of *Homo* in member I of the Swartkrans formation. South Afr J Hum Evol 7:159–178.

Olson T. 1985. Cranial morphology and systematics of the Hadar Formation hominids and *Australopithecus africanus*. In: Delson E, editor. Ancestors: The hard evidence. New York: Liss. p 102–119.

Omar G and Steckler M. 1995. Fission track evidence on the initial rifting of the Red Sea: Two pulses, no propagation. Science 270:1341–1344.

Oms O, Parés J, et al. 2000. Early human occupation of western Europe: Paleomagnetic dates from two paleolithic sites in Spain. Proc Nat Acad Sci USA 97:10666–10670.

Ovchinnikov I, Götherström A, et al. 2000. Molecular analysis of Neanderthal DNA from the northern Caucasus. Nature 404:490–493.

Owen R. 1858. On the characters, principles of division, and primary groups of the class mammalia. J Linn Soc London Zool 2:1–37.

Owens K and King M-C. 1999. Genomic views of human history. Science 286:451–453.

Paciulli LM. 1995. Ontogeny of phalangeal curvature and positional behavior in chimpanzees. Am J Phys Anthropol Suppl 20:165.

Pagani M, Freeman K, et al. 1999. Late Miocene atmospheric CO_2 concentrations and the expansion of C_4 grasses. Science 285:876–879.

Panchen AL. 1992. Classification, evolution, and the nature of biology. Cambridge, UK: Cambridge University Press.

Parés J and Pérez-González A. 1999. Magnetochronology and stratigraphy at Gran Dolina section, Atapuerca (Burgos, Spain). J Hum Evol 37:325–342.

Parés J, Pérez-Gonzalez A, et al. 2000. On the age of the hominid fossils at the Sima de los Huesos, Sierra de Atapuerca, Spain: Paleomagnetic evidence. Am J Phys Anthropol 111:451–461.

Parés JM and Perez-Gonzalez A. 1995. Paleomagnetic age for hominid fossils at Atapuerca archaeological site, Spain. Science 269:830–832.

Parsons T, Muniec D, et al. 1997. A high observed substitution rate in the human mitochondrial DNA control region. Nature Gen 15:363–368.

Partridge T. 1986. Paleoecology of the Pliocene and Lower Pleistocene hominids of southern Africa: How good is the chronological and paleoenvironmental evidence? South Afr J Sci 82:80–83.

Partridge T, Granger D, et al. 2003. Lower Pliocene hominid remains from Sterkfontein. Science 300:607–612.

PARU (Palaeo-Anthropology Research Unit). 1994. Twenty-eighth annual report. Johannesburg: University of the Witwatersrand.

PARU (Palaeo-Anthropology Research Unit). 1995. Twenty-ninth annual report. Johannesburg: University of the Witwatersrand.

Patterson B and Howells W. 1967. Hominid humeral fragment from early Pleistocene of northwestern Kenya Science 156:64–66.

Patterson B, Behrensmeyer A, et al. 1970. Geology and fauna of a new Pliocene locality in north-western Kenya. Nature 226:918–921.

Patterson C, ed. 1987. Molecules and morphology in evolution: Conflict or compromise? Cambridge, UK: Cambridge University Press.

Patterson H. 1986. Environment and species. South Afr J Sci 82:62–65.

Pavlov P, Svenden J, et al. 2001. Human presence in the European Arctic nearly 40,000 years ago. Nature 413:64–67.

Pearson O. 2000. Postcranial remains and the origin of modern humans. Evol Anthropol 9:229–247.

Peterhans JC, Wrangham RW, et al. 1993. A contribution to tropical rain forest taphonomy: Retrieval and documentation of chimpanzee remains from Kibale Forest, Uganda. J Hum Evol 25:485–514.

Peters C. 1987. Nut-like oil seeds: Food for monkeys, chimpanzees, humans and probably ape-men. Am J Phys Anthropol 73:333–363.

Peters C and O'Brien E. 1981. The early hominid plant-food niche: Insights from an analysis of plant exploitation by *Homo, Pan,* and *Papio* in eastern and southern Africa. Curr Anthropol 22:127–140.

Pfeiffer S and Zehr M. 1996. A morphological and histological study of the human humerus from Border Cave. J Hum Evol 31:49–59.

Pickering T, White T, et al. 2000. Cutmarks on a Plio-Pleistocene hominid from Sterkfontein, South Africa. Am J Phys Anthropol 111:579–584.

Pickford M. 1981. Preliminary Miocene mammalian biostratigraphy for western Kenya. J Hum Evol 10:73–97.

Pickford M. 1982. New higher primate fossils from the middle Miocene deposits at Majiwa and Kaloma, Western Kenya. Am J Phys Anthropol 58:1–19.

Pickford M. 1983. Sequence and environments of the lower and middle Miocene hominoids of western Kenya. In: Ciochon R, Corruccini R, editors. New interpretations of ape and human ancestry. New York: Plenum. p 421–440.

Pickford M, Johanson D, et al. 1983. A hominoid humeral fragment from the Pliocene of Kenya. Am J Phys Anthropol 60:337–346.

Pickford M, Senut B, et al. 1991. Correlation of tephra layers from the western rift Valley (Uganda) to the Turkana Basin (Ethiopia/Kenya) and the Gulf of Aden. CR Acad Sci Paris 313:223–229.

Pickford M, Mein P, et al. 1994. Fossiliferous Neogene karst fillings in Angola, Botswana and Namibia. South Afr J Sci 90:227–230.

Pickford M, Senut B, et al. 1994. Phylogenetic position of *Otavipithecus:* Questions of methodology and approach. In: Thierry B, Anderson JR, et al., editors. Current primatology: Ecology and evolution. Strasbourg, France: Universite Louis Pasteur. p 265–272.

Pickford M and Senut B. 2001. The geological and faunal context of late Miocene hominid remains from Lukeino, Kenya. CR Acad Sci Paris 332:145–152.

Pilbeam D. 1969. Tertiary Pongidae of East Africa. Evolutionary relationships and taxonomy. Peabody Mus Nat Hist Yale Univ Bull 31:1–185.

Pilbeam D. 1982. New hominoid skull material from the Miocene of Pakistan. Nature 295:232–234.

Pilbeam D. 1992. What makes us human? In: Jones S, Martin R, et al., editors. The Cambridge encyclopedia of human evolution. Cambridge, UK: Cambridge University Press. p 1–5.

Pilbeam D. 1996. Genetic and morphological records of the Hominoidea and hominid origins. Mol Phylogen Evol 5:155–168.

Pilbeam D. 2002. Perspectives on the Miocene Hominoidea. In: Harrison T, editor. The primate fossil record. Cambridge, UK: Cambridge University Press. p 303–310.

Pilbeam D and Gould S. 1974. Size and scaling in human evolution. Science 186:892–901.

Pilbeam D, Meyer G, et al. 1977. New hominoid primates from the Siwaliks of Pakistan and their bearing on hominoid evolution. Nature 270:689–695.

Pilbeam D, Rose M, et al. 1980. Miocene hominoids from Pakistan. Postilla 181:1–94.

Pilbeam D and Smith R. 1981. New skull remains of *Sivapithecus* from Pakistan. Mem Geol Surv Pakistan 2:1–13.

Pilbeam D, Rose M, et al. 1990. New *Sivapithecus* humeri from Pakistan and the relationship of *Sivapithecus* and *Pongo*. Nature 348:237–239.

Pilbeam D, Morgan M, et al. 1997. European MN units and the Siwalik faunal sequence of Pakistan. In: Bernor R, Fahlbusch V, et al., editors. The evolution of western Eurasian Neogene mammal faunas. New York: Columbia University Press. p 96–105.

Pitulko V, Nikolsky P, et al. 2004. The Yana RHS site: Humans in the Artic before the last glacial maximum. Science 303:52–56.

Plavcan JM and Van Schaik C. 1994. Canine dimorphism. Evol Anthropol 2:208–214.

Plavcan JM, Van Schaik CP, et al. 1995. Competition, coalitions and canine size in primates. J Hum Evol 28:245–276.

Plavcan JM and Kelley J. 1996. Evaluating the "dual selection" hypothesis of canine reduction. Am J Phys Anthropol 99:379–387.

Ponce de León M and Zollikofer C. 1999. New evidence from Le Moustier 1: computer-assisted reconstruction and morphometry of the skull. Anat Rec 254:474–489.

Ponce de León M and Zollikofer C. 2001. Neanderthal cranial ontogeny and its implications for late hominid diversity. Nature 412:534–538.

Pope G. 1983. Evidence on the age of the Asian Hominidae. Proc Nat Acad Sci USA 80:4988–4992.

Pope G. 1988. Recent advances in Far Eastern Paleoanthropology. Ann Rev Anthropol 17:43–77.

Pope G. 1991. Evolution of the zygomaticomaxillary region in the genus *Homo* and its relevance to the origin of modern humans. J Hum Evol 21:189–213.

Pope G. 1992. Craniofacial evidence for the origin of modern humans in China. Year Phys Anthropol 35:243–298.

Pope G and Cronin J. 1984. The Asian Hominidae. J Hum Evol 13:377–396.

Pope G and Keates S. 1994. The evolution of human cognition and cultural capacity: A view from the Far East. In: Corruccini RS, Ciochon RL, editors. Integrative paths to the past. Englewood Cliffs, NJ: Prentice Hall. p 531–567.

Porat N and Schwarcz HP. 1994. ESR dating of tooth enamel. In: Corruccini RS, Ciochon RL, editors. Integrative paths to the past. Englewood Cliffs, NJ: Prentice Hall. p 521–530.

Porter AMW. 1993. Sweat and thermoregulation in hominids. Comments prompted by the publications of P. E. Wheeler 1984–1993. J Hum Evol 25:417–423.

Potts R. 1984. Home bases and early hominids. Am Sci 72:338–346.

Potts R. 1987. Transportation of resources: Reconstructions of early hominid socioecology: A critique of primate models. In: Kinzey WG, editor. The evolution of human behavior: Primate models. Albany: SUNY Albany. p 28–47.

Potts R. 1989. Olorgesailie: New excavations and findings in Early and Middle Pleistocene contexts, southern Kenya rift valley. J Hum Evol 18:477–484.

Potts R. 1992. The hominid way of life. In: Jones S, Martin R, et al., editors. The Cambridge encyclopedia of human evolution. Cambridge, UK: Cambridge University Press. p 325–334.

Potts R. 1993. Archeological interpretations of early hominid behavior and ecology. In: Rasmussen DT, editor. The origin and evolution of humans and humanness. Boston: Jones & Bartlett. p 49–74.

Potts R. 1998. Variability selection in hominid evolution. Evol Anthropol 7:81–96.

Potts R, Shipman P, et al. 1988. Taphonomy, paleoecology, and hominids of Lainyamok, Kenya. J Hum Evol 17:597–614.

Potts R, Behrensmeyer A, et al. 2004. Small Mid-Pleistocene hominin associated with East African Acheulean technology. Science 305:75–78.

Poulianos A. 1978. Correction of the English text on the summary article "Stratigraphy and Age of the Petralonian Archanthropus." Anthropos 5:264–266.

Prell W and Kutzback J. 1992. Sensitivity of the Indian monsoon to forcing parameters and implications for its evolution. Nature 360:647–651.

Prentice M and Denton G. 1988. The deep-sea oxygen isotope record, the global ice sheet system and hominid evolution. In: Grine FE, editor. Evolutionary history of the "robust" australopithecines. New York: Aldine de Gruyter. p 383–403.

Preuschoft H and Witte H. 1991. Biomechanical reasons for the evolution of hominid body shape. In: Coppen Y, Senut B, editors. Origine(s) de la bipedie chez les hominides. Paris: CNRS. p 59–77.

Pringle H. 1997. Ice age communities may be earliest known net hunters. Science 277:1203–1204.

Pritchard J and Feldman M. 1996. Genetic data and the African origin of humans. Science 274:1548.

Prossinger H, Seidler H, et al. 2003. Electronic removal of encrustations inside the Steinheim cranium reveals paranasal sinus features and deformations, and provides a revised endocranial volume estimate. Anat Rec 273B:132–142.

Protsch R. 1981. The Kohl-Larsen Eyasi and Garusi hominid finds in Tanzania and their relation to *Homo erectus*. In: Sigmon BA, Cybulski JS, editors. *Homo erectus:* Papers in honor of Davidson Black. Toronto: University of Toronto Press. p 217–226.

Puech P-F, Cianfarani F, et al. 1986. Reconstruction of the maxillary dental arcade of Garusi Hominid 1. J Hum Evol 15:325–332.

Qi G. 1990. The Pleistocene human environment of North China. Acta Anthropol Sinica 9:340–349.

Quade J, Cerling T, et al. 1989. Development of Asian monsoon revealed by marked ecological shift during the latest Miocene in northern Pakistan. Nature 342:163–166.

Radosevich SC, Retallack GJ, et al. 1992. Reassessment of the paleoenvironment and preservation of hominid fossils from Hadar, Ethiopia. Am J Phys Anthropol 87:15–27.

Rak Y. 1978. The functional significance of the squamosal suture in *Australopithecus boisei*. Am J Phys Anthropol 49:71–78.

Rak Y. 1983. The australopithecine face. New York: Academic Press.

Rak Y. 1985. Australopithecine taxonomy and phylogeny in light of facial morphology. Am J Phys Anthropol 66:281–287.

Rak Y. 1986. The Neanderthal: A new look at an old face. J Hum Evol 15:151–164.

Rak Y. 1991. Lucy's pelvic anatomy: Its role in bipedal gait. J Hum Evol 20:283–290.

Rak Y and Clarke R. 1979. Aspects of the middle and external ear of early South African hominids. Am J Phys Anthropol 51:471–474.

Rak Y, Kimbel WH, et al. 1994. A Neandertal infant from Amud Cave, Israel. J Hum Evol 26:313–324.

Rak Y, Kimbel W, et al. 1997. Insights from the new faces of *Australopithecus afarensis*. Am J Phys Anthropol Suppl 24:192.

Ramirez-Rozzi FV. 1993. Tooth development in East African *Paranthropus*.. J Hum Evol 24:429–454.

Ramirez-Rozzi FV. 1994. Enamel growth markers in hominid dentition. Eur Microscopy Anal. 21–23.

Rampino M and Self S. 1992. Volcanic winter and accelerated glaciation following the Toba super-eruption. Nature 359:50–52.

Ranov V, Carbonell E, et al. 1995. Kuldara: Earliest human occupation in Central Asia in its Afro-Asian context. Curr Anthropol 36:337–346.

Raymo M and Ruddiman W. 1992. Tectonic forcing of late Cenozoic climate. Nature 359:117–122.

Rayner R, Moon B, et al. 1993. The Makapansgat australopithecine environment. J Hum Evol 24:219–231.

Raza S, Barry J, et al. 1983. New hominoid primates from the middle Miocene, Chinji Formation, Potwar Plateau, Pakistan. Nature 306:52–54.

Reed K. 1997. Early hominid evolution and ecological change through the African Plio-Pleistocene. J Hum Evol 32:289–322.

Reed K, Kitching JW, et al. 1993. Proximal femur of *Australopithecus africanus* from member 4, Makapansgat, South Africa. Am J Phys Anthropol 92:1–15.

Reed K and Eck G. 1997. Paleoecology of the Plio-Pleistocene Hadar hominid localities. Am J Phys Anthropol Suppl 24:194.

Relethford J. 1995. Genetics and modern human origins. Evol Anthropol 4:53–63.

Relethford J. 1998. Genetics of modern human origins and diversity. Ann Rev Anthropol 27:1–23.

Relethford J. 1999. Models, predictions, and the fossil record of modern human origins. Evol Anthropol 8:7–10.

Relethford J. 2001a. Absence of regional affinities of Neandertal DNA with living humans does not reject multireigonal evolution. Am J Phys Anthropol 115:95–98.

Relethford J. 2001b. Ancient DNA and the origin of modern humans. Proc. Nat. Acad Sci USA 98:390–391.

Relethford J. 2001c. Genetic history of the human species. In: Balding D, Bishop M, et al., editors. Handbook of statistical genetics. Chichester, UK: Wiley. p 813–846.

Relethford J and Harpending H. 1994. Craniometric variation, genetic theory, and modern human origins. Am J Phys Anthropol 95:249–270.

Relethford J and Harpending H. 1995. Ancient differences in population size can mimic a recent African origin of modern humans. Curr Anthropol 36:667–674.

Relethford J and Jorde L. 1999. Genetic evidence for larger African population size during recent human evolution. Am J Phys Anthropol 108:251–260.

Renne P, Sharp W, et al. 1997. ^{40}Ar/^{39}Ar dating into the historical realm: Calibration against Pliny the Younger. Science 277:1279–1280.

Renne P, WoldeGabriel G, et al. 1999. Chronostratigraphy of the Miocene–Pliocene Sagantole Formation, Middle Awash valley, Afar rift, Ethiopia. GSA Bull 111:869–885.

Reno P, Meindl R, et al. 2003. Sexual dimorphism in *Australopithecus afarensis* was similar to that of modern humans. Proc Natl Acad Sci USA 100:9404–9409.

Retallack GJ, Dugas DP, et al. 1990. Fossil soils and grasses of a Middle Miocene East African grassland. Science 247:1325–1328.

Retallack GJ, Bestland EA, et al. 1995. Miocene paleosols and habitats of *Proconsul* on Rusinga Island, Kenya. J Hum Evol 29:53–91.

Reynolds TEG. 1991. Revolution or resolution? The archaeology of modern human origins. World Archaeol 23:155–166.

Richards DA, Smart PL, et al. 1994. Maximum sea levels for the last glacial period from U-series ages of submerged speleothems. Nature 367:357–360.

Richards M, Pettitt P, et al. 2000. Neanderthal diet at Vindija and Neanderthal predation: The evidence from stable isotopes. Proc Natl Acad Sci USA 97:7663–7666.

Richmond B and Jungers WL. 1995. Size variation and sexual dimorphism in *Australopithecus afarensis* and living hominoids. J Hum Evol 29:229–245.

Richmond B and Strait D. 2000. Evidence that humans evolved from a knuckle-walking ancestor. Nature 404:382–385.

Richmond B, Begun D, et al. 2001. Origin of human bipedalism: The knuckle-walking hypothesis revisited. Am J Phys Anthropol 44:70–105.

Richmond B and Strait D. 2001. Did our ancestors knuckle-walk? Nature 410:324–326.

Richmond B, Aiello L, et al. 2002. Early hominin limb proportions. J Hum Evol 43:529–548.

Ricklan DE. 1987. Functional anatomy of the hand of *Australopithecus africanus*. J Hum Evol 16:643–664.

Ridley M. 1986. Evolution and classification: The reformation of cladism. New York: Longman.

Rigaud J-P. 1989. From the Middle to the Upper Paleolithic: Transition or convergence? In: Trinkaus E, editor. The emergence of modern humans. Cambridge, UK: Cambridge University Press. p 142–153.

Rightmire G. 1981a. *Homo erectus* at Olduvai Gorge, Tanzania. In: Sigmon BA, Cybulski, JS, editors. *Homo erectus:* Papers in honor of Davidson Black. Toronto: University of Toronto Press. p 189–192.

Rightmire G. 1981b. Patterns in the evolution of *Homo erectus*. Paleobiology 7:241–246.

Rightmire G. 1983. The Lake Ndutu cranium and early *Homo sapiens* in Africa. Am J Phys Anthropol 61:245–254.

Rightmire G. 1984. Comparisons of *Homo erectus* from Africa and Southeast Asia. Cour Forsch Inst Senckenberg 69:83–98.

Rightmire G. 1988. *Homo erectus* and later Middle Pleistocene humans. Ann Rev Anthropol 17:239–259.

Rightmire G. 1989. Middle Stone Age humans from eastern and southern Africa. In: Mellars P, Stringer C, editors. The human revolution. Princeton, NJ: Princeton University Press. p 109–122.

Rightmire G. 1990. The evolution of *Homo erectus*. Cambridge, UK: Cambridge University Press.

Rightmire G. 1992. *Homo erectus:* Ancestor or evolutionary side branch? Evol Anthropol 1:43–49.

Rightmire G. 1993. Variation among early *Homo* crania from Olduvai Gorge and the Koobi Fora region. Am J Phys Anthropol 90:1–33.

Rightmire G. 1996. The human cranium from Bodo, Ethiopia: Evidence for speciation in the Middle Pleistocene? J Hum Evol 31:21–39.

Rightmire G and Deacon H. 1991. Comparative studies of Late Pleistocene human remains from Klasies River Mouth, South Africa. J Hum Evol 20:131–156.

Rightmire G and Deacon H. 2001. New human teeth from Middle Stone Age deposits at Klasies River, South Africa. J Hum Evol 41:535–544.

Rink W, Schwarcz H, et al. 1995. ESR ages for Krapina hominids. Nature 378:24.

Rink W, Schwarcz H, et al. 1996. ESR dating of Micoquian industry and Neanderthal remains at Külna Cave, Czech Republic. J Archaeol Sci 23:889–901.

Riscutia C. 1975. A study on the Modjokerto infant calvarium. In: Tuttle RH, editor. Paleoanthropology, morphology and paleoecology. The Hague: Mouton. p 374–375.

Roberts M. 1994. How old is "Boxgrove man"? Nature 371:751.

Roberts M, Stringer C, et al. 1994. A hominid tibia from Middle Pleistocene sediments at Boxgrove, UK. Nature 369:311–313.

Roberts N. 1992. Climatic change in the past. In: Jones S, Martin R, et al., editors. The Cambridge encyclopedia of human evolution. Cambridge, UK: Cambridge University Press. p 174–178.

Roberts R, Jones R, et al. 1990. Thermoluminescence dating of a 50,000-year-old human occupation site in northern Australia. Nature 345:153–156.

Roberts R, Bird M, et al. 1998. Optical and radiocarbon dating at Jinmium rock shelter in northern Australia. Nature 393:358–362.

Robinson J. 1956. The dentition of the Australopithecinae. Pretoria: Transvaal Museum Memoirs.

Robinson J. 1960. The affinities of the new Olduvai australopithecine. Nature 186:456–458.

Robinson J. 1961. The australopithecines and their bearing on the origin of man and of stone tool-making. South Afr J Sci 57:3–16.

Robinson J. 1963. Adaptive radiation in the australopithecines and the origin of man. In: Howell FC, Bourliere F, editors. African ecology and human evolution. Chicago: Aldine. p 385–416.

Robinson J. 1965. *Homo "habilis"* and the australopithecines. Nature 205:121–124.

Robinson J. 1972. Early hominid posture and locomotion. Chicago: University of Chicago Press.

Roche H, Delagnes A, et al. 1999. Early hominid stone tool production and technical skill 2.34 myr ago in West Turkana, Kenya. Nature 399:57–60.

Rodman P and McHenry H. 1980. Bioenergetics and the origin of hominid bipedalism. Am J Phys Anthropol 52:103–106.

Roebroeks W. 1994. Updating the earliest occupation of Europe. Curr Anthropol 35:301–305.

Roebroeks W. 2001. Hominid behaviour and the earliest occupation of Europe: An exploration. J Hum Evol 41:437–461.

Roebroeks W, Conard N, et al. 1992. Dense forests, cold steppes, and the Palaeolithic settlement of Northern Europe. Curr Anthropol 33:551–586.

Roebroeks W and Kolfschoten T. 1994. The earliest occupation of Europe: A short chronology. Antiquity 68:489–503.

Rogers A. 1995. Genetic evidence for a Pleistocene population explosion. Evolution 49:608–615.

Rogers A and Jorde L. 1995. Genetic evidence on modern human origins. Hum Biol 67:1–36.

Rogers J. 1994. Levels of the genealogical hierarchy and the problem of hominoid phylogeny. Am J Phys Anthropol 94:81–88.

Rogers J and Comuzzie A. 1995. When is ancient polymorphism a potential problem for molecular phylogenetics? Am J Phys Anthropol 98:216–218.

Rohling E, Fenton M, et al. 1998. Magnitudes of sea-level low stands of the past 500,000 years. Nature 394:162–165.

Romm J. 1994. A new forerunner for continental drift. Nature 367:407–408.

Roosevelt A, da Costa M, et al. 1996. Paleoindian cave dwellers in the Amazon: The peopling of the Americas. Science 272:373–384.

Roper M. 1969. A survey of the evidence for intrahuman killing in the Pleistocene. Curr Anthropol 10:427–459.

Rosas A. 1987. Two new mandibular fragments from Atapuerca/Ibeas (SH site). A reassessment of the affinities of the Ibeas mandibles sample. J Hum Evol 16:417–427.

Rosas A. 1997. A gradient of size and shape for the Atapuerca sample and Middle Pleistocene hominid variability. J Hum Evol 33:319–331.

Rosas A. 2001. Occurrence of Neanderthal features in mandibles from the Atapuerca-SH site. Am J Phys Anthropol 114:74–91.

Rosas A, Bastir M, et al. 2002. Sexual dimorphism in the Atapuerca-SH hominids: The evidence from the mandibles. J Hum Evol 42:451–474.

Rose L and Marshall F. 1996. Meat eating, hominid sociality, and home bases revisited. Curr Anthropol 37:307–338.

Rose M. 1984. A hominine hip bone, KNM-ER 3228, from East Lake Turkana, Kenya. Am J Phys Anthropol 63:371–378.

Rose M. 1986. Further hominoid postcranial specimens from the late Miocene Nagri Formation of Pakistan. J Hum Evol 15:333–367.

Rose M. 1988. Another look at the anthropoid elbow. J Hum Evol 17:193–224.

Rose M. 1989. New postcranial specimens of catarrhines from the middle Miocene Chinji Formation, Pakistan: Descriptions and a discussion of proximal humeral functional morphology in anthropoids. J Hum Evol 18:131–162.

Rose M. 1992. Kinematics of the trapezium-1st metacarpal joint in extant anthropoids and Miocene hominoids. J Hum Evol 22:255–266.

Rose M. 1994. Quadrupedalism in some Miocene catarrhines. J Hum Evol 26:387–411.

Rose M, Leakey M, et al. 1992. Postcranial specimens of *Simiolus enjiessi* and other primitive catarrhines from the early Miocene of Lake Turkana, Kenya. J Hum Evol 22:171–237.

Rosenberg K. 1988. The functional significance of Neandertal pubic length. Curr Anthropol 29:595–617.

Rosenberg K. 1992. The evolution of modern human childbirth. Yearbk Phys Anthropol 35:89–124.

Rosenberg K and Trevathan W. 1996. Bipdalism and human birth: The obstetrical dilemma revisited. Evol Anthropol 4:161–168.

Rosenberg K and Lu D. 1997. The pelvis of the Jinniushan specimen. Am J Phys Anthropol Suppl 24:199.

Rosenberg N, Pritchard J, et al. 2002. Genetic structure of human populations. Science 298:2381–2385.

Ross C and Henneberg M. 1995. Basicranial flexion, relative brain size, and facial kyphosis in *Homo sapiens* and some fossil hominids. Am J Phys Anthropol 98:575–593.

Rouhani S. 1989. Molecular genetics and the pattern of human evolution: Plausible and implausible models. In: Mellars P, Stringer C, editors. The human revolution. Princeton, NJ: Princeton University Press. p 47–61.

Ruano G, Rogers J, et al. 1992. DNA sequence polymorphism within hominoid species exceeds the number of phylogenetically informative characters of a HOX2 locus. Mol Biol Evol 9:575–586.

Ruff C. 1991. Climate and body shape in hominid evolution. J Hum Evol 21:81–105.

Ruff C. 1993. Climatic adaptation and hominid evolution: The thermoregulatory imperative. Evol Anthropol 2:53–60.

Ruff C. 1994. Morphological adaptation to climate in modern and fossil hominids. Yearbk Phys Anthropol 37:65–107.

Ruff C. 1995. Biomechanics of the hip and birth in early *Homo*. Am J Phys Anthropol 98:527–574.

Ruff C. 2003. Long bone articular and diaphyseal structure in Old World monkeys and apes. II: Estimation of body mass. Am J Phys Anthropol 120:16–37.

Ruff C, Walker A, et al. 1989. Body mass, sexual dimorphism and femoral proportions of *Proconsul* from Rusinga and Mfangano Islands, Kenya. J Hum Evol 18:515–536.

Ruff C and Walker A. 1993. The body size and body shape of KNM-WT 15000. In: Walker A, Leakey RE, editors. The Nariokotome *Homo erectus* skeleton. Cambridge, MA: Harvard University Press. p 234–265.

Ruff C, Trinkaus E, et al. 1997. Body mass and encephalization in Pleistocene *Homo*. Nature 387:173–176.

Ruff C, McHenry H, et al. 1999. Cross-sectional morphology of the SK 82 and 97 proximal femora. Am J Phys Anthropol 109:509–521.

Russ J, Hyman M, et al. 1990. Radiocarbon dating of prehistoric rock paintings by selective oxidation of organic carbon. Nature 348:710–711.

Ruvolo M. 1994. Molecular evolutionary processes and conflicting gene trees: The hominoid case. Am J Phys Anthrop 94:89–113.

Ruvulo M. 1995. Seeing the forest and the trees. Am J Phys Anthropol 98:218–232.

Ryan A. 1979. Wear striation direction on primate teeth: A scanning electron microscope examination. Am J Phys Anthropol 50:155–168.

Sage R and Wolff J. 1986. Pleistocene glaciations, fluctuating ranges, and low genetic variability in a large mammal (*Ovis dalli*). Evolution 40:1092–1095.

Saitou N. 1991. Reconstruction of molecular phylogeny of extant hominoids from DNA sequence data. Am J Phys Anthropol 84:75–85.

Samollow P, Cherry L, et al. 1996. Interspecific variation at the Y-linked RPS4Y locus in hominoids: Implications for phylogeny. Am J Phys Anthropol 101:333–343.

Sanders W. 1998. Comparative morphometric study of the australopithecine vertebral series Stw-H8/H41. J Hum Evol 34:249–302.

Santa Luca A. 1978. A re-examination of presumed Neanderal-like fossils. J Hum Evol 7:619–636.

Santa Luca A. 1980. The Ngandong fossil hominids. Yale Univ Publ Anthropol 78:1–175.

Santayana G. 1905. The life of reason. New York: Scribner's.

Sarich V. 1971. A molecular approach to the question of human origins. In: Dolhinow P, Sarich V, editors. Background for man. Boston: Little, Brown. p 60–81.

Sarich V and Wilson A. 1967. Immunological time scale for hominid evolution. Science 158:1200–1203.

Sarich V and Cronin J. 1976. Molecular systematics of the primates. In: Goodman M, Tashian R, editors. Molecular anthropology. New York: Plenum. p 141–170.

Sartono S. 1975. Implications arising from *Pithcanthropus* VIII. In: Tuttle RH, editor. Paleoanthropology, morphology, and paleoecology. The Hague: Mouton. p 327–360.

Schenk ET and McMasters JH. 1936. Procedure in taxonomy. Stanford, CA: Stanford University Press.

Schick KD and Zhuan D. 1993. Early paleolithic of China and Eastern Asia. Evol Anthropol 2:22–35.

Schick KD. 1994. The Movius line reconsidered. In: Corruccini RS, Ciochon RL, editors. Integrative paths to the past. Englewood Cliffs, NJ: Prentice Hall. p 569–596.

Schlosser M. 1903. Die fossielen saugetiere Chinas. Abhandl Bayerische Akad Wissenschaften 22:1–221.

Schmid P. 1991. The trunk of the australopithecines. In: Coppens Y, Senut B, editors. Origine(s) de la bipedie chez les hominides. Paris: CNRS. p 225–234.

Schoeninger M. 1995. Stable isotope studies in human evolution. Evol Anthropol 4:83–98.

Schrag D, Hampt G, et al. 1996. Pore fluid constraints on the temperature and oxygen isotopic composition of the glacial ocean. Science 272:1930–1932.

Schrenk R, Bromage TG, et al. 1993 Oldest *Homo* and Pliocene biogeography of the Malawi Rift. Nature 365:833–835.

Schultz A. 1968. The recent hominoid primates. In: Washburn S, Jay P, editors. Perspective on human evolution. New York: Holt, Rinehart & Winston. p 122–195.

Schultz A. 1969. The Life of Primates. New York: Universe Books.

Schwarcz H. 1992a. Uranium series dating in paleoanthropology. Evol Anthropol 1:56–62.

Schwarcz H. 1992b. Uranium-series dating and the origin of modern man. Phil Trans R Soc Biol Sci 337:131–137.

Schwarcz H, Grün R, et al. 1988a. The Bilzingsleben archaeological site: New dating evidence. Archaeometry 30:5–17.

Schwarcz H, Grün R, et al. 1988b. ESR dates for the hominid burial site of Qafzeh in Israel. J Hum Evol 17:733–737.

Schwarcz H, Buhay W, et al. 1989. ESR dating of the Neanderthal site, Kebara Cave, Israel. J Archaeol Sci 16:653–659.

Schwarcz H, Bietti A, et al. 1991. On the reexamination of Grotta Guattari: Uranium-series and electron-spin-resonance dates. Curr Anthropol 32:313–316.

Schwarcz H and Grün R. 1992. Electron spin resonance (ESR) dating of the origin of modern man. Phil Trans R Soc Biol Sci 337:145–148.

Schwarcz H, Grün R, et al. 1996. ESR dating studies of the australopithecine site of Sterkfontein, South Africa. J Hum Evol 26:175–181.

Schwarcz H, Simpson J, et al. 1998. Neanderthal skeleton from Tabun: U-series data by gamma-ray spectrometry. J Hum Evol 35:635–645.

Schwarcz H and Rink W. 2000. ESR dating of the Die Kelders Cave 1 Site, South Africa. J Hum Evol 38:121–128.

Schwartz G. 1997. Patterning of enamel thickness in the postcanine dentition of *A. africanus*, *P. robustus* and early *Homo* from South Africa. Am J Phys Anthropol Suppl 24:206–207.

Schwartz J. 1990. *Lufengpithecus* and its potential relationship to an orang-utan clade. J Hum Evol 19:591–605.

Schwartz J and Tattersall I. 1996. Significance of some previously unrecognized apomorphies in the nasal region of *Homo neanderthalensis*. Proc Natl Acad Sci USA 93:10852–10854.

Schwartz J and Tattersall I. 2000. The human chin revisited: What is it and who has it? J Hum Evol 38:367–409.

Semah F, Semah A-M, et al. 1992. Did they also make stone tools? J Hum Evol 23:439–446.

Semaw S, Harris JWK, et al. 1995. New results from the Plio-Pleistocene deposits of the Gona area during the 1994 field season. Paper presented at the Paleoanthropology Society Conference, Oakland, CA.

Semaw S, Renne P, et al. 1997. 2.5-million-year-old stone tools from Gona, Ethiopia. Nature 385:333–336.

Semaw S, Rogers M, et al. 2003. 2.6-million-year-old stone tools and associated bones from OGS-6 and OGS-7, Gona, Afar, Ethiopia. J Hum Evol 45:169–177.

Senut B. 1989. Climbing as a crucial preadaptation for human bipedalism. OSSA 14:35–44.

Senut B and Tardieu C. 1985. Functional aspects of Plio-Pleistocene hominid limb bones: Implications for taxonomy and phylogeny. In Delson E, editor: Ancestors: The hard evidence. New York: Liss. p 193–201.

Senut B, Pickford M, et al. 2001. First hominid from the Miocene (Lukeino Formation, Kenya). CR Acad Sci Paris 332:137–144.

Sept J. 1992. Was there no place like home? A new perspective on early hominid archaeological sites from the mapping of Chimpanzee nests. Curr Anthropol 33:187–207.

Shackleton N. 1987. Oxygen isotopes, ice volume and sea level. Q Sci Rev 6:183–190.

Shackleton N, Backman J, et al. 1984. Oxygen isotope calibration of the onset of ice-rafting and history of glaciation in the North Atlantic region. Nature 307:620–623.

Shapiro H. 1974. Peking man. New York: Simon & Schuster.

Shapiro H. 1981. Davidson Black: An appreciation. In: Sigmon BA, Cybulski JS, editors. *Homo erectus:* Papers in honor of Davidson Black. Toronto: University of Toronto Press. p 21–26.

Shapiro L. 1993. Evaluation of "unique" aspects of human vertebral bodies and pedicles with a consideration of *Australopithecus africanus.* J Hum Evol 25:433–470.

Shea J. 1998. Neandertal and early modern human behavioral variability. Curr Anthropol 39:S45–S78.

Shea J. 2003. Neandertals, competition, and the origin of modern human behavior in the Levant. Curr Anthropol 12:173–187.

Shen G and Jin L. 1991. Restudy of the upper age of Beijing man site. Acta Anthropol Sinica 10:277.

Shen G, Teh-Lung K, et al. 1996. Preliminary results on U-Series dating of Peking man site with high precision TIMS. Acta Anthropol Sinica 15:216–217.

Shen G, Ku T, et al. 2001. High-precision U-series dating of Locality 1 at Zhoukoudian, China. J Hum Evol 41:679–688.

Shen G, Wang W, et al. 2002 U-series dating of Liujiang hominid site in Guangxi, southern China. J Hum Evol 43:817–829.

Shipman P. 1983. Early hominid lifestyle: Hunting and gathering or foraging, and scavenging? In: Clutton-Brock J, Grigson C, editors. Animals and Archaeology. Oxford, UK: BAR International Series. p 31–49.

Shipman P. 1987. An age-old question: Why did the human lineage survive. Discovery, Apr, 60–64.

Shipman P. 1994. Those ears were made for walking. New Scientist, July 30:26–29.

Shipman P and Phillips J. 1976. On scavenging by hominids and other carnivores. Curr Anthropol 17:170–172.

Shipman P and Phillips-Conroy J. 1977. Hominid tool-making versus carnivore scavenging. Am J Phys Anthropol 46:77–86.

Shipman P, Bosler W, et al. 1981a. Butchering of giant geladas at an Acheulian site. Curr Anthropol 22:257–268.

Shipman P, Walker A, et al. 1981b. The Fort Ternan hominoid site, Kenya: Geology, age, taphonomy and paleoecology. J Hum Evol 10:49–72.

Shipman P and Rose J. 1983. Early hominid hunting, butchering, and carcass-processing behaviors: Approaches to the fossil record. J Anthropol Archaeol 2:57–98.

Shipman P and Harris J. 1988. Habitat preference and paleoecology of *Australopithecus boisei* in eastern Africa. In: Grine FE, editor. Evolutionary history of the "robust" australopithecines. New York: de Gruyter. p 343–381.

Sibley C. 1992. DNA-DNA hybridisation in the study of primate evolution. In: Jones S, Martin R, et al., editors. The Cambridge encyclopedia of human evolution. Cambridge, UK: Cambridge University Press. p 313–315.

Sibley C and Ahlquist J. 1984. The phylogeny of the hominoid primates as indicated by DNA-DNA hybridization. J Mol Evol 20:2–15.

Sibley C and Ahlquist J. 1987. DNA hybridization evidence of hominid phylogeny: Results from an expanded data set. J Mol Evol 26:99–121.

Sighinolfie GP, Sartono S, et al. 1993. Chemical and mineralogical studies on hominid remains from Sangiran, central Java (Indonesia). J Hum Evol 24:57–68.

Sikes NE. 1994. Early hominid habitat preferences in East Africa: Paleosol carbon isotopic evidence. J Hum Evol 27:25–45.

Sillen A. 1992. Strontium-calcium ratios (Sr/Ca) of *Australopithecus robustus* and associated fauna from Swartkrans. J Hum Evol 23:495–516.

Sillen A. 1996. Physiological variability and Sr/Ca at Swartkrans. J Hum Evol 30:381–384.

Sillen A and Hoering T. 1993. Chemical characterization of burnt bones from Swartkrans. In: Brain CK, editor. Swartkrans: A cave's chronicle of early man. Pretoria: Transvaal Museum. p 243–249.

Sillen A, Hall G, et al. 1995. Strontium calcium ratios (Sr/CA) and strontium isotopic ratios (^{87}Sr/^{86}Sr) of *Australopithecus robustus* and *Homo* sp. from Swartkrans. J Hum Evol 28:277–285.

Sillen A and Morris A. 1996. Diagenesis of bone from Border Cave: Implications for the age of the Border Cave hominids. J Hum Evol 31:499–506.

Silverman N, Richmond B, et al. 2001. Testing the taxonomic integrity of *Paranthropus boisei sensu stricto*. Am J Phys Anthropol 115:167–178.

Simmons T, Falsetti AB, et al. 1991. Frontal bone morphometrics of southwest Asian Pleistocene hominids. J Hum Evol 20:249–269.

Simons E. 1972. Primate evolution. New York: Macmillan.

Simons E and Pilbeam D. 1965. Preliminary revision of the Dryopithecinae (Pongidae, Anthropoidea). Folia Primatol 3:81–152.

Simons E and Pilbeam D. 1978. *Ramapithecus*. In: Maglio VJ, Cooke HBS, editors. Evolution of african mammals. Cambridge, MA: Harvard University Press. p 147–153.

Simpson G. 1953. The major features of evolution. New York: Columbia University Press.

Simpson G. 1963a. The meaning of taxonomic statements. In: Washburn S, editor. Classification and human evolution. Chicago: Aldine. p 1–31.

Simpson G. 1963b. Principles of animal taxonomy. Oxford, UK: Oxford University Press.

Simpson G. 1975. Recent advances in methods of phylogenetic inference. In: Luckett W, Szalay F, editors. Phylogeny of the primates: A multidisciplinary approach. New York: Plenum. p 3–19.

Singer R. 1958. The Rhodesian, Florisbad and Saldanha skulls. In: von Koenigswald GHR, editor. Hundert Jahre Neanderthaler. Utrecht: Kemink & Zoon. p 52–62.

Singer R and Wymer J. 1982. The Middle Stone Age at Klasies River mouth in South Africa. Chicago: University of Chicago Press.

Skelton R, McHenry H, et al. 1986. Phylogenetic analysis of early hominids. Curr Anthropol 27:21–43.

Skelton R and McHenry H. 1992. Evolutionary relationships among early hominids. J Hum Evol 23:309–349.

Skinner J and Smithers R. 1990. The mammals of the southern African subregion. Pretoria: University of Pretoria.

Skinner M. 1991. Bee brood consumption: An alternative explanation for hypervitaminosis A in KNM-ER 1808 (*Homo erectus*) from Koobi Fora, Kenya. J Hum Evol 20:493–503.

Sládek V, Trinkaus E, et al. 2002. Morphological affinities of the Sal'a 1 frontal bone. J Hum Evol 43:787–815.

Slowey N, Henderson G, et al. 1996. Direct U-Th dating of marine sediments from the two most recent interglacial periods. Nature 383:242–244.

Smith B. 1986. Dental development in *Australopithecus* and early *Homo*. Nature 323:327–330.

Smith B. 1993. Physiological age of KNM-WT 15000. In: Walker A, Leakey R, editors. The Nariokotome *Homo erectus* skeleton. Cambridge, MA: Harvard University Press. p 195–220.

Smith B. 1994. Patterns of dental development in *Homo, Australopithecus, Pan,* and *Gorilla.* Am J Phys Anthropol 94:307–325.

Smith B, Brandt K, et al. 1995. Developmental age of the KMN-WT 15000 *Homo erectus* in broad perspective. Am J Phys Anthropol Suppl 20:196–197.

Smith C, Chamberlain A, et al. 2003. The thermal history of human fossils and the likelihood of successful DNA amplification. J Hum Evol 45:203–217.

Smith F. 1978. Some conclusions regarding the morphology and significance of the Krapina Neandertal remains. Jugoslav akad znan umjet 1:103–118.

Smith F. 1982. Upper Pleistocene hominid evolution in south-central Europe: A review of the evidence and analysis of trends. Curr Anthropol 23:667–686.

Smith F. 1992. Models and realities in modern human origins: The African fossil evidence. Phil Trans R Soc Biol Sci 337:243–250.

Smith F. 2002. Migrations, radiations and continuity: Patterns in the evolution of Middle and Late Pleistocene humans. In: Hartwig W, editor. The primate fossil record. Cambridge, UK: Cambridge University Press. p 437–456.

Smith F, Falsetti A, et al. 1989. Modern human origins. Yearbk Phys Anthropol 32:35–68.

Smith F and Paquette S. 1989. The adaptive basis of Neandertal facial form, with some thoughts on the nature of modern human origins. In: Trinkaus E, editor. The emergence of modern humans. Cambridge UK: Cambridge University Press. p 181–210.

Smith F and Ahern J. 1994. Additional cranial remains from Vindija cave, Croatia. Am J Phys Anthropol 93:275–280.

Smith F, Trinkaus E, et al. 1999. Direct radiocarbon dates for Vindija G1 and Velika Pecína Late Pleistocene hominid remains. Proc Nat Acad Sci USA 96:12281–12286.

Smith R, Gannon P, et al. 1995. Ontogeny of australopithecines and early *Homo:* Evidence from cranial capacity and dental eruption. J Hum Evol 29:155–168.

Smith S. 1995. Pattern profile analysis of hominid and chimpanzee hand bones. Am J Phys Anthropol 96:283–300.

Smith T, Martin L, et al. 2003. Enamel thickness, microstructure and development in *Afropithecus turkanensis.* J Hum Evol 44:283–306.

Soffer-Bobyshev O. 1988. Late Paleolithic. In: Tattersall I, Delson E, and Van Couvering JA, editors. Encyclopedia of human evolution and prehistory. New York: Garland. p 304–309.

Sohn S and Wolpoff MH. 1993. Zuttiyeh: A view from the East. Am J Phys Anthropol 91:325–347.

Solan M and Day M. 1992. The Baringo (Kapthurin) ulna. J Hum Evol 22:307–313.

Sorensen M and Leonard W. 2001. Neandertal energetics and foraging efficiency. J Hum Evol 40:483–495.

Spencer F. 1990. Piltdown: A scientific forgery. London: Oxford University Press.

Spencer L. 1997. Dietary adaptations of Plio-Pleistocene Bovidae: Implications for hominid habitat use. J Hum Evol 32:201–228.

Spencer MA and Demes B. 1993. Biomechanical analysis of masticatory system configuration in Neandertals and Inuits. Am J Phys Anthropol 91:1–20.

Speth J. 1989. Early hominid hunting and scavenging: The role of meat as an energy source. J Hum Evol 18:329–343.

Sponheimer M and Lee-Thorp J. 1999. Isotopic evidence for the diet of an early hominid, *Australopithecus africanus.* Science 283:368–370.

Spoor F. 1993. The comparative morphology and phylogeny of the human bony labyrinth. Utrecht: Universiteit Utrecht.

Spoor F, Hublin J, et al. 2003. The bony labyrinth of Neanderthals. J Hum Evol 44:141–165.

Spoor F, Wood B, et al. 1994. Implications of early hominid labyrinthine morphology for evolution of human bipedal locomotion. Nature 369:645–648.

Spoor F and Zonneveld F. 1999. Computed tomography-based three-dimensional imaging of hominid fossils: Features of the Broken Hill 1, Wadjak 1, and SK 47 crania. In: Koppe T, Nagai H, et al., editors. The paranasal sinuses of higher primates: Development, function, and evolution. Chicago: Quintessence. p 207–226.

Stanford C. 1995. The hunting ecology of chimpanzees: Implications for Pliocene hominid behavioral ecology. Am J Phys Anthropol Suppl 20:201.

Stanford C. 1996. The hunting ecology of wild chimpanzees: Implications for the evolutionary ecology of Pliocene hominids. Am Anthropol 98:96–113.

Stanford C and Allen J. 1991. On strategic storytelling: Current models of human behavioral evolution. Curr Anthropol 32:58–61.

Stanford C, Wallis J, et al. 1994. Patterns of predation by chimpanzees on red colobus monkeys in Gombe National Park, 1982–1991. Am J Phys Anthropol 94:213–228.

Stanley S. 1992. An ecological theory for the origin of *Homo*. Paleobiology 18:237–257.

Stefan V and Trinkaus E. 1998. Discrete trait and dental morphometric affinities of the Tabun 2 mandible. J Hum Evol 34:443–468.

Stern J and Susman R. 1981. Electromyography of the gluteal muscles in *Hylobates, Pongo,* and *Pan:* Implications for the evolution of hominid bipedality. Am J Phys Anthrop 55:153–166.

Stern J and Susman R. 1983. The locomotor anatomy of *Australopithecus afarensis*. Am J Phys Anthropol 60:279–317.

Stern J and Susman R. 1991. "Total morphological pattern" versus the "magic trait"? In: Coppens Y, Senut B, editors. Origine(s) de la bipedie chez les hominides. Paris: CNRS. p 121–131.

Steudel K. 1994. Locomotor energetics and hominid evolution. Evol Anthrop 3:42–48.

Steudel K. 1996. Limb morphology, bipedal gait, and the energetics of hominid locomotion. Am J Phys Anthropol 99:345–355.

Steudel-Numbers K. 2003. The energetic cost of locomotion: Human and primates compared to generalized endotherms. J Hum Evol 44:255–262.

Stewart C and Disotell T. 1998. Primate evolution—In and out of Africa. Curr Biol 8:R582–R588.

Stewart T. 1960. Form of the pubic bone in Neanderthal man. Science 131:1437–1438.

Stewart T. 1961. The skull of Shanidar II. Sumer 17:97–106.

Stewart T. 1962. Neanderthal scapulae with special attention to the Shanidar Neanderthals from Iraq. Anthropos 57:779–800.

Stiner M. 1991. The faunal remains from Grotta Guattari: A taphonomic perspective. Curr Anthropol 32:103–117.

Stiner M, Munro N, et al. 1999. Paleolithic population growth pulses evidences by small animal exploitation. Science 283:190–194.

Stokes S, Thomas D, et al. 1997. Multiple episodes of aridity in southern Africa since the last interglacial period. Nature 388:154–158.

Stone T and Cupper M. 2003. Last glacial maximum ages for robust humans at Kow Swamp, southern Australia. J Hum Evol 45:99–111.

Stoneking M. 1993. DNA and recent human evolution. Evol Anthropol 2:60–73.

Stoneking M, Bhatia K, et al. 1986. Rate of sequence divergence estimated from restricted maps of mitochondrial DNAs from Papua New Guinea. Cold Sprint Harbor Symp Quant Biol 51:433–439.

Stoneking M and Cann RL. 1989. African origin of human mitochondrial DNA. In: Mellars P, Stringer C, editors. The human revolution. Princeton, NJ: Princeton University Press. p 17–30.

Stoneking M, Sherry ST, et al. 1992. New approaches to dating suggest a recent age for the human mtDNA ancestor. Phil Trans R Soc Biol Sci 337:167–175.

Storey BC. 1995. The role of mantle plumes in continental breakup: Case histories from Gondwanaland. Nature 377:301–308.

Strait D. 2001. Integration, phylogeny, and the hominid cranial base. Am J Phys Anthropol 2001:273–297.

Strait D, Grine F, et al. 1997. A reappraisal of early hominid phylogeny. J Hum Evol 32:17–82.

Straus L. 1994. Upper Paleolithic origins and radiocarbon calibration: More new evidence from Spain. Evol Anthropol 2:195–198.

Straus L. 1995. The Upper Paleolithic of Europe: An overview. Evol Anthropol 4:4–16.

Straus W and Cave A. 1957. Pathology and the posture of Neanderthal man. Q Rev Biol 32:348–363.

Strauss E. 1999. Can mitochondrial clocks keep time? Science 283:1435–1438.

Streeter M, Stout S, et al. 2001. Histomorphometric age assessment of the Boxgrove 1 tibial diaphysis. J Hum Evol 30:331–338.

Stringer C. 1984. The definition of *Homo erectus* and the existence of the species in Africa and Europe. Cour Forsch Inst Senckenberg 69:131–143.

Stringer C. 1985. Middle Pleistocene hominid variability and the origin of late Pleistocene humans. In Delson E, editor. Ancestors: The hard evidence. New York: Liss. p 289–295.

Stringer C. 1986. The credibility of *Homo habilis*. In: Wood B, Martin L, et al., editors. Major topics in primate and human evolution. Cambridge, UK: Cambridge University Press. p 266–294.

Stringer C. 1989. Documenting the origin of modern humans. In Trinkaus E, editor. The emergence of modern humans. Cambridge, UK: Cambridge University Press. p 67–96.

Stringer C. 1992. Evolution of early humans. In Jones S, Martin R, et al., editors. The Cambridge encyclopedia of human evolution. Cambridge, UK: Cambridge University Press. p 241–251.

Stringer C. 1993a. New views on modern human origins. In Rasmussen DT, editor. The origin and evolution of humans and humanness. Boston: Jones & Bartlett. p 75–94.

Stringer C. 1993b. Secrets of the pit of the bones. Nature 362:501–502.

Stringer C, Howell F, et al. 1979. The significance of the fossil hominid skull from Petralona, Greece. J Archaeol Sci 6:235–253.

Stringer C and Trinkaus E. 1981. The Shanidar Neanderthal crania. In: Stringer CB, editor. Aspects of human evolution. London: Taylor & Francis. p 129–165.

Stringer C, Hublin J, et al. 1984. The origin of anatomically modern humans in Western Europe. In Smith F, Spencer F, editors. The origins of modern humans: A world survey of the fossil evidence. New York: Liss. p 51–135.

Stringer C, Andrews P. 1988. Genetic and fossil evidence for the origin of modern humans. Science 239:1263–1268.

Stringer C, Grün R, et al. 1989. ESR dates for the hominid burial site of Es Skhul in Israel. Nature 338:756–758.

Stringer C and Grün R. 1991. Time for the last Neanderthals. Nature 351:701–702.

Stringer C and Gamble C. 1993. In search of the Neanderthals. New York: Thames & Hudson.

Stringer C, Trinkaus E, et al. 1998. The Middle Pleistocene human tibia from Boxgrove. J Hum Evol 34:509–547.

Stringer C and Hublin J. 1999. New age estimates for the Swanscombe hominid, and their significance for human evolution. J Hum Evol 37:873–877.

Sugden DE, Marchant DR, et al. 1995. Preservation of Miocene glacier ice in east Antarctica. Nature 376:412–414.

Sugiyama Y. 1994. Tool use by wild chimpanzees. Nature 367:327.

Susman R. 1983. Evolution of the human foot: Evidence from Plio-Pleistocene hominids. Foot & Ankle 3:365–376.

Susman R. 1988. Hand of *Paranthropus robustus* from member 1, Swartkrans: Fossil evidence for tool behavior. Science 240:781–784.

Susman R. 1989. New hominid fossils from the Swartkrans Formation (1979–1986 excavations): Postcranial specimens. Am J Phys Anthropol 79:451–474.

Susman R. 1993. Hominid postcranial remains from Swartkrans. In Brain CK, editor. Swartkrans: A cave's chronicle of early man. Pretoria: Transvaal Museum. p 117–136.

Susman R. 1994. Fossil evidence for early hominid tool use. Science 265:1570–1573.

Susman R. 1998. Hand function and tool behavior in early hominids. J Hum Evol 35:23–46.

Susman R, Stern J, et al. 1984. Arboreality and bipedality in the Hadar hominids. Folia Primatol 43:113–156.

Susman R and Brain T. 1988. New first metatarsal (SKX5017) from Swartkrans and the gait of *Paranthropus robustus*. Am J Phys Anthropol 77:7–15.

Susman R and Stern J. 1991. Locomotor behavior of early hominids: Epistemology and fossil evidence. In Coppens Y, Senut B, editors. Origine(s) de la bipedie chez les hominides. Paris: CNRS. p 121–131.

Susman R, de Ruiter D, et al. 2001. Recently identified postcranial remains of *Paranthropus* and early *Homo* from Swartkrans Cave, South Africa. J Hum Evol 41:607–629.

Suwa G. 1988. Evolution of the "robust" australopithecines in the Omo succession: Evidence from mandibular premolar morphology. In Grine FE, editor. Evolutionary history of the "robust" australopithecines. New York: de Gruyter. p 199–222.

Suwa G, Wood BA, et al. 1994. Further analysis of mandibular molar crown and cusp areas in Pliocene and Early Pleistocene hominids. Am J Phys Anthropol 93:407–426.

Suwa G, White T, et al. 1996. Mandibular postcanine dentition from the Shungura Formation, Ethiopia: Crown morphology, taxonomic allocations, and Plio-Pleistocene hominid evolution. Am J Phys Anthropol 101:247–282.

Suwa G, Asfaw B, et al. 1997. The first skull of *Australopithecus boisei*. Nature 389:489–492.

Svoboda J. 1987a. Lithic industries of the Arago, Vértesszöllös, and Bilzingsleben hominids: Comparison and evolutionary interpretation. Curr Anthropol 28:219–227.

Svoboda J. 1987b. A new male burial from Dolni Vestonice. J Hum Evol 16:827–830.

Swisher C. 1997. A revised geochronology for the Plio-Pleistocene hominid-bearing strata of Sangiran Java, Indonesia. J Hum Evol 32:A23.

Swisher C, Curtis G, et al. 1994. Age of the earliest known hominids in Java, Indonesia. Science 263:1118–1121.

Swisher C, Rink W, et al. 1996. Latest *Homo erectus* of Java: Potential contemporaneity with *Homo sapiens* in Southeast Asia. Science 274:1870–1874.

Swisher C, Rink W, et al. 1997. Dating the Ngandong hominids. Science 276:1575–1576.

Swofford DL. 1991. PAUP: Phylogenetic analysis using parsimony, version 3.1. Champaign: Illinois Natural History Survey.

Szabo B, Ludwig KR, et al. 1994. Thorium-230 ages of corals and duration of the last interglacial sea-level high stand on Oahu, Hawaii. Science 266:93–96.

Szalay F. 1977. Ancestors, descendants, sister groups and testing of phylogenetic hypotheses. Syst Zool 26:12–18.

Szymborska W. 1993. View with a grain of sand (selected poems). New York: Harcourt Brace (translated by Baranczak S and Cavanagh C).

Tague R. 1991. Commonalities in dimorphism and variability in the anthropoid pelvis, with implications for the fossil record. J Hum Evol 21:153–176.

Tague R. 1992. Sexual dimorphism in the human bony pelvis, with a consideration of the Neandertal pelvis from Kebara Cave, Israel. Am J Phys Anthropol 88:1–21.

Tague R and Lovejoy C. 1986. The obstetric pelvis of A.L. 288-1 (Lucy). J Hum Evol 15:237–255.

Tague R and Lovejoy C. 1998. AL 288-1—Lucy or Lucifer: Gender confusion in the Pliocene. J Hum Evol 35:75–94.

Tallon P. 1978. Geological setting of the hominid fossils and Acheulian artifacts from the Kapthurin Formation, Baringo District, Kenya. In: Bishop WW, editor. Geological background to fossil man. Edinburgh, UK: Scottish Academic Press, p 361–373.

Tanner N. 1987. Gathering by females: The chimpanzee model revisited and the gathering hypothesis. In Kinzey WG, editor. The evolution of human behavior: Primate models. Albany: SUNY Albany. p 3–27.

Tappen M. 1995. Savanna ecology and natural bone deposition. Curr Anthropol 36:223–260.

Tardieu C. 1991. Etude comparative des deplacements du centre de gravite du corps pendant la marche par une nouvelle methode d'analyse tridimentionnelle. Mise a l'epreuve du'une hypothese evolutive. In: Coppens Y, Senut B, editors. Origine(s) de la bipedie chez les hominides. Paris: CNRS. p 49–58.

Tardieu C. 1999. Ontogeny and phylogeny of femoro-tibial characters in humans and hominid fossils: Functional influence and genetic determinism. Am J Phys Anthropol 110:365–377.

Tardieu C, Aurengo A, et al. 1993. New method of three-dimensional analysis of bipedal loco-motion for the study of displacements of the body and body-parts centers of mass in man and non-human primates: evolutionary framework. Am J Phys Anthropol 90:455–476.

Tarling D. 1980. The geologic evolution of South America with special reference to the last 200 million years. In: Ciochon R, Chiarelli A, editors. Evolutionary biology of the New World monkeys and continental drift. New York: Plenum. p 1–41.

Tattersall I. 1986. Species recognition in human paleontology. J Hum Evol 15:165–175.

Tattersall I. 1992. Species concepts and species identification in human evolution. J Hum Evol 22:341–349.

Tattersall I. 1994. Morphology and phylogeney. Evol Anthropol 3:40–41.

Tattersall I and Eldredge N. 1977. Fact, theory, and fantasy in human paleontology. Am Sci 65:204–211.

Tattersall I, Delson E, et al., editors. 1988. Encyclopedia of human evolution and prehistory. New York: Garland.

Tattersall I and Schwartz J. 1999. Hominids and hybrids: The place of Neanderthals in human evolution. Proc Nat Acad Sci USA 96:7117–7119.

Tattersall I and Schwartz J. 2000. Extinct humans. New York: Westview Press.

Tavaré S, Marshall C, et al. 2002. Using the fossil record to estimate the age of the last common ancestor of extant primates. Nature 416:726–729.

Taylor C, Heglund N, et al. 1982. Energetics and mechanics of terrestrial locomotion 1. Metabolic energy consumption as a function of speed and body size in birds and mammals. J Exp Biol. 97:1–21.

Taylor K, Lamorey G, et al. 1993. The "flickering switch" of late Pleistocene climate change. Nature 361:432–436.

Taylor R. 1996. Radiocarbon dating: The continuing revolution. Evol Anthropol 4:169–181.

Taylor R, Schmidt-Nielsen K, et al. 1970. Scaling of energetic cost of running to body size in mammals. Ann J Physiol 219:1104–1107.

Taylor R and Rowntree V. 1973. Running on two or on four legs: Which consumes more energy? Science 179:186–187.

Teaford M, Walker A, et al. 1993. Species discrimination in *Proconsul* from Rusinga and Mfangano Islands, Kenya. In: Kimbel WH, Martin LB, editors. Species, species concepts, and primate evolution. New York: Plenum. p 373–392.

Teaford M and Ungar P. 2000. Diet and the evolution of the earliest human ancestors. Proc Nat Acad Sci USA 97:13506–13511.

Teilhard de Chardin P and Pei W. 1932. The lithic industry of the *Sinanthropus* deposits in Choukoutien. Bull Geol Soc China 11:315–365.

Templeton A. 1984. Phylogenetic inference from restriction endonuclease site maps with particular reference to the evolution of humans and apes. Evolution 37:221–244.

Templeton A. 1985. The phylogeny of the hominoid primates: A statistical analysis of the DNA-DNA hybridization data. Mol Biol Evol 2:420–433.

Templeton A. 1989. The meaning of species and speciation: A genetic perspective. In: Otte D, Endler J, editors. Speciation and its consequences. Sunderland, MA: Sinauer. p 3–27.

Templeton A. 1991. Human origins and analysis of mitochondrial DNA sequences. Science 255:737.

Templeton A. 1993. The "Eve" hypothesis: A genetic critique and reanalysis. Am Anthropol 95:51–72.

Templeton A. 1994. "Eve": Hypothesis compatibility versus hypothesis testing. Am Anthropol 96:141–147.

Templeton A. 1996. Gene lineages and human evolution. Science 272:1363.

Templeton A. 1999. Human races: A genetic and evolutionary perspective. Am Anthropol 100:632–650.

Templeton A. 2002. Out of Africa again and again. Nature 416:45–51.

Thackeray A. 1992. The Middle Stone Age south of the Limpopo River. J World Prehist 6:385–440.

Thackeray F. 1995. Do strontium/calcium ratios in early Pleistocene hominids from Swartkrans reflect physiological differences in males and females? J Hum Evol 29:401–404.

Thackeray F. 2002. Palaeoenvironmental change and re-assessment of the age of Late Pleistocene deposits at Die Kelders cave, South Africa. J Hum Evol 43:749–753.

Thieme H. 1997. Lower Palaeolithic hunting spears from Germany. Nature 385:807–810.

Thoma A. 1978. Some notes on Wolpoff's notes on the Vértesszöllös occipital. J Hum Evol 7:323–325.

Thoma A. 1981. The position of the Vértessozöllös find in relation to *Homo erectus*. In: Sigmon BA, Cybulski JS, editors. *Homo erectus:* Papers in honor of Davidson Black. Toronto: University of Toronto Press. p 105–114.

Thomas H. 1985. The early and middle Miocene land connection of the Afro-Arabian plate and Asia: A major event for hominoid dispersal? In: Delson E, editor. Ancestors: The hard evidence. New York: Liss. p 42–50.

Thompson J and Nelson A. 2000. The place of Neandertals in the evolution of hominid patterns of growth and development. J Hum Evol 38:475–495.

Thomson R, Pritchard J, et al. 2000. Recent common ancestry of human Y chromosomes: Evidence from DNA sequence data. Proc Natl Acad Sci 97:7360–7365.

Thoreau, H.D. 1854. Walden. Boston: Ticknor and Fields.

Thorne A. 1980. The longest link: Human evolution in Southeast Asia and the settlement of Australia. In: Fox JJ, Earnaut RG, et al., editors. Indonesia: Australian perspectives. Canberra: Australian National University Research School of Pacific Studies. p 35–43.

Thorne A, Grün R, et al. 1999. Australia's oldest human remains: Age of the Lake Mungo 3 skeleton. J Hum Evol 36:591–612.

Tiemei C, Quan Y, et al. 1994. Antiquity of *Homo sapiens* in China. Nature 368:55–56.

Tishkoff S, Dietzsch E, et al. 1996. Global pattterns of linkage disequilibrium at the CD4 locus and modern human origins. Science 271:1380–1387.

Tobias P. 1964. The Olduvai Bed I hominine with special reference to its cranial capacity. Nature 202:3–4.

Tobias P. 1965a. *Australopithecus, Homo habilis,* tool-using and tool-making. South Afr Arch Bull 20:167–192.

Tobias P. 1965b. New discoveries in Tanganyika: Their bearing on hominid evolution. Curr Anthropol 6:391–411.

Tobias P. 1966. The distinctiveness of *Homo habilis*. Nature 209:953–960.

Tobias P. 1967a. The cranium and maxillary dentition of *Australopithecus boisei.* Olduvai Gorge. Cambridge, UK: Cambridge University Press.

Tobias P. 1967b. Olduvai Gorge. Cambridge, UK: Cambridge University Press.

Tobias P. 1980. "*Australopithecus afarensis*" and *A. africanus:* A critique and an alternative hypothesis. Palaeontol Afr 23:1–17.

Tobias P. 1984. Dart, Taung, and the "missing link." Johannesburg: University of the Witwatersrand Press.

Tobias P. 1987. The brain of *Homo habilis:* A new level of organization in cerebral evolution. J Hum Evol 16:741–761.

Tobias P. 1988. Numerous apparently synapomorphic features in *Australopithecus robustus, Australopithecus boisei* and *Homo habilis:* Support for the Skelton-McHenry-Drawhorn hypotheses. In: Grine FE, editor. Evolutionary history of the "robust" australopithecines. New York: de Gruyter. p 293–309.

Tobias P. 1989a. The gradual appraisal of *Homo habilis* Hominidae. In: Giacobini G, editor. Proceedings of the Second International Congress of Human Paleontology Milan: Editoriale Jaca Book. p 151–154.

Tobias P. 1989b. The status of *Homo habilis* in 1987 and some outstanding problems: Hominidae. In: Giacobini G, editor. Proceedings of the Second International Congress of Human Paleontology. Milan: Editoriale Jaca Book. p 141–149.

Tobias P. 1991. Olduvai Gorge IV: The skulls, endocasts and teeth of *Homo habilis*. Cambridge, UK: Cambridge University Press.

Tobias P. 1992. Piltdown: An appraisal of the case against Sir Arthur Keith. Curr Anthropol 33:243–293.

Tobias P. 1993a. Earliest *Homo* not proven. Nature 361:307.

Tobias P. 1993b. One hundred years after Eugene Dubois: The Pithecanthropus Centennial at Leiden. J Hum Evol 25:523–526.

Tobias P. 1994. The craniocerebral interface in early hominids. In: Corruccini RS, Ciochon RL, editors. Integrative paths to the past. Englewood Cliffs, NJ: Prentice Hall. p 185–203.

Tobias P and von Koenigswald G. 1964. A comparison between the Olduvai hominines and those of Java and some implications for hominid phylogeny. Nature 204:515–518.

Tobias P and Falk D. 1988. Evidence for a dual pattern of cranial venous sinuses on the endocranial cast of Taung (*Australopithecus africanus*). Am J Phys Anthropol 76:309–312.

Tobias P, Vogel J, et al. 1993. New isotopic and sedimentological measurements of the Thabaseek deposits (South Africa) and the dating of the Taung hominid. Quaternary Res 40:360–367.

Tobias P and Baker G. 1994. Palaeo-anthropology in South Africa. South Afr J Sci 90:203–204.

Tomaskova S. 1995. A site in history: Archaeology at Dolni Vestonice/Unterwisternitz. Antiquity 69:301–316.

Tompkins R and Trinkaus E. 1987. La Ferrassie 6 and the development of Neandertal pubic morphology. Am J Phys Anthropol 73:233–239.

Tooby J and DeVore I. 1987. The reconstruction of hominid behavioral evolution through strategic modeling. In: Kinzey W, editor. The evolution of human behavior: Primate models. Albany: SUNY Press. p 183–237.

Toth N. 1985a. Archaeological evidence for preferential right-handedness in the lower and Middle Pleistocene and its possible implications. J Hum Evol 14:607–614.

Toth N. 1985b. The Oldowan reassessed: A close look at early stone artifacts. J Archaeol Sci 12:101–120.

Toth N. 1987. Behavioral inferences from early stone artifact assemblages: An experimental model. J Hum Evol 16:763–787.

Toth N and Schick K. 1993. Early stone industries and inferences regarding language and cognition. In: Gibson K, Ingold T, editors. Tools, language and cognition in human evolution. Cambridge, UK: Cambridge University Press. p 346–362.

Toth N, Schick KD, et al. 1993. Pan the tool-maker: Investigations into the stone tool-making and tool-using capabilities of a bonobo (*Pan paniscus*). J Archaeol Sci 20:81–91.

Toussaint M, Macho G, et al. 2003. The third partial skeleton of a Late Pliocene hominin (Stw 431) from Sterkfontein, South Africa. South Afr J Sci 99:215–223.

Trinkaus E. 1981. Neanderthal limb proportions and cold adaptation. In: Stringer CB, editor. Aspects of human evolution. London: Taylor & Francis, p 187–224.

Trinkaus E. 1983. The Shanidar Neandertals. New York: Academic Press.

Trinkaus E. 1984a. Neandertal pubic morphology and gestation length. Curr Anthropol 25:509–514.

Trinkaus E. 1984b. Western Asia. In: Smith FH, Spencer R, editors. The origins of modern humans. New York: Liss. p 251–293.

Trinkaus E. 1985. Cannibalism and burial at Krapina. J Hum Evol 14:203–216.

Trinkaus E. 1987. The Neandertal face: Evolutionary and functional perspectives on a recent hominid face. J Hum Evol 16:429–443.

Trinkaus E. 1989a. Issues concerning human emergence in the later Pleistocene. In: Trinkaus E, editor. The emergence of modern humans. Cambridge, UK: Cambridge University Press. p 1–17.

Trinkaus E. 1989b. Olduvai hominid 7 trapezial metacarpal 1 articular morphology: Contrasts with recent humans. Am J Phys Anthropol 80:411–416.

Trinkaus E. 1989c. The Upper Pleistocene transition. In: Trinkaus E, editor. The emergence of modern humans. Cambridge, UK: Cambridge University Press. p 42–66.

Trinkaus E. 1993. Femoral neck-shaft angles of the Qafzeh-Skhul early modern humans, and activity levels among immature Near Eastern Middle Paleolithic hominids. J Hum Evol 25:393–416.

Trinkaus E and Zimmerman MR. 1982. Trauma among the Shanidar Neandertals. Am J Phys Anthrop 57:61–76.

Trinkaus E, Churchill SE, et al. 1991. Robusticity versus shape: The functional interpretation of Neandertal appendicular morphology. J Anthropol Soc Nippon 99:257–278.

Trinkaus E and Shipman P. 1992. The Neandertals: Changing the image of mankind. New York: Knopf.

Trinkaus E and Shipman P. 1993. Neandertals: Images of ourselves. Evol Anthropol 1:194–201.

Trinkaus E, Churchill SE, et al. 1994. Postcranial robusticity in *Homo*. II: Humeral bilateral asymmetry and bone plasticity. Am J Phys Anthropol 93:1–34.

Trinkaus E and Ruff C. 1996. Early modern human remains from eastern Asia: The Yamashita-cho 1 immature postcrania. J Hum Evol 30:299–314.

Trinkaus E, Churchill S, et al. 1997. Robusticity and body proportions of the Saint-Césaire 1 Neandertal. Am J Phys Anthropol Suppl 24:229.

Trinkaus E, Stringer C, et al. 1999. Diaphyseal cross-sectional geometry of the Boxgrove 1 Middle Pleistocene human tibia. J Hum Evol 37:1–25.

Trinkaus E, Milota S, et al. 2003a. Early modern human cranial remains from the Pestera cu Oase, Romania. J Hum Evol 45:245–253.

Trinkaus E, Moldovan O, et al. 2003b. An early modern human from the Pestera cu Oase, Romania. Proc Natl Acad Sci USA 100:11231–11236.

Turekian K and Bada J. 1972. The dating of fossil bones. In: Bishop WW, Miller JA, editors. Calibration of hominoid evolution. Edinburgh, UK: Scottish Academic Press. p 171–185.

Turner A and Chamberlain A. 1989. Speciation, morphological change and the status of African *Homo erectus*. J Hum Evol 18:115–130.

Turner S, Hawkesworth C, et al. 1993. Timing of Tibetan uplift constrained by analysis of volcanic rocks. Nature 364:50–54.

Turner A and Wood B. 1993a. Comparative palaeontological context for the evolution of the early hominid masticatory system. J Hum Evol 24:301–318.

Turner A and Wood B. 1993b. Taxonomic and geographic diversity in robust australopithecines and other African Plio-Pleistocene larger mammals. J Hum Evol 24:147–168.

Tuttle R. 1967. Knuckle-walking and the evolution of hominoid hands. Am J Phys Anthropol 26:171–206.

Tuttle R. 1970. Postural, propulsive and prehensile capabilities in the cheiridia of chimpanzees and other great apes. In: Bourne GH, editor. The chimpanzee: Physiology, behavior, serology and diseases of chimpanzees. Basel: Karger. p 167–253.

Tuttle R. 1974. Darwin's apes, dental apes, and the descent of man: Normal science in evolutionary anthropology. Curr Anthropol 15:389–398.

Tuttle R. 1981. Evolution of hominid bipedalism and prehensile capabilities. Phil Trans R Soc London B 292:89–94.

Tuttle R. 1985. Ape footprints and Laetoli impressions: A response to the SUNY claims. In: Tobias PV, editor. Hominid evolution: Past, present, and future. New York: Liss. p 129–134.

Tuttle R. 1987. Kinesiological inferences and evolutionary implications from Laetoli bipedal trails G-1, G-2/3, and A. In: Leakey MD, Harris JM, editors. Laetoli, a Pliocene site in northern Tanzania. Oxford, UK: Clarendon Press. p 503–523.

Tuttle R. 1994. Up from Electromyography. In: Corruccini RS, Ciochon RL, editors. Integrative paths to the past. Englewood Cliffs, NJ: Prentice Hall. p 269–284.

Tuttle R, Webb D, et al. 1991. Laetoli footprint trails and the evolution of hominid bipedalism. In: Coppens Y, Senut B, editors. Origine(s) de la bipedie chez les hominides. Paris: CNRS. p 187–198.

Underhill P, Jin L, et al. 1997. Detection of numerous Y chromosome biallelic polymorpisms by denaturing high-performance liquid chromatography. Gen Res 7:996–1005.

Ungar P and Grine F. 1991. Incisor size and wear in *Australopithecus africanus* and *Paranthropus robustus*. J Hum Evol 20:313–340.

Ungar P, Walker A, et al. 1994. Reanalysis of the Lukeino molar (KNM-LU 335). Am J Phys Anthropol 94:165–173.

Valladas H, Reyss JL, et al. 1988. Thermoluminescence dating of Mousterian "Proto-Cro-Magnon" remains from Israel and the origin of modern man. Nature 331:614–616.

Valladas H, Joron JL, et al. 1987. Thermoluminescence dates for the Neanderthal burial site at Kebara in Israel. Nature 330:159–160.

Valladas H, Cachier H, et al. 1992. Direct radiocarbon dates for prehistoric paintings at the Altamira, El Castillo and Niaux caves. Nature 357:68–70.

Vallois H. 1954. Neandertals and praesapiens. J R Anthropol Inst 84:111–130.

Vallois H. 1956. The pre-Mousterian human mandible from Montmaurin. Am J Phys Anthropol 14:319–323.

Van Couvering J and Miller J. 1969. Miocene stratigraphy and age determinations, Rusinga Island, Kenya. Nature 221:628–632.

Van Couvering J and Van Couvering J. 1976. Early Miocene mammal fossils from East Africa: Aspects of geology, faunistics and paleoecology. In: Isaac GL, McCown ER, editors. Human origins: Louis Leakey and the East African evidence. Menlo Park, CA: Benjamin. p 155–207.

Van Couvering J and Kukla G. 1988. Pleistocene. In: Tattersall I, Delson E, et al., editors. Encyclopedia of human evolution and prehistory. New York: Garland, p 459–464.

Van Der Burgh J, Visscher H, et al. 1993. Paleoatmospheric signatures in Neogene fossil leaves. Science 260:1788–1790.

Van der Hamman T, Wijmstra TA, et al. 1971. The floral record of the late Cenozoic of Europe. In: Turekian KK, editor. The late Cenozoic glacial ages. New Haven, CT: Yale University Press. p 391–424.

van der Merwe N. 1982. Carbon isotopes, photosynthesis, and archaeology. Am Sci 70:596–606.

van der Merwe N, Thackeray F, et al. 2003. The carbon isotope ecology and diet of *Australopithecus africanus* at Sterkfontein, South Africa. J Hum Evol 44:581–597.

Van Valen L. 1973. A new evolutionary law. Evol Theory 1:1–30.

Vekua A, Lordkipanidze D, et al. 2002. A new skull of early *Homo* from Dmanisi, Georgia. Science 297:85–89.

Vigilant L, Stoneking M, et al. 1991. African populations and the evolution of human mitochondrial DNA. Science 253:1503–1507.

Vignaud P, Duringer P, et al. 2002. Geology and palaeontology of the upper Miocene Toros-Menalla hominid locality, Chad. Nature 418:152–155.

Villa P. 1992. Cannibalism in prehistoric Europe. Evol Anthropol 1:93–104.

Vogel J. 1985. Further attempts at dating the Taung tufas. In: Delson E, editor. Ancestors: The hard evidence. New York: Liss. p 189–194.

von Koenigswald G. 1971. The evolution of man. Ann Arbor: University of Michigan Press.

von Koenigswald G. 1975. Early man in Java: Catalogue and problems. In: Tuttle R, editor. Paleoanthropology, morphology and paleoecology. The Hague: Mouton. p 303–309.

von Koenigswald G. 1981. Davidson Black, Peking man, and the Chinese dragon. In: Sigmon BA, Cybulski JS, editors. *Homo erectus:* Papers in honor of Davidson Black. Toronto: University of Toronto Press. p 27–39.

Vrba E. 1974. Chronological and ecological implications of the fossil Bovidae at the Sterkfontein australopithecine site. Nature 250:19–23.

Vrba E. 1975. Some evidence of chronology and paleoecology of Sterkfontein, Swartkrans and Kromdraai from the fossil Bovidae. Nature 254:301–304.

Vrba E. 1980a. Evolution, species and fossils: How does life evolve? South Afr J Sci 76:61–84.

Vrba E. 1980b. The significance of bovid remains as indicators of environment and predation patterns. In: Behrensmeyer A, Hill A, editors. Fossils in the making: Vertebrate taphonomy and paleoecology. Chicago: University of Chicago Press. p 247–271.

Vrba E. 1981. The Kromdraai australopithecine site revisited in 1980; recent investigations and results. Ann Transvaal Mus 33:17–60.

Vrba E. 1982. Biostratigraphy and chronology, based particularly on Bovidae of southern African hominid-associated assemblages: Makapansgat, Sterkfontein, Taung, Kromdraai, Swarkrans: Also Elandsfontein, Broken Hill and Cave of Hearths. Pretirage, 1er Cong Int Paleontol Hum Nic CNRS:707–752.

Vrba E. 1985a. Ecological and adaptive changes associated with early hominid evolution. In: Delson E, editor. Ancestors: The hard evidence. New York: Liss. p 63–71.

Vrba E. 1985b. The Kromdraai australopithecine site. Johannesburg: University Witwatersrand Press.

Vrba E. 1988. Late Pliocene climatic events and hominid evolution. In: Grine F, editor. Evolutionary history of the "robust" australopithecines. New York: de Gruyter. p 405–426.

Vrba E. 1994. An hypothesis of heterochrony in response to climatic cooling and its relevance to early hominid evolution. In: Corruccini RS, Ciochon RL, editors. Integrative paths to the past. Englewood Cliffs, NJ: Prentice Hall. p 345–376.

Wada A. 1995. A space-time slide rule. Nature 373:35–36.

Waddle DM. 1994. Matrix correlation tests support a single origin for modern humans. Nature 368:452–454.

Wagner G. 1996. Fission-track dating in paleoanthropology. Evol Anthropol 5:165–171.

Wainscoat JS, Hill AVS, et al. 1989. Geographic distribution of alpha- and beta- globin gene cluster polymorphisms. In: Mellars P, Stringer C, editors. The human revolution. Princeton, NJ: Princeton University Press. p 31–38.

Walker A. 1969. Lower Miocene fossils from Mount Elgon, Uganda. Nature 223:591–593.

Walker A. 1981. The Koobi Fora hominids and their bearing on the origins of the genus *Homo*. In: Sigmon BA, Cybulski JS, editors. *Homo erectus:* Papers in honor of Davidson Black. Toronto: University of Toronto Press. p 193–215.

Walker A. 1992. Louis Leakey, John Napier and the history of *Proconsul.* J Hum Evol 22:245–254.

Walker A. 1993. The origin of the genus *Homo*. In: Rasmussen DT, editor. The origin and evolution of humans and humanness. Boston: Jones & Bartlett. p 29–47.

Walker A and Rose M. 1968. Fossil hominoid vertebra from the Miocene of Uganda. Nature 217:980–981.

Walker A and Leakey R. 1978. The hominids of East Turkana. Sci Am 239:54–66.

Walker A and Leakey R, eds. 1993. The Nariokotome *Homo erectus* skeleton. Cambridge, MA: Harvard University Press.

Walker A, Zimmerman M, et al. 1982. A possible case of hypervitaminosis A in *Homo erectus*. Nature 296:248–250.

Walker A, Falk D, et al. 1983. The skull of *Proconsul africanus:* Reconstruction and cranial capacity. Nature 305:525–527.

Walker A and Pickford M. 1983. New postcranial fossils of *Proconsul africanus* and *Proconsul nyanzae*. In: Ciochon R, Corruccini R, editors. New interpretations of ape and human ancestry. New York: Plenum. p 325–352.

Walker A, Leakey R, et al. 1986. 2.5 myr *Australopithecus boisei* from west of Lake Turkana, Kenya. Nature 322:517–522.

Walker A and Leakey R. 1988. The evolution of *Australopithecus boisei*. In: Grine FE, editor. Evolutionary history of the "robust" australopithecines. New York: de Gruyter. p 247–258.

Walker A, Teaford MF, et al. 1993. A new species of *Proconsul* from the Early Miocene of Rusinga/Mfangano Islands, Kenya. J Hum Evol 25:43–56.

Wall J. 2000. Detecting ancient admixture in humans using sequence polymorphism data. Genetics 154:1271–1279.

Wallace DC, Garrison K, et al. 1985. Dramatic founder effects in Amerindian mitochondrial DNA's. Am J Phys Anthropol 68:149–155.

Wallace J. 1972. The dentition of the South African early hominids: A study of form and function. Ph.D. thesis. Johannesburg: University of the Witwatersrand.

Walter R, Buffler R, et al. 2000. Early human occupation of the Red Sea coast of Eritrea during the last interglacial. Nature 405:65–69.

Walter RC. 1994. Age of Lucy and the first family: Single-crystal $^{40}Ar/^{39}Ar$ dating of the Denen Dora and lower Kada Hadar members of the Hadar Formation, Ethiopia. Geology 22:6–10.

Walter RC Manega PC, et al. 1991. Laser-fusion $^{40}Ar/^{39}Ar$ dating of Bed I, Olduvai Gorge, Tanzania. Nature 354:145–149.

Walter RC. and Aronson JL. 1993. Age and source of the Sidi Hakoma Tuff, Hadar Formation, Ethiopia. J Hum Evol 25:229–240.

Wang C, Shi Y, et al. 1982. Dynamic uplift of the Himalaya. Nature 298:553–556.

Wang W, Crompton R, et al. 2003. Energy transformation during erect and "bent-hip, bent-knee" walking by humans with implications for the evolution of bipedalism. J Hum Evol 44:563–579.

Wanpo H, Ciochon R, et al. 1995. Early *Homo* and associated artefacts from Asia. Nature 378:275–278.

Wanyong C, Yufen L, et al. 1986. On the paleoclimate during the period of *Ramapithecus* in Lufeng County, Yunnan Province. Acta Anthropol 4:88.

Ward C. 1993. Torso morphology and locomotion in *Proconsul nyanzae*. Am J Phys Anthropol 92:291–328.

Ward C. 2002. Interpreting the posture and locomotion of *Australopithecus afarensis:* Where do we stand? Am J Phys Anthropol 45:185–215.

Ward C and Latimer B. 1991. The vertebral column of *Australopithecus*. Am J Phys Anthropol 12:180.

Ward C, Walker AC, et al. 1991. *Proconsul* did not have a tail. J Hum Evol 21:215–220.

Ward C, Walker A, et al. 1993. Partial skeleton of *Proconsul nyanzae* from Mfangano Island, Kenya. Am J Phys Anthropol 90:77–111.

Ward C, Walker A, et al. 1997. New fossils of *Australopithecus anamensis* from Kanapoi and Allia Bay, Kenya. Am J Phys Anthropol Suppl 24:235.

Ward C, Leakey M, et al. 1999. The new hominid species *Australopithecus anamensis*. Evol Anthropol 7:197–205.

Ward C, Leakey M, et al. 2001. Morphology of *Australopithecus anamensis* from Kanapoi and Allia Bay, Kenya. J Hum Evol 41:255–368.

Ward J. 1983. On the antiquity of the Namib. South Afr J Sci 79:175–183.

Ward S and Kimbel W. 1983. Subnasal alveolar morphology and the systematic position of *Sivapithecus*. Am J Phys Anthropol 61:157–171.

Ward S and Pilbeam D. 1983. Maxillofacial morphology of Miocene hominoids from Africa and Indo-Pakistan. In: Ciochon R, Corruccini R, editors. New interpretations of ape and human ancestry. New York: Plenum. p 211–238.

Ward S and Hill A. 1987. Pliocene hominid partial mandible from Tabarin, Baringo, Kenya. Am J Phys Anthrop 72:21–38.

Ward S, Brown B, et al. 1999. *Equatorius:* A new hominoid genus from the Middle Miocene of Kenya. Science 285:1382–1386.

Ward S and Duren D. 2002. Middle and late Miocene African hominoids. In: Hartwig W, editor. The primate fossil record. Cambridge, UK: Cambridge University Press. p 385–398.

Washburn S and Lancaster C. 1968. The evolution of hunting. In: Lee RB, DeVore I, editors. Man the hunter. Chicago: Aldine. p 293–303.

Watson V. 1993. Composition of the Swartkrans bone accumulations, in terms of skeletal parts and animals represented. In: Brain CK, editor. Swartkrans: A cave's chronicle of early man. Pretoria: Transvaal Museum. p 35–73.

Weaver AJ and Hughes TMC. 1994. Rapid interglacial climate fluctuations driven by north Atlantic ocean circulation. Nature 367:447–450.

Weaver K. 1985. Stones, bones, and early man. Natl Geogr Mag 168:560–623.

Weidenreich F. 1937. The dentition of *Sinanthropus pekenensis:* A comparative odontography of the hominids. Palaeon Sinica 1:120–180.

Weidenreich F. 1939. On the earliest representatives of modern mankind recovered on the soil of East Asia. Peking Natl Hist Bull 13:161–174.

Weidenreich F. 1943. The skull of *Sinanthropus pekinensis:* A comparative study on a primitive hominid skull. Palaeontol Sinica 10:1–484.

Weidenreich F. 1951. Morphology of Solo man. Anthropol Papers Am Mus Nat Hist 43:205–290.

Weiner J. 1955. The Piltdown forgery. London: Oxford University Press.

Weiner S, Xu Q, et al. 1998. Evidence for the use of fire at Zhoukoudian, China. Science 281:251–253.

Weinert H. 1937. Hominidae (palaozoolgie). Fortschr Palaontol 1:337–344.

Weinert H. 1950. Uber die neuen vor-und fruhmenschenfunde aus Afrika, Java, China und Frankreich. Zeit Morph Anthropol 42:113–148.

Weiss G and von Haeseler A. 1996. Estimating the age of the common ancestor of men from the ZFY intron. Science 272:1359–1360.

Weiss M. 1987. Nucleic acid evidence bearing on hominoid relationships. Yearbk Phys Anthropol 30:41–73.

Wesselman H. 1985. Fossil micromammals as indicators of climatic change about 2.4 myr ago in the Omo Valley, Ethiopia. South Afr J Sci 81:260–261.

West J. 1997. Reptiles, fat, and early *Homo* at Olduvai Gorge, Tanzania. Am J Phys Anthropol Supply 24:238.

Wheeler P. 1991a. The influence of bipedalism on the energy and water budgets of early hominids. J Hum Evol 21:117–136.

Wheeler P. 1991b. The thermoregulatory advantages of hominid bipedalism in open equatorial environments: The contribution of convective heat loss and cutaneous evaporative cooling. J Hum Evol 21:107–115.

Wheeler P. 1992a. The influence of the loss of functional body hair on the water budgets of early hominids. J Hum Evol 23:379–388.

Wheeler P. 1992b. The thermoregulatory advantages of large body size for hominids foraging in savannah environments. J Hum Evol 23:351–362.

Wheeler P. 1993. The influence of stature and body form on hominid energy and water budgets; A comparison of *Australopithecus* and early *Homo* physiques. J Hum Evol 24:13–28.

Wheeler P. 1994a. The foraging times of bipedal and quadrupedal hominids in open equatorial environments. J Hum Evol 27:511–517.

Wheeler P. 1994b. The thermoregulatory advantages of heat storage and shade-seeking behavior to hominids foraging in equatorial savannah environments. J Hum Evol 26:339–350.

Wheeler P. 1996. The environmental context of functional body hair loss in hominids. J Hum Evol 30:367–371.

White R. 1993. The dawn of adornment. Nat Hist 5:61–67.

White T. 1977. New fossil hominids from Laetolil, Tanzania. Am J Phys Anthropol 46:197–230.

White T. 1981. Primitive hominid canine from Tanzania. Science 213:348–349.

White T. 1984. Pliocene hominids from the Middle Awash, Ethiopia. Cour Forschungsinst Senckenb 69:57–68.

White T. ed. 1985. Acheulian man in Ethiopia's Middle Awash valley: The implications of cutmarks on the Bodo cranium. Netherlands: Enschede & Haarlem.

White T. 1986a. *Australopithecus afarensis* and the Lothagam mandible. Anthropos 23:79–90.

White T. 1986b. Cut marks on the Bodo cranium: A case of prehistoric defleshing. Am J Phys Anthropol 69:503–509.

White T. 1987. Cannibals at Klasies? Sagittarius 2:6–9.

White T. 1988. The comparative biology of "robust" *Australopithecus:* Clues from context. In: Grine F, editor. Evolutionary history of the "robust" australopithecines. New York: de Gruyter. p 449–484.

White T. 1992. Prehistoric Cannibalism at Mancos 5MTUMR-2346. Princeton, NJ: Princeton University Press.

White T. 2000. Cutmarks on the Bodo cranium: A case of prehistoric defleshing. Am J Phys Anthropol 69:503–550.

White T. 2002. Earliest hominids. In: Hartwig W, editor. The primate fossil record. Cambridge, UK: Cambridge University Press. p 407–417.

White T. 2003. Early hominids—Diversity or distortion. Science 299:1994–1997.

White T and Harris J. 1977. Suid evolution and correlation of African hominid localities. Science 198:13–21.

White T, Johanson D, et al. 1981. *Australopithecus africanus:* Its phyletic position reconsidered. South Afr J Sci 77:445–470.

White T and Suwa G. 1987. Hominid footprints at Laetoli: Facts and interpretations. Am J Phys Anthrop 72:485–514.

White T and Toth N. 1991. The question of ritual cannibalism at Grotta Guattari. Curr Anthropol 32:118–138.

White T, Suwa G, et al. 1993. New discoveries of *Australopithecus* at Maka in Ethiopia. Nature 366:261–265.

White T, Suwa G, et al. 1994. *Australopithecus ramidus,* a new species of early hominid from Aramis, Ethiopia. Nature 371:306–312.

White T, Suwa G, et al. 1995. *Australopithecus ramidus,* a new species of early hominid from Aramis, Ethiopia. Nature 375:88.

White T, Suwa G, et al. 2000. Jaws and teeth of *Australopithecus afarensis* from Maka, middle Awash, Ethiopia. Am J Phys Anthropol 111:45–68.

White T, Asfaw B, et al. 2003. Pleistocene *Homo sapiens* from Middle Awash, Ethiopia. Nature 423:742–747.

Whiten A, Goodall J, et al. 1999. Cultures in chimpanzees. Nature 399:682–685.

Whitfield L, Sulston J, et al. 1995. Sequence variation of the human Y chromosome. Nature 378:379–380.

Wildman D, Uddin M, et al. 2003. Implications of natural selection in shaping 99.4% nonsynonymous DNA identity between humans and chimpanzees: Enlarging genus *Homo.* Proc Natl Acad Sci 100:7181–7188.

Willermet C and Clark G. 1995. Paradigm crisis in modern human origins research. J Hum Evol 29:487–490.

Willerslev E, Hansen A, et al. 2003. Diverse plant and animal genetic records from Holocene and Pleistocene sediments. Science 300:791–795.

Williams B and Kay R. 1995. The taxon Anthropoidea and the crown clade concept. Evol Anthropol 3:188–190.

Williamson P. 1985. Evidence for Plio-Pleistocene rainforest expansion in east Africa. Nature 315:487–489.

Wills C. 1995. When did Eve live? An evolutionary detective story. Evolution 49:593–607.

WoldeGabriel G, White TD, et al. 1994. Ecological and temporal placement of early Pliocene hominids at Aramis, Ethiopia. Nature 371:330–333.

WoldeGabriel G, Heiken G, et al. 2000. Volcanism, tectonism, sedimentation, and the paleoanthropological record in the Ethiopian rift system. In: McCoy R, Heiken G., editors. Volcanic hazards and disasters in human antiquity. [special paper 345] Boulder, CO: Geological Society of America. p 83–99.

WoldeGabriel G, Haile-Selassie Y, et al. 2001. Geology and palaeontology of the late Miocene Middle Awash valley, Afar rift, Ethiopia. Nature 412:175–178.

Wolpoff M. 1971a. Competitive exclusion among Lower Pleistocene hominids: The single species hypothesis. Man 6:601–614.

Wolpoff M. 1971b. Is Vértesszöllös II an occipital of European *Homo erectus?* Nature 232:567–568.

Wolpoff M. 1979. The Krapina dental remains. Am J Phys Anthrop 50:67–114.

Wolpoff M. 1980. Cranial remains of Middle Pleistocene European hominids. J Hum Evol 9:339–358.

Wolpoff M. 1982. *Ramapithecus* and hominid origins. Curr Anthropol 23:501–510.

Wolpoff M. 1984. Evolution in *Homo erectus:* The question of stasis. Paleobiology 10:389–406.

Wolpoff M. 1989a. Multiregional evolution: The fossil alternative to Eden. In: Mellars P, Stringer C, editors. The human revolution. Princeton, NJ: Princeton University Press. p 62–108.

Wolpoff M. 1989b. The place of the Neandertals in human evolution. In: Trinkaus E, editor. The emergence of modern humans. Cambridge, UK: Cambridge University Press. p 97–141.

Wolpoff M. 1994. Time and phylogeny. Evol Anthropol 3:38–39.

Wolpoff M, Wu X, et al. 1984. Modern *Homo sapiens* origins: A general theory of hominid evolution involving the fossil evidence from east Asia. In: Smith F, Spencer F, editors. The origins of modern humans: A world survey of the fossil evidence. New York: Liss. p 411–483.

Wolpoff M and Caspari R. 1990. Metric analysis of the skeletal material from Klasies River mouth, Republic of South Africa. Am J Phys Anthropol 81:319.

Wolpoff M, Thorne A, et al. 1993. The case for sinking *Homo erectus:* 100 years of Pithecanthropus is enough! Cour Forschinst Senckenberg 171:341–361.

Wolpoff M and Caspari R. 1997. Race and human evolution. New York: Simon & Schuster.

Wolpoff M, Hawks J, et al. 2001. Modern human ancestry at the peripheries: A test of the replacement theory. Science 291:293–297.

Wolpoff M, Hawks J, et al. 2000. Multiregional, not multiple origins. Am J Phys Anthropol 112:129–136.

Wolpoff M, Senut B, et al. 2002. *Sahelanthropus* or "Sahelpithecus"? Nature 419:581–582.

Woo J. 1957. *Dryopithecus* teeth from Keiyuan, Yunnan Province. Vertebr Palasiat 1:25–32.

Woo J. 1964. Mandible of *Sinanthropus lantianensis*. Curr Anthropol 5:98–101.

Woo J. 1966. The skull of Lantian man. Curr Anthropol 7:83–86.

Wood B. 1984. The origin of *Homo erectus*. Cour Forsch Inst Senckenberg 69:99–112.

Wood B. 1985. Early *Homo* in Kenya, and its systematic relationships. In: Delson E, editor. Ancestors: The hard evidence. New York: Liss. p 206–214.

Wood B. 1991. Koobi Fora Research Project IV: Hominid cranial remains from Koobi Fora. Oxford, UK: Clarendon.

Wood B. 1992a. Early hominid species and speciation. J Hum Evol 22:351–365.

Wood B. 1992b. Evolution of australopithecines. In: Jones S, Martin R, et al., editors. The Cambridge encyclopedia of human evolution. Cambridge, UK: Cambridge University Press. p 231–240.

Wood B. 1992c. Origin and evolution of the genus *Homo*. Nature 355:783–790.

Wood B. 1993. Rift on the record. Nature 365:789–790.

Wood B. 1994. The oldest hominid yet. Nature 371:280–281.

Wood B. 1997. The oldest whodunnit in the world. Nature 385:292–293.

Wood B. 2002. Hominid revelations from Chad. Nature 418:133–135.

Wood B and Chamberlain A. 1986. *Australopithecus:* Grade or clade? In: Wood B, Martin L, Andrews P, editors. Major topics in primate and human evolution. Cambridge, UK: Cambridge University Press, p 220–248.

Wood B and Xu Q. 1991. Variation in the Lufeng dental remains. J Hum Evol 20:291–311.

Wood B and Van Noten F. 1986. Preliminary observations on the BK 8518 mandible from Baringo, Kenya. Am J Phys Anthropol 69:117–127.

Wood B, Wood C, et al. 1994. *Paranthropus boisei:* An example of evolutionary stasis? Am J Phys Anthropol 95:117–136.

Wood B and Collard M. 1999a. The changing face of genus *Homo*. Evol Anthropol 8:195–207.

Wood B and Collard M. 1999b. The human genus. Science 284:65–71.

Wood B and Richmond B. 2000. Human evolution: taxonomy and paleobiology. J Anat 197:19–60.

Wood B and Lieberman D. 2001. Craniodental variation in *Paranthropus boisei:* A developmental and functional perspective. Am J Phys Anthropol 116:13–25.

Wrangham R, Jones J, et al. 1999. The raw and the stolen. Curr Anthropol 40:567–593.

Wu M. 1983. *Homo erectus* from Hexian, Anhui found in 1981. Acta Anthropol Sinica 2:115.

Wu R. 1985. New Chinese *Homo erectus* and recent work at Zhoukoudian. In: Delson E, editor. Ancestors: The hard evidence. New York: Liss. p 245–248.

Wu R, Han D, et al. 1981. *Ramapithecus* skulls found first time in the world. Kexue Tongbao 26:1018–1021.

Wu R and Dong X. 1982. Preliminary study of *Homo erectus* remains from Hexian, Anhui. Acta Anthropol Sinica 1:2–13.

Wu R and Lin S. 1983. Peking man. Sci Am 248:86–94.

Wu R, Qinghua X, et al. 1983. Morphological features of *Ramapithecus* and *Sivapithecus* and their phylogenetic relationships—morphology and the comparison of the crania. Acta Anthropol 2:6.

Wu R, Qinghua X, et al. 1984. Morphological features of *Ramapithecus* and *Sivapithecus* and their phylogenetic relationships—morphology and comparison of the mandibles. Acta Anthropol 3:9.

Wu R and Yuerong P. 1985. Preliminary observations on the cranium of *Laccopithecus robustus* from Lufeng, Yunnan with reference to its phylogenetic relationship. Acta Anthropol 4:12.

Wu R, Qinghua X, et al. 1986. Relationship between Lufeng *Sivapithecus* and *Ramapithecus* and their phylogenetic position. Acta Anthropol 4:1–31.

Wu R and Qian F. 1991. The first study of the age of Yuanmou man by the method of amino acid racemization geochronology. Acta Anthropol Sinica 10:199.

Wu X. 1990. The evolution of humankind in China. Acta Anthropol Sinica 9:320–321.

Wu X and Bräuer G. 1993. Morphological comparison of archaic *Homo sapiens* crania from China and Africa. Z Morph Anthrop 79:241–259.

Wu X and Poirier F. 1995. Human evolution in China. Oxford, UK: Oxford University Press.

Wyss A and Flynn J. 1995. "Anthropoidea": A name, not an entity. Evol Anthropol 3:187–188.

Xu Q and Lu Q. 1979. The mandibles of *Ramapithecus* and *Sivapithecus* from Lufeng, Yunnan. Vertebr Palasia 17:1–13.

Xu Q and You Y. 1984. Hexian fauna: correlation with deep-sea sediments. Acta Anthropol Sinica 3:66–67.

Yamei H, Potts R, et al. 2000. Mid-Pleistocene Acheulean-like stone technology of the Bose Basin, South China. Science 287:1622–1626.

Yellen JE, Brooks AS, et al. 1995. A middle stone age worked bone industry from katanda, upper Semliki Valley, Zaire. Science 268:553–556.

Yu N, Chen F, et al. 2002. Larger genetic differences within Africans than between Africans and Eurasians. Genetics 161:269–274.

Yuan S, Chen T, et al. 1991. Study on uranium series dating of fossil bones and teeth from Zhoukoudian site. Acta Anthropol Sinica 10:193.

Zachos J, Breza J, et al. 1992. Early Oligocene ice-sheet expansion on Antarctica: Stable isotope and sedimentological evidence from Kerguelen Plateau, southern Indian Ocean. Geology 20:569–573.

Zachos J, Flower B, et al. 1997. Orbitally paced climate oscillations across the Oligocene/Miocene boundary. Nature 388:567–570.

Zavada MS and Cadman A. 1993. Palynological investigations at the Makapansgat Limeworks: An australopithecine site. J Hum Evol 25:337–350.

Zeuner FE. 1958. The replacement of Neanderthal man by *Homo sapiens*. In: von Koenigswald GHR, editor. Hundert Jahre Neanderthaler. Utrecht: Kemink & Zoon. p 312–315.

Zhang Y. 1991. Examination of temporal variation in the hominid dental sample from Zhoukoudian locality 1. Acta Anthropol Sinica 10:95.

Zhisheng A, Kutzbach J, et al. 2001. Evolution of Asian monsoons and phased uplift of the Himalaya-Tibetan plateau since late Miocene times. Nature 411:62–66.

Ziegler R and Dean D. 1998. Mammalian fauna and biostratigraphy of the pre-Neandertal site of Reilingen, Germany. J Hum Evol 34:469–484.

Zihlman A. 1983. A behavioral reconstruction of *Australopithecus*. In: Reichs K, editor. Hominid origins: Inquiries past and present. Washington, D.C.: University Press of America. p 207–238.

Zihlman A. 1985. *Australopithecus afarensis:* Two sexes or two species? In: Tobias PV, editor. Hominid evolution: Past, present and future. New York: Liss. p 213–220.

Zihlman A, Cronin J, et al. 1978. Pygmy chimpanzee as a possible prototype for the common ancestor of humans, chimpanzees and gorillas. Nature 275:744–746.

Zihlman A and Tanner N. 1978. Gathering and the hominid adaptation. In: Tiger L, Fowler H, editors. Female hierarchies. Chicago: Beresford Books. p 163–194.

Zihlman A and Brunker L. 1979. Hominid bipedalism: Then and now. Yearbk Phys Anthropol 22:132–162.

Zischler H, Geisert H, et al. 1995. A nuclear "fossil" of the mitochondrial D-loop and the origin of modern humans. Nature 378:489–492.

Zollikofer C, de León M, et al. 2002. Evidence for interpersonal violence in the St. Césaire Neanderthal. Proc Natl Acad Sci USA 99:6444–6448.

Index

Note: Page numbers in *italics* refer to figures.